Law and Literature

Law and Literature

~ *Revised and Enlarged Edition*

RICHARD A. POSNER

HARVARD UNIVERSITY PRESS
Cambridge, Massachusetts, and London, England 1998

For Emeline and Nathaniel

Excerpts from "Easter 1916," "The Second Coming," "The Wild Swans at Coole," and "Leda and the Swan" by William Butler Yeats are reprinted with the permission of Simon & Schuster from *The Collected Works of W.B. Yeats, Volume 1: The Poems*, Revised and edited by Richard J. Finneran, copyright 1919, 1924 and 1928 by Macmillan Publishing Company, renewed 1947 and 1952 by Bertha Georgie Yeats and 1956 by Georgie Yeats; and by permission of A. P. Watt Ltd. on behalf of Michael Yeats.

Excerpts from "The Waste Land" and "Burnt Norton" by T. S. Eliot are reprinted from T. S. Eliot, *Collected Poems 1909–1962*, copyright 1936 by Harcourt Brace & Company, copyright © 1964, 1963 by T. S. Eliot, and *Four Quartets*, copyright 1943 by T. S. Eliot and renewed 1971 by Esme Valerie Eliot, by permission of Faber and Faber Ltd. and Harcourt Brace & Company.

The excerpt from *The Sweeniad* by Victor Purcell is reprinted by permission of Routledge Ltd.

Library of Congress Cataloging-in-Publication Data
Posner, Richard A.
Law and literature / Richard A. Posner. — Rev. and enl. ed.
    p.   cm.
Includes bibliographical references and index.
ISBN 0-674-51470-X (cloth : alk. paper).
ISBN 0-674-51471-8 (pbk. : alk. paper)
1. Law in literature.   2. Law and literature.   I. Title.
809'.93355—dc21   97-28244

Contents

Preface

THE FIRST EDITION of this book was published a decade ago. I have continued to teach, reflect about, read about, and write about the interdisciplinary field of "law and literature." I welcome this opportunity to crystallize my current thinking in the form of a substantially revised and enlarged edition.

The field has grown in the past decade. The number of courses, in law schools alone, has doubled. Elizabeth Villers Gemmette, "Law and Literature: Joining the Class Action," *29 Valparaiso Law Review* 665, 666–667 (1995). (Gemmette reports that the first edition of this book is the most frequently assigned or recommended nonfiction work in such courses. Id. at 671 n. 46.) A number of notable monographs have appeared, including Thomas Grey's *The Wallace Stevens Case: Law and the Practice of Poetry* (1991), and Martha Nussbaum's *Poetic Justice: The Literary Imagination and Public Life* (1995). That scholars of such distinction as Grey and Nussbaum have enlisted in the law and literature movement attests to its vitality. The continued spate of symposia, anthologies, and general works on law and literature is illustrated by *Adversaria* (special issue of *Mosaic,* Dec. 1994); *The Happy Couple: Law and Literature* (J. Neville Turner and Pamela Williams eds. 1994); Ian Ward, *Law and Literature: Possibilities and Perspectives* (1995); and *Law and Literature Perspectives* (Bruce L. Rockwood ed. 1996). (See also *Interpreting Law and Literature* [Sanford Levinson and Steven Mailloux eds. 1988], published the same year as the first edition of this book.) A first-class law and literature scholarship by practicing lawyers has emerged. See Daniel J. Kornstein, *Kill All the Lawyers? Shakespeare's Legal Appeal* (1994); William Domnarski, *In the Opinion of the Court* (1996). And two new journals have been started, *Cardozo Studies in Law and Literature* and the *Yale Journal of Law and Humanities,* the first wholly, the second partly, devoted to law and literature. Nourished by the law's continuing fascination for American writers, the field of law and literature is prospering and its status as a school of interdisciplinary legal scholarship seems secure. See Gary Minda, *Postmodern Legal Movements: Law and Jurisprudence at Century's End,* ch. 8 (1995).

The field has developed pretty much along the lines described in the first edition of this book, with two major exceptions. First, interest in the application of literary methods to the interpretation of statutes and constitutions has diminished in the face of a growing sense that interpretation is relative to purpose and therefore unlikely to raise the same issues for different interpretanda (dreams, operas, labels, constitutions, sonnets), and is also one of those activities that is not much, if at all, improved by being pursued self-consciously. My own thinking about interpretation has changed, the changes being reflected in the revisions to the chapter on interpretation.

Second, there is increased interest in using imaginative literature and its techniques to address issues remote from the jurisprudential issues—such as, How does law grow out of revenge? What is natural law? What is objective interpretation of a text? How "literary" are or should be judicial opinions? What is the relation between rhetoric and justice?—that had been the focus of the movement. James Boyd White, in his review of the first edition ("What Can a Lawyer Learn from Literature?" 102 *Harvard Law Review* 2014 [1989]), took me to task for failing to understand that the important thing is that a lawyer have a *literary* education, not that he or she read works of literature that are *about* law. Id. at 1028. Imaginative literature unrelated, or at least seemingly unrelated, to law is used by White, Nussbaum, and others as the basis for a new model of legal scholarship, which I have made the subject of Part Three of this edition. The new model emphasizes narration and reminiscence rather than analysis, prefers judicial biography to the study of judicial opinions, promises fresh insights into the plight of people (blacks and women, for example) with whom American law has had troubled encounters, and in general seeks to promote compassion and empathy by enlarging the imagination of lawyers and judges.

The chapters in Part Three are the only entirely new ones, but a number of the others have been considerably augmented, one consequence being that Chapter 2 in the first edition is now three chapters—1, 3, and 4, with old 1 having become new 2. There are discussions of works by writers not discussed in the first edition, including works by Shelley, Manzoni, Stendhal, Forster, Duerrenmatt, Gaddis, and Richard Wright; discussions of additional works by writers that were discussed in the first edition; and discussions of several works of popular fiction. All the chapters have been revised or reorganized (or both) and bibliographical references brought up to date. Some of the new material is borrowed from books and articles of mine published since the first edition: *Cardozo: A Study in Reputation* (1990); *The Problems of Jurisprudence* (1990); *Overcoming Law* (1995); "When Is Parody Fair Use?" 21 *Journal of Legal Studies* 67 (1992); "Judicial Biography," 70 *New York University Law Review* 502 (1995); "Judges' Writing Styles (And Do They Matter)," 62 *University of Chicago Law Review* 1421 (1995); "Legal Narratology," 64 *University of Chicago Law Review* 737 (1997).

I have tried conscientiously to rethink the interpretations and other opinions expressed in the first edition. This process of reconsideration, in which I have been aided by the extensive scholarship on pertinent issues that has been published since 1988, has led to a number of changes. In addition, errors have been corrected and extraneous materials deleted.

I thank my editor at Harvard University Press, Michael Aronson, for encouraging me to undertake this new edition; Jennifer Canel, Kevin Cremin, Sorin Feiner, Simon Gilbert, Matthew Jackson, Christopher Keller, Geoffrey Manne, Neil Petty, David Sommers, and Andrew Trask for excellent research assistance; and Paul Abramson, Albert Alschuler, Michael Aronson, Jack Balkin, Wayne Booth, Richard Craswell, Joseph Epstein, Stephen Holmes, Lawrence Lessig, Catharine MacKinnon, Martha Nussbaum, Robert Pippin, Charlene Posner, Eric Posner, Richard Stern, Dan Subotnik, and participants in a Work in Progress Luncheon at the University of Chicago Law School and in the university's Rhetoric Workshop for many helpful criticisms and suggestions, and Anita Safran for expert copyediting. I take this opportunity also to acknowledge again the very helpful research assistance on the first edition of Darren Fortunato, Michael Keane, Laura Neebling, and Richard Zook, and the many helpful comments on the manuscript of that edition by Michael Aronson, David Bevington, Robert Ferguson, David Friedman, Michael Gagarin, Harrison Hayford, Stephen Holmes, Peter Jansen, Clayton Koelb, John Langbein, L. H. LaRue, Saul Levmore, Kenneth Northcott, Richard Porter, Charlene Posner, Eric Posner, James Redfield, Lawrence Rosen, Edward Rosenheim, Eva Saks, Cass Sunstein, Richard Weisberg, Robin West, and James Boyd White.

Introduction

E. M. Forster was not a lawyer, and his novel *Howards End* (1911) is not a "legal novel" even to the extent to which *A Passage to India,* which has a notable trial scene, could be said to be one. *Howards End* pivots on the contrast in style and values between a pair of German-born but Anglicized sisters, Margaret and Helen Schlegel—cultured, sensitive, high-minded heiresses of German Romanticism—and the Wilcoxes, a thoroughly English family whose men personify philistine commercial values. Margaret Schlegel marries Henry Wilcox after the death of his first wife. The unmarried Helen becomes pregnant by a pathetic young man of the working classes named Leonard Bast. Bast's wife, as it happens, had been Henry Wilcox's mistress at a time when he was married to his first wife but living in a different part of the world because of his work; and he had failed to make any provision for the mistress after leaving her.

Henry Wilcox regards the pregnancy of his unmarried sister-in-law as a deep scandal to which only two responses are possible. If the seducer is unmarried, he must be forced to marry her; if he is married, he "must pay heavily for his misconduct, and be thrashed within an inch of his life" (p. 305).[1] Wilcox questions his wife in an effort to discover the seducer's identity. Margaret doesn't want to reveal it, so she changes the subject. She asks whether Helen may stay at their house (Howards End), as Helen wants very much to do, this last night before she goes off to Munich to have the baby in seclusion. Henry is appalled, but responds mildly enough by questioning Helen's reasons for wanting to stay at Howards End. He gets nowhere—Margaret insists that the only important thing is that Helen wants to stay—and he quickly changes tack. "If she wants to sleep one

1. Page references are to the Vintage Books edition (1954).

night, she may want to sleep two. We shall never get her out of the house, perhaps" (p. 306). A lawyer's ears should prick up. This is a familiar lawyer's gambit—the "slippery slope." If you accept claim *a*, you must consider whether that commits you to accept *b, c* . . . *n* on the ground that there is no principled distinction among the claims, therefore no logical stopping point; and then you must consider the consequences of the entire set of claims. To suppose that this principle of argument obliterates the distinction between a visit of one night and a visit of indefinite length is absurd; and we may begin to wonder whether Henry Wilcox isn't an inflexible, rule-obsessed, in short *legalistic* reasoner, and whether his insistence that the only possible responses to Helen's pregnancy are a shotgun marriage or a criminal assault on the seducer isn't of a piece with his "slippery slope" argument in point of obtuse rigidity. Henry's legalistic bent shows up in another context. The first Mrs. Wilcox, who had been the legal owner of Howards End, had wanted to leave the house to Margaret but had expressed her intention in a note that did not comply with the formalities required for a will. Henry, standing on his legal rights, had torn up the note, perpetrating an injustice in the name of legal justice.

The impression of his obtuseness is reinforced when he fails to catch the meaning of Margaret's remark, "Will you forgive her—as you hope to be forgiven, and as you actually have been forgiven?" (p. 307). The reference is to Henry's relationship, which Margaret *had* forgiven, with the woman who is now Leonard Bast's wife. But the remark has a further significance, as an appeal to mercy over against strict legal justice. Henry rejects the appeal, saying, "I know how one thing leads to another." When he fails to react to her further remark, "May I mention Mrs. Bast?" Margaret becomes enraged. "Margaret rushed at him and seized both his hands. She was transfigured. 'Not any more of this!' she cried. 'You shall see the connection if it kills you, Henry! You have had a mistress—I forgave you. My sister has a lover—you drive her from the house . . . Only say to yourself: "What Helen has done, I've done."'" (p. 308). Even this sally has no effect. Committed to the fundamental precept of legal justice that like cases must be treated alike, Henry insists that "the two cases are different." But not being a clear thinker he is unable to identify the difference, so again he changes tack. He accuses Margaret of trying to blackmail him, thus placing her words in a legal category that he can offset against his own wrongful conduct. The charge of blackmail is false. Margaret has neither expressly nor by implication threatened Henry that unless he lets Helen stay the night at Howards End she will expose his old relationship with Mrs. Bast (and expose to whom? Who would care?). Henry is a very poor legal reasoner, but the interesting thing is that a novelistic setting remote from a trial or any other identifiably legal scene resounds with the echo of legal rhetoric and reasoning.

The implication is that Forster associates the legal style of thinking with the failure to connect heart and mind. ("Only connect . . ." is the epigraph of *Howards End* and in effect Forster's motto.) The human tragedy, as Forster sees it, is that people become enmeshed in structures of thought that prevent them from leading emotionally satisfying lives and from being fair to one another. For example, Victorian sexual morality had, by its condemnation of homosexuality, contributed, Forster believed, to making his own life miserable. In *Howards End* this condemnation is displaced onto Henry's rejection of Helen for her lesser violation of the Victorian code. The code itself Forster would have associated with the legal mentality, for he wrote *Howards End* only a decade after the trial, conviction, and imprisonment of Oscar Wilde for homosexual acts. The implied opposition between Romantic values (those of the Schlegel sisters) and legal values is a recurrent one in literature, as we shall see; and while the excesses of Romanticism are also a theme of *Howards End*—Helen's irresponsible behavior with Leonard Bast is a factor in his destruction—Forster is more critical of legalism than of Romanticism. He imagines legal thinking to be committed to rigid dichotomies and inhuman abstractions that are insensitive to the complexities of emotion and as a result inflict needless suffering. A common literary reaction to law, it undervalues rule and abstraction as methods of bringing order out of the chaos of social interactions. But that is not the point I want to make. I want rather to suggest the ubiquity of law as a theme of literature.

Law's techniques and imagery have permeated Western culture from its earliest days. The law has engaged the attention of imaginative writers as an object of fascination in its own right, as we see in "legal" works of literature ranging from *Eumenides* and *Antigone* to *The Caine Mutiny, The Bonfire of the Vanities,* and *A Frolic of His Own;* as a dramatic and rhetorical mode, as in *Howards End;*[2] and also as a symbol of the orderly everyday world that is foil and backdrop to the disruptive situations that are the stock in trade of literature. (Most literature is about screwing up one's life in one way or another.) Law in the courtroom is agonistic, but the spirit of law is irenic and conciliatory. The first aspect of law, the forensic, provides an analogy to the troubled lives encountered in works of literature. We see

2. On the effect of legal devices, specifically the trial, on literary forms, specifically the novel, see the interesting discussion in Alexander Welsh, *Strong Representations: Narrative and Circumstantial Evidence in England* (1992); also the review of Welsh's book by Barbara Shapiro, "Circumstantial Evidence: Of Law, Literature, and Culture," 5 *Yale Journal of Law and the Humanities* 219 (1993).

this in the punning title of Kafka's novel *The Trial,* which in both English and German *(Der Prozess)* means both a legal proceeding and a personal crisis. The second aspect, law as the condition for social peace, provides contrast with those troubled lives. In recent years, a number of literary scholars have trained their sights on texts lying far outside the traditional literary canon. This enlargement of interest has brought statutes, contracts, and judicial opinions within the literary field of vision.

If the law has fascinated writers and literary scholars, literature has fascinated judges and other lawyers, lately including law professors, as a possible model for their judicial, forensic, and scholarly efforts respectively, as a possible source of insight into the social problems that arise in legal cases, and as a rich source of quotations.[3] A number of distinguished authors of literary works have *been* lawyers (or law-trained), including Donne, Fielding, Sir Walter Scott, Balzac, James Fenimore Cooper, Flaubert, Tolstoy, Kafka, Galsworthy, Wallace Stevens, and possibly Chaucer. Even Henry James was for a time a student at the Harvard Law School. Some of today's most popular writers of fiction, such as John Grisham and Scott Turow, are lawyers.[4] And literature has been drawn directly into the orbit of the law as a subject of legal regulation under such rubrics as libel, copyright, and obscenity.

Although the overlap between law and literature is ancient, as a field of organized study "law and literature" hardly existed before the publication in 1973 of James Boyd White's textbook *The Legal Imagination.* The field remained tiny until well into the 1980s. For until very recently both legal scholarship and literary scholarship were autonomous fields defined by a specific, narrowly circumscribed, and nonoverlapping body of texts (the literary canon in the case of literary scholarship, and, in the case of legal scholarship, texts ranging from statutes, constitutional provisions, and opinions to articles and treatises—all written by lawyers) that were to be mastered by the application of a specific, narrowly conceived methodology. Literary texts lay outside the field of vision of the legal scholar, legal texts outside that of literary scholars. A recent blurring of the lines that separate different academic disciplines, and a growing professionalism and intellectual ambition in "soft" fields such as literature and law, got legal scholars interested in parallel fields,

---

3. See William Domnarski, "Shakespeare in the Law," 67 *Connecticut Bar Journal* 317 (1992).

4. No discussion of law in popular culture would be complete without examining the depiction of law in movies and television dramas; but to attempt this would extend this book unduly. Anyone interested in these topics will want to read Paul Bergman and Michael Asimov, *Reel Justice: The Courtroom Goes to the Movies* (1996), which synopsizes and analyzes 69 movies about law, and *Legal Reelism: Movies as Legal Texts* (John Denvir ed. 1996), a collection of critical essays.

including literature, while literary scholars, as I have mentioned, have become interested in nonliterary texts, including those of law.

Although a field that at its best can engage the interest of the serious student or practitioner of law and the serious student of literature, law and literature is also full of false starts, tendentious interpretations, shallow polemics, glib generalizations, and superficial insights. This does not distinguish it sharply from most other fields of scholarship outside the domain of the exact sciences. But the point is nonetheless worth emphasizing. The proper perspective on the law and literature movement is critical as well as sympathetic.

In Part One I shall be discussing works of literature that are in some sense "about" law, broadly defined to include natural law and revenge—normative systems that are parallel to positive law and influence it. This body of literature contains many of the monuments of Western culture, including works by Homer, the Greek tragedians, Shakespeare, Dostoevsky, Melville, Kafka, and Camus, as well as by innumerable writers of popular fiction. Yet I shall argue that we cannot learn a great deal about the day-to-day operations of a legal system from works of imaginative literature even when they depict trials or other activities of the formal legal system. The reason is bound up with the "test of time" as the touchstone of literary distinction, of which more shortly. But we can learn a great deal of *jurisprudence* from some works of literature; indeed, a well-chosen set of such works would be a close substitute for discursive works of jurisprudence. In addition, as we saw in considering *Howards End,* works of literature that do not deal overtly with the law or parallel normative systems can sometimes be better understood by being approached from a jurisprudential perspective.

The second part of the book examines two kinds of legal text—the legally operative document (whether a legislative enactment, statutory or constitutional, or a contract) and the judicial opinion—from the perspective of literature. Legislative enactments that become the subjects of celebrated or controversial judicial decisions are often deeply ambiguous texts, as are many works of imaginative literature. Such enactments raise the question of objectivity in interpretation, a question that has long preoccupied literary critics and scholars as well as judges and legal scholars. The specter of hopeless indeterminacy, of rampant subjectivity, hovers over the key texts of both fields.

Judicial opinions, although sometimes opaque too, are not canonical texts and can therefore be clarified or modified in subsequent opinions without much fuss or bother. The literary issue raised by the judicial opinion is not that of meaning but that of style. Is style an integral, or merely an ornamental, characteristic of the judicial opinion? Are there fruitful stylistic or rhetorical parallels between judicial opinions and works of imaginative literature? Is there such a thing as a "literary" judge, and is such a judge an improvement over the nonliterary judge? Have the "great" judges been more the former or the latter?

The relations between law and literature discussed in the first two parts of the book illuminate a number of topics in jurisprudence and legal theory; but, for an increasing number of legal scholars, inspired in part by philosophers and literary scholars, this is not enough. They want to reclaim law as a humanity from economists and economics-minded lawyers, who view law as a social science. They want to do this both by giving lawyers a literary education and by shifting the emphasis in legal scholarship—any legal scholarship, however remote the subject matter may seem from literature—from analysis to narrative and metaphor. Some want to bring works of imaginative literature into the legal classroom in order to present vivid pictures of the despised, the overlooked, and the downtrodden, and by fostering empathy for them to encourage legal reform along egalitarian or even revolutionary lines. This novel turning of the law and literature movement, one manifestation of which is an increased interest in biography and autobiography, is the subject of Part Three of this book. I am deeply skeptical about this branch of the law and literature movement. It has all the drawbacks of the didactic or moralistic school of literary criticism founded by Plato—of which, indeed, it is the continuation into legal studies—and more.

The single chapter of Part Four examines several topics in the regulation of literature by law. (An allied topic, the regulation of pornographic literature, is taken up in the chapter in Part Three on moralistic criticism, Chapter 9.) I discuss defamation by fiction and some implications of literary theory and scholarship for copyright protection, with particular emphasis on creative imitation (a term that only seems like an oxymoron) and on parodies. In the interest of literature itself, I caution against expanding the present scope of copyright protection of authors of imaginative literature.

It is in the areas discussed in Part Four, the areas in which the law regulates literature, that the law and literature movement can be expected to have its greatest impact on law. But there is just a chance that in the long run the movement will affect even more strongly ways of thinking about justice, interpretation, the judicial opinion, legal education, and legal scholarship, though this impact is bound to be more diffuse and only obliquely related to practice.

A curious thing about the works of literature that constitute the ever-shifting canon of great literature[5] is their mysterious capacity to speak to people who live in different times, which often means in different cultures, from the time and culture in which the work was written. These works have a measure of *universality*—it is what enables them to pass the test of time, to survive into cultures remote from those of their creation. "The poet," as the critic Cleanth Brooks put it in words that are equally applicable to any writer of what comes to be considered great literature, "is constantly relating the human predicament of his time to the universal qualities of human nature through all the ages. His view of a situation, however sharp and immediate, is nevertheless always part of a long view."[6] If this is right, and I think it is, it has several cautionary implications for the law and literature movement. It implies that the movement will make a greater contribution to illuminating jurisprudential issues than to understanding or improving law at the operating level, that it will contribute little to statutory or constitutional interpretation, and that it will not guide legal scholars, judges, and other members of the legal profession to a resolution of any of the burning issues that confront American law today.

Readers should not infer from my emphasis on the limitations of the law and literature movement that my overall attitude toward it is negative. I support it and wish to see it flourish—not necessarily on my own terms, but with due consideration both for the drawbacks of some of the approaches that have been taken and for the advantages of the approach taken in this book. I want it to flourish but not to be overrated. Law and literature have significant commonalities and intersections, but the differences are as important. Law is a system of social control as well as a body of texts, and its operation is illuminated by the social sciences and judged by ethical criteria. Literature is an art, and the best methods for interpreting and evaluating it are aesthetic. There is no inconsistency between being a formalist in literature and an antiformalist, a pragmatist, in law—which happens to be my position. But that is a detail. My principal aim in this book is not polemical. It is to describe this still-new field of interdisciplinary scholarship and to mine it for fresh insights.

5. More precisely canons, since people from different cultures have different conceptions of the body of great literature. This is an issue examined in Chapter 1.

6. Quoted in Robert Penn Warren, "A Conversation with Cleanth Brooks," in *The Possibilities of Order: Cleanth Brooks and His Work* 1, 10 (Lewis P. Simpson ed. 1976).

part I

*L*ITERARY
TEXTS *as* LEGAL TEXTS

ONE

The Reflection of Law in Literature

Law is so common a subject of literature that one is tempted to infer a deep affinity between the two fields, giving the lawyer privileged access if not to the whole body of literature then at least to those works that are explicitly about law. But I shall argue that the frequency of legal subjects in literature is partly a statistical artifact and that law figures in literature more often as metaphor than as an object of interest in itself, even when the author is a lawyer (like Kafka) or a law "buff" (like Melville). This is in general, however, not in every case. Moreover, the validity of the generalization depends on the precise sense in which the word "law" is used—and also the word "literature."

Theoretical Considerations

In matters of aesthetic judgment, even more than in other normative discourse, there is no "objective" procedure for resolving disagreements. The strongest defender of the possibility of reasoning to consensus on difficult political and moral questions—namely, Jürgen Habermas—acknowledges that aesthetic criticism, while it can be held to high standards of rationality, could not be expected to produce an evaluative consensus even if critics had forever to debate their evaluations.[1] I am persuaded by George Orwell, here following Samuel Johnson and David Hume, that literature can be judged great only by its ability to survive in the competition of the literary "marketplace."[2] (The quotation marks are to make clear that I am

---

1. See the interesting discussion in Georgia Warnke, "Communicative Rationality and Cultural Values," in *The Cambridge Companion to Habermas* 120, 126–129 (Stephen K. White ed. 1995).

2. "In reality there is no kind of evidence or argument by which one can show that Shakespeare, or any other writer, is 'good'. Nor is there any way of definitely proving that—for

speaking of reputation rather than the sale of commodities.) This is not to say that literary merit cannot be debated profitably, as a preference for blackberries over raspberries cannot be; the vast body of evaluative literary criticism, much of it of great distinction, shows that it can be; I offer my own aesthetic judgments from time to time in this book. But the debate achieves closure only with regard to very old works—suggesting that even the critics, in their hearts, accept only the verdict of time. Except by some radical critics, of whom more in a moment, the greatness of Homer or Dante or Shakespeare is no longer questioned. Tolstoy's attack on Shakespeare[3] and T. S. Eliot's on Hamlet ("most certainly an artistic failure")[4] are curiosities that do not invite emulation. The effort of some New Critics to devalue Milton along with much Romantic and Victorian literature achieved a temporary success but eventually flopped; their efforts to revalue the Metaphysical and Augustan poets upward have succeeded. Feminist literary critics are trying to boost the reputation of a number of women writers, some hitherto unknown, but it is too early to say whether their efforts will succeed. That is always the case with literature and the arts; it takes many years to separate the wheat from the chaff.

The impression that many intellectuals today have of living in an age of trash may be an illusion produced by the fact that the winnowing effects of time have not had a chance to operate on contemporary literature. No doubt the English Renaissance produced a richer literature than has twentieth-century England, but the contrast is less stark than readers acquainted with only a handful of the best works of Shakespeare, Donne, Jonson, and a few others think. Plenty of literary trash was produced by the Elizabethans; most of it has disappeared (the original *Hamlet* [see next chapter] may be an example); what has survived physically is read today only by specialists. Some of the Elizabethan plays discussed in the next chapter,

---

instance—Warwick Deeping is 'bad'. Ultimately there is no test of literary merit except survival, which is itself merely an index to majority opinion." Orwell, "Lear, Tolstoy, and the Fool," in *The Collected Essays, Journalism and Letters of George Orwell*, vol. 4, pp. 287, 290 (Sonia Orwell and Ian Angus eds. 1968). See Samuel Johnson, "Preface to the Plays of William Shakespeare," in *Samuel Johnson: Selected Poetry and Prose* 299, 300 (Frank Brady and W. K. Wimsatt eds. 1977); David Hume, "Of the Standard of Taste," in Hume, *Essays: Moral, Political, and Literary* 226, 231–233 (Eugene F. Miller ed. 1985); Anthony Savile, *The Test of Time: An Essay in Philosophical Aesthetics* (1982).

3. See Tolstoy, *Shakespeare and the Drama* (1903), the subject of the Orwell essay cited in note 2.

4. Eliot, "Hamlet and His Problems," in Eliot, *Selected Essays* 121, 123 (new ed. 1950). Of that verdict C. S. Lewis remarked, "If this is failure, then failure is better than success. We want more of these 'bad plays.'" Quoted in Arthur Kirsch, "Between Bardolatry and Bardicide," *Times Literary Supplement*, April 20, 1990, p. 421.

such as *The Spanish Tragedy,* have only modest merit and make a striking contrast to Shakespeare's mature works—as indeed does his early *Titus Andronicus.* It may not have been until Samuel Johnson brought out his edition of Shakespeare's plays in 1765 that it was settled as certain (as certain as these matters can be) that Shakespeare was great—that his best plays must have extraordinary qualities to be so riveting almost two centuries after their composition despite the intervening changes in language, taste, and social milieu. It is only today, more than seventy years after major writings by Kafka, T. S. Eliot, Joyce, Proust, and Mann, that we can say with some confidence, though more provisionally than in the case of Homer, Dante, Milton, and Shakespeare, that these men have written classics. And about some writers who only a few decades ago had the status of classic writers, such as Anatole France, John Dos Passos, and André Gide, there are growing doubts; their work is starting to date in a way that some of their contemporaries' is not.

Orwell's endorsement of the test of time rested partly on a preference for the judgment of the many over the expert few and partly on skepticism about the possibility of making objective judgments of literary merit. These are two reasons why few professional literary critics are enthusiastic about the test of time.[5] A third, which is related to the first, is that specialists acquire a taste for obscure writers. Orwell's skepticism mirrored that of the logical positivists concerning the possibility of objective normative judgments, anticipated the skepticism about interpretation that I shall discuss in Chapter 7, and is supported empirically by the amazing vicissitudes in literary and artistic taste. His skepticism, in combination with his democratic sentiments, led him to suppose that aesthetic disputes should be settled by a form of majority vote; the significance of time is that it broadens and diversifies the franchise—making the test of time an application of sampling theory. Samuel Johnson, himself a skeptic in many areas with a surprisingly egalitarian attitude toward aesthetic judgments,[6] had reached the same conclusion much earlier. But his ground was that the longer the perspective in which a work of art can be evaluated, the greater the possibility of comparison, and it is from comparisons that judgments of artistic greatness, which are judgments of less and more, emerge. "Of the first building that was raised, it might be with certainty determined that it was round or

5. "Criticism conceived as magistrate kills the dead or breathes on the face of what is very much alive anyway . . . I would like to ask whether critics have been responsible for establishing the greatness of Dante, Shakespeare, or Michelangelo, or, on the contrary, the great number of their readers and spectators." Benedetto Croce, *Guide to Aesthetics* 68 (1965 [1913]).

6. See William K. Wimsatt, Jr. and Cleanth Brooks, *Literary Criticism: A Short History* 325, 327–328, 331–333 (1957).

square, but whether it was spacious or lofty must have been referred to time."[7]

We might say, joining Johnson's and Orwell's points, that when a work of literature demonstrates appeal to diverse audiences familiar with many other works with which to compare it, it must "have something." So understood, the test of time illustrates epistemic democracy rather than mere nose-counting. (By the same token, it is a criterion, not a definition.) It is not the sheer number of people who have esteemed a work of literature but the cultural diversity of its readership that is telling. The more diverse the readership, the larger the range of potential objections and criticisms; if the work survives them all, this is robust evidence of merit.

Or is it? It is one thing to believe with Habermas, here following Charles Sanders Peirce, that if you give a community of disinterested and uncoerced inquirers enough time, they will reach a consensus that can fairly be regarded as "the truth." But we have seen that Habermas himself does not believe that *aesthetic* disagreement lends itself to this method of resolution. The real skeptic will repose no greater confidence in majority vote than in expert opinion. Neither Orwell nor Johnson specified the conditions necessary for democratic opinion to come within miles of yielding reliable aesthetic judgments.

To state this problem in another way, if passing the test of time shows that a work of literature has something, why is the identification of that something so elusive? If the survivors in the marketplace of literary reputation have nothing in common, this suggests that reputations are bestowed for reasons unrelated to the actual quality of the works. And so it is claimed, especially by literary scholars of a radical bent. These scholars march today under many different banners, including neo-Marxism, radical feminism, critical theory, and poststructuralism, but I shall lump them all together under the label of "postmodernists." They have in common a commitment to radical egalitarianism, hostility to the Enlightenment's faith in the power of reason, insistence on the primacy of politics—radical politics[8]—and skepticism about the traditional literary canon dominated by "dead white European males," whom the test of time favors because they were the ones doing almost all the writing in past centuries. This last point echoes the law's concern with practices, not discriminatory in themselves, that perpetuate past discrimination: for example, a union apprenticeship program that favors the children of current members, who may have become mem-

---

7. Johnson, note 2 above, at 300.

8. So John Beverley, in his book of literary criticism *Against Literature* (1993), thinks it germane to inform readers in his preface that he "had been involved since 1978 in solidarity work with Central American revolutionary movements." Id. at ix.

bers at a time when nonwhites were excluded. The literary canon may be biased in the same way.

The test of time has been called circular, because a work that endures shapes critical opinion and meets a social demand for cultural monuments.[9] But this does not explain *why* the work endures, only why its durability may eventually become self-sustaining as the text becomes an influential and admired "survivor." Gary Taylor has tackled this question, arguing that Shakespeare's reputation is a product of such lucky accidents as the number of people who speak English (itself a result, Taylor contends, of British imperialism), the variety of dramatic genres to which Shakespeare contributed (making his *oeuvre* a diversified portfolio more likely therefore to withstand the vicissitudes of taste), the closing of the theaters by the Puritans between 1642 and 1660, which reduced the output of plays that might have competed with Shakespeare's, the fact that in the eighteenth century Shakespeare was "taken up" by a prominent English publisher, and even erotic titillation, for women were permitted to act on the Restoration stage, as they had not been in Shakespeare's time, and a number of Shakespeare's heroines are disguised as men.[10] Taylor's argument is overstated, contradictory, tendentious, implausible, in places inaccurate, at best highly speculative.[11] But he is right that the survival of works of literature is, broadly speaking, Darwinian, that Darwinian processes produce fitness but may not produce goodness, and that literary reputation—the mark of that survivorship—is something bestowed upon a writer for the purposes of the people doing the bestowing, rather than something earned by pure merit.[12] So one expects many inflated reputations. But is Shakespeare's one of them? Read his plays and then read the plays of his predecessors and contemporaries and then the representative plays of his successors and, if you can, plays in other languages. Few people who have taken this— Johnson's comparative or perspectival—route doubt that Shakespeare's reputation as the preeminent dramatist since (and probably including) Sophocles is earned. The opinion of the strong majority of informed read-

9. See David Parker, *Ethics, Theory and the Novel* 21–22 (1994).

10. Gary Taylor, *Reinventing Shakespeare: A Cultural History, from the Restoration to the Present* (1989). See also Barbara Herrnstein Smith, *Contingencies of Value: Alternative Perspectives for Critical Theory* (1988). Taylor claims that this enabled actresses to appear in tight-fitting trousers that were more revealing of the female form than the dresses of the period. Taylor, above, at 18–19.

11. See Michael Shapiro, *Gender in Play on the Shakespearean Stage: Boy Heroines and Female Pages* 201, 270 n. 4 (1994); Laurence Lerner, "The New Shakespeareans," 44 *Comparative Literature* 194 (1992); Kirsch, note 4 above; Anne Barton, "Inventing Shakespeare," *New York Review of Books*, Feb. 1, 1990, p. 15.

12. Richard A. Posner, *Cardozo: A Study in Reputation*, ch. 4 (1990). Taylor elaborates his Darwinian view of cultural survival in a later book, *Cultural Selection* (1996).

ers over several centuries and across different cultures, an opinion defended not as ineffable or inspired but by rational arguments albeit not conclusive ones, provides some basis for a confident, though not an infallible, let alone a permanent, evaluation.

It is possible to be *too* skeptical about the value of evolutionary products. No more in literature than in biology can variation, adaptation, and selection guarantee a good result. Yet biological evolution has produced creatures of dazzling complexity, many of which seem beautiful to us; why should the more deliberate competitive process that shapes the literary canon do worse, merely because accidental and political factors enter into the quest for beauty and meaning? But as the proof of the pudding is in the eating, an alternative method of attacking the test of time is to challenge the greatness of classic authors, such as Shakespeare, which Taylor, however, does only implicitly, for the most part,[13] by ascribing Shakespeare's reputation to factors unrelated to the merit of his work. If it can be shown that these authors are not as good as they are cracked up to be—if even at this late date they can be dethroned—the test of time cannot be a reliable guide to aesthetic value.

The attack (I shall continue to use Shakespeare as my example) proceeds in two steps. The first is to reject aesthetic criteria of literary merit as subjective and implicitly political and to claim that the only value of literature is its contribution to the struggle for equality.[14] The second step is to argue, for example from the depiction of Caliban in *The Tempest,* or Edmund in *King Lear,* or Kate in *The Taming of the Shrew,* or the Roman mob in *Coriolanus* or *Julius Caesar,* that Shakespeare was a reactionary—a royalist, a racist, an imperialist, a misogynist.[15]

The first step is a peculiarly uncompromising version—reminiscent of Stalinist "socialist realism"—of the didactic school of literary criticism (see more on this in Chapter 9). The second step rests on a one-sided reading of the plays. The previous generation of critics had depicted Shakespeare as a subversive writer, evading Elizabethan censorship to question the val-

---

13. He does make clear that he considers Shakespeare greatly overrated. Taylor, note 10 above, ch. 7.

14. See, for example, Beverley's book, note 8 above; Louis A. Montrose, "Professing the Renaissance: The Poetics and Politics of Culture," in *The New Historicism* 15 (H. Aram Veeser ed. 1989). The pretensions of the postmodernist literary theorists to be engaged in revolutionary political action are ridiculed by Stanley Fish, the Mirabeau or Kerensky of radical literary theory, in his book *Professional Correctness: Literary Studies and Political Change* (1995). Here is a representative sally: "The language of literary theory is not subversive, but irrelevant; *it cannot be heard* except as the alien murmurings of a galaxy far away." Id. at 91.

15. For cogent criticisms of these attacks on Shakespeare, see Graham Bradshaw, *Misrepresentations: Shakespeare and the Materialists* (1993); Brian Vickers, *Appropriating Shakespeare: Contemporary Critical Quarrels* (1993).

ues of his society with respect to Christianity, monarchy, Henry V's victorious war with France, homosexuality, commerce, and the status of women, blacks, and Jews.[16] Oddly, it is quite possible, though unrewarding, to read Shakespeare either way—as reactionary or as radical. Little is known about Shakespeare's personal life and nothing of his private opinions. There is no authoritative text of the plays. None of the original manuscripts, that is, Shakespeare's autograph texts, survives. The copies from which printers worked were probably inaccurate, and the printers made many errors. It is not even clear that any of the plays ever *had* a single, definitive text, as different versions may have been prepared for different performances. The text of *Hamlet,* which is much longer than that of any of the other plays, may have been a kind of master text from which abridged versions were spun off for performance. And it is possible that the actors were authorized to ad lib lines, which would give the original text an inherently open-ended quality. The quest for authorial intentions is defeated by these textual uncertainties.[17] A play, moreover, lacks a narrator to tell the reader what to think. And Shakespeare's plays were written in an era of social transitions and questioning of values. All plays had to be approved by the public censor as politically and religiously inoffensive, and such censorship both implies that there is dissent from orthodox beliefs and induces ambiguity and obliquity of expression.[18] Shakespeare's "compul-

16. The generation before *that,* the generation of E. M. W. Tillyard, had portrayed Shakespeare as an orthodox spokesman of medieval Christian values. See Tillyard, *The Elizabethan World Picture* (1943). Yet Marx and Engels had greatly admired Shakespeare. See, for example, Letter from Engels to Marx, Dec. 10, 1873, in *Collected Works of Karl Marx and Frederick Engels,* vol. 44, p. 548 (Galina Kostryukova, Galina Voitenkova, and Natalia Sayenko eds. 1989): "The first act of the *Merry Wives* alone contains more life and reality than all German literature." See also David McLellan, *Karl Marx: His Life and Thought* 15, 113, 267, 327, 456–457 (1973).

17. See David Bevington, "General Introduction," in *The Complete Works of Shakespeare* lxxxiv–xcii (David Bevington ed., 4th ed. 1992); Jeffrey A. Masten, "Beaumont and/or Fletcher: Collaboration and the Interpretation of Renaissance Drama," in *The Construction of Authorship: Textual Appropriation in Law and Literature* 361 (Martha Woodmansee and Peter Jaszi eds. 1994); Jonathan Hope, *The Authorship of Shakespeare's Plays: A Socio-Linguistic Study* 3–5 (1994).

18. Bradshaw, note 15 above, at 297 n. 49; Janet Clare, *'Art Made Tongue-Tied by Authority': Elizabethan and Jacobean Dramatic Censorship* 214 (1990). Taylor could adduce this as another example of Shakespeare's good luck in the marketplace of reputations. One way that censorship fosters ambiguity in literary expression, as Clare points out, is by encouraging the writer to set his work in a culturally or temporally remote setting, such as ancient Rome, prehistoric England *(King Lear),* Italy, Vienna, or medieval (hence Catholic) Denmark. The exotic locale enables the writer to exercise a critical freedom that he would not enjoy if he were writing about contemporary events and institutions in his own society. At the same time, it reduces the topicality, and so enhances the universality, of the work. There is a parallel to the practice of Renaissance and Victorian artists in "us[ing] distance to deflect the censors—that is, they used mythical, legendary, or exotic personages and locales to disguise any implication that the artist was depicting the erotic behavior of his own society." Richard A. Posner, *Sex and Reason* 361 (1992).

sive habit of creative interiorization,"[19] moreover, gives his characters the kind of complexity that we encounter in living persons and that makes it difficult to classify most people as either "hero" or "villain." For all these reasons, it is impossible to determine where Shakespeare "stood" on most issues.

This discussion shows the silliness of trying to pin an ideological tail on the Shakespearean donkey, but it also flags another objection to the test of time: ambiguous works of literature are more likely to pass it though they may be no better than unambiguous ones. They provide a challenge to readers that is independent of the quality of a work, and they are more adaptable to political and ideological change. *The Merchant of Venice* has been performed both in Yiddish theaters (once with Shylock speaking German and the Christian characters Yiddish!) and in Nazi ones.[20] But there is a quality of literature that is like ambiguity but distinct from it, and that is universality. I suggested earlier that the quest for a quality common to all great literature has failed. That is correct if what we are looking for is some particular structure, theme, or verbal texture to be the touchstone of literary greatness. But if what we are looking for is the property that enables a writing to pass the test of time and be received into the canon, a plausible candidate is an adaptability to new and different cultural settings that is a product sometimes of ambiguity but more often of the writer's having succeeded in dramatizing in a particularly striking way some universal aspect of the human condition that science has not yet been able to domesticate, such as love, fear of death, emotional maturation, and social maladjustment. Such a dramatization is less likely to "date," more likely to "travel," than a more topical work.

Universality should not be confused with abstraction. Most great literature is highly textured, richly particular, and even (an implication of the test of time) exotic. The world of Homer, for example, is presented to the reader in great detail; and it is emphatically not our world. Ancient literature, especially, is often rich in anthropological or historical interest. But that is different from literary interest. The great author makes us *at home* in his fictive world; that is his universality.

Other criticisms of the test of time should be noted.[21] The first is that it privileges current aesthetic standards—the only works that survive into the

---

19. Bradshaw, note 15 above, at 132.

20. John Gross, *Shylock: A Legend and Its Legacy* 241, 276–282, 319–322 (1992). For a parallel example—Antigone played by both the Nazi occupiers of France and the French Resistance—see Theodore Ziolkowski, *The Mirror of Justice: Literary Reflections of Legal Crisis* 145–146 (1997).

21. The first two are made in Anita Silvers, "The Story of Art Is the Test of Time," 49 *Journal of Aesthetics and Art Criticism* 211, 213–214 (1991).

present are the works esteemed great by current standards. The second is that it is made indeterminate by the vicissitudes of literary reputation: if the timeline of a writer's reputation exhibits troughs as well as peaks, what significance can be assigned to a current peak? Next year there may be another trough, and if the test of time is applied to the writer then, he will flunk it. The third criticism is that the test of time is biased in favor of works that are written in widely read languages and works that are easily translated; it is therefore biased in favor of drama and against poetry. This means that the test of time will yield different results—different lists of canonical literature—when administered in different cultures, as well as at different times. When *I* speak of the literary canon, therefore, it is the canon primarily as it is understood in England and America, and secondarily in Europe; not the canon as it is understood in India or China. Fourth—but this is really a limitation rather than an objection—the test of time doesn't tell us what we *should* read, because an ephemeral work, say of political satire, may be more important given our current interests than a classic. But this is just to say that our reading interests, even our fiction-reading interests, extend beyond literature.

I do not consider the objections to the test of time disabling—they just show that it is an imperfect test, but there is none better. But for present purposes all I need to show is that it is the *operational* test of greatness; for if so, it becomes easy to see why law is a common literary subject. It is a brute fact, whatever its normative significance, that a work of literature will survive in places and times remote from those in which it was created only if it deals with permanent (equivalently, "universal") features of the human condition. This was Samuel Johnson's explanation for Shakespeare's greatness.[22] It echoes Aristotle's distinction in the *Poetics* between history (concerned with particulars, with what actually happened) and poetry (concerned with probabilities, with the universal features of the human condition). Like love, maturation, accident, adventure, religion, friendship, alienation, death, war, and art itself, law is a permanent feature of human experience. Specific doctrines and procedures have changed greatly since distinct legal institutions first emerged in Western society, but not the broad features of law. The legal systems of Elizabethan England and even of Periclean Athens are readily accessible to a modern understanding. Between, on the one hand, the Austro-Hungarian procedures reflected in Kafka's *Trial* or the nineteenth-century Russian criminal procedures reflected in *Crime and Punishment* and *The Brothers Karamazov,* and, on the other hand, modern European and even American criminal procedure, the differences, while important to lawyers,

---

22. Johnson, note 2 above, at 301.

would seem small to most lay people.

So between two otherwise similar works of literature of a time remote from our own, one about law and the other about burial customs or tool making, the first is more likely to be still read in the twentieth century. But one must be careful about "about." Literature may contain many details of vanished social customs without being "about" them, or without being just about them. The Homeric epics explore the heroic code and contain a wealth of specific information, though much of it garbled, about Mycenaean culture. But if they were merely a depiction of vanished customs they would be read today just as historical or sociological source documents, as the Icelandic sagas largely are. And so would *Moby-Dick,* if it were just about the whaling industry and the pre-Darwinian understanding of the natural history of the whale.

John Ellis makes what turns out to be the related point that the question "what is literature?" is misleading.[23] There is no satisfactory analytical or definitional procedure for deciding whether a comic strip, Lincoln's second inaugural address, Pepys' diary, Gibbon's *Decline and Fall,* the Homeric epics, the Bible, Orwell's journalism, or *Guys and Dolls,* is literature. Literature is a label that we give to texts, of whatever character or provenance, that are meaningful for readers who were not in the writer's contemplation. Lincoln made a political address; we who may have no interest in the political setting and purpose of the speech—we eavesdroppers, as it were—value it for its imagery and cadences. *Gulliver's Travels* was written as a satire on eighteenth-century English politics; it is read today without reference to its satirical purpose. *Alice in Wonderland* was written for children and is read today by a great many adults as well. College courses with such titles as "The Bible as Literature" tell the whole story. The authors of the Bible did not think they were writing for future readers of "literature." Even Shakespeare may not have thought so, at least when writing plays, as he made no effort to revise them for publication or to get them published.[24] He may have thought of them as strictly quotidian produc-

23. Ellis, *The Theory of Literary Criticism: A Logical Analysis,* ch. 2 (1974).

24. See Bevington, note 17 above, at lxxxiv; S. Schoenbaum, *William Shakespeare: A Compact Documentary Life* 159, 188, 220 (1977). Shakespeare retired to Stratford several years before his death, a rather wealthy man, and could have taken steps to see to the preservation or publication of his plays. Absence of secure copyright protection, however, which I discuss in Chapter 11, may have been a factor. Shakespeare's sonnets, which were published in his lifetime, contain expressions—though possibly ironic ones—of a desire for the immortality of print. See the discussion of his Sonnet 65 at the end of Chapter 7. Ben Jonson, who greatly admired Shakespeare, published an edition of his own plays the year of Shakespeare's death. The first edition of Shakespeare's plays was published seven years later. Shakespeare died young (at 52); had he lived a few more years he might have arranged for their publication himself.

tions, a way of making money.

Ellis's definition must not be taken literally. If I use a Babylonian sacred text as a source for a history of Babylonia, I am not making a literary use of it. (I will be making a nonliterary use of *Njal's Saga* in the next chapter.) Aristotle wasn't writing for twentieth-century Americans; we read him, but not as literature. Ellis is right, however, to shift our attention from the intrinsic properties of the text to the uses made of it and to emphasize, as a necessary condition of a text's being literature, that it be read in a setting different from that of its creation. That is what I am calling "universality," and it invites us, as we begin to think about the "legal" novel or play, to distinguish between concrete legal problems, which lawyers are expert at solving, and broader issues of legality, governance, and justice that are grist for moral, political—and literary—examination rather than for technical legal analysis. Every society has machinery for resolving serious disputes in accordance with rules or customs deemed authoritative, in some sense official. Every such machinery runs into problems of "fit" between formal rules and application. These problems include the difficulty of ascertaining the facts that constitute the predicate for applying a rule, and the tendency of a rule to take a dichotomous cut at a continuous problem: classifying a person as disabled or not disabled, literate or illiterate, distinguishing between a business gift and a personal gift, distinguishing "speech" from "action"—in short, drawing clear lines where there are no lines.[25] Related problems are the inflexibility of rules, which creates an irresistible demand for principles of "equity" (see Chapter 3) to reduce the rigidity of the purely "legal" rules, and the problem with officials' discretion that arises if rules cannot be bent and have to be changed (who shall be authorized to change them, and on what grounds?), or if it is infeasible or undesirable to enforce a rule in all cases to which the rule applies. Closely related is the problem of the gap between the ethical or political principle that underlies a rule and the rule itself, which for purposes of administrability is likely to be much cruder than the principle. Thus, from the principle that there ought to be an end to disputes, the legal system may derive a rule that a particular type of claim is extinguished forever unless sued on within two years, no matter how meritorious the claim is or how trivial would be the inroads on the principle if a particular late suit (late by just a day, maybe) were allowed.

The frequent discontinuity between the spirit and letter of the law, or between its general aim and its concrete application, is one reason why law

---

25. At common law, burglary was breaking into a house *at night* with the intention of committing theft or some other crime in the house. At what moment does day become night?

so often strikes laymen as arbitrary. And law's apparently arbitrary and un-deniably coercive character, combined with the inevitable errors of fact and law in the administration of justice and the resulting miscarriages of justice, and with law's "otherness" (law, like language, the state, and the market economy, is a human institution frequently perceived as external to man, like a natural phenomenon), makes law a superb metaphor for the random, coercive, and "unfair" light in which the human condition—"life"—ap-pears to us in some moods.

Moreover, literature is characteristically dramatic, and thus traffics in conflict. As a system for managing conflict, law provides a rich stock of metaphors for writers to use. It also provides a ready-made dramatic tech-nique in the trial—especially the Anglo-American trial, which is more ad-versary, more theatrical, than its Continental counterpart.[26] Whether his-torically the trial is modeled on the theater and offers the litigants and society (the audience) the type of catharsis that the theater does, or vice versa, or whether both the trial and the drama have a common origin in religious rituals, few social practices are so readily transferable to a literary setting and so well suited to the literary depiction of conflict as the trial.[27] Particularly close is the parallel between the trial in literature and the play within the play (for example, in *Hamlet*). Both are techniques for creating an audience within the work of literature—the tribunal and spectators, in the case of the trial, the playgoers in the internal play—to play off against the audience for the work itself.

It does not follow that what is transferred when law is adapted for liter-ary use must retain its legal character. Vittoria's trial for adultery in Webster's play *The White Devil* begins with the prosecuting lawyer mum-bling incomprehensible legal jargon. The Cardinal, who is presiding, quickly shoos him off the stage and takes over the prosecutor's role. There is no more law talk in the trial. An analogy can be drawn to "academic"

---

26. The ancient Greek trial, incidentally, is more like the Anglo-American trial than the Continental European trial (the roots of which are Roman): more in the nature of a private con-test, a struggle, a drama, than an official inquiry.

27. Literal merger of trial and drama was achieved in a medieval "biblical drama in which a criminal playing the role of Hollophernes was actually beheaded on stage." Jody Enders, *Rhetoric and the Origins of Medieval Drama* 103 (1992). On the theatricality of trials and the forensic char-acter of drama, see Milner S. Ball, "The Play's the Thing: An Unscientific Reflection on Courts under the Rubric of Theater," 28 *Stanford Law Review* 81 (1975); Kathy Eden, *Poetic and Legal Fiction in the Aristotelian Tradition* (1986); see also my discussion of John Brown's trial in Chapter 10, and the discussion of the isomorphism between litigation and drama in ancient Athens in S. C. Todd, *The Shape of Athenian Law* 9 (1993). It may even be helpful to an understanding of judicial behavior to think of the judge as a more informed, more detached spectator of a drama staged by the lawyers. Richard A. Posner, *Overcoming Law* 126–130 (1995).

novels by such writers as Mary McCarthy, Bernard Malamud, C. P. Snow, and David Lodge. Despite these writers' first-hand familiarity with academic life, their novels convey little sense of what academics do that is different from what other people do. The focus—understandably, since the novelist is reaching out to an audience composed primarily of nonacademics—is on personal rivalries, foibles of character, comic predicaments, sexual adventures, and other aspects of conduct and character that academics share with other people, rather than on the things that set them apart.

And while the legal trial may have a dramatic structure, and some celebrated trials may have performed a cathartic role comparable to what Aristotle assigned to tragedy, the essential spirit of the law is not dramatic. Law's aim is to mediate, often to diffuse, but rarely if ever to aggravate, conflict. Most statutes represent compromises, and the vast majority of legal disputes are settled out of court. Judges in their decisions seek to reduce rather than increase social tensions. The resemblance between drama and trial may be superficial, making it all the more likely that any borrowing by the first from the second will be metaphoric.

Probably there is more great revenge literature than there is great literature about "official" law. Revenge has a form that can be imitated (in Aristotle's sense) by literature. Law is a complex of rules and institutions from which a writer can borrow but which does not lend itself to being imitated.

The American Legal Novel from Twain to Grisham

The elaboration and qualification of these theoretical points will occupy me intermittently throughout this book, beginning in this chapter with a discussion of several works of fiction, American and French, old and new, popular and classical, that are overtly about law. I aim to give some sense of the variety of the genre that we might call "imaginative literature with a legal subject." My sample is necessarily a small one and excludes interesting works by Auchincloss, Dreiser, Faulkner, Melville, Wouk, and Wright, to name only Americans, although I discuss Melville's *Billy Budd* in Chapter 5 and Richard Wright's *Native Son* in Chapter 9.

James Gould Cozzens's novel *The Just and the Unjust* (1942) is so pervasively and accurately "about" law that one might think the author an experienced lawyer. In fact he had no legal training and the book is not about law in any interesting sense. The novel is set in a small town in an unimportant rural county. A trio of repulsive hoodlums—Howell, Basso, and Bailey—has kidnapped Zollicoffer, a drug dealer. After the ransom has been paid, Bailey, deciding that it would be unsafe to return Zollicoffer alive, shoots him.

Howell and Basso help Bailey weight Zollicoffer's body down with leg irons and dump him into a river. Bailey later dies fleeing the police. Although Howell and Basso do not deny having taken an active part in the kidnapping, it never becomes clear whether they authorized, knew about in advance, or participated in the murder. They are prosecuted by the county's assistant district attorney, Abner Coates, who is young and able, but a bit priggish. He emphasizes to the jury, in urging a verdict of first-degree murder (which would mean the electric chair), that the defendants' lack of participation in the actual murder is irrelevant. So long as they took part in the kidnapping, as unquestionably they did, they are guilty of first-degree murder because Zollicoffer was killed in the course of a felony in which they participated. To the disgust of Coates and the judge (who dresses down the jury afterward), the jury convicts Howell and Basso only of second-degree murder. The author leads us to understand, through one of the wise old codgers who people the novel, that the jury has exercised its prerogative of nullifying a law that it considers unjust—the felony-murder rule, a legal fiction that punishes a felon who is not a murderer as if he were one.

While the trial is wending its way to its surprising conclusion—for the reader is given no clue that the jury might fail to return a verdict of first-degree murder—Coates is both getting engaged and agreeing to run for district attorney (the incumbent is leaving for another job). It is understood that Coates cannot lose the election; he is a Republican, and Republicans always win in this county. But to agree to run, Coates must overcome his aversion to the local Republican boss, who Coates fears will interfere in the D.A.'s office, though in fact the boss is pretty straight. The suspense in the novel is focused not on the trial, which seems a foregone conclusion, but on whether Coates will overcome his priggish scruples against marrying his utterly charming childhood sweetheart and accepting the tremendous career opportunity opened up by the D.A.'s impending departure.

From this brief summary it should be plain that *The Just and the Unjust* is not really about trial strategy, the legal profession, the felony-murder rule, or the power of juries to acquit lawlessly, and thus that critics miss the point when they accuse Cozzens of "belligerent legalistic conservatism."[28] This is a rite-of-passage novel, a *Bildungsroman*. The hero is a prissy kid at the beginning and a man at the end, having assumed family responsibilities and learned the difference between pure forms (of law, of career advancement) and sordid realities (law may diverge from the lay sense of justice, politics

---

28. John P. McWilliams, Jr., "Innocent Criminal or Criminal Innocence: The Trial in American Fiction," in Carl S. Smith, John P. McWilliams, Jr., and Maxwell Bloomfield, *Law and American Literature: A Collection of Essays* 45, 114 (1983).

influences promotions), as well as the need to compromise, to moderate demands, to scale down ideals, to trim absolutes, to empathize—with the Republican boss, and above all with his sweetheart, to whose feelings Coates is remarkably insensitive at the beginning of the novel. The work has none of the resonance of *Hamlet* or the *Iliad* but is recognizably part of the same broad category of works in which (as we shall see in the next chapter) youthful idealism becomes tempered with realism through a series of crises.

That the law is rather a detail in all this can be made clearer by a comparison with another and finer novel by Cozzens, *Guard of Honor,* possibly the finest American novel about World War II. Set in Florida, it recounts a brief period in the administration of an air base by a young major general. He is champing at the bit to be sent overseas to do more fighting (he had held a major command in the North African campaign). But we soon understand that his command of the base, which involves dealing with domestic crises that have no martial dimension (race relations, a training accident), is an important preparation for the major combat command that he is slated to assume next—and that, with nice irony, is the command of fighter cover for the invasion of Japan, which of course never took place. Again it is a rite-of-passage novel, with the professional setting, in this case military, again incidental. The hero, at first insufficiently worldly-wise to handle senior administrative responsibilities, like Coates matures in the course of the novel by meeting the challenges of everyday life.

If either novel were about the *professional* challenges of its protagonists—if either one showed lawyers correcting their legal errors or generals correcting their military errors—neither would have much appeal even to members of those professions. A novelist with neither legal nor military training is unlikely to have significant insights to impart at the level of practice.

Written toward the end of the nineteenth century, Mark Twain's *Pudd'nhead Wilson* is set in Dawson's Landing, an imaginary Missouri town on the Mississippi River. The title character moves to the town as a young man in 1830, hoping to practice law. His hopes are dashed by a joke he makes. A dog is annoying people with its barking. Wilson says that he would like to buy half the dog, and kill his half. The townspeople (extremely gullible hicks to a one) think Wilson is serious, pronounce him a "pudd'nhead," and refuse to give him any legal business. He bides his time, doing some surveying and accounting, and pursuing his hobby of fingerprinting (a novelty in 1830).

At about the same time that Wilson arrived in Dawson's Landing, Roxana, a slave in the household of the town's leading citizen, had given birth to a son. Roxana is fifteen parts white and one part black, while the child's father (another leading citizen) is all white; so the son, whom she names Chambers, is only one thirty-second black. The wife of Roxana's master had given birth to a son, Tom, at the same time as Roxana and died a week later, so Roxana must take full care of both children. Fearful that her child might one day be "sold down the river" (that is, to owners of cotton plantations, who treat their slaves much worse than the slaveholders in Missouri), Roxana switches the babies. Her inattentive master does not notice. Roxana brings up her son, Chambers, as "Tom," a white, and the real Tom as "Chambers," a black. "Chambers," the supposed black, turns out to be a sweet and noble character. "Tom," the supposed white, is a devil. His principal vice is gambling, and it leads him to theft—and worse. Roxana's master has meanwhile died in debt, and "Tom" has been adopted by his (supposed) uncle, a wealthy man. Roxana's master had freed her in his will, yet "Tom," with terrible, unconscious irony (considering the reason his mother had switched the babies in the first place), sells her down the river. "Tom's" career of crime reaches its culmination when he kills the uncle with a stolen knife during a botched attempt at theft.

Meanwhile the town had recently become home to—of all people—twin Italian counts. Bad blood has arisen between them and "Tom's" uncle, and they have the misfortune to be passing by the uncle's house when he is murdered. They hear his screams and rush in and are still there when the neighbors arrive. The murder weapon, which "Tom" has discarded in his flight, had been stolen from one of the twins. They are suspected of the murder and put on trial. Wilson defends them—it is his first big case. The evening before he is to put on what we are led to expect will be a hopeless defense, "Tom" is visiting him and happens to place his thumb on a glass slide from Wilson's fingerprint collection, leaving a print that Wilson immediately recognizes as the same one he had taken from "Tom" when "Tom" was seven months old. Wilson discovers the baby switch by examining the set of prints he had taken of Tom and Chambers when they were a few weeks old—for in that set Chambers has the same print as "Tom" and Tom, the real Tom, the same print as "Chambers."

The next day in court, Wilson presents blowups of the fingerprints. The twins are immediately released, and "Tom" (who was in the audience) is arrested. He is convicted of murder and sentenced to life imprisonment. But the uncle's creditors (the uncle, too, died poor) insist that he is their property and should be sold, and he is—down the river. "Chambers" is restored to his status as a white man. But because his accent, gait, and manners are incurably those of a slave, he cannot adjust happily to his new lot. Roxana, who had regained her freedom and was in the courtroom when

"Tom" was exposed as a slave and a murderer, is brokenhearted.

Although written a half-century before *The Just and the Unjust,* Mark Twain's novel seems more modern because of its irony, surrealism, and open-textured quality; it has a resonance (perhaps the serendipitous result of its author's careless revising![29]) and a fascination that Cozzens's novel lacks. The presence not only of the twin Italian counts but of Wilson himself in a southern backwater town is entirely incongruous; the townspeople are comically absurd; the treatment of white people as Negro slaves (first Roxana and Chambers, then Tom) as if it were the most natural thing in the world—no one in the novel remarks on the oddness of treating a person who to all appearances is white as if he were black—is sinisterly absurd. Yet there is no overt criticism of slavery or racism; and maybe the reader is being invited to agree with Roxana that the false Tom's one thirty-second part Negro ancestry is responsible for his villainous behavior. But maybe instead it is his spoiled "white" upbringing that is responsible. And the fact that environment makes white "Chambers" more Negro than "Tom" may be intended as a mordant commentary on bigotry.[30] Roxana is the most impressive character in the novel, while the white people, except for Wilson, are yokels or freaks. Yet I wonder whether the book is essentially about slavery or racism at all, let alone about law, rather than about the debate—very lively in the late nineteenth century—over Nature versus Nurture (or genetics versus environment); about how easily people are taken in by appearances; and about the triumph of science and rationality, in the person of Wilson, over rural ignorance and complacency.

Robin West believes that the novel contains an implicit criticism of legalism.[31] Wilson proves not only that the Italians are innocent (because the fingerprint on the murder weapon is "Tom's") but also that the murderer is a slave. West argues that by exposing "Tom," Wilson goes further than necessary to save his clients, and does so because, like most lawyers, he accepts uncritically the legal system, which happens to classify some people as slaves. Yet in light of what "Tom" had done to his mother, his being sold down the river is poetic justice; it is also a lighter punishment than he could have expected. And it is better that "Tom" should be exposed so that "Chambers" can be freed rather than being condemned to a lifetime

29. On which see Hershel Parker, *Flawed Texts and Verbal Icons: Literary Authority in American Fiction* 139–143 (1984).

30. On the difficulty of extracting Twain's views of race from *Puddn'head Wilson,* see Brook Thomas, *American Literary Realism and the Failed Promise of Contract* 199–208 (1997).

31. West, "Adjudication Is Not Interpretation: Some Reservations about the Law-as-Literature Movement," 54 *Tennessee Law Review* 203, 219–244 (1987) (reprinted as chapter 3 of her book *Narrative, Authority, and Law* [1993]).

of slavery, as he will be if the secret of the baby switching is buried with "Tom." In order to clinch the case for his clients, moreover, Wilson must produce not just a discrepant fingerprint but the real murderer—and "Tom" as the slave who usurped the real Tom's place is a more plausible candidate than if he were believed to be the victim's nephew. It is hard to find in any of this a basis for criticizing Wilson or his profession. In any case the novel places no emphasis on Wilson's legal skills or his acculturation as a lawyer; he owes his triumph in the Italians' trial to his scientific hobby. He is the American as garage tinkerer, not as lawyer. Maybe the reader is meant to look askance at Wilson for having become so well assimilated (at long last) into the hick society of Dawson's Landing that he has come to internalize its dubious values of chivalry, slavery, and racism. But there is no indication that we are meant to infer that his legal education and scarcely employed legal skills are responsible.

The Just and the Unjust and *Pudd'nhead Wilson* are a half century and a century old, respectively, and I turn now to some contemporary American legal novels, beginning with Tom Wolfe's satiric *The Bonfire of the Vanities* (1987). The novel depicts its protagonist, Sherman McCoy, enmeshed in the coarse, dingy, and sordid operation that is, according to Wolfe, the Bronx criminal justice system today. McCoy had picked up his mistress, Maria Ruskin, at Kennedy Airport in his sports car and on the way back to Manhattan had gotten lost in the South Bronx. A couple of teenagers—one a drug dealer ("The Crack King of Evergreen Avenue")—had thrown a tire in front of the car, and when McCoy got out to move it, they approached him in a menacing fashion. A scuffle ensued. Maria took the wheel. McCoy jumped back into the car, which as it pulled away hit the Crack King's companion. Maria didn't stop, and neither she nor McCoy reported the incident to the police. Eventually, McCoy is investigated, questioned, arrested, and indicted for vehicular manslaughter. The prosecutors, abetted by self-appointed black leaders, knee-jerk liberals and radicals (such as the "Gay Fist Strike Force Against Racism"), and a scandal-mongering press, portray the victim of the homicide to a credulous public as the honor student that he is not. After the first indictment of McCoy is dismissed because of false testimony before the grand jury, he is reindicted. An epilogue briefly recounts his trial, which ends in a hung jury; when the novel ends he is about to be retried.

Since *The Bonfire of the Vanities* was published so recently, it can't have passed the test of time. That test excludes the literature of the present day, whether it belongs to "popular" culture (as Shakespeare's plays originally did) or is aimed at a cultural elite. Today's popular culture is saturated with law, however, and there is no reason why the treatment of law in it should be less illuminating than the treatment of law in literary classics. But it is unlikely to be much more illuminating. The author of a classic accretes a large audience over time; the author of a best seller accretes a large audience in a short time; in either case the display of an esoteric or technician's interest in the workings of a social institution, even one as interesting and important as law, will reduce the appeal of the work, making it less likely that it will be either a best seller or a classic. But there is an important difference between these two classes of work. The legal system depicted in a best seller is almost always going to be the *contemporary* legal system, which suggests that popular literature about law may play a role in shaping popular understanding of law. It is teacher rather than just mirror, and we can ask whether it is a good teacher or, instead, presents either too pollyannish or too cynical a picture. The popular television series *L.A. Law* made the practice of law seem more exciting than it is. The dominant mood of today's popular novels about law is realism verging on cynicism.

The Bonfire of the Vanities is attentive to the criminal process and its personnel. Larry Kramer, the assistant D.A. who prosecutes McCoy, is one of the principal supporting characters in the novel, along with Kovitsky, the judge in the case. The novel's gallery of minor characters includes the publicity-seeking D.A. himself, other lawyers, other defendants, court officers, and a juror, "the Girl with Brown Lipstick," whom Kramer pursues with a comic ineptness that culminates in scandal when he tries to rent for their trysts the rent-controlled "love nest" in which McCoy and Maria Ruskin had held *their* trysts. In addition to the proceedings directly involving McCoy, Wolfe treats us to an extended episode of plea bargaining and to a portion of a homicide trial.

Wolfe's novel makes several points that ought to interest lawyers in their professional capacity, as well as the broader public. These include the danger of misusing the legal process for political ends; the radicalizing effect (on McCoy) of being prosecuted (as the old saw goes, if a conservative is a liberal who has been mugged, a liberal is a conservative who has been arrested); the capacity of a public arrest to inflict profound, life-altering humiliation, making the actual outcome of the criminal process almost a side issue;[32] the effect

32. The mistreatment by the American criminal justice system of persons charged but not yet convicted of crime is an international scandal. People accused of white-collar crimes are arrested in the most public and shaming manner possible and led in handcuffs to jail to be booked, but are then released on bond. People accused of crimes of violence are generally though not always drawn from social strata in which a public arrest is not a conspicuous badge of shame, but neither are they released on bond; they are thrown into jail to languish, sometimes for many months and often in horrible conditions, while awaiting trial. It is curious that the arrest of Joseph K. in the first chapter of *The Trial* is more *civilized* than arrests in the land of freedom at the threshold of the twenty-first century.

of racial hostility on the rule of law; the difficulty of attaining justice across large differences in social class; even the difficulty of reconstructing history by the methods of litigation. Wolfe writes about the contemporary American legal system with something approaching prophetic insight—the sort of thing we tend to ascribe to Kafka—although as yet it is short-term. Often today the stage on which American legal justice is played is a bizarre intersection of race, money, publicity, and violence, an intersection perfectly described in *The Bonfire of the Vanities* even though the book was written before the intersection had come into view.

The legal theme fits nicely with Wolfe's evident desire to skewer the diverse social classes and ethnic groupings that coexist uneasily in New York City. The book exploits to the hilt New York's most arresting characteristic—the juxtaposition of grotesque extremes of opulence and squalor, the former symbolized by McCoy and his Park Avenue-Wall Street set, the latter by the Bronx County Criminal Court with its crummy and overcrowded facilities, its clientele of black and Hispanic criminals, and its harried, underpaid, precariously middle-class personnel. Shuttling between the extremes is a rich cast of hustlers, social climbers, toadies, hangers-on, and con men, seeking to share in the opulence and avoid sinking into the squalor. There is an *egregious* quality about New York that provides a field day for a sharp-eyed and sharp-tongued social satirist. Wolfe has a particularly keen eye for prices and for how people dress, and for dialect. True, he exaggerates the sordidness of New York, and, prophet though he is, failed to predict the recent dramatic improvements in the quality of life in New York. But he exaggerates less by misdescribing—I am told on good authority that his portrayal of the Bronx County Criminal Court is essentially accurate, although its environs are not *quite* so hellish as he describes, and indeed that the entire book is a *roman à clef* populated by institutions and characters instantly recognizable to knowledgeable New Yorkers—than by suppressing complexity. And that is the satirist's privilege. Wolfe is in the tradition of Bosch and Swift in portraying humanity at its worst. It is therefore part of his method to present a one-sided view of his subject,

The Bonfire of the Vanities is not a "great" novel, if one's touchstone is Dickens or Dostoevsky. Its plot is merely a thread connecting a series of tableaux. Its characters are shallow and are revealed to the reader by the simplistic device of making him privy to their thoughts. The writing is pedestrian. And about two-thirds of the way through the novel the author's energy flags. Satire increasingly gives way to broad and eventually tedious burlesque. The scene in which a courtroom mob attacks Judge Kovitsky for dismissing the indictment against McCoy is overdone and implausible;

the halo around Kovitsky's head at this point shines too brightly. And the hints of redemption for McCoy that Wolfe starts to drop are maudlin. The book peters out; Wolfe seems to have had no idea how to end it.

But this, the collapse of the book two-thirds of the way through, is the only criticism that counts. That the book lacks a rich plot and multidimensional characters and distinguished prose merely identifies it as a certain type of novel; for the same observations could be made about *Nineteen Eighty-Four*. The "novel" is not a closed genre. The satirical or political novel—*The Bonfire of the Vanities* is both—should not be judged by its resemblance to novels of a psychological or philosophical character—or to novels *deeply* interested in law or justice. The depiction of the criminal process in *The Brothers Karamazov* is designed, as we shall see in Chapter 5, not merely to provide local color or narrative suspense, or to be a caricature or an exposé, but to contrast rational inquiry, exemplified by the criminal justice system, with religious insight—to the disadvantage of the former. The only religions in *The Bonfire of the Vanities* are the Reverend Bacon's extortion racket and the Wall Streeters' worship of Mammon. The law for Wolfe is simply another setting—no different in any material respect from a dinner party on Park Avenue, or a dinner at a fancy restaurant, or the "ant colony" where Larry Kramer lives with his wife, infant, and au pair girl on his meager civil servant's salary—in which to observe the comic pratfalls of trivial people. Although the politicization of prosecutors' offices and the assembly-line character of criminal justice in the nation's big cities are genuine social problems that the novel vividly depicts, there is no suggestion that any of these problems might be alleviated, let alone solved.[33] On the contrary, the reader is led to believe that the present criminal justice system of the Bronx will soon give way to one dominated by the minority that is already a majority in the Bronx and that *that* system will be even worse than the present one, for there will be no Kovitskys in it. To stimulate social reform (other than by proposing some "invisible hand" mechanism that will turn private greed into social benefit) an author must convey the impression that there are *some* good people in the society. If there are none, not only is reform unlikely to succeed but there is no reason we should *want* it to succeed. New Yorkers, as depicted by Tom Wolfe, are mostly freaks and monsters who neither deserve a better system nor would profit from it, save in the mercenary sense.

Although we expect popular literature about law to tell us a lot about how lay people view law, we learn nothing from *The Bonfire of the Vanities* on this score that the classic legal novels, such as *The Brothers Karamazov*

---

33. This is also a limitation of Dickens's satire, as we'll see in Chapter 4.

and *Pickwick Papers,* had not taught us already. We learn that lay people expect technicalities to matter (and it is on a technicality that the first indictment against McCoy is dismissed) and are not surprised when miscarriages of justice occur (McCoy, remember, is innocent of the homicide charge, and the real culprits are used as false witnesses by the prosecution), and that they expect legal proceedings to be interminable and excruciatingly expensive and are unillusioned about the moral and intellectual shortcomings of judges, lawyers, jurors, and other participants in the machinery of legal justice and about the corrosion of that machinery by political and personal ambitions. Judge Kovitsky does get to make a Law Day speech to Larry Kramer: "What makes you think you can come before the bench waving the banner of community pressure? The law is not a creature of the few or of the many. The court is not swayed by your threats."[34] But he is duly punished for his independence: he is denied renomination. The public is more cynical about law than the profession is, and it is useful for legal professionals to be reminded of this from time to time.

William Gaddis's legal novel, *A Frolic of His Own,* is even more recent (1994) than *The Bonfire of the Vanities.* It is not, however, a work of popular culture. Allusive, erudite and even esoteric, syntactically complex, "high modernist" in style, it is a difficult read—the most difficult of any of the books discussed in this chapter. And yet, in tension with my discussion of the polarity between literature and topicality, it is even more saturated with contemporary American law than is Wolfe's novel. It depicts many more lawsuits and contains far more of the texture of the law. There are three long judicial opinions, a set of elaborate jury instructions, and a deposition. And all the litigation is civil litigation. Wolfe took the easy way out of public ignorance about law by using as the spine of his novel a criminal case. Criminal law and criminal procedure are more familiar to the lay person than civil law and civil procedure and generally less complex.

The legal theme is announced in the title. A "frolic," as one of the characters explains, is a concept in the law of agency. An employer is not liable for a tort committed by an employee, even if it occurs during working hours, if the employee was on a "frolic," that is, was engaged in an activity unrelated to his employment. Oscar Crease is on a "frolic" in a different sense, though a sense that turns out to be charged with legal significance. He is a disheveled, reclusive, unmarried, eccentric, selfish, childless, middle-aged skinflint who lectures on the history of the American Civil War at a small college and lives on a ramshackle but pricey

---

34. Page 676 in the 1988 paperback edition of the novel.

property in Long Island, mainly on the income from a trust fund. His grandfather was, like Oliver Wendell Holmes, a Civil War veteran and Supreme Court Justice. His father is a 97-year-old federal district judge in South Carolina who has been nominated for the federal court of appeals. (Nonagenarian district judges are not promoted, so here is an early clue that the novel has fantasy elements, along with a good deal of gritty realism— a combination familiar from *Bleak House*.) Oscar had years earlier written a play about his grandfather (the play was his "frolic"), who after being slightly wounded fighting for the South in the Civil War moves north to claim a coal mine in Pennsylvania that he has inherited. He hires a substitute to take his place in the Confederate army and then, threatened with being drafted into the Union army after his move to Pennsylvania, hires another substitute to fight for the Union. The two substitutes find themselves in opposing regiments at the battle of Antietam—and (in the play anyway, a wonderful Faulknerian mishmash garnished with passages lifted almost verbatim from Plato's dialogues on the trial and condemnation of Socrates) they kill each other, which grandfather regards as a kind of spiritual suicide of himself. The play, naturally, has never been produced.

When Oscar hears about a new movie that seems to bear a striking resemblance to his play, a copy of which he had sent many years ago to the movie's producer, he decides to sue for copyright infringement. The case looks absolutely hopeless. Oscar has not seen the movie and can't even find the letter from the producer acknowledging receipt of the play years earlier. He can't claim copyright protection for the Civil War or his grandfather's life,[35] let alone for his plagiarisms of Plato (presumably not reproduced in the movie, however). Oscar's lawyer, moreover, turns out to be an impostor and vanishes during the course of the litigation. Oscar is up against one of the biggest law firms in New York, and is ripped apart at his deposition by the brilliant young comer at the firm. Sure enough, summary judgment is granted against Oscar. But then his father takes a hand in the case (not for love of his son, but for love of the law—his only love), actually drafting the appeal brief. The appeal succeeds. The appellate court (the U.S. Court of Appeals for the Second Circuit, no less) recognizes the hand of a fellow judge, and the circuit judge who writes the opinion reversing the district judge dislikes female judges—the district judge in Oscar's case is a woman. Yet the opinion the circuit judge writes is very fine, and we understand that Oscar really did have a strong case all along. But another peripeteia is in store. The suit was for the profits of the movie and now they must be calculated. Through imaginative accounting the producer is able to convince

35. See Matthews v. Wozencraft, 15 F.3d 432, 437–439 (5th Cir. 1994).

the court that although the movie grossed almost $400 million there are no profits, and if there were, they would be attributable not to Oscar's stolen play but to the "Nordic-Eurasian tits" of the female star.

The copyright suit is one of more than a dozen suits described or mentioned in the book.[36] In another one of the suits Oscar is suing himself for an injury that he sustained when his car ran over him while he was jump-starting it. (He was too cheap to repair the ignition.) In another, his father is presiding over a wrongful-death suit brought against a minister by the family of a child who drowned while the minister was baptizing him. Judge Crease's instructions to the jury in that case intimate a possible liability of God, as the minister's principal. Judge Crease also presides over a series of suits arising from a bizarre accident in a hick town in his district. A sculptor—the sort of sculptor whom the National Endowment for the Arts likes to support—has erected a huge and hideous structure (it is meant to mock its setting, but the locals eventually discover and happily exploit its tourism potential), and a dog has wandered in and got stuck. The dog's owner summons the fire department to dismantle the structure with acetylene torches, but the sculptor obtains a preliminary injunction from Judge Crease.[37] Then lightning strikes the sculpture and kills the dog, ruining the chances for Judge Crease's promotion and even leading to calls for his impeachment.

The moral center of the novel is Oscar's stepsister, Christina, who tries to keep him and his dumb-blonde girlfriend out of trouble and whose description of the legal profession as a "self regulating conspiracy" appears to state the author's view. Christina's husband, Harry Lutz, a partner in the firm that represents the producer in Oscar's suit, and a nice guy, works himself literally to death. For nowadays being a partner in a large law firm is, as he explains, "like sailing through the strait of Messina between Scylla and Charybdis. You make partner, make senior partner with a fine old reputable white shoe firm used to mean you were set for life, now you've got the sea monster's cave on one side and a whirlpool on the other, liability as a partner you're on board risking being devoured by these monstrous suits and government regulators or sucked under and drowned in the unemployment pool" (p. 422). Christina is counting on Harry's $500,000 life

---

36. See Larry M. Wertheim, "Law as Frolic: Law and Literature in *A Frolic of His Own*," 21 *William Mitchell Law Review* 421, 425–445 (1995).

37. Although ruling ultimately for the sculptor, the judge rejects the sculptor's defense of animal trespass, on the ground that the town's leash law "appears more honored in the breach, in that on any pleasant day well known members of the local dog community are to be observed in all their disparity of size, breed, and other particulars ambling in the raffish camaraderie of sailors ashore down the Village main street and thence wherever habit and appetite may take them undeterred by any citizen or arm of the law" (p. 31 of the paperback edition).

insurance policy to tide her over. His firm tells her it's worried he may have committed suicide, a cause of death excluded from the policy's coverage. Christina provides the firm with convincing evidence that her husband's death was not suicide—only to discover that the beneficiary of the policy is not she, but the firm.

The paperback jacket copy describes *A Frolic of His Own* as "Swiftian." That is accurate to the extent that Gaddis has a bleak vision of a nation devoured by greed, a nation whose legal system is completely characterized by Ambrose Beirce's definition of litigation as a process that you go into as a pig and come out of as a sausage. But the presiding spirits are Sterne and Joyce rather than Swift. One cannot help liking the nutty Uncle Toby-style Oscar, whose suit against the movie industry is, in its own crazy and lucre-tinged fashion, a quest for justice and a challenge to the hideous wave of popular culture that is engulfing his exurban world. But the quest is a failure, and not only because Hollywood gets to keep its profits. The television is always on in Oscar's house. He orders a fish tank, provoking this reflection from Christina—

a fish tank? when they could better be watched in living colour and much wilder variety spawning and feeding, fin ripping and vacant staring glassy eyed from far grander submarine vistas and exotic plant and coral strewn habitats right on his nature program, spared those custodial concerns for wind and wave, temperature and salinity, aeration, pH balance, light and filtration and the daily toll of all those mouths to feed confined, best of all, where they could be summoned and banished in an instant like those hordes of his own species crowding the channels elsewhere rather than actually having them all over the house here firing guns, spouting news events, telling jokes, doing pushups, deep knee bends, shuddering with diarrhea, howling half dressed and full of passionate intensity humping guitars like the monkey with the greased football loosing mere anarchy upon the world where three's a crowd even in a house as large as this one. (pp. 282–283)

The movie stolen from Oscar's book is finally shown on television, and he watches it—rapt. The hyperrealistic battle scenes—the movie's producer is the king of gory special effects—enchant him. Gaddis's rendition of the battle scenes, like his descriptions of television programming (which are a leitmotif of the book), is dazzling.

Greed, litigiousness, media that lack any decorum or restraint, false values—all this sounds much like *The Bonfire of the Vanities.* Both Wolfe's and Gaddis's works are satiric novels, funny but bleak, that portray the contemporary American legal system, viewed as a microcosm of American (in *Bonfire,* of New York) culture, in unflattering colors. But the resemblance between the two novels is superficial. They reflect different sensibilities. Wolfe's characters are cardboard figures, and their lack of depth reflects the author's style—for the most part pedestrian journalese. The characters elicit no sympathy from the reader. The satire is also localized to New York City. Gaddis's characters, at least the main ones,[38] are human victims of a tawdry, frenetic, spiritually empty culture dominated by mind-destroying media and a Darwinian legal system. It is the culture of America circa 1990 as seen by Gaddis's too-jaundiced eye, but it could equally be the London of "The Waste Land" or even one of the circles of Dante's Inferno. The humor is often as broad as in Wolfe's novel, but *A Frolic of His Own* has greater depth, resonance, and humanity.

The legal detail is extraordinarily dense (it must be hard going for a reader who is not a lawyer), and except for the deliberate comic touches is realistic and accurate. Not only the copyright case, which raises issues that I'll be discussing in the last chapter, but also the cases arising from the immurement and subsequent death of the dog trapped in the sculpture, could be made the basis of law-school exam questions. The deposition of Oscar, in which the opposing lawyers spend most of their time interrupting each other, could be used in a course in pretrial procedure. And there is a marvelous description by Harry Lutz, forecasting the young hot shot's losing the case brought by Oscar, of what it can be like to argue a case before an appellate court:

> I don't think he's ever handled a case before the Second Circuit Appeals Court. Probably march in there with a twenty page brief ready to read every word of his brilliant legal analysis to these three old black robes sitting up there looking down at him and I mean looking down, he's standing at a lectern down in the well and they're up in their highbacked thrones behind this polished mahogany sort of horseshoe courteous, relaxed, really forbidding, almost informal and that's what's formidable about it. He starts off with something like in order to fully understand this case one of them cuts him right off. We're familiar with the case, Counsel, is there anything you wish to add to what is contained in your brief? Your honour, if I may be allowed to outline the facts . . . I believe we understand the facts, Counsel. If it please the court, the public interest in the far reaching cultural implications of this case and [Judge] Bone cuts right in, I remind Counsel that we are here to serve the public interest. Your case is thus and so, goes right to the heart of it, sums up the argument in a couple of sentences and asks counsel to sit down, poor bastard's got himself up for a real performance and the place, the whole atmosphere's like a theatre but they're not there for a matinee and his whole star turn goes out the window, a few more questions and down comes the curtain.   (p. 347)

---

38. Trish, Christina's very wealthy, very madcap old school chum, could have stepped straight out of *The Bonfire of the Vanities*.

But as with most other works of imaginative literature that take law for their theme, the heart of this fascinating novel lies elsewhere than in its critique of law. The impression that lingers is of the hapless characters caught in the webs of modern American trash culture (of which law is one), rather than of the webs themselves.

At the border between the legal novel and the detective story—either a mystery proper, or a crime story in which the culprit is known to the reader at the start and the "mystery" is how he will be brought to justice—is the "legal thriller." This is the most popular subgenre of the American legal novel. *The Bonfire of the Vanities* and even *Pudd'nhead Wilson* revolve around an unsolved crime, but in neither case is the process by which it is solved (in Wolfe's novel it is never solved) central to the reader's interest in the work. In contrast, Scott Turow's novel *Presumed Innocent*,[39] though written by an able and experienced lawyer and full of accurate legal detail, is *au fond* a murder mystery. In the popular novels of John Grisham, another lawyer, although the focus is on the solution of the crime, the law is such a pervasive presence that these novels are properly classified as legal thrillers rather than as detective stories. True mass-market best sellers, moreover, they provide insight into the depiction of law in popular fiction.

In Grisham's novel *The Client* (1993), an eleven-year-old boy, Mark, stumbles upon the attempted suicide of a "mob" lawyer. Before he finally succeeds in killing himself, the lawyer reveals to Mark the location of the body of a U.S. Senator assassinated by the mob. The mobster who did the "hit" has been indicted, but because the evidence against him is weak, the absence of the body is a major embarrassment to the prosecution. The U.S. Attorney and the FBI are desperate to find the body, and the mob is equally desperate to conceal its whereabouts. Mark, a street-smart lower-class son of an abused (now divorced) wife, is caught between two almost equally unsavory adversaries—federal law enforcement authorities led by a ruthless, publicity-mad, even sadistic U.S. Attorney (who "loved those moments when the power of the federal government shifted into high gear and landed hard on small, unsuspecting people"[40]) and staffed by thuggish, lawless FBI agents, versus the tentacular, vengeance-obsessed Mafia. But with the aid of a divorced, middle-aged, formerly drug-addicted woman lawyer who devotes herself to representing juveniles who

39. Perceptively discussed in Carol Sanger, "Seasoned to the Use," 87 *Michigan Law Review* 1338 (1989).
40. Page 261 of the paperback edition.

are in legal trouble, Mark triumphs over both the law and the outlaws. He produces the body to the FBI in circumstances that enable him to negotiate a uniquely favorable package of witness-protective provisions— not only plenty of money and new identities but also psychiatric care for his younger brother. En route a gruff, shrewd, heart-of-gold black juvenile-court judge modeled on Thurgood Marshall resists, for a time successfully, the efforts of the feds to obtain custody of Mark so that they can grill him about the whereabouts of the senator's body. The novel raises but does not resolve the question whether a subpoena issued to a witness by a federal district court can wrest a juvenile from the custody of a state juvenile court (it can).

The theme of *The Client* is the triumph of the underdog. A lower-class kid—a modern Huck Finn—and his déclassée female lawyer outwit the rich and powerful, including an unsavory legal establishment and its illegal counterestablishment. The novel thus is egalitarian and politically correct, even to the extent that the lawyer's secretary is a wimpish man. But these whiffs of ideology, along with the legal details, are minor variations on the standard adventure-yarn theme of the innocent hero who is being pursued by two sets of bad guys and manages eventually to turn the tables on both. The author's object in such a yarn is to keep the reader wondering how on earth the hero is going to triumph against such long odds. At this level, *The Client* succeeds. But at no other. The book is written at a child's reading level. Every character speaks alike, but it is uncertain whether Mark sounds just like the other characters because Grisham does not have an ear for an eleven-year-old's diction, or because the other characters have the diction of an eleven-year-old. The opening scene—the protracted attempted suicide—is so flat and preposterous that it is laughable. Neither the good guys nor the bad guys have any depth. The novel is set in Memphis and New Orleans, but it has no sense of place, and therefore cannot be read as a plausible or informed commentary on actual conditions in those cities or the nation as a whole.

Grisham's best-known novel, *The Firm* (1991), is tauter, more ingenious, more suspenseful than *The Client*. The story line, though, is basically the same. The innocent—this time an associate in a law firm—is pursued by the FBI and the mob and eventually negotiates a deal with the FBI that (along with a theft from the mob) enables him and his family to live in safety on $8 million. Mitch McDeere, a newly minted top-ranking graduate of the Harvard Law School, is hired by a small, discreet Memphis law firm that unexpectedly pays the highest salaries and offers the most generous perks of any law firm in the country. At first we think it is just the usual Faustian pact with a law firm: you get hooked on the money and don't realize till too late that in exchange you are going to have to work like a dog on dull and unrewarding projects and your marriage will break up because you are never at home. We soon discover that something far more sinister is involved. The law firm is owned by the Chicago mob (whose power, incidentally, the novel greatly exaggerates). The firm's function is to launder the money that the mob takes in from its illegal enterprises. The firm also has legitimate clients in order to maintain a respectable front. Brand-new associates work only on those clients' matters. But after a few years the associate is informed of the true nature of the firm. By then he is hooked by his high income; the law firm is careful always to hire young men who are married and come from poor backgrounds, and it encourages them to have children—so that they cannot afford to quit. Our hero is also compromised by having worked, all unknowingly, on illegal matters. No one has ever quit the firm. Anyone who tries is killed in a staged accident; there have been five such deaths. The FBI approaches Mitch and tells him what is going on and asks him to work for them as a confidential informant. He agrees, in part because he is told that otherwise he will be prosecuted as soon as the FBI gathers enough evidence to bust the firm. But, like Mark, he distrusts the FBI. The wisdom of his distrust is confirmed when it turns out that the FBI has a high-ranking mole who informs the mob that Mitch is working against it.

The Firm could be read as an allegory of professional greed and amorality, but is better read as an engaging potboiler. Its simple vocabulary and syntax, stick-figure good guys—always from the lower or lower-middle class, such as Mitch's brother, a convicted attempted murderer who saves the day for Mitch and Mitch's wife at the end of the book—and bad guys, cinematically swift pace, and raised lettering on the cover proclaim it a book aimed at the lowest common denominator of literary taste. The questions about today's legal profession at which *The Firm* glances—whether there are too many lawyers and whether their ethical standards are too low and their pay too high and the working conditions of young lawyers too exploitative despite the high pay—are difficult and are not illuminated by the novel. The people who will read it with real absorption are not likely to be influential on matters of professional regulation, and the highly educated and influential people who read it—and many will—will do so only to rest their brains when a television set is not at hand.

If you compare the depiction of law in sophisticated modern novels like *The Bonfire of the Vanities* and *A Frolic of His Own* with its depiction in Grisham's popular (and populist) fiction, you will not see much difference. In both sets of novels the depiction is negative: the law is a racket and lawyers are shysters. Here and there a ray of sunlight penetrates the fog.

Wolfe has Judge Kovitsky, and Grisham has both Judge Roosevelt (the black juvenile-court judge) and Mark's lawyer, but both novelists emphasize the marginality of their "good" judges or lawyers to the profession. The negative depiction of lawyers in the modern American novel taps into a very old vein of hostility to the legal profession, a hostility strongly marked, for example, in Dickens, and a newer hostility to authority generally. The number and wealth of American lawyers today, their role in well-publicized miscarriages of justice, and the difficulty that lay people have grasping the social function of representation of criminals and other bad people may explain why lawyers have become such an attractive target for the darts of the satirist and the mass-market novelist. Lawyer-baiting in fiction belongs to the same genre as lawyer jokes, and is growing with them.[41]

Camus and Stendhal

Camus's celebrated short novel (novella) *The Stranger* (1940)[42] was written at about the same time as *The Just and the Unjust* and is also centered on a trial for homicide. Yet the two works could not be more different morally and aesthetically, and this is a clue to the heterogeneous character of the genre ("imaginative literature on legal themes") that I am examining. *The Stranger* is narrated by its protagonist, Meursault, a *pied noir* (a European as distinct from an Arab resident of Algeria, then still a part of France). It opens with the death of Meursault's mother. Through his reaction to her death we learn that he does not think about past or future, does not form deep emotional attachments, lacks ambition, piety, pretension—and for that matter a conscience. He is innocent, but as an animal is innocent. He's a loner, and amoral, but his passive, anesthetized manner belies any suggestion that he might be either a pagan sensualist or a rebel and nonconformist.

41. Carl T. Bogus, "The Death of an Honorable Profession," 71 *Indiana Law Journal* 911, 914–922 (1996), argues plausibly that the depiction of the lawyer in popular fiction is a good index to vicissitudes in the public respect for lawyers. See also David Ray Papke, "The Advocate's Malaise: Contemporary American Lawyer Novels," 38 *Journal of Legal Education* 413 (1988). On the depiction of law in popular culture generally, see Lawrence M. Friedman, "Law, Lawyers, and Popular Culture," 98 *Yale Law Journal* 1579 (1989); Sanger, note 39 above; *Law and Literature: A Collection of Essays on John Grisham's* The Rainmaker, 26 *University of Memphis Law Review* 1251 (1996). *The Rainmaker* (1995), a novel about the awful ethics of lawyers engaged in civil litigation, is less garish and sensationalistic than Grisham's other novels.

42. A misleading translation. The primary meaning of *étranger*, and the meaning that fits the novella, is "outsider," "alien," or "foreigner" (it is the word translated as "foreign" in "French Foreign Legion"). Meursault is an outsider or (spiritual) foreigner to his society.

The day after his mother's funeral, Meursault begins sleeping with a new girlfriend, Marie. He later accepts her proposal of marriage, while admitting to her that he does not love her and would probably have accepted the same proposal from any number of other women. But before he and Marie get around to marrying, he and his pals get into a fight with a group of Arabs as a result of some disreputable business in which one of the pals had been involved—and had received Meursault's help, characteristically given with neither enthusiasm nor reluctance, but simply because he had been asked. Later that day Meursault finds himself walking alone on the beach, still carrying the friend's revolver lent him during the fight (in which no shots had been fired). He sees one of the Arabs lying ahead of him on the beach. The sun is beating down mercilessly. Meursault continues walking toward the Arab, without knowing why. The Arab draws a knife but makes no threatening gesture with it. There is no suggestion that Meursault feels endangered. Nevertheless he shoots the Arab, once—and, after a pause, four more times.

He is arrested, and in accordance with French procedure is questioned by an examining magistrate, a kind of cross between a judge and a prosecutor. The questioning brings out what the examining magistrate considers Meursault's disgusting callousness, demonstrated by his lack of emotional response both to his mother's death and the Arab's, his beginning his affair with Marie the day after his mother's funeral, and his rejection of Christianity. The prosecutor harps skillfully on these features of Meursault's character at the trial, and the jury brings in a verdict of first-degree murder. Meursault is sentenced to be guillotined. In prison, awaiting execution, Meursault fiercely rejects the efforts of the prison chaplain to convert him to Christianity. He has lost his earlier inarticulateness. Awareness of impending death has given him a voice and made him for the first time fully conscious, fully human, and (paradoxically—since he's imprisoned and about to die) fully in control of his life.[43]

The contrast with the other novels discussed in this chapter (even Grisham's), so far as the author's "take" on the criminal justice system is concerned, is striking. Camus tells his story through the eyes of the criminal and makes the trial a sinister farce in which the defendant is condemned not for committing murder but for rejecting bourgeois Christian values. The murder victim is nameless and faceless. The impending execution of Meursault—the only fully realized character in the novella—is made to seem a far worse crime than the murder, which indeed is made to seem an unimportant incident on a par with Meursault's having forgotten how

43. See the excellent discussion in Robert C. Solomon, *"L'Étranger* and the Truth," 2 *Philosophy and Literature* 141 (1978).

old his mother was when she died.

What will strike an American lawyer as particularly odd is how evidence of Meursault's "bad" character (bad in the conventional sense rejected by the novella) is allowed into the trial and indeed becomes the decisive factor in his condemnation. In an American trial the character evidence so damaging to Meursault's chances would not have been let in. Character evidence is not admissible in our courts to show that the defendant acted in conformity with his character in the incident for which he is being prosecuted.[44] It is admissible to prove motive, knowledge, and other dispositions or facts that bear directly on an issue in the case rather than on the defendant's general propensity to do bad things, but Meursault's behavior toward his mother and his rejection of Christianity are too remote from the crime to be admissible for any of these purposes.[45] Yet the admission of this evidence was probably not a violation of French criminal procedure. French law does not limit evidence of bad character.[46] On the contrary, the French Code of Criminal Procedure provides that "witnesses shall testify only either on the facts charged against the accused *or on his character and morals.*"[47] And consistent with the inquisitorial tradition of Continental procedure, a French criminal trial begins with the interrogation of the defendant by the presiding judge in open court and so in the hearing of the jury, and no details of the defendant's personal history—many of which will be in a dossier compiled during the investigation of the crime—are out

44. See Rule 404 of the Federal Rules of Evidence and the accompanying Note of Advisory Committee.

45. Inquiry into a defendant's religious beliefs or lack thereof would be unthinkable in an American court.

46. Roger Merle and André Vitu, *Traité de Droit Criminel*, vol. 2, pp. 155, 165–166 (3d ed. 1979).

47. *The French Code of Criminal Procedure* 116 (Gerald L. Kock trans. 1964) (article 331) (emphasis added). At the time Camus wrote *The Stranger*, the code did not contain any restriction on the scope of a witness's testimony. See *Code d'Instruction Criminelle* art. 317 (1932). The type of character evidence introduced in Meursault's trial would be admissible even today in a French criminal trial. Maurice Payrot, "Aux assises de Paris: Un accusé qui s'affirme non-violent repond d'une tentative de viol," *Le Monde*, Sept. 12, 1987, at 11, describes a trial in the Cour d'Assises, the French felony court, for attempted rape. The tribunal consisted of three professional judges and nine lay judges (that is, jurors) sitting together, with a majority vote of the lay judges being required for conviction. There was extensive testimony about his character and personality—that he was nervous, sensitive, nonviolent, accommodating, suggestible, impulsive, and emotional. The *pièce de résistance* was the testimony of a popular singer, who had never met the defendant, but who, having been informed that the defendant was one of his fans, testified as follows: "I am opposed to all forms of violence. Those who care for me do so because this is my philosophy. What strikes me about the accused is his concern over being accused of an act of which he totally disapproves. If I am present today, it is because I am absolutely convinced that he is innocent." Nevertheless the defendant was convicted.

of bounds.[48] It is true that rules of evidence are less important in Continental legal systems than in the U.S. system because the rules are designed primarily for the control of juries, which are much less important in those systems. But this is irrelevant; the French use juries in criminal trials.

It does not seem to have been Camus's purpose to criticize the only type of criminal procedure that he knew anything about, although the novella is sometimes taken as a polemic against capital punishment.[49] The author disapproves of the verdict,[50] but not because of any procedural irregularity. He accepts the legal relevance of Meursault's character. What he rejects is the ethical system that pronounces that character bad. We the readers can, however, find in the novella a reason, not of course a conclusive one, for preferring the Anglo-American system of criminal justice (that it avoids demeaning and largely irrelevant inquiries into character); and this shows that the law and literature movement can contribute to the study of comparative law. But if one wanted to make a comparative evaluation of American and French criminal procedure, one would not do so primarily on the basis of novelistic depictions; one would study actual trials. Besides, the trial of Meursault is, in at least one respect, profoundly unrealistic—not in the admission of but in the weight given to the character evidence. It is unlikely that a French colonial court would have convicted, and inconceivable that it would have condemned to death, a Frenchman who killed an armed "native."[51]

All this is not to suggest that Meursault would have been acquitted, or even convicted of a lesser offense, in an American trial from which the character evidence would have been excluded. Although the Arab displays a knife, Meursault is not in reasonable fear of death or serious bodily injury when he shoots him, so there would be no basis for an acquittal on grounds of self-defense. An actual but unreasonable fear of death or serious bodily injury would at least mitigate his guilt; but Meursault has no fear. And those four shots fired after a pause are highly indicative of premeditation. It is true that Meursault shot the Arab in a sort of trance

48. See Merle and Vitu, note 46 above, vol. 2, at 165; A. V. Sheehan, *Criminal Procedure in Scotland and France: A Comparative Study, with Particular Emphasis on the Role of the Public Prosecutor* 27 n. 14, 28–29, 48–49, 73 (1975); cf. Fernand Chapar, *Manuel de la Cour d'Assises* 141 (1961).

49. Robert R. Brock, "Meursault the Straw Man," 25 *Studies in the Novel* 92, 98 (1993).

50. More precisely the *implied* author, that is, the authorial personality that we reconstruct from the work itself, without reference to the author's personal opinions or biography, disapproves of the verdict. I do not consider the author the authoritative interpreter of his work, and often he is downright unreliable (see Chapter 7). In the case of *The Stranger*, however, the actual and the implied author coincide. See Albert Camus, "Preface to the American University Edition of *L'Etranger*," in *Albert Camus: A Study of His Work, Lyrical and Critical* 251 (Philip Thody ed. 1967).

51. Brock, note 49 above, at 96.

brought on by the fierce sun beating down on the beach, and did not intend to kill him, and that absence of lethal intent should reduce the killing to second-degree murder. But would a jury believe this version of what happened? Meursault testified at his trial but was unable to give a coherent account of the circumstances of the killing. And there were no witnesses.

"In a sort of trance . . ." Until he is imprisoned, Meursault goes through life in a kind of trance. He lacks that rich interiority which we find in Shakespeare's characters. That lack invites reflection on what we mean by "premeditation" and by criminal responsibility more broadly. If we could peer into Meursault's mind shortly before, and during, and shortly after the shooting, we would see nothing. If we could peer into the mind of a more reflective, articulate murderer, we would usually find not a focused malignity but instead an elaborate superstructure of rationalization and excuse.[52] Maybe the law does not really care about what is in the murderer's mind.[53] Maybe it is the deed rather than the state of mind that matters, that invites condemnation—the deed that in Meursault's case comprises not just the initial shot but also the four shots that followed it: four shots into an inert body.

That is one interesting legal angle to *The Stranger;* another, which turns out to be related, has to do with how the legal professionals—the prosecutor, the defense lawyer, and the judge—tell Meursault's story at the trial. Neither the accused nor the reader recognizes Meursault in the legal profession's retelling. Meursault implicitly rejects, and the reader is invited by the implied author of the novella to reject, "the state's ideology: that men are primarily spiritual beings endowed with souls and that men's actions possess a coherence."[54] The law has its own purposes, which are not those of psychology. The basic purpose is to enforce social norms, and it requires a judgmental stance alien to the values of a Meursault. There is such a thing as being excessively judgmental, however, which leads Ernest Simon to argue that "what invalidates the prosecutor's interpretation of Meursault's reality is not its wrongness, for it does fulfill a prime requirement of both legal and literary discourse: it is 'plausible.' What invalidates it is its ease, its rhetorical glibness, its blindness to ambiguities, and its exclusion of any feeling for the accused. These are lit-

---

52. For evidence, see Jack Katz, *Seductions of Crime: Moral and Sensual Attractions in Doing Evil,* ch. 1 (1988).

53. See A. D. Nuttall, "Did Meursault Mean to Kill the Arab?—The Intentional Fallacy Fallacy," in Nuttal, *The Stoic in Love: Selected Essays on Literature and Ideas* 191 (1989); Richard A. Posner, *The Problems of Jurisprudence* 168–179 (1990). See also the discussion in the next chapter of moral luck and strict liability.

54. Patrick McCarthy, *Albert Camus: The Stranger* 67 (1988).

erary more than judicial failures."[55] They may not be judicial failures at all. And notice that Simon's argument can be applied to Camus's own interpretation of Meursault's reality, an interpretation that while plausible is rhetorically glib, blind to ambiguities, and devoid of any feeling for the victim of a murder.

Simon helps us see that *The Stranger* supports a point of James Boyd White's, that law is (among other things—a qualification that White might not accept) a way of talking, and a way of talking that can be truer or less true to the things that it talks about. But descriptive accuracy, a cogent phenomenology of the criminal mind, is not necessarily the important thing for the law. The "literary" failures of the prosecution cannot excuse Meursault—a psychopath who is incapable of remorse for his action, indeed incapable of any feeling for a human being, whether it his mother, his lover, or the Arab. Is it not then *shameful* of Camus to invite the reader to take Meursault's part, despite the crime and despite the criminal's lack of remorse, by depicting him as victim rather than killer and by depersonalizing the real victim? Not only shameful, but incoherent? As René Girard puts it, "If the murderer is not held responsible for his actions, why should the judges be held responsible for theirs?"[56] In other words, why is not the court's action in condemning Meursault as "innocent" as his action in killing the Arab?

Girard points out that since no reader would believe that Meursault would be sentenced to death for not crying at his mother's funeral, he must commit a capital offense, but must do so in circumstances that preserve his essential innocence, so that the reader will believe that Meursault's failing to cry at his mother's funeral, and his other defiances of bourgeois pieties, were the real reasons for the conviction and sentence (p. 87).[57] *The Stranger* flirts with the form of neoromanticism which makes heroes out of criminals, as does André Gide's novel *Les Caves du Vatican,* whose hero, Lafcadio, shoves an inoffensive pilgrim to his death from a railroad carriage just for the hell of it. Meursault is another spokesman for, in Girard's words, "a new and radical variety of Romantic solipsism" (pp. 96–96).

Camus can be accused not only of taking murder too lightly but also of taking colonialism too lightly.[58] Not only is the Arab victim left nameless;

---

55. Simon, "Palais de Justice and Poetic Justice in Albert Camus' *The Stranger*," 3 *Cardozo Studies in Law and Literature* 111, 123 (1991).

56. René Girard, "Camus's Stranger Retried," in *Albert Camus* 79, 86 (Harold Bloom ed. 1989).

57. "How could Meursault premeditate murder, since he cannot premeditate a successful career in Paris or marriage with his mistress?" (p. 84).

58. See Conor Cruise O'Brien, *Albert Camus of Europe and Africa* 25–26 (1970); Jerry L. Curtis, "Cultural Alienation: A New Look at the Hero of *The Stranger*," *Journal of American Culture,* Summer 1992.

Arab customs and culture are occluded. Mosques, souks, Arabic, the milling throngs of Arabs in the streets—all are ignored even though Arabs outnumbered Europeans in French Algeria by more than ten to one. *The Stranger* is a novella of "white bourgeois alienation."[59]

But wait a minute. All these criticisms are political or moral in character. They are wide of the mark unless the proper criteria for judging a work of literature are political or moral or unless *The Stranger* belongs to the order of ethical, political, or legal commentary rather than to that of imaginative literature. *The Stranger* is not just the best known of the books discussed so far in this chapter; it is, in my opinion, the best, even though it is the only one with an implied value structure that is odious to a civilized person. It dramatizes with great vividness and emotional force, and considerable subtlety (as in the tricks that Girard describes— dramatic artifice does not lose its emotional power by being exposed), a mood that overcomes most of us, the young especially, from time to time. It is the feeling of disgust with the "system," that complex of mature values and established institutions that curbs the boundless egoism of the childlike "inner man." Meursault's Nietzschean rejection of religion, introspection, guilt, and remorse; his refusal to cry at his mother's funeral; his refusal to accept a promotion that would take him to Paris (hence his rejection of the capitalist ethic); and his refusal to acknowledge the moral authority of law and religion and the terror of death (the foundation, according to Hobbes, of the social impulse in man)—these rejections culminate in a final wish, rich in exalted self-assertion and Achillean defiance, that "on the day of my execution there should be a huge crowd of spectators and that they should greet me with howls of execration."[60] Through the power of literary art Camus makes all this crazy negativity wholly sympathetic to the reader.

And maybe it's not so crazy, or at least not so negative. The end of the novel evokes the Nietzschean doctrines of self-overcoming and eternal recurrence: "I . . . felt ready to start life over again. It was as if that great rush of anger had washed me clean, emptied me of hope, and, gazing up at the dark spy spangled with its signs and stars, for the first time, the first, I laid my heart open to the benign indifference of the universe. To feel it so like

59. Alice Yaeger Kaplan, "The American Stranger," 91 *South Atlantic Quarterly* 87, 92 (1992). But I can find no warrant in the text for Edward Said's argument that the sense of "tragically unsentimental obduracy" in *The Stranger* is due to Camus' having accepted the French overlordship of Algeria: "We have done what we have done here, and so let us do it again." Said, *Culture and Imperialism* 185 (1993).

60. Albert Camus, *The Outsider*, in *Collected Fiction of Albert Camus* 1, 68 (Stuart Gilbert trans. 1960).

myself, indeed so brotherly, made me realize that I'd been happy, and that I was happy still" (p. 68). The triumphalist mood in which Meursault awaits his imminent death reminds one of the similar mood of Yeats's late poetry, also Nietzschean in flavor. In "Death," for example, Yeats writes: "Nor dread nor hope attend / A dying animal . . . / A great man in his pride / . . . Casts derision upon / Supersession of breath; / He knows death to the bone— / Man has created death."

If we want to keep mining *The Stranger* for jurisprudential rather than metaphysical or psychological nuggets, we can compare Meursault to law's other great doomed refuser—the eponymous protagonist, a lawyer's office clerk whom today we would call a paralegal, of Melville's story "Bartleby the Scrivener." Meursault and Bartleby are alike in not wanting to be a part of the normative system of their society. (Another literary example is Barnabas—whose name "Bartleby" may faintly be echoing—in *Measure for Measure*. The earliest example may be Achilles.) The "consent of the governed" is a powerful legitimating slogan; but 99 percent of the legal and social norms that pen us in, even those of us who are fortunate enough to live in this most democratic of large nations, the United States, have been imposed upon us rather than—given the costs of emigration or even of moving to another state to escape unwanted laws—consented to by us in any meaningful sense. The refusers, the internal exiles, the nonconformists impress us by the strength and independence of their character, their "spirit of defiance and protest,"[61] and also challenge us to develop principled justifications for legal coercion.

Behind Meursault stands not only Lafcadio but also Julien Sorel, the protagonist of *The Red and the Black* (1830). At first glance, Stendhal's hero is the opposite of Camus's. Meursault, until sentence is passed on him, is affectless and unambitious, whereas Sorel is highly emotional and boundlessly ambitious (his hero is Napoleon). But both young men come from the lower class and are afflicted by an extreme egocentrism that expresses itself in a sense of profound estrangement from their society—a society that in both cases is despicable. Both are convicted for the wrong reasons—their nonconformity. Both are sentenced to death, and in both cases the sentences, though lawful, are made to seem excessive; and only in part is this because the convictions are motivated by hostility to the doer rather than to the deed. Sorel lightly wounds his former lover in a mad act of attempted revenge, and she promptly forgives him. (Under French law at the time,

---

61. Graham Seal, *The Outlaw Legend: A Cultural Tradition in Britain, America and Australia* 197 (1996). "Outlaw" literature could well be classified as a subgenre of imaginative literature about law.

attempted murder was punishable by death, but it is unlikely that the punishment would have been imposed in the circumstances.) Both authors imply that life achieves dignity, value, and savor only in the contemplation of imminent, premature, and unjust death.

The establishment that crushes Julien Sorel is more garish and odious than that which does in Meursault—or so it will seem to a modern reader, though perhaps only because the bourgeois French (including *pied noir*) society of the 1930s is more like our society than is the France of the Bourbon Restoration. The variety of human and social types is also greater in Stendhal's novel, as is the emphasis on social class, clericalism, and love; and the author maintains a far more critical perspective on his protagonist than Camus does on his.

The Red and the Black is almost over before Julien commits the crime that results in his trial, sentence, and execution. As a result of the different balance in the two works between legal and nonlegal themes, *The Stranger,* a lesser work, holds greater interest for law—greater interest, indeed, than any other work discussed in this chapter. Yet its heart, as is true for those other works, as in general for works of literature "about" law, lies elsewhere. That is an implication, I have argued, of the test of time, and it is supported by a close reading of "legal" literature.

TWO

Revenge as Legal Prototype
and Literary Genre

Holmes argued, I think correctly (I'll give some evidence in this chapter), that law grows out of revenge.[1] Law's origin in revenge has left its stamp on a number of legal doctrines and procedures, as well as on such overarching legal principles as corrective justice and retribution. And vengeful feelings play an important role in the administration of law even today. No general theory of law could be complete without attention to revenge. Revenge is also, as it happens, a theme of some of the greatest monuments of the Western literary tradition—works by Homer and the Greek tragedians, by Shakespeare and the other Elizabethan and Jacobean tragedians, by Kleist, Dumas, Melville, Faulkner, and many other important writers.[2] Literary depictions of revenge can tell us something about revenge and about the issues of law and justice that revenge adjoins or subtends; the lawyer's and the social scientist's analyses of revenge can tell us something about revenge literature.

Revenge as a Practice

I begin, far from the splendidly dramatic works that are my principal texts in this chapter, by sketching the logic of revenge, the sense that it makes. My sketch employs the vocabulary of rational choice (economics in a broad sense),[3] but it is consistent with the historical and anthropological literature

---

1. Oliver Wendell Holmes, Jr., *The Common Law* 2–25 (1881).
2. For a recent survey, see John Kerrigan, *Revenge Tragedy: Aeschylus to Armageddon* (1996).
3. See, for example, Richard A. Posner, *The Economics of Justice,* ch. 8 (1981) ("Retribution and Related Concepts of Punishment"); Robert Axelrod, *The Evolution of Cooperation* (1984); Robert H. Frank, *Passions within Reason: The Strategic Role of the Emotions* 1–70 passim (1988); Marla Radinsky, "Retaliation: The Genesis of a Law and the Evolution toward International Cooperation: An Application of Game Theory to Modern International Conflicts," 2 *George Mason*

describing the practice of revenge in a variety of social settings.[4] Yet the passion for revenge may seem the antithesis of rational, instrumental thinking—may seem at once emotional, destructive, and useless. It flouts the economist's commandment to ignore sunk costs, to let bygones be bygones. When there is no possibility of legal redress to deter an aggressor, potential victims will be assiduous in self-protection. But self-protection can be extremely costly—indeed impossible for someone who lacks the wealth necessary to surround himself with a wall and moat, trusty guards, and so forth. The remaining possibility is retaliation against the aggressor after he has victimized you. But if you are "rational man" you will realize that the harm is a sunk cost. No matter how much harm you do to the aggressor in return, the harm you have suffered will not be annulled; whatever dangers or other burdens you take on in order to retaliate will merely increase the cost to you of the initial aggression. The high cost of retaliation will make the aggressor all the more likely to attack, since if he thinks that his victim is "rational man"—coolly balancing costs and benefits and treating bygones as bygones—he will infer that the victim may well decide not to retaliate. This calculation will lower the anticipated costs of committing aggression.

Granted, I have omitted from the victim's calculus the potential benefits of retaliating in deterring future aggression. But I have done so because the current aggressor may be so well protected that the costs of revenge would exceed the benefits in reducing the probability of future aggression. A potential victim who seeks to deter aggression against himself thus must convince potential aggressors that he will retaliate even if the expected benefits of retaliation, calculated *after* the aggression has occurred, are smaller than the expected costs at that time. In other words, potential victims must make a credible commitment to act in a way that may be irrational when the time to act comes. The making of such a commitment may be perfectly rational: it may deter enough aggression to generate benefits in excess of the costs of having sometimes to honor the commitment—regardless of the costs of honoring it—by retaliating against the aggressor instead of cutting one's losses after the aggression. Commitment can be rational in the same way that acting according to rule, rather than always making ad

University Law Review 53 (1994). The idea of using notions of rational behavior to explain or understand better the behavior of characters in fiction, as I shall be doing in this chapter, is defended in Paisley Livingston, *Literature and Rationality: Ideas of Agency in Theory and Fiction* (1991).

4. Some good examples of this literature are Christopher Boehm, *Blood Revenge: The Enactment and Management of Conflict in Montenegro and Other Tribal Societies* (1984); David Cohen, *Law, Violence, and Community in Classical Athens* (1995); Stephen Wilson, *Feuding, Conflict and Banditry in Nineteenth-Century Corsica* (1988).

hoc maximizing decisions, can be rational, or that rule-utilitarianism can be preferred on utilitarian grounds to act-utilitarianism. Legal and political analogies to the commitment to revenge include the self-destructive defensive measures that corporate managers sometimes take to deter hostile takeovers, such as the "poison pill," which may result in the acquirer's finding itself owning a firm that is crushed by debt, or the commitment of the United States and the former Soviet Union to massive nuclear retaliation, parodied in the "Doomsday Machine" in the movie *Dr. Strangelove.*

In a society that has no formal legal institutions, it is by definition impossible to make a legally enforceable commitment to retaliate against an aggressor. The commitment has to come from instinctual or cultural reflex reactions to aggression. In the long prehistory of the human race, people who were endowed with an instinct to retaliate would have tended to be more successful in the struggle for survival than others. The desire to take revenge for real or imagined injuries, without calculating the net benefits of revenge at the time when it is taken, may therefore have become a part of the human genetic makeup.[5] The emotionality and universality of vengefulness are evidence for this speculation.

More than instinct may be necessary to make threats to retaliate fully credible, however. Cultures in which revenge plays a significant role in the regulation of social interactions place great emphasis on honor.[6] Shame, the reaction to being dishonored, helps overcome fear and so makes it more likely that a victim will retaliate if attacked or abused. Out of the interplay of honor, shame, and revenge grow notions of exchange, balance, reciprocity, "keeping score"[7]—notions later taken up by law, initially under the rubric of "corrective justice."

Another cultural overlay on the genetic impulse to revenge is the extended family. A potential victim of aggression in a revenge society must have allies; otherwise there would be no deterrence to murder. The natural place to seek allies in a society with rudimentary political structures is among one's kin. So important is kinship in a revenge society that a person without kin is little better than an outlaw. In the early period of law,

5. Robert L. Trivers, "The Evolution of Reciprocal Altruism," 46 *Quarterly Review of Biology* 35, 49 (1971); J. Hirshleifer, "Natural Economy versus Political Economy," 1 *Journal of Social and Biological Structures* 319, 332, 334 (1978).

6. On the relation of honor to revenge, see Frank Henderson Stewart, *Honor,* ch. 5 (1994). Jon Elster, "Norms of Revenge," 100 *Ethics* 862, 883–885 (1990), argues that revenge is caused by the pursuit of honor, rather than honor being ancillary to revenge. Emphasis on honor increases the likelihood of revenge—that is its function. But vengeful feelings are common even in societies—ours for example—that do not cultivate a sense of honor in the traditional sense.

7. The close connection between repayment and revenge is emphasized in Peter Singer, *The Expanding Circle: Ethics and Sociobiology* 39 (1981).

the period in which its roots in revenge show clearly, murder is a purely private offense, to be rectified by what today we would call a tort suit for wrongful death brought by the kin of the murder victim. There is then no legal sanction for murdering a kinless person, though a supernatural sanction may be feared.[8] It is almost as if an individual were believed to exist only by virtue of being embedded in a web of kinship.

Kinship increases not only the number of potential avengers but also the number of potential targets for revenge. By doing this it lowers the cost of revenge. If X kills Y, Y's family may decide to go after X's brother rather than after X himself—maybe the brother is not as well protected as X. And, with responsibility thus collective, people have an incentive to police their kin lest a kinsman's misbehavior lead to retaliation against them rather than against him.

A revenge society places a premium on rhetorical skill. Even your kin may be reluctant to risk their necks on your behalf, so you have to be able both to put the offender in the wrong in their eyes and to convince them of the importance of retaliation, with all the risks that it entails, to the future security of the kin group.

While revenge is thus a system of social control, like law itself, rather than a sign of the absence of all social control, it is a costly and clumsy system. To begin with, it retards specialization of the labor force. Instead of some people working full time at law enforcement, leaving the rest of the community free to work full time in other occupations, every man (for revenge cultures assign a distinctly circumscribed and subordinate role to women) must spend part of his time as investigator, prosecutor, judge, sheriff, and executioner. The avenger's role is a difficult and dangerous one. Every man has to equip himself with the skills and equipment necessary to play the role well, and this will limit his ability to engage in normal productive activities. And because not everyone has the same aptitudes, the duty of revenge may fall on someone who is not well suited to carry it out.

An ethic of revenge makes large-scale cooperation difficult. Everyone nurses his ego, knowing that the more prone to retaliate against slights he is known to be, the less likely it is that anyone will dare inflict a slight on him. Big egos have difficulty cooperating. An overdeveloped sense of honor, leading to a crazy act of revenge, is the undoing of Julien Sorel. The qualification "large scale" is important; a revenge culture breeds intense loyalty within the extended family. But powerful loyalties within small

---

8. On both points, see S. C. Todd, *The Shape of Athenian Law* 272–273 (1993); but Todd believes it possible, though not certain, that under ancient Athenian law murder could be prosecuted at the behest of a person not related to the victim. Id. at 273.

groups retard the formation of larger loyalties, to the tribe, the *polis,* or the nation. This seems to have been Plato's objection, in the *Republic,* to the portrayal of Achilles in the *Iliad.*

Acts of revenge tend to be too frequent and too savage, both because they proceed from emotion and because the avenger, being a judge in his own cause, is likely to misjudge the balance of right and wrong in his own favor, sensing a slight when none is intended or believing that to maintain credibility he must interpret every injury to himself in the worst possible light. A related point is that acts of revenge beget feuds. Aggressors become victims whose culturally sharpened instinct for revenge, activated by the revenge taken (perhaps rightfully) against them, is directed toward the original victim or the victim's avenger.[9] Such a response is especially likely because—people being adept at rationalizing their conduct—the aggressor may not realize that he is a wrongdoer. The fact that vengeance may be taken against the aggressor's family rather than against the aggressor himself (if he is hiding or well protected) increases the likelihood that the aggressor will escape retribution and view himself as a victim obliged to take revenge. And it further strengthens the family at the expense of the broader community.

The possibility of the wrongdoer's evading immediate punishment may engender destructive, interminable *intergenerational* feuds, as descendants of the original victim pursue the original aggressor or his descendants, and vice versa. Yet the revenge mechanism of a blood feud fails to cover cases of crime between family members; the father who kills his son or the son who kills his father would be the natural avenger of the crime. *Beowulf* contains a lament over the inadequacy of vengeance in such a situation. The plot of *Oedipus Tyrannus* turns on an alternative "enforcement" device— the "pollution" visited on Thebes as a result of Oedipus's crimes of parricide and incest.

For the threat of revenge to be an effective deterrent, the natural psychological tendencies of victims and aggressors have somehow to be reversed. Putative victims must have an unshakable commitment to retaliate violently for wrongs done to them, regardless of cost, while putative aggressors must be prudently self-restrained by rational calculation of the costs of aggression, which include the possibility of retaliation by the victim. Relying on revenge for justice can thus yield too little as well as too much punishment. An additional reason for this is that revenge depends on

---

9. So Odysseus expresses concern that if he kills the suitors their families will avenge them, and in fact it requires a *deus ex machina* to prevent this. *Odyssey,* bk. 20, ll. 42–43; bk. 24, ll. 531–540.

anger—the emotion that ensures our carrying out our genetic-cultural commitment to take revenge regardless of the present balance of costs and benefits. Because the average person's anger fades rapidly, revenge may not provide sufficient motivation to track down and punish—perhaps at a high cost in time and danger—an aggressor who has managed to elude swift capture. A system of revenge thus places a premium on implacable anger, the harboring of grudges, and the hatred of one's enemies.

This observation buttresses the point that revenge is inimical to large-scale cooperation. Revenge encourages the cultivation of a cluster of emotions—such as wrath and touchiness and unforgivingness and, above all, the refusal to behave "rationally" in the face of slights—that retard the emergence of such forms of social cooperation as the market economy. Cooperation depends on a willingness to compromise desires (the market translates our subjective valuations of goods and services into finite prices) and thus to accept limitation and commensurability as fundamental norms of social interaction.

Yet even in a modern capitalist society, revenge remains an important supplement to formal law enforcement. Vengefulness in the form of righteous indignation and justified anger motivates victims of crime and their families to assist in the apprehension and punishment of the criminal—rarely is there any financial incentive. And it deters aggressions and infringements, ranging from the mistreatment of friends and family members to breaches of faith by political leaders, that are too minor to activate law's cumbersome and expensive machinery of sanctions but that are cumulatively costly. People who always turn the other cheek do not thrive in our or any other society. But the mean between having an overdeveloped sense of honor and having no sense of honor is fragile. Cultures in which the sense of honor is highly developed, such as the traditional American South or America's inner cities today, are, despite the deterrent effect of a known willingness to revenge slights, on balance more violent than cultures in which honor is taken less seriously.[10] A preoccupation with honor creates a touchiness that senses slights where none are intended.

Justice as vengeance is crude from a moral standpoint once one steps outside the moral framework of the vengeance system itself. Not only do the sanctions bear no systematic relation to the gravity of the harms inflicted; they are imposed regardless of fault. Lacking as it does differentiated institutions for making and applying rules of law, justice as vengeance has no means

---

10. Richard E. Nisbett and Dov Cohen, *Culture of Honor: The Psychology of Violence in the South* (1996), esp. pp. 88–91; David Hackett Fischer, *Albion's Seed: Four British Folkways in America* 892 (1989).

of distinguishing between culpable and justifiable injuries or even for developing the distinction. Liability tends therefore to be absolute. The avenger is as "guilty" as the original aggressor. This feature of justice as vengeance makes the feud logical rather than pathological. Vengeance is a duty—and since the avenger's act is the same kind of wrong as that of the original aggressor, it imposes the same duty of revenge on the avenger's victim.

A revenge system is potentially unstable. The bigger a man's kin group, the less he will be restrained by fear of retaliation.[11] So there will be competition to form protective groups large enough not to be overawed by any man or his kin; fictive kinship may be used to expand the group beyond its "natural" limits. The Icelandic sagas, an important literary source for our knowledge of how a revenge society works, depict this transition.[12] Iceland, previously uninhabited, was settled by Norwegians in the tenth century A.D. For three hundred years the Icelanders managed to get by with a rudimentary political and legal system in which revenge was lawful and was the fundamental basis of public order. Iceland faced no threats of invasion until Norway began throwing its weight around toward the end of the period of Icelandic independence. Until then the benefits of a large protective association would have been slight and the costs great. The poverty of the country made it difficult for anyone to support an entourage of feudal-style retainers, who in exchange for food and shelter would place an armed force at the disposal of their liege. Lacking such an armed force, a magnate had little to offer in the way of protection to other people in the society. Little, but not nothing; there were chieftains. But the small forces at their disposal—a handful of relatives, dependents, and clients taking the afternoon off from tending their flocks—limited their power to the execution of piecemeal revenge. None was able to offer a king's peace to the entire society.

A community needs an economic surplus to support specialists in coercion. Toward the end of the period of Icelandic independence, the Roman Catholic Church was able at last to collect substantial taxes from the population. But the Church was unable to keep the bulk of the tax revenues out of the coffers of a handful of major chieftains. Six of them grew powerful enough to engage in civil war on a respectable scale, at which point the population was happy to turn to the King of Norway for protection, and Icelandic independence ended.[13] Civil war was not inevitable. Not all arms' races end in war. But where the potential gains from obtaining a mo-

---

11. See Boehm, note 4, at 168.

12. See William Ian Miller, *Bloodtaking and Peacemaking: Feud, Law, and Society in Saga Iceland* (1990), discussed in Richard A. Posner, *Overcoming Law*, ch. 14 (1995); also Theodore Ziolkowski, *The Mirror of Justice: Literary Reflections of Legal Crisis*, ch. 3 (1997).

13. Thráinn Eggertsson, *Economic Behavior and Institutions* 309–310 (1990).

nopoly of political power are great and seem attainable, a miscalculation can lead to war. So here is still another problem with the efficacy of revenge as a deterrent: it depends on a nice calculation of the strength and fortitude of the potential victims of your aggression.

All this is not to say that vengeance is a *bad* system of justice. That depends on the alternatives. The *Odyssey* depicts vengeance as thoroughly normal and normally righteous, and the reader, unfazed by disproportionality, thrills when Odysseus slaughters the scores of suitors and hangs the dozen maids who had slept with them. There is no other system of justice in the world of the *Odyssey,* just as during the Cold War world peace could be maintained only by the threat of vengeance, and concretely by the Soviet Union's belief that the United States would retaliate in kind to a nuclear attack even if the attack so devastated the United States as to deprive retaliation of any benefits to the few left alive.

Even before there is a nation or other organized community to take over from the victims of aggression and their families the responsibility for catching and punishing aggressors, customs evolve that alleviate some of the problems of revenge practices. Among these is the principle of retribution, that is, exact retaliation for a wrong—an eye for an eye. Rather than being bloodthirsty, which is the modern connotation of the word, retribution reduces the likelihood of overreactions (your life for my eye) that are likely to engender feuds.[14] Another moderating principle is "composition" (blood money, wergeld), whereby the victim or the victim's family is required, or at least encouraged, to accept payment in compensation for an injury, discharging the injurer's liability. A transfer of money or goods is less costly to society as a whole than an act of violence, which besides inflicting a net social loss rather than merely transferring wealth from one person to another may provoke further violence. In addition, composition fosters market values—it is a kind of trade—and, more broadly, an ethic of cooperation. Another meliorating institution is bilateral kinship. Icelanders reckoned kinship through both the father and the mother (many societies reckon it only through the father and some only through the mother). This not only increased the credibility of revenge as a deterrent to aggression by strengthening the family; it made it more likely that a disputant would have kin on both sides of the dispute. Caught in the middle, these kinsmen were naturals to try to make peace between the disputants. The *Iliad* hints at the further possibility that pity and empathy might limit the savagery of revenge.

As centralized institutions for the enforcement of law emerge and grow

14. This is a major theme of Axelrod, note 3 above; see, for example, pp. 121–122.

strong, the tendency is for vengeance, even as mitigated by principles of retribution, composition, or compassion, to come to be regarded, though not everywhere or always or by everyone, as an archaic and destructive passion. Retribution does not work well. It is not feasible for all wrongs—for defamation, for instance, or where victim and aggressor are not identically circumstanced (for example where *A,* who has only one eye, puts out one of *B*'s eyes). The threat of retribution is not an adequate deterrent in situations where an aggressor is unlikely to be caught and punished every time, so that punishment does not equal crime when all his punishments and all his crimes are summed. And a commitment to limited retaliation, or to accepting money or goods in settlement of any wrong, is hard to stick by in the highly emotional circumstances in which revenge is provoked and administered.

So vengeance falls out of favor, not only in ethics but in law. Taking the law into one's own hands becomes itself a crime. Practices are adopted that direct vengeful feelings into socially less disruptive channels, such as giving the victim his day in court, whether as plaintiff in a civil case or as prosecuting witness in a criminal case, in lieu of private vengeance. (Granted, the damages recoverable in a private case may no more slake the desire for revenge than the composition obtainable under customary law.) Revenge by victims and their relatives gives way to retribution by disinterested persons—with advantages made transparent, as we shall see, by *Hamlet.* Yet revenge tends to break out whenever legal remedies are blocked, as when the evildoer controls the legal machinery (*Hamlet* again) or is otherwise above the law, or when public law enforcement is very lax.

Intermediate stages in the evolution from revenge to public enforcement include the duel[15] and, closely related, the trial by battle, and ritualized medieval warfare.[16] Like retribution, these are devices for heading off feuds by establishing a natural end to a dispute. Trial by battle leads to the modern trial—also a form of combat but one that is much less expensive if a high value is placed on life and bodily integrity, and more likely to produce

---

15. For an excellent case study, see R. S. Radford, "Going to the Island: A Legal and Economic Analysis of the Medieval Icelandic Duel," 62 *Southern California Law Review* 615 (1989); also Eric A. Posner, "Law, Economics, and Inefficient Norms," 144 *University of Pennsylvania Law Review* 1697, 1736–1740 (1996), and references cited there. The duel between Menelaus and Paris in Book 3 of the *Iliad* is an example of an attempt (in that instance unsuccessful) to substitute the cheaper alternative of a duel for full-scale revenge. See also Bertram Wyatt-Brown, *Southern Honor: Ethics and Behavior in the Old South* 352 (1982).

16. "The vision of the Agincourt war, as presented both by Shakespeare [in *Henry V*] and by contemporary sources, is that of a law suit culminating in trial by battle, which will establish justice." A. W. B. Simpson, "The Agincourt Campaign and the Law of War," 16 *Michigan Journal of International Law* 653, 656 (1995).

accurate results. The development of codes of dueling that made it progressively less likely that a duel would result in death further illustrates the economizing character of the evolution from revenge to law.

I have simplified the evolution. Feuds, duels, trial by battle or ordeal, and "rational" litigation coexisted for a long time.[17] Especially in aristocratic circles the duel persisted long after an essentially modern legal system was in place. The persistence of norms of revenge in American gangster culture is a parallel phenomenon. Aristocrats and gangsters are disinclined or unable to submit their disputes to the formal legal system, which "belongs" to a different social or political class.

As I have already suggested, law channels rather than eliminates revenge—replaces it as system but not as feeling.[18] In early Roman law, as also in Anglo-Saxon and early Germanic law, a thief caught in the act ("manifest theft") was subject to capital punishment or enslavement, whereas if he escaped and was caught later ("nonmanifest theft") the punishment was lighter.[19] This pattern makes little sense from a strictly deterrent or retributive standpoint.[20] But it makes a lot of sense if criminal law tracks revenge, since the desire for revenge cools with the passage of time.

Corrective justice—the idea that the task of the legal system is to restore a preexisting balance between persons—reflects the revenge-inciting feeling of indignation caused by the infringement of one's rights. But the right to corrective justice is conceived in individual rather than group terms; the family falls out of the picture. This is not an accident. A central element of the concept of corrective justice is adjudicating disputes without regard to the status of the disputants. The social contract that legitimates the state and formal law, supplanting justice as revenge with corrective justice, is thus not a means of overcoming the selfishness and atomistic individualism of man in nature, but virtually the opposite. Revenge is not a selfish emotion, and a revenge ethic breeds powerful family and small-group loyalties. The state creates the conditions in which selfish behavior will not endanger social order. The state, as a collective, is hostile to competing collectives.

The relation between revenge and law is illustrated by the rudimentary legal system of medieval Iceland. The formal institutions of government were limited to courts and to an assembly, all staffed by ordinary citizens

17. See, for example, *The Settlement of Disputes in Early Medieval Europe* (Wendy Davies and Paul Fouracre eds. 1986).

18. The continuity between law and revenge—with litigation often amounting to feuding by other means—is emphasized in Cohen, note 4 above, esp. ch. 5.

19. Henry Sumner Maine, *Ancient Law* 387–388 (1861).

20. Not no sense, however; doubt of guilt is less when the criminal is caught redhanded, and that reduces the error costs of heavy punishment.

rather than by professionals. In effect there were jurors but no judges; there were no appeals, either. The speaker of the assembly was the only salaried official in Iceland. There were virtually no taxes, the speaker being paid out of a marriage fee. There was, crucially, no executive branch of government, so there were no sheriffs, police, soldiers, or prosecutors. All lawsuits, including criminal suits, were prosecuted by private individuals. What was the greater innovation in the art of minimizing government—for a number of societies that would not be called stateless, including those of ancient Greece and Rome and Anglo-Saxon England, left prosecution of criminal cases to private individuals[21]—all judicial decrees were enforced, if at all, privately.

Icelanders were great amateur lawyers. Their law codes were as complex and ingenious as most of the rest of their culture was simple and monotonous. (Njal, the eponymous hero of the best-known saga, was one of those amateur lawyers.) The procedures for finding facts were more rational than those used in other medieval legal systems, little reliance being placed on supernatural methods. But the system was inflexible on the remedial side. The only sanctions that the Icelandic courts meted out, other than for the most trivial infractions (which were punished by a fixed fine), were outlawry, which made a man an outlaw in the literal sense—anyone could kill him with impunity—and lesser outlawry, which meant banishment from Iceland for three years. The feud was lawful. So was private arbitration, in which a dispute was submitted for binding resolution to one or more men selected by the disputants. The inflexible character of the legal remedies made arbitration an attractive alternative to ordinary litigation. Arbitrators could impose fines or fashion what we would call equitable decrees, tailored to the particular circumstances of the case. Refusal to obey an arbitral decree was punishable like other serious wrongdoing.

Even feuds were governed by norms—for example, that the killing of an outlaw should not be avenged, should not, that is, occasion a feud. Despite the absence of formal sanctions, these norms were obeyed with some, though far from complete, regularity. (Where these norms came from, and what the source of their normative force was, is unclear.) Kinship was, as I have explained, highly elaborated, as one would expect in a system in which the threat of a feud was the ultimate backing of law.

Law played the same role in the Icelandic bloodfeud system as graphite

21. See, for example, Cohen, note 4 above, passim; Todd, note 8 above, at 272–273; Douglas M. MacDowell, *The Law in Classical Athens* 237–240 (1978). The history of private criminal prosecution in the Anglo-American legal system is summarized in Harold J. Krent, "Executive Control over Criminal Law Enforcement: Some Lessons from History," 38 *American University Law Review* 275, 290–295 (1989).

rods play in the core of a nuclear reactor: to slow down the chain reaction. (Bilateral kinship played this role too.) It is true that legal judgments were not self-executing, so that if the convicted defendant thumbed his nose at a judgment the plaintiff would have to rally his kin to enforce it by force, much as if he had decided to retaliate directly against the defendant for whatever wrong had precipitated the suit. But a legal judgment might have enough suasive force to enable the plaintiff to rally his allies and also make it easier for the defendant's potential allies to beg off, thus isolating the defendant and so vindicating the plaintiff's decision to go to law rather than fight.

Ancient Athens had a legal system not unlike that of saga Iceland. Prosecutions even for such serious offenses as murder and treason were instituted and conducted by private persons ("denouncers") and tried before panels of citizens chosen at random. There were no professional judges and no appeals. There were no lawyers as such, though litigants hired rhetoricians to write speeches for them. Criminal judgments were enforced by public officers, unlike the procedure in Iceland; and the juries were larger. There were other differences. But the parallels are striking, and even include the frequent use of banishment as a sanction and the propensity, emphasized by David Cohen, to protracted and repetitive litigation by "feuding" factions.[22] Yet even closer to saga Iceland is the society depicted in the Homeric epics (I set to one side the problem, equally serious in the case of the Icelandic sagas, of distinguishing fact from fiction in literary sources), which reveal only rudimentary government institutions and exhibit the same emphasis found in the sagas on revenge as the basic principle of social order. Other effectively stateless regimes operate this way, such as the mining communities that sprang up during the California Gold Rush to maintain order at a time and in a place where governmental authority was virtually nonexistent.[23]

Revenge Literature

The literature both of ancient Greece and of Renaissance England is preoccupied with the theme of revenge. The plot of Aeschylus's *Oresteia* is based on a revenge story, the legend of the House of Atreus.[24] Thyestes

22. Cohen, note 4 above. For a comprehensive description of Athenian law, see Todd, note 8 above.

23. See, for example, Robert C. Ellickson, *Order without Law: How Neighbors Settle Disputes* (1991); Gary D. Libecap, *Contracting for Property Rights* (1989).

24. For a full account of the legend, see Timothy Gantz, *Early Greek Myth: A Guide to Literary and Artistic Sources,* ch. 15 (1993).

had wronged his brother Atreus in retaliation for wrongs done to him by Atreus. Inviting Thyestes to a banquet, ostensibly of reconciliation, Atreus killed Thyestes' sons and fed their flesh to their unknowing father. (The banquet scene is described in hideous detail in Seneca's tragedy *Thyestes*.) One of Thyestes' sons remained alive, however—Aegisthus. (In some versions of the legend he is Thyestes' grandson rather than son.) Aegisthus kills Atreus and drives away Atreus's sons, Agamemnon and Menelaus. They eventually regain power. But then they go off to fight the Trojan War— itself a war to avenge Paris's seduction of Helen, Menelaus's wife. In their absence Aegisthus becomes the lover of Agamemnon's wife, Clytemnestra. She is nursing her own grievance: Agamemnon had sacrificed their daughter Iphigenia on the way to Troy, to appease the goddess Artemis. When Agamemnon returns at last from the Trojan War, Aegisthus and Clytemnestra kill him. To avenge Agamemnon's death, his son, Orestes, kills Aegisthus and Clytemnestra. Pursued by supernatural beings, the Furies—for Orestes himself would be the natural avenger of his mother's murder, were he not the murderer—Orestes is eventually tried for the murder of his mother, and acquitted, by the Court of the Areopagus in Athens, presided over by Athena. The cycle of vengeance is broken, since there is no avenger of Aegisthus. Indeed, *Eumenides*, the last play of the *Oresteia*, ascribes the founding of the Court of the Areopagus, reputed to be the first formal court in the classical world, to a desire to end the cycle— thus making transparent the relation between vengeance and the absence of regular institutions of criminal justice. The problem of subjecting royal personages of independent city-states to those institutions is circumvented by making Athena the chief judge, but it persists to this day in the international "community." Until the trial, it is assumed that Orestes' killing of Clytemnestra, though justifiable and indeed inescapable, must itself be avenged, just as it is assumed that Agamemnon had to be killed for sacrificing his daughter, even though he had to do it to get on with the war against Troy—a war ordained by Zeus. Hence the pursuit of Orestes by the Furies. And recall that although the *Odyssey* presents Odysseus's revenge against the suitors as wholly justifiable, it is understood that were it not for Athena's intervention, the suitors' families would have a duty to avenge them (Bk. 24, ll. 531–548).

Since revenge is associated with so uncompromising a form of strict liability for harms inflicted however justifiably, one is not surprised that early legal systems, in which the roots of law in revenge still show, rely on strict liability more heavily than modern legal systems do. Oedipus is guilty of parricide and incest and must be punished terribly, even though he had no reason to know that the man he had killed was his father and the woman he had married was his mother. Oedipus's punishment is an effective metaphor of the human condition. We frequently suffer as a result of acts that we do in warranted ignorance of the possible consequences; in other words, we may be "punished" for "innocent" or, in the case of Agamemnon, justified (or at least compelled, involuntary, and hence, in modern legal systems, often excused) violations of the order of things. The implied system of liability in *Oedipus Tyrannus,* as in the *Oresteia,* is crude from a modern legal standpoint, yet this crudeness is bound up with its dramatic effectiveness. Absolute liability makes law a more effective metaphor of necessity—of the external world that bears down on people and ruins their dreams. This is especially true when, as in *Oedipus Tyrannus,* "nature" and "law" are not clearly distinguished.[25]

We must not exaggerate the ethical gulf between the world of *Oedipus Tyrannus* and our world. Jocasta kills herself and Oedipus blinds himself, but these are effects of horror and remorse rather than punishments. The only punishment that is clearly required is that Oedipus leave Thebes; until he does so, the plague will continue. We would not formally punish a modern officeholder who, without knowledge or reason to know, committed Oedipus's offenses. But we must ask what similar revelations would do to the modern officeholder's tenure, let alone to his and his wife-mother's psychological state. If, like Agamemnon, a modern military or political leader killed his own daughter for the greater good of society (the atomic-age variant of this theme is explored in the movie *Fail Safe*), we would be horrified even if we concluded that the leader had been justified in doing what he did (maybe he had ordered a prison camp bombed where he knew she was being held). Kantian morality, which judges the person rather than the act and so equates wrongfulness with blameworthiness, is not the whole of our morality. If two drivers drive with equal carelessness, and one has an accident and injures someone and the other does not, the first will receive greater moral as well as legal condemnation even though the conduct of the two drivers, as distinct from the consequences of that conduct, was blameworthy to the same extent. "In the story of one's life there is an authority exercised by what one has done, and not merely by what one has intentionally done."[26]

We puzzle over this; and so does Oedipus, in *Oedipus at Colonus,* the sequel to *Oedipus Tyrannus,* written many years later. Notions of liability may

25. See Lloyd L. Weinreb, *Natural Law and Justice,* ch. 1 (1987).
26. Bernard Williams, *Shame and Necessity* 69 (1993). See also Williams, "Moral Luck," in his book *Moral Luck: Philosophical Papers 1973–1980* 20, 28–30 (1981); Robert B. Pippin, "Morality as Psychology, Psychology as Morality: Nietzsche, Eros, and Clumsy Lovers," in Pippin, *Idealism as Modernism: Hegelian Variations* 351, 367–368 (1997).

have been changing, for the later play suggests that there is a moral difference between strict liability and liability based on personal blameworthiness. At Colonus, Oedipus asserts his moral innocence, founded on lack of premeditation, or even of carelessness; and perhaps as a result, or partial result, of that innocence, his death on Athenian soil becomes a blessing to Athens rather than, as might have been expected, a curse. An emergent sense of free will—an influential ground for distinguishing between cause and fault as grounds of liability[27]—is also apparent in the difference between the curse that doomed Oedipus in the earlier play, a curse delivered by Oedipus against the then unknown murderer of his father, and the curse delivered by Oedipus in the later play against his son Polynices. Oedipus could have done nothing to escape the consequences of his unwitting self-cursing, but Polynices could have escaped the consequences of Oedipus's curse just by abandoning his attack on Thebes. (The disastrous consequences of that attack are the subject of *Antigone,* which I discuss in the next chapter.) Polynices rejects this escape route because he would lose face if he took it, and in particular because he would be humiliated before a younger brother, Eteocles, the defender of Thebes. So he may be said to choose his fate, and hence to be culpable in a way that Oedipus had not been.

Yet even in the earlier play, and in the *Oresteia,* one senses a recoil from the punishment of a subjectively innocent person who happens merely to be unlucky. Oedipus was impious in trying to evade his fate. It had been prophesied at his birth, as he well knew, that he would kill his father and marry his mother; what he did not know, in his arrogant finitude, was that he was a foundling. The fury with which Agamemnon kills Iphigenia, as well as his impiety in accepting Clytemnestra's invitation to walk into the palace on a purple carpet (the original "red-carpet treatment")—as if he were too good to touch the goddess earth—mark him as more than a merely involuntary transgressor.[28]

The trial of Orestes in *Eumenides* dramatizes the transition from a system of absolute liability, enforced by revenge, to one of legal liability based on

27. But not the only ground. As Holmes emphasized, negligence, the central concept of fault in tort law, has an element of strict liability because the concept of negligence is an objective one; negligence is the failure to exercise average care, whether or not the defendant is capable of that level of care. If he is not, then the effect of subjecting him to liability for negligence is to make him legally responsible for accidents that he can't avoid, and that's strict liability. See Holmes, note 1 above, lect. 3.

28. Martha C. Nussbaum, *The Fragility of Goodness: Luck and Ethics in Greek Tragedy and Philosophy* 35–46 (1986). Of course death is too severe a punishment, by modern lights, for not having an exemplary character.

blameworthiness in something approaching the modern sense.[29] Hounded by the Furies, Orestes takes refuge with Apollo, who had encouraged him to kill his mother. Orestes thinks it unfair that he should be punished for having done what a god ordained. Apollo agrees, and comes up with the idea of a trial ("the first trial of bloodshed," as Athena says, line 694), to sort out blame; and the procedure at trial, apart from the presence of divine personages, is an approximation to Athenian trial procedure in fifth century B.C. The Furies argue that if Clytemnestra's murder of her husband is punishable, which of course is the premise of Orestes' defense, so should his murder of his mother be. The reply that leaps to mind is that the killing of Clytemnestra was justifiable because it was punishment for her deed; an executioner is not a murderer. But Clytemnestra, with some justification, had regarded her deed as punishment for Agamemnon's killing their daughter. So Orestes would have to argue either that *that* killing, too, was justified—an unattractive argument of "the end justifies the means" variety—or, more subtly, that Clytemnestra's act, being not just murder but also usurpation, had a political resonance that made it a disproportionate punishment for Agamemnon's misconduct.

Orestes takes a different tack. He asks the Furies why they had failed to punish Clytemnestra, which would have made it unnecessary for him to shed her blood. They reply that they punish only people who kill a blood relative—a son who kills his mother but not a wife who kills her husband.[30] This reply sets the stage for Apollo, Orestes' advocate, to deliver the crushing rebuttal that persuades Athena and thereby assures Orestes' acquittal.[31] Apollo says that Orestes is not really a blood relative of Clytemnestra, because a mother is merely the incubator of the father's child; the father is the only real parent. The modern reader, incredulous, asks how the Greeks could have failed to notice the physical resemblance between mothers and children, which shows (without any need to know anything about genetics) that the mother is as much a parent as the father. But it doesn't show this. Environmental as well as genetic factors determine the constitution of an organism. The taste of wine is affected by the soil in which the grapes are grown. Before the rise of modern science it was believed that what a

---

29. For good discussions of the trial, and more broadly of the themes of law, justice, and revenge, in the *Oresteia,* see Michael Gagarin, *Aeschylean Drama,* ch. 3 (1976); Lois Spatz, *Aeschylus,* ch. 5 (1982); David Cohen, "The Theodicy of Aeschylus: Justice and Tyranny in the *Oresteia,*" 33 *Greece and Rome* 129 (1986).

30. So why didn't they go after Agamemnon for killing his daughter? I am not aware that this question is answered anywhere in the trilogy.

31. Either by a tie vote, if the jury consists of eleven Athenians plus Athena, or by a majority vote, if the jury consists of an even number of Athenians plus Athena—it is unclear which.

mother saw during pregnancy could exert a decisive influence on the off-spring. We shall see an example of this belief when we discuss *The Merchant of Venice*. People who believe these things will easily believe that even if the mother is merely an incubator of the father's clone, the womb environment will affect the child's appearance.[32]

Apollo's argument is apt in its dramatic context. It comes right after the Furies have said they punish only the shedding of relatives' blood. This limitation on the Furies' jurisdiction is not completely arbitrary. Murder within the family creates, as I noted earlier, serious problems for a system in which revenge is a duty of family members. A supernatural agency is needed to avenge such murders, and in the *Oresteia* the Furies are that agency, corresponding to the plague sent by Apollo in *Oedipus Tyrannus*. However, for the Furies to exclude from their jurisdiction relatives by marriage creates open season on such relatives. Clytemnestra can kill Agamemnon with relative impunity, knowing that the Furies will not punish her and hoping that their children, his natural avengers, will be deterred by the knowledge that the Furies will punish *them* if they avenge him.

The litigant who takes his stand foursquare on technicality invites his opponent to do the same. Having asserted a distinction, arbitrary in the circumstances, between relatives by blood and by marriage, the Furies open the way for Apollo to make a technical distinction between the male and the female parent. They are hoist by their own forensic petard. They play doubly into Apollo's hands: his belittlement of the woman's role in procreation makes Agamamnon's wrong, the killing of Iphigenia, seem less serious than Clytemnestra's wrong in killing him, as well as distinguishing parricide from matricide.

Arguments based on legal technicalities, such as Apollo's in *Eumenides* or Portia's in *The Merchant of Venice,* tend to be more dramatic, and hence more suitable for imaginative literature, than complex, finely balanced, well-reasoned arguments from legal principles and public policy. Technicalities dazzle and surprise, flatter the audience's expectations of what law is *really* like, and take less time to expound. *Eumenides* would be

---

32. See Lesley Dean-Jones, *Women's Bodies in Classical Greek Science* 149 n. 8 (1994). Apollo's genetic theory, as Dean-Jones points out, appears to have been a minority view even in fifth-century B.C. Athens, although it was later adopted by Aristotle. Like the humbling of the Furies (who are female) at the end of *Eumenides,* and the presentation of Clytemnestra as the sole killer of Agamemnon (rather than jointly with Aegisthus, as in most of the previous treatments, see Gantz, note 24 above, at 664–675), Apollo's theory seems intended to disparage any claim that women might have to the rights of a citizen, rights unrelated to the role of a woman as a breeder. Cf. James Redfield, "Homo Domesticus," in *The Greeks* 153, 162 (Jean-Pierre Vernant ed. 1995): "marriage, by turning the sexual power of women to the end of inheritance, restrains that power and thus secures both the civic order and a right relation with the god."

a bore as drama if Aeschylus had made the trial a serious investigation of the arguments pro and con various conceptions of justifiable or excusable homicide. Dramatic exigency is a reason why readers should not bring to literature too high hopes of finding legal meat.

The greatest work of revenge literature since the Greeks is *Hamlet*.[33] Before Shakespeare's *Hamlet* there was another *Hamlet,* which has been lost, and Kyd's *Spanish Tragedy,* which has many parallels to *Hamlet,* although the avenger in *The Spanish Tragedy,* Hieronimo, is the victim's father rather than his son. The problem for Hieronimo, which will recur in a somewhat different form in *Hamlet,* is that even though he is a Spanish general and thus a man of power in the state, the man who killed his son and whom he wishes to kill in return—Lorenzo—is the nephew of the King of Spain. At first Hieronimo is hopeful that either God or the authorities will punish Lorenzo. But gradually he is driven to accept that the duty of revenge must fall on him. He pretends to be crazy in order to buy time in which to devise and carry out a suitable plan of revenge. Eventually, by staging a play in which both he and Lorenzo have parts, he is able to stab Lorenzo to death. Bellimperia, Lorenzo's sister, takes the opportunity to stab to death her own oppressor and then kills herself. In a nice Senecan touch, Hieronimo bites off his own tongue to prevent himself from giving away secrets under torture (what secrets, the play gives no hint) and then kills Lorenzo's father and himself. *The Spanish Tragedy* ends with Revenge saying that he "shall hale" the villains killed by Hieronimo and Bellimperia "down to deepest hell, / Where none but Furies, bugs and tortures dwell, / . . . For here though death hath end their misery, / I'll there begin their endless tragedy" (IV.5.27–28, 47–48).

The death of Hieronimo is no accident; the avenger dies in virtually every Renaissance revenge play. (*Julius Caesar* and *Macbeth* are exceptions.) This may reflect not only Christian ambivalence about the morality of revenge, which we shall encounter in *Hamlet,* but also recognition that every act of revenge is a fresh wrong that requires punishment in turn. Were the avenger left alive, the audience would be left wondering who would be gunning for him.

The character of *Julius Caesar* as a revenge play is obscured by the fact that Caesar, the victim to be avenged, does not die until the beginning of

---

33. For some recent discussions of Elizabethan and Jacobean revenge drama, see Peter Mercer, Hamlet *and the Acting of Revenge* (1987); Harry Keyishian, *The Shapes of Revenge: Victimization, Vengeance, and Vindictiveness in Shakespeare* (1995); Carol Bishop, "Introduction," in Bishop, *A Critical Edition of Massinger and Field's* The Fatal Dowry 1, 3–25 (1976); Paul N. Siegel, "'Hamlet, Revenge!': The Uses and Abuses of Historical Criticism," 45 *Shakespeare Survey* 15 (1993).

Act III. When that finally happens, Antony utters a blood-curdling vow of revenge over Caesar's body (III.1.265–277):[34]

> Domestic fury and fierce civil strife
> Shall cumber all the parts of Italy;
> Blood and destruction shall be so in use
> And dreadful objects so familiar
> That mothers shall but smile when they behold
> Their infants quartered with the hands of war,
> All pity choked with custom of fell deeds;
> And Caesar's spirit, ranging for revenge,
> With Ate by his side come hot from hell,
> Shall in these confines with a monarch's voice
> Cry havoc and let slip the dogs of war,
> That this foul deed shall smell above the earth
> With carrion men, groaning for burial.

These lines express to perfection the boundlessness of vengeful feelings. Indeed, the Renaissance sense of the infinitude of human will may explain some of the attraction of the theme of revenge to Elizabethan dramatists.

Julius Caesar establishes an opposition, typified by the attitudes of the main characters toward the duty of revenge, between two approaches to keeping order in the state. Brutus's approach is "modern," rationalistic, high-minded, impersonal. It appeals to ideals of civic virtue, individual freedom, and self-government, and disdains "primitive" emotions such as vengefulness. Caesar's and Antony's approaches are personalistic. They are based on a realistic insight (exemplified by Caesar's assessment of Cassius, and by his stated preference for men who are fat and sleek-headed to those with a lean and hungry look) into the sway that personal and familial ties, emotion generally, and superstition hold over men's minds. Both Caesar and Brutus make fatal mistakes, and in both cases this is due to a failure (in Caesar's case, a failure that marks his loss of grip—his failing insight, which is making him more like Brutus) to appreciate the emotional side of human nature. Caesar fails to understand how accepting a crown, which would bring no increase in his political power, already complete, would affront the proud Senators. And he displays excessive rationalism in the manner of Brutus in disregarding the repeated warnings of the soothsayer, the augurs, the elements, and Calpurnia. The play links Brutus and Caesar in small ways as well as large. Both have wives who want to be consulted (no other character's wife appears in the play). Both are susceptible to flattery. Both

---

34. All Shakespeare quotations in this book are from *The Complete Works of Shakespeare* (David Bevington ed., 4th ed. 1992).

see themselves as occupying a higher plane than other men. Both claim exemption from ordinary human weaknesses, a claim undercut in Caesar's case by his superstitiousness and his physical ailments and in Brutus's case by political ineptitude. Both see themselves as embodiments of pure political principle—absolutism in Caesar's case, liberty in Brutus's. Both suffer from hubris.

Brutus's mistakes, which mark him as a political naif, include failing to enlist Cicero in the conspiracy, sparing Antony and then letting him speak at Caesar's funeral, quarreling with Cassius, and ignoring Cassius's military advice. His overarching mistake, reflecting his ignorance of human nature, is to assume that the conspiracy must succeed because all right-thinking men will recognize that Caesar's ambition is a threat to liberty. Brutus doesn't realize that the other conspirators are not acting out of high motives, that the Roman mob is not high-minded and does not care about liberty but does care about the terms of Caesar's will (which left both money and public lands to the Roman citizenry), that Antony cares nothing about either his word or the merits of Brutus's cause but is mad for revenge out of personal loyalty to Caesar and will be able to turn the mob against Brutus, in part by stressing Brutus's ingratitude—Caesar had treated Brutus like a son—and that Caesar's ghost will hound Brutus. The ghost is the eruption of the nonrational into the political plans of a hyperrational statesman.

The impersonal conception of political justice that Brutus espouses is either too advanced for the world depicted in *Julius Caesar* or makes unrealistic demands on human nature. Brutus's obtuseness to the fact that personal bonds trump loyalty to principles is marked by such little things as his refusing to bind the conspirators to him by an oath and by his remark that Caesar's own son, if he had had one, would have approved of the assassination once he was acquainted with the grounds and motives of the conspirators,[35] and by such big things as his inability to understand what makes men like Cassius and Antony tick. Brutus cannot understand the emotional context in which he is operating, in which the assassination of Caesar is certain to trigger a passion for revenge.

The play gives us three views of Caesar. One is as a man past his prime. This is marked not only by the recklessness with which he disregards supernatural portents but also by his indecision and inconsistency—despite his expressed disdain for superstition, his first remark in the play is a request for a magical cure for Calpurnia's sterility—and by the bluster and hol-

---

35. The idea that willingness to condemn a member of one's own family is the acid test of devotion to justice recurs in *Measure for Measure*. See next chapter.

lowness of his rhetoric. He compares himself to Mount Olympus, and shortly after he has twice changed his mind about going to the Capitol he calls himself as "constant as the northern star" (III.1.60). Brutus, however, a dealer in abstractions, sees in Caesar not the aging, slipping tyrant but ambition personified.

For Antony, in contrast, Caesar is simply "the noblest man / That ever lived in the tide of times" (III.1.257–258), an uncritical but unshakable view based on Caesar's record and the personal relationship between the two men. From *Antony and Cleopatra* we learn that if Brutus's theory of governance was premature, and would perhaps be too idealistic for any era, Antony's was becoming outmoded and would soon give way to the calculating methods of Octavius, methods more suitable for governing an empire.[36] The powerful emotional loyalties that characterize a society in which vengeance is an organizing principle are dysfunctional in a large polity.

I do not wish to leave the impression that the Greeks and the Elizabethans shared a monopoly of revenge literature. It is a rich and durable genre. Consider Heinrich von Kleist's great novella *Michael Kohlhaas* (1810). The eponymous hero (the fictionalized version of a historical figure) is a prosperous horse trader in sixteenth-century Brandenburg. A Saxon nobleman extorts two beautiful black horses from Kohlhaas, mistreats them, and refuses to return them. Kohlhaas tries to sue the nobleman, but the man is too influential and Kohlhaas gets nowhere. He attacks the nobleman's home with a band of armed followers, kills everyone except the nobleman himself (who escapes), and burns the place down. His thirst for vengeance is unslaked; and meanwhile, as a by-product of his fruitless legal proceedings, his beloved wife has died, which further inflames him. With a growing band, he cuts a swath of destruction through Germany, burning down cities in his futile search for the nobleman and the still-missing horses. But now Martin Luther, the only man in all of Germany to whom Kohlhaas will listen, intervenes. Although furious at Kohlhaas for the destruction he is wreaking, Luther recognizes that Kohlhaas has been wronged and promises him an amnesty and a renewed effort at legal redress if he will stop the slaughter and turn himself in—which Kohlhaas does. Tangled judicial proceedings follow, but it proves impossible to recover the horses

---

36. I am not suggesting that this was the actual course of Roman history. *Julius Caesar* is broadly consistent with historical fact, but many of the details are inaccurate or fanciful. See, for example, P. A. Brunt, *The Fall of the Roman Republic and Related Essays* 499–500 (1988); Lily Ross Taylor, *Party Politics in the Age of Caesar* 174–175 (1949).

and Kohlhaas is unwilling to accept their monetary worth in damages from the nobleman, who is now terrified and contrite.

Because members of Kohlhaas's band are continuing to maraud, the Holy Roman Emperor decides that the terms of the Luther amnesty have been violated and that Kohlhaas must stand trial for treason. He is tried, convicted, and sentenced to death. Kohlhaas could get his sentence commuted by giving the Elector of Saxony a piece of paper entrusted to him (and that he now wears in a locket around his neck), on which the Elector's destiny is inscribed. But he refuses; he holds the Elector responsible for having failed to bring the nobleman, a subject of the Elector, to justice. Learning that the Elector is planning to search his body after the execution to retrieve the paper, Kohlhaas, with an air of triumph (and a strange echo of *The Spanish Tragedy*), swallows it moments before his execution, to the horror of the Elector, who is in the audience. Kohlhaas dies a happy man.

Clearly Kohlhaas allowed the passion for revenge to run away with him. The incident with the horses, which at the beginning of the novella makes the reader's blood boil and makes him want to spur Kohlhaas on, by the end is recognized to be disproportionate to the destruction, both of others and of self, that is set in train. This is one of the central problems of revenge. And, writing as he was shortly after the subjugation of Germany by Napoleon, Kleist also seems to be commenting on the consequences of German disunity. One reason Kohlhaas has such trouble getting justice is that his oppressor lives in a different German state from him. The political violence and disorder, to which Kohlhaas's band contributes its share, are attributed to divided authority (confusingly shared by the Emperor, the Electors, and Martin Luther—the last representing a "higher law" whose principles the temporal authorities are unable to enforce) and to the absence of an effective system of justice. The ineffectuality of "public revenge," as the Elizabethans would have called it, forces Kohlhaas to assume the avenger's role. Like Hamlet, and like Achilles in the *Iliad,* he is carried away (notably in refusing to accept damages in lieu of the lost horses—and thus symbolically in refusing to accept civil law as a substitute for revenge), becomes a kind of monster (though also hero), and is killed. His death, like Hamlet's, blends triumph and tragedy.

E. L. Doctorow, in his novel *Ragtime* (1975), transposes the story of Michael Kohlhaas to New York at the beginning of the twentieth century. Coalhouse Walker (*Kohle* is the German word for "coal"), a black man who refuses to behave in the submissive manner prescribed for blacks in that period of American history, is the proud owner of a Model T Ford. En route to New York City he is stopped by a rowdy group of firemen who try to make him pay a toll for use of the public street. When he refuses, they deface his car. He tries to obtain legal redress but is blocked by racial prejudice. His fiancée is accidentally killed while trying to petition the President of the United States for assistance in the matter. Giving up on the law, Walker organizes a band of marauding black men, and they conduct a ferocious campaign of revenge that includes blowing up the firehouse (but the fire chief is away at the time) and killing firemen. When Walker and his band barricade themselves in J. Pierpont Morgan's library and threaten to destroy its contents, which include a five-page letter from George Washington—the counterpart of the message that Michael Kohlhaas carried in a locket around his neck—the authorities enlist the aid of Booker T. Washington, the most famous black man of the day and thus the counterpart to Martin Luther in *Michael Kohlhaas*. With Washington's assistance a settlement is negotiated. The Model T is to be restored to its pristine state, the fire chief undergoes a public humiliation, and Coalhouse Walker surrenders—only to be shot down by the police as he leaves the Morgan library.

Doctorow is a skillful writer, and *Ragtime*—with its complex plot and large gallery of historical figures—is a tour de force. The transposition of *Michael Kohlhaas* to a most unlikely venue is accomplished with great panache. But the spirit of the original is lost. Doctorow is unable to invest the Model T Ford with the powerful symbolism of the black horses, is unable to achieve either supernatural or political resonance (despite the ready-at-hand theme of racism), and is unable to make credible the fear that Coalhouse Walker and his band inspire in the white community. In Doctorow's hands, *Michael Kohlhaas* becomes farce or fantasy rather than a meditation on the moral ambiguity of revenge.

The Iliad *and* Hamlet

It is the tenth year of the Trojan War. Apollo has sent a plague on the Greek camp in response to the prayers of his priest, Chryses, for the return of the priest's daughter, Chryseis, captured in a Greek raid and allotted to Agamemnon in the division of the spoils. The intelligent thing would be to return Chryseis to her father. Achilles—young, headstrong, and tactless—insultingly advises Agamemnon to do just that. But in Homeric society, which lacks formal institutions of law and governance, this advice is problematic. The extent of Agamemnon's authority over the allied army is not well defined. Nor is the legitimacy of his position established by the kind of "rule of recognition" that determines the identity of the English Prime Minister or the American President. Were Agamemnon a man of great personal force, the ambiguities in his formal authority would not matter so much. But he is an insecure blusterer. Because his position is inherently unstable, he can ill afford to lose face. If he is to give up Chryseis, he must retaliate for the affront. He cannot retaliate against Apollo, so he chooses Apollo's agent, as it were, in the council—Achilles. He takes away the prize that Achilles had been allotted in the same raid that had netted Agamemnon Chryseis—Briseis.

This is a grievous error. One has only to compare Agamemnon's action in stealing Briseis with Paris's in stealing Helen—the *casus belli*—to see the point. And since Achilles is stronger than Agamemnon and, as events will prove, even more fiercely protective of his personal honor, Agamemnon's gambit is reckless. One of many signs of his unfitness to lead the allied army, it helps explain why the war is still going on after ten years. Achilles' first impulse is to kill Agamemnon on the spot, and he would have done so had not Athena swept down from Mount Olympus and grabbed him by the hair and told him to stay his hand, assuring him that she would arrange an even better revenge. And she does. He sits out the battle, and the Trojans make mincemeat of the Greeks in his absence and almost drive them into the sea. A desperate Agamemnon dispatches emissaries to Achilles with instructions to promise him not only Briseis back, untouched, but also Agamemnon's (surviving) daughter and countless gifts of high value, if only he will rejoin the fighting. Yet conscious that if he fights he will die young, and beginning to question the heroic ethic, in which glory is considered ample compensation for dying young, Achilles does not return to the fight until Hector kills Achilles' beloved companion, Patroclus, who wearing Achilles' armor to fool the Trojans had gone too near Troy. When Achilles does rejoin the fighting, he pursues Hector with a savagery marked by the poet as excessive even by the standards of heroic culture, kills him, and mutilates his body. Hector, also wearing Achilles' old armor, which he had stripped from the slain Patroclus, momentarily and fatally forgot his own limitations, just as Patroclus had done. But at the end of the poem Achilles relents and returns Hector's body, miraculously unmutilated, to Priam. We are given to understand that, by killing Hector, Achilles has sealed both Troy's fate and his own.

At one level, the level one might suppose would be most interesting to a lawyer, the *Iliad* is "about" revenge as a system of justice. We learn that revenge works. Troy will be destroyed in revenge for Paris's having stolen Helen, a deed in violation of the norms of hospitality that are so important in primitive and ancient cultures (norms emphasized even more strongly in the *Odyssey*). But we are also made aware of the high costs of this method of maintaining law, and perhaps invited to wonder whether there might not be a cheaper method of dealing with the likes of Paris. We are also made to understand that revenge ought to have some limits—that Achilles goes too far in mutilating Hector and that the return of Hector's body to Priam is necessary to prevent the Greeks from crossing the line that separates lawful revenge from barbarism.

The *Iliad* also provides a glimpse of composition, both in Agamemnon's elaborate offer to compensate Achilles and in one of the scenes on Achilles' new shield (XVIII.580–592):[37]

> And the people massed, streaming into the marketplace
> where a quarrel had broken out and two men struggled
> over the blood-price for a kinsman just murdered.
> One declaimed in public, vowing payment in full—
> the other spurned him, he would not take a thing—
> so both men pressed for a judge to cut the knot.
> The crowd cheered on both, they took both sides,
> but heralds held them back as the city elders sat
> on polished stone benches, forming the sacred circle,
> grasping in hand the staffs of clear-voiced heralds,
> and each leapt to his feet to plead the case in turn.
> Two bars of solid gold shone on the ground before them,
> a prize for the judge who'd speak the straightest verdict.

But composition is not a perfect substitute for revenge, at least not in the heroic, wartime world, in contrast to the peaceable world depicted on the shield. Or at least not for Achilles—not yet, anyway—when, in refusing Agamemnon's offer, he articulates one of the recurrent problems of a revenge ethic, that of emotional excess (IX.470–473): "No, not if his gifts outnumbered all the grains of sand / and dust in the earth—no, not even then could Agamemnon / bring my fighting spirit round until he pays me back, / pays full measure for all his heartbreaking outrage!" Like Michael Kohlhaas, who refuses the nobleman's offer of damages, Achilles cannot be "bought." Until his anger runs its course or is deflected to another object, there is no possibility of a peaceful settlement. Until then, nothing is bad enough for Agamemnon. The *reductio ad absurdum* of this attitude is Atreus's regret (in Seneca's *Thyestes*) that he did not make Thyestes drink his sons' blood while they were still living. We shall meet the problem again in *Hamlet*.

The *Iliad* teaches not only the excessive character of the passion for revenge but also its fragility as a principle of social order. The vindication of the norms of hospitality through the successful completion (but at what cost!) of the siege of Troy is retarded by the vendetta between Achilles

---

37. All my Homeric quotations in this book are either from Robert Fagles's 1990 translation of the *Iliad* or his 1995 translation of the *Odyssey*. Line references are to the translation rather than to the original.

and Agamemnon. Until the last book of the *Iliad* Achilles acts entirely out of concern for his personal honor and, something that is not clearly distinguished from it, his personal possessions, including Briseis and Patroclus. (This is his "unsociability," which troubled Plato.) It is made to seem almost an accident that at the critical moment Achilles' private incentive to fight Hector becomes aligned with the needs of the Greek alliance, for which Achilles cares not a fig. We know that he will not throw up the game and go home to Phthia, but we also know that he easily could, and knowing this we may be led to wonder whether a social order based on a heroic code and the violent defense of personal honor is stable; the collision between Agamemnon and Achilles in Book I suggests that it is not. Not only Achilles' own questionings of the heroic code, but the events of the *Iliad,* which ends before the fall of Troy and depicts the Greek alliance in disarray, reinforce the suggestion. And beginning with the symbolic death of Achilles when Hector kills Patroclus, who is wearing Achilles' armor (and at first is taken for Achilles), images of death progressively enshroud Achilles,[38] foreshadowing his actual death, which is to occur shortly after the close of the *Iliad,* and contributing to a sense, very strongly marked in the *Odyssey,* that the heroic code is being depicted in its twilight.

Against this reading can be placed the sense the *Iliad* conveys that it is only the prospect of death that gives dignity and value to life. The gods are immortal, yet frivolous and primitive; no god depicted in the *Iliad* has the dignity of Achilles at his best. But when is that? When he is being "modern"? Although we are made acutely conscious of the negative side of the heroic ethic, the poem seems also to be telling us that Achilles' tragic mistake was not the refusal to yield to the entreaties of Agamemnon's emissaries, a refusal solidly grounded in the absolutism of heroic character, but the compromise of permitting Patroclus to fight in Achilles' place wearing Achilles' armor to fool the Trojans. The compromise has the earmarks of modern instrumental reasoning. It is antithetical to the code of honor that defines the vengeance ethic epitomized by Achilles, and it marks his doom and perhaps that of the ethic itself. The ethic of pity glimpsed at the end of the poem has no place for Achilles.

James Boyd White, in a major book on law and literature—the field, indeed, that White did more than anyone else to create—devotes one of his longest chapters to the *Iliad* yet does not discuss the prelegal institutions

---

38. For example, when Achilles kills Hector, Hector is wearing Achilles' old armor; symbolically Achilles kills himself, which is symbolically appropriate since we know that Achilles will die shortly after Hector.

that the poem depicts or the theme of justice that it develops.[39] He makes only two attempts to relate the poem to law. Concerning the wrangle between Achilles and Agamemnon in Book I, he says: "The issue is stated with the directness of a modern legal case: there are apparently two accepted conceptions of what is 'fitting,' only one of which can be satisfied. It is like what happens in law when two lines of precedent, both solidly established, are seen to point opposite ways when a case that no one ever thought of comes up or when two rules of law are suddenly found to be in conflict" (p. 34). Most any argument can be analogized to a legal dispute, as we saw in discussing *Howards End.* What is significant from a lawyer's standpoint about the disputes in the *Iliad,* but does not engage White's interest, is that the society depicted in the poem lacks public agencies for resolving disputes and must therefore fall back on custom, ritual, and the gods (as in Athena's grabbing Achilles by the hair) to minimize the costs of purely private methods of dispute settlement, such as the feud.

White says that "the best analogue" to the language of heroic poetry "in our own experience might be the language of the law, which from some points of view may seem similarly discrete and bounded, similarly constitutive of a certain set of clear social relations and expressive of a certain set of clear values" (p. 55). It is true that both the Homeric dialect and the language of law are artificial languages. All languages are artificial. White's observation will not help us understand what is distinctive about either Homer or law.

In fact it is merely an accident, from White's standpoint, that the *Iliad* is a poem about justice. He has no interest in works of literature that are *about* law or justice, as such. He believes that literature edifies the reader; the readers whom he wants to edify are judges, lawyers, and law students; any great work of literature will do for this purpose. He says rather grandly and vaguely that what we should be seeking from the law and literature movement is "the perpetual affirmation of the individual mind as it seeks community with others."[40] He belongs, in short, to the didactic or moralizing school of literary criticism. The interests of that school, which I treat at length in Part Three of this book, are remote from anything that I discuss here.

In Shakespeare's best-known play we encounter three avengers besides Hamlet himself (so a total of four), all, as it happens, avenger sons. Fortinbras is seeking to avenge his father's death at the hands of Hamlet's father. Laertes is seeking to avenge the death of his father and sister. And a speech by one of

39. White, *When Words Lose Their Meaning: Constitutions and Reconstitutions of Language, Character, and Community,* ch. 2 (1984).

40. James Boyd White, "Law and Literature: 'No Manifesto,'" 39 *Mercer Law Review* 739, 751 (1988).

the players describes the killing of Priam by Achilles' son in revenge for the death of his father at the hands of Priam's son Paris. In Act I the ghost of Hamlet's father commands Hamlet to avenge his murder by his brother Claudius, and the rest of the play revolves around Hamlet's efforts to carry out the ghost's injunction (and as a preliminary thereto to determine the ghost's bona fides) and the counterplots of Claudius.

The central puzzle of this puzzling play is why Hamlet takes so long to carry out his assignment and makes so many mistakes along the way. The mistakes result in the death of seven people (besides Claudius)—Polonius, Ophelia, Laertes, Rosencrantz and Guildenstern, Hamlet's mother, and Hamlet himself, none of whom should have had to die in order for justice to be done. There is the purely mechanical necessity of spinning the play out to a proper length, so that the audience gets its money's worth. Hamlet's simulation of madness is less clearly motivated than Hieronimo's in *The Spanish Tragedy,* making the delay in the later play seem less natural; there are, as we shall see, other loose ends as well. But we suppose that more is involved in the protraction and clumsiness of Hamlet's revenge than authorial unimaginativeness or incompetence. Shakespeare could, as in *Julius Caesar,* have lengthened the play, while shortening the revenge, by starting the action before the death of Hamlet's father and the remarriage of his mother. The *Odyssey* shows that a revenge story does not have to be short even if the revenger is supremely competent.

The medieval Denmark the play depicts has, unlike the society depicted in the *Iliad,* a formal legal system. But Claudius certainly, and Hamlet and the other principals probably, are effectively above the law. There is little likelihood that Hamlet would be punished for killing Polonius and trying to conceal his body. Claudius raises the issue briefly, only to reject it on the ground that Hamlet is too popular. And there is no hint that Claudius might be deposed or otherwise brought to book for murdering the rightful king and making an "incestuous" marriage, as Elizabethans considered marriage with a brother's widow to be, except possibly under the strict conditions of a Levirate marriage.[41] The only way for Hamlet to obtain justice against Claudius, or for Laertes to obtain justice against Hamlet, is by revenge.

---

41. That is, if the deceased brother did not have a son, a condition not satisfied in *Hamlet.* That *Hamlet*'s first audiences would have been horrified by the remarriage, both because of its incestuous character and because of its haste, is strongly argued in Roland Mushat Frye, *The Renaissance Hamlet: Issues and Responses in 1600* 77–82 (1984). But Graham Bradshaw, *Misrepresentations: Shakespeare and the Materialists* 294 n. 25 (1993), does not think that the audience would have been greatly troubled by the "incestuous" character of the marriage. In the play itself, only Hamlet and the ghost describe the marriage as incestuous, though the very name "Claudius," Roman rather than Danish, would remind some in the audience of the incestuous Roman emperor.

Yet the play contains a good deal of implicit criticism of revenge. Those seven more or less innocent deaths mark it as an expensive way of doing justice, reminding us that revenge can place responsibilities on people who are not temperamentally suited to bear them, unlike a system of formal justice, whose personnel—judges, police, prosecutors, and so forth—are self-selected and full-time. Their training and experience, plus whatever aptitudes or bent made them choose a career in law enforcement, give some assurance of their having the necessary skills and, what is almost as important, the necessary callousness for doing society's dirty work efficiently and contentedly. As Hamlet puts it, "the hand of little employment hath the daintier sense" (V.1.69–70). And when he says at the end of Act I, having just received his marching orders from the ghost, "The time is out of joint. O cursèd spite / That ever I was born to set it right!" (1.5.197–198), the emphasis falls on "I." It will soon become plain that Hamlet is not a fit instrument for the ghost's plan; only there is no one else. Hamlet kills Claudius after having given up active, and thus far bungling and ineffectual, efforts to do so. And it is only by chance that he discovers what is afoot and is able to kill Claudius before he himself dies. His failure to check the foils before beginning the match—knowing what he knows of Claudius's previous effort to kill him and of Laertes' rage against him—is negligent in the extreme.

Claudius, implicitly commenting on Hamlet's dilatoriness in making an attempt on his life, warns Laertes that anger may cool with time, a traditional problem with revenge as a method of law enforcement. Claudius is also eloquent on the problem of many a slip 'twixt cup and lips, another of Hamlet's problems. They are not Laertes' problems. Hamlet acts too slowly and cools; Laertes acts too quickly while still red hot. Hamlet wastes time building an unnecessary case against Claudius, though it may not have appeared unnecessary to Hamlet. (I shall come back to this important point.) Laertes, who as Polonius's son has the same duty of vengeance as Hamlet does toward his own father, leaps to the wrong conclusion—thus underscoring the dangers of being a judge in one's own cause.

Hamlet also illustrates the problem of the avenger's emotional excess. He forgoes an opportunity to kill Claudius while the king is praying. Had he taken the opportunity, those seven lives would have been spared, but he wants to make sure that Claudius burns in hell. (Notice the parallel to *The Spanish Tragedy*.) Similarly, though characteristically more crudely, when Claudius says to Laertes, "Hamlet comes back. What would you undertake / To show yourself in deed your father's son / More than in words?" Laertes answers, "To cut his throat i'th' church." Claudius replies, "No place, indeed, should murder sanctuarize; / Revenge should have no bounds" (IV.7.128–129). But it should; that must be one of the points that we are meant to bring away from the play.

Hamlet stands to its contemporary revenge literature, in point of ambivalence as well as of quality, as the *Iliad* presumably stood to the lost heroic epics on which it built. In many Elizabethan and Jacobean revenge plays the violence and the revenger's emotional excess are so grotesque that any social or ethical observation is submerged in melodramatic effect, as in that strange cross between *Thyestes* and *The Spanish Tragedy*, Shakespeare's early play *Titus Andronicus*. Among other horrors, Titus, the avenger (like Hieronomo a high official who cannot obtain justice through lawful means because the villains are royal personages), borrowing a leaf from Atreus, kills Queen Tamora's two sons and serves them to her in a pie. He remarks to someone who asks him to fetch the boys (V.3.60–63),

> Why, there they are, both baked in this pie,
> Whereof their mother daintily hath fed,
> Eating the flesh that she herself hath bred.
> 'Tis true, 'tis true; witness my knife's sharp point

—whereupon he stabs the queen and is stabbed in turn. Or consider Tourneur's *Revenger's Tragedy*, written a few years after *Hamlet*. The pattern is familiar. The evildoer is the king; so Vindice, to avenge his wife's murder by the king, must act outside the law. Vindice has kept his wife's skull, and now he covers it with poison. He lures the lecherous king to a dark bower on the pretense of supplying him with a woman. The king embraces the skull in the dark; to make the king's death still more painful, Vindice has lured the queen and her lover to the bower so that the last thing the king will see before the poison kills him is his wife in an act of adultery. When the king tries to shout, Vindice cuts his tongue out. In Webster's *White Devil*, the method of revenge against Bracchiano is to smear poison on the inside of the lower visor of his helmet, causing him hideous agonies which go on for pages; finally the avengers get impatient and strangle him.

The most dramatic rejection of the revenge ethic is found in the New Testament; and we must consider whether *Hamlet,* and perhaps the gorier revenge plays as well, are trying to remind the audience of *Romans* 12:19–20: "Avenge not yourselves, but rather give place unto wrath: for it is written, Vengeance is mine; I will repay, saith the Lord. Therefore if thine enemy hunger, feed him; if he thirst, give him drink: for in so doing thou shalt heap coals of fire on his head."[42] There are two ways to take

---

42. The King James Bible, from which I have quoted, had not yet been written when Shakespeare wrote *Hamlet*. But the bibles he would have known—the Coverdale Bible (1535),

this. The first, suggested by the reference to "coals of fire," is that God will straighten out all the accounts in the afterlife. It is not a practical formula for living. No society can maintain order just by appeals to posthumous rewards and sanctions. The second interpretation, equally impractical, is, in its purest form—leave it to God to punish the wrongdoer in this life; do not even try to get the help of God's delegate, the king—embraced in the last act of *Hamlet*. Hamlet abandons active efforts to kill Claudius, trusting in providence to arrange time, place, and manner. "There's a divinity that shapes our ends, / Rough-hew them how we will . . . The readiness is all" (V.2.10–11, 220). Providence obliges. By Act V the ghost has been forgotten—a scary, pagan figure.[43] The revenge ethic that the ghost embodies is made to seem primitive, pre-Christian. Hamlet's death is suffused with a tragic dignity that it would have lacked had he carried out with smooth efficiency the task assigned him by his father's ghost.

Yet within the dramatic structure and implied values of the play as a whole, quietistic resignation would not have been an adequate response by Hamlet to the ghost's urgings. The play portrays with consummate art the negative aspects of private revenge as a method of vindicating rights and maintaining public order—in the stupid bloodthirstiness of Laertes and the destructive ineffectuality of Hamlet's schemes of revenge—but leaves us with the abiding sense that Hamlet had no choice but to try to avenge his father. "Honour has duties which Christianity refuses to recognise."[44] Euripides sought to debunk the Orestes legend by situating his *Orestes* in a society with a fully operative legal system, in which—as Clytemnestra's father reminds Orestes—Orestes did not have to kill his mother; he could have turned her over to the authorities for punishment. Hamlet had no such option.

The ambivalence about revenge that one senses in *Hamlet* reflects the ambivalence of Shakespeare's society about this issue.[45] The Bible made re-

---

the Geneva Bible (1583), and the Bishop's Bible (1588)—do not differ materially from the King James version in the relevant passage. Here for example is the same passage in the Coverdale Bible: "Avenge not yourselves, but give room unto the wrath of God. For it is written: Vengeance is mine, and I will reward, sayeth the Lord. Therefore if thine enemy hunger, feed him. If he thirst, give him drink. For in so doing thou shalt heap coals of fire upon his head."

43. "The king dies for the murder of Gertrude and the prince, not for a poisoning in the orchard. Old Hamlet does not return to triumph over the corpses of his enemies." Kerrigan, note 2 above, at 187.

44. William Empson, "Hamlet," in Empson, *Essays on Shakespeare* 79, 121 (David B. Pirie ed. 1986).

45. See Frye, note 41 above, ch. 2; Catherine Belsey, "The Case of Hamlet's Conscience," 76 *Studies in Philology* 127 (1979). This ambivalence was mirrored in the career of James I, the patron of Shakespeare's company (the King's Men). As king of Scotland before he ascended the

venge problematic in a way that it had not been for the Greeks. The or-thodox Elizabethan solution was to distinguish three forms of revenge—God's revenge, public revenge, and private revenge—and to link the first two in the notion that the rulers of political society, as God's agents in the political sphere, were to "Smite as God Smites," wielding powers "or-dained by God to fill the seat of vengeance."[46] The criminal justice system was thereby reconciled with the divine monopoly of vengeance. This was an important move but left unresolved cases in which the criminal justice system was inoperative, as in *Hamlet*. That was the domain of private re-venge.

The dual interpretation of God's revenge results in four possible meth-ods of dealing with wrongdoers, of which the fourth—private revenge—is the most problematic:

(1) Divine revenge—afterlife	(3) Public revenge (divine delegation)
(2) Divine revenge—this life	(4) Private revenge

For us, the choice is likely to be between (3) and (4). For Hamlet, it is be-tween (2) and (4). When Hamlet call himself heaven's "scourge and min-ister" (III.4.182), we see the possibility of linking private revenge to God's revenge in the same way that public revenge is linked to it, by constitut-ing the private revenger God's delegate. We also see the impracticality of leaving wrongdoers to the judgment of heaven merely because the official system of temporal punishment has been rendered impotent. The case for Hamlet's taking revenge against Claudius is strengthened by the fact that Claudius, besides being a murderer (and of his own brother—like Cain),

---

English throne, James had tried to control the blood feuds that were rampant in his country; yet at the same time he was a determined and ruthless avenger of his father's murder and of other wrongs done to his family. See Alvin Kernan, *Shakespeare, the King's Playwright: Theater in the Stuart Court 1603–1613* 37–44 (1995); cf. Jenny Wormald, "An Early Modern Postscript: The Sandlaw Dispute, 1546," in *The Settlement of Disputes in Early Medieval Europe*, note 16 above, at 191.

46. Lily B. Campbell, "Theories of Revenge in Renaissance England," in *Collected Papers of Lily B. Campbell* 153, 163 (1968).

and an "adulterate beast," is a tyrant and a usurper. Tyrannicide is a more defensible form of private revenge than regicide based purely on the king's private misconduct.[47]

Hamlet makes its strongest case against private revenge on the practical rather than on the conceptual level. Hamlet commits the standard revenger's mistake of allowing himself to get carried away by emotion and then of cooling.[48] Remember that the train of unnecessary deaths is set in motion when he forgoes the opportunity to kill Claudius at prayer because he wants to make sure that Claudius's punishment is eternal. The prayer soliloquy reveals to the audience that Hamlet is mistaken in believing that if he kills Claudius at prayer, the king may be saved. It was an odd mistake for Hamlet to make. Since he never deludes himself that Claudius might voluntarily relinquish the fruits of his crimes—the kingship and the queen—he should have realized that Claudius's "repentance" must be false and would not save Claudius from damnation. There is no textual basis for thinking that Hamlet could not be so bloodthirsty as to wish to damn Claudius for eternity and that therefore the reason he gives for sparing him must be a pretext. Not only is excessive bloodthirstiness the occupational hazard of a revenger, but it is a marked characteristic of Hamlet in Act III. What the text fairly implies is that Hamlet is a bungler at revenge and spares Claudius for a bad reason. And having done so, and though now fully convinced of Claudius's guilt, Hamlet continues to dither (as he accuses himself in Act IV), with disastrous results. The excess of heat that caused him to stay his hand when he had Claudius in his sights gives way to an excess of coldness that induces passivity.

A difficult question is whether the concern earlier expressed by Hamlet that the ghost might be a devil—the concern that leads him initially to delay his revenge until he can verify Claudius's guilt, which he does eventually by means of the play he stages—is a pretext for delay. Hamlet tumbles to the idea in the midst of reflections on his inexplicable and unpardonable tardiness in carrying out the ghost's command. And doubt about the ghost's bona fides is a convenient rationalization for past delay and an excuse for more delay. Yet from the concerns expressed by Horatio and the nightwatchmen at the beginning of the play, as well as from the general reputation of ghosts among Elizabethans, we can infer that Hamlet had reason to fear that the purported ghost of his father might be a devil. A

47. Frye, note 41 above, at 38–40.
48. The mistake is standard; obviously I do not mean that Hamlet is a standard revenger—the characterization attributed to me in Peter Read Teachout, "Lapse of Judgment," 77 *California Law Review* 1259, 1277–1278, 1280 (1989).

modern audience, because it does not believe in ghosts or devils, does not think to question the bona fides of the ghost, regarding it as just a piece of stage machinery to be taken at face value, like a talking mouse. *Hamlet's* original audiences would have considered the status of the ghost (Hamlet's father? Or a devil disguised as Hamlet's father?) a live issue, one that would naturally trouble Hamlet.[49]

Claudius, moreover, has such a civil and plausible demeanor—he is the Stanley Baldwin of Shakespearean villains—that Hamlet could well be skeptical about the ghost's uncorroborated accusation. Claudius's soliloquies are necessary to make his wickedness convincing to the audience, and Hamlet is not in the audience. So Hamlet's sudden doubt about the ghost's bona fides has some foundation. And it is reinforced by the pronounced interrogative mood of the play, announced in literally the first line— "Who's there?"—and carried forward by such seemingly peripheral scenes as the one in which Polonius sets Reynaldo to spy on Laertes in Paris, and by the abundance of misunderstandings that plague the characters (for example, Hamlet's belief that the person behind the arras is Claudius, or Laertes' belief that Claudius killed Polonius).[50] Hamlet's doubt also illustrates the problem of proof that plagues a revenge system of justice (a problem also stressed in *Othello*) because there is no machinery of investigation and adjudication, a problem that plagued sixteenth-century adjudication as well.[51] Yet the doubt proceeds from Hamlet's character as much as from objective circumstances. He repeatedly blames himself for his delay in acting on the ghost's instructions. And as late as Act V, long after the ghost's veracity has been confirmed to Hamlet's satisfaction, he is wondering whether he has enough evidence to proceed against Claudius.[52]

A sufficient motive for delay might seem to be the possibility that Claudius is armed, or surrounded by guards, or that someone might seek to avenge *his* killing. But these conjectures have scant basis in the text of the play (in contrast to *The Spanish Tragedy*)—and in fact no one lifts a fin-

---

49. See Frye, note 41 above, at 14–17.

50. Among the oddest of the misunderstandings is the belief, which is not supported in the text, that Ophelia committed suicide, rather than having drowned in an accident to which her insanity contributed.

51. See Alexander Welsh, *Strong Representations: Narrative and Circumstantial Evidence in England* 132–134 (1992).

52. Even today there are readers who believe that the ghost is a devil and Hamlet either his witting or unwitting accomplice. See, for example, Arthur McGee, *The Elizabethan Hamlet* (1987). If we accept such readings, however, "We [are] left with a period piece which shows how immoderate grief is every bit as sinful as Claudius suggests, and how melancholy is a weapon taken into Satan's hand." Graham Bradshaw, "Hamlet in the Prison of Arden," *London Review of Books,* Sept. 2–15, 1992, p. 12.

ger when Hamlet stabs Claudius at the end of the play and then makes him drink from the poisoned cup to boot. Although the royal trappings are necessary both to elevate the characters in an Elizabethan audience's esteem and to put them far enough above the law to make the duty of revenge plausible, the political overtones so prominent in Shakespeare's Roman and history plays are muted. Cassius needs to organize a conspiracy in order to assassinate Caesar. There is little indication that Hamlet has a political problem in dealing with Claudius.

It may be that an Elizabethan audience, more impressed than a modern one with the majesty of kingship and the New Testament's injunction against vengeance, would have taken for granted that the ghost's command could not be carried out quickly and easily. The mention of the king's Swiss guards; the fact that Polonius, and later Rosencrantz and Guildenstern, have been set to watch over Hamlet; Rosencrantz's "cess of majesty" speech (III.3.15–23); and Claudius's remark to Gertrude (deeply ironic though it is), "Do not fear [for] our person. / There's such divinity doth hedge a king / That treason can but peep to what it would, / Acts little of his will" (IV.5.126–129), may have been all the hints that such an audience required. Yet Hamlet himself voices no concerns along these lines. His words and deeds suggest that the basic cause of his delays and pratfalls is that he is temperamentally unsuited to play the avenger's role. He is not a Vindice, Titus, Hieronimo (who does hesitate a little), Kohlhaas, or Orestes.[53] As his father's ghost tells him when it returns in Act III, and as Hamlet keeps telling himself, he does not have the implacable rage, the single-minded fury, the towering wrath, that a proper avenger has. The "To be, or not to be" soliloquy is the *locus classicus* of the mind in equipoise—the mind that sees both sides of every question—as well as an ingenious rationalization for inaction. More than a habit of mind is involved. Hamlet is labile; his strongly marked impulsiveness is the other side of his quickness to cool. When he asks the ghost to make haste to acquaint him with the details of the murder so that "I, with wings as swift / As meditation or the thoughts of love, / May sweep to my revenge" (1.5.30–33), it is as if he realizes that unless he acts quickly he may fail to act at all—his initial anger may give way to his characteristically detached and reflective posture.

---

53. This is not to deny the interesting parallels between Orestes and Hamlet, first pointed out by Gilbert Murray. For a recent discussion, see A. D. Nuttall, *The Stoic in Love: Selected Essays on Literature and Ideas* 34–38 (1989); and cf. Kerrigan, note 2 above, at 173–174. Yet an even better classical predecessor of Hamlet may be Telemachus, who until his father turns up alive is acutely conscious of his duty to punish the suitors for their disrespect for his parents but is too young to carry out his duty and therefore frets and sulks.

Neither does Hamlet have that overdeveloped—and also automatic, un-hesitating—sense of honor so well illustrated by Fortinbras's willingness to sacrifice thousands of lives for a worthless bit of land. A prey to the teem-ing imagination revealed in his soliloquies, Hamlet becomes distracted by what from the standpoint of vengeance is a side issue: his mother's adul-tery and incest. (It is a side issue because his mother is innocent of his fa-ther's murder and because his father has told him not to harm her.) Hamlet is a thinker, but not a planner like Antony. Maybe he assumes an "antic disposition" because he knows that he is no dissembler, either, again un-like Antony. Hamlet seems more interested in the implications of his uncle's and mother's behavior for the human condition than in getting on with the task given him by his father's ghost. The only thing that "works" for Hamlet in the first four acts is the escape from the trap set for him by Claudius in the voyage to England. And because that is due to luck or Providence—a vague unease prompts Hamlet to search Rosencrantz and Guildenstern's things for the fatal commission, and the fight with the pi-rates the next day enables him to get back to Denmark before Claudius dis-covers his couriers' fate—Hamlet is encouraged to assume a fatalistic stance in Act V.

I hope it doesn't sound as if I'm criticizing Hamlet. That he should be such a *thoughtful* person—bookish (books are an important prop in *Hamlet*[54]), a university student, a questioner of his corrupt society, a per-son who wants to *deliberate* before he acts[55]—that he should lack the grim single-mindedness of his father and of Fortinbras, both comfortable denizens of a traditional honor-bound vengeance-based society—is alto-gether to his credit, especially given the ambivalence with which his soci-ety (more precisely, the society of *Hamlet*'s original audiences) viewed re-venge. But if so sympathetic, so ultimately admirable a character as I think we are intended to find Hamlet—not to mention such a brave man and so good a swordsman, as we learn in the last act—cannot negotiate the shoals of a revenge culture, it tells us a lot about such a culture.

So *Hamlet* is a criticism of revenge. Should this be taken to be Shakespeare's "position" on revenge? Just to ask the question is to make three mistakes: that of projecting the implied moral values in a work of lit-erature onto the author; that of wanting literature to be edifying or didac-tic; and that of trying to evaluate the morality of revenge without regard to circumstances. Shakespeare's works display a range of attitudes toward

54. Alastair Fowler, "The Case against Hamlet: Understanding the Multiple Viewpoints of Shakespeare's 'Renaissance Realism,'" *Times Literary Supplement,* Dec. 22, 1995, pp. 6, 7.
55. Frye, note 41 above, at 170–177.

revenge, with *Hamlet* lying midway between plays like *Titus Andronicus, Julius Caesar, King Lear,* and *Macbeth* on the one hand, which depict it more or less uncritically, and *The Merchant of Venice* and *Romeo and Juliet* on the other hand, which reject it resoundingly. The "ancient grudge" between the Montagues and the Capulets is made absurd, though not funny, by the fact that the origin of the feud has been forgotten (unlike the origin of the Jews' "ancient grudge" against the Christians in *The Merchant of Venice*) and that the feud is taking place in what is depicted as a civilized, modern, and well-governed city-state; by the lack of motive for Tybalt's malignancy; by the speed with which the feud is ended when the heads of the feuding families are finally brought to their senses by the deaths of Romeo and Juliet; and by the love between Romeo and Juliet, which makes the murderous antipathy between their families seem all the more irrational.

Hamlet's dilemma is resolved, in a curious fashion, in William Faulkner's story "An Odor of Verbena," the last chapter of his loosely knit novel *The Unvanquished.* The story is set in Mississippi shortly after the Civil War. Colonel Sartoris, a violent and quarrelsome man in the tradition of the Old South,[56] has had a long-standing quarrel with a local businessman, Redmond. A duel is inevitable. But Sartoris is "growing tired of killing men" and tells his son Bayard, a law student and a symbol of the New South that will rise from the ashes of the old, that he intends to confront Redmond unarmed. The next day Sartoris goes to Redmond's office, and Redmond kills him. It turns out that Sartoris was armed, and although apparently he did not draw his gun, Sartoris's supporters pronounce it a fair duel. Yet they expect Bayard to avenge his father's killing. Bayard, however, is determined to put the revenge ethic behind him. The day after his father's death he goes to Redmond's office, unarmed; enters; and walks toward the desk where Redmond is seated. Redmond fires twice, but deliberately aims wide and misses. When Bayard reaches the desk, Redmond gets up, puts on his hat, walks bravely through the throng of the Sartoris supporters outside—his bravery lies in the fact that he knows they will think he has killed Bayard—and keeps walking straight to the train station, where he takes the next train out of Mississippi (with no baggage—nothing), never to return. The Sartoris hangers-on, who serve a choral function, speaking as in a Greek tragedy the conventional wisdom, had been insistent that Colonel Sartoris's death had to be avenged. But when they

56. See Wyatt-Brown, note 15 above, ch. 2 and p. 352 (1982); Jack K. Williams, *Dueling in the Old South: Vignettes of Social History* (1980); Edward L. Ayers, *Vengeance and Justice: Crime and Punishment in the 19th Century American South* (1984).

find out what Bayard has done, they are impressed by his bravery. He has made his point; Redmond has seconded it.

"Bayard, who fears the imputation of cowardice, has done a braver thing than the code demanded: he has gone to the assassin's office, thus honouring the code, but has transcended the code by having determined, at the risk of his own death, that he would not shoot Redmond."[57] Hamlet, too, can be thought to have transcended his father's simple code of honor by having resisted its implications and yet in the end having achieved the goal set for him. Claudius does die, just as Redmond does exile himself.

Colonel Sartoris had a young wife, Drusilla, who was only a few years older than Bayard, and she and Bayard had fallen in love. (It is as if Gertrude had been Hamlet's young stepmother!) Bayard had been on the verge of telling his father about his relationship with Drusilla when his father had said he was going up against Redmond the next day unarmed; Bayard kept silent. (Did he expect him to be killed? Want him to be killed?) When the colonel is killed, Drusilla is desperately eager for Bayard to avenge him. She presses him to take two huge dueling pistols, which appear to have phallic significance for her. When Bayard returns home after having spared Redmond, Drusilla has gone, apparently forever. In rejecting the revenge ethic (for the Rule of Law? Bayard is a law student, after all), Bayard has rejected, not entirely willingly, a whole complex of traditional southern values, in which masculinity is correlated with readiness to kill in defense of honor.

If Bayard is unwilling, Hamlet is unable, to play the role scripted for a revenger. Richard Weisberg disagrees. He attributes Hamlet's hesitations and mistakes not to the problematics of revenge but to Hamlet's envying Claudius as a man of action who has succeeded where Hamlet has failed—namely, in a plot to kill—and to Hamlet's resentment at having to play up to Claudius in order to ensure his own succession to the throne when Claudius dies.[58] Hamlet in this analysis personifies the weak, ineffectual verbalizer confronted with the Nietzschean "master" or *Übermensch,* who, as we shall see in Chapter 5, is above revenge.

Hamlet is resentful, and naturally so. But the play presents Claudius as a sneak, liar, tippler, mediocrity, and weakling, who dispossessed a much superior man (Hamlet senior) of position, wife, and life and has dispossessed

57. Cleanth Brooks, "The Criticism of Fiction: The Role of Close Analysis," in Brooks, *A Shaping Joy: Studies in the Writer's Craft* 143, 148 (1971).

58. See Richard Weisberg, "Hamlet and Ressentiment," 29 *American Imago* 318 (1972); Weisberg, *The Failure of the Word: The Protagonist as Lawyer in Modern Fiction* 8–9, 27 (1984).

another superior man, young Hamlet, of his expectancy of the kingship in succession to his father (not an automatic succession as in a hereditary monarchy, but, apparently, presumptive). Claudius has a pleasant manner and is politically astute—he deftly turns aside the threats to his throne posed successively by Fortinbras and Laertes—but these are an old man's qualities that Hamlet does not admire. He could hardly envy Claudius, and the play contains no hint of such envy. Nor is it suggested that Claudius either controls the succession or has a rival candidate to Hamlet; he seems happy to let Hamlet succeed him so long as he can continue to reign and enjoy Gertrude in peace. And Hamlet makes no efforts to ingratiate himself with Claudius—quite the opposite.

As Weisberg puts it, Hamlet's reaction to the situation in which he finds himself as a result of the encounter with his father's ghost is one of "generalized negativity."[59] Hamlet becomes disgusted with women, himself, indeed all of humanity; and this disgust, rather than the task that the ghost has set him, becomes the focus of his attention until he returns to Denmark, resigned but no longer disgusted, after the aborted voyage to England. But Hamlet's generalized negativity cannot be equated with envy of Claudius; and Hamlet himself—with all his hesitations and impetuosities the undoubted hero of the play—is not one of Nietzsche's "priestly men" or "last men." On the contrary, by the last act of the play Hamlet has become Nietzsche's self-overcoming man, too "big" to plot revenge. Hamlet kills Claudius on impulse when he discovers that his mother has drunk a poisoned chalice intended for him. He had said, very Nietzsche-like, "praised be rashness" (V.2.7), and Claudius had described him as being "remiss, / Most generous and free from all contriving" (IV.7.135–136), which could as well be said of Zarathustra. Earlier, when Polonius directed that the players be "used" (housed and fed) according to their "desert," Hamlet had reproved him: "God's bodikin, man, much better. Use every man after his desert, and who should scape whipping? Use them after your own honour and dignity. The less they deserve, the more merit is in your bounty" (II.2.529–532). In this passage, which looks forward to his fatalism and magnanimity in the last act, Hamlet rejects the concern with balance, reciprocity, and accounts-keeping that underlies a revenge system (and much more). This is Hamlet *transcending* the system of resentful revenge later criticized by Nietzsche. The same thing happens in *The Merchant of Venice,* with Shylock the resentful revenger and Bassanio (notably in his choice of the lead casket over the gold or silver) rejecting the ac-

---

59. "Hamlet and Ressentiment," note 58 above, at 325.

counts-keeping approach. In *The Merchant of Venice* "the graspers and hoarders lose; the givers gamble and win."[60]

Just as there are affinities between Nietzsche and Freud, there are affinities between Weisberg's Nietzschean interpretation of *Hamlet* and Freud's interpretation, which attributed Hamlet's delays to the Oedipus complex.[61] By killing Hamlet's father and marrying Hamlet's mother, Claudius has done what Hamlet himself (a Freudian would say) unconsciously wanted to do. Therefore Hamlet identifies with Claudius and is made doubly uncomfortable at the thought of killing him. It would be like killing himself; and supplanting Claudius as king would imply, in a symbolic sense, marrying Gertrude. There is no textual support for these conjectures, and yet they (and Weisberg's) are tame compared to what can be found in much *Hamlet* criticism.[62] Consider the fantastic conjectures that have been built on one of the lesser puzzles in the play: Claudius's failure to catch on to the play within a play when it is first performed in dumb show (pantomime), even though, as described in what apparently are Shakespeare's stage directions, the dumb show depicts Lucianus, its villain, pouring poison into the king's ear—just as Claudius had done to Hamlet's father—and then successfully wooing the queen. One conjecture is that Claudius is not surprised by the dumb show because he had seen the play before and indeed got his method of murdering Hamlet's father from it.[63] In this view the only thing that alarms Claudius is that in the spoken version Lucianus turns out to be the player-king's nephew instead of brother, which implies that Hamlet may go after Claudius. The changing of the murderer from brother to nephew does pull Hamlet into the play within the play, and by thus suggesting that he is a murderer of sorts it presages his imminent killing of Polonius, which in turn will place Hamlet in the approximate relationship to Laertes that Claudius bears to Hamlet. But the idea that Claudius had seen the play before is baseless.

One critic has said that in staging the play within the play Hamlet "is

60. Joseph Pequigney, "The Two Antonios and Same-Sex Love in *Twelfth Night* and *The Merchant of Venice*," in *Shakespeare and Gender: A History* 178, 190 (Deborah Barker and Ivo Kamps eds. 1995). Despite the title of this article, the author argues convincingly against the hypothesis advanced by some modern critics that the relation between Antonio and Bassanio is an erotic one. See id. at 187.

61. The Freudian interpretation of *Hamlet,* first suggested in 1900 in *The Interpretation of Dreams,* was elaborated in Ernest Jones, *Hamlet and Oedipus* (1949).

62. See, for example, Jacques Lacan, "Desire and the Interpretation of Desire in *Hamlet*," *Yale French Studies,* nos. 55/56, p. 11 (1977); Ned Lukacher, *Primal Scenes: Literature, Philosophy, Psychoanalysis,* ch. 6 (1986); *Shakespeare and the Question of Theory,* pt. 4 (Patricia Parker and Geoffrey Hartman eds. 1985).

63. Lukacher, note 62 above, at 231–232.

trying to recreate his infantile glimpses of his parents' coitus."[64] Another "that the manner of Claudius's crime reveals symbolically that Claudius poisoned his brother with words, and more particularly, words that revealed to old Hamlet that he, Claudius, knew of his brother's treachery in poisoning old Fortinbras" with the help of Polonius.[65] There is no basis in the text for suspecting foul play in the death of old Fortinbras. He died in a fair duel—which he had provoked—with Hamlet's father.[66] The excesses of *Hamlet* criticism, in suggesting the degree to which some literary critics feel free to range far beyond the text—even to contradict it—in seeking to "interpret" literature, provide a foretaste of current fashions in both literary and legal theory, discussed in later chapters.

There are interesting parallels between Achilles and Hamlet. Both completely dominate their fictive worlds because of a natural authority sensed by the other characters and because of their unsurpassed detachment and insight. Both are young and impulsive yet mature rapidly near the end of their brief lives. In both the transition from youth to maturity is signified by a period of absence—Achilles' sitting out the fighting in his tent, Hamlet's aborted voyage to England. Hamlet's return—he was brought naked (or so he writes his uncle) onto the shore of Denmark—is a symbolic rebirth that helps the reader accept his abrupt maturing. Both characters resist the tasks that character and fate have set them—fighting Trojans, in the case of Achilles, and avenging his father's death and mother's dishonor, in the case of Hamlet—and interrupt the tasks while reflecting on them. Both are inadvertently responsible for the death of the person or persons who are nearest and dearest to them, plus an assortment of bystanders.

Man is the animal that can imagine a life of triumph but cannot achieve it; that can imagine eternal bliss but knows that he will die; that can imagine a better world but learns that the improvements, if any, will be modest in his lifetime; that can imagine a life of ease but lives a life of frustration. As Shakespeare's Troilus said, the will is infinite but the execution

---

64. Id. at 225, n. 70, summarizing a theory of Otto Rank's. This theory is also defended in Stanley Cavell, *Disowning Knowledge in Six Plays of Shakespeare,* ch. 5 (1987). In a similar vein Cavell argues that Othello killed Desdemona because he was "horrified by human sexuality." Id. at 137. "The torture of logic in his [Othello's] mind we might represent as follows: Either I shed her blood [on our wedding night] and scarred her or I did not. If I did not then she was not a virgin and this is a stain upon me. If I did then she is no longer a virgin and this is a stain upon me. Either way I am contaminated." Id. at 135.

65. Lukacher, note 62 above, at 225–226, summarizing a theory of Nicolas Abraham's.

66. Notice that after being deflected from seeking revenge against the Danes, young Fortinbras will—we are led to believe at the end of the play—succeed Claudius as king of Denmark. This can be taken as another implied criticism of the ethic of revenge.

confined; the desire boundless but the act a slave to limit. It takes a while for these unpleasant truths—the "narcissistic wound" in Freudian terms, the shocking "recognition of our essential helplessness and aloneness"[67]— to sink in. Most young people inhabit the fool's paradise of thinking they can live their dreams and could set right all of the world's imperfections but for the fears and hesitations of the old men who run things. Their imagination has not been chastened by experience.

Distinctly young men at the outset,[68] Achilles and Hamlet receive a sudden, rude awakening at the hands of distinctly adult figures concerning the nature of the world—Achilles from Agamemnon's snatching away his prize and Hamlet from the overhasty and incestuous remarriage of his mother and from the encounter with the ghost. They react to these revelations with the innocent indignation of youth. "Hamlet's dangerous subversive humour—which is neither madness nor sanity, but a denial of the authority of the society that holds him—permanently defines a freedom and impotence of the young."[69] Afterward comes the painful process of coming to terms with reality, of learning to live in the world, of learning the inevitability of mistakes and disasters.[70]

The character of these works as literature about maturing is signaled by the global reflections to which the opening shocks provoke the protagonists. Achilles begins to think about the choice that is not a choice: although he is free to decide whether to have a short glorious life or a long inglorious one, his character makes the choice a foregone conclusion. We die after a short time but as participants in a human community can live on indefinitely in the memory of our successors. Achilles' exploits will be sung by Homer hundreds of years later,[71] but only if the exploits are glorious, implying risk-taking and a high probability of early death. So the short glorious life is actually longer than the long inglorious one; we can

67. Martha Grace Duncan, *Romantic Outlaws, Beloved Prisons: The Unconscious Meanings of Crime and Punishment* 96 (1996). This is the germ of a Freudian interpretation of *Hamlet* that would remain more firmly tethered to the text of the play than the interpretations proposed by the other Freudian critics whom I have cited.

68. The impression of their youth is reinforced by the prominence in both works of an old man—Nestor in the *Iliad* and Polonius in *Hamlet*. Lear—who despite his great age is a parallel figure not to Nestor or Polonius but to Achilles and Hamlet—is in his second childhood: his effort to divest himself of responsibility and his demand for infinite love are behaviors characteristic of a child.

69. Barbara Everett, *Young Hamlet: Essays on Shakespeare's Tragedies* 22 (1989).

70. So one way to explain the disappearance of the ghost in the latter part of *Hamlet* is that Hamlet has *become* his father—and, like his father, will be killed by Claudius. Id. at 126.

71. On the Greeks' belief in the importance of fame *(kleos)* activated by the spoken word, see Jesper Svenbro, *Phrasikleia: An Anthropology of Reading in Ancient Greece*, chs. 3–4 (1993).

cheat death only by inviting death. This is a more limited triumph than the young are willing to settle for.

Hamlet's reflections follow a different path, his discovery being of different aspects of the human dilemma: the existence of radical evil—Claudius's deep-seated malignity and Gertrude's lack of taste and of sexual propriety, reflecting the animal in man; the role of chance in human affairs; the difficulty of translating motive and desire into effective action;[72] the ease with which we evade responsibilities and rationalize our evasions; and lack of candor in human relations (a lack displayed by Polonius, Claudius of course, Gertrude, Rosencrantz and Guildenstern, and even Ophelia). Hamlet learns that everybody is acting, in the disreputable sense of the word, and that he, too, must become an actor, even a stage manager, if he is to be effective. The deeply rooted nature of the vices and deficiencies exhibited to Hamlet is underlined by the characters' allusions to the Garden of Eden and to Cain's murder of *his* brother, by the plausibility of the villains—Claudius and particularly Gertrude lack the surface malignity of a Iago or a Goneril (indeed, Gertrude's love for Hamlet is extremely touching)—and by the atmosphere of drunkenness and sexual intrigue in which the play's fictive Denmark is wrapped from the beginning, an atmosphere set off by the one completely straightforward major character in the play, Horatio. The resignation that Hamlet displays in Act V reflects a hard-won understanding of the nature of the human condition and a resolution to face it with readiness (which Hamlet characteristically fails to do, however, when he accepts a foil without checking whether it is bated) rather than with elaborate plans sure to go awry, as Hamlet's plan with the players went awry and Claudius's plans with Rosencrantz and Guildenstern and later with Laertes went awry. We do not live our dreams. Those who do, like Macbeth and Faustus, find they are nightmares.

Another way to describe the thematic development in the *Iliad* and *Hamlet*, particularly the latter, is as the process of becoming at home in the world. At the beginning of the play and especially in the throne-room scene, in which Hamlet is set off from the others by his black mourning cloak and responds to his uncle and mother in bitter quips, he is distinctly not at home in his world. This not-at-homeness remains strongly marked through the third act. But then, and especially in the last act, whether Hamlet is jawing with Horatio or wrestling with Laertes in Ophelia's grave

---

72. One of the themes of *Hamlet* is the equal fatality of delay and impetuosity. Hamlet usually does badly when he delays, as in failing to kill Claudius in the prayer scene, *and* when he acts impulsively, as in stabbing Polonius. The play places particular emphasis on the futility of planning, and hence on the importance of contingency in human affairs. No happy medium, no optimum tempo of deliberation, is suggested.

or fencing verbally with Osric or fatally with Laertes, he seems quite at home and his at-homeness gives a sense of completion to his short life. Centuries later, the idea that you are not fully alive until, giving up your plans for the future, you take life day by day will recur in *The Red and the Black.* When, shortly before his execution, Julien Sorel renounces ambition and begins to live "a life without past and future, a life always in the present moment, a life which is lived from day to day," he becomes "a being worthy of Stendhal."[73] Julien is not "himself" when he is acting out the script for an ambitious poor boy that he got from Napoleon's memoirs. Hamlet is not himself when he is attempting to be the instrument of his father's vengeance.

To place the *Iliad* and *Hamlet* in a bin labeled "revenge literature" and leave it at that would thus be a fearful oversimplification. Nevertheless, revenge literature is a coherent literary category—indeed a "supergenre," embracing many specific genres such as Elizabethan and Jacobean revenge drama—to which these two works belong; and an understanding not only of the category, but of revenge as a radically imperfect but sometimes inescapable social practice, can help us make sense of both works. Achilles and Hamlet are more than avengers, but that is part of what they are and is important to an understanding of why they act as they do or, in Hamlet's case, why he does not act as he is told to do by the ghost. These works offer a critical perspective on justice as vengeance, though the authors were after even bigger game. It is a critical perspective that foreshadowed and dramatizes the social scientific critique sketched in the first part of this chapter.

73. Georges Poulet, "Stendhal and Time," in *Stendhal, Red and Black: A Norton Critical Edition* 470, 473 (Robert M. Adams ed. 1969).

THREE

The Antinomies of Legal Theory

Jurisprudential Drama from
Sophocles to Shelley

Law considered reflectively can be seen, in both its conceptual and its in-stitutional aspects, as riven by a series of antinomies, such as law versus eq-uity, rule versus discretion, positive law versus natural law, customary law versus enacted law, judge versus jury—even, it may be, male versus female. These antinomies give structure and subject to jurisprudence. They also in-form a number of distinguished works of imaginative literature, discussed in this and the next chapter, that constitute in the aggregate a supplemen-tal course of reading, of unsurpassed vividness, to the philosophical and legal literature of jurisprudence.

Consider Euripides' dramatization of historical jurisprudence in *Hecuba*. The Trojan War has just ended, and the Greek fleet, carrying Hecuba and the other Trojan women as slaves, has stopped in Thrace on its way back from Troy. Hecuba learns that the king of Thrace, Poly-mestor, has killed her only surviving son, Polydorus, whom Priam had entrusted, along with a large quantity of gold, to Polymestor in the hope of preserving the boy and the gold from the perils of war. Poly-mestor admits the killing. But he argues that he did it to protect the Greeks from the danger that Polydorus might have rebuilt Troy and sought revenge for his father's death and for the other disasters that had befallen his family. This if true would not be a negligible argument. But Hecuba is certain that it is false, that Polymestor killed Polydorus for the gold. She implores Agamemnon, in the first of two informal "trial" scenes in the play, to punish him:

give me my revenge on that treacherous friend
who flouted every god in heaven and in hell
to do this brutal murder.
    At our table he was our frequent guest; was counted first
among our friends, respected, honored by me,
receiving every kindness that a man could meet—
and then, in cold deliberation, killed
my son . . .
    I am a slave, I know,
and slaves are weak. But the gods are strong, and over them
there stands some absolute, some moral order
or principle of law more final still.
Upon this moral law the world depends;
through it the gods exist; by it we live,
defining good and evil.
    Apply that law
to me. For if you flout it now, and those
who murder in cold blood or defy the gods
go unpunished, then human justice withers,
corrupted at its source.   (ll. 790–805)[1]

It is natural for Hecuba, a slave, having none of the rights of a citizen, to appeal to the law of nature[2] rather than to the positive law of a specific political community. It is natural too for her to speak of revenge, which has roots in instinct, rather than of criminal punishment, which is part of positive law. In any case there are no formal institutions of justice in the martial society depicted in the play. We are invited to consider that the fundamental social norms that condemn unwarranted killing precede the institutions of positive law and may set bounds to a purely positivistic conception of law. Euripides' audience knew, moreover, that Agamemnon

---

1. My quotations are from William Arrowsmith's translation of *Hecuba* in *The Complete Greek Tragedies,* vol. 3: *Euripides* 495 (David Grene and Richmond Lattimore eds. 1955).

2. If that is what she is doing; for *nomos,* which Arrowsmith translates as "some absolute, some moral order," has a variety of meanings, of which natural law is only one, and not necessarily the one intended. Martha Nussbaum, *The Fragility of Goodness: Luck and Ethics in Greek Tragedy and Philosophy* 400 n.* (1986), argues that it is "a human and not an eternal *nomos.*" Yet her own translation of the sentence in which the word appears—"The gods are strong, and so is convention *(nomos)* which rules over them" (id. at 400)—suggests a divine underwriting (unless Hecuba thinks the gods a creation of the human imagination, though if she thought that, she would be unlikely to say it to Agamemnon, as it would weaken her plea). For how could a purely human artifact rule over the gods? Nussbaum's interpretation of *nomos* is questioned in John Kerrigan, *Revenge Tragedy: From Aeschylus to Agamemnon* 352 (1996), and in the references cited in id. at 352 n. 14. Euripides was, however, notably unorthodox and sometimes put unorthodox speeches into the mouths of his characters.

would feel the lash of natural law—that he would be killed for having killed his daughter in violation of that law.

Although sympathetic to Hecuba's plea, Agamemnon is unwilling to take action against Polymestor. Cassandra, Hecuba's surviving daughter, is Agamemnon's mistress. He would be suspected of partiality in taking the Trojan side of the dispute between Hecuba and Polymestor, an ally of the Greeks. He explains (ll. 852–861):

> So far as justice is concerned, god knows,
> nothing would please me more than to bring
> this murderer to book.
>   But my position
> here is delicate. If I give you your revenge,
> the army is sure to charge that I connived
> at the death of the king of Thrace because of my love
> for Cassandra. This is my dilemma. The army
> thinks of Polymestor as its friend,
> this boy as its enemy. You love your son,
> but what do your affections matter to the Greeks?
> Put yourself in my position.

Two aspects of Agamemnon's reply are noteworthy. The first is his setting entirely expedient considerations against the precepts of natural law; evidently he believes that the law as enforced by human beings should reflect or at least flatter public opinion, here that of the Greek army. His outlook is not entirely remote from that of the modern judge. A standard judicial flourish is to concede the natural justice of a litigant's case yet decide against him on the ground that positive law, which is on one view simply crystallized public opinion, entitles his opponent to judgment. And one characteristic of modern American positive law, as of ancient Greek positive law (indeed of all positive law), is that citizens have greater rights than aliens.

The second noteworthy aspect of Agamemnon's "ruling" is the difficulty of doing justice when the judicial function is commingled with the executive. Agamemnon cannot confine his attention to issues of right and duty on the ground that the political implications of rendering judgment for an enemy national are the business of another branch of government; he *is* that other branch. Justice under law is facilitated when judges are able credibly to deny that the politics of the case are their business, and when the political branches of government are able to say with equal credibility that they are forbidden to interfere in judicial decision making. By that Alphonse-Gaston shuffle legal justice is secured.

Although he refuses to help Hecuba directly, Agamemnon places no obstacles in the way of her attempting private revenge on Polymestor—and with the aid of her female attendants she succeeds in blinding him and in killing all his children. Now it is Polymestor's turn to appeal to Agamemnon for justice, in the second informal trial scene in the play. With the damage done, Agamemnon can assume a more judicial stance: "No more of this inhuman savagery now. / Each of you will give his version of the case / and I shall try to judge you both impartially" (ll. 1129–1131). They give their competing versions of why Polymestor killed Polydorus. Persuaded by Hecuba, Agamemnon finds Polymestor guilty of murder and tells him that he must therefore bear the consequences that Hecuba has visited on him.

In the course of delivering his judgment, Agamemnon makes two revealing remarks. The first is that "I should cut a sorry figure in the world / if I allowed this case to come to court / and then refused or failed to give a verdict." The second is that since "We Greeks call [killing a guest] murder . . . [how] could I acquit you now / without losing face among men?" (ll. 1242–1249). One's initial reaction is that this just proves that Agamemnon is playing a political game. He is interested in the ultimate justice of Hecuba's case only insofar as it might move public opinion against him if he acquits Polymestor. By standing aloof from the actual punishment of Polymestor he has managed to avoid the appearance of siding with a Trojan against a Greek ally, while at the same time permitting a sort of justice to be done—although with the great violence and excess that typify revenge as a method of doing justice; Polymestor's children had not been complicit in their father's crime.[3]

But this assessment of Agamemnon's position is incomplete. In appealing to what "we Greeks" believe on the subject of killing a guest, he is invoking a concept of law distinct from either natural law in a transcendental or universal sense or law as public opinion. This is the concept of law as deep-rooted custom fulfilling powerful social needs. Although the reasons for regarding the murder of guests with special abhorrence are not spelled out in the play, they are plain enough. In a society in which trade is both valuable and, because there are no public institutions of law enforcement, precarious, the duty of hosts to protect guests, especially guests

---

3. The sense of Hecuba's having gone too far, like so many revengers, is strongly marked in the play, which tells us that she is going to be punished for her excesses by being turned into a dog. See Nussbaum, note 2 above, ch. 13; Judith Mossman, *Wild Justice: A Study of Euripides' Hecuba,* ch. 6 (1995). (*Hecuba,* incidentally, was a popular play during the Renaissance, id. at 236–243; and recall that Hecuba figures in the player's speech in *Hamlet.*) Nussbaum, while emphasizing the dehumanization of Hecuba, recognizes that Hecuba's actions are "in some sense justified, even extenuated, by the circumstances." Nussbaum, note 2 above, at 418.

from afar bearing precious commodities (such as the gold that Polydorus—whose name means either "Giver of Much" or "Receiver of Much"—had brought with him to Thrace), is a potent customary norm. It is a norm more plausibly justified by practical social need than by supernatural edict, although it may be given supernatural backing to make it more impressive and therefore more likely to be obeyed. And it is local—"we Greeks," not necessarily "we Greeks and you Trojans too," especially since it was a Trojan abuse of hospitality that had touched off the Trojan War.

In both respects—local application and pragmatic basis—customary norms are different from natural law, which is based on the existence of a normative order in nature and can thus be said to be universal and compulsory rather than merely expedient. But because a customary norm has deep public support, it is not subject to the same rapid shifts in public opinion as ordinary legislation. It thus resembles a constitutional norm.

All this leaves unexplained, however, Agamemnon's change of heart between the first and second trials. In suggesting that he could switch sides without causing an uproar among the Greeks because Hecuba had done his dirty work for him (punishing Polymestor), I was casting his motives in a disreputably "political" light, consistent with his reiterated concern with saving face. Yet instead we might see in Agamemnon's performance of the judicial function legality tempered by prudence. He is the leader, not the tyrant, of the Greek expeditionary force. It behooves him, just as it would a democratic leader, to heed public opinion. He must balance Hecuba's claims against the larger public interest that he is charged with protecting. The effectiveness of his leadership, and hence his ability to protect that larger public interest, depends upon his prestige, so he must be protective of that too. We catch here a glimpse of the jurisprudence of prudence or practicality, of interest-balancing—something that legal formalists abhor but that American judges, at least, frequently practice.

The transition depicted in *Hecuba* from a system of private vengeance to a system of public enforcement of laws shaped by public opinion and administered by persons expressly charged with civic and political responsibilities is also visible in Sophocles' *Antigone,* with Antigone corresponding to Hecuba and Creon to Agamemnon. With governmental institutions as undifferentiated as they are in the world depicted in the Greek tragedies, we should not expect, and do not find, that the judicial function is performed well. The dominant impression both Agamemnon and Creon project is that of political trimmers deaf to the claims of natural law. They are the first legal positivists, and it is not surprising that in its earliest stage positivism cuts a poor figure on the social and ethical stages. Legal positivism depends on institutions that take a long time to evolve, although even in its earliest and crudest form it marks an advance over the system of private vengeance.

A distant descendant of Euripides' Hecuba is Beatrice Cenci, the protagonist of Shelley's lurid and powerful poetic drama *The Cenci* (1819). It is a pastiche of Elizabethan and Jacobean revenge tragedy, with many echoes of Shakespeare (especially *Macbeth*), though the mood is closer to that of Webster or Tourneur; but thematically it is closest to *Hecuba* and *Michael Kohlhaas*. Count Cenci, a Roman magnate of the sixteenth century (and a real historical figure, whose misdeeds Shelley seems not to have exaggerated), is a true monster; he puts Polymestor to shame. Insanely avaricious, sadistic, and sexually perverted, he throws a banquet to celebrate the deaths of two of his sons. When Beatrice, his daughter, remonstrates, he retaliates by raping her. She knows that he plans to do away with his remaining sons and with his wife (Beatrice's stepmother) and to continue to use her sexually—he even threatens to impregnate her so that she may have a child whose physical appearance will be to her a lifelong hateful reminder of him. Despairing of legal justice—for the legal system, administered by the Pope, is depicted as totally corrupt, and the Pope rejects Beatrice's plea to take action against her father—Beatrice arranges for the murder of her father. She is arrested, tried, and convicted when her brother and stepmother, both of whom were in on the plot, confess under torture, and the play ends with all three awaiting execution. (The Pope is not as forbearing to Beatrice as Agamemnon was to Hecuba.) Beatrice hurls magnificent defiance at the evil judge who presides over the trial and over the use of the rack to extract confessions from her accomplices, and yet we are left with the sense that she exhibited a deep flaw in character in giving way to the impulse, understandable as it was, to take revenge against her father. At the beginning of the play she is a figure of saintly patience, as her name suggests. When she decides to kill her father, she hardens, and while her defiance of the judge and of the repulsive legal establishment that he serves is, as I said, magnificent, the play appears to disapprove of her having taken the law, Hecuba-fashion, into her own hands. For one thing, right after the murder, an officer of the Pope appears with a warrant to arrest Count Cenci—so maybe human justice is not so hopeless as it seemed to Beatrice. For another, by making her stepmother and brother complicit in the plot, Beatrice condemns them—and what is more, she refuses to confess while they (and the "triggerman," whom she later persuades to retract the confession he gave under torture) are being tortured.

Antigone requires a closer examination. It is set in Thebes, now ruled by Creon after the fall of Oedipus. Polynices, one of Oedipus's sons, has revolted and attacked the city, defended by his other son, Eteocles. Both are killed in the fighting. Creon orders an honorable burial for Eteocles but decides that Polynices shall remain unburied—a hideous punishment in the theology of the ancient Greeks and a recurrent motif in Greek literature (it figures in both the *Iliad* and *Hecuba*). Antigone, a daughter of Oedipus by his incestuous marriage and therefore a sister of Polynices and Eteocles, defies the order and buries her dishonored brother. This is discovered and in a brief trial scene in which she asserts the primacy of divine law and Creon the inviolability of his decrees, he condemns her to death for having violated his burial interdiction. Horrible things ensue, including the death of Creon's wife and of his son, who is betrothed to Antigone and decides to die with her. We are made to understand that in failing to honor the claims of the gods of the underworld, who insist on proper burial without which the souls of the dead cannot be received into the underworld, Creon has acted with dreadful impiety and must be terribly punished.

Yet it would be a mistake to think Creon simply a moral monster who gets his just deserts. Polynices, the traitor, and Eteocles, the hero, were both killed in the revolt. To give them both honorable burial would, by blurring the moral distinction between them, encourage future revolts. Having therefore decreed that Polynices shall remain unburied—a decree with all the presumptive legitimacy of a modern statute or court order—and having prescribed the death penalty for anyone who violates the decree, Creon is confronted by a blunt challenge to his authority, and the authority of law, in Antigone's actions. It does not help that Antigone is a woman, that she is the daughter of the former ruler and the sister of the rebel, and that she states her position with uncompromising self-righteousness rather than asking for mercy—she gives Creon no way to avoid condemning her without a severe loss of face. (Notice the parallel to the confrontation between Achilles and Agamemnon in Book I of the *Iliad*.) It is a "no win" situation for him, and he is punished terribly; the play is his tragedy as well as Antigone's.

The natural law that Antigone sets up in opposition to Creon's positive law is not only, and perhaps not primarily, a decree from on high commanding proper burial even for traitors. The natural law most emphasized in the play is the tie of blood between sister and brother. Like Clytemnestra and the Furies in *Eumenides,* Antigone places blood relationships above the political relationship (loyalty to Thebes, to the *polis*) that Creon's decrees are intended to cement. The harshness of her challenge to Creon may reflect the persistence of the revenge ethic in the rudimentary city-state political culture depicted in the play.[4] We have seen how that ethic encourages the

---

4. R. P. Winnington-Ingram, *Sophocles: An Interpretation* (1980), especially ch. 6.

formation of tightly knit family units and discourages loyalty to impersonal social groups. Modern people balance loyalty to family and to state; Antigone is incapable of that.

We moderns can look back, as Sophocles could not, to a long history of religious wars, and to the efforts of Enlightenment thinkers to defuse religious strife, from a perspective shaped by the concept, mentality, and institutions of what has come to be known as the liberal state. History has taught us that intense religious feeling can undermine civic virtue and social peace. We can therefore see, more sharply than Sophocles could, perhaps, that justice is not all on Antigone's side. Civil disobedience motivated by obedience to a "higher law" can be admirable as well as heroic. But depending on the nature of the *civitas* and of the "higher" law set in opposition to it, it can also be a formula for anarchy and civil war. The tragedy of Antigone and Creon can be seen from a modern perspective as caused by their inability to compromise,[5] to achieve the sort of via media attempted by the religion clauses of the First Amendment to the U.S. Constitution.

And which, by the way, *is* "higher"—a law based on nature or a law based on culture? Blood relationships—that is, close genetic relationships—are an aspect of our biological nature. Antigone exalts them over civic relationships, such as that of the citizen to the state, which are social rather than biological in character. We are less likely than were the Greeks to look to biological nature as a source of norms. We don't think that ties of blood entitle people to defy positive law, though we make some allowances for them, for example by requiring judges to recuse themselves from cases in which their close relatives are involved as parties or counsel.

The normative ambiguities of "nature" are at the heart of *King Lear*. Although not usually considered one of Shakespeare's "legal" plays, it has three trial scenes and they help to focus the audience's attention on the themes of nature and natural law. The first is the mock trial of Lear's evil daughters by Lear and his disheveled entourage on the heath. The second is the trial of Gloucester on false charges of treason ginned up by his bastard son Edmund. That trial ends in a verdict of guilt and Gloucester's punishment by blinding. The third trial is the trial by battle in which Edgar, Gloucester's legitimate son, kills Edmund. Only the second trial complies with the forms of law in a modern sense (modern to Shakespeare as well as to us)—and it is a sinister farce. The first, an ostensible farce, renders true though ineffective justice by denouncing the evil daughters.

---

5. See Th. C. W. Oudemans and A. P. M. H. Lardinois, *Tragic Ambiguity: Anthropology, Philosophy and Sophocles' Antigone* 160–169 (1987).

The third trial harks back to medieval English law, when God was believed to decide legal disputes by awarding victory to the combatant whose cause was just. But to conclude—not incorrectly—from Edgar's victory that natural law is vindicated in *Lear* would conceal the play's ambivalence toward "nature." The ambivalent note is sounded early, in Edmund's soliloquy (I.2.1–22) that begins "Thou, nature, art my goddess; to thy law / My services are bound." From the standpoint of nature Edmund is *more* legitimate than Edgar. His conception "in the lusty stealth of nature" partook more of nature's vital essence than conception "within a dull, stale, tired bed" of married persons.[6] So he resolves to supplant Edgar, and later their father, by whatever means lie to hand. And if Regan and Goneril are unnatural in their lack of filial piety, they are only too natural—in the sense in which animals are natural—in their selfishness, pitilessness, and unbridled sexuality. Although both are married women, they compete shamelessly for Edmund's bed, and Goneril has an affair with her servant Oswald. Finally, if Lear is unnatural in his initial rejection of Cordelia, he is all too natural in his childish desire to be loved without any limits and to enjoy the pleasures of life free of its responsibilities.

The depiction of nature in *King Lear* thus is modern; it is the nature red in tooth and claw that Darwinism teaches us to expect. The sense of justice to which Lear (when the scales fall from his eyes) and Gloucester appeal is not a normative order in nature, as we find in the Greek tragedies. It is a complex of civilized values built on property, piety, and hierarchy—the complex that fixes, against the riotous claims of nature, the status and correlative rights and duties of Lear, Edmund, Edgar, Oswald, and the rest. And yet an Elizabethan audience, heavily imbued with medieval values which were the orthodox values of Renaissance England as well—perhaps even a modern audience—would consider the behavior of Edmund, Regan, and Goneril (like that of Lear in initially rejecting Cordelia) "unnatural," and Edmund's defeat by Edgar therefore a vindication of natural law. Those three were behaving like animals, which is contrary to *human* nature. This is not an absurd distinction; nor one that modern science has erased. Man is an animal, secular moderns believe, but not every animal has the same nature. It is in the nature of a bear to hibernate, but a man who hibernates is not acting naturally.

Aquinas, from whom the orthodox Renaissance conception of nature derives, had claimed that human nature is distinguished from animal nature

---

6. Marriages of aristocrats—Gloucester is an earl—could be assumed to be loveless, since they were arranged by the fathers of the bride and groom.

by the presence of a capacity for reason not found in animals.[7] However, the capacity to reason does not dictate its use for good ends. Edmund, Iago, and other Shakespearean villains use their reason to commit their villainies, so if we call them unnatural, there is no escape from dividing human nature into a good and a bad nature. But this makes naturalistic morality impossible, because "nature" will no longer tell us where to make the cut. The "good" human nature is what God implanted in us. It is normative because it is divinely underwritten—because it is an *idealized* conception of nature—rather than because it is an accurate description of human beings.

If we abandon physical nature as a source of norms, we are likely to be forced back upon social conventions. Much is lost by this retreat, which is why it seems odd that Hecuba should be appealing merely to "convention" in her plea to Agamemnon for justice. It is always possible to criticize law, but the concept of a divinely underwritten natural law perceptible to human reason had offered the possibility of a securely objective criticism. In *King Lear* we see the "object" beginning to disappear (I say "beginning" because Edmund's defeat by Edgar can be taken as a sign of divine justice). We learn that social life offers the vantage point from which to perceive nature as amoral, instead of nature offering the vantage point from which to judge human law; and social life lacks fixity. It is the defiance of convention, notably of bonds feudal, contractual, and quasi-contractual (such as marriage), more than of anything found "in nature," that marks the behavior of the wicked characters as unnatural. The filial ingratitude of Edmund, Goneril, and Regan is only a partial exception. The filial instinct is weaker than the parental. Cordelia puts it on a par with marital duty— and among the acts of defiance of convention committed by the characters in the play are not only Regan's and Goneril's refusal to honor the conditions under which they each received a half of the kingdom from Lear, but also Lear's initial rejection of Cordelia's promise to love him in accordance with her *duty* to a father rather than to shortchange her husband by giving *all* her love to her father.

Despite the emphasis that *King Lear* places on the duty of promise-keeping, a cornerstone of a commercial society, and although no play of Shakespeare contains a stronger warning against imprudence in the management of one's affairs,[8] Edmund and possibly even the bad daughters ap-

---

7. See Thomas Aquinas, *Summa Theologica,* vol. 1, pp. 1009–1010 (1947) (question 94, articles 2–3).

8. As Barbara Everett points out in her book *Young Hamlet: Essays on Shakespeare's Tragedies* 61 (1989), Lear is imprudent in dividing his kingdom, in thinking that he can retain the perquisites of power without the power, and in relying on public protestations to judge his daughters' love.

pear to represent the values of nascent capitalism, and Lear and his party the vanishing feudal values.[9] The duties approved of in the play are based on ascriptive status rather than free contracting. No one has ever accused Lear of engaging in cost-benefit analysis, while on the other side Edmund, Oswald, and the bad daughters are paragons or rather parodies of instrumental rationality, busily maximizing a wholehearted, and incidentally rather short-sighted, self-interest. This is another way in which they are "natural" in a modern sense.

Feudal values have gone out of fashion; and, monster that he is, Edmund, in defending bastards in his "Thou, nature, art my goddess" soliloquy, anticipates by more than 350 years a series of decisions in which the Supreme Court has held that governmental discrimination against persons born out of wedlock must be shown to be justified by important social interests in order to pass constitutional muster.[10] If we put Edmund's soliloquy together with Shylock's "Hath not a Jew eyes" speech and Hamlet's references to the injustices that result from the accidents of birth,[11] we have impressive rhetorical support for something like the modern notion of the equal protection of the laws. This is not to say either that it was Shakespeare's notion or that it is the dominant notion in the plays. Shakespeare's private opinions are unknown, and the plays are not united by a single perspective on any of the larger ethical and political issues.

The current center of legal debate over nature and the natural is the criminalization of sodomy, which the Supreme Court upheld against constitutional challenge in *Bowers v. Hardwick*.[12] Sexual activity is as "natural" as anything that people do; and we now know that same-sex sexual activity is found among animals as well as human beings and that homosexual orientation probably is genetic rather than psychological in origin.[13] Yet the Roman Catholic Church insists that same-sex activity is profoundly unnatural because it is not oriented toward procreation and employs organs in ways that God did not intend them to be employed. The Church does not deny, or even disapprove of, the orientation, but it insists that it

9. See, for example, Paul Delany, "*King Lear* and the Decline of Feudalism," in *Materialist Shakespeare* 20 (Ivo Kamps ed. 1995).

10. See Weber v. Aetna Casualty and Surety Co., 406 U.S. 164 (1972); Gomez v. Perez, 409 U.S. 535 (1973); Jimenez v. Weinberger, 417 U.S. 628 (1974); Trimble v. Gordon, 430 U.S. 762 (1977).

11. As when he says, ". . . oft it chances in particular men, / That for some vicious mole of nature in them, / As, in their birth—wherein they are not guilty, / Since nature cannot choose his origin— / . . . [Their] virtues else, be they as pure as grace, / As infinite as man may undergo, / Shall in the general censure take corruption / From that particular fault" (I.4.23–36).

12. 478 U.S. 186 (1986).

13. Richard A. Posner, *Sex and Reason* 101–105 (1992).

not be translated into action. There is no inconsistency between the biological and the theological positions on homosexuality. They use "nature" and "natural" in different senses—the very senses, the biological and the normative respectively, in which they are used in *King Lear.*

The most celebrated of Shakespeare's "legal" plays, *The Merchant of Venice,* is also the one most concerned with commerce,[14] and the association of positive law with commercial values is no accident. The aristocrat Bassanio needs money to woo an heiress, Portia, in proper style. But he is a spendthrift and has no assets to pledge as security for a loan. His friend Antonio, the merchant of the title, is wealthy and generous, but at the moment illiquid, all his assets being on board ships at sea. The two men approach Shylock for the loan. As it happens, there is no love lost between Antonio and Shylock. Antonio lends money but charges no interest, thus competing unfairly, as it seems to Shylock, with the Jewish moneylenders. In the world of the play, lending at interest is no longer illegal for Christians, as it had been during the Middle Ages, but it is not quite respectable. That was approximately the situation in Shakespeare's England as well. Since 1571 the lending of money at interest had been de facto legal,[15] provided that the interest rate did not exceed 10 percent. Shakespeare's father had been prosecuted for charging more.[16]

Besides underselling Shylock, Antonio has made no secret of his contempt for Jews—has indeed kicked and spat on Shylock. Shylock hates Antonio both because he is a Christian and because of the specific wrongs, commercial and personal, that Antonio has done to him. Nevertheless he agrees to lend him the money Bassanio wants and demands no interest—just Antonio's pledge of a pound of his flesh as security against a default. The text suggests that Shylock is hoping that Antonio *will* default, so that Shylock can kill him, and is "buying" this chance by forgoing interest. Shylock refers to the bond as a "merry bond," leading a school of revisionists to argue that his intentions are benign, at least initially. The long-standing effort to cast Shylock as the "real" hero of the play and Shakespeare as a cryptic Semitophile crests in Richard Weisberg's claim that "Jewish commitment finally prevails over Christian mediation in *The Merchant of Venice.*"[17] In fact the play depicts Shylock as a villain, though a

---

14. Everett, note 8 above, at 41, calls the play "a romance of millionaires."

15. See Norman Jones, *God and the Moneylenders: Usury and Law in Early Modern England* 77–80, 145 (1989); P. S. Atiyah, *The Rise and Fall of Freedom of Contract* 66 (1979) ("a reasonable return on a loan was coming to be given a grudging acquiescence").

16. James Shapiro, *Shakespeare and the Jews* 99 (1996).

17. Weisberg, *Poethics and Other Strategies of Law and Literature* 103 (1992). Weisberg regards Portia as the avenger, and Shylock deficient only in moderation. Id. at 209–210.

villain not without tragic dignity.[18] "The seeds of sympathy are there . . .
He [Shakespeare] simply tried to imagine, within the confines of the plot,
and within the limits that his culture set him, what it would be like to be
a Jew. But dramatic imagination, when it is pitched at the Shakespearean
level, becomes a moral quality, a form of humanism."[19] This is an aspect
of the fundamental point that "Shakespeare's greatness, his 'impersonality'
. . . in his best plays, lies in the fact that, whatever univocal insights or
affirmations may be expressed within any work, they are thoroughly *dramatised*—that is, set within a complex interlocutory process such that they are
never the 'final vocabulary' of individual works."[20] There is a saying among
actors that no man is a villain in his own eyes. You need this adage to act
a villain's role convincingly. Shakespeare, himself an actor, internalized the
adage.

Soon after the deal is struck, Shylock, inexplicably abandoning his rule
of never having social intercourse with Christians, goes to dinner at
Bassanio's house. While he is there, his daughter, Jessica, runs off with her
Christian lover, taking the family jewels with her. (She later marries him
and converts to Christianity.) This incident makes Shylock desperate for
revenge. By a happy coincidence the ships carrying Antonio's goods are
just then lost at sea and as a result the loan goes into default. Shylock brings
suit to enforce the bond. Antonio asks him for mercy (not forcefully, however—he is "half in love with easeful death"). Shylock refuses. The Duke
of Venice also urges mercy, to no avail. Bassanio has succeeded in marrying Portia and as a result has enough money to repay the loan with generous interest, and he offers to do so. Shylock refuses the offer.

In the nick of time Portia appears, disguised as a (male) doctor of laws.
At first she pretends to be a legal stickler, and wins Shylock's praise. This
interlude serves two purposes. It puts Shylock on record as accepting her
as an authoritative exponent of the law, and it hardens his resolve not to
accept Bassanio's offer—which Portia had funded—of double Shylock's
principal back. Then she turns on him. She points out that the bond refers
to flesh, not blood, and says that if Shylock sheds a drop of Antonio's blood
while executing the bond he will not be protected by the bond and therefore will be guilty of murder. Which means that Shylock is already guilty

---

18. For excellent discussions of the relation of the play to anti-Semitism, see John Gross,
Shylock: A Legend and Its Legacy (1992); Shapiro, note 15 above; Thomas Moisan, "'Which is the
merchant here? and which the Jew?': Subversion and Recuperation in *The Merchant of Venice*,"
in *Shakespeare Reproduced: The Text in History and Ideology* 188 (Jean E. Howard and Marion F.
O'Connor eds. 1987).

19. Gross, note 18 above, at 349.

20. David Parker, *Ethics, Theory and the Novel* 60 (1994).

of a capital crime—plotting the death of a Venetian citizen—and should be executed! Everyone is astonished by Portia's legal sagacity, and no one offers a counterargument. But to demonstrate that Christians are more merciful than Jews, the Duke offers to pardon Shylock if he will surrender all his wealth and convert to Christianity. He protests, and either half or maybe the whole forfeiture is then remitted,[21] except that he must leave all his wealth at his death to Jessica, whom he had disinherited when she ran away. He accepts the modified offer, and departs.

The legal aspects of *The Merchant of Venice* are on one level absurd; and the trial, with its imposture (by Portia) and its technicalities, could almost be a satire on law and lawyers, except that it does not have the feel of satire. No justification is ever offered for the pound-of-flesh bond—for example, that it is intended to incite Antonio to greater than usual efforts to safeguard his assets so that he does not default. The bond recalls and is no doubt meant to remind the audience that Jews were thought to drink the blood of Christians at Passover; and the reminder is apropos, since Shylock seems motivated by the long-shot chance of eliminating his hated Christian competitor. But no civilized sixteenth-century legal system (and Venice is presented as a civilized state) would enforce a penalty bond of this character. Indeed, by the end of the sixteenth century the English court of equity was relieving some debtors against merely pecuniary penalties in bonds.[22]

A defaulting borrower has a right, moreover, called the "equity of redemption," to recover his forfeited property by coming up with the money that is due on the loan, even though it is overdue, within a reasonable time. So even if Antonio's life was in a sense forfeited to Shylock, a real court would have relieved Antonio from the forfeiture if before it took place the money due Shylock was tendered.[23] And since Shylock's loan to Antonio

21. Half is returned to Shylock outright, half is to be held by Antonio in "use" (trust) for Jessica upon Shylock's death. If Shylock is to be the beneficiary of the trust during his lifetime, then the whole forfeiture has been remitted subject only to Jessica's rights on Shylock's death. If the income of the trust is to accumulate for Jessica, only half of the forfeiture has been remitted. It is as difficult as it is unimportant to determine which interpretation is correct.

22. See A. W. B. Simpson, "The Penal Bond with Conditional Defeasance," 82 *Law Quarterly Review* 392, 416 (1966); Simpson, *A History of the Common Law of Contract: The Rise of the Action of Assumpsit* 118–119 (1975); William H. Loyd, "Penalties and Forfeitures," 29 *Harvard Law Review* 117, 123 (1915); Theodore Ziolkowski, *The Mirror of Justice: Literary Reflections of Legal Crisis* 167–172 (1997). The Roman Law of the Twelve Tables allowed creditors to cut up a defaulting debtor into as many pieces as there were creditors—but that is a law of the fifth century B.C. Under modern law, penalty clauses in contracts are unenforceable even if the penalty is only pecuniary.

23. The term "equity of redemption" and its application to mortgages come later in English legal history. But the use of the concept to relieve against other types of forfeiture appears to have been established by the end of the sixteenth century, and perhaps much earlier. See George E. Osborne, *Handbook on the Law of Mortgages* 12–15 (2d ed. 1970).

was for only three months, Bassanio's offer to double Shylock's principal implies interest at an annual rate of 400 percent. Shylock's refusal of this magnificent offer proves conclusively that the bond was not a commercial guarantee at all but a gamble, with Antonio's life as the stake. Yet no one in the play doubts the legality of Shylock's demand for the pound of flesh until Portia comes up with her hypertechnical argument—which Shylock does not attempt to rebut by pointing out that the bond must have implicitly authorized him to shed Antonio's blood, since otherwise he could not get his pound of flesh.

The absence of any reference to equity jurisprudence or to any other basis for the amelioration of penalties and forfeitures in contracts is unrealistic, but a literary imperative. The audience must take seriously the possibility that Antonio will be killed. It would not do so if the law as depicted in the play refused to enforce penalty clauses. True, the additional rabbit that Portia pulls out of her hat—the law making it a capital offense to plot to kill a Venetian—undermines that possibility because it makes Shylock's bond illegal. Why didn't Antonio, Shylock, and the others know about the law when the bond was signed, or at the latest when the trial began? But there are plenty of obscure laws; and, realistic or not, the invocation of this law is dramatically necessary in order to cap Shylock's defeat. If it were merely that he could not enforce the bond, he would be disappointed but would keep his wealth, except maybe for the money he had lent to Antonio, and he would not have to convert to Christianity to save his life. Here as elsewhere Shakespeare sacrifices plausibility to dramatic effect.[24]

The lack of realism in the play's treatment of law extends to the procedures as well as the substance of law. Portia not only is an impostor but has an undisclosed interest in the outcome of the trial; the parties have no lawyers; Venice has no professional judges; a civil case ends in a criminal conviction.[25] And yet the play *is* about law. The character of Shylock is a suggestive combination of three dispositions: the commercial ethic (Shylock as "economic man"[26]); vengefulness; and legal formalism in its lay sense of using the letter of the law to accomplish an unjust end. Shylock is at once the Jew stereo-

24. Another example in *The Merchant of Venice* is the simultaneous loss at sea of all the ships carrying Antonio's cargoes, and their miraculous reappearance. And no one asks why Antonio did not protect himself from default by insuring his cargoes, as he could have done. See C. F. Trenerry, *The Origin and Early History of Insurance,* ch. 25 (1926); H. A. L. Cockerell and Edwin Green, *The British Insurance Business: A Guide to Its History and Records* 4–5 (2d ed. 1994).

25. The fact that the Duke of Venice has to send to Padua to find an expert on the law of Venice may seem to be another unrealistic aspect of the law in the play, but it is not. Padua was both a center of legal studies and a possession of Venice, although Shakespeare does not bother to tell the audience either of these things.

26. I discuss this aspect of Shylock further in Chapter 5.

typed as modern, commercial man and the Jew stereotyped as Old Testament avenger ("an eye for an eye") who rejects the New Testament's command to "forgive thine enemy." He actually prefers taking lethal revenge on Antonio to receiving extravagant interest on his loan. Yet he is moved by avarice as well as vengeance: "I will have the heart of him if he forfeit, for were he out of Venice I can make what merchandise I will" (III.1.119–121).

When the Christians "steal" Shylock's daughter—and really do steal his jewels—he is wrought to a furious pitch of vengefulness. But unlike Achilles or Hamlet, Shylock is subject to law and tries to use his legal rights as the agency for revenge. Michael Kohlhaas tried it too, and only after failing turned to private revenge. We are made to see how law is a substitute for revenge, and could in principle provide a basis for obtaining it in as gruesome a form as the avenger might desire.

I noted in the last chapter that revenge molts into corrective justice; the commission of a wrong creates a right to redress, though it is a right channeled through law rather than left in the hands of the victim or his family. Equivalently, it creates a debt of sorts by the wrongdoer to the victim, enabling us to see that tort and criminal law, on the one side, and contract law, on the other, deal with forced and voluntary exchanges respectively and are thus twin halves of a unified theory of legal rights and duties modeled on reciprocal exchange in the marketplace.

Antonio is in some respects Shylock's opposite. A melancholy bachelor and a foe of interest-charging moneylenders, Antonio is generous to the point of improvidence, heedless of danger, and altogether willing to die to save Bassanio. "I am a tainted wether of the flock, / Meetest for death. The weakest kind of fruit / Drops earliest to the ground, and so let me" (IV.1.114–116). In his debate with Shylock over whether there is biblical authority for lending at interest we may sense an analogy to the temptation of Christ by a plausive Satan; Antonio even complains about the devil quoting Scripture. In rejecting Old Testament vengefulness and Pharisaic preoccupation with formal, rigid observances of "the Law" (what Aquinas and others called "the Old Law"), Antonio rejects Shylock's dominant characteristics. Had Shylock gotten his pound of flesh, this would have been the reenactment of the crucifixion of Jesus at the behest of the Jewish priestly establishment.[27] Or a diabolical taking literally of St. Paul's argument against the Jewish ritual of circumcision that "circumcision is of the heart."[28]

Yet there is something Shylock-like, not altogether wholesome, about

27. Other Christological features of the depiction of Antonio are his bachelorhood and his abuse of Shylock—an echo of Christ's driving the money changers from the Temple.
28. Shapiro, note 16 above, at 126–128.

Antonio.[29] Not only has Shakespeare given Shylock some pretty good lines against Antonio—one is not likely to forget the comparison to a "fawning publican" (I.3.38)—but in his joylessness, wifelessness, melancholy, anti-Semitism, and essential solitariness, he is almost the Christian mirror of Shylock. And they are both in business. Portia may represent the *via media*. Worldly—even sensual, in comparison with the frugal, chaste, and self-denying natures of both Shylock and Antonio—she is not above using legal technicalities, and even ethically dubious tricks, to save a life, just as she is not above bending the terms of her father's will to help the debonair and easygoing Bassanio win her hand in competition with the other suitors, or above tricking Shylock out of settling his dispute with Antonio for double his principal back, which would have come out of her fortune. (The ring trick in Act V provides still another example of Portia's fluent manipulation of contracts.) Whatever the law might say, the enforcement of the bond would be absurd, and Portia does what is necessary to prevent it. Yet she is explicitly concerned to accomplish this without establishing a bad precedent or damaging Venice's commercial standing, which, as Shylock repeatedly points out, requires that an alien (a Jew could not be a Venetian citizen in the sixteenth century) receive the same justice as a citizen.

Portia personifies the spirit of equity—the prudent recognition that strict rules of law, however necessary to a well-ordered society, must be applied with sensitivity and tact so that the spirit of the law is not sacrificed unnecessarily to the letter. The evolution of a legal system is often and perhaps typically from strict and simple rules to looser, more flexible standards. The former are easier to create, articulate, and enforce. This is important in a society in which the absence of literacy and of reliable techniques for factual inquiry and complex administration necessitates extreme simplification of legal rights and duties. We should not be surprised that a member of a primitive society would side with Shylock against Portia.[30] As techniques for a more supple and nuanced administration of law emerge, the price of applying simple rules

---

29. That a Christ figure should be depicted ambivalently is a challenge to the argument of the school of Tillyard (see Chapter 1) that Shakespeare's plays endorse orthodox Christian values. There is a remarkable absence of piety from his plays.

30. The Somali tribesman Farah, to whom Isak Dinesen told the story of *The Merchant of Venice*:

"Did the Jew give up his claim? He should not have done that. The flesh was due to him, it was little enough for him to get for all that money."

"But what else could he do," I asked, "when he must not take one drop of blood?"

"Memsahib," said Farah, "he could have used a red-hot knife. That brings out no blood."

"But," I said, "he was not allowed to take either more or less than one pound of flesh."

"And who," said Farah, "would have been frightened by that, exactly a Jew? He might have taken little bits at a time, with a small scale at hand to weigh it on, till he had got just

to situations in which that application denies substantive justice comes to seem too high. In a number of societies, not just the English, the upshot has been to overlay strict "legal" rules with flexible "equitable" principles.[31]

The "spirit" of equity in the play, it must be emphasized, is just that—spirit, not legal substance. No equitable principles actually inform the law of Venice as it is presented in the play. Portia's great "quality of mercy" speech (IV.1.182–203) is cast as an appeal to Shylock's sense of pity (he has none), not as a legal argument. Her reference to mercy as proceeding from heaven and "enthroned in hearts of kings" hints at the royal and ecclesiastical origins of the English court of equity,[32] but in the world of the play no one is empowered to trump law with equity. So when her appeal to Shylock for mercy fails, she is forced to argue in the legalistic terms that are the only ones available in the legal culture depicted in the play. Within those terms her argument is stronger than may at first appear. To rebut it by pointing out in good lawyer's fashion that the bond *must* have authorized whatever acts were necessary to execute it, and therefore the shedding of Antonio's blood, Shylock would have had to appeal to the spirit rather than the letter of the bond; for the bond is silent on the matter of shedding blood. But once he had done that he would have found it hard to maintain his legal position. The spirit of the bond is to make sure that Shylock is repaid in full, and Bassanio has offered to repay him double, or even more if Shylock insists—but Shylock suffers from the revenger's standard vice of immoderateness.

Yet Shylock's insistence on the principle of literal interpretation need not be viewed merely as the product of a primitive and vengeful spirit. As an unpopular alien (a point that he harps on and that the Christians do not deny), he naturally would mistrust a jurisprudence that gave judges a broad discretion to mitigate the rigors of legal rules, for he could expect any discretion to be exercised against him. A punctilious legalism is the pariah's protection. But he who lives by the letter of the law may perish by it.

Another famous depiction of contract in Elizabethan drama is the pact with the devil in Marlowe's *Doctor Faustus*. Faustus conjures Mephostophilis,

---

one pound. Had the Jew no friends to give him advice? . . . He could have done that man a lot of harm, even a long time before he had got that one pound of his flesh."

I said: "But in the story the Jew gave it up."

"Yes, that was a great pity, Memsahib," said Farah.

Out of Africa and Shadows on the Grass 269–270 (1985).

31. See Henry Sumner Maine, *Ancient Law* (1861).

32. Stephen A. Cohen, "'The Quality of Mercy': Law, Equity and Ideology in *The Merchant of Venice*," *Mosaic,* Dec. 1994, p. 35.

and after brief negotiations signs in blood a deed conveying his soul to Mephostophilis's master in exchange for various undertakings. The document states in full (I.5.95–114):[33]

> On these conditions following:
> First, that Faustus may be a spirit in form and substance.
> Secondly, that Mephostophilis shall be his servant, and be by him commanded.
> Thirdly, that Mephostophilis shall do for him, and bring him whatsoever.
> Fourthly, that he shall be in his chamber or house invisible.
> Lastly, that he shall appear to the said John Faustus at all times, in what shape and form soever he please.
> I, John Faustus of Wittenberg Doctor, by these presents, do give both body and soul to Lucifer, Prince of the East, and his minister Mephostophilis, and furthermore grant unto them that four and twenty years being expired, and these articles above written being inviolate, full power to fetch or carry the said John Faustus, body and soul, flesh, blood or goods, into their habitation wheresoever.
> By me, John Faustus.

At the end of the play the twenty-four years are up and a posse of devils appears and carries Faustus off to hell.

As the maker of an immoral contract, Faustus is a parallel figure to Shylock. Shylock's bond has a diabolical quality, and both characters are damned, unless Shylock is saved by his conversion. Shylock, with his Old Testament vengefulness, is the less modern man, yet there are hints of the proto-capitalist in him. Faustus, despite his fascination with magic, is thoroughly modern, individualistic man. He recognizes no limitations on human autonomy and man's quest for knowledge and control of his physical and social environment. In contrast to the orthodox Christian view that the soul belongs to God, Faustus thinks he owns his soul and therefore can transfer it for appropriate consideration. And being a man of honor and in his own way a hero, he makes no effort to break the contract when the time comes for him to fulfill his obligations under it. He substitutes the sanctity of contract for the sanctity of God; this shows his modernity. To put it differently, he cannot imagine a God of mercy, but only one of justice.[34]

Faustus's adherence to the contract may seem all the more striking be-

---

33. All my quotations from Marlowe in this book are from Christopher Marlowe, *The Complete Plays* (J. B. Steane ed. 1969).
34. Cleanth Brooks, "The Unity of Marlowe's *Doctor Faustus*," in *Christopher Marlowe* 97, 105–106 (Harold Bloom ed. 1986).

cause arguably Mephostophilis failed to honor his side of the bargain, and the contract expressly conditions Faustus's grant of body and soul to Lucifer on "these articles above written being inviolate." Shortly after signing and delivering the contract Faustus had asked Mephostophilis for a wife. Mephostophilis had temporized, then produced "a DEVIL *dressed like a woman, with fireworks,*" whom Faustus spurns: "A plague on her for a hot whore." Mephostophilis comments, "Tut, Faustus, marriage is but a cere-monial toy. / If thou lovest me, think no more of it" (1.5.149–156). The matter is dropped—and Faustus's failure to pursue it could be thought a ratification of the breach. Daniel Yeager may be correct, moreover, that the contract is best described as a "relational" contract,[35] one that estab-lishes a long-term relationship not every contingency in the performance of which can be foreseen. It is understood that the parties will act in good faith to resolve problems as they arise rather than standing on the letter of the contract. That appears to be the spirit in which the issue of a wife for Faustus is resolved. What is more, since marriage is a sacrament under any version of Christianity plausibly attributable to the world of the play, a devil could not procure a wife for Faustus, and this impossibility may be part of an implicit background understanding that qualifies the literal terms of the contract. Under the doctrine of substantial performance, moreover, even if Mephostophilis's failure to produce a wife for Faustus was a breach of the contract and was not forgiven, it would not have justified Faustus in repu-diating the contract; it was too minor a breach.[36]

Faustus would have been on stronger ground in seeking to repudiate the contract because of its illegality. The law refuses to enforce contracts that are against public policy, and a contract with the devil fits the bill. Yet even a court of cold-blooded agnostics might be reluctant to let Faus-tus off on this ground. The lawyer's distinction between an executory and a half-executed contract shows why. An executory contract is one in which neither party has begun to perform his contractual undertak-ing; it is a bare exchange of promises. If the contract is illegal or other-wise contrary to public policy, the law will not enforce it. But what if after one party has performed his side of the bargain, or at least a good part of it, the other party asks to be excused from having to perform, because the contract is illegal, or on some other ground? Maybe party *A* has, as agreed, built a house for *B,* and now it is time for *B* to pay, and *B* refuses. The court is apt to be less sympathetic to a defense of illegal-

---

35. Yeager, "Marlowe's Faustus: Contract as Metaphor?" 2 *University of Chicago Law School Roundtable* 599, 611–612 (1995).

36. See Jacob & Youngs, Inc. v. Kent, 129 N.E. 889 (N.Y. 1921) (Cardozo, J.).

ity in such a case, because *B* will be unjustly enriched.[37] That is Faustus's case. His part of the bargain was not to be performed until the devil had finished performing *his* part. For Faustus to be allowed to repudiate the contract after having enjoyed its benefits for twenty-four years—benefits less ample than he had expected but considerable nevertheless[38]—would be to let him off scot-free after all those years of grossly immoral behavior. In these circumstances a sincere repentance, though feared by Mephostophilis, who keeps trying to intimidate Faustus into keeping his side of the bargain, is hard to visualize.

When a court does hold a half-performed illegal contract unenforceable, it may mitigate the hardship to the party who has performed by requiring the other party to restore to him the value of that performance.[39] But how could Faustus have restored to Mephostophilis the value (with interest!) of the goods and services that Mephostophilis had provided over the twenty-four years that the pact was in force? Penance would be of no benefit to Mephostophilis—quite the opposite. Faustus's inability to make restitution might make a court less likely to let him escape his contractual obligations.

But a critical qualification has been overlooked. The devices that courts use to minimize the injustices that unbending enforcement of the defense of illegality would produce are available only in cases in which the party seeking to enforce the contract was excusably ignorant of its illegality or less responsible for the making of the contract than the other party.[40] The devil could not argue either that he didn't know that contracts with him are illegal or that the primary wrongdoer was not himself but Faustus. So Faustus could have wiggled out of his contract, as a matter of contract law, even if there was no breach (or serious breach) by the devil. But not too much should be made of this. It is time we reminded ourselves that a pact with the devil is not subject to the law of contracts at all. The literary function of Faustus's pact is not to invoke that law but to symbolize the irrevocability of Faustus's choice. With eyes wide open he chooses a course of

---

37. See *Kelly v. Kosuga*, 358 U.S. 516 (1959); E. Allan Farnsworth, *Farnsworth on Contracts*, vol. 2, § 5.1, p. 6 (1990).

38. Just being guaranteed 24 more years of life meant a lot in plague-plagued London when *Doctor Faustus* was written. Christopher Ricks, "*Doctor Faustus* and Hell on Earth," in Ricks, *Essays in Appreciation* 1, 7 (1996). But Faust expected more, and, just like a modern intellectual, was disappointed when the world failed to live up to the expectations of his book-inflamed imagination. Ian Watt, *Myths of Modern Individualism: Faust, Don Quixote, Robinson Crusoe* 40 (1996).

39. See American Law Institute, *Restatement of Contracts (Second)* § 197 and comment b, § 198 (1979); Farnsworth, note 37 above, § 5.9.

40. Id., § 5.1, p. 6; § 5.9, pp. 76–77.

conduct that leads inevitably to his damnation. In *Doctor Faustus,* contract is a metaphor for commitment.

Vienna, where *Measure for Measure* is set, is depicted as having very strict laws, including the death penalty for fornication. But the laws are not enforced. The Duke of Vienna is unhappy with this situation—prostitution, adultery, and fornication are flourishing—but unwilling to crack down in person. As he explains (1.3.19–36),

> We have strict statutes and most biting laws,
> The needful bits and curbs to headstrong steeds,
> Which for this fourteen years we have let slip;
>
> . . . So our decrees,
> Dead to infliction, to themselves are dead;
> And liberty plucks justice by the nose . . .
>
> Sith 'twas my fault to give the people scope,
> 'Twould be my tyranny to strike and gall them.

The Duke arranges to take a leave of absence, leaving his strict and ascetic deputy, Angelo, in charge. Angelo promptly sentences Claudio, a young man who has impregnated his fiancée, to death for fornication. Claudio has a sister, Isabella, a novice in a nunnery. She goes to Angelo and pleads for her brother's life. He is smitten with her and offers to spare her brother if she will go to bed with him. She indignantly refuses. When she reports all this to Claudio, to her astonishment he urges her to accept Angelo's offer. She is dismayed by her brother's thinking his life more important than her immortal soul, whose salvation might be jeopardized by sex with Angelo. Why it would be is not made clear. Would not fornication, the least deadly of deadly sins (as Claudio points out to her), be excused if necessary to save an innocent life? But since fornication is also a crime, Isabella would not be sacrificing her chastity to save an innocent man—in fact she would be committing two crimes herself, bribery and fornication. Fortunately, the Duke, who is lurking about in his guise as a friar, comes up with a solution for their problems: Isabella is to tell Angelo that she accepts his offer but to insist that their sexual encounter be brief and in the dark. The friar will substitute in her place Mariana, Angelo's former fiancée, whom Angelo had jilted because her dowry had been lost in a shipwreck.

All is done as arranged. But to compound his perfidy Angelo decides to execute Claudio anyway lest Claudio seek revenge when he finds out what Angelo has done to his sister. (This is another example of the ubiquity of the revenge motif in Elizabethan drama.) Angelo orders Claudio's head sent to him, but the Duke-friar arranges the substitution of the head of a prisoner who has just died of natural causes. The Duke now sends word that he is returning to Vienna and will want an accounting of Angelo's stewardship. When the Duke and Angelo meet outside the city's gates, Isabella steps forward and accuses Angelo, who at first denies everything but is quickly exposed and confesses. Showing mercy, like his counterpart in Venice, the Duke pardons Angelo after making him marry Mariana. Claudio is freed and marries his fiancée. It seems that the Duke is going to marry Isabella, though this is not completely certain because she does not say anything when he tells her that he plans to marry her.[41]

Parallels to *The Merchant of Venice* abound. Like Shylock, Angelo is at once austere, a stickler for law, and (beneath his cold exterior) prey to a lawless, violent passion which drives him to attempt on Isabella the very crime that he sentenced Claudio to die for. He misuses his legal authority in much the same way that Shylock misuses the law of contracts. Less obvious is the affinity within *Measure for Measure* between Angelo and Isabella. It is poetic justice for Angelo that Isabella is the first woman to awaken his sensuality; they are alike in being moral fanatics.[42] Probably we are meant to think capital punishment for fornication absurd and (though this is less clear) to laugh at Isabella's indignant refusal to sacrifice her virginity for her brother's life.[43] After all, the Duke incites Mariana to commit the same crime for which Claudio is to be executed.

Karl Zender points out that Isabella displays an adolescent sensitivity to public humiliation and treats Claudio's imminent death not as a reality but "as a limit term for the desire for withdrawal from the world."[44] Young people have difficulty understanding death (or maybe it's just that as we become older we become more attached to life, almost as a matter of habit). Isabella has difficulty distinguishing between her impending with-

41. See Karl F. Zender, "Isabella's Choice," 73 *Philological Quarterly* 77, 88–91 (1994).

42. David J. Gless, *Measure for Measure, the Law, and the Convent,* ch. 2 and p. 97 (1979), places Shakespeare's portrayal of Isabella's "spiritual overreaching" in the context of Elizabethan anti-monasticism.

43. Shakespeare's first child was conceived before he married the mother. The Duke's pardoning Angelo on condition that he marry Mariana reflects what apparently in Elizabethan England, as until recently in this country, was the standard "punishment" for fornication. See Gless, note 41 above, at 108. Although the Puritans made adultery a capital offense, as it is also under Islamic law, I am not aware of a legal system that has made fornication a capital offense.

44. Zender, note 41 above, at 83. "Only the young can so detachedly if tormentedly survey the prospect of adult existence as to believe that they have the option 'To be or not to be'; the adult, with 'promises to keep', more often has to shrug and trudge on." Everett, note 8 above, at 22–23.

drawal from the world by becoming a nun and Claudio's by dying. So this is another *Bildungsroman*. Poetic justice for Isabella is being made an accomplice in the Duke's scheme of arranging a sexual encounter between Angelo and Mariana and being snatched from the nunnery to become the Duke's wife, which is why I think the better interpretation of the somewhat ambiguous ending is that she and the Duke are indeed to marry. I don't wish to transform *Measure for Measure* into *Emma,* however. There is grandeur in Isabella's appeals to Angelo, giving point to Brian Vickers' remark that "it is obvious to anyone who has studied the place of women in Elizabethan society that [Shakespeare's] heroines enjoy a degree of independence and a mastery of language and eloquence that are totally untypical of his age."[45]

The most difficult legal question in the play is the status of the two marriage contracts. Claudio calls his fiancée his "wife" in Act I. Under the law of Elizabethan England, a marriage contract probably created a valid, though irregular and perhaps sinful, marriage even if it was not solemnized, although the legal picture is very obscure. Yet no one in the play doubts that Claudio is guilty of fornication, including Claudio. But then the Duke tells Isabella that it would be fitting, in light of the marriage contract with Mariana that Angelo had broken, to substitute Mariana for Isabella in the sexual encounter with Angelo. This might seem to imply that the law of Vienna is the same in this respect as English law—but if so, why does the Duke and everyone else in the play insist that Claudio is guilty of fornication? Margaret Scott points out that the Council of Trent had outlawed informal marriage in 1563, and she notes that the play represents Vienna as an emphatically Roman Catholic state, in this respect wholly unlike England.[46] So what exactly is going on?

Scott's eminently sensible suggestion is that the legal world of the play is not to be identified with any real-life legal regime, whether English or Continental. Since fornication is a capital crime in the world of the play but nowhere else, there should be no difficulty in accepting that informal or clandestine marriages are illegal in the play regardless of the legal position outside. The required suspension of disbelief is less than in imagining that Shylock's bond would have been enforceable if only it had been drafted more carefully, for example to provide for death by strangulation so that no blood would have to be shed. Yet that is the contract law of *The Merchant of Venice*. Shakespeare is not concerned with depicting law realis-

---

45. Vickers, *Appropriating Shakespeare: Contemporary Critical Quarrels* 414 (1993).

46. Scott, "'Our City's Institutions': Some Further Reflections on the Marriage Contracts in *Measure for Measure,*" 49 *English Legal History* 790 (1982).

tically in either its substantive or its procedural aspects. Angelo points out that a jury verdict is not invalid just because one of the jurors is a thief; but there are no juries in the legal world depicted in *Measure for Measure,* where Angelo is attorney general, judge, jury, and court of appeals all in one.

Scott has not solved the problem of the Duke's treating the two marriage contracts inconsistently. But that problem is superficial. The Duke does not deny that Angelo and Mariana will be committing fornication; the idea rather is that turnabout is fair play. The Duke must know that he is going to pardon both couples, and he is not worried that fornication is a deadly sin. What might be thought a more serious inconsistency is Isabella's failing to raise any objection to the Duke's scheme. She does not say, "Hold on—Mariana's immortal soul will be jeopardized, just as mine would have been." Instead her reaction is, what a nifty idea ("the image of it gives me content already," III.1.261). That the source of the suggestion is a friar, as she thinks the Duke is, may alleviate her theological concerns. But we may also be meant to treat her reaction as further evidence that she is priggish rather than principled—or as evidence that she is beginning to share the Duke's pragmatic outlook. Another possibility is that she may think that Mariana's marriage contract, although illegal under the law of Vienna as presented in the play, will mitigate Mariana's deed in Heaven's eye; this ties in with the apparent clerical sponsorship of the deed. Isabella could raise no such "defense" if she yielded her body to Angelo. So Mariana can save Claudio with less jeopardy to her soul than Isabella to hers. The law, whether of Shakespeare's England or Catholic Austria, has little to do with any of this; the play's jurisprudential interest is not trivial, but it lies elsewhere.

The Duke plays a role in the play that is similar to Portia's in *The Merchant of Venice*—arranging things to come out right through a series of none-too-creditable stratagems. The Duke's apparent withdrawal from Vienna, leaving Angelo to enforce the laws strictly, to take the blame, and to get humiliated on the Duke's return, recalls Machiavelli's *The Prince.* The Duke, when disguised as a friar, puts a terrible scare into Claudio by repeatedly telling him that he is going to be executed; frightens Isabella by telling her that Claudio *has* been executed and by ordering her to be arrested for slandering Angelo; arranges an apparently illicit sexual encounter between Angelo and Mariana; and seems bent on luring a nun aspirant into the marriage bed. But it all works. Angelo's reign of terror succeeds, we are led to believe, in curtailing prostitution without impairing the Duke's popularity. Angelo is taught a lesson. Mariana obtains justice at long last. Moderate officials, like Escalus (Angelo's deputy) and the keeper of the jail, are vindicated. And Isabella, a cold and priggish young lady, becomes a woman fit for a glorious marriage.

Angelo on the one hand, and the bawds who provide the "low" comic relief on the other, represent at the opening of the play the extremes—angel and animal—between which man, in the medieval and Elizabethan world view, is intermediate; and the "angel" turns out to be an animal after all. Extremes of particular interest to the law-trained reader are the law that is never enforced and the law that is enforced too strictly. We are made to understand that attempting to outlaw fornication would be as quixotic in the culture of the play as it would be in our own culture, and that the Duke, though not a fully exemplary character, achieves the prudent mean—law enforced in moderation, which apparently means that the "punishment" for fornication is marriage and that prostitution, even if not completely suppressed, is no longer flaunted.

Angelo's insistence on enforcing law to the hilt reflects a conception of law that he shares not only with Shylock and Isabella but also with many lawyers and judges of the present day—the conception of law as something existing apart from man. It is a conception particularly congenial to people like Shylock, Angelo, and Isabella, who lack warmth in human relationships. Angelo cannot understand acting leniently toward Claudio just because there are extenuating circumstances; that would imply tampering with the law, to him a set of rigid rules inflexibly applied. When Isabella pleads for her brother's life, Angelo replies, "It is the law, not I, condemn your brother. / Were he my kinsman, brother, or my son, / It should be thus with him" (II.2.84–86). The image of a judge condemning his own son expresses the sharpest possible cleavage between law and human feeling. Angelo is glancing ahead to Robert Louis Stevenson's *Weir of Hermiston: An Unfinished Romance* (1896), the climax of which was to be a judge's condemning his own son to death. Angelo's "angelism" is the unattainable and unnatural divorce of body from spirit—something Brutus attempted (an ancestor of his was famous for having condemned his own son to death). Isabella shares Angelo's conception of law as a thing apart from man. The ground on which she pleads with the Duke for Angelo's life before she discovers that Claudio is alive is that since her brother was, after all, guilty, his execution was not wrongful despite the judge's corruption.

Marxist critic Terry Eagleton takes the side of Shylock and Angelo against Portia and the Duke of Vienna: "It is Shylock who has respect for the spirit of law and Portia who does not. Shylock's bond does not actually state in writing that he is allowed to take some of Antonio's blood along with a pound of his flesh, but this is a reasonable inference from the text, as any real court would recognize . . . Portia's ingenious quibbling would be ruled out of order in a modern court, and Shylock (given that his bond were legal in the first place) would win his case."[47] As any *real* court would recognize? No real court would have enforced Shylock's bond, either in the sixteenth century or since. The enforcement of such a bargain is not, as Eagleton believes, entailed by commitment to the rule of law. A rule against penalty clauses in contracts is—a rule. Eagleton might, but does not, argue that any compromise with freedom of contract, as in refusing to enforce a bond agreed to by consenting adults in full possession of their faculties and all relevant information, undermines the premises of a capitalist system. We shall consider that issue in Chapter 5.

Equity, moreover, has been a part of the Western concept of law since Aristotle, a point that Eagleton ignores when he says, Angelo- or Shylock-fashion, that "for law to be law its decrees must be general and impartial, quite independent of and indifferent to any concrete situation" (p. 36). Law does not only consist of unbendable rules that must be enforced to the hilt regardless of consequences; meliorative doctrines are a part of law too. Eagleton's suppositions that not punishing Claudio to the maximum extent authorized by law fatally undermined the law's generality (pp. 55–57), and that justice can never be tempered by mercy because "how is mercy to break the vicious circle of prosecutions when it must somehow spring from inside that circle, from a humble solidarity with vice?" (p. 57), assume incorrectly that legality entails always imposing the maximum punishment. On the contrary, the existence of a *maximum* implies that lawful punishment is a range, not a point. Anglo-American law has always given law enforcement officials discretion not to prosecute every offense and within each category of offenses (for example, fornication) has usually allowed the judge to vary the punishment according to aggravating or mitigating circumstances of the defendant's conduct.

There are solid utilitarian reasons, independent of any "solidarity with vice" felt by judges, for the mixture of rule and discretion in criminal justice. Because the legislature lacks information about the particular circumstances in which its laws might be violated, it fixes only the outer limits of punishment and leaves to the prosecuting, the judicial, and sometimes the correctional authorities the task of fitting the punishment to the conduct and circumstances of each criminal. This is a rational division of labor, and does not contradict the idea of law.

Eagleton's view of legality rests on a misunderstanding that *The Merchant*

---

47. Eagleton, *William Shakespeare* 36–37 (1986). See also Roberto Mangabeira Unger, *Knowledge and Politics*, ch. 2 (1975); Unger, *The Critical Legal Studies Movement* 64 (1986) (discussing *The Merchant of Venice*); John Denvir, "William Shakespeare and the Jurisprudence of Comedy," 39 *Stanford Law Review* 825, 827–835 (1987).

of Venice and *Measure for Measure* can help dispel. It is false that Shylock, Angelo, Isabella, and Eagleton represent law, and Portia and the Duke of Vienna not-law. The first four represent one end of a spectrum while the last two are closer to the other end. The left-hand column of the table below lists a number of different terms—jurisprudential, philosophical, psychological, institutional—in which to describe law as an abstraction, a thing apart from the people charged with responsibility for enforcing the law and adjudicating disputes. The terms suggest ways of minimizing discretion and the human factor and maximizing "ruledness" or "legalism." The emphasis is on professionalism, logic, strict rules, sharp distinctions, positive law, and "hard" cases (meaning, not as it has come to mean, cases that are difficult, but cases that reach harsh results, showing that head and heart are firmly separated), and on abstracting from the specific circumstances of a case, from the tug of emotion, and from the personalities of the disputants.

TABLE OF LEGAL ANTINOMIES

government of laws	government of men
formalism	realism
law	politics
law	equity
law	mercy
law	justice
rule	discretion
rule	standard
rule	principle
legal rule	equity maxim
per se rule	rule of reason
logic	policy
rigid	flexible
right answers	good answers
positive law	natural law
decision by precedent	arbitration
judge	Qadi, jury
strict liability	negligence
objective theory of contracts	subjective theory
objectivity	subjectivity

impersonality	personalism
principled	result-oriented
rights	needs
right	might
statute law	common law
statute law	constitutional law
interpretivism	noninterpretivism
strict construction	flexible or loose construction
letter	spirit
judge finds law	judge makes law

No civilized society has ever embraced the legalist position in undiluted form. Every such society softens the rigors of strict legalism by some or all of the items listed in the right-hand column. It is because the strict enforcement of rules is intolerable ("working to rule" is a device by which workers disrupt their employer's operations) that law is the *art* of governance by rules, not just an automated machinery of enforcement. Both the extreme of hyperlegalism and the opposite extreme of a purely discretionary system of justice are found only in primitive societies. Mature societies mix strict law with discretion. Every cell in the table is a feature of modern American law. The mixture is not inconsistent with the idea of law; it *is* the idea of law—as literature can help us see.

Has Law Gender?

Some feminists believe that the legalistic approach to law reflects a distinctively male style of thinking.[48] It is remarkable how often in literature the view of law expressed by the terms on the right-hand side of my table is personified by a woman and the opposing view by a man. Recall the pleas of mercy by Portia and Isabella. Recall Hecuba, Beatrice Cenci, and Antigone all confronting a male embodiment of legal positivism. Compare Orestes, who is avenging a civic as well as a personal wrong (regicide as well as parricide), with Clytemnestra, who is avenging a purely personal wrong. The Furies are female avengers—and of familial rather than civic

48. See, for example, Carol Gilligan, *In a Different Voice: Psychological Theory and Women's Development* 105 (1982) (discussing *The Merchant of Venice*); Robin West, "Jurisprudence and Gender," 55 *University of Chicago Law Review* 1 (1988).

wrongs.[49] In Chapter 5 we shall see Captain Vere instructing the court-martial in *Billy Budd* to disregard "the feminine in man" in favor of strict, hard justice. If Portia is literature's exemplary female lawyer—though we must not overlook the negative features in her portrayal[50]—male lawyers and judges in literature are more often than not cruel, bloodless enemies of life, such as Jaggers, Tulkinghorn, Ivan Ilich, and Judge Crease.

Susan Glaspell's story "A Jury of Her Peers" (1917) illustrates the gender contrast.[51] The story, loosely based on a real case,[52] is set in the rural Midwest, probably Iowa. A farmer is found dead in his bedroom, strangled by a rope. Because there is no indication of forced entry or of suicide, the widow is suspected. She is arrested and carted off to jail. Sheriff Peters returns to the scene of the crime to investigate, accompanied by the county attorney and by Hale, the man who had discovered the body. Peters and Hale bring their wives, who remain downstairs while the men search the bedroom for clues. Poking about in the kitchen—the quintessential "woman's room," which the men had not thought to search carefully—the women discover the body of a pet bird, its neck broken. Mrs. Hale understands in a flash that the bird had been the only bright spot in the bleak life of this lonely, childless farm woman; that the husband—a cold, hard man—had killed the bird; and that his deed had driven her to kill him. Mrs. Hale decides that the men must not be told about her find. The sheriff's wife has qualms about withholding evidence, but goes along.

The men are smug and patronizing. It would never occur to them that the women might have discovered something they had overlooked. That is the irony in the story, as well as a telling point against the virtual exclusion of women from the legal system, whether as lawyers, judges, or jurors, at the time Glaspell was writing.[53] The story makes another point about law. Obviously the breaking of a bird's neck is not the sort of provo-

49. See Paul Gewirtz, "Aeschylus' Law," 101 *Harvard Law Review* 1043 (1988). Bernard M. W. Knox, *The Heroic Temper: Studies in Sophoclean Tragedy* 77–78 (1964), compares Antigone to the Furies, emphasizing that the natural law that she expounds is one of familial obligation, as we have seen.

50. Oddly paralleled by the ambivalent portrayal of female lawyers in American movies, on which see Carole Shapiro, "Women Lawyers in Celluloid: Why Hollywood Skirts the Truth," 25 *University of Toledo Law Review* 995 (1995).

51. The story is a rewrite of her one-act play *Trifles* (1916). See generally *Susan Glaspell: Essays on Her Theater and Fiction* (Linda Ben-Zvi ed. 1995).

52. State v. Hossack, 89 N.W. 1077 (Iowa 1902). See Marina Angel, "Criminal Law and Women: Giving the Abused Woman Who Kills *A Jury of Her Peers* Who Appreciate *Trifles*," 33 *American Criminal Law Review* 230, 241–244 (1996).

53. See Leonard Mustazza, "Gender and Justice in Susan Glaspell's 'A Jury of Her Peers,'" 2 *Law and Semiotics* 271 (1988).

cation that excuses a murder in the eyes of the law. (Look what happened to Beatrice Cenci, whose provocation was a thousand times greater.) But those are not the eyes the women train on the matter. More sensitive, we are made to understand, than men would be to the full particulars—the total context—of the crime, less committed to the "legalistic" view that guilt should be determined in accordance with rules that abstract from those particulars (which may be considered only at the sentencing stage of the criminal proceeding), the women are prepared to become accessories after the fact to the murder by suppressing vital evidence.

Men, Glaspell implies, abstract from the circumstances of a dispute a few salient facts and make them legally determinative. This is law by rules—that is what rules *do*. Women prefer to base judgment on all the circumstances of a case, unhampered by rules that require a blinkered vision, untroubled by a felt need to conform decision to general, "neutral" principles. Emphasis on particulars links the feminist and literary approaches to law. Literary expression is characteristically concrete, and many feminists are critical of abstraction, regarding it as a masculine method of apprehending reality.

There is more to the story, including a very distant echo of *Antigone*. In both the play and Glaspell's story there is a strong sense that the family or household is the woman's domain, and politics and law the man's; and that the woman's authority in her domain must be recognized. Mrs. Hale, like Antigone, vindicates the woman's authority within her proper sphere, though she does so nonconfrontationally. But I want to focus on the suggestion that women think differently about law, think about it concretely rather than abstractly—and to point out its lack of the supposed feminine virtue of nuance. The suggestion is excessively dichotomous both in its strict gendering of the polar conceptions of law and in its assumption that law does or can embrace one of the poles to the exclusion of the other. The traditional personification of impersonal justice is a blindfolded goddess, and the preeminent spokesman for law and order in *Eumenides* is Athena, though, lacking a mother, she is not the most feminine of goddesses. Faulkner's Gavin Stevens, on the other hand, is a male Portia. Agamemnon in *Hecuba* equivocates between the rival conceptions of law. And the principal female exemplars, in literature, of the alleged feminine outlook on law are the creation of men who depicted the so-called masculine outlook in an unfavorable, and even an unmasculine, light. The Shakespearean men who embrace the "male" conception of law with the most ardor, Shylock and Angelo, are weak rather than strong figures. Shylock is a pariah; and we have seen how a legalistic conception of law can be the pariah's refuge. Angelo is presented to the reader as naturally submissive. When the Duke tells him he's in charge now, Angelo protests that he's not ready. Rather than take responsibility for his decisions, he retreats behind the law; the law becomes his master in lieu of the absent Duke. Angelo's legalism is connected with his being a born underling as well as with his desire to transcend the body and become all spirit. Excessive legalism has been associated with immature, weak, and father-fixated personalities.[54]

Glaspell's suggestion that there is more than an adventitious connection between genders on the one hand and styles of law and justice on the other has been elaborated by Carol Gilligan.[55] Her influential book *In a Different Voice*—the nonfiction counterpart to "A Jury of Her Peers"—distinguishes between an "ethic of justice" (a better term might be "ethic of rights") that Gilligan deems distinctively masculine and an "ethic of care" that she deems distinctively feminine. Her principal evidence is the different attitudes of boys and of girls toward the "enforcement" of rules in games. Boys are quick to "adjudicate" alleged violations and condemn the violator. Girls tend to evaluate the alleged infraction in its specific context, with particular attention to the importance of preventing a disruption of relationships.[56] And being more empathetic than boys, girls will often stop playing when an infraction is charged, fearing that an attempt to decide the merits of the charge would cause hurt feelings. The ethic of rights corresponds to the formalistic style of law and the ethic of care to the contextual, personal, and discretionary style. Gilligan's theory thus contains the germ of a full-fledged feminist jurisprudence—a jurisprudence that is not limited to women's legal issues such as comparable worth, rape, pornography, and sexual harassment in the workplace, but seeks to make over all law so that it will be less masculine (formalist, rule-bound).

Yet whatever may be the attitudes of male and female children toward rule infractions in games, the "ethic of care" of which Gilligan speaks is no more a female preserve in law than it is in literature. Men have controlled the legal system from the beginning, yet that system has never been as dominated by formalism, strict rules, relish for hard cases, and the like, as feminism, Marxism, and the legal establishment have claimed. For every Langdell there has been a Cardozo, for every Frankfurter a Murphy, for

---

54. This is the burden of Jerome Frank's famous denunciation of legal formalism, *Law and the Modern Mind* (1930).

55. See note 48 above.

56. Lisa Weil, "Virginia Woolf's *To the Lighthouse*: Toward an Integrated Jurisprudence," 6 *Yale Journal of Law and Feminism* 1 (1994), points out that the principal characters in Woolf's novel, Mr. and Mrs. Ramsay, are anticipatory personifications of Gilligan's ethic of rights and ethic of care, respectively.

every Rehnquist a Brennan, for every Scalia a Blackmun, and for every Easterbrook a Reinhardt. If we want to emphasize not the epistemological virtues of case-specific legal reasoning but instead sympathy for the underdog (one aspect of the ethic of care), then we have only to list the many male judges who have worn that sympathy on their sleeve. Even the emphasis on maintaining ongoing relationships is not special to feminism; it is the stock in trade of those legal scholars, most of them male, who emphasize the relational aspects of long-term contracts. It may be that, as Gilligan believes, more women than men have the characteristics that feminists regard as distinctively feminine. It would not follow that more female judges had these characteristics than male judges, since neither female nor male judges are a random draw from the population.[57] But even if female judges are likely to be on average closer than male judges to the "care" end of the spectrum, this need imply no more than a shift along a known spectrum; it need not portend the transformation of law.

What is true is that if society goes too far in making the administration of law flexible, particularistic, "caring," the consequence will be anarchy, tyranny, or both, which is why "people's justice" is rightly deprecated. This was the problem with Athenian justice, and is illustrated by the trial of Socrates, which Plato implicitly compared to the trial of a physician before a jury of children upon an accusation by a cook.[58] There is a hint of the anarchic in the way the Duke of Vienna conducts state affairs in *Measure for Measure,* lending point to Graham Bradshaw's observation that the contrast between Angelo and the Duke is the contrast between "unbenevolent principle and unprincipled benevolence."[59] The inhuman formalism of an Angelo is the abuse of a good thing rather than the essence of a bad. Impersonality is one of the features that distinguishes law from revenge, and the fusion of the victim's and the law enforcer's roles is one of the drawbacks of a revenge system. Read literally, "A Jury of Her Peers" en-

---

57. In the early years of Sandra Day O'Connor's service on the Supreme Court, some legal scholars thought they detected in her opinions "a feminine jurisprudence" that "might thus be unlike any other contemporary jurisprudence." Suzanna Sherry, "Civic Virtue and the Feminine Voice in Constitutional Adjudication," 72 *Virginia Law Review* 543 (1986). See also Frank I. Michelman, "The Supreme Court, 1985 Term: Foreword, Traces of Self–Government," 100 *Harvard Law Review* 4, 17 n. 68, 33–36 (1986). It has been many years since anyone has said that about O'Connor. It is even less likely to be said of Justice Ruth Bader Ginsburg, whose opinions are notably emotionless and formalistic. What is true is that these Justices, like most female judges, are highly sympathetic to women's rights; but this does not imply a distinctive feminine style of legal reasoning.

58. Plato, *Gorgias* 100–101 (W. C. Helmbold trans. 1952).

59. Bradshaw, *Misrepresentations: Shakespeare and the Materialists* 143 (1993). Ziolkowski, note 22 above, draws a similar contrast between Shylock and Portia.

dorses a "battered wife" defense to murder so encompassing as to place most husbands outside the protection of the law.

The Shakespearean characters who urge flexible justice do not embrace the untenable extreme of wholly discretionary, personalistic law, which is no law.[60] Portia realizes that a measure of impersonality in the administration of the laws—and thus a willingness to provide justice to aliens—is necessary to preserve Venice's commercial position. The Duke of Vienna is concerned with the breakdown of law and order in his state, although he is not scrupulous about the means of restoring them. It is not true that "abstraction is the first step down the road of androcentric ignorance" because "the abstract principle that women as the weaker sex belong in a separate sphere, protected and cared for by men, supported the rule preventing married women from owning property."[61] Abstraction is a precondition of thinking, and a rule distinguishing women from men on the ground that women are weaker is less rather than more abstract than a rule treating men and women alike regardless of any difference in strength between them.

60. For a good novelistic treatment of discretionary justice run wild, see Robert Graves, *Claudius the God* 327–336 (1935).

61. Mari J. Matsuda, "Liberal Jurisprudence and Abstracted Visions of Human Nature: A Feminist Critique of Rawls' Theory of Justice," 16 *New Mexico Law Review* 613, 619 (1986).

FOUR

The Limits of Literary Jurisprudence

Kafka

No author of imaginative literature seems to have had more to say about law than Kafka, himself a lawyer, whose great novel *The Trial* opens with the arrest of the protagonist, Joseph K., and ends with K.'s execution one year later, and whose short stories and fragments frequently have law for their theme. In Chapter 6 I shall examine Robin West's claim that Kafka's fiction is a criticism of the economic model of human behavior which lies at the heart of the influential school of legal studies known as law and economics. Here I take up *The Trial* and "In the Penal Colony," a short story Kafka wrote in 1914, interrupting his work on the novel.

An explorer (as the German word *Reisende* is usually rendered in translations of the story, although it just means traveler) has been invited to the penal colony of an unnamed European power to witness an execution that is to be conducted in the manner traditional in the colony, and to report his impressions to the colony's newly appointed commandant. A soldier on guard duty had fallen asleep, and an officer had struck him with his riding whip. Waking up, the soldier had grabbed the officer by the legs and threatened to devour him. For this act of insubordination the soldier has been sentenced to death. The officer in charge of the execution, who is the unnamed protagonist of Kafka's story (there are no proper names), explains to the explorer in loving detail the manner of execution. Devised by the former commandant of revered memory (revered by the officer, in any event), it works as follows. The condemned is stripped naked and placed on the table-like surface, covered with cotton, of the execution machine—a kind of giant sewing machine. The moving part of the machine, suggestively nicknamed the "harrow," inscribes the judgment—which in the case of this condemned is "Honor your superiors"—with many curlicues and flourishes, by means of moving needles that jab deeper and deeper while the bed of the machine rotates the body and the cotton sops up the blood. The turning point in the execution comes in the sixth hour, when, as the officer explains to the explorer, the condemned, who has not been told what the judgment is, comes to understand it in his body through the repeated jabbing of the needles. In the twelfth hour, having had six hours to reflect on the judgment, the condemned man dies and the machine tosses him into a pit dug next to it.

The explorer expresses surprise that the condemned is not told the judgment or given any opportunity to defend himself against the charge. But the officer explains that as he is prosecutor, judge, and executioner all in one, the problem of error that plagues complex justice systems is avoided; to give the accused a chance to speak in his own defense would merely precipitate a stream of lies. The officer pours his heart out to the explorer, knowing that the new commandant dislikes the traditional mode of execution and hoping the explorer will render a positive report on it. The officer is particularly distressed by the decline in appropriations and public interest in executions—the whole population of the colony, including children, once used to attend them, all solemnly awaiting the climactic moment when the condemned man would comprehend the judgment.

After being laid on the machine, the condemned man vomits because standing orders not to feed the condemned too near the time for execution have been disobeyed, and because lack of funds has forced the officer to use the same gag over and over again. This incident, which results in soiling the machine, combined with the explorer's refusal to join in a zany scheme by which the officer hopes to recapture public support for the method of execution, is the last straw for the officer. He sets the condemned man free, changes the judgment in the machine to "Be just," undresses, climbs on the machine, and takes the filthy gag into his mouth. As if by magic, before he can press the start lever the machine begins to operate—at first smoothly, but after a while it goes crazy. Instead of just tattooing the judgment on the officer's body, it stabs him through the forehead with a single spike, killing him instantly and denying him his moment of illumination. The back of the machine opens up and spills out hundreds of gears. Stopping briefly at the cafe where the old commandant is buried under a table in the patio, the explorer then takes the first ship leaving the colony. With the death of the officer and the disintegration of the machine, there is no need to make his report.

Kafka is often regarded as an oracular figure, like George Orwell; "In the Penal Colony" is considered a prophecy of the Nazi concentration camps, *The Trial* a prophecy of the state terrorism practiced by Hitler and Stalin. A lawyer might be tempted to read "In the Penal Colony" as a commentary on due process and on cruel and unusual punishments. But what I find most striking, and most characteristic of Kafka, about the story is the juxtaposition of the repulsive absurdity of the mode of punishment with the gravity with which the officer expounds its sublime virtues. The officer's problem, a recurrent one in Kafka's fiction, is his inability to get anybody to take seriously what he believes to be the most important thing in the world. This inability is signaled by the officer's devotion to a machine that attempts to communicate legal judgments without—communication. The condemned man is an imbecile (or worse—remember the nature of his threat) for whom there would have been no ray of insight at the sixth or any other hour. He does not understand the language spoken by the officer and would not understand the machine's "body language" either. The soldier who guards the condemned man is also a clod. The only other observer is the explorer. He affects a glacial detachment modulating into polite distaste, but eventually makes clear his lack of sympathy for the officer's obsession. With the spatial clarity that is so striking a feature of Kafka's fiction, we are made to feel the officer's total isolation in the grim desert setting—the pathos of the obsession that has cut him off from all human contact. We come to feel sorry for this monster, sensing in him the pathological extreme of the ordinary human inability to get others to share our plans and passions. Despite the overt theme of justice perverted, the heart of the story is further from law than the Elizabethan plays discussed in the preceding chapter.

Thus I am not persuaded by Lida Kirchberger's effort to depict "In the Penal Colony" as an allegory of law,[1] with the torture machine symbolizing the "machinery of justice" and its destruction the impossibility of a "mechanical" jurisprudence, a jurisprudence from which all discretion has been banished—the very jurisprudence that Terry Eagleton might think entailed by the concept of law. This interpretation cannot explain the officer's personality or pathos or account for the fact that the torture machine does not formulate rules, find facts, render judgments, or do anything else that a justice system does except announce and administer the sentence.

The Trial, also written in 1914, faithfully reproduces many details of

---

1. Kirchberger, *Franz Kafka's Use of Law in Fiction: A New Interpretation of* In der Strafkolonie, Der Prozess, *and* Das Schloss, ch. 2 (1986).

Austro-Hungarian criminal procedure.[2] Yet law is not at the heart of this work either. Joseph K.—a finicky bachelor, at once a successful bank executive and a modest boarding-house resident, of bureaucratic outlook, rule-abiding, insecurely self-important, alternatively abject and self-assertive, commonplace, urban rather than urbane, *l'homme moyen sensuel*— is arrested at his boarding house on the morning of his thirtieth birthday by two plainclothesmen and an inspector. They produce no identification and give no hint of what agency they work for or what the charge against K. is. Since he has committed no offense and is a respectable member of the middle class, naturally he is indignant. "Who could these men be? What were they talking about? What authority could they represent? K. lived in a country with a legal constitution, there was universal peace, all the laws were in force; who dared seize him in his own dwelling?" (p. 7).[3] He asks the inspector, "'Who accuses me? What authority is conducting these proceedings? Are you officers of the law? None of you has a uniform, unless your suit'—here he turned to Franz [one of the arresting officers]— 'is to be considered a uniform, but it's more like a tourist's outfit'" (p. 16). But they say nothing to the point.

The remark about the tourist's outfit is a clue that something stranger than a critique of the denial of due process of law is in the offing. From the outset K. had been fascinated by Franz's outfit. He had noticed that Franz "wore a closely fitting black suit, which was furnished with all sorts of pleats, pockets, buckles, and buttons, as well as a belt, like a tourist's outfit, and in consequence looked eminently practical, though one could not quite tell what actual purpose it served" (p. 4). K. is preoccupied with precisely those aspects of his predicament that are *not* related to due process. Meanwhile the arresting officers have taken K.'s underwear, allegedly for safekeeping, and are busy wolfing down his breakfast, while through the

2. See Martha S. Robinson, "The Law of the State in Kafka's *The Trial*," 6 *ALSA Forum* 127 (1982). A better translation of *Prozess* would be "case" or "proceeding" because what is depicted in parodic form is the stretched-out, nonadversarial Continental criminal proceeding rather than an Anglo-American trial. Theodore Ziolkowski, in *The Mirror of Justice: Literary Reflections of Legal Crisis* 235–239 (1997), argues that the real subject of *The Trial* is the difference between turn-of-the-century Prussian and Austrian criminal law, the latter, he argues, being, like the court that condemns Joseph K., more concerned with the criminal's state of mind than with the criminal act. Ziolkowski supports this interpretation by reference to uncompleted chapters and excised passages in *The Trial*. See id. at 308 n. 55. A dubious interpretive procedure from a literary standpoint, it makes *The Trial* esoteric, a historical relic, and a bore—but as I noted in the Introduction, that is not Ziokowski's standpoint. He is interested in quarrying works of literature for traces of legal controversies contemporary with the work.

3. My quotations from *The Trial* are from the 1960 edition of Willa and Edwin Muir's translation.

open window of his room people living across the alleyway are staring at the goings-on in the room "with truly senile inquisitiveness" (p. 5). K. asks the inspector whether he can call his friend the public prosecutor (*Staatsanwalt*—mistranslated by the Muirs as "lawyer"). Certainly, the inspector says, but it's pointless. K. becomes furious and petulantly announces that he won't call the prosecutor after all, as if by this refusal he is scoring a point off the inspector.

The atmosphere of the book is dream-like but until the last chapter not nightmarish. Having arrested K., the mysterious trio informs him that he is free to go about his business—the court will get in touch with him in due course—and they leave. K. is not "booked" and does not have to post bond. There is next a mysterious interlude in which K. makes advances to another boarder, Fraülein Bürstner, who then disappears; later we are led to understand that K. is mistakenly seeking the aid of women in dealing with the court.

Next (Kafka never finished the book; it is choppy and episodic) K. is summoned for his first interrogation by the examining magistrate of the court, never named, that ordered his arrest. The court turns out to occupy a rabbit warren of musty rooms in a tenement building. When K. at last finds the courtroom—there are no signs or other trappings of an official enterprise—the scene is like a cross between the Court of Chancery in *Bleak House* and a circle of hell in the *Divine Comedy*. It gradually dawns on us that no one obtains justice from this court; one just attends until broken by old age, or killed. Needless to say, there is no interrogation. When K. returns the next week (unbidden, but he is trying to expedite his case, or at least find out what the charge is), the place is deserted. He rummages through the books on the judges' bench, but they are not law books—they are dirty novels. He has a brief flirtation with a woman washing clothes and a run-in with a law student. What follows is a scene reeking of sadomasochism: K. opens a storage room at the bank where he works—and finds the two officers who had arrested him being whipped for having stolen his underwear.

K.'s uncle, who has heard about the mysterious judicial proceeding against his nephew, refers K. to an eminent lawyer, Huld (German for "grace"). Huld turns out to be the Austro-Hungarian counterpart of a "Washington lawyer." He lets it be known that he has inside knowledge about the workings of the mysterious court, knows the judges, has heard about K.'s case, has clout, finesse—just leave everything to him. "The most important thing was counsel's personal connection with officials of the Court; in that lay the chief value of the Defense" (p. 146). Nothing happens. K. becomes distracted by Huld's maid, Leni, and has a flirtation with her similar to the one with Fraülein Bürstner earlier.

K. is becoming mesmerized by the case. Not that anyone from the court is bothering him; after that first, abortive summons to an interrogation the court has made no effort to get in touch with him. But K. is distracted at work and fears that his principal rival at the bank, the deputy director, is gaining on him, though there is no suggestion that the arrest and ensuing proceeding have stigmatized K. A client of K.'s puts him in touch with a painter, Titorelli, who turns out to be the court's official portraitist. After escaping a clutch of faintly sinister teenage girls, K. finds Titorelli's tenement apartment. It is in the court's building; all roads lead K. to the court. Titorelli explains that, assuming K. is innocent, there are three possibilities: real acquittal (which is out of the question), ostensible acquittal (where the accused is liable to rearrest and reprosecution at any time), and indefinite postponement. The impression conveyed is that K. will never get free from the clutches of the court. It is as if he had a chronic, incurable disease which, if carefully managed, might not shorten his life.

Feeling that he is making no progress with his case, K. decides to fire Huld, who all this time has been working laboriously (or so he says—doubtless lying) on a draft of K.'s first plea. The question of how the plea can be made when neither K. nor Huld has the faintest idea of what the charge is does not faze Huld in the least, and is one of the many jokes in this unexpectedly funny book. It happens that Huld has another client, Block, whose case is now five years old and has utterly devoured him, more even than K's case has devoured K. (but it is still less than a year old). Block has actually moved into Huld's house, and Leni has taken to locking him in her room during the day to keep him out of her hair. In an effort to dissuade K. from firing him, Huld gives a wonderful rendition of the lawyer's trick of intimidating a client by making the law seem wholly beyond lay comprehension. He reports a conversation he has recently had with a judge of the court about Block. Huld says, quoting the judge, "'Block is merely cunning . . . But his ignorance is even greater than his cunning. What do you think he would say if he discovered that his case had actually not begun yet, if he were to be told that the bell marking the start of the proceeding hadn't even been rung?'—'Quiet there, Block,' said the lawyer, for Block was just rising up on trembling legs, obviously to implore an explanation" (p. 244). One can imagine how poor Block feels—he has spent all his money on the case only to discover that the case hasn't even begun. The time is ripe for Huld to assert his mastery:

"That remark of the Judge's has no possible significance for you . . . Don't get into a panic at every word. If you do it again I'll never tell you anything . . . All that I said was to report a remark by a Judge. You know quite well that in these matters opinions differ so much that the confusion is impenetrable. This judge, for instance, assumes that the proceedings begin at one point, and I assume that they begin at another point. A difference of opinion, nothing more. At a certain stage of the proceedings there is an old tradition that a bell must be rung. According to the Judge, that marks the beginning of the case, I can't tell you now all the arguments against him, you wouldn't understand them, let it be sufficient for you that there are many arguments against his view." In embarrassment Block sat plucking at the hair of the skin rug lying before the bed . . . "Block," said Leni in a tone of warning, catching him by the collar and jerking him upward a little. "Leave the rug alone and listen to the lawyer." (pp. 245–246)

One day K. is supposed to show an Italian client of the bank the sights of the city. They are to meet at the cathedral. K. goes there, but the client does not show up. It is dark in the almost empty cathedral. A priest mounts the pulpit. K. does not want to hear a sermon and begins sidling out. All at once "he heard the priest lifting up his voice. A resonant, well-trained voice. How it rolled through the expectant Cathedral! But it was no congregation the priest was addressing, the words were unambiguous and inescapable, he was calling out: 'Joseph K.!'" (p. 262). The priest turns out to be another functionary of the court—the prison chaplain. He tells K. a parable (separately published by Kafka as "Before the Law"). Before the law stands a doorkeeper. A man from the country comes and asks to be admitted. The doorkeeper says it is impossible. The man sits down on a stool provided by the doorkeeper, to wait. He waits for years, continually imploring the doorkeeper for admittance. Finally he is an old man, dying, and he says to the doorkeeper, "'Everyone strives to attain the Law . . . How does it come about, then, that in all these years no one has come seeking admittance but me?' The doorkeeper perceives that the man is nearing his end and his hearing is failing, so he bellows in his ear: 'No one but you could gain admittance through this door, since this door was intended for you. I am now going to shut it.'" (p. 269). The chaplain and K. debate the meaning of the parable inconclusively. As K. is about to leave, he asks, "Don't you want anything more from me?" The chaplain answers, "I belong to the Court . . . So why should I want anything from you? The Court wants nothing from you. It receives you when you come and it dismisses you when you go" (p. 278).

Nevertheless, in the next and last chapter. K. is executed. (Apparently Kafka intended to write additional chapters between it and the cathedral chapter.) Like the prisoner in "In the Penal Colony," he is not told the sentence. On the evening before K.'s thirty-first birthday, "two men came to his lodging . . . in frock coats, pallid and plump, with top hats that were apparently irremovable" (p. 279). They escort him on foot to the country, and when they get to an isolated spot they place him against a boulder and take out a knife. He understands, without anything being said, that he is expected to plunge the knife into his own chest, but

> he could not completely rise to the occasion, he could not relieve the officials of all their tasks; the responsibility for this last failure of his lay with them who had not left him the remnant of strength necessary for the deed. His glance fell on the top story of the house adjoining the quarry. With a flicker as of a light going up, the casements of a window there suddenly flew open; a human figure, faint and insubstantial at that distance and that height leaned abruptly far forward and stretched both arms still farther. Who was it? A friend? A good man? Someone who sympathized? Someone who wanted to help? Was it one person only? Or was it mankind? Was help at hand? Were there arguments in his favor that had been overlooked? Of course there must be. Logic is doubtless unshakable, but it cannot withstand a man who wants to go on living. Where was the Judge whom he had never seen? Where was the High Court, to which he had never penetrated? He raised his hands and spread out all his fingers.
>
> But the hands of one of the partners were already at K.'s throat, while the other thrust the knife deep into his heart and turned it there twice. With failing eyes K. could still see the two of them immediately before him, cheek leaning against cheek, watching the final act. "Like a dog!" he said; it was as if the shame of it must outlive him. (pp. 285–286)

People often think that the point of *The Trial* is how awful it is to be arrested, charged with an unspecified offense by a secret court whose inscrutable proceedings tend to drag on interminably, and then clandestinely and summarily executed; that in short it is a book about the perversion of legal justice. I don't read it so. The legal proceeding that provides the novel's skeleton seems rather to be a typically Kafkaesque "sick joke" on the protagonist, akin to the transformation of Gregor Samsa into a giant bug in the opening sentence of "The Metamorphosis." Imagine waking up one morning and discovering you've been turned into a giant bug. Imagine waking up one morning to be arrested on unspecified charges and discovering it is impossible to find out what the charges are—and anyway you have done nothing that could be thought to violate any law.[4] That potent

---

4. The mirror image in Kafka's writings of the defendant who is unable to discover the charges against him is the eponymous hero of "The Stoker," the first chapter of Kafka's unfinished novel *Amerika* but published separately. The stoker has a grievance against his superior that he is unable to articulate in the hilarious "trial" scene that forms the centerpiece of the story. (Compare the officer's failure of communication in "In the Penal Colony.") The mob of witnesses whom his antagonist summons to confute the stoker's mindless babble is wonderfully comic overkill. Inability to get anyone to listen and understand is one of Joseph K.'s problems, too.

symbol of life's unfairness, strict liability—legal responsibility for the consequences of conduct that may not be blameworthy, indeed may be completely unavoidable—is bad enough. Joseph K. is not punished for anything he does, whether blameworthy or not. He has *done* nothing.[5] In his world not only will or desert and punishment, but action and punishment, have been severed from one another.

In both *The Trial* and "The Metamorphosis" something at once awful, incomprehensible, and absurd happens to the protagonist and we watch him struggle absurdly and pathetically and finally go down to ignominious defeat. At the same time we are made to feel, as with the torturer in "In the Penal Colony," that the protagonist's grotesque dilemma is somehow emblematic of the human condition. This is easier to accept in the novel than in the story because Joseph K. is colorless and mediocre, very much an Everyman—or less. Most of Kafka's protagonists have something of the *schlemiel* about them.

I do not mean that *The Trial* is devoid of legal interest. By focusing on the chapters in which Huld appears, the reader can experience the novel as a layman's nightmare of being a party to a lawsuit yet unable to figure out what is going on because of the legal mumbo-jumbo. Lawyers, like other professionals, wish to draw a veil of mystery around their activity in order to bolster their self-esteem and strengthen their claim to a legally privileged status. One may also be reminded of Judge Learned Hand's remark that "after some dozen years of experience I must say that as a litigant I should dread a lawsuit beyond almost anything else short of sickness and death."[6] For Joseph K. it *is* sickness and, literally, death. Or one can note that the "law" under which Joseph K. is tried is discretionary justice gone crazy. Or that Block (like Oscar Crease and Dickens's Richard Carstone) is that familar and pathetic figure, the obsessed litigant. More fancifully, one may conclude that both Joseph K. and the man from the country are seeking natural law, symbolized, perhaps, by the glow from behind the door in "Before the Law."

The heart of *The Trial* lies elsewhere, however—in K.'s futile efforts to find a human meaning in a universe, symbolized by the court, that has not been created to be accommodating or intelligible to man but is arbitrary, impersonal, cruel, deceiving, and elusive. This universe is like the doorkeeper in "Before the Law," who not only thwarts the effort of the man

---

5. In *The Trial,* "guilt is *produced* by the legal apparatus" instead of being discovered by it. Mark Anderson, *Kafka's Clothes* 192 (1992).

6. Hand, "The Deficiencies of Trials to Reach the Heart of the Matter," 3 *Lectures on Legal Topics 1921–1922* 89, 105 (Association of the Bar of the City of New York 1926).

from the country to reach the source of the "radiance that streams inextinguishably from the door of the Law" (p. 269) but makes the man's effort ridiculous and pathetic. It is a universe whose reigning deities have descended from the starry heavens to tenement attics,[7] a universe in which all is unintelligibility, dislocatedness, alienation, human isolation, in which all of K.'s moves are wrong but there is nothing he could have done that would have changed the outcome, because human agency is ineffectual. Not only is K. unable to master (in both senses—understanding and control) the logic of the events that disrupt his life and lead to his humiliating death; like the officer of "In the Penal Colony," he cannot get anybody to listen to his "defense"—his *apologia pro vita sua.*

Kafka wrote *The Trial* at the same time that Joyce was beginning *Ulysses* and a few years before T. S. Eliot wrote "The Waste Land." These three classics of modernism depict the urban culture of the twentieth century as an ironically diminished pastiche of high Western culture.[8] In *Ulysses,* Homer's hero reappears as a cuckolded Jewish advertising solicitor in twentieth-century Dublin. In "The Waste Land," St. Augustine, Spenser, Shakespeare, Dante, Marvell, and Wagner become the voices of urban decay and "flapper era" sexual dysfunction, and the quest for the Holy Grail becomes an aimless wandering through the purlieus of modern London. In *The Trial,* Dante, who at age 30 escapes from a leopard and travels through Hell and Purgatory to the portals of Heaven, and Christ, who at age 30 is arrested, executed, and resurrected, reappear in the guise of a petit bourgeois who at age 30 is arrested, undertakes a journey that takes him no higher than a tenement attic, and dies like a dog. Satires on modernity, these works evoke what some intellectuals consider the social, cultural, and even metaphysical isolation and mediocrity of the modern urbanite.

Joseph K.'s isolation is particularly marked, and not only in the execution scene. As Ritchie Robertson points out, "in social life we learn, usually in a casual and unsystematic way, how to place other people by their appearance, their clothes, their vocabularies, and their accents."[9] K. cannot

---

7. A number of Kafka's works invite religious interpretations. "In the Penal Colony," for example, could be thought an allegory of the supersession of Judaism by Christianity—of the "Old Law" by the "New Law;" see Thomas Aquinas, *Summa Theologica,* vol. 1, pp. 999–1000 (1947) (question 91, article 5)—with the retributive harshness of the old commandant's system of justice corresponding to the Old Law, and the feminized gentleness of the new commandant's system to the New Law. Of course this interpretation is greatly complicated by the death of the officer, who is the old commandant's spiritual son, and could thus be thought a blasphemous symbol for Jesus Christ.

8. "The Metamorphosis"—a takeoff on Ovid—is another example.

9. Robertson, "Reading the Clues: Franz Kafka, *Der Prozess,*" in *The German Novel in the Twentieth Century: Beyond Realism* 59, 71 (David Midgley ed. 1993).

use these clues to "read" the court, and his inability dooms his quest for meaning. "The Court operates a different semiotic system" (p. 72), one in which, for example, power is inverse to space and opulence; for remember that the court's quarters are cramped and shabby. "K.'s habit of interpreting his surroundings by bold and self-flattering hypotheses which are not confirmed by observation" (p. 74) results in "the dismantling of a personality" (p. 64). "Beyond the semiotics of Realism K. has occasional glimpses of another world with its own system of meaning, different from and in some ways antithetical to his everyday reality . . . [*The Trial*] suggests the . . . alarming possibility that the Law may be real, and that human life may be going on against the background of a wholly other reality. Everyday life permits only occasional glimpses of this other reality, which inhabits the forgotten corners, the garrets and lumber-rooms, of the familiar world" (p. 72).

I do not mean to deny the parallels between the legal process depicted in *The Trial* and the legal processes employed by Hitler's Germany, Stalin's U.S.S.R., and other totalitarian regimes in dealing with political crimes. I mentioned the absence of definitive acquittal—how no accused is given a clean bill of health, but if released is subject to rearrest and reprosecution at any time, and thus to double jeopardy. The prohibition against placing a person in double jeopardy, resting as it does on the principle that the state is bound by law just as private citizens are, is central to the rule of law but contrary to the premises of totalitarianism. (So it is no surprise that Athens had a rule against double jeopardy and Sparta did not.[10]) By placing the accused beyond the power of the state to reprosecute, definitive acquittal would undermine the totalitarian state's pretensions to infallibility and omnipotence. Then there is the secrecy of the court in *The Trial*, its labyrinthine bureaucracy, its existence apart from but parallel to the public organs of the state, its punishing for unspecified, even nonexistent, offenses, its apparent concern with the character and thoughts of people rather than with their actions. These are all premonitions of totalitarian "justice," as well as echoes of the medieval church militant and therefore aspects of the novel's theological symbolism.

But the essential features of a totalitarian system are missing. To see this, one has only to compare *The Trial* with *Darkness at Noon,* Arthur Koestler's novel of the Soviet purge trials of the 1930s. Rubashov, the protagonist of Koestler's novel, is an "old Bolshevik." Although he is not in fact plotting against Stalin ("No. 1" in the novel), he arouses Stalin's paranoid fears and

10. Douglas M. MacDowell, *Spartan Law* 143–144 (1986).

is arrested in the middle of the night and hauled off to Lubyanka prison, where he is subjected to subtle psychological pressures (there is no physical torture) until he signs a confession to having plotted the death of No. 1. He comes to believe that his confession is his last act on behalf of the Bolshevik cause, and at his show trial he repeats it with complete sincerity though he knows it is false, after which he is executed by a shot behind the ear in the cellars of Lubyanka.

The novel is chilling, and though in reality most of the confessions used in the purge trials were extracted by less fancy means—for example, by threats to kill the defendants' families—it conveys an authentic impression of totalitarian justice, Soviet style.[11] It might even interest people professionally concerned with interrogation, as might Porfiry's interrogations of Raskolnikov in *Crime and Punishment* or Mikulin's interrogation of Razumov in *Under Western Eyes*. But *Darkness at Noon* belongs to the genre of twentieth-century documentary novels by Malraux, Orwell, Dos Passos, and others, while *The Trial,* despite its authentic legal details, does not have the feel of a documentary novel. More than feel is involved; the essential difference is the lack of any *political* point. Joseph K. has no politics and the mysterious court that condemns him has no political mission and is no more a part of some official system of intimidation than is the English Court of Chancery in *Bleak House*—from which, as we are about to see, Kafka borrowed for his depiction of the court in *The Trial*.

The documentary novels of the 1920s and 1930s have sunk into obscurity; the reason, which will be obvious from the discussion of the test of time in Chapter 1, is their topicality. Unlike *The Trial,* they are historically local; they do not speak to the permanent elements of the human condition. *Nineteen Eighty-Four* is an exception. Although intended as a political allegory, and when so considered was rendered obsolete and indeed was falsified by the collapse of the Soviet Union,[12] it engages vividly with issues, such as the relation of language and popular culture to thought, that have survived the fall of communism.

---

11. Robert Conquest, *The Great Terror: Stalin's Purge of the Thirties* 189–191 (rev. ed. 1973). Rubashov apparently is a composite of Bukharin, Trotsky, and Radek. See id. at 190n. Nathan Leites and Elsa Bernaut, *Ritual of Liquidation: The Case of the Moscow Trials* (1954), emphasizes the undertone of resistance and the covert messages of defiance in the confessions at the Moscow trials. The brainwashing of the defendants was far less complete than Koestler's novel suggests. In Bukharin's case, it was a total failure. Stephen F. Cohen, "Introduction," in Anna Larina, *This I Cannot Forget: The Memoirs of Nikolai Bukharin's Widow* 11, 17–19 (1993).

12. Like Koestler, Orwell exaggerated the effectiveness of brainwashing. This is a tendency of intellectuals—the class that is engaged, in a sense, in brainwashing.

The Trial has been linked to *Michael Kohlhaas*.[13] Kafka admired Kleist's writings and may have borrowed details from them. Joseph K.'s interview with the prison chaplain echoes Kohlhaas's interview with Martin Luther, while the "shadowy establishment network"[14] against which Kohlhaas struggles in his vain quest for justice resembles the attic court with which Joseph K. struggles. Everywhere Kohlhaas turns he finds connections with the nobleman who wronged him; everywhere K. turns he finds connections with the court, as in his encounters with Titorelli and the prison chaplain. But the mood and outlook of the two works are completely different. Kohlhaas is a traditional revenger, with the revenger's standard problem of going too far, and Kleist wants to make a point about the breakdown of justice in a divided Germany. Joseph K. is a fly caught in a spiderweb partly of his own spinning, who reacts to his predicament not with the revenger's implacable fury but with comically futile gestures.

Closer in spirit is Friedrich Duerrenmatt's novella *Die Panne* (1956),[15] a suggestive conflation of *The Trial* and Kafka's story "The Judgment" (see Chapter 6). Traps is a traveling salesman with a taste for adultery reminiscent of K.'s weekly visits to a prostitute. When his car breaks down he is offered lodging with a retired judge who, together with his equally ancient cronies—a retired prosecutor, a retired defense lawyer, and a retired executioner—amuse themselves by staging trials with any visitor willing to play the game. Traps is happy to play. Amidst much laughter and generous imbibing of fine wines, the prosecutor wheedles out of Traps a confession to "murder." Traps's superior, Gygax, whose position he has now taken, had had a fatal heart attack shortly after learning that Traps was having an affair with his wife. Traps admits that he hated Gygax, who was blocking his advancement, and that he was glad he died. But the defense lawyer points out, plausibly enough, that the fatal heart attack was probably a consequence of the heat (Gygax was known to have heart disease) rather than of the discovery of his wife's infidelity. Traps is indignant. He insists that he *is* guilty of murder. The web of supposition woven by the prosecutor, in which adultery is the crucial move in a deliberate and suc-

---

13. J. M. Lindsay, "Kohlhaas and K.: Two Men in Search of Justice," 13 *German Life and Letters* 190 (1959); Eric Marson, "Justice and the Obsessed Character in *Michael Kohlhaas, Der Prozess* and *L'Etranger*," *Seminar (A Journal of Germanic Studies)*, Fall 1966, p. 21; F. G. Peters, "Kafka and Kleist: A Literary Relationship," 1 *Oxford German Studies* 114 (1966).

14. John M. Ellis, *Heinrich von Kleist: Studies in the Character and Meaning of His Writings* 74 (1979). Compare Charles Bernheimer, "Crossing Over: Kafka's Metatextual Parable," 95 *Modern Language Notes* 1254, 1263 (1980).

15. The title means *The Breakdown* or *The Mishap*, but the novella was translated into English under the title *Traps* (Richard and Clara Winston trans. 1960).

cessful campaign to kill Gygax and take his place, invests Traps's life with a shape and meaning which heretofore it had lacked. The judge obligingly sentences Traps to death. The sentence is intended and understood as a joke, but Traps goes up to his room and hangs himself.

Traps is an even more thoroughgoing mediocrity than Joseph K. He is incapable of anything big, including murder. He is guilty only of the petty cheats and meannesses of the ordinary man. The mock trial lifts him out of his mediocrity, ennobling him with the status of murderer that requires for its confirmation the execution of the sentence prescribed for murderers. Joseph K. is "guilty" in the same sense as Traps, but is denied even a spurious ennoblement. These characters' incapacity for anything as "big" as a capital offense is their capital offense.

Dickens

Dickens chose fog to be the symbol of the Court of Chancery in *Bleak House,* a novel framed by a fictional equity case finally dismissed when the estate that was its subject has been entirely consumed by legal fees and other costs. The impenetrable mystery and futility of its proceedings resemble those of the court in *The Trial.* This should not be a surprise, and not only because Kafka greatly admired Dickens's novels.[16] The traditional procedure of the English chancery court, with its leisurely course, its emphasis on documentary evidence, and its somewhat "inquisitorial" tone, is closer to Continental procedure than is the procedure of the classic Anglo-American trial at law. It may not be an accident that the centerpiece of Dickens's other and much sunnier law novel, *Pickwick Papers*—the trial in the breach of promise case of *Bardell v. Pickwick*—is a case at law rather than in equity, though equity takes some knocks in *Pickwick Papers* too.[17]

The judicial proceedings themselves are mainly in the background in *Bleak House,* just as they are in *The Trial* (this may be connected with the attenuation or dilution of adversary procedure in an inquisitorial system). The courtroom drama of a *Bardell v. Pickwick* is missing, along with the sheer legal *variety* of *Pickwick Papers,* a novel that touches on bankruptcy and estate law as well as on breach of promise, and whose gallery of lawyers

---

16. George H. Ford, *Dickens and His Readers* 254–256 (1965); Ronald Gray, *Franz Kafka* 72 (1973); Ernst Pawel, *The Nightmare of Reason: A Life of Franz Kafka* 159 (1984). Specific parallels between *Bleak House* and *The Trial* are discussed in Mark Spilka, *Dickens and Kafka: A Mutual Interpretation,* ch. 10 (1963), and in Deborah Heller Roazen, "A Peculiar Attraction: *Bleak House, Der Prozess,* and the Law," 5 *Essays in Literature* 251 (1978).

17. For a survey of Dickens's "legal" novels, see Larry M. Wertheim, "Law, Literature and Morality in the Novels of Charles Dickens," 20 *William Mitchell Law Review* 111 (1994).

includes the sympathetic figure of solicitor Perker. But *Bleak House* is particularly rich in unforgettable portraits of repellent lawyers—particularly Tulkinghorn and Guppy—and also of the crazy court buffs who follow litigation, their own or others', with paranoid intensity (for example, Miss Flite), and other, soberer unfortunates who nevertheless become obsessed and eventually ruined by their hope of scoring big in litigation, such as Richard Carstone, the counterpart of Block in *The Trial* and Oscar Crease in *A Frolic of His Own.*

Although there is exaggeration and even fantasy in *Bleak House,* and although the chancery court is not merely a target of criticism but also a metaphor for broader problems of human selfishness and indifference that preoccupied Dickens, the novel was intended to be (more precisely, to include) a serious criticism of a particular legal procedure, that of chancery. The criticism is unfair. Chancery procedure was reformed before *Bleak House* was written, and the novel confuses will contests with guardianships.[18] *Jarndyce v. Jarndyce* is a will contest and should therefore have been tried in the probate court rather than in the chancery court. And the protractedness of chancery cases was due in major part to the innocent fact that chancery exercised supervision over guardians and trustees of minors (hence the expression "a ward in Chancery"). The supervision had to continue until the minor reached adulthood.

Pickwick Papers is more on the mark as legal criticism. The centerpiece of that novel is Mrs. Bardell's groundless suit against Pickwick for breach of a marriage promise (which he had never made), and her futile efforts to collect the large judgment the jury awards her. The proceeding is likely to strike a modern reader—even, or perhaps especially, one with legal training—as a farce. Neither Mrs. Bardell nor Mr. Pickwick testifies in the trial, so the best evidence of whether there was a promise of marriage is withheld from the jury. And no procedure exists for levying execution of the judgment against Pickwick's considerable assets; all that Mrs. Bardell can do is have him imprisoned for contempt of court when he refuses to pay up.[19] But all this is fact, not farce. When Dickens wrote *Pickwick Papers* par-

---

18. Allen Boyer, "The Antiquarian and the Utilitarian," 56 *Tennessee Law Review* 595, 597, 617–624 (1989). Boyer also points out that Dickens's criticisms of the English legal system were greatly influenced by Bentham's, id. at 598–599—making it rather a puzzle why Dickens pilloried Bentham as Gradgrind in *Hard Times.*

19. This is an inefficient remedy, as game theorists understand, because it sets the stage for a game of chicken: Bardell threatens to keep Pickwick incarcerated for the rest of his life if he refuses to pay; Pickwick threatens to remain incarcerated for the rest of his life (in which event Bardell will collect nothing) unless Bardell agrees to accept a steep discount from the amount of the judgment. Cf. Linda S. Beres, "Games Civil Contemnors Play," 18 *Harvard Journal of Law and Public Policy* 795 (1995).

ties to lawsuits were not permitted to testify; and securities—the form in which Pickwick's wealth was held—could not be levied against to satisfy a judgment.[20]

The problem with the preformed chancery proceedings was not that they were encrusted with the kind of legal barnacles that *Bardell v. Pickwick* scraped up against—equity, as we know already, is more flexible, less hidebound and rule-bound, than law—but that they were slow and costly.[21] The chancery court had a monopoly of important classes of potentially complex and protracted litigation, not only suits involving trusts and guardianships but also suits seeking equitable relief—an injunction, a receivership, a complex accounting, or the specific performance of a contract[22]—rather than the standard "legal" remedy, which was (and is) an award of damages. Equitable remedies often require continuing judicial supervision. The chancery court made greater use of written evidence than did the regular law courts, and this slowed down proceedings too, as did the fact that the Lord Chancellor personally reviewed virtually all the cases in his court.[23] Chancery's sluggishness was particularly conspicuous because trials in the regular English courts had traditionally been very swift (they still are); few lasted more than a day. Chancery was expensive, too. Judges were compensated out of the court fees paid by the litigants, and the fees in chancery were very high, in part because the classes of litigation that the court monopolized were lucrative ones. The Lord Chancellor had one of the highest incomes in England.

Bleak House is a powerful, if belated, satire on a seriously flawed, though already reforming, legal institution. But someone who wanted to learn about nineteenth-century English chancery court would not spend time reading *Bleak House*. There are fuller and soberer sources of data; Dickens's novel is not like the Homeric epics or the Old Norse sagas, which are the main sources of our knowledge of their societies' legal institutions. Viewed merely as description and critique of the Court of Chancery, *Bleak House* is a century-and-a-half-old piece of fictionalized journalism—whose au-

---

20. William S. Holdsworth, *Charles Dickens as a Legal Historian*, ch. 4 (1928).

21. Id., ch. 3; John P. Dawson, *A History of Lay Judges* 170–172 (1960); G. W. Keeton, *An Introduction to Equity* 18–20, 35 (6th ed. 1965); D. M. Kerly, *An Historical Sketch of the Equitable Jurisdiction of the Court of Chancery*, ch. 13 (1890).

22. That is, an order to the contract breaker than he perform the contract on pain of being held in contempt of court if he does not. An order of specific performance is thus a type of injunction.

23. John H. Langbein, "Fact Finding in the English Court of Chancery: A Rebuttal," 83 *Yale Law Journal* 1620, 1629 (1974). This had changed, however, by 1851 (see George W. Keeton and L. A. Sheridan, *Equity* 73–74 [1969])—like so many of the chancery abuses depicted in *Bleak House*.

thor, moreover, for all his keen sense of injustice, was not a practical reformer.[24] Though acutely aware of the large amount of evil in the world and not in the least quietistic or resigned, Dickens had no suggestions for reducing it. He was greatly distressed by the delays and expense of chancery but seems to have accepted these things as part of the natural order. He is warning the reader to avoid falling into the clutches of the court, rather than trying to make those clutches less fell.

The negativity of the picture of equity in *Bleak House* is in striking contrast to the rosy hues in which equity jurisprudence is painted in *The Merchant of Venice* and *Measure for Measure*. The jurisdiction of the Lord Chancellor—the original equity jurisdiction in England—had arisen in the Middle Ages in response to the rigidity and hypertechnicality of the common law courts, which, like many primitive adjudicators, were unable to render substantive justice in a large class of cases. They would enforce a contract even if it had been procured by fraud; they could not protect the legal rights of children and the insane; they had no procedures by which litigants could obtain pretrial discovery of essential facts; they could not enjoin a litigant who filed a torrent of redundant suits in order to wear out his opponent. *Bardell v. Pickwick* illustrates the persistence of the quirky deficiencies of common law procedure well into the nineteenth century.

The Lord Chancellors, originally clerics (such as Thomas à Becket and Cardinal Wolsey), dispensed justice according to conscience rather than strict legal forms. Later, the rules and remedies of equity jurisprudence, as the jurisprudence developed by the Lord Chancellors came to be known, were institutionalized in the Court of Chancery. It is the *spirit* of equity that Portia symbolizes. The irony so effectively exploited by Dickens in *Bleak House* is that the court of conscience had become the nation's worst example of legal abuses. This made it the perfect target for a moralist who believed (very much in the spirit of the Romantic movement) that institutions pervert the inborn goodness of people. A lawyer might want to point out, however, that equity had the weakness of its strengths, just as law had the strength of its weaknesses. It is the old dilemma of rule versus discretion. Equity started out as a truly discretionary jurisdiction. This proved intolerable, and *rules* of equity emerged; nevertheless equity procedure remained relatively formless, and the result eventually was tremen-

---

24. George Orwell, "Charles Dickens," in *The Collected Essays, Journalism and Letters of George Orwell*, vol. 1, p. 413 (Sonia Orwell and Ian Angus eds. 1968); Joseph I. Fradin, "Will and Society in *Bleak House*," in *Critical Essays on Charles Dickens's* Bleak House 40, 63 (Elliot L. Gilbert ed. 1989); Robert A. Donovan, "Structure and Idea in *Bleak House*," 29 *Journal of English Literary Theory* 175 (1962).

dous delays and uncertainty. Proceedings at law were full of crotchets and traps but at least moved along at a smart pace. The underlying dilemma may be inescapable.

Wallace Stevens

Stevens was a lawyer, like Kafka, and indeed both did insurance law. Kafka often worked law into his fiction; Stevens never worked law into his poetry. Until law professor Thomas Grey wrote a book on Stevens, no one had supposed that his poetry had anything to do with his "day job" as a lawyer and executive.[25]

Grey argues that legal thought oscillates between unrealistic extremes—the "official" position that legal conclusions follow deductively from sound general principles, and the "opposition" line that law is really just politics—and in his poetry Stevens is "a kind of therapist for the habitual and institutional rigidities of binary thought" that generate this oscillation (p. 7). I agree with the first point; it is silly to think that the issue in jurisprudence is whether law is all logic or all politics, all the left-hand side of the Table of Legal Antinomies or all the right-hand side. I also agree that the "law and lit" types who believe that the choice is between conceiving of the judge as a poet (their preference) and conceiving of him as an economist are embracing a precious and irrelevant aestheticism.[26] I am also persuaded by Grey's suggestion that to the extent that Stevens is a "philosophical" poet, the philosophy is pragmatism; and this enables Grey to draw some interesting parallels between Stevens and Oliver Wendell Holmes. But I disagree that Stevens's poetry is a useful corrective for the type of rigidly dichotomous thinking of which Grey rightly accuses major schools and figures in jurisprudence.

In "The Motive for Metaphor,"[27] Stevens contrasts the world of metaphor ("The obscure moon lighting an obscure world / Of things that would never be quite expressed") with what we today would call the "real" world: "Steel against intimation . . . / The vital, arrogant, fatal, dominant

---

25. Thomas C. Grey, *The Wallace Stevens Case: Law and the Practice of Poetry* (1991). Short poems that take law as their subject have been rare. A notable exception is the poems of Lawrence Joseph, a contemporary poet who, like Stevens, was a trained and professional lawyer, but who, unlike Stevens, has made law a subject of his poetry. See David A. Skeel, "Practicing Poetry, Teaching Law," 92 *Michigan Law Review* 1754 (1994), reviewing Lawrence Joseph, *Before Our Eyes* (1993).

26. "Strategically, to accept the separation of heart and head and align with the heart in the ensuing party struggle [with, for example, the law and economics movement] is to relegate oneself to marginal, weekend, after-hours status—and to losing." Grey, note 25 above, at 89.

27. *The Collected Poems of Wallace Stevens* 288 (1955).

X." The algebraic symbol is an effective metaphor for the nonmetaphoric, depersonalized, efficient, Gradgrindian, "bottom line" orientation that characterizes the world of "primary noon, / The A B C of being, / The ruddy temper, the hammer / Of red and blue, the hard sound." Grey sees Stevens as contrasting the poet with the hard-headed, practical, decisive lawyer who disdains ambiguity and metaphor and, in Holmes's famous words, "thinks things, not words" (and we might also recall here Holmes's aphorism that law is the calling of thinkers, not of poets). So read, the poem "cleanly separates—as Stevens did in his life, and as Judge Posner tells us [in the first edition of *Law and Literature*] we should do in our legal scholarship—the realms of poetry and law" (p. 59).

Grey thinks that, read closely, the poem is trying to blur the dichotomy between the metaphoric and real worlds. He notes, for example, that while spring, a transitional season, is an apt metaphor for the nuanced, tentative, elusive (and allusive) world of poetry or metaphor, Stevens chose as his symbol for the clear-eyed world of quotidian reality not summer, as the reader is expecting, but a moment—noon—that lasts only an instant and occurs in every season. The contrast between the world of metaphor and the world of action is further blurred, Grey argues, by the fact that the poem's opening lines ("You like it under the trees in autumn, / Because everything is half dead"), while describing the world of metaphor, are uncharacteristically flat, clear, and literal for Stevens. Grey concludes that Stevens is denying that the metaphoric world is all a dreamy mist and the real world all hard-edged masculine clarity (life according to Henry Wilcox). Both are a mixture of hard and soft, clear and blurred, masculine and feminine. "The primary reading [of the poem] has 'The Motive for Metaphor' warning of the dangers of lawyers' locating their subject too much in literature's obscure world of rustling leaves and melting clouds, too little in the harsh smithy of noonday sweat and violence. The secondary reading, the other side that Stevens brings us to hear after resisting our intelligence almost successfully, warns of an opposed jurisprudential danger" (p. 64).

I am skeptical about Grey's association of the world of "primary noon," "the ruddy temper," "steel against intimation," "X," and so forth with law, as where he says that "'Steel against intimation' then juxtaposes two aspects of law: its sharp rigidity . . . and its flexibility before the imagination" (p. 67). Stevens's text lacks the clues that enabled us to read Henry Wilcox's arguments against Helen's being permitted to stay overnight at Howards End as legalistic, and the scene in which he makes them as a criticism of the legal sensibility. True, Stevens was a lawyer. But people can play multiple roles with pretty tight bulkheads between them.[28] Grey himself acknowledges, indeed emphasizes, that Stevens succeeded in dichotomizing the practice of law and the writing of poetry.[29]

Since poetry is a metaphoric medium, any "statement" that it makes is likely to be couched in metaphoric terms. And since a fresh metaphor implies the yoking of dissimilar terms, it is easily taken ironically, as did the New Critics, for whom irony was a pervasive feature of the poetry they most admired. But this tells us more about poetry than about law. The specific examples that Grey uses to demonstrate the inescapably metaphoric character of daily reality are unconvincing. An example is the substitution of noon for summer (or winter) to signify that reality. The word "summer" has complex associations; "noon" brings straight to mind the sun's brightness[30] and thus complements the "harsh sound" and "sharp flash" with which Stevens extends the image of the real world in the next stanza.

I doubt that "The Motive for Metaphor" will lead judges, lawyers, or law students to find "binary thought" in jurisprudence uncongenial. If Stevens could separate the practice of law from poetry, should we expect his readers to be less successful in doing so? Might not the reading of poetry be a relief from practicing or writing about law rather than a source of professional guidance? Yet lawyers might be able to derive some professional utility from studying the poetry of Wallace Stevens simply because his poetry is dense and difficult; that is what tempts the reader (it tempted Grey) to seek aids to understanding in the poet's biography. Reading a poem by Stevens requires the reader not only to attend carefully to every word but also to consider the extent to which guidance to meaning can be appropriately sought from sources outside the text itself ("legislative history," for example) and to make use of the linguistic and cultural competence that Stevens would have expected his readers to bring to their reading of his poetry. To be a good lawyer one must be a careful and resourceful reader, and immersion in poetry and other difficult imaginative literature is therefore not the worst preparation for the study of law.

As part of my general hostility to the so-called "canons of construction" by which judges pretend to be able to find "the" meaning of contracts, statutes, wills, constitutional provisions, and other legal rules and instruments, I have long criticized as unrealistic the principle that the reader of a statute or contract or other legal rule or instrument should assume that every meaning was placed there for a purpose—that there is no surplusage,

28. Erving Goffman, *The Presentation of Self in Everyday Life* (1959).

29. This conclusion is questioned, however, in David A. Skeel, Jr., "Notes toward an Aesthetics of Legal Pragmatism," 78 *Cornell Law Review* 84, 94–104 (1992).

30. That is why the title of Arthur Koestler's novel *Darkness at Noon* is so arresting even for readers who do not recognize the allusion to the Crucifixion.

inconsistency, mistake, or irrelevance. I now see, with the aid of my own interpretive struggles with the poems of Wallace Stevens discussed by Grey, that there is another and more favorable light in which to regard this principle: as an antidote to hasty, careless, lazy reading. If we assume that every word is there for a purpose, we are made to read and ponder—every word, as we would be led to do by a good teacher of poetry. It is only when that principle of interpretation is transformed from a discipline to an algorithm that it is aptly criticized as unrealistic and misleading.

FIVE

The Literary Indictment of Legal Injustice

My focus in this chapter is on *Billy Budd* and *The Brothers Karamazov*—
though I discuss, more briefly, several other works of literature as well—
and on romantic and neoromantic, including Nietzschean, currents in contemporary legal thought. My jumping-off point is Richard Weisberg's *The
Failure of the Word*.[1] Using the methods of both literary criticism and legal
reasoning, Weisberg—a professor of law who was once a professor of literature—tries to show how a lawyer's knowledge can enrich our understanding of such fiction and how a critic's knowledge of such fiction can
enrich our understanding of law.

Law and Ressentiment

Weisberg's central theme is *"ressentiment."* A word whose currency is due
to Nietzsche,[2] it means the rancorous envy of the naturally weak toward
the naturally strong. Weak men manage to overcome strong ones—the
strong man being highly vulnerable to certain forms of attack because he
is open, trusting, nonverbal, unsubtle, indeed unreflective—by spinning
conceptual webs. The three most important webs are Christianity, legalism, and the translation of experience into words, which falsifies the experience.[3] The last two are Weisberg's own variations on Nietzsche's theme,
but it is worth pausing to notice how Nietzsche himself had related *ressentiment* to law. He was on both sides of the question. The side more con-

---

1. Weisberg, *The Failure of the Word: The Protagonist as Lawyer in Modern Fiction* (1984). Unless
otherwise indicated, page references in this chapter are to Weisberg's book.
2. See, for example, Friedrich Nietzsche, *On the Genealogy of Morals* 73–75 (II.11), 121–129
(III.14–16) (Walter Kaufmann and R. J. Hollingdale trans. 1967).
3. "Word" in Weisberg's title is an ironic echo of the Christian "Word" in the Gospel according to St. John *(Logos)*. On Weisberg's equation of legalism and religion, see p. 116 of his
book.

genial to Weisberg is summarized in the sentence, "And when they say, 'I am just,' it always sounds like 'I am just—revenged.'"[4] *Ressentiment*, the bitter mood in which the weak and defeated nurse grievances and plot revenge, is in the realm of psychology what revenge itself is in the realm of action; and the person who seeks to vindicate his legal rights, like the revenger, is deformed by ressentiment. Shylock thus exemplifies ressentiment. (Hamlet, too, according to Weisberg, as we saw in Chapter 2.) The *Übermensch* is above envy, takes no notice of slights, and therefore has no use for revenge or indeed for law. Elsewhere, however, Nietzsche describes law as an effort to overcome *ressentiment*—indeed, as a substitute for *ressentiment*, for vengeful feelings, and even for conscience (a faculty that Nietzsche despised)—rather than as an expression of *ressentiment*.[5] If the analysis in Chapter 2 is sound, Nietzsche was right to sense a relation of substitution between law and vengeance.

Weisberg usefully emphasizes differences between Anglo-American and Continental criminal procedure that an American reader of such works as *Crime and Punishment, The Stranger,* and *The Trial* might miss. The Continental examining or investigating magistrate has a relationship with a suspect or accused different from that of any in Anglo-American criminal justice systems—more intimate, more paternalistic, more invasive of privacy, less structured, less adversary.[6] As Weisberg explains, this relationship provides a convenient vehicle for the exploration of character. But he does not pursue the implications of this insight. In particular, he does not consider the possibility that the purpose of the criminal investigation in a Continental novel may be to reveal character rather than to criticize law.

The other emphatic intervention of Weisberg the lawyer comes in the discussion of *Billy Budd*. He asserts that the drumhead court-martial and execution of Billy Budd are marred by serious procedural and substantive errors. They could not be Melville's errors, he says, because Melville, though not a lawyer, was well versed in the law of the sea. Yet if there are legal errors in *Billy Budd* (a question I take up later), it is far from certain that Melville would have been aware of them. Although he had served on an American warship for fourteen months beginning in 1842 and had a

---

4. Friedrich Nietzsche, *Thus Spoke Zarathustra: A Book for All and None* 95 (pt. II) (Walter Kaufmann trans. 1966). The translation is a confusing attempt to render a pun. The German is: *Und wenn sie sagen: "ich bin gerecht," so klingt es immer gleich wie: "ich bin gerächt." Recht* means justice, *Rache* revenge.

5. Nietzsche, note 2 above, at 73–76 (II.11).

6. The contrast should not be overdrawn: the legal proceedings in *The Brothers Karamazov* resemble a modern English or American trial, while, as I noted in the last chapter, English equity procedure resembles Continental procedure.

long-standing interest in naval discipline, he may have known little about eighteenth-century British law; and *Billy Budd,* though written between 1888 and 1891, is set in the British navy of 1797. Anyway, since Melville was writing a novella rather than a law review article, he may have departed from legal accuracy for literary reasons.[7] Nothing in the text of *Billy Budd* would alert a lay reader to the possibility that the court-martial and execution of Billy were legally flawed. Not even a lawyer reading it (and it was not written mainly for lawyers) would find any such clues unless he happened to be an antiquarian. Weisberg has gone outside the proper frame of reference.

This is also what he did when he ascribed to Hamlet envy of Claudius. Yet more than idiosyncrasy is involved. Writings in which the writer seems unwilling or unable to achieve closure invite the reader to become a collaborator in the creation of meaning. This tempting open-endedness is characteristic of much literature. That is an implication of the test of time. And both *Hamlet* and *Billy Budd* are illustrations. But when emphasis on the indeterminacy of literature is pushed to the point at which every work of literature turns into a Rorschach test, literary criticism becomes navel-gazing. We shall see Weisberg pulling out of *Billy Budd* what he himself put in it. He should cut out the middleman and make his points directly.

His main point is that the legalistic or formalistic conception of law, for example Angelo's conception in *Measure for Measure,* fosters injustice—indeed, leads straight to the Nazi extermination of the European Jews. Shylock, brimming over with *ressentiment,* is a perfect symbol of legalism as injustice, but it is one that Weisberg avoids, as it would blur the connection that he is trying to make between *ressentiment* and anti-Semitism. The legalistic cast of mind can indeed be exasperating and lead to, or more commonly blind one to, injustice. But the suggestion that it fosters genocide is sufficiently *outré* to require evidence. Little is forthcoming, and the opposite thesis could be argued from Weisberg's own analysis of *Billy Budd.* For if he is right about eighteenth-century British naval law, Billy Budd would not have been executed (not so soon, anyway) had Captain Vere been a stickler for legal niceties. And recall what I said in the last chapter about legalism being the pariah's friend. Furthermore, the insinuating style of the European examining magistrate illustrates not the operation of legal technicalities but the power of informal, discretionary procedures. A system of criminal justice like the American, which throws greater protections (many

---

7. Melville in his fiction often took great liberties with the facts. See, for example, the editors' "Explanatory Notes" in Herman Melville, *Omoo: A Narrative of Adventures in the South Seas* 341–348 (Harrison Hayford and Walter Blair eds. 1969). We *expect* that in fiction.

highly legalistic) around the criminal suspect, would have made it harder for the examining magistrate in *Crime and Punishment* to push Raskolnikov toward confessing or for the jury in *The Stranger* to convict Meursault.

Romantic Values in Literature and Law

Behind the concept of *ressentiment* lies an opposition between two human types—"natural" man, and "social" or "civilized" man (for Nietzsche, resentful man). The first type, whose prototype is Achilles, is the heroic individual, whose devotion to personal honor and indifference to the claims of the community place him on a collision course with the herd of ordinary men living in supine conformity to collective norms. Although Achilles himself expresses doubts about the heroic code, the claims of society in the *Iliad* are weak; that he places his own honor entirely above the welfare of the Greek cause in the Trojan War is shown as admirable rather than treasonable.[8] The Greek and Elizabethan tragedies temper admiration for individualism with a sharp awareness of the competing claims of society (*Prometheus Bound* and *Tamburlaine the Great* may be exceptions), and often present the great protagonists as evil (Macbeth), greatly deluded (Oedipus, Lear, Brutus, Othello), or initially immature (Hamlet). The excesses of individualism are especially vivid in Edmund in *King Lear*. In works of Christian literature, such as the *Divine Comedy* and *Paradise Lost*, great individuals often are consigned to hell, and the social virtues (what Nietzsche called the herd instinct or slave morality) receive their most powerful literary celebration.[9]

The First Part of Tamburlaine the Great depicts the triumph of an indomitable will, which carries a Scythian shepherd to the heights of power. Tamburlaine explains his philosophy to the Persian king whom he has just overcome in battle (II.7.12–29):

> The thirst of reign and sweetness of a crown,
> That caus'd the eldest son of heavenly Ops
> To thrust his doting father from his chair,
> And place himself in the imperial heaven,
> Mov'd me to manage arms against thy state.
> What better precedent than mighty Jove?

8. On Achilles as Nietzsche's "blond beast," see W. Thomas MacCary, *Childlike Achilles: Ontogeny and Phylogeny in the Iliad* 249 (1982).

9. C. S. Lewis, *A Preface to Paradise Lost,* ch. 11 (1942). On Milton's Satan as an inversion of the epic hero, see John M. Steadman, *Milton and the Renaissance Hero* (1967), and on Renaissance ambivalence about the heroic (illustrated by Marlowe's plays), see *Concepts of the Hero in the Middle Ages and the Renaissance* (Norman T. Burns and Christopher J. Reagan eds. 1975).

> Nature, that fram'd us of four elements
> Warring within our breasts for regiment,
> Doth teach us all to have aspiring minds.
> Our souls, whose faculties can comprehend
> The wondrous architecture of the world,
> And measure every wandering planet's course,
> Still climbing after knowledge infinite,
> And always moving as the restless spheres,
> Will us to wear ourselves and never rest,
> Until we reach the ripest fruit of all,
> That perfect bliss and sole felicity,
> The sweet fruitition of an earthly crown.

Tamburlaine's "precedent" is successful rebellion, and his goal the possession of an earthly, not a heavenly, crown. It is a subversive as well as a blasphemous goal. The suggestion that "all of us" can aspire to an earthly crown is a frontal thrust at the divine right of kings. And notice how Tamburlaine relates pride and worldly ambition to scientific curiosity and the growth of scientific knowledge. The vision is of the individual who takes control of his destiny instead of accepting his place in a hierarchical universe. Not even on his deathbed, in *The Second Part of Tamburlaine the Great,* does Tamburlaine display awareness of human finitude.

The hero of Marlowe's other great drama of self-assertion, *Doctor Faustus,* is at first as self-confident and aspiring as Tamburlaine. But, like Macbeth, he dies a wiser man, having discovered the resistance that reality, including the social reality of opposed wills, puts up to the transformative efforts of the human imagination. Both Macbeth, with the help of the weird sisters, and Faustus, with the help of Mephostophilis, get most of what they ask for, but it turns out to be not what they want. The difference between them is that Faustus's aspirations for sexual freedom, scientific knowledge (though conflated with magic), and control of his environment make him a more distinctively modern figure than the usurper-murderer-tyrant Macbeth.

Whether the audience of *Doctor Faustus* was intended to take an orthodox Christian view of the pact with the devil or to identify with Faustus's Promethean aspirations has been much debated.[10] The best capsule sum-

---

10. Wilber Sanders, *The Dramatist and the Received Idea: Studies in the Plays of Marlowe and Shakespeare,* ch. 11 (1968). George Santayana argued in *Three Philosophical Poets: Lucretius, Dante, and Goethe* 133–135 (1910), that Marlowe's play marks the beginning of the rehabilitation of the Faust figure's image, a process that culminates in Part II of Goethe's *Faust.* See also Ian Watt, *Myths of Modern Individualism: Faust, Don Quixote, Don Juan, Robinson Crusoe,* ch. 2 (1996).

mary of Faustus may be Robert Potter's: "magnificent villainy."[11] By his pact with the devil Faustus seeks to annul the limitations that God imposes on human aspiration; when made forcibly aware of those limitations, he refuses to yield to them even at the price of damnation.

Tamburlaine's "aspiring minds" speech could serve as a manifesto of Romanticism, except that the Romantics lacked the Renaissance's enthusiasm for science. William Blake, who thought Satan the real hero of *Paradise Lost,* inverted the conventional values, just as Marlowe's Tamburlaine had done and Nietzsche would do. Natural man is good, society and religion evil, as Blake explains in "The Garden of Love":

> I went to the Garden of Love . . .
> That so many sweet flowers bore;
> And I saw it was filled with graves,
> And tomb-stones where flowers should be;
> And Priests in black gowns were walking their rounds,
> And binding with briars my joys and desires.

Although the word "Romanticism," if it is to be used with any precision, should be confined to a cluster of literary, artistic, and philosophical movements of the late eighteenth and early nineteenth centuries,[12] the romantic impulse or temperament is one of humankind's fundamental moods.[13] It is the expression, reflection, or residue of the boundless egoism of early childhood, the beauty and innocence of the child, the sense of loss that accompanies growing up, and the nostalgia for lost youth which that sense produces. Interdisciplinary scholarship—this book—is romantic in the broad sense that I have indicated because it rejects Max Weber's dictum that "limitation to specialized work, with a renunciation of the Faustian universality of man which it involves, is a condition of any valuable work in the modern world."[14]

An early rejection of the romantic impulse can be found in the false tale

---

11. Potter, *The English Morality Play: Origins, History and Influence of a Dramatic Tradition* 128 (1975).

12. Arthur O. Lovejoy, *English Romantic Poets: Modern Essays in Criticism* 3 (M. H. Abrams ed., 2d ed. 1975). Even so confined, the term conceals tremendous diversity. The Romanticism of Byron or Stendhal is more realistic than that of Shelley. I shall generally ignore these nuances. Rousseau is is the most consistent exponent of Romanticism in the sense in which I'll be using the word.

13. The continuity with twentieth-century neo-Romantic poets, notably Yeats, is well discussed in George Bornstein, *Transformations of Romanticism in Yeats, Eliot, and Stevens* (1976), especially chs. 1 and 2. See also Frank Kermode, *Romantic Image* (1957). I use "Romantic" to denote the movement, "romantic" the mood.

14. Weber, *The Protestant Ethic and the Spirit of Capitalism* 180 (Talcott Parsons trans. 1958).

of his life that Odysseus, who after twenty years of war and wandering has just returned to Ithaca disguised as a beggar, tells his swineherd Eumaeus in Book 14 of the *Odyssey* (ll. 199–359). He was born in Crete—the story begins—the bastard son of a wealthy man who had many legitimate sons. The father honored him equally with his half brothers. But when the father died, the arrogant sons divided his property by lots, assigning only a small holding to the narrator. He was nevertheless able to get a wife from a wealthy family because of his prowess—he was good at the ambush, loved to charge the fleeing foe, and so forth. (Here he interrupts himself to remark that if Eumaeus will look at him closely he will see the shadow of the man he once was.) Such was he in battle, but farming and domestic management were not for him. His world was that of ships and battles and the like, things other people dreaded. Before the Trojan War he led nine sea raids against foreigners, won a lot of booty, and was feared and respected by his fellow Cretans.

Then Zeus decreed that awful journey—as the narrator calls the Trojan War—which killed many men. The people kept urging the narrator and Idomeneus, in the *Iliad* the leader of the Cretan contingent in the allied Greek force, to lead the ships to Troy. There was no way to get out of it, so harsh would the verdict of public opinion have been. After Troy fell, the narrator managed to reach home. But he remained there for only a month before his spirit moved him to sail to the Nile. He anchored and sent some men out as scouts, ordering the rest to stay by the ships. They were cocky, however, and trusting to their strength ravaged the Egyptians' fields. The Egyptians sallied forth from their town and routed the Cretans, sparing only the narrator (who interrupts the story at this point to say, "Would that I had died there in Egypt!"). He clasped and kissed the Egyptian king's knees in supplication. The king pitied him and shielded him from the angry populace.

The narrator spent seven years in Egypt and gained wealth. But in the eighth year he was persuaded to accompany a deceitful merchant to Phoenicia. After a year his patron sent the narrator with a cargo to Libya, ostensibly to trade, but actually intending to sell him into slavery when the ship arrived. The ship was wrecked in a storm; after floating for ten days clinging to the mast, the narrator was washed ashore in the land of the Thesprotians. The son of Pheidon, their ruler, found him, exhausted from his ordeal, and led him to his home and clothed him. Pheidon asked the crew of a Thesprotian ship that was sailing in the direction of Crete to take the narrator with them. As soon as they were out of sight of land they took away his good clothes and gave him beggar's clothes. When the ship stopped that evening at Ithaca, the crew bound him in the hold while they went ashore to eat, but he slipped his bonds and swam to shore.

The extensive commentary on the false tale[15] overlooks its artistic purpose: not, as one might think, to glorify Odysseus by contrasting his career with that of the narrator, but rather to bring the story and character of Odysseus down to earth by retelling his life, and reinterpreting his character, in terms appropriate to the comparatively realistic setting and events of the poem's dénouement. The *Odyssey* has many romantic elements—the tale of Odysseus's adventures at Troy and of his wanderings before he lands in Ithaca is shot through with them. But the movement of the poem is antiromantic. The significance of Odysseus's rejection at the beginning of the poem of Calypso's offer of a sensual and luxurious immortality on the island of Ogygia in favor of his minor kingship, mortal span of years, grown son, and middle-aged wife is underscored by the fact that the Ogygian idyll was for Odysseus the culmination of a career of near-superhuman achievement at Troy and adventures of mythic proportions afterward (with the Cyclops, with Circe, in the land of the dead, and so on). Ogygia is a kind of one-man Valhalla and thus a fitting climax, one might suppose, to Odysseus's doings at Troy—which have already passed into legend and song—and his subsequent wanderings. Nevertheless, Odysseus leaves Ogygia, and the end of the poem presents him as a hero on a human rather than superhuman scale. He has been outwitted by his wife and, disguised as a beggar, has suffered intolerable indignities at the hands of the suitors. He finishes the suitors off neatly, but they are a poor match for his fabulous adversaries in the first half of the poem; and it is only with the help of his son and several faithful retainers that he comes into his own as the restored king of his small realm, and as husband, son, and father. We are made to understand that reintegration into human society, though not itself a heroic destiny, is the best culmination of a heroic career.

This lesson is reinforced by the many references to the unhappy fate of Agamemnon and other heroes of the Trojan War and by the "everyman" character of Odysseus. He is no ordinary man, but neither is he the strongest or the noblest of the Greek heroes. He is merely the most intel-

---

15. For recent discussions, see Chris Emlyn-Jones, "True and Lying Tales in the *Odyssey*," 33 *Greece and Rome* 1 (1986); Louise H. Pratt, *Lying and Poetry from Homer to Pindar: Falsehood and Deception in Archaic Greek Poetics* 90–91 (1993); Karl Reinhardt, "The Adventures in the *Odyssey*," in *Reading the Odyssey: Selected Interpretive Essays* 63, 66–68 (Seth L. Schein ed. 1996); Frederick Ahl and Hanna M. Roisman, *The Odyssey Re-Formed* 161–166 (1996). Many critics regard the false tale as one of the *longueurs* of the *Odyssey*. Ahl and Roisman's book, a strange deconstruction (or am I being redundant?) of the *Odyssey*, while agreeing that the false tales are indeed false, argues that Odysseus's narration to the Phaeacian court of his adventures after he left Troy is also false; that no one knows where he was or what he was doing during those ten years.

ligent—his intelligence, his skill at what today we would call instrumental or practical reasoning, is emphasized throughout the *Odyssey*—and intelligence is the defining trait of the human animal, making Odysseus perhaps the most *representative* human figure in Homer.

The parallels between the true story of Odysseus's life before he returns home from Troy and the false tale are numerous, though the latter is the story of an average, restless, disappointed, and unlucky man—a minor, and now rather soured, adventurer. The narrator's service at Troy was apparently without distinction and his subsequent wanderings certainly so. Instead of being rescued like Odysseus by a beautiful princess (Nausicaa) who promptly falls in love with him, he is rescued by a prince. Instead of returning to Ithaca on a ship that rows itself, supplied by the king of a magic kingdom (Scheria), the narrator is conveyed by a bunch of thugs who rob him, and he must scramble furtively ashore and hide in a thicket. And he is not really home; supposedly he lives in Crete, not Ithaca. He is stranded far from home, a beggar.

The false tale thus accentuates a basic movement in the *Odyssey,* which is to make Odysseus more distinct and, correlatively, more recognizably human. At first he is a vague offstage presence, and although we know that he's alive, most of the characters in the poem do not. When he first appears he is quasi-human, eating ambrosia in Calypso's cave; then he is shown as the fabulous hero of the Trojan War and the wanderings. Reborn in Ithaca, dealing with the members of his household, attending to domestic chores, recalling his life before the Trojan War, he is a more fully realized human character, and the Odysseus of the earlier books becomes a memory.[16]

Often one can get a deeper understanding of a work of literature by distinguishing between foregrounded and total stories. In one sense the *Odyssey* is the story of Odysseus's career after the end of the Trojan War, just as the *Iliad* is the story of the Trojan War, *Oedipus Tyrannus* the story of the Oedipus legend, and *Hamlet* the story of the murder and revenge of Hamlet's father. But in all four works the foreground story is a truncated version of the whole story.[17] In the *Odyssey* it is the story of Odysseus's return not from Troy but from Ogygia. He moves from west to east, from

16. See Pierre Vidal-Naquet, "Land and Sacrifice in the Odyssey: A Study of Religious and Mythical Meanings," in *Myth, Religion and Society: Structuralist Essays* 80, 83 (R. L. Gordon ed. 1981) (discussing "Odysseus's return to normality . . . [and] his deliberate acceptance of the human condition"); Charles Paul Segal, "The Phaeacians and the Symbolism of Odysseus' Return," *Arion,* Winter 1962, pp. 17, 25, 29 n. 13.

17. In both *Oedipus* and *Hamlet* because these are plays of discovery—precursors, in a sense, of the detective story—and would lose their drama and suspense if the horrors discovered were revealed to the audience at the outset.

immortality to mortality, from a life of ease to a life of struggle, and he does so through a liquid medium (the sea) and is symbolically reborn in a cave in Ithaca. He chooses life over death, reality over imagination, earth over heaven, work over retirement.

An intersecting movement in the poem is the maturing of his son, Telemachus. At the beginning of the poem father and son are worlds apart. Their physical separation symbolizes the emotional gulf between the shallow youth of Book 2 and the hero of the Trojan War. The rapid maturing of Telemachus through a series of adventures constituting, much like the false tale told to Eumaeus, a scaled-down version of Odysseus's career, coupled with the redefinition of Odysseus as a human hero, enables father and son to join as approximate equals in the three-generation tableau that ends the poem. Family continuity is presented as an alternative form of immortality both to fame—Achilles' way in the *Iliad*—and personal immortality, which Odysseus rejects in leaving Ogygia. A notable contrast between the world of the *Iliad* and that of the *Odyssey* is revealed in Achilles' pleasure when Odysseus tells him, in the course of the visit to the underworld, of the exploits of the dead hero's son.[18]

In contrast to the critical perspective on attempts to transcend human finitude that a work such as the *Odyssey* offers, Romantic literature laments the loss of the child's sense of unlimited, even superhuman potential. Wordsworth's "Ode: Intimations of Immortality from Recollections of Early Childhood" tells us that

> Our birth is but a sleep and a forgetting:
> The Soul that rises with us, our life's Star,
>   Hath had elsewhere its setting,
>   And cometh from afar:
>   Not in entire forgetfulness,
>   And not in utter nakedness,
> But trailing clouds of glory do we come
>   From God, who is our home:
> Heaven lies about us in our infancy!
> Shades of the prison-house begin to close
>   Upon the growing Boy . . .

> Thou [six-year-old], whose exterior semblance doth belie
>   Thy Soul's immensity;
> Thou best Philosopher, who yet dost keep

18. "So I said and / off he went, the ghost of the great runner, Aeacus' grandson / loping with long strides across the fields of asphodel, / triumphant in all I had told of him of his son, / his gallant, glorious son" (14.612–616).

Thy heritage, thou Eye among the blind . . .

Mighty Prophet! Seer blest!
On whom those truths do rest,
Which we are toiling all our lives to find.

This is magnificent poetry, although the surface meaning is absurd; six-year-olds do not have the knowledge that we spend our whole lives trying to recapture. What is true is that well-treated and well-beloved children, and young people generally, have vitality and enthusiasm, warmth and idealism, a sense of infinite horizons and limitless power to do good—all things that aging and experience gradually rub off, leaving in some people a sense of profound loss. "The sunshine is a glorious birth; / But yet I know, where'er I go, / That there hath past away a glory from the earth": so Wordsworth. Others have thought differently. Here is Aristotle on youth: "They look at the good side rather than the bad, not having yet witnessed many instances of wickedness. They trust others readily, because they have not yet often been cheated. They are sanguine . . . [because] they have as yet met with few disappointments . . . [Their] hot temper prevents fear, and the[ir] hopeful disposition creates confidence . . . They have exalted notions . . . They think they know everything, and are always quite sure about it."[19]

The Romantic poets' cult of the child leads to the rejection of institutional Christianity, with its doctrine of original sin,[20] and to the rejection of the natural sciences, because of their realism, and of economics, because of its emphasis on constraints—an emphasis particularly marked in the age of Malthus, which coincided with the Romantic age. Romanticism transfers the attributes of divinity from God to man, and by doing so holds out the promise that man (like God) can create his own reality by an act of imagination. It teaches that natural man, the child spirit, is good as well as full of latent power but becomes corrupted and weakened by institutions, by "the system"—the domain of the adult, the experienced, the cynical,

---

19. Aristotle, *Rhetoric*, bk. 2, ch. 12, in *The Complete Works of Aristotle*, vol. 2, pp. 2213–2214 (Jonathan Barnes ed. 1984) (W. Rhys Roberts trans.) (1389a–1389b). Aristotle's view is echoed in Michael Oakeshott, "On Being Conservative," in his book *Rationalism in Politics and Other Essays* 168, 195 (1962): "Everybody's young days are a dream, a delightful insanity, a sweet solipsism. Nothing in them has a fixed shape, nothing a fixed price; everything is a possibility, and we live happily on credit. There are no obligations to be observed; there are no accounts to be kept. Nothing is specified in advance; everything is what can be made of it. The world is a mirror in which we seek the reflection of our own desires."

20. The qualification *institutional* Christianity is important. Romanticism shares with Christianity (and Marxism) a hope of transcending the normal human condition (albeit in different ways) that is foreign to the outlook of the *Odyssey*.

the worldly—as if maturation and aging were social phenomena rather than personal and biological ones.

Nietzsche hated Romanticism, but was romantic in the generic sense, "elevat[ing] to new heights the characteristically modern aspirations to conquer fortune, to master nature, and to actualize freedom."[21] His "consistent preference is clear: he is always for the single man against the herd, for genius against justice, for grace against deserts; he favours inspiration against the rule of rules and professional competence, and the heroic in every form against all that is 'human, all too human.'"[22]

Nietzsche amplifies the Romantic hostility to institutions in general and organized Christianity in particular by attacking the Christian religion root and branch and the Jews as the inventors of Christianity:

> The priests are the *most evil enemies* [of "powerful physicality, a flourishing, abundant, even overflowing health, together with that which serves to preserve it: war, adventure, hunting, dancing, war games, and in general all that involves vigorous, free, joyful activity"]—but why? Because they are the most impotent. It is because of their impotence that in them hatred grows to monstrous and uncanny proportions, to the most spiritual and poisonous kind of hatred [compare Blake's "Garden of Love"]. The truly great haters in world history have always been priests . . . All that has been done on earth against "the noble," "the powerful," "the masters," "the rulers," fades into nothing compared with what the Jews have done against them; the Jews, that priestly people, who in opposing their enemies and conquerors were ultimately satisfied with nothing less than a radical revaluation of their enemies' values, that is to say, an act of the *most spiritual revenge* . . . With the Jews there begins *the slave revolt in morality;* that revolt which has a history of two thousand years behind it and which we no longer see because it—has been victorious.[23]

This passage does not give a complete picture of Nietzsche's attitude toward the Jews, for alongside it must be placed passages of lyrical philo-Semitism[24] together with diatribes against anti-Semitism and German nationalism (indeed, against Germans, period). Nietzsche did give currency

---

21. Peter Berkowitz, *Nietzsche: The Ethics of an Immoralist* 2 (1995).

22. J. P. Stern, *A Study of Nietzsche* 127 (1979).

23. Nietzsche, note 2 above, at 33–34 (I.7). See also id. at 35 (I.8).

24. For some examples, see *Beyond Good and Evil: Prelude to a Philosophy of the Future* 185–189 (§§ 250, 251) (Walter Kaufmann trans. 1966); *Daybreak: Thoughts on the Prejudices of Morality* 124–125 (§ 205) (R. J. Hollingdale trans. 1982); *Human, All Too Human: A Book for Free Spirits* 228–229 (§ 475) (Marion Faber trans. 1984); *Joyful Wisdom* 288–289 (§ 348) (Thomas Common trans. 1960). Yet in *Beyond Good and Evil* (§ 195) Nietzsche again speaks of the Jews as "a people 'born for slavery'" (quoting Tacitus approvingly) and again says "they mark the beginning of the slave rebellion in morals" (p. 108). And in *Daybreak* he says (§ 377), "The command 'love your enemies' had to be invented by the Jews, the best haters there have ever been" (p. 170).

to, although he did not coin, the word *Übermensch,* which was to play so large a role in Nazi racial doctrine. But he did not use it in a racial sense; that is, he did not believe that there was a race of *Übermenschen.* Nor did he ever refer to people who were not *Übermenschen* as *Untermenschen.* Only rarely—but the qualification should be noted—did he speak approvingly of slavery or of racial purity.[25] Much, maybe most, of what appears to be vicious in Nietzsche's writings can be interpreted figuratively as designed to promote "positive thinking." He is trying to get people to "say 'Yes' to life" by encouraging them to smash the shackles of custom and habit, stop being craven and weak, cultivate a healthy ego, ignore slights, take responsibility for their life, give shape and meaning to it—what Joseph K. failed to do, what Meursault finally did, what Alfredo Traps succeeded in doing only in parodic form. The *Übermensch* is a self-overcomer rather than a "Superman." Nietzsche admired much in the Old Testament and praised the assimilated Jews of the diaspora.[26] Yet he repeatedly asserted that the Jews were ultimately responsible, though perhaps not culpably so, for virtually everything that is bad in the modern world, and he continuously advocated pagan values in opposition to the gentler Christian ones. "You say it is the good cause that hallows even war? I say unto you: it is the good war that hallows any cause."[27] Nietzsche considered both anti-Semites and Jews, especially Jews like Paul, the architect of Christianity, to be consumed by *ressentiment.* Nietzsche was "an anti-anti-Semite *and* a critic of

25. Walter Kaufmann, *Nietzsche: Philosopher, Psychologist, Antichrist,* chs. 10–11 (4th ed. 1974); Richard Schacht, *Nietzsche,* ch. 7 (1983). Yet we read in *Daybreak,* note 24 above, at 1491 (§ 272), "Crossed races always mean at the same time crossed cultures, crossed moralities; they are usually more evil, crueller, more restless . . . Races that have become pure have always become *stronger* and more *beautiful.*" And in *Human, All Too Human,* note 24 above, at 211 (§ 439): "A higher culture can come into being only where there are two castes of society: the working caste and the idle caste, capable of true leisure; or, to express it more emphatically, the caste of forced labor and the caste of free labor." For other examples of Nietzsche's flirtations with racism, exploitation, and genocide, see Ofelia Schutte, *Beyond Nihilism: Nietzsche without Masks,* ch. 7 (1984).

26. Sander L. Gilman, "Nietzsche, Heine, and the Otherness of the Jew," in *Studies in Nietzsche and the Judaeo-Christian Tradition* 206 (James C. O'Flaherty, Timothy F. Sellner, and Robert M. Helm eds. 1985). To the same effect, see Michael F. Duffy and Willard Mittleman, "Nietzsche's Attitudes toward the Jews," 49 *Journal of the History of Ideas* 301 (1988). Gilman points out that all these characterizations of the Jews are stereotypes, "reduc[ing] the perception of a group of single individuals to the generalities of a class." Gilman, above, at 206.

27. Nietzsche, note 4 above, at 47 (I.10). "What Nietzsche's song of praise to war and strength expressed was the adoption by wide sectors of the middle class of his time of a warrior code which had at first belonged to the nobility." Norbert Elias, *The Germans: Power Struggles and the Development of Habits in the Nineteenth and Twentieth Centuries* 118 (Michael Schröter ed. 1996). Nietzsche transformed elements of the warrior code "into a middle-class nationalist doctrine." Id. at 119.

ancient Judaism, the cradle of Christianity."[28] The Nazis ignored the first part of this condemnation. Weisberg ignores the second.

I shall not turn Weisberg on his head by blaming Nietzsche for the rise of Hitler. Yet much of the Nazi program could be stitched out of passages from Nietzsche's *oeuvre,* justifying Aschheim's description of Nazism as "a kind of Nietzschean Great Politics."[29] The German *Volk* united in the person of Adolf Hitler, the triumph of the will over material constraints, the glorification of war, the cultivation of pitilessness and cruelty, the replacement of bourgeois by barbarian values, the creation of a master race of the strong and the beautiful, and the release of Satanic energies align Nietzsche, along with reactionary neoromantic modern poets such as Yeats, who was greatly influenced by Nietzsche, with fascism at a number of points, not just anti-Semitism. But what is more, as a cultural rather than a religious anti-Semite[30]—a critic not of Jews from a Christian standpoint, but of Judaism and Christianity from a pagan standpoint—Nietzsche pointed the way to Hitler's particular brand of anti-Semitism; for Hitler too was an anti-Christian who bracketed Christianity and Judaism.

No more than Nietzsche's philosophy does romanticism lead in a straight line to Hitler. The Romantic emphasis on organic unities supports the radical communitarianism of neo-Marxists and the conservative communitarianism of Edmund Burke, as well as the organicism of a Mussolini or a Hitler.[31] But T. S. Eliot's *antir*omanticism led him in the direction of fas-

28. Yirmiyahu Yovel, "Nietzsche, the Jews, and *Ressentiment*," in *Nietzsche, Genealogy, Morality: Essays on Nietzsche's Genealogy of Morals* 214, 215 (Richard Schacht ed. 1994) (emphasis added).

29. Steven E. Aschheim, *Culture and Catastrophe: German and Jewish Confrontations with National Socialism and Other Crises* 81 (1996). Consider the following passage from *Human, All Too Human,* note 24 above, at 230–231 (§ 477): "*War essential*. It is vain rhapsodizing and sentimentality to continue to expect much (even more, to expect a very great deal) from mankind, once it has learned not to wage war . . . Such a highly cultivated, and therefore necessarily weary humanity as that of present-day Europe, needs not only wars but the greatest and most terrible wars (that is, occasional relapses into barbarism) in order not to forfeit to the means of culture its culture and its very existence." Or this passage from *The Anti-Christ,* in *Twilight of the Idols and The Anti-Christ* 115–116 (§ 2) (R. J. Hollingdale trans. 1968): "What is good?—All that heightens the feeling of power, the will to power, power itself in man. What is bad?—All that proceeds from weakness . . . The weak and ill-constituted shall perish: first principle of our philanthropy. And one shall help them to do so. What is more harmful than any vice?—Active sympathy for the ill-constituted and weak—Christianity." Or this from *Joyful Wisdom,* note 24 above, at 250 (§ 325): "Who can attain to anything great if he does not feel in himself the force and will to *inflict* great pain? . . . Not to perish from internal distress and doubt when one inflicts great suffering and hears the cry of it—that is great, that belongs to greatness." This could be the text of one of Himmler's pep talks to the SS officers involved in the program to exterminate the Jews.

30. A. D. Nuttall, *Why Does Tragedy Give Pleasure?* 63 (1996).

31. See Roger Eatwell, *Fascism: A History* 6–7 (1995).

cism, while Benthamite utilitarianism, anathema to romantics, has been used to argue both for socialism and for laissez-faire capitalism. As these examples show, even the relation between individualism and romanticism is ambiguous. Although in one sense the extreme of individualism, in another sense romanticism is the annihilation of the boundaries between individuals. It is law—unromantic, indeed antiromantic—that patrols those boundaries.

Romantic unease with law is reflected in the literary tradition of the "romantic outlaw."[32] One of the aphorisms in Blake's "Marriage of Heaven and Hell"—"Sooner murder an infant in its cradle than nurse unacted desires"—could be the epigraph of twentieth-century neoromantic novels by Gide, Genet, Camus, and others. Nietzsche's celebration of war is consistent with this sentiment, although he did not go so far as to approve murder. (Nor for that matter did Blake.) Nietzsche's complaint about Christian values is not that they repress homicidal impulses but that they are "anti-life." Weisberg, however, interprets several of the novels he discusses as taking Nietzsche's philosophy a step further and depicting, with profound disapproval, the repression of homicidal *Übermenschen.* Raskolnikov commits two murders, one of which would be first-degree murder in our system. Meursault, we saw, is a murderer. Billy Budd commits what in civilian law (an essential qualification, as we shall see) would be manslaughter. Weisberg condones the inversion of values that he thinks these works celebrate. He repeatedly expresses sympathy for the criminal act and antipathy toward the people who bring criminals to justice—those people, he thinks, are consumed by *ressentiment*. He says that "the perception of the criminal act as a declaration of freedom from *ressentiment* is a fundamental contribution of modern literature," that "the criminal is not prone to *ressentiment*," and that "almost diametrically opposed to the case of the criminal is that of the intellectual" (pp. 27–28). Meursault rebels against "an arbitrary value system" because he has "his own system of what are, on balance, positive values. Meursault stands, as an individual, for the total rejection of verbal sentimentality. As such, he partakes of the free flow of human existence with honesty, if not perfect Cartesian rationality" (pp. 119–120). The witnesses at Meursault's trial "fail to convey the benignity of the defendant's moral system" (p. 120). Criticized for "almost willfully ignoring" what Meursault has actually done,[33] Weisberg replies

---

32. For an excellent discussion, see Martha Grace Duncan, *Romantic Outlaws, Beloved Prisons: The Unconscious Meanings of Crime and Punishment,* pt. 2 (1996).

33. Susan Sage Heinzelman and Sanford Levinson, "Words and Wordiness: Reflections on Richard Weisberg's *The Failure of the Word,*" 7 *Cardozo Law Review* 453, 465 (1986).

irrelevantly that among a group of fictional characters who include both Meursault and one character falsely accused of murder (Dmitri Karamazov) "none, taken alone, is meant to be a *sterling* moral paradigm."[34] In discussing how the examining magistrate in *Crime and Punishment* uses lawyer's wiles in an effort to entrap Raskolnikov into confessing, Weisberg compares Raskolnikov's plight to that of Joseph K. in *The Trial,* overlooking that Raskolnikov has murdered two people while Joseph K. has committed no crime at all. And in calling Billy Budd "an innocent man" and a "joyful innocent" (pp. 155, 162), Weisberg makes light of the fact that Billy Budd struck a lethal blow to a superior officer at sea in wartime; after doing that, Billy was innocent no longer. The legally guilty and the legally innocent are both innocent in Weisberg's eyes; the law and its agents are guilty.

A society in which criminals are free to roam without threat of sanction leaves little freedom for the rest of the population. Dostoevsky and Melville understand this.[35] Readers of *Crime and Punishment* are, and are intended to be, appalled at Raskolnikov's conduct—and not because he fails to live up to his self-billing as *Übermensch.* The efforts of Porfiry, the examining magistrate—described by Weisberg as "coercing Raskolnikov into confession and moral conformity" (p. xii; see also p. 54)—to catch Raskolnikov off guard are standard, albeit dramatized, interrogative tactics. Porfiry does not coerce Raskolnikov into confessing. The confession is not even the result of Porfiry's interrogation. Raskolnikov confesses to another official after Porfiry has given up on trying to pin the crime on him—confesses from internal pressures rather than from the strain of the interrogation.

His concluding apologetic for Meursault lays Weisberg open to the accusation of not taking crime seriously: "When the defendant declares that 'the sun' produced the homicide, we know that within a system based on openness to sensual experience, the natural environment on the day of the murder—coupled with the slight drunkenness from the luncheon wine, a condition never revealed by the legal ratiocination—did in effect rob him of free will. Indeed, in an American court, Meursault's lack of real premeditation would have formed the basis of a viable defense; with the 'personality' issue virtually inadmissible there as well, Meursault might have received a relatively light sentence for manslaughter" (pp. 121–122; footnotes

---

34. Richard H. Weisberg, "More Words on *The Failure of the Word*: A Response to Heinzelman and Levinson," 7 *Cardozo Law Review* 473, 483 (1986) (emphasis added). More recently he has said that Meursault, whom he calls "heterodox," was "convicted of *being different.*" Weisberg, *Vichy Law and the Holocaust in France* 7 (1996) (emphasis in original).

35. Camus is another matter, as I noted in Chapter 1.

omitted). The unedifying message is obscured by evasive locutions ("in effect," "real," "viable," "relatively") and by neglecting to mention that Meursault shot his (unnamed, un-French, depersonalized, even dehumanized) victim five times and never expressed regret or remorse.[36] Evidently the tendency to inhuman abstraction that some forms of legal reasoning foster is a danger not only to criminal defendants but also to the victims of crime, when the victim's humanity is ignored while the criminal is portrayed as richly human.[37] Although a consistent commitment to legalism might have saved Meursault from the death penalty, a consistent commitment to viewing his case in its full human dimensions—and thus with due regard for the Arab's humanity as well as for Meursault's—might have condemned him.

Weisberg fails to see that if "justice" depends on who the victim and the injurer are, the popular man will get justice and the unpopular one will not. If the nonconformist is likely to end up an outlaw (one interpretation of the trial and condemnation of Socrates under the Athenian system of popular justice), the pressure on people to conform to community norms will be intensified. The essence of legal justice, as formulated by Aristotle in the concept of corrective justice, is ignoring the personal merits of the litigants. Romantic self-assertion, by rejecting legal justice, can lead to the deadliest conformity.

I hope I made clear in Chapter 1 my admiration for *The Stranger* as a work of literature. And later in this book I shall argue against the view that immoral literature causes immoral behavior. But viewed as a moral treatise, as Weisberg views it, *The Stranger* is vicious. Exhausted by the mass murder of Jews, Weisberg's fund of indignation has nothing left for the ordinary murder of an Arab.

---

36. Similarly evasive of the moral issue posed by Meursault's act is Peter Read Teachout's claim that *The Stranger* is "a deeply moral work" simply because it asks the big questions about life. Teachout, "Lapse of Judgment," 77 *California Law Review* 1259, 1287 (1989).

37. A modern example is the murder of a female student at Yale by a young man from a poor home who not only received great sympathy from the Catholic Church but was given only a short prison sentence for his crime. Willard Gaylin, *The Killing of Bonnie Garland: A Question of Justice* (1982); Peter Meyer, *The Yale Murder* (1982). See generally Lynne N. Henderson, "Legality and Empathy," 85 *Michigan Law Review* 1574 (1987). Might not the charge of lack of empathy for victims of crime be leveled against "A Jury of Her Peers" (Chapter 3)? Could not that story, too, have been told from the victim's standpoint? Maybe the murdered husband had been jealous of his wife's bird, like Harry in John Steinbeck's story "The White Quail," who kills, apparently out of jealousy, the bird that his wife loves. In Chapter 9 we shall note the law's effort to redress the forensic balance between murderer and (absent) victim by means of "the victim impact statement."

Billy Budd *and* The Brothers Karamazov

Weisberg's *pièce de résistance* is an unorthodox reading of *Billy Budd*.[38] The eponymous hero is a young seaman impressed onto a British man-of-war during the war between Britain and the French Directory (the interregnum between the Revolutionary regime and Napoleon). The British navy has recently experienced a serious mutiny and everyone is on the lookout for a recurrence, especially among impressed seamen. John Claggart, the petty officer in charge of security on the ship, decides, for reasons that are never made clear, to frame Billy. He tells the ship's captain that Billy is a mutineer. Captain Vere does not believe Claggart, and summons Billy to confront his accuser in the captain's cabin. Billy, who has a speech impediment, is unable to respond to Claggart's accusations. Vere puts his arm on Billy's shoulder in a fatherly way and tells him there's no hurry about speaking. Speechless and enraged, Billy responds by striking Claggart dead with a single punch. Vere convenes a drumhead (that is, summary) court-martial. The members are inclined to leniency until Vere reminds them that striking one's superior in wartime is a capital offense and that any leniency might encourage mutiny. They reluctantly sentence Billy to death and he is hanged the next morning—his last words being, "God save Captain Vere." Vere, fatally wounded in a battle shortly afterward, dies whispering "Billy Budd."

In Weisberg's interpretation, Billy is Rousseau's noble savage, Nietzsche's "master"[39] or "blond beast," Wordsworth's Seer blest, while Vere as well as Claggart are consumed by *ressentiment* and the execution of Billy is a grave injustice. Weisberg argues that the court-martial was irregular because Claggart was not "in the execution of his office" when Billy struck him (pp. 154–155). But he was; ferreting out mutiny was his foremost task as the ship's security officer. He was abusing his office in accusing Billy, not abandoning it. Vere and the members of the court-martial believe merely that Claggart was mistaken in accusing Billy. Weisberg argues that the death penalty is excessive for Billy Budd's offense, but misreads the historical record: a seaman in the eighteenth-century British navy who struck and killed a superior officer might indeed be executed. Seaman John Cumming was tried in 1784 for striking the boatswain of his ship and

---

38. Besides the discussion in *The Failure of the Word*, see Weisberg, *Poethics and Other Strategies of Law and Literature* 104–116 (1992). For other examples of the extensive scholarly literature on the legal aspects of *Billy Budd*, see Symposium on *Billy Budd*, 1 *Cardozo Studies in Law and Literature* 1 (1989); *Critical Essays on Melville's* Billy Budd, Sailor (Robert Milder ed. 1989); Susan Weiner, *Law in Art: Melville's Major Fiction and Nineteenth-Century American Law*, ch. 8 (1992).

39. On the difference between the "masters" and the *"Übermenschen,"* see John Richardson, *Nietzsche's System* 52–72 (1996). The master is naturally noble; the *Übermensch* overcomes the slave morality within himself.

was found guilty and sentenced to be hanged, with no recommendation for mercy, even though there is no indication that the boatswain died.[40] The procedural irregularities identified by Weisberg reflect the differences between the formality of a regular court-martial and the informality of a drumhead court-martial. Weisberg also argues that under English law Vere should have waited until the ship rejoined the fleet before proceeding against Billy and should then have asked the admiral commanding the fleet to convene a regular court-martial; the summary procedure was proper only if Billy's striking Claggart could be construed as mutinous. But striking a superior officer in wartime was mutinous per se.[41]

Even if Weisberg were correct about eighteenth-century law and practice, his interpretation of the novella would be refuted by the absence of any suggestion in the text—nor could the reader be assumed to know from other sources—that the court-martial and execution of Billy were illegal. Harsh, maybe horrible, maybe even precipitate (the ship's surgeon, a member of the court-martial, thought that so unusual a case should have been referred to the admiral); but not illegal. Not Vere but the narrator tells the reader that the drumhead court-martial was proper in the circumstances.[42] Nor does Melville scatter clues that the narrator himself might be unreliable or that the reader must research eighteenth-century British naval law in order to understand the book.

It is, moreover, a literary imperative that Billy Budd should be tried on the ship. A delay to rejoin the fleet, followed by a shift of the action to a court-martial in which Vere would play no role, would blur the plot and delay the dénouement to no artistic purpose. And to give Billy a punishment obviously lawful for a drumhead court-martial—a lashing, say—would have robbed the novella of its tragic overtones. It is also a literary imperative that Vere be prosecutor, jury, and judge rolled into one; it is necessary in order to maintain the brisk pace of the narrative. Art trumps due process. An understanding of literature on legal themes as a coherent literary genre, rather than as a branch of legal doctrine, can help to prevent misunderstandings about the literary meaning of departures from legal regularity.

The misgivings that the members of the court-martial exhibit—one of

---

40. John MacArthur, *Principles and Practices of Naval and Military Courts Martial*, vol. 2, p. 437 (4th ed. 1813); see id. at pp. 419–451 for a survey of cases.

41. Thomas Simmons, *The Constitution and Practice of Courts Martial* 79 (7th ed. 1875).

42. "In wartime on the field or in the fleet, a mortal punishment decreed by a drumhead court—on the field sometimes decreed by but a nod from the general—follows without delay on the heel of convicting, without appeal." Herman Melville, *Billy Budd, Sailor (An Inside Narrative)* 114 (Harrison Hayford and Merton M. Sealts, Jr., eds. 1962). My page references to *Billy Budd* are to this edition.

them even questions Vere's sanity—are based not on legal reservations but on the fact that Billy is such an attractive person and the provocation (in a layman's, not a lawyer's, sense) for striking Claggart was great. The opposition portrayed is between the sympathies of subordinate officers of narrow outlook and limited understanding and the responsibilities that rest on the captain's shoulders alone. Vere is isolated by his intelligence, role, and perspective. There is no one with whom he might take counsel or share responsibility for dealing with the consequences of Billy's crime.

Assuming the role of devil's advocate in almost a literal sense, Weisberg argues that Billy Budd is Nietzsche's "blond beast" and Claggart is Jesus Christ: "Claggart-Christ," Weisberg absurdly calls him (p. 174). Billy does have the qualities of natural man according to Nietzsche—robust health and high animal spirits, primal rage but no rancor or vengefulness, heedlessness for the future (he does not worry about being impressed onto a warship in wartime), guilelessness, and inarticulateness (symbolized by the speech impediment that conveniently silences him at the critical moment), a trait he shares with Meursault. Empathy, sensitivity, forward planning, and other characteristic features of human mentality are in Nietzsche's view devices by which the members of the herd seek to overcome their weakness and express their will to power. "He who possesses strength divests himself of mind."[43] But Billy is also associated with Adam before the fall (Christ is frequently referred to in Christian literature as "the second Adam") and with the Lamb of God; heavenly portents attend his execution; and he forgives Vere. Vere's fatherly attitude toward Billy resonates with God's sacrifice of His Son to save mankind (and "bud" is the vegetable counterpart of "child"). Claggart, in contrast, is repeatedly likened to a serpent, putting one in mind of Satan rather than of Jesus Christ. The name "Claggart" has a clanging sound, recalling the traditional association of devils with noise. He has the same initials as Christ and dies at about the same age, but even a rabid anti-Christian—even a Nietzsche—could not find any similarity in character or deeds between Christ and Claggart. And is it a surprise that the Antichrist should have the same initials as the Christ? Isn't it just the sort of thing you'd *expect* of the devil?

Nietzsche, too, believed that Christianity had destroyed the Roman Empire (others might think it extended the Empire's longevity). But he distinguished between Jesus Christ, whom he thought admirable and even "pagan," and institutional Christianity.[44] It was Nietzsche who said "there

---

43. *Twilight of the Idols: or How to Philosophize with a Hammer,* in *Twilight of the Idols and The Anti-Christ,* note 29 above, at 76 ("Expeditions of an Untimely Man," 14). See also *Daybreak,* note 24 above, at 90 (§ 142).

44. See *The Anti-Christ,* note 29 above, at 139–153, 179–183 (§§ 27–40, 58–59).

has been only one Christian, and he died on the Cross."[45] There is neither textual nor biographical evidence that Melville outdid Nietzsche in hostility to Christianity.[46]

Most "liberals," in the sense current today, dislike the military and abhor capital punishment. (How contemptible Nietzsche would find them!) They do not find Vere a sympathetic figure and some of them project their lack of sympathy onto Melville. Brook Thomas, for example, unimpressed by Weisberg's procedural criticisms, which he thinks reflect a Vere-like "legalistic point of view that focuses on technicalities,"[47] thinks Melville's point is that law—to Thomas a means by which the upper classes oppress the lower—is such a beguiling idealogy that it persuades even its victims that it is just. "Vere projects such an image of fairness that not even Billy himself protests the call for his execution" (p. 219). But if Vere's ideology is so beguiling, it is difficult to resist the conclusion that Melville is himself beguiled. Thomas assumes rather than argues that the reader is meant to pierce the image of fairness to the underlying reality of oppression.[48]

Weisberg goes these critics one better not only by accusing Vere of having violated military law to obtain a death sentence against Billy but also by charging him with having done so out of rancorous envy of Admiral Nelson. His thesis is that Vere, though a competent officer, is not in Nelson's league (which is true but, as we shall see, misleading); that Vere resents the comparison (for which there is no evidence); and that because Nelson and Billy Budd share the quality of perfectly uniting thought and action, Vere identifies one with the other[49] and condemns Billy out of envy of Nelson—

45. Id. at 161 (§ 39).

46. See generally Rowland A. Sherrill, "Melville and Religion," in *A Companion to Melville Studies* 481 (John Bryant ed. 1986).

47. Brook Thomas, *Cross-Examinations of Law and Literature: Cooper, Hawthorne, Stowe, and Melville* 211–212 (1987).

48. Not all liberal critics project their dislike of Vere onto Melville. Stephen Vizinczey, "Engineers of a Sham: How Literature Lies about Power," *Harper's*, June 1986, at 69, 71–73, argues both that the novella approves of Vere and that it is wrong to do so. He considers *Billy Budd* a paean to authoritarian values. Robert P. Lawry, "Justice in Billy Budd," in *Law and Literature Perspectives* 169 (Bruce L. Rockwood ed. 1996), argues that Vere was deficient in courage and moral imagination, but rejects Weisberg's reading on grounds similar to mine.

49. The identification is far-fetched. Weak and sickly to begin with, only 5 feet 2 inches tall, Nelson had by 1797 lost both an eye and an arm in combat. And, far from being a free spirit, he apotheosized duty, as in the famous signal to the fleet before Trafalgar: "England expects every man to do his duty." At once physically unprepossessing, indeed crippled, and an eloquent man of authority, Nelson is the opposite of Billy Budd. And he talks just like Vere. "Our country has the first demand for our services; and private convenience or happiness must ever give way to the public good. Duty is the great business of a sea officer: all private considerations must give way to it, however painful." Quoted in Robert Southey, *The Life of Nelson*, vol. 1, p. 69 (1813).

which is preposterous. And in so arguing Weisberg makes aesthetic hash out of *Billy Budd* (another reason to question his interpretation) by breaking the novella into two unrelated stories: a struggle between paganism and Christianity that ends with the death of Claggart (which dooms Billy—that is, Rome); and the acting out of Vere's envy of Nelson, which begins with Claggart's death and ends with Vere's death.

The novella presents Vere to the reader with high accolades: "a sailor of distinction even in a time prolific of renowned seamen," Vere "had seen much service, been in various engagements, always acquitting himself as an officer mindful of his men, but never tolerating an infraction of discipline; thoroughly versed in the science of his profession, and intrepid to the verge of temerity, though never injudiciously so" (p. 60). To take Vere down a peg Weisberg quotes a description from the same page: "Ashore, in the garb of a civilian, scarce any one would have taken him for a sailor." But Weisberg omits the words that immediately follow: ". . . more especially that he never garnished unprofessional talk with nautical terms, and grave in his bearing, evinced little appreciation of mere humor . . . His unobtrusiveness of demeanor may have proceeded from a certain unaffected modesty of manhood sometimes accompanying a resolute nature" (p. 60). It is true that Vere is no Nelson, but neither was Nelson in 1797, for that was before the battles of the Nile, Copenhagen, and Trafalgar—the victories for which he is mainly remembered. Within the world of the novella, the world of 1797, there was no reason for Vere to be envious of Nelson unless gifted with prevision. In Weisberg's hands *Billy Budd* becomes a postmodernist fantasy in which a character acts on the basis of knowledge available to the readers of the book in which he appears, but not to him. Not for nothing was Weisberg a student of Paul de Man, the fallen angel of deconstruction.

I do not consider the mention in chapter 5 of *Billy Budd* of Nelson's having prevented a possible mutiny on the *Theseus* by his mere presence an implicit criticism of Vere. No acts of violence on the *Theseus* are mentioned, and we can be sure that had there been any Nelson would have responded with the utmost severity: he once congratulated another admiral for hanging four seamen on a Sunday and said he would have approved hanging them on Christmas.[50] The purpose of the references to Nelson may be to lend verisimilitude, as with the insertion of Martin Luther into *Michael Kohlhass*. It may even be to suggest what Vere might have become had he not (like Nelson, incidentally) fallen in action, for someone remarks of him that, despite "the gazettes, Sir Horatio [Nelson] . . . is at bottom

---

50. *Dispatches and Letters of Vice Admiral Lord Viscount Nelson*, vol. 2, pp. 408–410 (1845).

scarce a better seaman or fighter" than Vere, albeit Vere is "pedantic" (p. 63).

The contrast between Billy and Vere is indeed the contrast between natural and civilized man. It is underscored by Billy's stammer and lack of education and by Vere's bookishness; the captain is no rough-and-tumble old salt. But Weisberg misses the narrative functions of Billy's stammer and Vere's bookishness. If Billy could have defended himself verbally against Claggart's accusations, his striking Claggart would be unintelligible, or at least out of character. Yet the striking of Claggart is necessary to the unfolding of the story. Vere's bookishness lends plausibility to the elaborate argumentation by which he seeks to persuade the court-martial that it must convict Billy and sentence him to death. It also elevates him intellectually above the officers of the court-martial, and, by presenting him as an introspective man rather than as merely a tough military commander, imparts tragic overtones to his decision to condemn Billy Budd and to his whispering Billy's name on his own deathbed. To Nelson the trial and hanging of Billy would have been all in a day's work and quickly forgotten.

The command of a major warship in a major war is an awesome responsibility; upon its proper discharge may depend many lives. When the most popular sailor kills the most hated petty officer in circumstances of provocation that do not, however, extenuate the capital nature of the offense under the Articles of War, the commander, a sensitive man and not a martinet, finds himself torn between private feeling and public duty. Vere chooses the latter. We are not meant to think he had no choice; but neither are we meant to think he was acting illegally or out of envy. His bookishness, his "pedantry," make us realize he *knew* he faced a tough choice.

Robert Ferguson points out that the commander's choice was between obedience to positive law and obedience to natural law, and notes the affinity between Vere's style of legal reasoning and the approach of legal positivists, which was making headway when Melville was writing *Billy Budd*.[51] Holmes's classic of legal positivism, *The Common Law,* had appeared in 1881; what better antidote to lofty natural-law conceptions of justice than to stress, as Holmes had done, that law originates in vengeance?[52] Vere refuses to allow the positive law governing naval discipline to be trumped by appeal to the higher law under which the killing of Claggart was just: "Before a court less arbitrary and more merciful than a martial one, that plea [that Billy Budd

---

51. See Ferguson, *Law and Letters in American Culture* 288–290 (1984).

52. Vengeance is perfectly "natural," as we saw in Chapter 2; but it is no part of the "good" nature of the natural lawyers (see Chapter 3).

intended neither mutiny nor homicide] would largely extenuate. At the Last Assizes it shall acquit. But how here? We proceed under the law of the Mutiny Act . . . The heart . . . sometimes the feminine in man . . . must here be ruled out" (p. 111). This reasoning places Vere firmly in the left-hand column of the Table of Legal Antinomies (Chapter 3). There is even a touch of Angelo in his reasoning when he says, "Would it be so much we ourselves that would condemn as it would be martial law operating through us? For that law and the rigor of it, we are not responsible" (pp. 110–111). And of Brutus when he adds, "Did [Billy] know our hearts, I take him to be of that generous nature that he would feel even for us on whom in this military necessity so heavy a compulsion is laid" (p. 113).

But Vere does not just invoke the letter of the law. He also argues policy, as a lawyer would say—the danger of mutiny. This is the most unsettling part of Vere's argument, even though it has no connection to legalism or *ressentiment*—even though it is the *rejection* of legalism in favor of utility or expediency. When Vere asks, "How can we adjudge to summary and shameful death a fellow creature innocent before God, and whom we feel to be so?" (p. 110), he puts the reader in mind of the most disturbing feature of utilitarianism—that, in principle anyway, it countenances the deliberate sacrifice of an innocent person for the sake of the general good. Utilitarianism treats the whole society as a single organism whose welfare is to be maximized, and this equation makes it as natural to kill one person for the greater good of society as it would be to remove a cancerous organ. But this type of utilitarian "balancing" owes nothing to legal formalism—to which Bentham was resolutely opposed.

Claggart had had a cabal of informers on the ship; what would they have thought and said had Billy Budd received lenient treatment for killing their boss? Vere explains to the court-martial that to the unsophisticated crew Billy's deed, "however it be worded in the announcement, will be plain homicide committed in a flagrant act of mutiny. What penalty for that should follow, they know. But it does not follow. *Why?* They will ruminate. You know what sailors are. Will they not revert to the recent outbreak at the Nore? Ay. They know the well-founded alarm—the panic it struck throughout England. Your clement sentence they would account pusillanimous. They would think that we flinch, that we are afraid of them—afraid of practicing a lawful rigor singularly demanded at this juncture, lest it should provoke new troubles" (pp. 112–113). Chapter 29 of *Billy Budd* provides corroboration for Vere's concerns. A newspaper widely circulated throughout the fleet is quoted as having given an inaccurate and sensational account of how Billy, the "ringleader" of a sinister plot (p. 130), had stabbed Claggart to death while being arraigned by him before the captain.

To disregard Vere's reasons for condemning Billy is like disregarding Creon's reasons for condemning Antigone—except that Vere has better reasons than Creon for acting as he does. In neither case, however, is it just a matter of upholding "the law" come what may. Although that is an important consideration to both Vere and Creon, neither is a prisoner of the impoverished jurisprudence that makes law impervious to the equity of the facts, to mercy, and to justice. Both think they have justice (granted, human rather than divine justice) on their side, and both have some basis for thinking this. Robert Cover compares Vere to the judges—including Melville's father-in-law, Chief Justice Lemuel Shaw of the Massachusetts Supreme Judicial Court—who before the Civil War enforced the fugitive-slave laws because they were "the law."[53] There is no comparison. The law enforced by Vere was harsh but, in the desperate circumstances in which it was invoked, not vicious.

I have said that Billy Budd is a Christ figure, and this may lend an air of paradox to my defending Vere; if Billy is Christ, Vere must be Pontius Pilate. But Pilate has always had his defenders, such as James Fitzjames Stephen, English criminal-law scholar and judge, foe of John Stuart Mill, friend of Oliver Wendell Holmes, uncle of Virginia Woolf:

> The position of Pilate was not very unlike that of an English Lieutenant-Governor of the Punjab . . . Pilate, more or less closely associated with a native ruler, was answerable for the peace probably of the most dangerous and important province of the empire . . . It is surely impossible to contend seriously that it was his duty, or that it could be the duty of anyone in his position, to recognize in the person brought to his judgment seat, I do not say God Incarnate, but the teacher and preacher of a higher form of morals and a more enduring form of social order than that of which he was himself the representative. To a man in Pilate's position the morals and the social order which he represents are for all practical purposes final and absolute standards. If, in order to evade the obvious inference from this, it is said that Pilate ought to have respected the principle of religious liberty as propounded by Mr. Mill, the answer is that if he had done so he would have run the risk of setting the whole province in a blaze.[54]

The nineteenth-century mind did not blanch at the implications of legal positivism, of which Pilate of the famous question "What is truth?" was a notable early spokesman.

---

53. Cover, *Justice Accused: Antislavery and the Judicial Process* 1–6 (1975). But he is properly critical of the use of formalistic techniques of legal reasoning to mask the character of those laws. Id. at 229–238.

54. Stephen, *Liberty, Equality, Fraternity* 113–115 (R. J. White ed. 1967). Stephen's book was first published in 1873.

The affinity between Vere's mode of thinking and that of Oliver Wendell Holmes is underscored by Holmes's opinion in *Buck v. Bell* and its famous aphorism "three generations of imbeciles are enough."[55] A Virginia statute authorized the compulsory sterilization of inmates of certain state institutions if the inmate had a hereditary form of insanity or imbecility. Holmes's opinion describes Carrie Buck, an inmate of a state institution for the "feebleminded," as the feebleminded daughter of another feebleminded inmate of the institution and the mother of an illegitimate feebleminded child. In holding that neither the equal protection clause nor the due process clause of the Fourteenth Amendment forbade the state to sterilize Carrie Buck, Holmes wrote: "We have seen more than once that the public welfare may call upon the best citizens for their lives. It would be strange if it could not call upon those who already sap the strength of the State for these lesser sacrifices, often not felt to be such by those concerned, in order to prevent our being swamped with incompetence" (p. 207). This passage mixes nationalism (in the allusion to conscription, used by this country not only in World War I but also in the Civil War, in which Holmes had been wounded three times), Darwinism, and utilitarianism—"isms" that have in common putting aggregates (nation, species, society) ahead of individuals—in a brew congenial to Captain Vere, as to much nineteenth-century thought, but distasteful to most modern students of law as well as of literature. It may have been distasteful to Melville as well. But would he not have thought that the Virginia authorities, like Captain Vere, had made a *permissible* choice?

The examples of Vere and Holmes underline the difficulty of holding the two sides of the Table of Legal Antinomies apart. We have seen that Vere appealed to both. Holmes, in emphasizing objective standards of liability and therefore the justice of sometimes sacrificing innocents, and in his positivism, was very much a man of the left-hand column (rule, formalism, and so forth); but in his rejection of any general principle of strict liability and in his insistence that the life of the law had been experience rather than logic, he was very much a man of the right-hand column. Indeed, he is the father of legal realism.[56]

The least plausible feature in Weisberg's account of *Billy Budd,* the equating of Claggart to Christ, prepares us for his finding in *The Brothers Karamazov*

---

55. 274 U.S. 200, 207 (1927). See Chapter 8 for further discussion of this opinion; and note that, in all probability, none of the "three generations" involved in the case was actually feebleminded. See Paul A. Lombardo, "Three Generations, No Imbeciles: New Light on *Buck v. Bell,*" 60 *New York University Law Review* 30 (1985).

56. See in particular his article "The Path of the Law," 10 *Harvard Law Review* 457 (1897). Thomas, note 49 above, at 232–236, in arguing that Holmes's jurisprudence undercuts Vere's

(1880) a rejection, rather than, as previous readers thought, a celebration of Christianity. This great "legal" novel (about one-fifth of it is given over to the interrogation and trial of Dmitri Karamazov)[57] is really two novels, skillfully interwoven. The first is the melodramatic detective story of the rivalry between Dmitri and his father, Fyodor, for the beautiful Grushenka; Fyodor's murder by his valet, Smerdyakov, who probably is his illegitimate son; and the arrest, interrogation, erroneous conviction, and sentencing of Dmitri for the crime. The second is a philosophical novel, in which the principals are Ivan and Alyosha, Fyodor's other legitimate sons; Alyosha's mentor, Father Zossima; the boy Ilusha; and Ivan's fictional creation, the Grand Inquisitor. The philosophical novel is not only more interesting and resonant but, paradoxically, more vivid than, though it could not exist without the narrative scaffolding provided by, the melodrama. The dependence is mutual. Ivan's atheism and its corollary (as it seems to Dostoevsky) that "everything is lawful," operating on Smerdyakov's warped mind, makes the murder possible, while Dmitri's assault on Ilusha's father—one of the causes of Ilusha's tragic death—suggests that the conviction of Dmitri, though a judicial error, is consistent with a higher justice, is part of the divine plan, is indeed the condition of Dmitri's redemption.

The philosophical novel is a theodicy—an effort to reconcile the existence of God with the prevalence of suffering in the world, and in particular the suffering of children, that is, of innocents. Ivan's inability to resolve the issue to his satisfaction drives him to atheism and then madness. The suffering of children is rendered with great vividness, culminating in the story of Ilusha. Many other challenges are offered to religious belief as well, ranging from the premature decay of Father Zossima's corpse to the powerful arguments of the Grand Inquisitor. But all the challenges are overcome by the end of the book. We come to understand that the suffering, the baseness, the horrors, and the scandals of the human condition are both redeemable and redemptive. They are a necessary condition of a religious faith that is chosen rather than imposed. For example, the premature decay of Zossima's corpse, by shaking Alyosha's faith, enables him to rebuild it on a foundation of free choice rather than supernatural coercion.

---

position, overlooks the "hard" side of that jurisprudence—Social Darwinism, the separation of law and morals, the emphasis on sacrifice, and disdain for natural law. Although it would be a gross oversimplification to regard Holmes as the reincarnation of Thrasymachus (see Book I of Plato's *Republic*), there is that element in him.

57. On the characteristics of Russian legal procedure in Dostoevsky's time—including the use of juries (a Western import) at a time when they were fast disappearing from the rest of the Continent—see Samuel Kucherov, *Courts, Lawyers, and Trials under the Last Three Tsars* (1953), especially pp. 74–86, 168–179.

The legal scenes belong to what I am calling the melodrama—yet not entirely. Dmitri is innocent of his father's murder in a legal sense. But both he and Ivan are guilty in a moral sense: Dmitri for wanting to kill his father and for being, in fact, quite capable of doing so in the right circumstances, and, more profoundly, for being, as he frequently and truthfully confesses, a scoundrel; Ivan for having inspired, if unwittingly, Smerdyakov to commit the actual crime. And Dmitri's conviction and sentencing are presented as stations on the way to his salvation.

Another connection between the legal scenes and the philosophical novel is the idea expressed by several of the characters that if God does not exist, anything goes. To the possible response that law by itself suffices to deter crime, making supernatural sanctions unnecessary, the trial and conviction of Dmitri provide rebuttal. The wrong man is convicted, while the murderer escapes through suicide. Since Smerdyakov does not believe in God or an afterlife and his life is a miserable one, suicide provides what seems to him a costless escape. It also seals Dmitri's fate, by making it impossible for the real murderer ever to confess (as did happen in the real murder case on which Dostoevsky modeled Dmitri's case, ten years after the conviction of the innocent defendant). We are made to feel the inadequacies of secular justice.

Amidst the cruelty, the passion, and the tears that saturate the rest of the novel, the legal scenes stand out as islands of humane rationality. The atmosphere is entirely different from that of the legal scenes in *The Stranger*. It is true that the authorities, and even Dmitri's own lawyer, do not understand him.[58] And we are led to understand that the members of the jury are hostile to Dmitri because of his outrageous behavior on many occasions during his sojourn in the town where his father lived and the events of the novel take place. Yet in point of solicitude for the rights of the accused and for finding the truth, both the preliminary interrogation in the hotel where Dmitri is arrested and the trial can stand comparison with modern American procedure. The basic reason for Dmitri's conviction is not that the jury is prejudiced against him because of his wild behavior (though it is), but that the evidence of his guilt is overwhelming; Smerdyakov framed him brilliantly and then killed himself. Not only is the trial basically fair, though the verdict is mistaken, but Dmitri's sentence—twenty years of

58. The problem recurs in a modern "legal" story, Katherine Anne Porter's "Noon Wine," perceptively discussed in James Boyd White, *Heracles' Bow: Essays on the Rhetoric and Poetics of the Law* 181–191 (1985). Pursuing this theme, one might suggest that Vere's commitment to rational methods of inquiry (suggested by, among other things, his name, with its echo of "veritas" and "verity") prevents him from understanding Billy Budd. Melville's short story "Benito Cereno" has a similar theme. One begins to see how seemingly disparate works of literature on legal themes compose an order of literature, repaying study together.

penal servitude in Siberia—is lenient for a crime that the judges and jury believe to be parricide in the course of theft.

The parallels that *The Brothers Karamazov* enables us to see between nineteenth-century Russian and twentieth-century American criminal procedure are underscored by the contrast between that novel and *Crime and Punishment*. The first depicts adversary procedure, the second inquisitorial procedure. Oddly, considering all the suffering in it, *The Brothers Karamazov* is a sunnier, more exhilarating novel. This impression may be connected with the freer give-and-take, and the greater drama, of adversary procedure. The inquisitorial method of Continental and chancery proceedings lends itself to novels of protraction, constraint, and obsession. *Crime and Punishment* (like *The Trial* and *Bleak House*) is one of them, but *The Brothers Karamazov*, like *Pickwick Papers* (another novel in which a jury renders an erroneous verdict), is not.

The Brothers Karamazov implies criticism of law, but criticism that has less to do with the particulars of Russian criminal justice than with the very idea of secular justice. Not only does the legal system get the facts wrong; the elaborate reconstructions of Dmitri's character which dominate the closing arguments by the prosecutor and by the defense lawyer get his character wrong. To Dostoevsky, reconciliation of the goodness of God with the fact of human suffering lies neither in authority (the miracles, expected but not forthcoming, at Zossima's death) nor in reason (where Ivan searches futilely). It lies in faith, deepened by that very suffering and affording insight into the divine plan. *Credo quia absurdum est*. The idea that law, despite or maybe because of its commitment to reason, misunderstands life is one that *The Brothers Karamazov* shares with *The Stranger*.[59] But in the

---

59. We can hear the echo of this theme in E. M. Forster's novel *A Passage to India*. Dr. Aziz, an Indian, is tried for a sexual assault against a young Englishwoman during a visit to the mysterious Marabar Caves. The assault did not in fact occur, and Aziz is acquitted. The most interesting thing about the trial—a colonial trial, like that of Meursault, but with the conventional alignment of native with defendant and European with victim and prosecuting witness—is the sense of an unbridgeable gap between Western rationality and Eastern mysticism. In the trial scene, the gap in understanding and the foreshadowing of independence are expressed by such devices as the Indianization of Mrs. Moore's name and by the low-caste Indian who pulls the fan that cools the courtroom and who hasn't the slightest comprehension of the proceedings. The Indianization of the Englishwoman's name symbolizes the absorption and transformation of the British presence in India and Indian resistance to Westernization while the fan puller personifies the massive indifference of traditional India to the alien intrusion. The British with all their bustle and power haven't made a deep impression on the subcontinent after all. The fan puller doesn't even know that he's operating a fan; he just knows that he's pulling a rope. His ignorance of his causal efficacy is a commentary on Western rationalism, as is the court's inability to discover what happened in the Marabar Caves on the day of the alleged assault, and possibly on Indian subservience—the Indians do not know their power.

earlier novel the law's shortsightedness reflects the inherent limitations of human reason and argues for religious values, while in the later one it is equated with the bourgeoisie's persecution of free spirits.

Weisberg thinks Dmitri and even Alyosha were noble pagans brought down by resentful, wordy, legalistic Christians (pp. 54–81). This picture is unconvincing even for Dmitri, the victim of a miscarriage of justice. As Dmitri says of himself many times, and for good reason, he is a man of unbridled, frequently vicious passions, a spendthrift and sponge, who treats women dishonorably, assaults his father, nearly kills his father's loyal servant (Grigory), and causes great suffering by dragging Ilusha's father by his beard through the streets of the town, right in front of Ilusha. Far from being inarticulate, Dmitri quotes great swatches of Schiller. Far from being natural man, he appears at his trial dressed like a dandy.

The Brothers Karamazov is unmistakably a work of Christian literature, perhaps the greatest since the *Divine Comedy* and *Paradise Lost*. This is what throws Weisberg. The suffering of children, the rationalism of Ivan and of the lawyers, the stench from Father Zossima's corpse, the utilitarian arguments of the Grand Inquisitor, the erroneous conviction of Dmitri—this formidable array of challenges and alternatives to the Christian faith is vanquished by Christ's silent kiss bestowed on the Grand Inquisitor, by the fates of Smerdyakov and Ivan, by the luminous teachings and personality of Father Zossima, by the parable of the onion[60] and Dmitri's dream of the babe, by the goodness and purity of Alyosha, and above all by the sense that everything will come right in the end—that real punishment is reserved for those who choose wickedness with their eyes open, like the woman in the parable of the onion. Weisberg's suggestion that Ivan is a priestly figure and that at the end of the book Alyosha has become "garrulous," signifying the triumph of Christian *ressentiment* and "organic men-

---

60. "Once upon a time there was a peasant woman and a very wicked woman she was. And she died and did not leave a single good deed behind. The devils caught her and plunged her into the lake of fire. So her guardian angel stood and wondered what good deed of hers he could remember to tell to God: 'she once pulled up an onion in her garden,' said he, 'and gave it to a beggar woman.' And God answered: 'You take that onion then, hold it out to her in the lake, and let her take hold and be pulled out. And if you can pull her out of the lake, let her come to Paradise, but if the onion breaks, then the woman must stay where she is.' The angel ran to the woman and held out the onion to her; 'Come,' said he, 'catch hold and I'll pull you out.' And he began cautiously pulling her out. He had just pulled her right out, when the other sinners in the lake, seeing she was being drawn out, began catching hold of her so as to be pulled out with her. But she was a very wicked woman and she began kicking them. 'I'm to be pulled out, not you. It's my onion, not yours.' As soon as she said that, the onion broke. And the woman fell into the lake and she is burning there to this day. So the angel wept and went away." *The Brothers Karamazov* 330 (Constance Garnett and Ralph E. Matlaw trans., Matlaw ed. 1976).

dacity" (p. 81), is dotty. *The Brothers Karamazov* would fail as Christian apologetics if Dostoevsky had failed to give sin, temptation, and apostasy their due. By not failing he gives purchase to readers who would like to make him, as Blake and many since have tried with better reason to make Milton, of the devil's party.

Another great nineteenth-century novel that plays law off against religion, though one that has been spared Weisberg's attentions, is Alessandro Manzoni's novel *I Promesi Sposi (The Betrothed)*. The novel is set in northern Italy (mainly the Duchy of Milan, owned by Spain) in the early seventeenth century. It is a time and place of great political turmoil. Powerful nobles, deploying armed bands of *bravi*, flout the laws and terrorize the countryside. The governor issues edict after edict outlawing the *bravi* and making them subject to impressively harsh punishments. The edicts are ignored and the *bravi* and their patrons flourish. Renzo, a young peasant, is engaged to Lucia, whom one of the riotous nobles, Don Rodrigo, covets. The don sends his *bravi* to intimidate the village curate so that he will refuse to marry the couple. The attempt at intimidation succeeds. Naively believing that law is law and innocently carrying the latest edict against the *bravi* with him, Renzo goes for help to the local lawyer, who is nicknamed Dr. Quibbler (*Azzeccagargugli*—literally, "fastener of tangled threads"). Quibbler assumes that Renzo is a *bravo* who wants him to find a loophole in the edict, and sets about this task with a lawyer's enthusiasm for technicalities. (Laypeople believe this to be lawyers' only enthusiasm.) When Quibbler discovers that Renzo wants help in enforcing the edict against Don Rodrigo and his gang, he is horrified and throws Renzo out of his office. The lawless nobles, including Don Rodrigo, have hired the lawyer to defeat the governor's pathetic edicts: Quibbler will not turn against a patron.

The picture is thus of a legal system entirely ineffectual despite its good intentions, in part because the legal profession is craven. But vengeance is not an option for Renzo. So how, if at all, is mankind's powerful impulse for justice to be expressed? An implied answer is offered by a change in emphasis, as in *The Brothers Karamazov*, from the defeat of law at the beginning of the novel to the triumph of religion in the middle and end. Driven from his village when his attempt to trick the curate into performing a marriage ceremony fails, Renzo eventually finds himself in Milan during a gruesome outbreak of plague. He survives, as does Lucia, who had escaped to Milan after being kidnapped by Don Rodrigo, and returns home to find Don Rodrigo dying of the plague. The curate's fear lifts. Renzo and Lucia are finally married.

The key figures who ward off disaster to the young couple and engineer the happy ending are two heroic clerics, Father Cristoforo and Cardinal

Borromeo. The Cardinal (a real historical figure) is also instrumental in mitigating the horrors of the plague. The sense conveyed is that religious faith enables dreadful conditions—plague and anarchy—to be, if not overcome, at least borne. Positive law may be hopeless. But a divinely sponsored natural law remains in the picture, at least as a criterion for evaluating positive law. And sometimes natural law is vindicated, against all odds.

Literature and the Holocaust

Weisberg's culminating thesis is that the kind of attitudes which he finds in the examining magistrates in *Crime and Punishment* and *The Stranger,* the lawyers in *The Brothers Karamazov,* and Captain Vere in *Billy Budd* pave the way for Hitler's effort to exterminate the Jews. This thesis rests not only on the very peculiar idea that punishing murderers and other criminals encourages Nazism, but also on the only slightly more plausible idea that the spiritual distance between Nietzsche and Nazism is greater than that between Christianity and Nazism; that Nietzsche, the anti-Christian, is the better anti-Nazi. It is true that the roots of European anti-Semitism are Christian; that conformity and submission played an important role in Nazism; that there was collaboration between organized Christianity and the fascist regimes; and that many individual Nazis appear to have been consumed by *ressentiment.*[61] Goebbels, for example, with his club foot, small stature, and warped intellectuality, could have been cast as Nietzsche's archetypal resentful man. But the Nietzschean celebration of barbarism and condemnation of Judeo-Christian values as worthy only of slaves were vital elements of National Socialist idealogy; Judeo-Christian values have nothing in common with that ideology, despite the instances of collaboration between institutional Christianity and fascism, a collaboration exaggeratedly described by Weisberg as "the participation of all Christian institutions in an unthinkable victimization of innocents" (pp. 69–70).

Perhaps because Weisberg associates *ressentiment* and anti-Semitism with forces neither admired by nor influential with Nazis, such as Christianity and legality, he is led to condemn French anti-Semitism more strongly than German. "France reveled in the racial possibilities brought onto its territory by the foreign conquerors . . . Western egalitarianism and liberality embraced racial ostracism and ultimate genocide more effusively than had the still seemingly neobarbarous and deeply romantic Germanic states" (p. 2). There was indeed a great deal of anti-Semitism in France before and

---

61. On the role of Christianity in the rise of Nazism, see George L. Mosse, *Toward the Final Solution: A History of European Racism,* ch. 9 (1985).

during World War II. But the proposition that France would have tried on its own, as it were, to exterminate the Jews, or that it embraced genocide more enthusiastically than Germany did, cannot be taken any more seriously than such other paradoxes asserted or implied in *The Failure of the Word* as that Nazism was the product of too much head and too little heart (p. 138), that *Mein Kampf* is in the line of descent from the Sermon on the Mount, and that people who investigate and punish murders are morally equivalent—even morally inferior—to murderers. Although Weisberg has presented evidence that the Vichy French racial laws were indeed more severe, and were interpreted more strictly, than the Nazi laws,[62] survival statistics refute his contention that France outdid Germany in viciousness toward the Jews. Even though France surrendered to Germany in the second year of the war and was not liberated until four years later, three-fourths of the Jews in France (many of them refugees from Nazism rather than French nationals) survived the war. The Vichy government, while anti-Semitic, tried to protect French Jews from the Nazis and to dissociate itself from the "Final Solution."[63]

Let us take a look at French lawyer Joseph Haennig, an article by whom "leaves us gasping" (p. 7). Entitled "What Means of Proof Can the Jew of Mixed Blood Offer to Establish His Nonaffiliation with the Jewish Race?" it argues that the decision of a court in Leipzig may provide guidance to interpreting Vichy's racial laws, which had been modeled on the Nuremberg laws.[64] Haennig obsequiously commends the court for "a largeness and objectivity of spirit" (p. 181) in allowing a Jewish woman of mixed blood to prove nonaffiliation with the Jewish "race" without having to show affiliation with a Christian denomination. He notes that "the Court affirmed the lower court judge's view that she had only attended

---

62. *Vichy Law and the Holocaust in France,* note 34 above.

63. See Michael R. Marrus and Robert O. Paxton, *Vichy France and the Jews* 361–362, 371 (1981); also W. D. Halls, *Politics, Society and Christianity in Vichy France* 143 (1995). Halls points out that many Christians helped Jews. Id., pt. 3. On Vichy and its racial policies, see also Tony Judt, "France without Glory," *New York Review of Books,* May 23, 1996, p. 39. Weisberg accepts the figure given by Marrus and Paxton and by Halls for the number of Jews in France who fell victim to the Holocaust: 75,000. *Vichy Law and the Holocaust in France,* note 34 above, at xiv. (This figure is only about 1.5 percent of the likely number of Holocaust victims.) Weisberg attributes the rigor of Vichy's anti-Semitic policies to French Catholicism. "Where there is a Joan of Arc, there must be an enemy; where there is Catholic suffering and the need to blame it on someone else, Jews will often suffer physical torment while Christians privately (and with far less actual discomfort) undergo spiritual Calvary." Id. at 145. I don't follow his reasoning.

64. There is more to the article (which may be found, in the original French, in 1943.1 *Gazette du Palais,* Doctrine 31), but that is the main part and the only one Weisberg translates (pp. 181–182). He repeats his discussion of Haennig, with immaterial changes, in *Vichy Law and the Holocaust in France,* note 34 above, at 77–81.

[Jewish] New Year's services in order to preserve family peace. The view that there was no sufficient tie to the Jewish community in the case was thus deemed correct." He concludes that the court's "analysis indicates a possible route, without risk of distorting the statute writers' intention, and in conformity with the principles which underlie the racial statutes and cases" (p. 182).

Is this the work of a man whose behavior raises questions described by Weisberg (p. 1) as "more potentially catastrophic in their resolution than those posed by the leaders of European repression and racism"?[65] Without knowing anything about Haennig except what Weisberg tells us—that he was a lawyer in German-occupied Paris and (rather inconsistently in light of Weisberg's summary characterization of him) that he "was clearly not a villain" and "earlier in the Occupation . . . had defended a Jew who was facing incarceration and death for a 'political' crime" (p. 1)—I can't accept Weisberg's verdict.[66] Although the article contains no hint of disapproval of the racial laws, it probably would not have been published if it had. It does not praise the laws. The only thing praised is a German decision that saved a woman who was half-Jewish from the gas chamber. The article may have saved some French half-Jews. Indeed, it may have saved more lives than if Haennig had thrown up his law practice and joined the Resistance, for which he may have been neither physically nor emotionally suited (how old was he?). Maybe he thought the racial laws grotesque but knew it would not help to let his feelings show in the article. What would Weisberg have had Haennig *do?* No doubt if most Frenchmen had refused to collaborate with the Nazis the Jews would have been better off than they were receiving small crumbs of assistance from the likes of Haennig. But the problem with mass defiance—a classic Prisoner's Dilemma problem—is, who shall step forward first?

Weisberg's treatment of Haennig, a man who under difficult circumstances did *something* for the Jews, even if not a great deal, illustrates the very *ressentiment* that Weisberg denounces, as does his hectoring prosecution of both Vere and Haennig in the dock of history and his lack of sympathy for people like Vere who are called upon to exercise power, and make painful choices, in defense of social order. Melville put it well in *Billy Budd* (p. 114): "Little ween the snug card players in the cabin of the responsibilities of the sleepless man on the bridge."

65. "Lawyers like Haennig, more than those few who relished the infliction of suffering upon the Jews, made that suffering possible." Id. at 80.

66. I have tried without success to find out more about Haennig.

SIX

Two Legal Perspectives on Kafka

The most influential movement in legal scholarship since legal realism petered out during World War II has been the "law and economics" movement. Proceeding on the assumption that human beings are rational (in a sense that will become clearer as this chapter unfolds) in every department of social life and not just when trading in markets, economic analysts of law have sought to explain the law as a system for shaping rational behavior in both marketplace and nonmarket settings. Every field of law, every legal institution, every practice or custom of lawyers, judges, and legislators, present or past—even ancient—is grist for the economic analyst's mill. The criminal, the prosecutor, the accident victim, the adulterer, the soapbox orator, the religious zealot, the con man, the monopolist, the arbitrator, the union organizer—all are modeled as "economic man." Economic analysis of law is critical as well as descriptive. It brims over with proposals for reforming the institutions of the law to make them more efficient, with "efficiency" defined in cost-benefit terms.

The movement is controversial. It challenges many assumptions that lawyers have held about their field. It challenges the very autonomy of law—the idea of law as a self-contained discipline that can be practiced without systematic study of any other field. It asks lawyers to learn an alien and difficult set of concepts. It rests or seems to rest on assumptions about human nature that many people, especially people trained in the humanities, find disturbing, even repulsive. It aspires to be scientific, not humanistic. It even uses math. And it is the flagship of the application of social science to law, while law and literature is the most humanistic field of legal studies. A collision was inevitable, though I hope to convince the reader by the end of this book that a proper understanding of the two movements dissolves the conflict.

On Reading Kafka Politically

Robin West uses Kafka's fiction to criticize the model of human behavior employed in economic analysis of law.[1] Her target is a principle basic to classical liberalism as well as to the law and economics movement: government should not interfere with voluntary transactions that impose no uncompensated costs on third parties—"Pareto-superior" transactions, as economists say. Which is not to say that every consensual transaction between informed and competent adults that has no uncompensated third-party effects is beyond ethical reproach; the purpose of the Pareto concept, when conceived as a principle of political philosophy, is to define the proper role of the state rather than to guide personal choice.

Mill and other classical liberals went further, arguing that some transactions and activities that are not Pareto-superior should be insulated from governmental control by an independent concept of liberty.[2] And some economic analysts of law believe that transactions which raise the aggregate wealth of society are entitled to respect even if there are uncompensated losers. I shall not dwell much on these extensions beyond the Pareto principle, since voluntary transactions are quite bad enough in West's view even if everyone affected by them is fully compensated. This is because she believes that our choices very often, perhaps typically, make us miserable—a belief that she grounds in Kafka's fiction.

West's enterprise may look passing strange. But Richard Weisberg, another "literary lawyer," found political significance in Dostoevsky, Melville, and Camus; and so enigmatic a writer as Kafka could easily be thought a political writer. Easily, but erroneously. For Kafka is not a topical writer like Zola or Dreiser, or a writer of political allegories like Swift or Orwell. Even though he was a lawyer, worked most of his adult life for an insurance institute, and borrowed scenes, symbols, and vocabulary from law and business, his fiction belongs primarily to the literature of private feeling. West reads Kafka so literally that the incidents and metaphors from

1. West, "Authority, Autonomy, and Choice: The Role of Consent in the Moral and Political Visions of Franz Kafka and Richard Posner," 99 *Harvard Law Review* 384 (1985) (reprinted as chapter 1 of her book *Narrative, Authority, and Law* [1993]). My page references to West in the text are to this article. See also West, "Submission, Choice and Ethics: A Rejoinder to Judge Posner," 99 *Harvard Law Review* 1449 (1986) (reprinted as chapter 2 of her book). She cites none of the extensive scholarly literature that questions the adequacy of the rational-choice model. See, for example, Jon Elster, *Sour Grapes: Studies in the Subversion of Rationality* (1983); Richard H. Thaler, *Quasi Rational Economics* (1991); Amartya Sen, "Rational Fools: A Critique of the Behavioural Foundations of Economic Theory," in Sen, *Choice, Welfare and Measurement* 84 (1982).

2. On illiberal Paretianism, see Amartya Sen, "The Impossibility of a Paretian Liberal," 78 *Journal of Political Economy* 152 (1970).

business and law in his fiction become its meaning. It is like reading *Animal Farm* as a tract on farm management or *Moby-Dick* as an exposé of the whaling industry. Kafka's fiction is not *really* a series of disquisitions on people who starve themselves for a living, sons who commit suicide at their father's direction, traveling salesmen who are fired because they have turned into giant insects, denials of due process, delay in court, torturers who kill themselves on their torture machine (which goes crazy in the process), singing mice, talking apes, introspective dogs, and famous horses who practice law.

Of "A Hunger Artist" West writes: "Kafka's hunger artist is the ultimate Posnerian entrepreneur, and the artist's audience consists of Posnerian consumers" (p. 393). This is an eccentric reading, mistaking Kafka for a lecturer at the Harvard Business School. The hunger artist is tormented not by commercial failure but by his inability to convince an indifferent world of his artistic integrity, inability to explain oneself being a recurrent theme of Kafka's fiction; people think he sneaks food on the side.[3] Eventually the hunger artist's spirit is so crushed that he either pretends or comes to believe that he fasted not because of the challenge but because he was too fastidious to eat. He dies, is buried unceremoniously together with the straw in his cage, and is replaced by a panther, which has no interior life; his fate links Kafka to Nietzsche, and "A Hunger Artist" to Thomas Mann's "Tonio Kröger," in the literature of intellectuals' self-hatred, their envy of the unreflective life of normal people. "A Hunger Artist" may also be about the world's indifference to Kafka's own artistic scruples, but only at the most superficial, most literal level is it about the pitfalls of entrepreneurship and the fickleness of consumers.

West quotes a passage from *The Trial* about Joseph K.'s rivalry with the Assistant Manager of the bank to show that "although K. suffers no physical abuse on the job, he is humiliated and dehumanized, not enriched, by his white-collar employment as Chief Clerk in a bank" (p. 396). Actually the passage merely reflects the standing rivalry between K. and the Assistant Manager[4]—in which K. gives as good as he gets. K. is not ground down by his job. He is a big shot at work; that

---

3. Mark Anderson, *Kafka's Clothes* 175 (1992), quoting Margot Norris, points out that in both "A Hunger Artist" and "In the Penal Colony" "a fanatical believer in meaningful suffering reenacts a spectacle that in an earlier age drew huge festive crowds but now results only in sordid death and burial."

4. The Muirs' translation is misleading. The "Assistant Manager" is the second in command at the bank (literally "deputy director"). Similarly, K. is an important executive, not a "clerk" in the American sense.

is one of the ironies of his situation. The passage shows not that K. is alienated from his work but how distracted he is by the mysterious "judicial" proceeding in which he has become enmeshed. *The Trial* is a novel about obsession.

A few sentences that West elides will make my point: "He [K.] glanced up slightly, but only slightly, when the door of the Manager's room opened, [and] disclosed the Assistant Manager, a blurred figure who looked as if veiled in some kind of gauze. K. did not seek for the cause of this apparition, but merely registered its immediate effect, which was very welcome to him. For the manufacturer at once bounded from his chair and rushed over to the Assistant Manager, though K. could have wished him to be ten times quicker, since he was afraid the apparition might vanish again."[5] Far from being "humiliated and dehumanized," K. welcomes the Assistant Manager's interruption. He wants to be rid of the manufacturer so that he can be free to think about the trial.

"The Metamorphosis" is Kafka's best-known story. Gregor Samsa, who lives with his parents and sister, wakes up one morning to find that he has turned into a giant insect, something like a beetle—hard back, many legs. Within this grotesque frame Gregor is initially unchanged. He thinks and speaks as always, only no one can understand what he says; he sounds like an insect. The family, particularly Gregor's father, reacts to his transformation with disgust. At first the family more or less puts up with Gregor, though at one point his mother has to intervene to prevent his father from killing him. But when Gregor's untimely appearance in the living room to hear his sister play the violin alerts the lodgers to his existence and they give notice, the family locks him up in his room. In the usual passive style of Kafka's protagonists (recall the execution of Joseph K. in the last chapter of *The Trial*), Gregor—dutiful, considerate, docile, and devoted to his parents and sister, all of whom indeed he had been supporting before he lost his job—accepts their unfeeling treatment of him and dies unshaken in his love for them. Relieved by his death, they make all sorts of new plans and celebrate with a train ride to the country. "And it was like a confirmation of their new dreams and excellent intentions that at the end of their journey

---

5. Franz Kafka, *The Trial* 163–164 (Willa and Edwin Muir trans., definitive ed. 1960). See also id. at 165. Kafka apparently did not think his own job humiliating or dehumanizing, though he did consider it a distraction from his primary interest, which was writing. Like Stevens and Eliot (and Joseph K.!), Kafka was not a rebel or a Bohemian, but a successful executive diligent in his work, highly regarded and well liked by his superiors and associates. Frederick R. Karl, *Franz Kafka: Representative Man* 221–224 (1991); Ernst Pawel, *The Nightmare of Reason: A Life of Franz Kafka* 188 (1984).

their daughter sprang to her feet first and stretched her young body" (p. 139).[6]

West does not discuss "The Metamorphosis," and this is odd, because it furnishes stronger evidence than any work she does discuss for thinking that Kafka's fiction is indeed about capitalist alienation.[7] Gregor is literally de-humanized—and could it not be by his work? And think of the grotesque scene in which, in a futile effort to save his job, he crawls toward the chief clerk of his firm while delivering an intricate but completely unintelligible apology for being late to work. Gregor's transformation, which renders him unemployable, has elements of a deliverance for him as well as for his family. They had lived parasitically on his earnings; he had been in the thrall of clock time; only after his transformation is he awakened to the beauty of music. But white-collar wage slavery is not at the heart of the story, which, like "A Hunger Artist" and "In the Penal Colony," drama-tizes the difficulty of communicating with other people (recall from Chapter 4 the inarticulateness of the stoker in Kafka's story of that name) and, a closely related point, the gap between how we perceive ourselves and how others perceive us. Gregor accepts notionally the fact that he is an embarrassment to his family, and he does not resist being locked up. Indeed, he expires by a kind of inanition brought on by awareness that he has become a burden to the family. But he cannot see himself through their eyes, and in his heart of hearts cannot accept his altered appearance.

We all have Gregor's problem, though in less acute forms. We cannot make our aspirations fully understood, or quite bring our self-conception into phase with the conception that others have of us. And looking at Gregor from the other side, his family's side, we can never completely pen-etrate the externals and enter the interior life of another person. Life goes on—the awakening love life of Gregor's sister, the life of the carnival man-agers and customers in "A Hunger Artist" and of the passersby in "The Judgment"—with complete, with shocking indifference to the inner life of

---

6. My page references to Kafka's stories are to Franz Kafka, *The Complete Stories* (Nahum N. Glatzer ed. 1971). The translations of the stories I discuss are all by the Muirs, with the excep-tion of "The Refusal," translated by Tania and James Stern.

7. See Robert Currie, *Genius: An Ideology in Literature* 143–150 (1974); also Blume Goldstein, "Bachelors and Work: Social and Economic Conditions in 'The Judgment', 'The Metamorphosis,' and 'The Trial,'" in *The Kafka Debates: New Perspectives for Our Time* 147, 156 (Angel Flores ed. 1977). Another work not discussed by West—*Amerika,* Kafka's unfinished novel (all his novels were unfinished) about a young European immigrant to the United States—is Kafka's most sustained exploration of business and labor, for it is about how Karl, the protag-onist, searches for, and finds, work. Still, it is not easy to find in it the theme of capitalist alien-ation, although Robert Alter argues that "the America of the novel . . . is at once the Promised Land and the house of bondage." Alter, *The Pleasures of Reading in an Ideological Age* 122 (1996).

a fellow human being. The other characters in "The Metamorphosis"— the members of Gregor's family, the charwoman, the clerk, and the lodgers—are all depicted not just as ordinary people but more particularly as nonneurotic people, defined (and faintly derided), but envied withal, as people without an interior, like the panther in "A Hunger Artist," and set over against the neurotic with his rich, tormented, and despairing inner life, of which Gregor's grotesque outward form is the projection. The healthy and beautiful, Nietzsche's masters or blond beasts, do not think. Thinking is the mode by which weaklings, natural slaves—those who believe themselves good because they have no claws—express their will to power.[8]

In another great story of Kafka's, "The Judgment," Georg, a young merchant who works for his father, feels guilt (only slightly tinged with *Schadenfreude*) about an unnamed friend who years earlier had gone abroad in pursuit of business opportunities that have not turned out well. Finally deciding to invite the friend to his wedding despite concern that the friend might be made envious by the invitation, Georg is suddenly, gratuitously accused by his vicious, loony father of having played the friend false all these years. Here is the father talking:

> "And now that you thought you'd got him down, so far down that you could set your bottom on him and sit on him and he wouldn't move, then my fine son makes up his mind to get married!" . . .
>
> "Because she lifted up her skirts," his father began to flute, "because she lifted up her skirts like this, the nasty creature . . . because she lifted her skirts like this and this you made up to her, and in order to make free with her undisturbed you have disgraced you mother's memory, betrayed your friend, and stuck your father into bed so that he can't move. But he can move, or can't he?"
>
> And he stood up quite unsupported and kicked his legs out. His insight made him radiant. (p. 85)

Eventually father—who is still standing upright on the bed, with one hand on the ceiling to steady himself—says to son, "I sentence you now to death by drowning!" Georg, "the crash with which his father fell on the bed behind him . . . still in his ears," rushes out and drowns himself. As he leaps from the bridge, he "called in a low voice: 'Dear parents, I have always loved you, all the same,' and let himself drop. At this moment an unending stream of traffic was just going over the bridge" (pp. 87–88). That is the end of the story.

Because Georg's friend, a brooding presence in the story, is an unsuc-

8. Friedrich Nietzsche, *Thus Spoke Zarathustra: A Book for All and None* 199 (pt. II) (Walter Kaufmann trans. 1966).

cessful businessman, West conceives the story to be about capitalism. She is led to argue, with considerable perversity, that Georg kills himself because of guilt over "his own self-imposed alienation from [his friend's] suffering" (p. 410; see also p. 411). Thus she takes the father's side in the story. There is no textual support for her interpretation. If the story is not about the Oedipus complex, Kafka's relationship with his own father, how adults appear to sensitive children, or why Kafka did not marry,[9] then it is about the sense of guilt, about the disproportion between cause and effect, about the surreal, about life's unfairness, about how people tend to accept the valuation placed on them by other people, about the dislocated feeling of modern life to highly sensitive souls, about the indifference of others to our inner turmoil—not only the passersby on the bridge but Georg's friend, who apparently knows nothing of Georg's attempts to avoid distressing him with reminders of his business failure. The story can even be regarded as a sketch for *The Trial* (which was written later) and thus pulled directly into the law and literature fold. Though indicted, convicted, and sentenced to death (*Das Urteil*—the title of the story—means "the judgment" in the sense of a legal decision or sentence), Georg, like Joseph K. in *The Trial*, is guilty of no crime; nor can he get the "tribunal" to listen to him. Notice, finally, the ironic twist that the story gives to the theme of the judge called upon to condemn his son.

Although business transactions figure in Kafka's fiction, they are far from its center. The penal colony's torture machine is not a capitalist plot; nor is K.'s arrest on unspecified charges. Kafka does not appear to have been a romantic who believed that people would be happy if only they could escape the clutches of the market and other social institutions, though there may be a hint of this in "The Metamorphosis," and one strand of romantic thought—the loneliness of genius, the alienation of the artist from the herd—is prominent in "A Hunger Artist." A mind preoccupied with politics can easily "find" political meaning in Kafka's fiction, overriding the feeble opposition put up by such enigmatic texts. But the more idiosyncratic an interpretation, the less authority it can draw from the author. If Kafka reminds Robin West of how much she dislikes capitalism and thereby stimulates her to critical reflections about it, that is fine, but she shouldn't wrap her criticisms in the mantle of Kafka's prestige.

---

9. In this interpretation Kafka's worldly self, symbolized by Georg, who was engaged (as Kafka was several times to be), dies so that Georg's friend (who stands for Kafka's writing self) can be redeemed from failure and exile. See Ronald Gray, *Franz Kafka* 61–65 (1973). Cf. Kurt Fickert, "Kafka's Addenda to 'In der Strafkolonie,'" 22 *University of Dayton Review* 115 (1993). I am not myself drawn to biographical interpretations of literature, for reasons explained in the next chapter.

I do not claim that great literature can never be trolled for social relevance. When the Duke of Venice asks Shylock why he would rather have a pound of worthless flesh than a large sum of money, Shylock answers with a commonplace of liberal theory—the subjectivity of value. He explains that value is determined by willingness to pay, which is a function of the preferences and resources of each individual, rather than by some external, objective, or governmental determination of merit or desert (IV.1.42–59):

> . . . I'll not answer that,
> But, say, it is my humor. Is it answered?
> What if my house be troubled with a rat
> And I be pleased to give ten thousand ducats
> To have it baned? What, are you answered yet?
> Some men there are love not a gaping pig,
> Some that are mad if they behold a cat . . .
> As there is no firm reason to be rendered
> Why he cannot abide a gaping pig,
> Why he a harmless necessary cat, . . .
> So can I give no reason, nor I will not.

Shylock further defends his position by reference to freedom of contract and the rule of law, and implies that the rejection of his claim for the pound of flesh would be redistributive, socialist (IV.1.90–102):

> You have among you many a purchased slave,
> Which, like your asses and your dogs and mules,
> You use in abject and in slavish parts,
> Because you bought them. Shall I say to you,
> "Let them be free, marry them to your heirs!
> Why sweat they under burdens? Let their beds
> Be made as soft as yours . . ." So do I answer you:
> The pound of flesh which I demand of him
> Is dearly bought, is mine, and I will have it.
> If you deny me, fie upon your law!
> There is no force in the decrees of Venice.

The audience is not expected to take Shylock's part in this debate! There are plenty of distinguished places in literature to find criticisms of bourgeois values, but Kafka's fiction is not one of them.

In Defense of Classical Liberalism

For the sake of argument, though, I shall now assume with Robin West that Kafka's works should be read literally as tracts on entrepreneurship, suicide, and so on. When read so, what do they tell us about bourgeois values and the legal order based on them? Nothing. Kafka's works are not realistic in the style of the nineteenth-century social novel; read literally, they provide as much insight into modern American life as would Dracula or "The Cask of Amontillado." (Or would West think Count Dracula a symbol of blood-sucking capitalism?) Maybe, though, her point is an ironic one—that economists have so unrealistic a conception of human nature (a common view) that even the literal Kafka, the Kafka who is "Kafkaesque," is more realistic than an economist. Even Kafka's strangest characters—the officer of "In the Penal Colony," for example—have a more recognizably human personality than a calculating machine. Indeed, such a tour de force is "In the Penal Colony" that a torturer becomes emblematic of suffering humanity.

It is true that most thieves, spouses, litigants, pedestrians, trespassers, rescuers, and other nonmarket actors encountered in the economic analysis of law do not consciously engage in cost-benefit analysis. But neither do most consumers consciously maximize consumer surplus or most businessmen consciously equate marginal revenue to marginal cost. Rational choice in economics does not mean self-consciously economic choice, or even conscious choice, let alone the articulation of choice in the language of economics, a language of scholarship rather than of everyday life, commercial or otherwise. The concern of economics is not with states of mind but with what people do.

But forget all this and assume that West's Kafka has presented a gallery of examples of real people transacting. We are now far from any meaningful engagement with Kafka's fiction, which she is treating as muckraking journalism. This is reductionism with a vengeance, but it is West's method, and let us see where it leads.

She groups all her illustrations together under the rubric of voluntary transactions that make people worse off, thereby obscuring the morally dissimilar ways in which an ostensibly voluntary transaction can disappoint one or both of the parties. Some of her transactions illustrate market failure, and so are not really voluntary, while others really are voluntary and increase happiness ex ante (before the fact) but turn out badly because of people's inability to predict and control the future. Others are completely unproblematic.

In the first group are West's own fictional creation—a bulimic tomato consumer[10]—and the hunger artist, who, on the literal plane to which

10. Who "on a daily basis...buys twelve tomatoes, eats five plates of spaghetti, and regurgitates it all, thus destroying her digestive tract" (p. 401). The purpose of this example is to show that even the simplest consumer transaction is fraught with potential disaster.

West confines Kafka, is anorectic. (Dying, the hunger artist had said, "I have to fast, I can't help it . . . I couldn't find the food I liked." P. 277.) Bulimia and anorexia are mental illnesses, and a mentally ill person cannot be expected to make the eating choices that will maximize his satisfactions; nor can a person who would commit suicide because his father said to him, "I sentence you now to death by drowning!" be expected to act rationally. But let us not be too quick to pronounce people who make weird and even self-destructive choices insane. The impersonality of market transactions protects privacy and freedom; West does not have to undergo a psychiatric examination before she can buy a tomato.

The market does not always work as well as we would like it to, even when consumers are competent. An example is when a woman is subjected to the sexual advances of a man who has power over her husband's career. Actually West has misunderstood the encounter in *The Trial* between K. and the woman washing clothes, from which this example is drawn. They are talking when the woman sees a law student who we are told may someday be a big shot. She goes over to the student. He begins kissing her. K. intervenes, but the student picks the woman up bodily and makes off with her. K. then attacks him but the woman tells K. to stop because the student is only obeying the orders of the Examining Magistrate. The student, puffing with fatigue, carries her up a stairway in the court's tenement. "The woman waved her hand to K. as he stood below, and shrugged her shoulders to suggest that she was not to blame for this abduction, but very little regret could be read into that dumb show . . . He was forced to the conclusion that the woman not only had betrayed him, but also had lied in saying that she was being carried to the Examining Magistrate. The Examining Magistrate surely could not be sitting waiting in a garret."[11] This is not, as West believes, a depiction of the exploitation of women. K. would *like* to believe that in yielding to the law student the woman is acting under compulsion, but gradually he realizes that this isn't true, that she and the student are playing with him. K., not the woman's husband, is the victim in this episode. Almost all the compulsion in *The Trial* is inside K.'s head.

West interprets the whipping scene in the novel as a commentary on employment relations. This interpretation strikes me as humorless and obtuse. (The points are related. Kafka is a humorous writer, though his sense of humor is morbid.) K. opens the door to a storage room in his bank and discovers the officers who had arrested him being whipped for having

---

11. Kafka, note 5 above, at 74.

stolen his underwear during the arrest.[12] The location, pretext, whipper's garb, and reaction by K. convey the impression of a sadomasochistic dream, which might be considered a microcosm of the entire novel. The employment context—the officers are being whipped on the orders of their superiors—is incidental.[13] It would be ridiculous to make the scene a basis for formulating public policy in the workplace.

Suppose, coming back to the incident between the law student and the washerwoman, that Kafka *was* trying to depict sexual harassment by supervisory employees. Such harassment (whether of a female worker or, as in *The Trial*, of a male worker's wife) is not, as West appears to believe, economically efficient and so proof of the Pareto principle's moral inadequacy. Sexual harassment by superiors of subordinates is a market failure caused by what economists call "agency costs." It is a form of extortion, which is nonconsensual, and it is inefficient because it reduces the output of both worker and supervisor and forces the employer to pay higher wages to workers to compensate them for the unpleasantness of the workplace, much as employers are forced to do when the workplace carries a risk of illness or injury.[14] Could the employer offset those additional costs by paying the supervisors less, on the theory that he has given them a valuable license to harass female workers? In other words, might the benefits to the harassers exceed the costs to the victims? It is unlikely. Sexual harassment, in our society anyway—but it is our society rather than Austro-Hungarian society that West is interested in—is generally a minor and guilty pleasure to the harasser but a source of anguish and indignation to the harassed. Because of the disparity between the pleasure and the pain and also because there are fewer supervisors than workers and most of them do not want to harass their subordinates sexually, cutting supervisors' pay is unlikely to compensate the employer fully for the higher wages he must pay his female employees to compensate them for the risk of harassment, and for the reduction in the productivity of those supervisors and workers who spend their time respectively making and fending off (or yielding to) sexual ad-

---

12. Id. at 6, 103–106.

13. For good discussions see Gray, note 9 above, 112–113; Henry Sussman, "The Court as Text: Inversion, Supplanting, and Derangement in Kafka's *Der Prozess*," 92 *Publications of the Modern Language Association* 41, 43 (1977).

14. That workers demand and receive wage premiums for assuming risks of physical injury or death is well documented. See, for example, Richard Thaler and Sherwin Rosen, "The Value of Saving a Life: Evidence from the Labor Market," in *Household Production and Consumption* 265 (Nestor E. Terleckyj ed. 1976); W. Kip Viscusi, *Risk by Choice: Regulating Health and Safety in the Workplace*, ch. 3 (1983); Jean-Michel Cousineau, Robert Lacroix, and Anne-Marie Girard, "Occupational Hazard and Compensating Wage Differentials," 74 *Review of Economics and Statistics* 166 (1992).

vances rather than working. Furthermore, if sexual harassment is common, women who are less sensitive or more compliant will have a competitive advantage; they will be slower to quit and quicker to be promoted. There is no reason to think they will be the better workers, so there will be an inefficient sorting of workers to jobs, just as when promotions are based on nepotism rather than merit.

The fact that sexual harassment is inefficient does not mean that competition and the profit motive will eliminate it without any assistance from law. The costs of detecting and proving it are high, and anyway not every potential efficiency is achieved in every market. Most business managers are male, and they may not evaluate issues of sexual harassment as clear-sightedly as a genderless robot would—although those who do will have lower costs than their competitors and may gradually supplant them. Probably the main reason why sexual harassment persists in the workplace, despite its doubly nonconsensual nature—being involuntary on the woman's part (as the word "harassment" connotes) and a source of incompletely compensated costs to the employer—is that it is often difficult to distinguish in practice from ordinary flirtations between coworkers. The costs to the employer of distinguishing between these externally similar behaviors may exceed the benefits in lower wages and greater productivity. The need to make distinctions could be eliminated by the employer's banning all fraternization in the workplace, but this would significantly increase the costs of sexual and marital search.

This analysis does not show that sexual harassment is either a voluntary practice (that is, one that is consented to) or a value-maximizing one. It is neither; it is a market abuse. Stealing from one's employer is not a voluntary or wealth-maximizing transaction even if the employer is unable to prevent it.

A further peculiarity of West's treatment of sexual harassment is her associating it with capitalism, rather than with authority generally. There is no basis for thinking that there is more sexual harassment in private profit-maximizing companies than in the armed forces, other government agencies, or nonprofit institutions. If anything, one expects the least amount of harassment (other things being equal) in profit-maximizing firms in highly competitive environments, for these are the employers who are under the most pressure to eliminate inefficient practices within their enterprise.

West says that "most of what happens to Kafka's fictional characters is fully consensual" (p. 390). This statement not only ignores what happens to Gregor when he is changed into a bug and to Joseph K. when he is arrested, but also ascribes meaningful consent to decisions made under the influence of a mental disease or extorted. Among the "fully consensual" transactions listed in the conclusion to West's article (p. 427), many are not consensual at all, and it is unclear whether the others are consensual because the reader is not told whether there is compensation. By definition, a woman does not consent to forcible rape, but whether a worker consents to working in a dangerous environment depends on whether he is paid to do so or tricked into doing so (the dangers may be concealed). The economic analysis of fraud and duress does not treat fraudulent or coerced choices as consensual. On the contrary, it teaches that fraud, duress, incapacity, and sometimes mistake are allowed as defenses to suits for breach of contract in order to deny legal protection to inefficient transactions.

Because consenting to work in a hazardous environment might seem much like consenting to work for an employer who finds it too costly to prevent sexual harassment by supervisory employees, the reader may wonder why I called sexual harassment a source of market failure. The reason is that although the employer may be blameless in both cases, there is always a blameworthy actor in the second case (harassment) but often not in the first (hazard). A workplace may be dangerous for reasons beyond any human being's control or ability to prevent at reasonable cost; but sexual harassment, like murder and theft, occurs only when there is a wrongdoer. Workplace hazards may also be due to wrongdoing—to carelessness, or worse. But they need not be; and when they are not, no blame attaches to anyone when a worker with adequate foreknowledge of a hazard is injured.

The second exhibit in West's case against the ethical significance of consensual transactions is the hard or risky choice, illustrated by my example of workplace hazards and by her example of a homosexual who continues to patronize homosexual bathhouses (while refusing to use, or insist that his sexual partners use, condoms) despite the high risk of contracting AIDS.[15] If homosexuality is considered to be a mental disease like bulimia or anorexia, this case can be assimilated to the first group. If not (the current view of most psychiatrists), the homosexual merely faces an unhappy but not uncommon choice: life style or life expectancy. West may believe that since the sex drive is instinctual, no choice that it influences can be a free one. But most human choices are influenced by preferences and aversions that have their roots in instinct—the instinct to survive, the instinct to reproduce. Many of these choices involve risk. If any risky choice rooted

---

15. West abstracts, as shall I, from the most problematic aspect of the homosexual's behavior from an economic standpoint: that one who puts himself at risk of catching a communicable disease is also imposing a risk on other people, namely those whom *he* may infect, and is thus creating an "external cost" that may warrant regulation even under a laissez-faire theory of the state. The bathhouse example is somewhat dated, but unsafe sex continues to be a major factor in the spread of the AIDS virus.

in our "animal instincts" is on that account to invite government intervention, then West must conceive of the problem of political governance on the analogy of the governance of a zoo.[16]

Furthermore, unless one believes that choice is free in a metaphysical sense, all choices can be said to be "coerced" or "involuntary." If I want to work but have only one job offer, I have "no choice" but to take it. The compulsion may be as great as when a gun-toting robber barks at me, "Your money or your life." The reason that the choice to give the robber my money is deemed coerced and the other not is that society as a whole would clearly be better off if this class of ostensibly "voluntary" transactions (extortion) were eliminated, and we do not have the same confidence with the other example; for if "bad" jobs are outlawed, what are people to do when they cannot get "good" jobs? Or consider the case of a spinal fusion operation intended to alleviate the agonizing pain of spinal disk disease. The operation may cause paralysis. Should a patient who is fully informed of the risk be forbidden to consent because it would be a choice made under uncertainty? If, coerced by pain as it were, the patient chooses the operation and becomes paralyzed, does that show that he lacked freedom of choice? That such choices should be reserved to physicians, or to the state? That risky operations should be forbidden altogether, so that the occasion for choice does not arise?

Since West wrote her article, the question whether physician-assisted suicide should be permitted has come to the forefront of public debate. The question raises in acute form the issue of the proper limits on choice. Not only can denying people a choice of when to die—the practical consequence, for many people, of forbidding physicians to assist patients to kill themselves—subject the sick or dying to horrible suffering; it can also actually *increase* the number of suicides. For it can induce some people to kill themselves in anticipation of becoming helpless to do so without assistance as their illness progresses, whereas they might have recovered or changed their minds had they been able to wait secure in the knowledge that they could obtain assistance later if they needed it.[17] Yet the suicide taboo, and fear that some people will be pushed by callous or self-seeking relatives or busy physicians into agreeing to end their lives without really wanting to do so, militate against physician-assisted suicide. There is no obviously correct answer to whether choice should be respected in this or the other areas

16. The distinction between, on the one hand, sexual orientation, sexual preference, and sexual drive, all aspects of the biology of sex, and, on the other hand, sexual acts, which are a matter of deliberate choice to commit or to refrain from committing, is fundamental to the economic analysis of sex. See my book *Sex and Reason*, ch. 5 (1992).

17. See my book *Aging and Old Age*, ch. 10 (1995).

in which difficult questions of freedom of choice have arisen, such as whether to allow the surrogate mother to renege on her promise to give up the child when it is born and whether to allow people to sell their organs. Each of these questions requires, if it is to be answered intelligently, a separate, careful inquiry and analysis rather than global reflection on the meaning and significance of consent.

Choice under uncertainty is not limited to the tragic choices that I have been discussing. The hunger artist, if Kafka's story is read literally as a marketing report on a declining industry,[18] failed to predict consumer preference correctly and found himself displaced by a panther, just as a comedian might find himself displaced in popular favor by a talking cat. In a figurative sense every failed entrepreneur "starves." But if he chose entrepreneurship with his eyes open, must we feel sorry for him? Do we feel sorry for the person who buys a lottery ticket and doesn't win? It is not an unexpected change in consumer preferences that makes us feel sorry for Kafka's hunger artist. Not that Kafka meant us just to feel sorry for the hunger artist; we are meant to feel for him and to laugh at him. No doubt in "The Metamorphosis" we are meant to see Gregor from his standpoint and from his family's standpoint—to feel sorry for him and disgusted by him. Kafka's art is affecting but not sentimental. It has a kind of Shakespearean impartiality, something that moralistic critics have trouble understanding.

West does not understand the social function of risk taking. Suppose you are a farmer who does not want to assume the risk of price fluctuations, and therefore you want to sell your crop for a fixed price before it is harvested. In other words, you want to hedge. To do so, you must find someone willing to speculate—someone who likes to take risks. The more this person likes risk the less he will charge you to compensate him for assuming it; he may even pay you to shift the risk of price fluctuations to him. Speculation thus facilitates hedging. It also reduces uncertainty about values by bringing more people into the market—speculators, on top of producers and consumers. Market price may not be a good predictor of market value when the market is very thin; speculators make it thicker.

The risk one takes when one buys a lottery ticket is somewhat unusual in not being compensated in pecuniary terms. The cost of the ticket exceeds the expected payoff (the prize if you win multiplied by the probability of winning). Lotteries appeal to people who like risk or uncertainty,

18. Not an *altogether* absurd idea. There really were "hunger artists" on the Continent in Kafka's day, and indeed as late as 1956. Breon Mitchell, "Kafka and the Hunger Artists," in *Kafka and the Contemporary Critical Performance: Centenary Readings* 236 (Alan Udoff ed. 1987); Meno Spann, *Franz Kafka* 191 n. 1 (1976).

to desperate people (it would make sense to spend your last dollar on a lottery ticket if you're going to starve unless you win the lottery), to people who cannot compute odds, to people who believe in their lucky star, to fools, and to daydreamers. In contrast, the risk that you take when you buy stock in a highly leveraged company or commit yourself to a risky career such as acting or marry someone whose qualities you are not sure about is compensated risk; you engage in the risky activity because the net expected payoff to you is positive. If you end up disappointed, that is the risk you assumed; and if the choice was a good one ex ante, we need not listen to your bellyaching ex post. Even if we feel for you, your plight, being of your own authorship, does not present a sympathetic case for using the power of government to bail you out. Government is coercion. The forced transfer of wealth from the frugal, the prudent, and the saving to a person who takes financial risks with his eyes open is not easy to justify on either practical or moral grounds. The feckless, the reckless, the remiss, the generous, the Hamlets and Bassanios, the people who take seriously what the Sermon on the Mount said about living as the birds do—these may be very charming people compared to your average M.B.A., but they have no moral claim on the taxpayer.

There is a deeper point. It is the paradox of commitment that to be able to surrender one's freedom can increase one's freedom. Laws that enable people to make binding commitments enable choices that would not otherwise be available. If the loser in the lottery could always redeem his ticket for the money he paid for it, there would be no lotteries and hence no lottery winners. If the surrogate mother cannot make a binding commitment to give up the baby when it is born, she will not be able to make a surrogacy contract, or will have to settle for a lower contract price. If I make a legally binding commitment to pay a builder to build a house for me, I enlarge my freedom, for without the commitment I could not get the house built unless I paid for it in advance. And the builder could not get me to agree to pay for it in advance unless he could commit himself to complete it without demanding additional money.

The fact that a choice may entail a commitment does not make choice illusory. Nor does the fact that it may be a choice of the lesser of two evils. The range of job choices open to a person who lacks highly marketable skills will be narrow; the best job he can get may be greatly inferior to the jobs of other workers. The feasible set of choices is always limited. It does not follow that people should not be allowed to make choices within their feasible set, or that the choices they make lack authenticity because other people have larger feasible sets. The wealthier the society, the larger is the feasible set for most people. A society does not become wealthy unless it allows people to make binding commitments that may turn out badly for them.

Freedom is not Utopia and will not prevent the dietary disorders and "bad sex" (p. 390) that loom so large in West's redaction of Kafka's fictional world. The need to choose the lesser of two evils will persist as long as there are evils. In denigrating such choices, West identifies herself as a utopian fantasist[19] who believes that "the future of community depends not just upon political or even revolutionary action. It also depends upon our imaginative, rational, spiritual, and moral freedom to break free of our present, and to conceive of other ideal worlds."[20] She points out that women frequently consent to sex without desiring it and asks rhetorically, "Why is it okay for her to have sex even though she does not want to, but not okay for him not to have sex even though he wants to?"[21] Either she does not understand barter, or in Utopia the male and female sex drives will be identical.

Between the incompetent choice of the mentally ill person and the merely hard choice lies the case of addiction. An alcoholic surrenders an important part of his freedom, and, it might seem, gets little in return. Yet to prohibit people from becoming alcoholics would infringe their freedom to choose a particular, if to the temperate a revolting, mode of life. If the choice to become an alcoholic or some other sort of addict is made on incomplete information or involves uncompensated costs to third parties (for example, in the form of accidents caused by drunk driving), then it is not a "free" choice in the Pareto sense; and perhaps that is the typical case of addiction. But the fact that it is a choice to pursue an unfree type of life does not make the choice itself unfree. It is another example of a choice that entails commitment, and such choices, as I have pointed out, are not inherently unfree.

Between the case of addiction and the merely hard choice lies the angry, impetuous, compulsive, "irrational" choice that all of us make from time to time.[22] Whether such behavior should be considered "free" is a pro-

19. A label she is proud to wear. West, "Law, Literature, and the Celebration of Authority," 83 *Northwestern University Law Review* 977 (1989).

20. West, "Jurisprudence as Narrative: An Aesthetic Analysis of Modern Legal Theory," 60 *New York University Law Review* 145, 202 (1985) (reprinted as chapter 7 of her book *Narrative, Authority, and Law*, note 1 above).

21. West, "Legitimating the Illegitimate: A Comment on 'Beyond Rape,'" 93 *Columbia Law Review* 1442, 1456 (1993).

22. Arrayed from least to most free, the different kinds of choice I am considering are: the insane person's choice, the addict's choice, the occasional "irrational" choice of the normal person, the hard choice (for example, a choice between a bad job and no job), and the easy choice (such as the risk preferrer's choice to bear risk).

found philosophical question. But being deeply ingrained in the human animal, such behavior is unlikely to be altered by changing the economic system or by authorizing the government to prevent individuals from deciding how to live. Government officials are not free from the weaknesses that afflict private persons. Granted, there are degrees of government interference with personal choice. Subsidizing clinics that help people break the smoking habit is not so intrusive as prohibiting the sale of cigarettes. Yet the taxes required to defray the expense of such a subsidy would reduce freedom in the functional sense noted earlier. Higher taxes reduce people's feasible choice sets. Government programs designed to reduce the number of bad choices that people make may end up reducing the number of their choices, period.

Even the least problematic choices are difficult in West's version of Kafka's fictive world because its denizens do not like to make choices; they crave submission to authority. Were this true of most Americans, we would have to rethink our national commitment to free markets and democratic government. But the characters in Kafka's fiction are not typical Americans.[23] Reflecting their creator's neuroticism and his historical situation as a German-speaking Czech Jew in the twilight, disintegration, and aftermath of the Austro-Hungarian Empire (Kafka died in 1924), they are marked by an extraordinary submissiveness. This is true not only of Georg Bendemann, Gregor Samsa, Joseph K., and the traveler in "Before the Law," but also of the citizens in another of Kafka's stories, "The Refusal," who are *relieved* when their petitions for exemption from onerous laws are denied.

"The Refusal" is set in an unimportant town in a large military empire. The town is far from either a frontier or the capital; it is a backwater. Authority is represented by the tax collector, who has the rank of colonel and in effect rules the town, and by the fierce-looking soldiers who intimidate the citizens. The public life of the town is limited to the occasions when the colonel receives petitions for tax exemption or for permission to cut timber from the imperial forests at a reduced price or for some other privilege or exemption. On these "occasions the colonel stood upright, holding in front of him two poles of bamboo in his outstretched hands. This is an ancient custom implying more or less [*etwa*—"approximately"] that he supports the law, and the law supports him" (p. 266). The petition

---

23. Incidentally, this appears to have been Kafka's own view, insofar as one can judge from *Amerika*. Although wonderfully inaccurate (hardly a surprise, since Kafka never visited America)—he's got the Statue of Liberty holding a sword, for example—the novel does convey a sense of America as the land of limitless opportunity and boundless energy.

is always refused, and when this happens, "an undeniable sense of relief passe[s] through the crowd . . . Without this refusal one simply cannot get along, yet at the same time these official occasions designed to receive the refusal are by no means a formality. Time after time one goes there full of expectation and in all seriousness and then one returns, if not exactly strengthened or happy, nevertheless not disappointed or tired" (p. 267). Only the young people—those between the ages of seventeen and twenty—are not content with these refusals.

The yearning for authority, the fear of change, and the masochistic submissiveness are palpable. Perhaps in the colonel's refusal to grant exemptions from the laws one can sense an ironic commentary on the theme of "a government of laws, not men." Perhaps the colonel (described as breathing like a frog when he is listening to the petition, and collapsing into his chair after delivering his judgment) is the stunted descendant of the oracle at Delphi or the Hebrew prophets. Perhaps he is Kafka's father—or everyone's father in some obscure and disturbing sense. The citizens' relief when their requests are denied puts one in mind of the emotionally anesthetized inhabitants of "The Waste Land" who fear life (and the epigraph of the poem reports the death wish of an oracle). "The Refusal" was written in 1920, two years before "The Waste Land." These are distinguished works of literature but they are also period pieces, written in the aftermath of World War I by a dying man and a man recovering from a nervous breakdown, respectively.

West argues that in another late story, "The Problem of Our Laws," "Kafka straightforwardly describes his vision of the nature of law and legal authority, and the mechanism of legitimation upon which it depends. The authority of law, Kafka tells us, is ultimately sustained not by force, but by the craving of the governed for judgment by lawful, 'noble' authority" (p. 422). This two-page parable describes a society in which the law is kept secret by the small group of nobles that rules the society. So people begin to wonder, how do we know there *are* any laws? Some decide the only law is: what the nobility does is law. Most reject this view, instead diligently searching the acts of the nobles for clues that those acts are manifestations of the secret laws, and hoping eventually to understand the laws—at which point, they believe, the nobility will vanish.

The deference and passivity of the population support West's interpretation, but "straightforward" the parable is not. One might for example read "judiciary" for "nobility" and interpret "The Problem of Our Laws" as a parable about legal formalism and legal realism, or about natural law and positive law. In a sense law *is* a secret of judges, for until they speak the law is unknown in detail. The realist or positivist regards the "law" that is behind the judges' decisions as an illusion. To him the law is merely an extrapolation, from past decisions, of what the judges are likely to do when confronted by a particular case; so there is nothing outside the decisions themselves to count as law. The formalist or natural lawyer—whose point of view, though contested, still dominates the society depicted in Kafka's parable—clings to the faith that there is some body of enduring and consistent principles generating the judges' decisions and that with enough insight we might discover it and maybe even dispense with the judges.

Hints of such a faith can be found in other works by Kafka, including a marvelous one-page parable, "The New Advocate," which begins: "We have a new advocate, Dr. Bucephalus. There is little in his appearance to remind you that he was once Alexander of Macedon's battle charger." Yet he "mount[s] the marble steps" to the courthouse "with a high action that made them ring beneath his feet . . . In general the Bar approves the admission of Bucephalus. With astonishing insight people tell themselves that, modern society being what it is, Bucephalus is in a difficult position . . . Nowadays—it cannot be denied—there is no Alexander the Great . . . So perhaps it is really best to do as Bucephalus has done and absorb oneself in law books" (pp. 414–415). Is this *just* an ironic commentary on the disappearance of the heroic from modern life, on a par with the descent of heaven into the attic court in *The Trial*? The last sentence of the parable makes me wonder: "In the quiet lamplight, his flanks unhampered by the thighs of a rider, free and far from the clamor of battle, he reads and turns the pages of our ancient tomes" (p. 415). Bucephalus is like the people in "The Problem of Our Laws," with their faith in the existence of natural law: he thinks that if he reads the ancient tomes carefully enough he may discover something worthy of his heritage. Only he is more dignified and enterprising than they. Yet whatever else he is, Bucephalus is a horse, so that his superior dignity and enterprise reinforce the reader's impression of Kafka's dyspeptic assessment of human potential.

Misled, perhaps, by the passivity of Kafka's characters, West confuses the desire to surrender the power of choice over the essential conditions of one's life (self-slavery, the pact with the devil, Antonio's bond, the abjectness of the population in "The Refusal") with the decision to submit through ordinary contracting to partial and temporary direction or instruction by others. She considers both types of decision inconsistent with free choice, but the second is not. A person will submit to hierarchical direction by going to work for a company, rather than remain an independent contractor, only if he expects to do better as an employee. The status is freely chosen, and since the choice is not irrevocable, there is no surrender of essential autonomy. West would not be surrendering her freedom by deciding to take piano lessons. Instruction is not coercion; the educated person is actually freer than the uneducated one.

The interesting question about freedom of contract is whether *every* contract, however *outré*, between consenting and adequately informed adults that does not have palpable adverse effects on third parties should be enforced to the hilt, not whether normal commercial and consumer bargains should be enforced. That many idiosyncratic contracts (the sale of body parts, or Antonio's bond, or a contract to duel, or to become a slave) are or would be denied enforcement may indicate only that the demand for enforcement is insufficiently strong to induce judicial action. A court will not create a new enforceable right, at some cost in burdening the court with a new class of cases, unless there is a substantial perceived social need for the right.

In our society as in every society not all adults are fully competent, capable, or autonomous. Apart from the insane and the severely retarded, there are many unhappy and neurotic people, many unlucky people, many stupid people, and many who are prone to self-deception and wishful thinking. The existence of such people makes adherence to the principle of free choice problematic for West even in normal market settings. The practical questions are as follows: How many of these unfortunates are there? What can be done to reduce their number? Are there so many that we should rethink our commitment to free markets? Is there a better system of allocating resources than the market? Consistent with her self-description as a utopian thinker, West has nothing to say about any of these questions, but her biggest mistake is to suppose that the answers might be found in the fiction of Kafka, distinguished as that fiction is. Utopian thinkers may have some social utility in drawing attention to problems and possibilities that practical people may overlook. But Kafka cannot aid them in their mission.

The Grand Inquisitor and Other Social Theorists

If West really believes that Americans have the same desire to be ruled with an iron hand as some of Kafka's fictitious characters express—if she believes that we have "cravings for judgment and punishment by noble authority" (p. 422) and are "attracted to the authoritarian structure of law" and "of fate" (p. 423) and "to the power and punitive authority of the state" (p. 424), and that our world, like Kafka's, "is peopled by excessively authoritarian personalities" (p. 387)—then one can understand why she is troubled by a political philosophy which assumes that people are on the whole competent judges of their self-interest. But if she believes these things she lives not in the world of present-day America but in the world of the Grand Inquisitor, who tells Jesus Christ that for the great mass of mankind freedom of choice is a source of profound misery; that what people crave is to be led around like sheep, by miracle, mystery, and authority. "Thou didst not come down from the Cross when they shouted to Thee, mocking and reviling Thee, 'Come down from the cross and we will believe that Thou are He.' Thou didst not come down, for again Thou wouldst not enslave man by a miracle, and didst crave faith given freely, not based on miracle. Thou didst crave for free love and not the base raptures of the slave before the might that has overawed him forever. But Thou didst think too highly of men therein, for they are slaves, of course, though rebellious by nature."[24]

The Grand Inquisitor's argument can be transposed into economic terms—indeed, there is more than a hint of this in his diatribe. Some people do not want the burden of choice. They want government to make their decisions, including their economic decisions, for them. "Dost Thou know that the ages will pass, and humanity will proclaim by the lips of their sages that there is no crime, and therefore no sin; there is only hunger? . . . In the end they will lay their freedom at our feet, and say to us, 'Make us your slaves, but feed us.' They will understand themselves, at last, that freedom and bread enough for all are inconceivable together" (pp. 233–234).

> We shall allow them even sin, they are weak and helpless, and they will love us like children because we allow them to sin. We shall tell them that every sin will be expiated, if it is done with our permission, that we allow them to sin because we love them, and the punishment for these sins we take upon ourselves . . . And they will have no secrets from us. We shall allow or forbid them to live with their wives and mistresses, to have or not to have children—according to whether they have been obedient or disobedient—and they will submit to us gladly and cheerfully. The most painful secrets of their conscience, all, all they will bring to us, and we shall have an answer for all. And they will be glad to believe our answer, for it will save them from the great anxiety and terrible agony they endure at present in making a free decision for themselves. And all will be happy, all the millions of creatures except the hundred thousand who rule over them . . . There will be thousands of millions of happy babes, and a hundred thousand sufferers who have taken upon themselves the curse of the knowledge of good and evil. Peacefully they will die, peacefully they will expire in Thy name, and beyond the grave they will find nothing but death. But we shall keep the secret, and for their happiness we shall entice them with the reward of heaven and eternity. (p. 240)

24. Fyodor Dostoevsky, *The Brothers Karamazov* 236 (Constance Garnett and Ralph E. Matlaw trans., Matlaw ed. 1976).

But whereas the Grand Inquisitor locates the human flight from freedom in the inherent and ineradicable weakness of the human creature, West believes that the institutions of bourgeois society have stunted an innate human capacity for freely chosen, rewarding, nonexploitive relationships, so that if by an effort of sheer will and insight we could overthrow these institutions we might transform the human condition. She is, in short, a romantic. When she claims that individuals are "capable of empathic nurturing in the public sphere," she quickly adds that "the origin of our capacity for public, empathic nurturing is a dimly remembered feeling of life-giving solidarity with others in our world"[25]—a Wordsworthian "Our birth is but a sleep and a forgetting." When she says that "to the communitarian scholar, the central concern of law is the tension between our present separateness and our remembered union with the world at large, particularly with the strangers in it,"[26] she both puts one in mind of Blake's metaphor of human society as a single human body and ties it to the infant's sense, stressed by Blake and Wordsworth, of oneness with the world (that is, its mother).[27]

The difference between a poet and a law professor is that we do not ask the poet to show us how to get from where we are to where in his imaginative vision he wants us to be. The urge to break free from conditions of scarcity, morality, hierarchy, and inequality is a permanent element of human psychology. No more is needed as a grounding for great literature. It may even be a necessary condition for social reform. But it is not a sufficient condition. The record of utopian social experiments is not encouraging.

West has written on Freud's legal theory.[28] It is natural to wonder, in view of Kafka's tormented relationship with his father and the amenability of Kafka's fiction to Freudian interpretations, why she doesn't apply that theory to Kafka. The reason may be that although paternal authority resembles legal authority, and although K., the citizens in "The Refusal," and other inhabitants of Kafka's fictional world are easily seen as seeking a missing father in their ostensible quest for law, the particulars of Freud's legal theory[29] do not fit the mood of Kafka's fiction. Freud thought law a father substitute brought into being by the remorse felt by powerful brothers who

25. West, "Law, Rights, and Other Totemic Illusions: Legal Liberalism and Freud's Theory of the Rule of Law," 134 *University of Pennsylvania Law Review* 817, 859 (1986) (footnotes omitted).

26. Id. at 861 (footnote omitted).

27. See Northrop Frye, "Blake's Treatment of the Archetype," in *English Romantic Poets: Modern Essays in Criticism* 55, 62 (M. H. Abrams ed., 2d ed. 1975); Frye, *Fearful Symmetry: A Study of William Blake,* ch. 1 (1947).

28. West, note 25 above.

29. Summarized in id. at 822–844.

had ganged up and killed their father (and did not want the same thing to happen to them); the function of law is thus to repress strong men. The people in Kafka's fiction on whom the law bears down, or who are searching for the law, are weak. To Freud, such people would be beneficiaries of law. To Kafka they are either its victims or its hopeless suppliants.

Freud's idea that the proper role of law and the state is to control the excesses of individualism is also uncongenial to the romantic view that these institutions have perverted man's natural goodness. West likes Freud's theory to the extent that it emphasizes the role of law in protecting the weak from the strong. She is disturbed by the traces of Social Darwinism in economic thought and believes that to use competition to allocate scarce resources favors the strong. She does not distinguish adequately between the role of law in preventing the use of force or fraud to reallocate those resources (the Freudian, and also, with certain refinements, the economic view) and its role in equalizing the distribution of resources (the left-wing aspiration for law). But she sees that in emphasizing innate human aggressiveness Freud's theory undermines her project of making empathic nurturing the organizing principle of society.

West's use of Kafka shows how far the legal academic left has strayed from its roots in the legal realist movement of the 1920s and 1930s. The legal realists were meliorists. They attacked a form of conceptualism that viewed law as a closed logical system which ideas of public policy must not be allowed to penetrate. In terms of the Table of Legal Antinomies in Chapter 3, they thought law had been pushed too far into the left-hand column (not left politically, of course). Some of the realists, notably Jerome Frank, were unduly hostile to "ruledness," which they associated, as Shakespeare may have done, with psychological insecurity. But they were not utopian dreamers; they did not believe in the perfectibility of human nature and society. And they had a clear idea of specific legal reforms that they wanted to and in large measure did achieve. They would have gotten little help from reading Kafka.

part II

*L*EGAL TEXTS

as LITERARY TEXTS

SEVEN

Interpreting Contracts, Statutes, and Constitutions

Interpretation Theorized

When I wrote this chapter for the first edition a decade ago, interpretation was a hot topic both in literary criticism, which had been deeply penetrated by deconstruction (whose premise has been waggishly described as "all texts are allegories of their own unreadability"[1]), and in legal scholarship. A strong conservative attack on the free-wheeling jurisprudence of liberal Supreme Court Justices was being mounted by Robert Bork and others under the banner of "original intent," and as vigorously rebutted by liberal legal scholars such as Ronald Dworkin. The bridge between legal and literary interpretive concepts was Stanley Fish, an interpretive skeptic as hostile to Dworkin as to Bork.

The topic of interpretation has cooled in both fields. The focus of literary theory has shifted to feminist and multiculturalist criticism of the literary canon, while a determinedly middle-of-the-road Supreme Court is busily defusing the debate between originalists and "noninterpretivists." Political change—the radicalization of English faculties, the "moderatization" of the Supreme Court—is not the only factor in the decline of interpretation as a topic. Another is the exhaustion of the subject. The harvest from all that has been written about interpretation is meager.[2] It comes down to two propositions. The first is that interpretation is always relative

---

1. Gerald Graff, *Professing Literature: An Institutional History* 241 (1987).
2. I do not denigrate the scholarship that by separating the wheat from the chaff has enabled a harvest to be gathered. See, for example, William N. Eskridge, Jr., *Dynamic Statutory Interpretation* (1994).

to a purpose that is not given by the interpretive process itself but that is brought in from the outside and guides the process. The purpose of interpreting a set of directions for assembling a stereo system is to assemble the system, and it is best achieved by using the directions to infer the procedure for assembly that the author of the directions had in mind. Whether the conductor of a piece of music written in the eighteenth century should try to recreate the experience of an eighteenth-century audience, and thus use the original instruments rather than their modern, improved successors, depends on whether the goal of musical interpretation is historical or aesthetic. And whether in interpreting a written contract the court should listen to the testimony of the parties as to what they intended when they negotiated the contract may depend on whether the purpose of contractual interpretation is to recreate the intentions of the parties or to encourage contracting parties to embody their agreement in a clearly written, comprehensive document.

Richard Weisberg and Robin West want to enlist Melville and Kafka, respectively, in a political cause because of the prestige of these writers. The proper interpretive focus of *that* endeavor is on what it is plausible to suppose that Melville and Kafka intended to get across in these works. That might require a biographical study. Biographical data may also be essential to determining whether a work of literature should be taken ironically. Someone who read Swift's "A Modest Proposal" without knowing anything about the author might conclude that he was advocating cannibalism. But it is the unusual case in which the text itself contains no clue that it is intended to be ironic. Irony can often be inferred without inquiring into the author's actual views. Cleanth Brooks, in interpreting Andrew Marvell's poem "An Horatian Ode upon Cromwell's Return from Ireland,"[3] wasn't interested in Marvell's conscious thoughts about Cromwell. Brooks's interests were aesthetic rather than polemical and as he noted, "the poet sometimes writes better than he knows."[4] Marvell may have admired Cromwell unqualifiedly yet been induced by unconscious reservations to qualify his admiration with the undercurrent of criticism that Brooks's interpretation brings to the surface. Maybe Shakespeare really did mean us to think that the ghost in *Hamlet* is a devil and Hamlet himself the Vice figure from medieval morality plays; we strain against this interpretation in part because it would diminish the aesthetic appeal of the play, and it is as an aesthetic object that the play interests us (or most of us).

---

3. Brooks, "Marvell's 'Horatian Ode,'" in *Seventeenth-Century English Poetry: Modern Essays in Criticism* 321 (William R. Keast ed. 1962).
4. Id. at 322.

Nothing in the nature of interpretation *requires* us to give primacy to a writer's conscious intentions, except, as I have said, when, as in the case of "A Modest Proposal," meaning inheres in the tension between the text and those intentions.

The second proposition is that interpretation is not much, and maybe not at all, improved by being made self-conscious, just as one doesn't become a better reader by studying linguistics. The interpretation of a written or an oral statement, a dream, a musical composition, a painting, a poem, or a legal document is a natural, intuitive, "instinctive" human (and not only human) activity, rather than one performed by consciously following rules. Not that these aren't rule-bound activities; modern linguistics has exposed the vast structure of implicit rules that constitute the actual grammar of speech. But you don't become a better speaker by bringing the rules to the surface. Competent interpretation may require a great deal of knowledge, skill, and practice (obviously so in the case of music), but it is not improved by algorithmic procedures or "theories" of interpretation. The relevant competences involve the study of the interpretenda rather than of "interpretation" at large. In the case of documents, whether literary or legal, "interpretation" just means reading to make whatever kind of sense one happens to be interested in. This might coincide with the writer's intended meaning, but equally it might be a sense that the reader wants to impress on the writing for reasons remote from anything the writer had in mind.

These two points seem to me to exhaust the theory of interpretation, as I shall try to show with reference to various approaches to literary and legal interpretation. The two points exhaust the theory of interpretation in a second sense as well: they suggest that interpretation is unlikely to be improved by being made a subject of theory or reflection.

What Can Law Learn in the Schools of Literary Criticism?

Although passé in literary studies, deconstruction retains a theoretical interest as the most skeptical of interpretive methods and continues to attract some legal scholars[5] and to alarm others—those who think it a synonym for destructive criticism or textual indeterminacy. So let me begin there, distinguishing first of all among deconstruction as philosophical theory, lit-

---

5. See, for example, *Deconstruction and the Possibility of Justice* (Drucilla Cornell, Michel Rosenfeld, and David Gray Carlson eds. 1992); J. M. Balkin, "Nested Oppositions," 99 *Yale Law Journal* 1669 (1990); Balkin, "Transcendental Deconstruction, Transcendent Justice," 92 *Michigan Law Review* 1131 (1994); Duncan Kennedy, *A Critique of Adjudication (Fin de Siècle)* 348–350 (1997).

erary practice, and legal practice.[6] The philosophical theory, so far as it bears directly on interpretation (some deconstructionists have even bigger game in their sights, such as the correspondence theory of truth), attacks orthodox language theory. According to that theory, we create from our perceptions concepts—for example, the concept of the tree that stands in front of my house—that are independent of time and space and distinct from the perceptions out of which they are made; the concept of the tree in front of my house exists apart from the particular angles and distances from which I have seen the tree. At first the concept is imprisoned in my mind. If I want to share it with another person I have to encode it in some physical form ("signifier")—writing, sound, or gesture. Upon hearing or seeing the signifier, the other person will decode it, recreating the identical concept in his own mind.

The orthodox theorist acknowledges that communication is not quite so simple as this. Understanding a communication requires more than simple decoding; it requires inference as well.[7] The metaphor of understanding as seeing something in the "mind's eye" obscures the interpretive element in communication. A language may, for example, lack a signifier for a particular signified. English, for example, lacks words for the concepts that lie behind such Greek words as *polis, basileus,* and *tyrannos.* The English words by which they are usually translated, "city," "king," and "tyrant," signify other concepts in our culture. So translation is often problematic. Even within the same language community, words have different shades of meaning for different speakers. Moreover, a sign carries more information than is necessary for communicating the concept. When I say "tree," my listener may be put in mind of family trees, decision trees, or shoe trees, as well as nature's trees; every word is a signifier of other concepts besides the one the speaker meant to convey by a particular use of the word. Since conversation is a two-way exchange, the person to whom I am speaking can seek clarification. This course is unavailable if the signifiers are written rather than spoken, and if the writer is dead or otherwise unavailable to be quizzed about his intentions. Hence Plato's distrust of written language (*Phaedrus* 275d–275e). Collaborative writing, which is more common in

6. For sympathetic descriptions of the theory, see Henry Staten, *Wittgenstein and Derrida* (1984), and Christopher Norris, *Derrida* (1987); for hostile descriptions, see John M. Ellis, *Against Deconstruction* (1989). For a useful overview, see J. Douglas Kneale, "Deconstruction," in *The Johns Hopkins Guide to Literary Theory and Criticism* 185 (Michael Groden and Martin Kreiswith eds. 1994).

7. Peter Carruthers, *Language, Thought and Consciousness: An Essay in Philosophical Psychology* 75 (1996).

literature than is generally believed,[8] further complicates the signifying process.

Orthodox language theory regards these impediments to conceptual transfer as impurities or corruptions to be overcome. This is the point against which deconstruction mounts its attack, insisting that to regard the properties of signifiers that impede communication as secondary is arbitrary and culture-bound rather than, as the orthodox theorists suppose, logical or "natural." It is just as logical, just as natural, deconstruction claims, to subordinate the communicative function of discourse to the communication-impeding effects of the signifiers that the speaker or writer uses, and thus to attend to the relation between the signifiers and other concepts besides the one intended to be signified. The practitioner of deconstruction may take an ostensibly serious prose passage and get hung up on the first word, which may be a homonym or a false cognate or may contain a secondary meaning (perhaps deeply buried in its root) at war with the surface meaning. He may become fascinated with the shape of the letters or the visual pattern they make on the page. He may juxtapose passages unrelated at the level of communication in order to jar the reader out of his conventional response, or even treat an earlier writing as a commentary on a later one.

Consistent with its program of redirecting attention to the concealed aspects of language, deconstruction insists on the problematic character of regarding an author as "present" in his text in the same way that we suppose a speaker to be present in his utterance. By virtue of its permanence in comparison to speech, writing can outlive the communicative occasion that brought it forth by outliving the author, the readers whom the author intended to address, and the writing's original linguistic and cultural context. All this is true and is the basis of John Ellis's (no friend of deconstruction) theory of literature (see Chapter 1). It is also true that much can be lost in clarity of communication when we move from spoken to written speech. Inflection, for example. Whether the commerce clause in Article I of the Constitution ("Congress shall have the power . . . to regulate [interstate and foreign] Commerce") forbids states to burden inter-

---

8. See, for example, Jonathan Hope, *The Authorship of Shakespeare's Plays: A Socio-Linguistic Study* 3–5 (1994); Jeffrey A. Masten, "Beaumont and/or Fletcher: Collaboration and the Interpretation of Renaissance Drama," in *The Construction of Authorship: Textual Appropriation in Law and Literature* 361 (Martha Woodmansee and Peter Jaszi eds. 1994). How common collaborative writing is depends, however, on how broadly "authorship" is defined. Jack Stillinger, *Multiple Authorship and the Myth of Solitary Genius* (1991), defines it very broadly and as a result finds multiple authorship ubiquitous.

state commerce unreasonably or merely empowers Congress to regulate commerce depends on whether one reads the clause with the emphasis on "Congress" or on "Commerce."

To say that the properties of signifiers that make them an imperfect medium of communication are as interesting or important as communication—even to say that the orthodox theory of language is ungrounded or incoherent—is not to say that no text can be interpreted in a way that will recreate in the reader's mind the concept that the author wished to convey. Deconstruction does not disestablish the interpretability of texts; if it did, how could the deconstructionists get their message across? But by emphasizing the impediments to effective written communication, it does invite a textual skepticism that can be corrosive, as we shall see.

Literature interests deconstructionists because it is not even *trying* to convey concepts in the most economical manner possible (in contrast, say, to an "executive summary"). The use of figurative language, rhyme, assonance, meter, fiction, parable, punning, the arrangement of words on a page (as in poetry), and other devices that call attention to the signifiers and thus decrease the transparency of the medium of communication fits the deconstructionists' program of placing the properties of language that impede forthright communication on a par with the properties that enable it. No wonder orthodox language theorists, beginning with Plato, have often been impatient with literature, though the real point about literature is not that it does not communicate, for obviously it does, but that concepts are not primarily what it communicates.

If practitioners of literary deconstruction were content merely to point out the dense and refractory character of much literature, they would be doing nothing new; the New Critics were pointing out the same things a half century ago, with particular reference to seventeenth- and twentieth-century poetry. It has long been understood that a work of literature is much more than its paraphrasable content. For most critics, however, the "more" is a depiction or evocation of some aspect of reality, such as love or war; and this makes literature "referential"—there are not just signifiers, there are things signified. So it was natural for the deconstructionists, being interested in signifiers rather than signifieds, to train their sights on the mimetic theory of literature—the theory propounded by Aristotle, Samuel Johnson, and Erich Auerbach, among many others, that literature presents an imitation or representation of reality (though not necessarily of existing particulars), understood as something "out there." Literary deconstruction, in contrast, presents literature as self-referential. In so doing it closes the loop with philosophical deconstruction by directing attention to the medium of communication and indeed making the subject of literature the problematics of reading for meaning.

"In the Penal Colony" is thus a work of particular resonance for deconstruction.[9] The torture machine is a writing machine, and one way of stating the officer's problem is that he puts too much faith in writing as a medium of communication, while an alternative interpretation is that, in good deconstructive fashion, it is the medium, not the communication, that obsesses him. And those fearful arabesques that the machine inscribes on the body of the condemned in order to protract the torture are a wonderful metaphor of overdetermination. Words live a life of their own, and an unruly life at that. But the relevance to law is obscure. Even if literary texts are self-referential, it does not follow that a legal text is; the techniques employed by authors of literary texts are different from those of the authors of legal texts. So one should not be surprised that deconstruction in law, except when the word is used merely as a synonym for text skepticism (we shall encounter such a use shortly), bears only a generic resemblance to deconstruction in philosophy or literary theory. Deconstruction in law means identifying latent contradictions in legal reasoning or legal doctrine.[10] In Balkin's formulation, "all conceptual oppositions can be reinterpreted as nested oppositions," a "nested opposition" being "a conceptual opposition each of whose terms contains the other, or each of whose terms shares something with the other."[11] For example, negligence and strict liability are, conventionally, opposite theories of liability for accidental injury. But negligence has an element of strict liability because a person is liable in negligence for failing to use the care of an average person even if he is incapable of doing so, while strict products liability has an element of negligence because the plaintiff has to prove that the product was defective, implying negligence somewhere in the chain of production.[12]

These were commonplaces of tort scholarship when Balkin was in high school. He does not claim otherwise. So what is gained by restating them in terms of nested opposition, besides the shock value of associating legal scholarship with a movement that uses extreme state-

9. See Clayton Koelb, "'In der Strafkolonie': Kafka and the Scene of Reading," 55 *German Quarterly* 511 (1982); Koelb, *Kafka's Rhetoric: The Passion of Reading* (1989); Arnold Weinstein, "Kafka's Writing Machine: Metamorphosis in the Penal Colony," 7 *Studies in Twentieth-Century Literature* 21 (1982–1983). Cf. Mark M. Anderson, *Kafka's Clothes* 185–193 (1992).

10. See, for example, Clare Dalton, "An Essay in the Deconstruction of Contract Doctrine," 94 *Yale Law Journal* 997 (1985), esp. 1007–1008.

11. "Nested Oppositions," note 5 above, at 1676–1677.

12. Id. at 1683–1686.

ment, willful obscurity, and unfamiliar terminology to convey an impression, however misleading, of revolutionary menace and excitement?[13] A little, perhaps: "nested opposition" is a cute phrase; I shall use it myself a little farther along in this chapter. But the only important point for this book is that legal deconstruction, as a distinct mode of analysis rather than a vogue word for text skepticism, has nothing specifically to do with the interpretation of texts (and so nothing to do with this book). Its focus is on concepts.

The opacity and sheer strangeness of much deconstructionist writing, notably but not only that of Derrida himself,[14] the appropriation of the term by leftist legal scholars, and its apparently if misleadingly radical implications for interpretation, a subject important to both literary criticism and the legal profession, have given deconstruction a notoriety that threatens to occlude other aspects of postmodernist thinking that might bear on legal interpretation. One, which we glimpsed in the first chapter, is the rejection of aestheticism in favor of social and political criticism in which works of literature are either mined for anticipations of modern leftist thought or exposed as accomplices in oppression. Another postmodernist gambit is refusing to recognize the interpretive authority of authors. Foucault argued that "authorship" is a cultural artifact rather than a natural or indispensable foundation of our response to a written work, and a cultural artifact whose "authoritarian" purpose is precisely to limit the range of possible interpretations by appointing the writer the single authorized interpreter.[15]

The rejection of aestheticism belittles the author by making him a politico; Foucault dethrones him; deconstruction denigrates the intelligibility and coherence of texts and joins Derrida in undermining authorial authority.[16] The net effect—a kind of reader's and critic's re-

---

13. See Ellis, note 6 above, ch. 6.

14. Here is a comment on an essay by Derrida: "for readers with a lifetime to spare, there is also a 100-page essay by Jacques Derrida, dealing with a subject yet to be determined." William E. Cain, *The Crisis in Criticism: Theory, Literature, and Reform in English Studies* 167 (1984). The translator's note at the end of Jacques Derrida, "Devant la Loi," in *Kafka and the Contemporary Critical Performance: Centenary Readings* 128, 149 (Alan Udoff ed. 1987), states: "Derrida's text continues; but, blind and weary, I shut the text-door here." The translator is alluding to the last sentence of "Before the Law": "I am now going to shut it [the door]."

15. Michel Foucault, "What Is an Author?" in *Textual Strategies: Perspectives in Post-Structuralist Criticism* 141 (Josué V. Harari ed. 1979). There is merit to Foucault's view, as we shall see in Chapter 11.

16. "A deconstruction is better understood as an artifact that 'works' in relation to another artifact (the deconstructed text), by dissolving the second artifact's 'effect' of impersonal compulsion, always in the name of an unrepresented something." Kennedy, note 5 above, at 349.

bellion[17]—gives aid and comfort to the advocates of free interpretation of legal texts. If statutes and constitutions lack definite author-given meanings, then judges in "interpreting" these texts must actually be exercising discretion. So the attack on interpretability and authors' authority is an attack on "ruledness" as well.

But the political and the epistemological aims of postmodernism clash. If objective textual interpretation is impossible, Robin West is wasting her time in trying to show that Kafka's fiction contains a radical message; she must have put it there herself.[18] A posture of radical skepticism, if adhered to consistently,[19] deprives the radical critic of firm ground for advocating social change. The critic's own proposals can be derided as culture-bound, historically contingent, subjective—even as implicated in the repressive discourse that the critic is attacking, as when Kafka's writings are treated as *authored* by Franz Kafka. Just by treating Kafka as an *authority,* a social prophet, a "genius" who speaks to the social problems of modern America across a cultural and temporal gulf, West is challenging the radical egalitarianism of postmodernists who want to bring the reader level with the author.

Postmodernism denies the givenness, singularity, and interpretability of the object (for example, a text), but also the autonomy of the subject (the knower—for example, the writer or reader of a text). Depending on which denial is emphasized, postmodernism can be either revolutionary or

17. The restiveness of the literary critic forced, in the traditional conception of the critic's role, to play second fiddle to the literary text is the plaintive theme of Geoffrey H. Hartman, *Criticism in the Wilderness: The Study of Literature Today* (1980); and see his preface to Harold Bloom et al., *Deconstruction and Criticism* vii (1979): "While teaching, criticizing, and presenting the great texts of our culture are essential tasks, to insist on the importance of literature should not entail assigning to literary criticism only a service function." The parallel to the restiveness of the judicial activist asked to play second fiddle to statutes and the Constitution is apparent, as is the relation of such attitudes, in both literature and law, to the tradition of romantic self-assertion examined in Chapter 5.

18. She is aware of this problem: "the infusion of a postmodern skepticism regarding universal accounts of our nature has led to a debilitating impasse in critical legal thought." West, "Introduction: Reclaiming Meaning," in West, *Narrative, Authority, and Law* 1, 18 (1993). Her "book is accordingly put forward not as an attack on traditional or enlightenment understandings of meaning, but quite the contrary, as an attempted reclamation of meaning from contemporary and postmodern critics of both the political Right and Left." Id. at 22. This represents a change of position for West, who four years before the publication of the passages I have just quoted was a Foucaldian. See Robin West, "Law, Literature, and the Celebration of Authority," 83 *Northwestern University Law Review* 977, 1003–1010 (1989).

19. Which it never is. Graham Bradshaw, *Misrepresentations: Shakespeare and the Materialists* (1993), points out that cultural materialists, new historicists, and other postmodernist literary critics do not relativize their own political and methodological stances but treat them as timeless and true.

quietistic. When the contingent, constructed character of social and in some versions even physical reality is emphasized,[20] radical transformation of the world and society is seen as possible and desirable, although authors can't be appealed to as authorities for the transformation. Much radical feminist thought is of this character, including the idea that sexuality itself is a social construction. When instead the ethnocentric, embedded, socially constructed character of the self is emphasized, the possibility of objective social criticism is nixed. Such criticism presupposes an external, ecumenical standard, such as "universal rights" or "our common humanity," that postmodernism denies exists.[21]

The postmodernist challenge to interpretability has been resisted, not least within literary criticism itself.[22] Critics who believe that their task in reading a literary work is to reconstruct the author's intentions[23] might be thought to provide ammunition for the "interpretivists" of legal texts, perhaps even for the "strict constructionists." Ronald Dworkin has taken an intermediate position and defended it in terms reminiscent of the New Criticism.[24] He claims that we choose between two interpretations of a work of literature by deciding which one makes the work better, more coherent, more pleasing, and that we should do the same with statutes and the Constitution, except that the criteria of goodness, of coherence, of integrity (a favorite concept for both Dworkin and the New Critics) would be legal and political rather than aesthetic. We should ask, for example, what interpretation of "equal protection of the laws" makes the Fourteenth Amendment the best, the most coherent expression of the principle of equality, the expression most consonant with the best legal and political thinking about law, rather than asking what the framers or ratifiers of the amendment had in mind. Inverting Shelley's dictum in *A Defence of Poetry*,

20. Preposterously so, in the case of physical reality. For incisive criticism of this most extreme version of postmodernism, see Paul Boghossian, "What the Sokal Hoax Ought to Teach Us: The Pernicious Consequences and Internal Contradictions of 'Postmodernist' Relativism," *Times Literary Supplement,* Dec. 13, 1996, p. 14.

21. See Sabina Lovibond, "Feminism and Postmodernism," 178 *New Left Review* 5 (1989).

22. See, for example, Robert Alter, *The Pleasures of Reading in an Ideological Age* (1996)—both an argument for and a demonstration of literary criticism as the imaginative but disciplined interpretation and evaluation of works of literature.

23. See, for example, E. D. Hirsch, Jr., *Validity in Interpetation* (1967); P. D. Juhl, *Interpretation: An Essay in the Philosophy of Literary Criticism* (1980); Steven Knapp and Walter Benn Michaels, "Against Theory," 8 *Critical Inquiry* 723 (1982).

24. See, for example, Dworkin, *Law's Empire,* ch. 2 (1986); Dworkin, *Freedom's Law: The Moral Reading of the American Constitution* 2 (1996); also the debate between Dworkin and his critics in 29 *Arizona State Law Journal* 353 (1997).

Dworkin hails judges and (other) legislators as the unacknowledged poets of the world.

New Critics treat a work of literature as an artifact, coherent in itself and not to be understood better by immersion in the details of the author's biography or in the other circumstances of its composition, except that some knowledge of those circumstances, including knowledge of the meanings that the words in the work bore at the time it was written, may be necessary.[25] New Criticism is thus a school of formalist criticism. Its approach corresponds not only to the coherentist jurisprudence of Dworkin, which downplays intentions, but also to the common practice of interpreting contracts without reference to "extrinsic" evidence such as testimony by the parties as to what they meant by ambiguous terms—that is, evidence other than the document itself and the cultural background necessary to understand the words and sentences in the document and the purposes of contract interpretation.[26] This comparison suggests a more far-reaching analogy between New Criticism and legal formalism, the latter like the former emphasizing the autonomy of its subject matter.

For an intentionalist judge, the task in interpreting a statute is to figure out from the words, the structure, the background, and any other available information how the legislators whose votes were necessary for enactment would have answered the interpretive question had it occurred to them. And a deconstructionist judge? He might argue that the provision in Article II of the Constitution that you must be at least 35 years old to be President of the United States could mean merely that you must have the maturity of the average 35-year-old.[27] To read the provision so, however, is to take the words

25. The New Critics' approach is well illustrated by Brooks's essay on Marvell's ode, note 3 above, and by his book *The Well Wrought Urn* (1947), and is particularly well explained in a later book of his, *A Shaping Joy: Studies in the Writer's Craft* (1971). See "Introduction," in id. at xi, and "The Uses of Literature," in id. at 1; also W. K. Wimsatt, Jr., *The Verbal Icon: Studies in the Meaning of Poetry* (1954). For overview and critique, respectively, see Leroy F. Searle, "New Criticism," in *The Johns Hopkins Guide to Literary Theory and Criticism*, note 6 above, at 528, and John Guillory, *Cultural Capital: The Problem of Literary Canon Formation*, ch. 3 (1993).

26. So one of the synonyms for formalist criticism, "intrinsic" criticism, is particulary apt. See Stein Haugom Olsen, *The Structure of Literary Understanding* 137–155 (1978).

27. See Gary Peller, "The Metaphysics of American Law," 73 *California Law Review* 1151, 1174 (1985); Mark V. Tushnet, "A Note on the Revival of Textualism in Constitutional Theory," 58 *Southern California Law Review* 683, 686–688 (1985). Notice that this is deconstruction as text skepticism, not deconstruction à la Dalton and Balkin as the bringing to the surface of latent doctrinal contradictions. Neither Peller nor Tushnet, incidentally, invokes the authority of Gilbert and Sullivan. The plot of *The Pirates of Penzance* turns on the circumstance that, having been born on February 29, Frederic, upon reaching the age of 21, is "legally" only 5 and therefore still apprenticed to the pirates.

of the Constitution ("neither shall any person be eligible to that Office who shall not have attained to the age of thirty five Years") out of their context. Words have reliable meaning only by virtue of their location in a sentence or larger verbal structure and often in a social practice as well. The relevant context of the age-35 provision includes a desire to establish orderly means of succession of officials, a practice of recording birth dates—and computing age, as not all societies do, from birth—and frequent use by lawmakers of arbitrary deadlines, as in statutes of limitations and in the age of majority. This context enables us to see that the Constitution lays down a flat rule for age of eligibility so that everyone will know in advance of an election whether the candidates are eligible. It would be absurd if after the election of a 40-year-old as President of the United States the loser could sue to void the election by showing that the winner was less mature than the average 35-year-old had been in 1787, when average life spans were much shorter. The age-35 provision, like laws fixing the drinking age, the driving age, the marriage age, and the voting age, is designed to avoid these absurdities.

One can imagine a cultural setting in which the provision would mean something different from what is obvious to us. Imagine a culture in which birth dates are not recorded or in which, as was common in ancient and medieval society, numbers are used for rhetorical emphasis rather than quantitative exactness ("an army of 100,000" to mean "a large army"). But these are just further illustrations that the meaning of a sentence depends on a context that may include a social practice.

One can also imagine that just as *force majeure* or "impossibility" can void a contract, extraordinary circumstances might require courts to let stand a violation of the age-35 provision—for example, if some epidemic, a kind of reverse AIDS, killed off all (or all but one or two?) persons 35 or older; or if, after the election of a President believed by everyone to be 35, a mistake was discovered in his birth certificate: he was really only 34. Perhaps the casuistic resources of the courts would be equal to the challenge of "interpreting" the provision to accommodate these affronts to its literal terms. Perhaps not; perhaps these cases show that context can alter meaning only so much. Either way, the essential judgment the courts would have to make would be political and prudential, and the insights of deconstruction would not help.

The choice between the New Critical and the intentionalist approach is less stark than I have suggested. New Criticism is less formalist than I have made it seem—and indeed more intentionalist—while intentionalism can be understood in formalist terms. The term "New Criticism" denotes a specific school of American literary criticism that arose in the 1920s, achieved great influence in American universities in the 1940s and 1950s, and then faded. Its trajectory coincided with that of logical positivism, with which it also shares an extraordinary tenacity that has enabled it to survive as mood and inclination long after it was reviled and refuted as doctrine. (The same is true of legal formalism.) The New Critics were committed to the close reading of works of literature viewed as more or less self-contained artifacts, and hence were drawn to works that best repaid such scrutiny by reason of their dense and complex (often in the sense of ironic) structure. In addition, these critics, taking their cue from T. E. Hulme and T. S. Eliot, expressed a preference for literature that reflects a mature, realistic, even disenchanted—and definitely unromantic—attitude toward life. This led many of them to disparage Romantic literature, with its cult of the child—and for the further reason that most of these critics were Christian and conservative and associated the Romantic cultivation of spontaneity, rebellion, transformative politics, the esemplastic power of the imagination, and egocentrism with atheism and populism. More, the New Critics' insistence on the complex particularity of the individual work of literature was connected to a characteristically modernist hostility to modernity viewed as the triumph of science and technology, products of "abstract thinking." The New Critics let "the 'integrity' of the literary work stand in for the 'integrity of all forms of endangered specificity.'"[28]

So there was a moral and political tincture to the ostensibly formalistic, ostensibly aestheticist, character of the New Criticism, just as legal formalism has usually had a political hue. Moralistic criticism today is much more likely to reflect a secular humanist, left-wing materialist, or radical feminist viewpoint than a Christian or conservative one. In retrospect it is apparent that by taking a politico-moral stance, the New Critics were exposing their reputation to the winds of political fashion; when the wind changed, they became the butt of left-wing critics.[29]

Some New Critics were aggressively uninterested in biographical or historical background and hence unwilling on principle to seek any clues to literary meaning in these things. Although none doubted that a piece of writing

28. Catherine Gallagher, "The History of New Criticism," *Dædalus,* Winter 1997, pp. 133, 134.
29. "New Criticism's high regard for 'ambiguity', its admiration of polysemous structures, represent no real leaning towards 'total' criticism so much as a bourgeois mistrust of singlemindedness and commitment: the stances it prizes most—sophistication, wit, poise—are those of a decaying aristocracy characteristically revered by a sycophantic middle-class." Terence Hawkes, *Structuralism and Semiotics* 155 (1977). There is unintended irony here, since methodologically, as we shall see, New Criticism has significant affinities with postmodernism, which Hawkes does not consider a product of bourgeois sycophancy. And would not sophistication, wit, and poise be prized in any civilized society?

is intelligible only in a context, that is, only in terms of presuppositions regarding language and culture that the reader brings with him rather than finds in the text, some thought that very little in the way of context was necessary to make literature intelligible. Cleanth Brooks, in contrast, thought it essential to the interpretation of Marvell's ode to know what the words in it meant in the seventeenth century, when it was written; what the poem owed to Horace; and something about Cromwell's career. But he didn't think it important to know Marvell's conscious opinion of Cromwell, since Brooks believed that a poet can write better than he knows. As Aldous Huxley once said, to admire a writer and want to meet him makes as much sense as loving paté de foie gras and wanting to meet the goose. Or as Auden apostrophized Yeats, "You were silly like us: your gift survived it all."

The history of literature contains countless obtuse or deceptive (often falsely modest) comments by creative writers on their own work. These include T. S. Eliot's description of "The Waste Land" as "only the relief of a personal and wholly insignificant grouse against life; it is just a piece of rhythmical grumbling," and Kafka's pronouncing "The Metamorphosis" a failure because of its ending.[30] Among the reasons for this obtuseness are not only the role of the unconscious in literary creativity and the author's lack of distance and perspective in judging his own work, but also the possibility that the writer may generate meaning as a by-product of his attempt to solve a technical problem, such as how to make what he wants to say conform to his chosen metrical scheme or how to provide the audience with essential information (recall the discussion in Chapter 2 of the dumb show in *Hamlet*). The inspiration that sets the writer going must be distinguished from the process of selection and revision necessary to complete the work. The meaning of the work will emerge from the interaction of these activities and thus in the act of creation, rather than having been completely thought out in advance.[31]

When Brooks says that the poet writes better than he knows, he does not mean that someone else's hand is pushing the pen or pressing the keys, or that the writing is random, accidental, or occult. The writing is being guided by the poet's mind, only not necessarily the conscious mind, aware of all the ramifications of meaning that are being created. Some literature

30. T. S. Eliot, *The Waste Land: A Facsimile and Transcript of the Original Drafts Including the Annotations of Ezra Pound* 1 (Valerie Eliot ed. 1971); Ronald Gray, *Franz Kafka* 91 (1973).

31. See Beardsley, "The Creation of Art," in *The Aesthetic Point of View* 239 (Michael J. Wreen and Donald M. Callen eds. 1982); Samuel Alexander, *Beauty and Other Forms of Value*, ch. 4 (1933). For a case study of the emergence of poetic meaning from the process of revision, see Jon Stallworthy, *Between the Lines: Yeats' Poetry in the Making* (1963).

is written in a state close to an unconscious blur. The great fifth part of "The Waste Land" spilled out in a rush and required virtually no correction, while "The Judgment" was written uninterruptedly in a single night.[32] "Automatic" writing of this sort is unusual, and most great works of literature undergo painstaking revision before the author will authorize publication. But often the revisions are made not according to conscious plan but instead out of an unconscious sense of feel and fitness. They are nonetheless *intended*, just as Meursault intended to shoot (though not necessarily to kill) the Arab even though he had no plan to do so before he pulled the trigger. Because we do not have unmediated access to another person's mind, intent is always something inferred or constructed; we're foolish to take people's statements of their intentions at face value. I think that all that the New Critics meant in rejecting what they called the "intentional fallacy" was that the materials for inference or construction should not include anything beyond the text itself except the *essential* contextual elements, which they did not think included the details of the author's biography or the author's conscious understanding of his intentions. This is surprisingly congruent with the view later expressed by Foucault about authorship. Like him, the New Critics thought authorship a construct, and they insisted that the author be constructed from his work rather than from his biography and his extraliterary opinions.

Why did they think it necessary to take this intermediate step of constructing an author (as they certainly did, for they are constantly talking about what Donne meant in this poem or Yeats in that one)? The reason is that we normally interpret a piece of writing as someone's action. So when we want to interpret a particular text, we construct an actor, the writer whose action we are trying to understand.[33] We are highly attuned to inferring people's intentions from their words, gestures, facial expressions, and deeds. It is the most natural thing in the world, therefore, when confronted with a human artifact in the form of writing, to seek to understand it by reference to the inferred intentions of the artificer. It would have been unnatural for me in the previous chapters, when talking about works of literature, to refrain from implying authorship, saying that Homer, for example, about whom nothing is known, including whether someone by that name wrote either of the Homeric epics, meant us to think thus and so about Achilles or Agamemnon.

32. Eliot, note 30 above, at 82–90, 129; Peter Ackroyd, *T. S. Eliot: A Life* 116–117 (1984); Gray, note 30 above, at 57.

33. Alexander Nehamas, "What an Author Is," 83 *Journal of Philosophy* 685 (1986); A. D. Nuttall, *The Stoic in Love: Selected Essays on Literature and Ideas* viii (1989).

The concept of the implied author is helpful here. One element of authorial intention is the intention that the reader consider the author a particular kind of person. The reader forms this belief by inference from the book itself. So the implied author—who might better be called the inferred author—stands between the real author and the reader. Formalists of legal as of literary interpretation—formalists of contractual interpretation, for example—stop their inquiry into authors' intentions with the implied author. One thing that makes Shakespeare's plays so difficult to interpret is that a play does not have an implied author, and we do not have the crutch of conscious intentions to fall back upon because nothing is known of Shakespeare's personal opinions.[34]

If formalist criticism is in this sense intentionalist, intentionalist criticism is in another sense formalist. As Frank Kermode explains, writing against the intentionalist P. D. Juhl,

> Somebody is quoted [by Juhl] as having maintained that [Swift's "Modest Proposal"] has "something to say" about the Vietnam War, and his application is permitted as an instance of significance. The *meaning* of the pamphlet, however, is [to Juhl] entirely a matter of Irish conditions in Swift's own time. But this is surely wrong: the most that could be claimed is that Swift so *planned* it. On Juhl's own argument, what Swift intended was what he wrote, and what he wrote is compact of ironies, opacities, interpretanda of many kinds, and the hermeneutic effort required to discover what they mean (and to so determine Swift's intention) is indistinguishable from that required for the elicitation of "significance." Swift's work reflects upon the desirability of massacring babies as a political expedient, and so what it says is not at all entirely a matter of Irish conditions in 1729, though it applies to those conditions, as no doubt it does to the Vietnam War; it would certainly be absurd to argue that Swift meant to discuss that war, and it would be absurd to say that he did not have Ireland in mind, but these considerations are insufficient to justify Juhl's retreat into an intentionalism far more primitive than the kind he is expounding.[35]

Similarly, if you know anything about Yeats's life, you know that most of his love poetry alludes to (without naming) Maud Gonne.[36] But the fact that he did not name her, and that he published his poetry knowing that most of

---

34. See, for example, the interesting discussion of Shakespeare's religious views by Patrick Collinson, "William Shakespeare's Religious Inheritance and Environment," in Collinson, *Elizabethan Essays* 219, 251–252 (1994), concluding that nothing is known about those views except what might be inferred (again nothing) from the fact that Shakespeare's father may well have been Catholic.

35. Kermode, *The Art of Telling: Essays on Fiction* 206–207 (1983), discussing Juhl, note 23 above.

36. For a fascinating discussion, see Deirdre Toomey, "Labyrinths: Yeats and Maud Gonne," in *Yeats Annual No. 9: Yeats and Women* 95 (Deirdre Toomey ed. 1991).

his readers would either not know or not care who the loved one in the poem was, suggests that he did not intend the poems to be just about Maud Gonne.[37] To put this point differently, he intended her to have a representative status. In the poetry she is changed from an individual into a type.

The real fight is not between formalists and intentionalists; that fight, fierce as it is, is largely, although as we shall see not entirely, semantic, academic, and sectarian. The real fight for which the dispute between formalism and intentionalism is mistaken is between critics whose interests are primarily aesthetic and those whose interests lie rather in the author's life or personality (biographical critics), his politics, his relation to his own or subsequent times, or his ethical views as expressed or implied in his works. But there is a second real fight as well. It is the fight between those (including formalists) who believe that literary texts are objectively interpretable and those who do not. The issue of the constructed character of authorship cuts across this divide. The construction of the implied author facilitates objective interpretation by assimilating the work of literature to other purposive human action which we interpret without being able to peek into the actor's mind. But noninterpretivists think it arbitrary (or worse) to try to construct an author. They think the effect is to conceal the truth about interpretation, which is that there are as many different interpretations as there are readers. The readers are the real authors. Anyone who has seen different productions of the same play realizes how much leeway the playwright leaves for competing interpretations; and when there is no performing intermediary—when the reader is alone with a novel or poem—the reader must play the mediating role himself. And there is more than one reader.[38]

It will sharpen the analysis to give legal and literary examples of intentionalist, New Critical, and postmodern interpretation—but New Criticism shorn of

---

37. A similar argument can be made about the equal protection clause of the Fourteenth Amendment: although the ratifiers' primary intention may have been just to prevent certain forms of discrimination against blacks, the omission to mention race in the clause is evidence of a secondary intention to give the clause a broader reach.

38. In addition to making general points of this sort, the reader-response school of literary criticisms has offered a number of arresting insights. For example, Wolfgang Iser, in his book *The Act of Reading: A Theory of Aesthetic Response* 191–192 (1978), points out that serial publication (as of Dickens's novels when first published) gives the reader a more creative role than book publication. Between installments the reader will be thinking ahead and considering alternative possibilities more thoroughly than if he is reading the novel uninterruptedly or with only brief, irregular interruptions. He may therefore put up greater resistance if the novel does not come out as he has been led to expect; and this prospect may in turn restrict the novelist's freedom as he composes the novel. The reader's collaborative role in creating literary meaning is made transparent by this example. An even clearer example is an unfinished novel, which forces every reader to compose his or her own ending.

the religious or political commitments of the New Critics themselves. Confronted by the provision in the Eighth Amendment that forbids "cruel and unusual punishments," the New Critic judge might ask, what ethically satisfying meaning might this verbal artifact be made to bear? Might not capital punishment be deemed cruel because taking life is cruel, and unusual because with the greater tenderness that modern people feel about human life, very few people who commit capital crimes are actually executed? (Moreover, capital punishment has been abolished in most Western countries.) Capital punishment is therefore cruel and unusual, and should be forbidden.[39] The intentionalist would be inclined to ask, rather, what the framers of the Bill of Rights were trying to accomplish by forbidding cruel and unusual punishments. Unfortunately, he would not get a completely clear answer. He might conclude either that they were just trying to forbid punishments that were barbaric or that they also wanted to forbid punishments too severe to fit the crime, along with all punishments, severe or lenient, for conduct that ought not be made criminal at all.[40] None of the intentionalist readings, however, supports a conclusion that capital punishment is unconstitutional.

By way of a literary example I offer Yeats's great poem "Easter 1916." Here are the last three of its four stanzas:

> That woman's days were spent
> In ignorant good-will,
> her nights in argument
> Until her voice grew shrill.
> What voice more sweet than hers
> When, young and beautiful,
> She rode to harriers?
> This man had kept a school
> And rode our wingèd horse;
> This other his helper and friend
> Was coming into his force;
> He might have won fame in the end,
> So sensitive his nature seemed,
> So daring and sweet his thought.

---

39. Paul Brest, "The Misconceived Quest for the Original Understanding," 60 *Boston University Law Review* 204, 220–221 (1980).

40. Compare Anthony F. Granucci, "'Nor Cruel and Unusual Punishments Inflicted': The Original Meaning," 57 *California Law Review* 839, 840–842 (1969), with Ingraham v. Wright, 430 U.S. 651, 664–667 (1977). See also Harmelin v. Michigan, 501 U.S. 957 (1991); Hugo Adam Bedau, *Death Is Different: Studies in the Morality, Law, and Politics of Capital Punishment* 105–110 (1987); Stephen E. Meltzer, "*Harmelin v. Michigan*: Contemporary Morality and Constitutional Objectivity," 27 *New England Law Review* 749 (1993).

This other man I had dreamed
A drunken, vainglorious lout.
He had done most bitter wrong
To some who are near my heart,
Yet I number him in the song;
He, too, has resigned his part
In the casual comedy;
He, too, has been changed in his turn,
Transformèd utterly:
A terrible beauty is born.

Hearts with one purpose alone
Through summer and winter seem
Enchanted to a stone
To trouble the living stream.
The horse that comes from the road,
The rider, the birds that range
From cloud to tumbling cloud,
Minute by minute they change;
A shadow of cloud on the stream
Changes minute by minute;
A horse-hoof slides on the brim,
And a horse plashes within it;
The long-legged moor-hens dive,
And hens to moor-cocks call;
Minute by minute they live:
The stone's in the midst of all.

Too long a sacrifice
Can make a stone of the heart.
O when may it suffice?
That is Heaven's part, our part
To murmur name upon name,
As a mother names her child
When sleep at last has come
On limbs that had run wild.
What is it but nightfall?
No, no, not night but death;
Was it needless death after all?
For England may keep faith
For all that is done and said.
We know their dream; enough
To know they dreamed and are dead;
And what if excess of love

Bewildered them till they died?
I write it out in a verse—
MacDonagh and MacBride
And Connolly and Pearse
Now and in time to be,
Wherever green is worn,
Are changed, changed utterly:
A terrible beauty is born.

The title and oblique references in the text reveal that the poem is in some sense about the Easter Rebellion in Ireland during World War I, which the British repressed with great firmness. A New Critic might deny that the reader needs to know any more about the circumstances in which the poem was composed and to which it refers in order to extract its full meaning as a work of art. (But at least this much he must know—and that green is the Irish national color, and probably also—to make sense of "England may keep faith"—that England had in 1914 agreed to create an Irish Free State but that the plans had been shelved with the outbreak of the war.) It might help to have read other poetry by Yeats, though this too is problematic—for why are not the poet's other poems considered extrinsic to this one, just like his biography? This is another aspect of the baffling but inescapable issue of the proper context in which to read a text. No text is intelligible in a vacuum; but once contextual factors are admitted (as they must be), it is unclear what the stopping point should be. Should it be at the point where the text is no longer gibberish? Or should the reader keep going, in search of a richer, fuller meaning—maybe a private, highly personal one? Who can say?

An intentionalist would think it important to point out that the four people discussed in the second stanza of the poem were real people and that three of them—the three men (Pearse, MacDonagh, and MacBride)—were executed; that one of them, MacBride, described in the poem as "a drunken, vainglorious lout," was the ex-husband of Maud Gonne; and that Yeats, like many of the Anglo-Irish (that is, Protestants), believed in Irish independence but did little for it and in fact lived most of his life in England.[41] Yeats was, or

41. James D. Boulger, "Yeats and Irish Identity," 42 *Thought* 185, 189–194 (1967); Elizabeth Cullingford, *Yeats, Ireland and Fascism* 91–98 (1981); Hugh Kenner, *A Colder Eye: The Modern Irish Writers* 180–182 (1983); C. K. Stead, "Politics as Drama," in *William Butler Yeats: A Collection of Criticism* 51 (Patrick J. Keane ed. 1973). I am not persuaded by Said's argument that the characteristic themes of Yeats's poetry can be referred to his having been a colonial engaged in a cultural rebellion against imperial oppression. Edward W. Said, *Culture and Imperialism* 237–238 (1993). As a member of the Protestant ascendancy, Yeats belonged to the colonizer, rather than the colonist, class, a little like Camus, although Yeats was less ambivalent about Irish independence than Camus was about Algerian independence—paradoxically, since Yeats was from birth a reasonably well-off member of the colonizer class, whereas Camus grew up in poverty.

at least pretended to be, obsessed with Maud Gonne, a firebrand for Irish independence, though herself English; many of his poems refer directly or indirectly to her, in this case through the reference to Major MacBride. The woman of the second stanza, Constance Markiewicz, was sentenced to death for her part in the Easter Rebellion, but her sentence was commuted to imprisonment and she was soon released. You can visit her home, Lissadell, near the Irish town of Sligo where Yeats was born, and see photographs of her. Yeats believed that she, like Maud Gonne, had become poisoned by an unwomanly preoccupation with politics. Padraic Pearse's school, referred to in the second stanza, was named St. Enda's.

All this is very interesting, and a consuming interest in Yeats's poetry makes it almost impossible to resist extending this interest to his life and times, so discovering the rest of the autobiographical references in his poems. It is this natural human curiosity about the person behind the work that drives the demand for biography of distinguished persons. You can visit Coole Park and see the lake where Yeats counted 59 swans in "The Wild Swans of Coole."[42] In the gift shop attached to Yeats's nearby summer home, Thor Ballylee, you can see photographs of Major Robert Gregory, the son of Yeats's patroness and friend Lady Augusta Gregory and the subject of two of his finest poems, "In Memory of Major Robert Gregory" and "An Irish Airman Foresees His Death." (You can also buy a toy leprechaun there.) You can visit Yeats's grave in Drumcliffe Churchyard, beneath Ben Bulben (Ireland's highest mountain), and read the magnificent epitaph that Yeats ordered carved on his headstone—"Cast a cold eye / On life, on death. / Horseman, pass by!"

But having done all these things and more, has one come closer, as it were, to the poetry? I don't think so. The physical and human landscape that is celebrated in Yeats's poetry seems, when encountered directly rather than as mediated through the poetry, rather commonplace—and I say this as one who has been reading Yeats's poetry with undiminished pleasure for forty years. Even the Easter Rebellion is generally thought to have been a harebrained scheme that would have been a political disaster had it not been for Britain's foolish decision to shoot the rebel leaders—and perhaps for Yeats's poem. Of course for some people a work of literature is merely a window on the author and his time and place, a historical document, as in Ziolkowski's book on law and literature, cited in previous chapters. They are entitled to this interest, but they are missing a lot. Genius is borne in frail vessels amidst drab surroundings. The only thing remarkable about

---

42. I counted one when I visited it.

Yeats or about his relatives and most of his acquaintances and friends, including Maud Gonne, was his poetry, which is certainly a good deal more than the projection of his life and times onto the printed page, and which is diminished, even trivialized, when used as a windowpane or telescope. "Easter 1916" is a challenging case for my thesis, since it is undoubtedly a notable document in the history of Yeats and of modern Ireland. But its major interest, for me at any rate, lies elsewhere—in the poem's dramatization, made emotionally compelling in part by the lilting rhythm, of the transformative effects of revolutionary movements on human personality. These effects are fearfully mixed (hence the refrain "terrible beauty"). On the one hand, the drunken, vainglorious lout has resigned his part in the casual comedy; on the other hand, a protracted sacrifice can make a stone of the heart and be futile to boot, for England may keep faith for all that is done and said. The penultimate stanza ("Hearts with one purpose alone . . .") is at once the least political and the most beautiful.

I have a similar reaction to Marvell's ode to Cromwell, another political poem. What is striking and memorable in the poem has nothing to do with Cromwell as such but rather with the figure of the representative Great Man, the idea of greatness (both in Cromwell and in Charles I) as bound up with theatricality,[43] the ambivalence displayed toward Cromwell in the poem, and the striking description of Charles—but it could be any noble figure—on the scaffold. "He nothing common did or mean / Upon that memorable scene," about which the poet comments, "This was that memorable hour / Which first assur'd the forced power," adding somberly in the closing couplet: "The same arts that did gain / A power must it maintain."

I cannot prove that an aesthetic or formalist approach to Yeats or Marvell is better than a biographical, historical, or political approach, or even that the aesthetic or formalist approach to literature is not covertly political. Some people are more interested in writers than in what is written and in the past more than the present, and some see everything in life through the lens of politics. All that I can say with any approach to certainty is that the interpretive issue with regard to the cruel and unusual punishments clause is different from the interpretive issue with regard to the poems that I have discussed, because the clause plays a different role in our lives than does poetry. The clause was added to the Bill of Rights, with little debate or discussion, to mollify people worried that the strong central government ordained by the Constitution might imitate the British practice of using criminal punishment to in-

---

43. Notice the parallel allusion in "Easter 1916" to resigning one's "part / In the casual comedy."

timidate political opponents. The concern was with methods of punishment that were barbarous and hence especially intimidating, and possibly with the making of inoffensive or only trivially offensive conduct criminal. No effort to particularize the prohibition was made; the framers were content to appropriate the term "cruel and unusual" from the English Declaration of Rights of 1689 as a general, summary formula. Particularizing would have been time-consuming and might have sparked debilitating controversy, since it is easier to agree on generalities than on particulars. The courts would be there to particularize the prohibition if that became necessary. Sufficient unto the day is the evil thereof might be the motto of the legislative process. The forging of a consensus, or even just of a majority agreement, in a diverse group may be impossible unless some disputes can be papered over with general language, leaving resolution to the courts. Another reason for not having particularized the prohibition against cruel and unusual punishments in the constitutional text, a reason that hindsight teaches was vital to the survival of the prohibition as a meaningful limitation on punishment, is that to do so would have reduced its adaptability to social and technological changes—changes in society's conceptions of cruelty, in the frequency of particular punishments, and in the technically feasible range of painful or humiliating methods of punishment.

General as the language of the clause is, we cannot be cavalier about the authors' or ratifiers' intentions. When a court reads the Constitution, it is looking for guidance. It would find none if it felt free to give "cruel and unusual punishments" any meaning that the words permit. A New Critical approach would thus let the Eighth Amendment delegate to the courts untrammeled power to regulate criminal punishments. True, the standards that Ronald Dworkin would use in interpreting legal enactments are philosophical rather than literary. But there is no more agreement on the important issues in political philosophy than there is in aesthetics. Regarding the specific issue of capital punishment, some philosophers and philosophically minded lawyers believe that justice requires capital punishment, which was Kant's view, and others that justice forbids it.[44] Besides being indeterminate, Dworkin's approach imposes an intellectual burden on judges—that they be philosopher kings—which none is fit to bear. (Significantly, he calls his model judge "Hercules.") New Critics could produce convergent interpretations of the great literary texts only to the extent that they shared aesthetic values that told them what interpretation of an ambiguous poem would make it the best aesthetic object it could be.

44. See, for example, Tom Sorell, *Moral Theory and Capital Punishment* (1987); Ernest van den Haag and John P. Conrad, *The Death Penalty: A Debate* (1983).

We cannot expect the legal counterpart to New Criticism to produce convergent interpretations of the great legal texts without a similar consensus on underlying value questions.

But can intentionalism do much better? A sophisticated legal intentionalism recognizes that the framers might intend to regulate a set of activities not all of which they could actually foresee—might intend that, within prescribed limits, the intentions of others (for example, of judges applying the legislators' handiwork in the distant future) should govern rather than the legislators' own mental pictures of the future.[45] This recognition may largely dissolve intentionalism as a usable interpretive strategy (no surprise in light of the earlier discussion of the mutual interpenetration of formalism and intentionalism—Balkin's "nested opposition"). Largely, but not entirely, since the problem of intention about intention mainly arises when legal provisions are couched in vague or general language. When, as in the age-35 clause, the provision is specific, the authors' intentions usually are obvious.

The effect of generality on interpretive freedom can be seen in poetry as well. Consider the famous couplet from Yeats's poem "The Second Coming": "The best lack all conviction, while the worst / Are full of passionate intensity." Although poetry tends to be concrete and particular, Yeats here uses general language to create an aphorism of broad applicability. Many people reading it for the first time are put in mind of the behavior of the appeasing democracies in the 1930s toward the fascist powers. Since the poem was written in 1919 Yeats could not have been thinking about the political situation in the 1930s. But there is no objection to saying that the poem is "about" that situation, just as there is no objection in principle to reading Kafka "prophetically." Swift's "Modest Proposal," in contrast to "The Second Coming," *purports* to be about Ireland, so it takes a bit of a wrench to think it is also about Vietnam (maybe it would be better to say "applicable to" rather than "about"). No similar wrench is necessary with Yeats's couplet, because it is not topical. Moreover, the tone of "The Second Coming" is prophetic; if one of its

45. Hirsch, the leading intentionalist literary critic, gets this exactly right in a brief discussion of statutory interpretation. Hirsch, note 23 above, at 124–125; also Hirsch, "Counterfactuals in Interpretation," 3 *Texte: Revue de critique et de théorie littéraire* 15 (1984). That the framers of the Constitution indeed meant to distinguish between the "intent" of the document and the "intentions" of the authors (that is, how the authors themselves would have decided a specific case arising under the Constitution, knowing only what they knew when they wrote it), and to allow only the former to guide interpretation, is argued in H. Jefferson Powell, "The Original Understanding of Original Intent," 98 *Harvard Law Review* 885 (1985). For counterargument, see Charles A. Lofgren, "The Original Understanding of Original Intent?" 5 *Constitutional Commentary* 77 (1988).

prophecies happens to come true, the poem is ready at hand to "mean" it.[46] Broadly drafted constitutional provisions have the same property of ready applicability to unforeseen situations.

The problematic nature of intentionalism is further illustrated by the debate[47] over the meaning of this untitled lyric by Wordsworth:

> A slumber did my spirit seal;
>   I had no human fears:
> She seemed a thing that could not feel
>   The touch of earthly years.
>
> No motion has she now, no force;
>   She neither hears nor sees;
> Rolled round in earth's diurnal course,
>   With rocks, and stones, and trees.

The debate is about whether the reader is meant to feel horror at the death of Lucy (the name of the young girl, as we may infer from the surrounding poems),[48] or to feel consoled. There is extrinsic evidence that at the time Wordsworth wrote the poem he was a pantheist. He thought that the rocks and stones and trees were alive, which suggests that he meant the reader to be consoled rather than distressed by the prospect of Lucy's being rolled around with them.[49] If this was his intention, it was imperfectly

46. Robert H. Bork prefaces his book *Slouching towards Gomorrah: Modern Liberalism and American Decline* (1996), a jeremiad of cultural pessimism, with "The Second Coming," reprinted in full, and comments: "The image of a world disintegrating, then to be subjected to a brutal force, speaks to our fears now . . . The rough beast of decadence, a long time in gestation, having reached its maturity in the last three decades, now sends us slouching towards our new home, not Bethlehem but Gomorrah." Bork, above, at vii. This is vivid, but misreads the poem. The "rough beast" ("And what rough beast, its hour come round at last, / Slouches towards Bethlehem to be born?") is not *impelling* anyone toward Bethlehem; "slouches" is not transitive. What is being depicted is the Second Coming of a de-Christianized Christ conceived not as the Prince of Peace but as the violent disturber of mediocrity and cowardice (". . . but now I know / That twenty centuries of stony sleep / Were vexed to nightmare by a rocking cradle"). The "rough beast" is a redemptive figure, though an unorthodox one. And decadence is smooth, not rough.

47. Discussed in (among other places) Hirsch, note 23 above, at 227–230, and Walter Benn Michaels, "Against Formalism: The Autonomous Text in Legal and Literary Interpretation," 1 *Poetics Today* 23, 29–30 (1979).

48. Efforts to find a historical model for Lucy have failed. Mary Moorman, *William Wordsworth: A Biography: The Early Years, 1770–1803* 423–428 (1957). This process of inference from surrounding poems, by the way, illustrates one of the functions of the author construct: to improve understanding by comparison with other works reasonably assumed to have the same general outlook or to be pieces in the same jigsaw puzzle of meaning.

49. See Michaels, note 47 above, at 30.

achieved. The image of the motionless, deaf, dumb Lucy being whirled around forever "with rocks, and stones, and trees" (the rhythm of the last line reinforcing the sense of circular, repetitive, perhaps dizzying motion) is grim. If we want to save the poem as an object of aesthetic value we can impute an unconscious intention at war with and overcoming Wordsworth's conscious desire to celebrate pantheism, or we can say that his primary intention was to write a good poem, or we can forget intentionalism and simply say that we are interested in the poem rather than the poet's biography—not in what the poet "could possibly have meant" but in what "could possibly be meant" by the poem.[50]

If intentions are to be disregarded when they contradict what the work itself seems to be saying—what in other words the implied author is saying—maybe they should not enter into interpretation at all. Richard Baines, a contemporary of Christopher Marlowe, wrote shortly after Marlowe's death that Marlowe had boasted of being an atheist. Although Baines may have been lying, there is corroboration for what he reported.[51] Yet it does not follow that *Doctor Faustus* is blasphemous rather than orthodox. Even if Marlowe was an atheist, he may have wanted to write an orthodox play. He may have thought that such a play would be better, more interesting, more dramatic, or more popular than an atheistic one—especially since a play believed to be atheistic would have been suppressed. He may simply have wanted to stay out of trouble; atheists were still being burned at the stake in late sixteenth-century England. Knowing that Marlowe probably was an atheist may make us more alert for un-Christian undertones in *Doctor Faustus*—more sensitive to Faustus's oscillation between skepticism and faith—than we would be if we thought Marlowe had been the Archbishop of Canterbury. But we cannot determine the meaning of the play by reference to his beliefs.

Wordsworth's lyric can also be used to point up the difference—and also the continuity—between New Criticism and (literary) deconstruction. Here are excerpts from a discussion of the poem by J. Hillis Miller:

> Lucy is both the virgin child and the missing mother, that mother earth who gave birth to the speaker and has abandoned him. Male and female, however, come together in the earth, and so Lucy and the speaker are "the same," though the poet is also the perpetually excluded difference from Lucy, an unneeded increment, like an abandoned child. The two women, mother and girl child, have jumped over the male generation in the middle. They have

50. Stein Haugom Olsen, *The End of Literary Theory* 37 (1987).

51. For a judicious summary of the evidence, see J. B. Steane, "Introduction," in Christopher Marlowe, *The Complete Plays* 9, 12–15 (J. B. Steane ed. 1969).

erased its power of mastery, its power of logical understanding, which is the male power *par excellence* . . . The poet has himself somehow caused Lucy's death by thinking about it. Thinking recapitulates in reverse mirror image the action of the earthly years in touching, penetrating, possessing, killing, encompassing, turning the other into oneself and therefore being left only with a corpse, an empty sign . . . Lucy's name of course means light. To possess her would be a means of rejoining the lost source of light, the father sun as logos, as head power and fount of meaning . . . In spite of the diurnal rotation of the earth that earth seems to have absorbed all the light. Even the moon, reflected and mediated source of sunlight at night, and so the emblem of Lucy, has set . . . This loss of the radiance of the logos, along with the experience of the consequences of that loss, is the drama of all Wordsworth's poetry, in particular of "A Slumber Did My Spirit Seal."[52]

In this kind of criticism the work of literature becomes a window into the critic's mind, just as in a narrowly intentionalist criticism the work of literature becomes a window into the author's mind. Notice, among other extravagances that give Miller's essay an air of free association, his emphasizing the etymology of "Lucy" even though the name does not appear in the poem itself or in its title (it has no title). This is a standard deconstructive move—all the more because practitioners of deconstruction are fascinated by imagery of light. Light puts them in mind of the metaphor of understanding as seeing, a metaphor that reflects the "metaphysics of presence," which deconstruction challenges.

To someone who had never heard of deconstruction, Miller's essay might seem just an extreme example of New Criticism. But in the word "extreme" lies an essential difference. The judicial interpretation of contracts is predominantly formalist; only in exceptional cases is extrinsic evidence admissible to alter the meaning that one would infer from the writ-

52. Miller, "On the Edge: The Crossways of Contemporary Criticism," in *Romanticism and Contemporary Criticism* 96, 108–110 (Morris Eaves and Michael Fischer eds. 1986). For another taste of literary deconstruction, see Barbara Johnson, "Melville's Fist: The Execution of *Billy Budd*," in Johnson, *The Critical Difference: Essays in the Contemporary Rhetoric of Reading* 79 (1980). When deconstructed, Melville's novella turns out to be about the crisis in reading, its characters are different types of reader, and the law being "critiqued" is the law of signification. The deconstruction of Kafka has led to such *aperçus* as that in "In the Penal Colony" "Kafka portrays the fall of *logos* into time with the gusto of a Harpo Marx." Allen Thiher, "Kafka's Legacy," 26 *Modern Fiction Studies* 543 (1980–1981). Then there is Derrida's deconstruction of "Before the Law," in which he finds sexual significance because "door" in French (not in German of course, the language in which Kafka wrote) is *porte;* the Latin phrase *ante portas* is a medical expression for premature ejaculation; and the man from the country never succeeds in entering the door to the law. See Derrida, "Devant la Loi," note 13 above, at 143. And I mentioned in Chapter 5 (note 15) the deconstructive interpretation of the *Odyssey* that has Odysseus fabricating the tale of his adventures after the Trojan War.

ten contract in the absence of such evidence. Yet there are better and worse interpretations of contracts, and likewise better and worse interpretations of "A Slumber Did My Spirit Seal." Miller's is among the worst.

Possible attitudes toward fidelity to an author's conscious intentions range, as we have seen, from a narrow intentionalism at one end, through formalism in the middle, to deconstruction (and postmodernism more generally) at the other end.[53] Generally, but as we shall see not invariably, the interpretation of statutes and constitutions should lie closer to the intentionalist end than literature should. A poet tries to create a work of art, a thing of beauty and pleasure. He either succeeds or fails. If he succeeds, we do not care how banal his intentions were, and if he fails, we do not care how elevated they were. A legislature is trying to give commands, not only to the persons whose conduct the legislation is intended to regulate but also to the judges who will be applying the legislation in specific cases. A command is designed to set up a direct channel between the issuer's mind and the recipient's. It is a communication, to be decoded in accordance with the sender's intentions. If a message is garbled in transmission you ask the sender to repeat it; that is intentionalism in practice. If you cannot reach the sender, you try to glean from everything you know about him and the circumstances of the failed message what he would have done had he been on the spot.[54] Again the correct analysis is an intentionalist one. One of the things that gives intentionalism its purchase in literary criticism, besides the misguided search for authoritative literary interpretations, is the Romantic fascination with the personality of the artist—with the work of art as emanation rather than artifact. That is why there is resistance to the idea that Shakespeare's plays were written by "the Stratford man" rather than by someone like Francis Bacon or the Earl of Oxford, who had a more impressive c.v.[55] That a statute is an emanation is condition of its authority.

Notice how in describing the legislative text as command or communication I am doing just what the deconstructionists denounce: I am privi-

---

53. The spectrum becomes a loop in the influential critical writings of William Empson, a free-reading close interpreter (too close, at times, according to John Crowe Ransom, *The New Criticism* 121–130 [1941]) who often based his readings on highly speculative reconstructions of authorial intent.

54. This is not a novel approach to interpretation. It was Aristotle's theory of statutory interpretation (see *Rhetoric,* bk. 1, ch. 13), and was articulated by John Adams with great clarity shortly before the Constitution was promulgated. See Leonard D. White, *The Federalists* 130 (1948), quoting John Adams, *Works,* vol. 8, pp. 11–12 (1853).

55. James D. A. Boyle, "The Search for an Author: Shakespeare and the Framers," 37 *American University Law Review* 625 (1988). These people are unaware of Huxley's dictum, which seems as applicable to Shakespeare as to any writer.

leging the spoken over the written word; that is, I am thinking of the written word on the model of speech, a less problematic form of communication than writing. At the same time I am doing what the New Critics denounced: refusing to treat the legal text as a fascinating multifaceted artifact, and instead treating it as an attempt to set up a path of clear communication between author and reader. But why not? Some statutes are open-ended but most are not, whereas open-endedness is characteristic of great literature. Remember that works of literature are called great because they transcend boundaries of period and culture. Their property of meaning different things to different people is not problematic because it is not the function of literature to lay down rules of conduct.

Much great literature—this is a central insight of the New Critics—achieves an equipoise, rather than a resolution, of opposing forces. Recall Marvell's exquisite ambivalence about Cromwell. To come down on one side or another—for Cromwell or against him—is not a response that the poem invites. Statutes may be ambivalent too, through failure of foresight or pressure to compromise. But when a statute is drawn into litigation, the court must adopt a reading that will favor one side of the lawsuit or the other. It cannot revel in statutory ambivalence.

Meaning and message are more likely to diverge in literature than in law. One can extract a clear and definite message from either type of writing by paraphrase. The message of *Doctor Faustus* is that if you sign a pact with the devil you will be sorry in the end. At the level of message most works of literature are clear, but also banal; what makes them unclear is that we are not interested in staying at that level; we seek a deeper meaning that may be inconsistent with the surface meaning. But the message level is the only interesting level of a statutory or constitutional text, unless the text is to be merely a launching pad for judicial flights of fancy. That is why the Peller-Tushnet interpretation of the age-35 provision in the Constitution seems obtuse or provocative rather than ingenious.

Many contemporary critics rebel against being chained to the text. They are "in it for what they can get out of it, not for the satisfaction of getting something right."[56] The public would be horrified at such a conception of the judicial role. The concern of literary intentionalists with the idea of authoritative interpretation (for them, the interpretation that is faithful to the author's intent) is displaced from its proper object. The problem of legitimacy need not arise in literary criticism, but it is central to law and government. The literary intentionalist is a lawyer *manqué;* the legal New

---

56. Richard Rorty, *Consequences of Pragmatism (Essays: 1972–1980)* 152 (1982). And recall the quotation from Hartman, in note 17 above.

Critic is a literary critic *manqué*. The former demands a type of constraint on interpretation that law rather than literature requires;[57] the latter seeks a freedom of interpretation that literature allows but law does not.

For an intentionalist like Juhl, who concedes the inexhaustibility of literature, the possibility of unconscious intention, and the dangers in relying too heavily on historical and biographical materials as clues to the author's intent,[58] almost the whole significance of intentionalism is to rule out interpretations that cannot be referred to the author's conscious or unconscious mind. Mainly these are interpretations that either imply prophetic gifts (for example, interpreting *The Trial* as an allegory of the police state, the "Fourth Eclogue" as an allegory of the birth of Christ, or "The Second Coming" as an allegory of the Munich Pact) or contradict unequivocal biographical or historical data. Juhl illustrates with a passage from "The Love Song of J. Alfred Prufrock": "Would it have been worth while . . . To have squeezed the universe into a ball." Suppose, says Juhl, that we knew Eliot had never read Marvell's "To His Coy Mistress," which contains the lines, "Let us roll all our strength and all / Our sweetness up into one ball." Then, Juhl argues, we could not regard the allusion to Marvell as part of the meaning of Eliot's poem.[59] Why not? Why not say that Eliot had made a lucky hit—had, by his choice of words, accidentally enriched the meaning of his poem for readers who remembered Marvell's poem and would contrast the vigor of the lover's solicitations in that poem with Prufrock's hesitations?

A related point is that because "the aim of literary interpretation is to reveal those features which make the work a good literary work[,] . . . coherence and complexity are criteria of an author's intention which override whatever the author himself may have to say about the emergent aesthetic features of a work after he has delivered the text."[60] The most im-

---

57. Hirsch points out that there is an "advocacy system in [literary] interpretation as in law. The advocates have the task of bringing forward evidence favorable to their side and unfavorable to their opponents . . . But without a judge all those relevant pieces of evidence float uselessly . . . [Therefore] unless advocates sometimes serve as judges, none of this activity will actually contribute to knowledge." Hirsch, note 23 above, at 197. But there is no mechanism for appointing authoritative judges of disputes over literary interpretation; nor would such a mechanism be welcome. And self-appointed judges with no authority are not a close analogue to official judges.

58. See Juhl, note 23 above, at 135, 151, 225–230; also Hirsch, note 23 above, at 22 ("it is very possible to mean what one is not conscious of meaning") and his discussion in "Counterfactuals in Interpretation," note 42 above, of the importance of distinguishing dominant from local intentions and the spirit from the letter of a work.

59. Juhl, note 23 above, at 58–59.

60. Olsen, note 50 above, at 51.

portant methodological innovation of the New Criticism was to adopt a hypothesis of total coherence—to assume that no detail of a work of literature is an accident, that everything contributes in some way to its meaning and emotional impact.[61] Through the study of the details of a work and their interrelations one begins to understand how great literature casts its spell. In "The Wild Swans at Coole" we are made to feel the mystery and remoteness of nature by a surprising yet somehow "right" juxtaposition of the words "cold" and "companionable" in a description of swans on a lake:

> Unwearied still, lover by lover,
> They paddle in the cold
> Companionable streams or climb the air;
> Their hearts have not grown old;
> Passion or conquest, wander where they will,
> Attend upon them still.

The same interpretive technique—that of attributing significance to every detail—is, when used on statutes, a familiar source of error. Statutes and constitutions are written in haste by busy people not always of great ability or diligence, and we are not privileged to ignore the hasty and the hackneyed provisions and reserve our attention for the greatest. They are the products of a committee, moreover, the legislature, rather than of a single mind—and a committee whose numerous members may have divergent objectives. So a statute may well contain meaningless repetitions and inconsistencies. To suppose that its every word probably has significance, that every statute is a seamless whole, may be a useful discipline (see Chapter 4), but taken literally it misconceives the nature of the legislative process and can lead to erroneous interpretations, at least if authorial intention is important in statutory interpretation, as I think it is. A similar mistake would be to suppose that the interpretive task for a court is to make the statute or constitutional provision in question the best rule of law the court can imagine, because legislators can be assumed to strive to make the best rule of law they can, as Yeats strove to make "The Wild Swans at Coole" the best poem he could. That is to be unrealistic about legislative intention, and the practical consequence is to substitute the judge's will for that of the legislature—which is more serious than the substitution of a critic's will for Wordsworth's or Yeats's. If the intended meaning of the

61. Robert Penn Warren, "A Conversation with Cleanth Brooks," in *The Possibilities of Order: Cleanth Brooks and His Work* 1, 15 (Lewis P. Simpson ed. 1976) (remark of Brooks). The presumption is rebuttable; there are radically imperfect works of literature, as argued in Hershel Parker, *Flawed Texts and Verbal Icons: Literary Authority in American Fiction* (1984).

legislation remains inscrutable after the court has made its best effort to determine that meaning, the court may have no choice but to impress a meaning upon the legislation, and in such a case Dworkin's approach may be best, for in that case the judges are, realistically, the legislators. But that is the exceptional case.

Literary critics operate in a more competitive market than judges. The extravagances of the former must pass a market test similar to that of literature itself—will they be accepted by other critics or perhaps by the reading public at large? The Supreme Court need convince no one of the rightness of its "interpretations"; its word is law. There is also a feedback loop between interpretation and legislation. If interpretation is too erratic, the making of new legislation is discouraged because legislators cannot predict the effects of the legislation they pass. There is no similar loop between critics and authors. Legislatures, moreover, usually produce a publicly available "legislative history" to help guide judicial interpretation. Writers of literature sometimes offer interpretations of their own works, but for reasons discussed earlier these interpretations tend to be unreliable. Sometimes writers preserve their unpublished drafts, which are comparable to the unenacted bills that often precede an enacted statute. But though invaluable in understanding the process of creative composition, writers' rough drafts rarely dispel interpretive fogs; this is the lesson of Stallworthy's fine study of the Yeats manuscripts. It is harder to extract the writer's intentions than those of the legislature. Often it is attempted by facile psychoanalyzing on incomplete data: the fate that has befallen Kafka, among many others.

And the legislature has at least decided to enact the law being interpreted. Many literary works (including *The Trial* and *Billy Budd*) were left unfinished at their authors' death, making it uncertain whether what we have was intended to be read. Kafka left instructions to destroy all his unpublished works, though how seriously these instructions were intended to be taken is unclear. We do not know which if any drafts of his plays Shakespeare regarded as authoritative. Intentionalism is deeply problematic in these instances.

Related to the obvious point that uniformity is more important in legal than in literary interpretation is the subtle point that multiple interpretations of the same work at the same time may be an equilibrium state for the literary marketplace and a source of disequilibrium in law. A reader's interpretation of a literary text is affected by what he knows; and different readers know different things. There is no way in which a person who has spent a lifetime studying Shakespeare can convey his entire understanding of the Shakespearean context to a nonspecialist; Shakespeare's plays will always mean different things to specialists and nonspecialists. Eliot's fourth quartet, "Little Gidding," will yield additional meaning to the reader who recognizes that "The dove descending breaks the air / With flame of incandescent terror" refers to the bombing of England in World War II, a reference not apparent from the poem itself but assumed by every student of Eliot's poetry. "The Wild Swans at Coole" will yield a richer meaning to a person who has read a lot of Yeats's poetry than to one who has read little or none of it, because the former will realize that "swan" has not just its ordinary meaning in Yeats's poetry but also an esoteric meaning as a symbol of pride, courage, and power.[62] *The Trial* takes on additional hues of meaning if read in conjunction with Kafka's legal parables, such as "The Problem of Our Laws," than if read in isolation. But it would be incorrect to say that you cannot understand a Yeats poem or a Kafka novel without having read extensively in, and having reflected profoundly upon, other works by these authors, and without, in addition, having immersed yourself in what *they* read. It would be a mistake to suppose that only the specialist possesses the authentic meaning of the great works of literature. The authors of those works would not have wanted it so; they were not writing for a tiny coterie of professors.

But while the judge thus has many reasons to feel less free than the literary critic, he has as many reasons to feel freer than the critic. A legislature is not a single mind, and the determination of collective intent is often problematic and sometimes impossible. Moreover, much legislation reflects compromise rather than consensus, and one way to achieve compromise is to use general language, in effect shifting to the courts the task of completing the legislation. Neither intentionalism nor New Criticism provides helpful analogies here. But I admit that the distinction that I am trying to draw between law and literature is blurred by the frequency of committee authorship in literature.[63] For example, *Hamlet* as we experience it is a collaboration of Shakespeare, the authors of the sources on which he drew, the early printers who garbled his texts, the actors whose ad libs may have become incorporated into the text,[64] modern editors of its various texts, and the producers, directors, and actors who put on performances of the play.

The principle of *stare decisis* (decision in accordance with precedent) also

---

62. Esoteric, but not unique: compare the lines on the dying swan in Yeats's poem "The Tower" with Socrates' explanation for the "swan song" in *Phaedo* 84e–85b.

63. See note 8 above.

64. Masten, note 8 above, at 371, notes Hamlet's request to the players to be allowed to interpolate some lines, apparently a common Elizabethan practice.

deflects statutory and constitutional interpretation from framers' intentions. When a particular interpretation has become entrenched in a long line of decisions, a court will be loath to abandon it, because of the reliance that has been engendered, because the court wants to maintain the appearance that law is objective and impersonal, or because the court does not want to encourage legislators to be hasty and careless by leading them to think that judges will make any needed legislative revisions simply by reinterpreting legislation to keep it abreast of the times. The result of a long period of judicial interpretation, such as that undergone by the Constitution (two centuries) or the Sherman Antitrust Act (one century), may be a body of doctrine that bears even less relation to the intentions of the framers than a modern interpretation of an old work of literature will bear to its author's intentions.

While the only, though not a bad, reason for an interpretation of a work of literature that makes it mean something different from what it meant to its original audience is to get greater pleasure and insight from the work, a free interpretation of a statute or the Constitution may be necessary to avert a catastrophe. The limitations that the Constitution appears to place on the powers of the President and the Congress have been relaxed by judicial interpretations of the Constitution in order to accommodate the perceived exigencies of modern government. The Second Amendment provides that "a well regulated Militia, being necessary to the security of a free State, the right of the people to keep and bear Arms, shall not be infringed." This language states pretty clearly that the federal government shall not forbid law-abiding citizens to keep military weapons. But the government has felt compelled to forbid this and the Supreme Court has not interfered. Lacking generality and hence adaptability, the Second Amendment, like a too topical work of (attempted) literature, has become obsolete and, rightly or wrongly, has been ignored, as I said might also happen to the age-35 provision if it began to bite too hard. The existence of Marxist and feminist literary criticism makes it no longer possible to say that there is no political pressure in this country to interpret literature freely (unconventionally, unexpectedly)—and perhaps the New Criticism illustrates the ubiquity of "political" criticism—but there is less pressure than in the case of legislation.

There is, moreover, a morality of rebellion as well as of obedience. Like Captain Vere in *Billy Budd*, I have stressed the latter, appropriately in a civilized democratic society such as ours. (Anyway, I'm a judge, so what can you expect?) In a wicked society, the proper course for a judge might be to defy the law. With power to deprive citizens of their property, liberty, or even lives comes responsibility for the wise exercise of this power as well as duty to obey the legal limitations on its exercise.[65] Even in a civilized legal system the circumstances of an individual case may rightly lead the judge to decide in a way that cannot easily be squared with the text of the statutory or constitutional provision being interpreted. This is another example of the force of discretionary, equitable, or political considerations in judicial decision making. Such considerations are elements of the law, just as rules handed down by higher authority are. Aristotle introduced the idea of equity *(epieikeia)* to justify judicial departures from the literal meanings of statutes.

And, strange as it may seem, ignoring historical context can sometimes do more damage to the understanding and enjoyment of works of literature than to the understanding of statutes and constitutions. The cultural distance between a work of literature and its reader usually is greater than that between a statute and the judge concerned with its meaning. The legal texts that are authoritative in the American legal system were written by American lawyers no earlier than 1787 and usually much later. Works of literature are often much older, often foreign, often written by inhabitants of a radically different cultural milieu from that of the modern American reader. To read literature composed in a different culture without being aware of the difference is reckless. Imagine trying to read *Hamlet* without knowing how such words as "brave" and "fat" have changed meaning (Gertrude's remark during Hamlet's duel with Laertes that Hamlet "is fat and scant of breath" does not mean that Hamlet is overweight but either that he is sweaty or, less probably, since he has been practicing fencing steadily, that he is out of condition), or that the English thought Danes given to excessive drinking (that is the "custom / More honored in the breach than the observance," that is, more honorably rejected than followed, to which Hamlet refers), or that marriage to a brother-in-law was deemed incestuous. Imagine trying to read *The Merchant of Venice* thinking that Jews had the same position in Elizabethan society as they do in ours. Imagine reading works of literature written half a century ago and thinking that when they used the word "gay" (as in the line from Yeats's poem "Lapis Lazuli": "They know that Hamlet and Lear are gay") they meant homosexual.

Some readings based on ignorance or error may be better, in the sense of imparting a greater resonance to the work of literature, than readings scrupulously confined by historical knowledge. I gave a few examples earlier; there are others. Several mistranslations in the King James version of the Bible seem superior on literary grounds to the originals, though maybe

65. Cf. Robert M. Cover, "Violence and the Word," 95 *Yale Law Journal* 1601 (1986).

it is only habit and tradition that make us think so. Mark Twain's careless revising of *Pudd'nhead Wilson* may be an example of serendipitous error.[66] The Duke's admonition to Claudio in *Measure for Measure*, "Be absolute for death," is more impressive if "absolute" is taken in its modern sense rather than in its Elizabethan senses of resolute or (as in Hamlet's outburst at the literalistic gravedigger, "How absolute the knave is") single-minded. But such serendipity is rare. The introduction of a random element is unlikely to improve a work of literature; and except in the rare instance where the reader is as talented as the author, the reader is unlikely to improve the work by using it as a mirror for his own insights.

Judges read statutes and the Constitution not for enjoyment but for help in deciding a lawsuit and in devising or refining a rule of conduct that may have a significant impact on the welfare of the community. The community is not always willing to allow its choices to be controlled by what people who lived two centuries ago wrote into the Constitution, talented as those people were; and the procedure for amending the Constitution is so cumbersome that the judges are under great pressure to use the interpretive process to keep the original document flexible. The framers themselves may not have wanted to control the future tightly even though flexible interpretation would be bound to impair the symmetry and elegance of what they wrote. Consequences are more important in legal than in literary interpretation and may tug the interpreter away from the words of a statute or constitutional provision or the framers' conscious intentions. Radical critics *want* their literary interpretations to have consequences in the political world,[67] but "as things stand now in our society, interpretations of literary works, no matter what their emphasis and independently of the motives of those who produce them, do not connect up strongly with the issues being debated in the larger political arena."[68]

Artificial interpretive rules, moreover, such as a rule that every word in

---

66. Herschel Parker disagrees. Parker, note 61 above, at 5. He asks, how can the chapters that Mark Twain wrote before he decided to make the false "Tom" a black, and included without change after making him black, be taken seriously as meditations on race, or genetics, or slavery? See id. at 135–145. The answer is that context shapes meaning. Mark Twain may have retained these chapters because, relocated in a work about blacks and whites, they acquired new meaning.

67. As one of them writes, "Literary theory has come to be identified with the political left . . . In one sense, theory has been the continuation of radical politics by other means." Terry Eagleton, "Discourse and Discos: Theory in the Space between Culture and Capitalism," *Times Literary Supplement,* July 15, 1994, p. 3. But Eagleton doubts that literary theory has any political consequences.

68. Stanley Fish, *Professional Correctness: Literary Studies and Political Change* 51 (1995).

a statute is to be deemed significant, can be defended as a way not of determining intentions but instead of curtailing judicial discretion and inducing clearer legislative drafting (and thus curtailing judicial discretion indirectly, by giving the judges less wiggle room in reading a statute). There is no counterpart pressure in literary criticism to adopt interpretive rules that obstruct the search for meaning. Last, because a basic goal of education is to give students a sense of other cultures, there is an argument for continuing to stress the original meaning of works of literature that, once again, has no counterpart in law.

All this said, I do think a judge should pay more intention to legislators' conscious intentions than a literary critic should pay to the author's conscious intentions; and this rules out Dworkin-style "New Critical" statutory and constitutional interpretation. But the judge should also pay attention to practical consequences in choosing between interpretations, and this rules out the kind of narrow textualism that I have just described, which is another kind of legal formalism though one remote from Dworkin's. I see no inconsistency between being a pragmatist judge who emphasizes legislative intention and practical consequences and a formalist literary critic in the style of the New Criticism. This just illustrates my opening point in this chapter about the field-dependence of interpretation.

I also have no quarrel with the law's adhering in the interpretation of *contracts* to a rather narrow textualism, placing strict limits on the use of extrinsic evidence, including testimony about the contracting parties' conscious intentions, to change the meaning suggested by the contractual text. Walter Benn Michaels and Stanley Fish have attacked this rule, arguing that because interpretation is inherently contextual, intrinsic interpretation is a fantasy.[69] Fish notes, for example, that a court will allow evidence that the trade to which the contract pertains (for example, maritime shipping or cotton factoring) attaches a special meaning to words used in the contract, a meaning that would not be apparent to an ordinary reader. So, says Fish, the parties are allowed to contradict the written contract after all.[70] A vital distinction is overlooked. Trade usage can be established by disinterested testimony to a reasonable degree of certainty; to consult trade usage is like consulting a dictionary. The concern behind the rule limiting extrinsic evidence in contractual interpretation is that written contracts would mean little if a party could try to persuade a jury that while the contract said X, the parties had actually agreed, without telling anybody or writing anything

69. Michaels, note 47 above, at 26–29; Fish, *There's No Such Thing as Free Speech, and It's a Good Thing, Too* 141–156 (1994).
70. Id. at 148.

down, that the deal was *Y*. That concern is not engaged by objective evidence, such as trade usage, and therefore such evidence is not barred. The principles of contractual interpretation depend on the purposes of contract law, rather than on any general theory—there is no such thing—of interpretation.

Chain Novels and Black Ink

Scholars who believe that legal texts can be analogized to literary texts rarely specify which literary genre provides the best analogy to law. Dworkin is the exception; he has specified the genre—the chain novel.[71] One author writes chapter 1. This sets a certain direction because the next author must write chapter 2 in such a way that it seems to grow out of chapter 1 so the two will seem like work of the same hand; likewise with subsequent chapters. Each author thus has less freedom than the one before. Dworkin suggests that the judge who must first interpret a constitutional text is like the author of chapter 2, while a judge asked to interpret a constitutional text on which additional meaning has been grafted by previous judicial interpretations is like the author of one of the subsequent chapters. Not so. First of all, the chain novel as Dworkin defines it places no constraint on authors of subsequent chapters. Each author can in the first sentence of his chapter kill off all the existing characters and start anew. Of course this would not be thought cricket, but that just means that the writing of a chain novel is a more complex practice than Dworkin's description of it. It is thus unclear to what exactly he is analogizing the legal interpretive process.

Dworkin's analogy is additionally defective because it puts the judges who interpret the Constitution on the same level as the framers of the Constitution: the framers just get the ball rolling. Even if the author of the first chapter of a chain novel could, despite my first point, exclude some possible sequels, all the chapters would be equally authoritative. But decisions interpreting an authoritative legal text, such as the Constitution or a statute, inherently stand on a different, and lower, level than the text. Only the text is fully authentic; all the interpretive decisions must return Antaeus-like to the text for life-giving strength. Dworkin's analogy equates the judges who interpret the Constitution to the framers of the Constitution.

Even as a description of common law rather than of statutory or constitutional law, the chain-novel analogy is misleading. First, "chapter 1" in

71. Dworkin, *Law's Empire,* note 24 above, at 228–250, 313.

the evolution of common law doctrine is likely to be highly tentative—more like a preface or introduction. Second, the "authors" of the subsequent chapters are not bound to adhere to the directions set by the author of chapter 1. If accumulating experience shows that chapter 1 took a wrong turn, the judges can discard it. Third, the common law is merely the set of legal concepts created by judicial decisions, and as with any concept, the precise articulation is mutable, can be refined, reformulated. The concept is inferred from the decision (more often from a sequence of decisions) but exists apart from it. The common law judge thus is not engaged in the exegesis of fixed, authoritative texts. The literary critic, the biblical exegete, and the judge engaged in statutory and constitutional interpretation all have the difficult task of interpreting a fixed text.

The skeptical vein in literary criticism, and the hermeneutic theories that nourish it, show how difficult the interpretation of texts can be and by doing so should make lawyers, judges, and legal scholars more cautious, more self-conscious, more tentative about the process of interpreting legal texts. But it has been the burden of the argument in this chapter that no specific techniques or discoveries of literary criticism, or literary analogies, such as that of the chain novel, are transferable to the law. Like law, literary criticism lacks a formalizable method or theory—a lack that all the theoretical endeavors since Aristotle show no signs of closing. A good literary critic is a careful, thorough, scrupulous, informed, logical, and practical reader of literary texts, and a good lawyer is a careful, thorough, scrupulous, informed, logical, and practical reader of legal texts. They are both close readers, but of different materials. Their strength as close readers comes from immersion in a voluminous, diverse, but particular body of texts rather than from mastery of a theory.

Sanford Levinson may be right that "there are as many plausible readings of the United States Constitution as there are versions of *Hamlet*, even though each interpreter, like each director, might genuinely believe that he or she has stumbled onto the one best answer to the conundrums of the texts."[72] But his dictum implies a relation between interpretive problems that does not exist. Among the things that open *Hamlet* to different interpretations are that it was written almost 400 years ago (and is thus almost 200 years older than the original U.S. Constitution and the Bill of Rights) and in another country; that the text is corrupt; that there is no evidence of the author's intentions beyond what is in the text; that it was written to be performed rather than to be read; that plays are inherently open-ended

72. Levinson, "Law as Literature," 60 *Texas Law Review* 373, 391 (1982).

because actors' inflection, timing, and body language, and details of the sets, are usually not prescribed by the text of the play and can alter the intrinsic meaning of the lines;[73] that great literature is, almost by definition, pitched at a level of generality that invites divergent interpretations; that part of the fascination of *Hamlet* is the number of interpretive puzzles it poses; and that we do not care much about what Shakespeare thought he was trying to accomplish—partly because we do not know, partly because we doubt that he fully knew. The things that make the Constitution open to different interpretations include multiple authorship, the apparent decision of the framers to leave certain issues open through the use of general language, the social, economic, legal, political, and institutional changes that have occurred since the Constitution was drafted, and the lack of agreement on how free a judge should feel in interpreting a constitutional provision and what weight he should give to previous interpretations of it. The puzzles about the Constitution are so different from those about *Hamlet* that it is unlikely that a *Hamlet* scholar will have anything useful to say about the Constitution or a constitutional scholar anything useful to say about *Hamlet*.

When, however, a law professor does resort to literary theory in these debates, he invites ripostes from literary theorists, such as Stanley Fish.[74] Fish is famous for claiming that meaning does not reside in a text but is imposed by the reader, and hence that the source of any interpretive agreement must be found in the training, experience, and power of the interpreters. If because of selection, training, or hierarchy, professional or official, people can be made to think alike or like-thinking people come to control the interpretive process, interpretations of the same text will converge, although the resulting consensus will not reflect any objective or determinate properties of the text: "there is nothing in principle to prevent the emergence of a unified legal interpretive community. All that

---

73. Consider the "reversal of values" achieved by the nineteenth-century English actor Henry Irving, who first made Shylock a thoroughly sympathetic character. "The elopement scene in his production [of *The Merchant of Venice*] closed in a whirl of music, lights and color, with Jessica and Lorenzo caught up in a crowd of masquers as it swept across the stage. The curtain dropped briefly; when it rose . . . 'the stage was empty, desolate, with no light but a pale moon, and all sounds of life at a great distance—and then over the bridge came the weary figure of the Jew.' He was bearing a lantern, returning (though he did not realize it yet) to a deserted house. Then the curtain fell again, without a word having been spoken." John Gross, *Shylock: A Legend and Its Legacy* 149 (1992).

74. See the essays collected in Fish, *Doing What Comes Naturally: Change, Rhetoric, and the Practice of Theory in Literary and Legal Studies* (1989), and in Fish, note 69 above; and, for criticism, Reed Way Dasenbrock, "Do We Write the Text We Read?" in *Literary Theory after Davidson* 18 (Reed Way Dasenbrock ed. 1993).

is required is that a number of assumptions be so firmly held that they are no longer regarded as assumptions, but as truths so unchallengeable that the determinations (of fact, constitutionality, etc.) they entail would be universally recognized and acknowledged. As an institution the law would then be in the happy state (if it is happy) enjoyed by certain branches of the physical sciences."[75] Since this "happy state" neither exists nor is foreseeable in American legal culture, Fish leaves us stranded on the skeptical shoals.

He is emphatic that theory cannot bring us to the happy state. Theory can have no effect on practice. For Fish, every area of human activity is a game that has rigid rules, like chess. You could have a theory *about* chess—about its origins, its fascination, even how it might be improved by a change in its rules. But you could not use the theory in playing chess. When you play chess you play by its rules, not theory's rules. So legal theory, including theories about interpretation, whether they originate in law itself, or in literary theory or practice, or anywhere else, could not be expected to alter the way judges decide cases, Fish argues, because judges play the judging game, which has its own rules. Although I am generally sympathetic to the argument, he misunderstands the stakes in legal debates over "originalism" and other legal interpretive theories. As with the extrinsic-evidence rule of contract law, the issue is not "theoretical" in Fish's sense. It is a question about a practice, about what evidence, arguments, and policies shall be admissible in the resolution of particular types of dispute—a concrete, discussable, and even answerable question but not one that theories of interpretation will shed any light on.

With Fish, a literary critic and theorist, gliding effortlessly between skepticism about the possibility (at least as things are, and can be expected to remain) of objective literary interpretations and skepticism about the possibility (subject to the same qualification) of objective legal interpretations, it is no wonder that Levinson should connect the multiplying interpretations of *Hamlet* with the multiplying interpretations of the Constitution. And, though different, the two phenomena do have a common cause. The 1950s were a period of consensus both in English departments and in law schools; and literary critics who share similar values, and lawyers who share

---

75. Fish, "Interpretation and the Pluralist Vision," 60 *Texas Law Review* 495, 498 (1982). Compare A. W. B. Simpson, "The Common Law and Legal Theory," in *Oxford Essays in Jurisprudence* 77, 95 (2d ser., A. W. B. Simpson ed. 1973), arguing that the determinacy of the English common law in its heyday was due to the extraordinary degree of social and educational uniformity among the judges.

similar values, are apt to generate in their respective fields interpretations that command wide agreement and therefore seem authoritative. Political and methodological consensus has eroded in both fields, generating an increase in interpretive divergence.

Consistent with my separation thesis—legal and literary interpretation have nothing *useful* in common—I take exception to Charles Fried's effort to infer the intelligibility of the Constitution from that of Shakespeare's Sonnet 65.

> Since brass, nor stone, nor earth, nor boundless sea,
> But sad mortality o'ersways their power,
> How with this rage shall beauty hold a plea,
> Whose action is no stronger than a flower?
> O, how shall summer's honey breath hold out
> Against the wrackful siege of battering days,
> When rocks impregnable are not so stout,
> Nor gates of steel so strong, but Time decays?
> O fearful meditation! Where, alack,
> Shall Time's best jewel from Time's chest lie hid?
> Or what strong hand can hold his swift foot back?
> Or who his spoil of beauty can forbid?
> > O, none, unless this miracle have might,
> > That in black ink my love may still shine bright.

Fried argues that the poem's premise is the intelligibility of writing, and that the premise has been triumphantly vindicated by time, for the poem is 400 years old, yet, he implies, it poses no interpretive problems for the contemporary reader.[76] He has overlooked those problems, and not only by *sub silentio* modernizing the spelling and punctuation.[77] In writing "spoil of beauty" he has (again without acknowledgment) used an emended version of Shakespeare's original text, which reads "spoil or beauty."[78] And he has overlooked the note of dubiety sounded by "un-

---

76. Fried, "Sonnet LXV and the 'Black Ink' of the Framers' Intention," 100 *Harvard Law Review* 751 (1987).

77. On the uncertainties of meaning created by the erratic punctuation of Shakespeare's sonnets as originally published, see Theodore Redpath, "The Punctuation of Shakespeare's Sonnets," in *New Essays on Shakespeare's Sonnets* 217 (Hilton Landry ed. 1976). To compare the original with the modern spelling and punctuation of Sonnet 65, see *Shakespeare's Sonnets* 58–59 (Stephen Booth ed. 1977), where the original and modern versions are printed side by side. I have quoted the version of the sonnet published in Fried's article.

78. Booth, in *Shakespeare's Sonnets,* note 77 above, at 247, argues against the emendation. On the inescapability of literary theory in textual emendation, see G. Thomas Tanselle, "Recent Editorial Discussion and the Central Questions of Editing," 34 *Studies in Bibliography* 23 (1981).

less" and "may" in the concluding couplet and by the possible pun in "might." Shakespeare is not so confident as Fried supposes that "black ink" can survive time's ravages.[79]

There may be a graver misinterpretation. It has been suggested that the reference to "black ink" is contemptuous and that Shakespeare, careless of publication, saw the "miracle" elsewhere: "The poet knows that through his poetry, or the poetic consciousness, he establishes, or focuses, a supernal reality, or truth, what we may call a 'poetic dimension', that cannot otherwise be attained; and of this the written poetry ('black ink'), though it be necessary, is really subsidiary, the carrot to the donkey, but not the journey's purpose."[80]

I will set aside these quibbles and concede that Fried has shown that a great work of literature can, because of the timelessness of its theme, be universal without being ambiguous. Still, the implications of this point for the interpretation of the Constitution are obscure. Some of Shakespeare's works may not pose acute interpretive difficulties, but others do, as do works of literature considerably more recent. If we pursue the misguided quest for literary analogies to problems of legal interpretation, we shall have to ask in every case whether the particular statutory or constitutional provision we're interested in is, in point of interpretive difficulty, more like Sonnet 65 (or what Fried thinks Sonnet 65 is like) or more like other and more ambiguous literary works, such as *Billy Budd*, written in this country a mere century ago. On such questions Fried is silent. Literary theory provides no more comfort for the legal Right than for the legal Left. One can no more argue the interpretability of the Constitution from Sonnet 65 than one can argue the inscrutability of the Constitution from *Hamlet*.

Interpretation as Translation

I said at the beginning of this chapter that the debate over interpretation, having reached white-hot intensity in the 1980s, has cooled considerably. There has been one new development of note, however, and that is the proposal to think of legal interpretation on the model of translations from

79. Compare Fried, note 76 above, at 756, with *Shakespeare's Sonnets*, note 77 above, at 247; Murray Krieger, *A Window to Criticism: Shakespeare's Sonnets and Modern Poetics* 170–172 (1964); Philip Martin, *Shakespeare's Sonnets: Self, Love and Art* 153–155 (1972); Kenneth Muir, *Shakespeare's Sonnets* 66 (1979); Rodney Poisson, "Unequal Friendship: Shakespeare's Sonnets 18–126," in *New Essays on Shakespeare's Sonnets*, note 77 above, at 1, 11.

80. G. Wilson Knight, *The Mutual Flame: On Shakespeare's Sonnets and* The Phoenix and the Turtle 86 (2d ed. 1982).

one language to another,[81] especially translations of literary works, where the problematics of translation are most conspicuous.

The proposal takes two forms. James Boyd White argues that since "no sentence can be translated into another language without change," translation can only be "the composition of a particular text by one individual mind in response to another text,"[82] and a judicial opinion interpreting a provision of the Constitution should be viewed in the same light. The premise is incorrect. Some sentences *can* be translated into another language without any loss of meaning: instructions for assembling a kitchen table, for example. The provision of the Constitution that the President must be at least 35 years old, or the provision that each state is entitled to two senators, can be "translated" from eighteenth-century linguistic, political, and social understandings into those of the twentieth century without loss of meaning, even though longevity has increased and the method of choosing senators has changed.

This is more than a quibble. It shows that literal translation is not an oxymoron, and places on White the burden of showing that legal enactments are more like poems than like instructions. It also suggests that translation involves the making of choices that may be neither "right" nor "wrong." Take Agamemnon's usual sobriquet in the *Iliad*: "*anax andron.*" A literal translation might be "supreme leader of the warriors," but that is stilted. If we wanted to make the *Iliad* sound modern we could translate the term as "Supreme Allied Commander" or even "Chief Honcho" (this would be like playing *Hamlet* in modern dress). Or if we wanted to preserve the sense of antiquity, of cultural distance, we could leave the term untranslated, as in "Kaiser Wilhelm" (versus "Emperor William"). We might compromise with "Lord Agamemnon," but this sounds a bit British Imperial. The choice among these myriad possibilities, none satisfactory, none right or clearly wrong, has to do with the effects the translator is aiming at and the intended use of the translation and hence the intended audience. Although White expects reflection on the difficulties of literary translation to engender humility in the judge faced with the task of "translating" an eighteenth-century document into the culture of today, an alternative inference to be drawn from the practice of literary translation is the translator's freedom. If a

81. See James Boyd White, *Justice as Translation: An Essay in Cultural and Legal Criticism* (1990); Lawrence Lessig, "Fidelity in Translation," 71 *Texas Law Review* 1165 (1993). For criticism of these "translation" theories, see Sanford Levinson, "Conversing about Justice," 100 *Yale Law Journal* 1955 (1991); Levinson, "Translation: Who Needs It?" 65 *Fordham Law Review* 1457 (1997).

82. White, note 81 above, at 250, 254.

translator can choose between a literal and a free translation, why not a judge between a literal and a free interpretation?

So one is not surprised that where White finds an injunction to humility, Lawrence Lessig finds a license for creativity. Building on the lawyerly intuition that constitutional and statutory interpretation, to be legitimate, must be faithful in some sense to the constitutional or statutory text, and adding that translation aims at preserving the meaning of the original text, Lessig argues that faithful translation cannot be literal because the cultural significance of words changes. In my example, "Lord" may be an adequate literal translation of *"anax andron,"* but it means something so different to modern Americans (Lord Peter Wimsey? Lord Haw-Haw? Lord Acton?) that to affix it to "Agamemnon" alters Homer's meaning for American readers. To preserve meaning in an altered social context we might have to choose a literal *mis*translation.[83] This shows that "the translator is empowered to *change text.*"[84] The same ought to be true, Lessig argues, for judicial interpretation of the Constitution.

But the translator is authorized to change text for two reasons, neither of which is applicable to law. The first is the lack of an equivalent word in the language into which a work is being translated. The second, which is related, is the need to make the translation a good "read." Translation thus involves two stages. In the first, the translator interprets the original, that is, decides the meaning. In the second, he expresses his interpretation in the language of the readers of the translation.[85] The first stage, interpretation, has a counterpart in law, of course, but I hope I have persuaded the reader that the interpretation of different kinds of text, specifically the literary and the legal, have few interesting commonalities. The second stage in translation, expression of the translator's interpretation in a new language, is no part of legal interpretation.

Consider what the best translation of some work of literature or philosophy would be if the only objective were to convey its full meaning clearly—including the shades of meaning conveyed by the form or style of the work—without regard for readability or emotional impact. It would probably be a literal translation with numerous footnotes explaining the

---

83. For dramatic examples, see Amel Amin-Zaki, "Religious and Cultural Considerations in Translating Shakespeare into Arabic," in *Between Languages and Cultures: Translation and Cross-Cultural Texts* 223 (Anuradha Dingwaney and Carol Maier eds. 1995).

84. Lessig, note 81 above, at 1191. This may not be very different from White's claim that the translator must produce a new text.

85. Raymond van den Broeck, "Literary Conventions and Translated Literature," in *Convention and Innovation in Literature* 57 (Theo D'haen, Rainer Grübel, and Helmut Lethen eds. 1989).

ways in which the translation might mislead. Untranslatable words and phrases (such as *anax andron*) might be left in the original and their meaning explained by bracketed paraphrases. Anachronisms, false cognates, conventions, changes in the cultural, linguistic, and historical context—all would be patiently explained. The result would be charmless and copious, but the loss of verbal meaning, of cognitive content narrowly defined, would be minimal. The problem of translation would not be "solved," however, and not only because an important part of the meaning of a work of literature is emotional and is killed by literal translation. The problem of translation is not achieving fidelity to the original but striking a compromise between the desire to preserve the original meaning of the translated work and the desire to interest, delight, stir, or even just economize on the time of, some target audience. The choice between a fluency that effaces the sense that one is reading a translation and so makes the author present to us, and a "translationese" that preserves the sense of the author's foreignness,[86] will depend upon the nature of the intended audience,[87] the character of existing translations, the translator's talents, and the author's preferences if he's alive and controls translation rights.[88] The choice has nothing to do with interpreting legally operative documents written in the interpreter's language.

An even deeper problem with the "translation" metaphor for statutory and constitutional interpretation, stressed by Levinson (see note 81), is that of verifiability. The accuracy of a translation can be determined by a person fluent in both languages, and such persons can be identified with considerable confidence. Whom do we trust to *know* the meaning of a disputed statutory or constitutional provision and thus to verify the accuracy of its "translation" into a modern setting? No one; if judges or professors were trusted to determine what such provisions mean, constitutional law and theory would not be such disputatious activities. The problem of conventional translation is not accuracy but readability; the *only* problem of legal "translation" is accuracy.

86. Lawrence Venuti, *The Translator's Invisibility: A History of Translation* (1995). Venuti argues against the tendency in translations into English to achieve fluency at the expense of accuracy, a tendency he attributes in typical leftist fashion to English cultural aggressiveness. He advocates "foreignizing" translations. See, for example, id. at 20.

87. Which is why careful translations of the same work into the same language can differ so greatly—as strikingly shown by the anthology *Homer in English* (George Steiner ed. 1996).

88. On the specific problems of literary translation, see Peter Green, "The Slampam Blues," *New Republic,* Feb. 19, 1996, p. 37 (reviewing *The Oxford Book of Classical Verse in Translation*); Joel Weinsheimer, *Imitation* 73–77 (1984); *Theories of Translation: An Anthology of Essays from Dryden to Derrida* (Rainer Schulte and John Biguenet eds. 1992).

EIGHT

Judicial Opinions as Literature

Meaning, Style, and Rhetoric

There is nothing eccentric about examining judicial opinions under the aspect of literature. Many distinguished works of literature began with a religious, political, or even utilitarian, rather than a literary, aim. I shall call the literary properties of the judicial opinion its "style," distinguishing "style" from conceptual content on the one hand and "rhetoric" on the other. The conceptual content of an opinion is its paraphrasable content, the part of the opinion's meaning that is not lost when it is put into different words from those employed by the author. The facts, the holdings, the dicta, the conclusion—these can all be paraphrased, and the paraphrase will convey a lot more than it would in the case of a short poem. If you paraphrased Keats's "Ode to a Nightingale" you might come up with the same trite summary as you would if you paraphrased "The Wild Swans at Coole": the narrator, contemplating avian beauty, is moved to the reflection that although people die, and individual birds too of course, nature as symbolized by the swan or the nightingale is immortal. But the force of the two poems lies elsewhere, and their effects on the reader are dissimilar. The beauty of the nightingale's song reconciles the narrator of the "Ode to a Nightingale" to death (something so much lovelier and happier will live on forever), while "The Wild Swans at Coole" presents nature as composing the cool, formal, aesthetic—and silent—pattern of a work of art. The imagery and tone of the poems are different, and as a result their meanings are different despite the similarity of their overt themes.

"Rhetoric," as I shall mainly use the term, refers to the subset of stylistic devices that is used to persuade readers or listeners to believe or to do something. Aristotle used the term to refer to all persuasive devices, not just the stylistic ones, found in fields of debate or inquiry in which logical or scientific proof is unavailable. By thus enlarging rhetoric's scope to the propositional meaning and truth value of a speech or writing as well as its form, he swept in authority, anecdote, analogy, and every other method of reasoning used to establish the probable truth of a proposition when exact demonstration is impossible.[1] Some law-and-literature scholars use "rhetoric" even more broadly, as a term of high approbation, inseparable from morality and signifying humanistic values set over against the supposedly cold rationality of social-scientific analysis.[2] This fusion of content and style, of the ethical and the aesthetic, is of a piece with the inclination of the law and literature movement toward ethical criticism (see next chapter). The commonest meaning of the word "rhetoric" in everyday speech, a meaning that can claim a remote ancestry in Plato's denunciation of rhetoric in *Gorgias,* carries the opposite valence: rhetoric as empty verbiage ("that's just rhetoric").

The first and last meanings of "rhetoric"—persuasive style and empty verbiage—connect to the meaning that I have assigned to "style." When defined as choice among the various options for encoding the paraphrasable content of a writing, style is the smooth capsule or the flavor additive that makes the medicine easier to swallow and hold down—or that makes some readers want to throw up. But it is also the earmark of "good" writing (that is, not "just rhetoric"), whether or not the writing has any persuasive purpose other than to keep the reader reading to the end. One judicial opinion might be better than another not because the argument was more persuasive but because by candidly disclosing the facts and authorities tugging against its result, by being tentative and concessive in tone, even by confessing doubt about the soundness of its result, it was a more credible, a more impressive judicial document, though not a more convincing defense of the outcome.

With the acknowledgment that there may be better or worse ways of writing up the same idea or other message, we enter the domain of handbooks of style.[3] These contain all sorts of useful precepts that judges, and

1. See discussion and references in *Essays on Aristotle's* Rhetoric (Amélie Oksenberg Rorty ed. 1996), and in Richard A. Posner, *Overcoming Law,* ch. 24 (1995) ("Rhetoric, Legal Advocacy, and Legal Reasoning").

2. See, for example, Peter Read Teachout, "Lapse of Judgment," 77 *California Law Review* 1259, 1290–95 (1989); Robert A. Prentice, "Supreme Court Rhetoric," 25 *Arizona Law Review* 85 (1983).

3. See, for example, Joseph M. Williams, *Style: Ten Lessons in Clarity and Grace* (1981). There actually are handbooks of judicial style, which parallel the general style handbooks and are largely ignored. American Bar Association, *Judicial Opinion Writing Manual: A Product of the Appellate Judges Conference, Judicial Administration Division,* ch. 3 (1991); Ruggero J. Aldisert, *Opinion Writing,* pt. 3 (1990); Federal Judicial Center, *Judicial Writing Manual* 21–26 (1991); Joyce J. George, *Judicial Opinion Writing Handbook,* ch. 4 (3d ed. 1993).

their ghostwriters, the law clerks, regularly ignore.[4] They ignore them partly because judges and lawyers tend to disdain "fine" writing, thinking it unprofessional, "literary," affected, overrefined. A distinguished federal judge begins his comment in a symposium volume on narrative and rhetorical methods by saying, "I am a judge. I know nothing of the theories of narrative and of literary criticism of law. I wondered why I was invited to contribute to this volume."[5] Then he tells a story, and very well too. But the point of the story as of his comment as a whole is that judges should forgo the "quest after persuasive power or beauty" in favor of "clear analysis and clear transmission of its message" (p. 207). He is caustic about judges who "see[ing] themselves brushing up against immortality . . . spurn the vulgar tongue and use sonorous forms that will resonate in history" (p. 208). Right on. But beauty and sonority are not synonyms; nor is clarity incompatible with rhetorical power. One can be as "professional" as one likes and still avoid infelicities that impair readability with no offsetting benefit.

Style as discretionary (as underdetermined by content, by meaning), and style as writing well, point to a third aspect of style—style as "literary." Writings count as literature when they are detachable from the specific setting in which they were created. Style is one of the features of written expression that facilitates this portability; for style is often less local, less time- and place-bound, than content (though sometimes more—style can be an impediment to understanding). Rhyme and meter, the most musical features of poetry, have an appeal that, being nonverbal, is not tied to the local culture out of which the poetry emerged. We might have lost interest in a particular legal issue discussed in a judicial opinion yet the style of the opinion may make us want to read it anyway; and then the opinion will have outlived the occasion of its creation.

The effect of style on portability is a factor in judicial reputations. Even a brilliant analysis of yesterday's legal problems is unlikely to hold much

---

4. Such precepts as: go easy on adjectives, adverbs, italics, and other modifiers, qualifiers, and intensifiers; alternate (irregularly, not metronome style) long and short sentences; don't end a paragraph with a preposition; don't use agentless passives; go easy on parenthetical and other qualifying phrases; try to begin and end sentences with important words, because the first and the last positions in a sentence are the most emphatic; avoid jargon and clichés; punctuate for clarity rather than to conform to grammarians' fusty rules for the placement of commas and other punctuation marks; be clear; go easy on quotations, especially long block quotations; pay some attention to the music of sentences; don't strain to avoid ever splitting an infinitive; disregard deservedly obscure and unobserved rules of grammar, such as never begin a sentence with "But" or "And."

5. Pierre N. Leval, "Judicial Opinions and Literature," in *Law's Stories: Narrative and Rhetoric in the Law* 206 (Peter Brooks and Paul Gewirtz, eds. 1996).

current interest, especially since a major effort at historical reconstruction may be required to determine that it *was* brilliant. The vivid and therefore memorable opinion is not chained to the immediate context of its creation. It can be pulled out and made to exemplify law's abiding concerns.[6]

Two writers' styles can resemble one another yet one will be better because the writer has avoided the pitfalls against which the handbooks warn or is a gifted writer—a person who writes well without regard to, and often while defying, the codified rules. Styles can differ in kind as well as quality. This is the domain of style as signature, as "voice." We recognize a person by his or her voice in both the literal and the figurative senses of the word. When judges were thought to be (and perhaps thought themselves to be) oracles, the ideal judicial voice would have sounded like the voice of God.

The idea of style as voice plays a rationalizing role in the contemporary scandal, as some think it to be, of the delegation of opinion writing to law clerks. If you try to embarrass a professor of constitutional law by saying, "What are you doing teaching 'opinions' written by your last year's law students? Why not just teach the answers they gave to your exam questions?" the professor is apt to reply defensively: "I know that Justice X or Justice Y delegates much of the opinion writing in his chambers to his law clerks, and yet each chambers has a distinctive 'voice.' X's opinions don't sound like Y's—they sound like X's, even though written by a constantly reshuffled deck of law clerks. The voice of the judge is audible." Everything in this imaginary quotation is true except the last sentence. Law clerks often prepare for their job by reading a bunch of their boss's old opinions (sometimes he tells them to do this), and they model their own style on that of the opinions they read. By this process a chambers style, not perhaps *very* distinctive but distinctive enough to be recognizable, evolves. All that this shows is that style, like intention, can be a corporate attribute.

To see what style can do, consider once again the couplet that concludes the first stanza of "The Second Coming." Here is the stanza in full:

> Turning and turning in the widening gyre
> The falcon cannot hear the falconer;
> Things fall apart; the centre cannot hold;
> Mere anarchy is loosed upon the world,
> The blood-dimmed tide is loosed, and everywhere
> The ceremony of innocence is drowned;

6. See, for example, Robert A. Hillman, "'Instinct with an Obligation' and the 'Normative Ambiguity of Rhetorical Power,'" 56 *Ohio State Law Journal* 775 (1995).

The best lack all conviction, while the worst
Are full of passionate intensity.

The concluding couplet, I noted in the last chapter, has seemed an uncanny prophecy of the relation between the fascists and the appeasing democracies in the 1930s. It could just as well describe the situation in American universities during the student uprisings of the late 1960s. Other readers will supply other referents.[7] Historical confirmation to one side, it strikes the reader with a self-evident sense of rightness. One reason is meter. The couplet, like most of the rest of the stanza, is in iambic pentameter. The slight lilt imparted by the meter gives the couplet a faintly incantatory quality that increases its power, as does its placement at the end of the stanza, that is, in the normal position for a conclusion, as if the poet had set forth premises that lead up to it. The preceding lines do nothing of the sort; instead they present a cascade of images. Nevertheless the "conclusion" gains authority from being presented as the culmination or resolution of an emotionally powerful vision. Its authority is enhanced by the absence of qualification. Yeats does not say that some of the best people are perhaps this and many of the worst doubtless that; he does not hedge. Few people dare to speak plainly, so when we hear a plain speaker we tend to give him a measure of trust. Only a big man, we might say, would put it so bluntly, without equivocations that he could retreat behind if attacked. At the same time, the subordinate-clause construction with the concessive "while" imparts a considered, judicious tone; imagine how the couplet's force would be diminished by replacing "while" with a superficially more forceful "but." And notice the absence of "poetic" diction in these two lines, in contrast to the preceding ones. It's as if the poet, overwhelmed with sudden insight, had been moved to drop all poetic craft in order to announce the simple truth that had been revealed to him. Notice also the contrast between the multisyllabic, sibilant richness of "passionate intensity" and the clipped matter-of-factness of "lack all conviction." We are made to *feel* the stronger emotions of the "worst" people, and this somehow makes us more convinced of the opposition asserted by the poet.

Well, you may say, a child might be taken in by such tricks, but surely an adult reader would not be persuaded of the truth of the proposition asserted by Yeats unless the reader believed it anyway, on other, more rationally probative evidence. Persuasion is not the issue. After all, it is not even clear who the "best" and the "worst" are. Yeats used poetic art to

---

7. One of the passages that I quoted from *A Frolic of His Own* in Chapter 1 contains two (unmarked) quotations from "The Second Coming."

create an emotionally powerful image which is then available to readers as a template for characterizing their own experiences.

The rhetoric of "The Second Coming" is not forensic, but the forensic tradition in literature is very old. It may be said to begin with Book I (ll. 19–24) of the *Iliad,* in Chryses' plea to Agamemnon to restore his daughter to him, a wonderfully compressed lawyer-type pleading:

> Agamemnon, Menelaus—all Argives geared for war!
> May the gods who hold the halls of Olympus give you
> Priam's city to plunder, then safe passage home.
> Just set my daughter free, my dear one . . . here,
> accept these gifts, this ransom. Honor the god
> who strikes from worlds away—the son of Zeus, Apollo!

The carrot and stick are neatly tendered—carrot first, the more courteous sequence. Chryses asks the gods to bestow victory and a safe return home on the Greeks in general and Agamemnon and his brother Menelaus in particular; and since Chryses is a priest, the invocation of divine assistance is not just an empty conventional gesture. To make assurance doubly sure, Chryses also offers a more tangible and immediate benefit, requiring no divine intervention—a ransom. The offer of the ransom comes immediately after the request to free Chryseis, thus underscoring the element of quid pro quo. Chryses ends his plea by pointedly, though as before courteously, suggesting that by accepting his offer the Greeks will be conciliating a powerful god, Zeus's son who shoots from afar, Apollo—who, not incidentally, is Chryses' patron. The Greek words for far-shooter Apollo, which are given emphasis by their placement at the end of a line and the end of Chryses' plea, have the ominous sound of a roll of thunder *(hekebolon Apollona).*[8]

Another splendid Homeric example of persuasive pleading is found in Book VI (ll. 163–203) of the *Odyssey.* Shipwrecked on his way home to Ithaca after his twenty-year absence, Odysseus is washed ashore near the mouth of a river on the island kingdom of Scheria—naked, filthy, exhausted, alone. He encounters the princess of the island, Nausicaa, who had come down to the river with her attendants to wash clothes. The attendants flee when they see this repulsive apparition but Nausicaa stands her ground. Odysseus addresses her. He wants clothing and eventually assistance in getting home. He has no way to prove who he is. How is he to persuade Nausicaa to help him? The norm of hospitality, and its abuse by both host and guest, are fundamental to the ethos and action of the

---

8. The pattern of stressed (–) and unstressed syllables (˘) in these two words is ˘ – ˘˘   – – – –.

Odyssey. Odysseus's speech to Nausicaa, which comes at the approximate midpoint of the poem, is therefore thematically central.

He begins with a heavy dose of flattery by asking her whether she is a goddess or a mortal; if the latter, then, so fair is she, "three times blest are your father, your queenly mother, / Three times over your brothers too." But "*he* is the one / more blest than all other men alive, that man / who sways you with gifts and leads you home, his bride! / I have never laid eyes on anyone like you, / neither man nor woman . . . / I look at you and a sense of wonder takes me." After more in this vein Odysseus finally mentions his plight: "pain has ground me down." He explains briefly that he was shipwrecked, adding that he doesn't think his torments are yet ended. Only then—three-fourths of the way through his speech—does he ask Nausicaa for compassion, pointing out that among other things he doesn't know anyone on the island. All he requests is that, assuming that the clothes she and her attendants brought to the river to wash were wrapped in something, she give him the wrapper to cover his nakedness, and that she show him where the city is. The request is stated briefly—the entire plea for pity and assistance takes up only six lines—and Odysseus then changes the subject from himself back to her: "may the good gods give you all your heart desires," specifically including a husband and a home.

Since Odysseus cannot pay Nausicaa for helping him, he must place her in a donative mood. A generous gift is likelier the more the donor's wealth exceeds the suppliant's. People usually set a much higher value on their own welfare than on that of a stranger, so only if they are much better off are they likely to gain more utility from the stranger's consumption of part of their wealth than they would from their own consumption of it. That may be why Odysseus devotes the first part of his speech primarily to establishing how wealthy Nausicaa will soon be because her loveliness will get her a wealthy husband, one who will outdo her other suitors in giving her fine bridal gifts. Odysseus doesn't have to spend much time persuading Nausicaa of his present poverty; that is evident from his appearance. Having established the disparity in their wealth, he emphasizes how slight the cost of the gift he is asking for (a rag and a bit of information) is to her. Even so, he offers some compensation for the modest gifts that he is asking for by ending his speech with wishes for Nausicaa's happiness. Good wishes are worth little, but a small benefit can offset a small cost.

The first part of Odysseus's speech has the additional function of reassuring Nausicaa concerning the speaker's character. By pretending to be unsure whether Nausicaa is mortal or divine, Odysseus is trying to allay any fear of this dirty and naked man that might cause Nausicaa, like her attendants, to flee from his presence; for a mortal, like himself, would be unlikely to attack a divinity. And by heaping praise on Nausicaa, Odysseus shows himself to be at once courteous, respectful, and articulate. He uses civilized words to offset his uncivilized appearance. By doing so he signals, moreover, that he may not be what he seems—he may be, as in fact he is, a powerful man temporarily down on his luck, hence someone who might in the future be in a position to repay Nausicaa's kindness to him. So there is the hint of the possibility of reciprocal altruism. And a little flattery never hurts—is in fact often enjoyed even when not believed.

Odysseus's speech is at once highly literary and, even though it conveys little information of a conventional sort, highly rational as well. The appearance of paradox in this statement (highly rational, but little information) comes from the familiar but exaggerated antithesis between reason and emotion.[9] Emotions direct and intensify attention (as in Samuel Johnson's quip that the prospect of being hanged concentrates the mind wonderfully), furnish motivation, nurture intuition, and stimulate the imagination (including the empathetic imagination, which enables us to enter into other people's feelings), while reason furnishes triggers to and disciplines, directs, and constrains emotion. Compassion is an emotion that can be activated by perceived disparities in wealth and by the size of the prospective transfer—more precisely by information about these things, information that Odysseus's speech conveys in a winning way by the weighting and ordering of the points that he needs to make in order to maximize the likelihood that he will be well treated.

The apogee of forensic oratory in literature is Antony's speech at the funeral of Julius Caesar in Act III of Shakespeare's play. Not Brutus's: his speech is a failure that highlights the qualities of Antony's and the difference in character between the two men. Although Brutus's speech is elaborately wrought, with careful use of repetition and antithesis—"Not that I loved Caesar less, but that I loved Rome more" (III.2.21–22), and so forth—the rhetorical structure is so conspicuous that the listener is made immediately aware that he is hearing an oration. This awareness opens an emotional gap between audience and speaker. The gap is widened by the oration's brevity, prose form, and chaste classical balance. Brutus—very much in character—forbears to stir the passions of the mob. He also fails to elaborate the charge of Caesar's ambition, saying merely, "but, as he was

---

9. An antithesis criticized in Nelson Goodman, *Languages of Art: An Approach to a Theory of Symbols* 245–252 (2d ed. 1976); Ronald de Sousa, *The Rationality of Emotion* (1987); Martha C. Nussbaum, *Upheavals of Thought: A Theory of the Emotions* (Cambridge University Press, forthcoming); and, with specific reference to judicial opinions, Paul Gewirtz, "On 'I Know It When I See It,'" 105 *Yale Law Journal* 1023 (1996).

ambitious, I slew him" (III.2.26–27). (And notice how he buries the charge in a subordinate clause.) This omission will make it easy for Antony to "refute" the charge. We are meant to understand, I think, that Brutus's speech, while elegant, is maladroit. One clue is that someone in the crowd shouts in response to the speech, "Let him be Caesar" (III.2.50)—showing that he's missed the point.

Antony's speech—much longer than Brutus's, and in verse rather than prose—begins with a double falsehood: "I come to bury Caesar, not to praise him" (III.2.76). He did come to praise Caesar, and also, in effect, to resurrect him by loosing Caesar's revenging spirit on the conspirators. Antony's rhetorical problem is that as he starts speaking the crowd is still with Brutus. His initial task is to win their confidence and undermine Brutus's standing. So right after saying that he will not praise Caesar he complains ever so gently about the unfairness of funeral obsequies in which only the faults of the dead man can be recited (III.2.77–79): "The evil that men do lives after them; / The good is oft interrèd with their bones. / So let it be with Caesar . . ." Antony continues to emphasize his own good faith by assuring the audience that "Brutus is an honorable man." But the repetition of this formula, mingled with reminders of Caesar's great accomplishments, causes the refrain to become increasingly, and eventually savagely, ironic (III.2.123–129):

> O masters! If I were disposed to stir
> Your hearts and minds to mutiny and rage,
> I should do Brutus wrong, and Cassius wrong,
> Who, you all know, are honorable men.
> I will not do them wrong; I rather choose
> To wrong the dead, to wrong myself and you,
> Than I will wrong such honorable men.

—by which point "honorable men" has become redefined as "ungrateful traitors."

Antony uses suspense to raise the crowd's emotional temperature even higher. He refuses at first to read Caesar's will and instead invites the crowd to gaze on Caesar's wounds. Still using suspense to good rhetorical effect, he describes the wounds in loving detail before exhibiting them. By stressing Brutus's ingratitude to Caesar, he makes it seem as if Caesar had died of a broken heart (III.2.182–187):

> For Brutus, as you know, was Caesar's angel.
> Judge, O you gods, how dearly Caesar loved him!
> This was the most unkindest cut of all;
> For when the noble Caesar saw him stab,

> Ingratitude, more strong than traitors' arms,
> Quite vanquished him. Then burst his mighty heart.

Lest the crowd tumble to the fact than Antony is playing on its emotions, he becomes ever more emphatic in denying any inflammatory design on them or breach of faith with those who gave him leave to speak (III.2.211–231):

> Good friends, sweet friends, let me not stir you up
> To such a sudden flow of mutiny.
> They that have done this deed are honorable.
> What private griefs they have, alas, I know not,
> That made them do it. They are wise and honorable,
> And will no doubt with reasons answer you.
> I come not, friends, to steal away your hearts.
> I am no orator, as Brutus is,
> But, as you know me all, a plain blunt man,
> That love my friend, and that they know full well
> That gave me public leave to speak of him.
> For I have neither wit, nor words, nor worth,
> Action, nor utterance, nor the power of speech
> To stir men's blood. I only speak right on.
> I tell you that which you yourselves do know,
> Show you sweet Caesar's wounds, poor poor dumb mouths,
> And bid them speak for me. But were I Brutus,
> And Brutus Antony, there were an Antony
> Would ruffle up your spirits and put a tongue
> In every wound of Caesar that should move
> The stones of Rome to rise and mutiny.

Almost everything in this passage is false. Brutus and the other conspirators will not be able to answer Antony with reasons if, as Antony hopes, by the time he finishes his speech the mob will be in a frenzy—and anyway Brutus had left before Antony began to speak. Antony is not a plain (in the sense of artless) speaker, and if Brutus were Antony he would not stir the mob on Caesar's behalf any more than he had done on the rebels' behalf. Antony did come to stir the crowd to mutiny and does not think the rebels honorable. Caesar's wounds are not "dumb mouths"; Antony makes them speak for him.

At last Antony lets the other shoe drop and tells the crowd what Caesar has left the citizenry of Rome in his will, ending his oration with: "Here was a Caesar! When comes such another?" (III.2.252). The crowd rushes off on cue to burn down the conspirators' houses. Yet Antony has not tried to refute the charge of ambition that Brutus laid against Caesar, except by misleadingly reminding the audience that Caesar had three times refused the crown that Antony had offered him the day before the assassination. Antony omits to add that Caesar was lured to the Capitol on the morning of the assassination by a message that the Senate would offer him a crown that day.

Not for nothing has Antony's speech been called "an exhibition of the destruction of reason by rhetoric."[10] It is not that he is insincere, or that he does not have a case; the irony of the conspirators' honorableness is genuine. It is that his rhetoric is dishonest. Yet while Shakespeare probably meant us to be critical of the Roman mob for being so easily swayed, he must also have meant us to admire Antony's consummate rhetorical skill; for there is no inconsistency in describing a piece of rhetoric as both skillful and dishonest.

A law school course in trial or appellate advocacy could be built on a comparison of Brutus's and Antony's speeches. The weaknesses in Brutus's speech, which are equally weaknesses in an oral argument to an appellate court or a closing argument to a jury, are its obtrusively rhetorical character (which puts the audience on its guard), its failure to engage the audience in dialogue, its lack of detail or anecdote, its failure to appeal to the concrete interests of the audience, and the decision to waive rebuttal. Antony ingratiates himself with an audience predisposed to be hostile to him, ticks off three arguments against Brutus's charge of ambition (they are far from airtight, but since Antony has the last word he doesn't have to worry that they will be picked apart), displays emotion, brandishes Caesar's will (his first use of a prop—and how judges and juries love physical evidence, so welcome a relief from words!), tells an anecdote about Caesar, displays Caesar's shrouded body (the second use of a prop), shows the gashes and bloodstains in Caesar's toga and then dramatically unveils the naked, mutilated body (the third prop, consisting of wounds more eloquent than words), disclaims oratorical ability in a successful effort to disarm the audience, uses the terms of the will to appeal to the audience's concrete interests and sense of gratitude, invites frequent interruption to create the illusion of conversational give and take, and ends in a state of high excitement. Antony's speech is concrete, vivid, personal, colloquial, versatile, dramatic, eloquent, blunt, emotional—and unscrupulous.

I have given examples of literary style used for persuasive ends. Here is an example of literary style in the service of legal description. It is from Philip Roth's novel *Operation Shylock* (1993). Someone is impersonating the narrator (confusingly named Philip Roth). The narrator confronts the impostor:

> "You're involved in a deceptive practice . . . You're breaking the law."
> "Which law? Israeli law, Connecticut state law, or international law?"

10. Nicholas Brooke, *Shakespeare's Early Tragedies* 157 (1968).

"The law that says that a person's identity is his private property and can't be appropriated by somebody else."

"Ah, so you've been studying your Prosser."

"Prosser?"

"Professor Prosser's *Handbook of the Law of Torts*."

"I haven't been studying anything. All I need to know about a case like this common sense can tell me."

"Well, still take a look at Prosser. In 1960, in the *California Law Review,* Prosser published a long article, a reconsideration of the original 1890 Warren and Brandeis *Harvard Law Review* article in which they'd borrowed Judge Cooley's phrase 'the general right to be let alone' and staked out the dimensions of the privacy interest. Prosser discusses privacy cases as having four separate branches and causes of action—one, intrusion upon seclusion; two, public disclosure of private facts; three, false light in the public eye; and four, appropriation of identity." (p. 75)

This is a deliciously terse and lucid introduction to the common law of privacy. Later the impostor acknowledges,

"Yes, the law *is* on your side. Who says no? I wouldn't have undertaken an operation on this scale without first knowing in every last detail the law that I am up against. In the case of *Onassis v. Christian Dior-New York, Inc.,* where a professional model, a Jackie Onassis look-alike, was used in advertisements for Dior dresses, the court determined that the effect of using a look-alike was to represent Jackie Onassis as associated with the product and upheld her claim. In the case of *Carson v. Here's Johnny Portable Toilets,* a similar decision was reached. Because the phrase 'Here's Johnny' was associated with Carson and his TV show, the toilet company had no right, according to the court, to display the phrase on their portable toilets. The law couldn't be any more clear: even if the defendant is using *his own name,* he may be liable to prosecution for appropriation if the use implies that some other famous individual of that name is actually being represented." (pp. 80–81)

If only lawyers and judges could write with such dash, grace, economy, and simplicity! It might not be the worst method of teaching legal writing to assemble an anthology of descriptions of legal doctrine found in works of imaginative literature.

There have been some fine legal stylists; and to go right to the top, I turn to Holmes's dissent in *Lochner v. New York.*[11] The Supreme Court's decision invalidated, as a deprivation of liberty without due process of law, a

11. 198 U.S. 45, 74 (1905). For other discussions of the rhetoric of *Lochner* (not limited to Holmes's dissent—and conceiving of "rhetoric" more broadly than I am inclined to do), see Forum, *Rhetorical Criticism of Legal Texts: Four Rhetoricians on* Lochner v. New York, 23 *Hastings Constitutional Law Quarterly* 619 (1996).

state statute limiting the hours of work in bakeries. The most famous sentence in Holmes's dissent—one of the most famous in the history of law and as precious to those who think the statute bad policy as it is to advocates of regulating the employment relation—is: "The Fourteenth Amendment does not enact Mr. Herbert Spencer's Social Statics." This proposition is offered without proof; and it is also possible to agree with it yet think the case correctly decided. Somehow these points seem not to detract from the authority of the dissent, now more than ninety years old. The number of opinions that survive from that period is minuscule, and a disproportionate number of them were written by Holmes. Yet, as we shall see, Holmes's opinion is not well reasoned.[12] What then is the source of its power?

Here is the full text of the opinion:

> I regret sincerely that I am unable to agree with the judgment in this case, and that I think it my duty to express my dissent.
>
> This case is decided upon an economic theory which a large part of the country does not entertain. If it were a question whether I agreed with that theory, I should desire to study it further and long before making up my mind. But I do not conceive that to be my duty, because I strongly believe that my agreement or disagreement has nothing to do with the right of a majority to embody their opinions in law. It is settled by various decisions of this court that state constitutions and state laws may regulate life in many ways which we as legislators might think as injudicious or if you like as tyrannical as this, and which equally with this interfere with the liberty to contract. Sunday laws and usury laws are ancient examples. A more modern one is the prohibition of lotteries. The liberty of the citizen to do as he likes so long as he does not interfere with the liberty of others to do the same, which has been a shibboleth for some well-known writers, is interfered with by school laws, by the Post Office, by every state or municipal institution which takes money for purposes thought desirable, whether he likes it or not. The Fourteenth Amendment does not enact Mr. Herbert Spencer's Social Statics. The other day we sustained the Massachusetts vaccination law. *Jacobson v. Massachusetts,* 197 U.S. 11. United States and state statutes and decisions cutting down the liberty to contract by way of combination are familiar to this court. *Northern Securities Co. v. United States,* 193 U.S. 197. Two years ago we upheld the prohibition of sales of stock on margins or for future delivery in the constitution of California. *Otis v. Parker,* 187 U.S. 606. The decision sustaining an eight hour law for miners is still recent. *Holden v. Hardy,* 169 U.S. 366. Some of these laws embody convictions or prejudices which judges are likely to

12. See also David P. Currie, *The Constitution in the Supreme Court: The Second Century: 1888–1986* 82 (1990).

share. Some may not. But a constitution is not intended to embody a partic-ular economic theory, whether of paternalism and the organic relation of the citizen to the State or of *laissez faire*. It is made for people of fundamentally differing views, and the accident of our finding certain opinions natural and familiar or novel and even shocking ought not to conclude our judgment upon the question whether statutes embodying them conflict with the Constitution of the United States.

General propositions do not decide concrete cases. The decision will de-pend on a judgment or intuition more subtle than any articulate major premise. But I think that the proposition just stated, if it is accepted, will carry us far toward the end. Every opinion tends to become a law. I think that the word liberty in the Fourteenth Amendment is perverted when it is held to prevent the natural outcome of a dominant opinion, unless it can be said that a rational and fair man necessarily would admit that the statute proposed [op-posed?] would infringe fundamental principles as they have been understood by the traditions of our people and our law. It does not need research to show that no such sweeping condemnation can be passed upon the statute before us. A reasonable man might think it a proper measure on the score of health. Men whom I certainly could not pronounce unreasonable would uphold it as a first instalment of a general regulation of the hours of work. Whether in the latter aspect it would be open to the charge of inequality I think it un-necessary to discuss.

After setting a properly serious and deferential tone in the first sentence, Holmes makes a startling accusation—"This case is decided upon an eco-nomic theory which a large part of the country does not entertain." He does not elaborate. The reader is told neither what the economic theory is nor the relevance of the fact (which is not elaborated either) that a large part of the country does not entertain it. The force of this opening sally lies in the assurance with which it is made. It puts the reader on the defensive; dare he question a statement made with such serene conviction? An ordi-nary judge would say something like, "I respectfully but earnestly dissent from the majority's unwarranted substitution of its own views of public policy for the more flexible mandate of the Constitution," and would fol-low up with pages of argument and citation. Holmes's method is more ef-fective because, as I pointed out in discussing "The Second Coming," in areas where our own knowledge is shaky we tend to take people at their own apparent self-evaluation and thus to give more credence to the confident statement than to the defensive one.

A speaker's effort, at the outset of the speech, to make himself seem like the kind of person who can be trusted to tell the truth is what classical rhetoricians called the ethical appeal. The next sentence in Holmes's dis-sent ("If it were a question whether I agreed with that theory, I should desire to study it further and long before making up my mind") continues the ethical appeal. The ordinary judge would say something like, "My personal views on the truth of the majority's economic theory are irrelevant." That is the paraphrasable content of Holmes's sentence. But by putting it this way he slips in the additional suggestion, which makes the sentence more credible, that he is slow to jump to conclusions. It is a masterful touch. And false. Holmes was not slow to jump to conclusions, and had as a matter of fact made laissez-faire his economic philosophy years earlier.[13] He doubtless thought the statute invalidated in *Lochner* was nonsense. Many judges, when voting to uphold statutes they dislike, will admit their dislike to make themselves sound impartial. That is also a type of ethical appeal, but of a crass and self-congratulatory sort. Holmes's is subtle and disarming. It is a version of the "simple man" style that George Orwell used so effectively. The "I" in Orwell's essays and journalism is not Eric Blair (Orwell's real name); it is the very model of a plain-speaking, decent, honest Englishman. The plain style is often, and in these examples, an artifice of sophisticated intellectuals.[14] The idea that if Holmes had thought that the case properly turned on an economic theory he would have studied the theory is a fantasy. The implied author of the *Lochner* dissent is not the real Oliver Wendell Holmes.

Meanwhile the reader's suspense is building to find out what Holmes thinks the "economic theory" of the majority is, since the majority opinion does not use any such term. (Holmes, like Antony, uses suspense to rhetorical effect.) We discover that it is indeed the theory of laissez-faire, "which has been a shibboleth for some well-known writers, [and which] is interfered with by school laws, by the Post Office, by every state or municipal institution which takes [the citizen's] money." Observe the nicely understated derision in "shibboleth" and how it is reinforced by characterizing the advocates of laissez-faire, with some exaggeration, as people who would abolish the Post Office. (Holmes does not say, who would privatize the Post Office.)

This derisive characterization provides the lead-in to the climactic sentence of the opinion, the one about Herbert Spencer—one of the "well-

13. See Robert W. Gordon, "Holmes' *Common Law* as Legal and Social Science," 10 *Hofstra Law Review* 719, 740 (1982); Joseph Frazier Wall, "Social Darwinism and Constitutional Law with Special Reference to *Lochner v. New York*," 33 *Annals of Science* 465, 475–476 (1976).

14. James Arnt Aune, "On the Rhetorical Criticism of Judge Posner," 23 *Hastings Constitutional Law Quarterly* 658, 668 (1996), remarks "the similarity of [Holmes's] prose style [in the *Lochner* dissent] to that of Emerson: they share the common characteristics of a lack of linear progression, a preference for the sentence rather than the paragraph as the unit of thought, and the simultaneous affectation of simplicity and cosmopolitan irony."

known writers"—which gains its force from its concreteness. How much weaker the sentence would have been if for "Mr. Herbert Spencer's Social Statics" Holmes had written "laissez-faire," or even if for "enacts" he had written "adopts." The absurdity of the idea that the Constitution would enact a book with a weird title, written by an Englishman, lends emotional force to the sentence and—my essential point—operates as a substitute for proof. Holmes makes Spencer's book a metaphor for laissez-faire. And metaphors, because of their concreteness, their vividness, and, when they are fresh, their unexpectedness, are more memorable than their paraphrases. That is one reason the dissent in *Lochner* not only contributed to the shift of opinion that culminated many years later in the repudiation of "Lochnerism" but also became the symbol of opposition to the judicial philosophy reflected in the majority opinion. Because Holmes's dissenting opinion is so short, there is no danger that the key sentence, the sentence about Herbert Spencer, will be missed. Brevity is a risk in persuasive speech, as we saw with Brutus, but also an opportunity. The brevity of Holmes's dissent focuses and commands the reader's attention. The varying lengths of the sentences and the graceful rhythm of the long sentences enhance the opinion's charm, while the concentrated power of the aphorisms—not only the one about Spencer, but also "general propositions do not decide concrete cases" and "every opinion tends to become a law"—gives the opinion a forcefulness that it would lack if the dissent were longer and more diffuse, burying the aphorisms under qualifications, citations, quotations, repetitions, and the other common padding of judicial opinions.

After dispatching Spencer, Holmes does at last marshal some support for his position, beginning with the case in which the Supreme Court had recently sustained a compulsory vaccination law *(Jacobson)*. That case is inapposite. Vaccination confers what economists call an external benefit; it protects not only the person vaccinated but also persons who might otherwise have caught the disease from him. Compulsory vaccination is therefore consistent with most versions of laissez-faire—as is an antitrust law *(Northern Securities)*—while a law fixing maximum hours of work is paternalistic and therefore inconsistent with it. The other two cases that Holmes cites are to the point, and he could have cited several more. But instead he returns to first principles, remarking that a constitution "is made for people of fundamentally differing views, and the accident of our finding certain opinions natural and familiar, or novel, and even shocking, ought not to conclude our judgment upon the question whether statutes embodying them conflict with the Constitution of the United States." The majority had never said it ought to. It had said that the statute was an unreasonable interference with freedom of contract. About this virtually all Holmes says is, "A reasonable man might think it a proper measure on the score of health."

Would the dissent in *Lochner* have received a high grade in a law school examination in 1905? I think not. It is not logically organized, does not join issue sharply with the majority, is not scrupulous in its treatment of the majority opinion or of precedent, is not thoroughly researched, does not exploit the factual record, and is highly unfair to Herbert Spencer, of whom most Americans nowadays know no more than what Holmes told them in the *Lochner* dissent. The dissent also misses an opportunity to take issue with the fundamental premise of the majority opinion, which is that unreasonable statutes violate the due process clause of the Fourteenth Amendment; the dissent is silent on the origin and purpose of the amendment. Indeed, at the end Holmes seems to concede the majority's fundamental (and contestable) premise that the due process clause outlaws unreasonable legislation and to disagree merely with the conclusion that New York's maximum-hours law is unreasonable. The sweeping assertions at the beginning of the dissent are thus discordant with its conclusion. Read as a whole, the opinion does not clearly challenge Lochnerism but just the abuses of Lochnerism. It is not, in short, a good judicial opinion. It is merely the greatest judicial opinion of the last hundred years.

To judge Holmes's dissent in *Lochner* by "scientific" standards is to miss the point. It is a rhetorical masterpiece, and rhetoric counts for a lot in law because many legal questions cannot be resolved by logical or empirical demonstration. After all these years it still is uncertain whether *Lochner* really was decided incorrectly.[15] By striking down paternalistic statutes (though only fitfully) until finally overwhelmed by political pressures in the late 1930s, the Supreme Court may have made the United States marginally more prosperous than it would otherwise have been. Granted, there is great doubt whether the Fourteenth Amendment was intended to authorize the kind of free-wheeling federal judicial intervention in the public policy of the states that *Lochner* has come to symbolize as a result of Holmes's dissent. But it is no greater than the doubt about the free-wheeling federal judicial intervention of recent decades in the public policy of the states in such areas as abortion, capital punishment, and obscenity—which is why *Roe v. Wade* is widely regarded as the second coming of *Lochner*. Those who think "Lochnerism" (a word whose currency is due to Holmes's dissent) bad law continue to draw comfort and support from the dissent's enchanting rhetoric.

15. See, for example, Bruce Ackerman, *We the People,* vol. 1: *Foundations* 66 (1991); Richard A. Epstein, *Takings: Private Property and the Power of Eminent Domain* 108–109, 128, 280–281 (1985).

The dissent in *Lochner* is more than a symbol, however, and more than a tour de force. The second sentence—"This case is decided upon an economic theory which a large part of the country does not entertain"—was one of the opening salvos in the legal-realist movement, which taught that many cases are decided on the basis not of legal principles but of the judges' own values and preferences and their intuitions about sound public policy. Holmes had said such things before he was appointed to the Supreme Court,[16] but for a Supreme Court Justice to say them carried greater weight. The characteristic abruptness of Holmes's opinions, including the dissent in *Lochner,* is consistent with his "realist" belief that the decision of a closely balanced case is a judgment of policy rather than a deduction. The dissent in *Lochner* does not make its points by carefully marshaling the facts and authorities, yet we do not miss these things. Maybe reason cannot decide the most difficult cases.

In comparing Holmes to Mark Antony I may seem to be suggesting a view of legal reasoning that is not so much realistic as cynical. I may seem to be saying that there are only two forms of persuasion: on the one hand logic, which cannot be used to decide the difficult and important cases, and on the other hand the tricks of rhetoric. Not quite. Between the extremes of logical persuasion and emotive persuasion lies a variety of methods for inducing justified true belief which are rational though not rigorous or exact. This is the domain of practical reason ("rhetoric" in the broad Aristotelian sense mentioned at the outset of this chapter).[17] It includes appeals to common sense, to custom, to precedents and other authorities, to tradition, to empiricism, to intuition, to institutional considerations, to history, to consequences, to the social sciences, to our just or good emotions, and to the "test of time" stressed throughout this book. Traces of these methods can be discerned in the *Lochner* dissent. But the power of the opinion lies in its rhetoric (narrowly defined), which compels the reader's attention and shocks him into reconsidering his constitutional intuitions.

I anticipate the objection that Holmes's rhetorical tricks in *Lochner* are tolerable only because we think his legal position either correct (the dominant view) or defensible, and that if he performed such tricks in support of an outrageous result, his skillful use of rhetorical devices would only make us more indignant. Yet *Buck v. Bell* is an eloquent and moving opinion even if one is revolted by the author's evident enthusiasm for the eugenic breeding of human beings, just as *The Triumph of the Will* is a beau-

---

16. See, for example, Holmes, "The Path of the Law," 10 *Harvard Law Review* 457 (1897).
17. See my book *The Problems of Jurisprudence,* chs. 2–3 (1990).

tiful movie even though it is Nazi propaganda. Here is the heart of Holmes's opinion in *Buck v. Bell*:

> We have seen more than once that the public welfare may call upon the best citizens for their lives. It would be strange if it could not call upon those who already sap the strength of the State for these lesser sacrifices, often not felt to be such by those concerned, in order to prevent our being swamped with incompetence. It is better for all the world, if instead of waiting to execute degenerate offspring for crime, or to let them starve for their imbecility, society can prevent those who are manifestly unfit from continuing their kind. The principle that sustains compulsory vaccination is broad enough to cover cutting the Fallopian tubes. Three generations of imbeciles are enough.[18]

This is beautiful prose—sparkling, passionate, topped off by a brilliant aphorism—but dubious legal and moral reasoning. The comparison to conscription is incomplete; the sacrifice demanded of draftees may be greater, but so is the need for their sacrifice. The analogy to compulsory vaccination depends on the unexamined assumption that feeblemindedness begets crime. Holmes does not try to show that compulsory sterilization is the only alternative to either executing degenerate offspring or letting them starve to death. And he drops the mask of judicial detachment and makes clear his personal approval of the Virginia statute, though on his view of the Fourteenth Amendment his opinion of the merits of the statute is irrelevant to the judicial function. *Buck v. Bell* would be a poorly reasoned, a brutal, and even, to a modern sensibility,[19] a vicious opinion even if Carrie Buck really had been an imbecile. But it is a first-class piece of rhetoric. Clear thinking about art, including literary art, including the literary art occasionally displayed in judicial opinions, requires distinguishing aesthetic from moral values.

Among other famous American judges, John Marshall, Benjamin Cardozo, Louis Brandeis, Learned Hand, and Robert Jackson all had interesting, and most had distinguished, styles, which I shall discuss briefly, returning to Holmes later. Because the law and literature movement is preoccupied

---

18. 274 U.S. 200, 207 (1927) (citation omitted). See also my discussion of the case in Chapter 5.

19. An important qualification: belief in eugenics, and in sterilization as a means to achieving the objectives of eugenics, was widespread in perfectly respectable intellectual circles in the period in which Buck v. Bell was decided. See index references to "eugenics" and "sterilization" in Elazar Barkan, *The Retreat of Scientific Racism: Changing Concepts of Race in Britain and the United States between the World Wars* (1992). It was the Nazi practice of eugenics, which Holmes could not have foreseen, that discredited the eugenics movement.

with the ethical dimension of judicial expression, the stylistic properties of judicial opinions have been neglected.[20]

Only John Marshall style's is magisterial, but it is not pompous. Patient, systematic, unadorned, unemotional, unpretentious, it is the calm and confident voice of reason—the quintessential Enlightenment style. A related characteristic of Marshall's opinions, remarkable in our legal culture, is the absence of citations to previous decisions, American or English, though there were plenty he could have cited. Also related and also remarkable is Marshall's avoidance of legal jargon. Whether such a style remains possible in a mature legal system is a matter of doubt; in any event Marshall has had no successful imitators. He had the advantage of interpreting the Constitution while it was still fresh, so that although he required (and fortunately possessed) great political wisdom, he did not face as severe an interpretive problem as his successors did. Nor did he have the modern judge's burden of negotiating a minefield of authoritative precedents.

The main issue in *McCulloch v. Maryland* was whether Congress had the power to create a bank as something "necessary and proper" to carry out the legislative powers enumerated in Article I of the Constitution. The Court held that it did. This conclusion required a flexible approach to constitutional interpretation, and Marshall's formulation of that approach remains canonical:

> A constitution, to contain an accurate detail of all the subdivisions of which its great powers will admit, and of all the means by which they may be carried into execution, would partake of the prolixity of a legal code, and could scarcely be embraced by the human mind. It would probably never be understood by the public. Its nature, therefore, requires, that only its great outlines should be marked, its important objects designated, and the minor ingredients which compose those objects be deduced from the nature of the objects themselves. That this idea was entertained by the framers of the American constitution, is not only to be inferred from the nature of the instrument, but from the language. Why else were some of the limitations, found in the ninth section of the 1st article, introduced? It is also, in some degree, warranted, by their having omitted to use any restrictive term which might prevent its receiving a fair and just interpretation. In considering this question, then, we must never forget, that it is *a constitution* we are expounding.[21]

20. For a notable exception, see William Domnarski, *In the Opinion of the Court* (1996).

21. 17 U.S. (4 Wheat.) 316, 407 (1819). Marshall's italicization in the last sentence shows that rules of style (for example, one should not italicize for emphasis)—like rules of grammar and, in a sense used in Chapter 3, rules of law—are made to be broken, though selectively. On Marshall's style, see Christopher L. Eisgruber, "John Marshall's Judicial Rhetoric," 1996 *Supreme Court Review* 439.

This is not flashy prose, but it is simple and logical, and builds nicely to the famous aphorism of the last sentence.

Here is how Holmes made a similar point about the need for flexibility in constitutional interpretation: "When we are dealing with words that also are a constituent act, like the Constitution of the United States, we must realize that they have called into life a being the development of which could not have been foreseen completely by the most gifted of its begetters. It was enough for them to realize or to hope that they had created an organism; it has taken a century and has cost their successors much sweat and blood to prove that they created a nation. The case before us must be considered in the light of our whole experience and not merely in that of what was said a hundred years ago."[22] Compared with Marshall, Holmes is racy. But Holmes was not Chief Justice, was not writing when the constitutional convention was a living memory, and, most important, did not have Marshall's eighteenth-century faith in the power of reason to resolve difficult legal questions. The passage from Holmes calls to mind another great eighteenth-century mind, that of Edmund Burke, who set definite limits on that power.

One might suppose from my comparison of Marshall to Holmes that Marshall would have escaped the kind of academic censure that opinions like the *Lochner* dissent and *Buck v. Bell* invite. Not so. Here is Professor Currie's report card on Marshall's constitutional opinions: ". . . great rhetorical power, invocation of the constitutional text less as the basis of decision than a peg on which to hang a result evidently reached on other grounds, a marked disdain for reliance on precedent, extensive borrowing of the ideas of others without attribution, an inclination to reach out for constitutional issues that did not have to be decided, a tendency to resolve difficult questions by aggressive assertion of one side of the case, and an absolute certainty in the correctness of his conclusions."[23]

It seems, then, that despite his more sedate style Marshall displays the same lack of judicial craftsmanship as Holmes. As these are probably the two greatest judges in our history, I am moved to ask whether it is the conception of craftsmanship that is deficient rather than the judges. Maybe the art of judging is inescapably rhetorical, and a failure to appreciate this is a shortcoming of the school of legal formalism, of which Currie is an illustrious member. Maybe some cases cannot be resolved otherwise than by "aggressive assertion of one side"—perhaps a balanced analysis would leave the court and reader in paralyzed equipoise, like Buridan's ass. Currie crit-

22. Missouri v. Holland, 252 U.S. 416, 433 (1920).
23. David P. Currie, *The Constitution in the Supreme Court: The First Hundred Years: 1789–1888* 74 (1985). Talk about disdain!

icizes Marshall for what are undoubtedly faults in academic writing. Are we to understand from this that the best judicial opinion is the one that most closely resembles a good law review article? Judges do not work under conditions conducive to the production of opinions of high academic quality. Because the subject-matter jurisdiction of most high courts is too broad to enable specialization, judges are bound to know less about each field than the professors in those fields know. The audience for judicial opinions, moreover, is not primarily an academic one. And the judge who wants to be effective is constrained for the most part to operate incrementally and thus to respect distinctions, traditions, colleagues' views, political realities, and whatnot that make the professor justifiably impatient, and sometimes disgust him. Most professors who become judges write (at least when writing opinions) like judges rather than like professors.

Although we should not expect a high order either of intellectual creativity or of analytical rigor in judicial opinions, we can expect in the best opinions a perspicuous, even dramatic, bodying forth of the judge's concerns; a lucid presentation of arresting particulars—fodder for academic analysis; a sense of the relatedness of these particulars to larger themes; a point of view that transcends the litigants' parochial concerns; a power of clear and forceful statement; and a high degree of sensitivity to the expectations of the audience. All are virtues associated with imaginative literature. Pursuing the literary analogy, we may say that a prime virtue of a judicial opinion is wit in the eighteenth-century sense of what oft was thought but ne'er so well expressed. The themes in a judicial *oeuvre* are not novel, and they are played in cases randomly served from the docket. The skill lies in making each of them a memorable exemplar of an issue, problem, or approach. It is an essentially literary skill, and lawyers are reluctant to acknowledge that so "unprofessional" a skill as literary writing ability could be an element of judicial greatness. A lawyer may admit that law may sometimes be poetry but is unlikely to admit that poetry may sometimes be law.

Of Brandeis one may say with more justice than T. S. Eliot said of Milton that his style has had a bad influence on his successors. Here is the central passage from one of his most famous opinions, the dissent in *Olmstead,* the case (later overruled) which held that wiretapping was not a search or seizure within the meaning of the Fourth Amendment: "The makers of our Constitution undertook to secure conditions favorable to the pursuit of happiness. They recognized the significance of man's spiritual nature, of his feelings and of his intellect. They knew that only a part of the pain, pleasure and satisfactions of life are to be found in material things. They sought to protect Americans in their beliefs, their thoughts, their emotions and their sensations. They conferred, as against the Government, the right to be let alone—the most comprehensive of rights and the right most valued by civilized men."[24] The jackhammer style (sentences of roughly equal length, starting the same way, and full of lists—"their beliefs, their thoughts, their emotions." and so on—and repetition, notably of "they" and of "their") conveys a distracting sense of Brandeis's own excitement, making readers wonder whether he may not have been projecting onto the long-dead framers his own vision of a just society. A hectoring style, it grabs the interlocutor by the lapels and shouts in his face, demanding assent rather than engaging in a discussion. A discordant style in which to celebrate the classical liberal ideal of personal autonomy, it is also easily imitable and is the model for the windy jeremiads found in so many modern judicial dissents.

Compare the style, at once more rational (less "rhetorical") and more pungent, of this passage from an opinion by Justice Jackson, protesting his colleagues' willingness to sit in judgment on state supreme court decisions involving the rights of criminal defendants: "Whenever decisions of one court are reviewed by another, a percentage of them are reversed. That reflects a difference in outlook normally found between personnel comprising different courts. However, reversal by a higher court is not proof that justice is thereby better done. There is no doubt that if there were a super-Supreme Court, a substantial proportion of our reversals of state courts would also be reversed. We are not final because we are infallible, but we are infallible only because we are final."[25] As with Marshall and Holmes, the aphorism toward which the passage builds gains force from the low-keyed manner in which it is introduced. These judges are masters of cadence and timing.[26]

24. Olmstead v. United States, 277 U.S. 438, 478–479 (1928). With Brandeis's dissent compare Holmes's characteristically terse and eloquent dissent describing the government's illegal wiretapping as "dirty business," and stating, "We have to choose, and for my part I think it a less evil that some criminals should escape than that the Government should play an ignoble part." 277 U.S. at 469–471. Notice the legal-realist flavor of "We have to choose, and for my part . . ."

25. Brown v. Allen, 344 U.S. 443, 540 (1953) (concurring opinion).

26. Jackson's opinion in the second flag-salute case is one of the most eloquent majority opinions in the history of American law. I quote its climactic passage: "Ultimate futility of such attempts to compel coherence is the lesson of every such effort from the Roman drive to stamp out Christianity as a disturber of its pagan unity, the Inquisition, as a means to religious and dynastic unity, the Siberian exiles as a means to Russian unity, down to the fast failing efforts of our present totalitarian enemies. Those who begin coercive elimination of dissent soon find themselves exterminating dissenters. Compulsory unification of opinion achieves only the unanimity of the graveyard . . . The First Amendment . . . was designed to avoid these ends by avoiding these beginnings . . . The case is made difficult not because the principles of its decision are obscure but because the flag involved is our own." West Virginia State Board of Education v. Barnette, 319 U.S. 624, 641 (1943).

Cardozo is the most criticized of the great judicial stylists, and we can see why by attending to his opinion in *Palko v. Connecticut*. The issue was whether carrying out Palko's sentence of death would be a denial of due process of law. The sentence had been imposed at a retrial after the state's successful appeal of Palko's original conviction, which was for second-degree murder, a crime that did not carry the death penalty. Cardozo assumed that, in a federal prosecution, to allow the prosecution to appeal in these circumstances would place the defendant in double jeopardy and therefore violate the Fifth Amendment. Even so, he concluded that Connecticut's decision to allow such an appeal was not so basic a deprivation of human rights that it violated the looser restraints imposed on the states by the due process clause of the Fourteenth Amendment.[27] For "if the trial had been infected with error adverse to the accused, there might have been [appellate] review at his instance, and as often as necessary to purge the vicious taint. A reciprocal privilege, subject at all times to the discretion of the presiding judge, has now been granted to the state. There is here no seismic innovation. The edifice of justice stands, its symmetry, to many, greater than before."[28] The metaphor is ingenious. As long as the innovation is not "seismic"—that is, as long as there is no earthquake—the "edifice" of justice will not be damaged. It will actually look more symmetrical, since now the state can appeal if it loses, as well as the defendant if he loses. The ingenuity of the figure, however, bordering as it does on cuteness, strikes a sour note in a death case. And the unqualified appeal to "symmetry"—to an aesthetic rather than a political or juridical concept—is out of place in a discussion of criminal procedure. That procedure is deliberately asymmetrical. The prosecution must prove guilt beyond a reasonable doubt; would the edifice of justice be grander or straighter if the burden of persuasion were reduced, so that, perhaps, if the evidence was in equipoise, the defendant's guilt would be determined by tossing a coin? Rabelais's Justice Bridlegoose might have thought so, but not Justice Cardozo. Rather than completing a thought, the geological metaphor is a substitute for thought—and so obvious is this that the figure fails as effective rhetoric.[29]

27. Years later the Supreme Court was to hold that the Fourteenth Amendment gives state criminal defendants the same rights under the Fifth Amendment's double-jeopardy clause as federal defendants have, even though the Fourteenth Amendment does not contain a double-jeopardy clause.

28. 302 U.S. 319, 328 (1937) (citation omitted).

29. Or maybe the American ear is simply not attuned to metaphysical wit. The earthquake metaphor dimly echoes Donne's great love poem "A Valediction: forbidding Mourning": "Moving of the earth brings harms and fears, / Men reckon what it did and meant; / But trepidation of the spheres, / Though greater far, is innocent." Notice how Donne "deconstructs" Cardozo *ante facto* by belittling earthquakes!

The danger, when judges try to be literary, is not that they will make pompous fools of themselves, though often they will, or make the worse appear the better cause. It is that they will muddy the law. Cardozo in *Palko* injected symmetry where it did not belong. If a judge says that pricing is "the central nervous system of the economy,"[30] literal-minded lawyers will begin thinking about antitrust law in terms of inappropriate biological analogies. The metaphor elides the reasoning process that might indicate both the aptness and the limits of the analogy (of the pricing system to the nervous system, of the criminal justice system to a building) that the metaphor conveys.[31]

Consider now a Cardozan gem. In *People v. Defore,* Cardozo's court reaffirmed that under New York law evidence illegally seized by the police is nevertheless admissible in a criminal trial.[32] He packed into eleven words the case against the exclusionary rule: "The criminal is to go free because the constable has blundered." Compression is not the only virtue of this sentence. The substitution of the slightly archaic (even in 1926) "constable" for "policeman" is inspired. It not only improves the rhythm of the sentence and, by its faintly exotic air, makes the sentence more memorable; it also makes the abuse of power by the police seem trivial, almost comical. The "constable" puts the reader in mind of the unarmed British policeman, so different (in legend anyway) from his rough American counterpart. And Cardozo's constable is not a uniformed thug but a blunderer—a Gilbert and Sullivan constable whose pratfalls are unlikely to strike anyone as a menace to personal liberty.

Inverting subject and predicate is a signature of Cardozo's style: "Negligent the act is, and wrongful in the sense that it is unsocial, but wrongful and unsocial in relation to other travelers, only because the eye of vigilance perceives the risk of damage."[33] The inversion puts the reader off at first but turns out to be an effective method of emphasizing key words ("negligent" and "wrongful," in the passage just quoted). Such departures from standard word order, and the frequent use of metaphor and aphorism, are what people have chiefly in mind when they criticize Cardozo's style as being "ornate." It is not ornate. An ornate style is one

30. United States v. Socony-Vacuum Oil Co., 310 U.S. 150, 226 n. 59 (1940).

31. See Michael Boudin, "Antitrust Doctrine and the Sway of Metaphor," 75 *Georgetown Law Journal* 395 (1986); Chad M. Oldfather, "The Hidden Ball: A Substantive Critique of Baseball Metaphors in Judicial Opinions," 27 *Connecticut Law Review* 17 (1994). See generally Bernard J. Hibbitts, "Making Sense of Metaphors: Visuality, Aurality, and the Reconfiguration of American Legal Discourse," 16 *Cardozo Law Review* 229 (1994).

32. 150 N.E. 585, 587 (N.Y. 1926).

33. Palsgraf v. Long Island R.R., 162 N.E. 99, 100 (N.Y. 1928).

rich in subordinate clauses, parentheses, digressions, redundancies, and other curlicues. Cardozo's inversions of standard word order and his use of metaphor and aphorism make for compression and vividness.

The style of Cardozo's nonjudicial writings is more florid than that of his judicial opinions, and this has colored impressions of his opinion writing. Here is an example: "Judges march at times to pitiless conclusions under the prod of a remorseless logic which is supposed to leave them no alternative. They deplore the sacrificial rite. They perform it, none the less, with averted gaze, convinced as they plunge the knife that they obey the bidding of their office. The victim is offered up to the gods of jurisprudence on the altar of regularity."[34] Extended—indeed extravagant—metaphor, a tone arch and coy, and staccato sentences lending a dramatic air to the proceedings—these are hallmarks of the overripe style found in many of Cardozo's nonjudicial writings. But there is plenty of good stuff in those writings as well, such as this graceful tribute to John Marshall: "He gave to the constitution of the United States the impress of his own mind; and the form of our constitutional law is what it is, because he moulded it while it was still plastic and malleable in the fire of his own intense convictions."[35]

Cardozo's style has a high sheen, an artifactual quality that makes the reader conscious of his opinions as works of judicial art and incidentally gives Cardozo a touch of Brutus. The opinions of his approximate contemporary Learned Hand are successful imitations of the judge's thinking process as he wrestles with a case. It twists and turns as the judge is pulled now hither, now yon, by the weight of opposing considerations as they present themselves to his mind. Hand is the Henry James of judicial stylists. Cardozo's style suggests a smoother surface, Hand's (of which I'll give an example later) a greater depth.

Unlike Cardozo, Holmes wrote as well off the bench as on. Here is a short passage from a speech that he gave in 1886 to students at the Harvard Law School: "The Professors of this School have said to themselves more definitely than ever before, We will not be contented to send forth students with nothing but a rag-bag full of general principles—a throng of glittering generalities, like a swarm of little bodiless cherubs fluttering at the top of one of Correggio's pictures."[36] Holmes makes his point memorable

---

34. Cardozo, *The Growth of the Law* (1924), in *Selected Writings of Benjamin Nathan Cardozo: The Choice of Tycho Brahe* 219 (Margaret M. Hall ed. 1947).

35. Cardozo, *The Nature of the Judicial Process* 169–170 (1921).

36. Oliver Wendell Holmes, "The Use of Law Schools," in *The Essential Holmes: Selections from the Letters, Speeches, Judicial Opinions, and Other Writings of Oliver Wendell Holmes, Jr.* 224, 227 (Richard A. Posner ed. 1992).

first by adopting a dramatic mode ("the Professors of this School have said to themselves . . . We will" rather than "the Professors of this School are not content to . . .") and then by heaping up images. Two metaphors ("a rag-bag full of general principles" and "a throng of glittering generalities"), the second employing consonance, precede the climactic simile ("like a swarm of little bodiless cherubs fluttering"). The "swarm of little bodiless cherubs" is a master stroke. Cherubs are in fact (if one can speak of them thus) little and bodiless; but describing them so makes them the very quintessence of ineffectuality. That they are in a picture, and, even more, that they are fluttering at the top of the picture and thus at the edge of the viewer's focus, makes the image even sharper. Notice also how the progression—general principles, glittering generalities, bodiless cherubs—enables the reader to accept a simile that, without any preparation, might have seemed grotesque. An abstraction ("general principles") is made perfectly visualizable.

Holmes's beat was not limited to law. Here is the end of one of his after-dinner speeches:

> . . . I think it not improbable that man, like the grub that prepares a chamber for the winged thing it never has seen but is to be—that man may have cosmic destinies that he does not understand. And so beyond the vision of battling races and an impoverished earth I catch a dreaming glimpse of peace.
>
> The other day my dream was pictured to my mind. It was evening. I was walking homeward on Pennsylvania Avenue near the Treasury, and as I looked beyond Sherman's Statue to the west the sky was aflame with scarlet and crimson from the setting sun. But, like the note of downfall in Wagner's opera, below the sky line there came from little globes the pallid discord of the electric lights. And I thought to myself the Götterdämmerung will end, and from those globes clustered like evil eggs will come the new masters of the sky. It is like the time in which we live. But then I remembered the faith that I partly have expressed, faith in a universe not measured by our fears, a universe that has thought and more than thought inside of it, and as I gazed, after the sunset and above the electric lights there shone the stars.[37]

This is prophecy expressed in prose poetry. It is, indeed, a distant cousin to "The Second Coming." Maybe not so distant. Like Yeats's poem, Holmes's peroration is about a rebirth at once sinister and thrilling. The house of the old gods is going up in flames, as in Wagner's opera. The new gods, the gods of technology, symbolized by the street lamps pregnant with fearful possibilities, appear just as the old gods are flaming out. But their reign is short. Immediately the stars—the symbols of the universe that con-

---

37. Holmes, "Law and the Court," in id. at 145, 148.

tains man and his projects along with everything else ("a universe not measured by our fears" is a lovely touch)—appear, the real rulers, dispelling the fear engendered by man's "evil eggs."[38]

Aesthetic Integrity and the "Pure" versus the "Impure" Style

Some law-and-literature scholars claim that judges can obtain insights from literature that have nothing to do with effective presentation, that have rather to do with the spirit, meaning, values, even information (the novel as news) found in literature. I shall discuss their views in the next chapter. Here I want to abstract from the moral and even the informational content of literature and direct attention to the craft values displayed in it, notably *impartiality* (detachment, balance, an awareness of the possibility of other perspectives than the writer's own), *scrupulousness,* and *concreteness.* These values, formalistic in character because independent of the content of the work, add up to aesthetic integrity and have relevance for judicial opinion writing.

To read *The Merchant of Venice* without preconceptions (as if such a thing were really possible!) is to have no doubt that Shylock is a villain; likewise Satan in *Paradise Lost,* though the contrary view has long been argued.[39] If you read the *Iliad* carefully you can have no doubt that you are meant to think it a fine thing that the Trojans are going to be slaughtered. And no reader of *For Whom the Bell Tolls* doubts that Hemingway sides with the Spanish Loyalists. But in none of these cases has the author loaded the dice by depriving the villains of their essential humanity (in the case of Satan, his "angelicity"). Forgoing the facile triumph, the author makes the reader see the situation from the villain's point of view too. To visualize a Jew as fully if wickedly human was something few Elizabethans could have done; Shakespeare's great contemporary Marlowe could not do it. To portray Satan as a heroic figure, Milton was bordering on blasphemy. The *Iliad* is the oldest surviving expression of awareness that foreigners who are your

---

38. Judges are not the only authors of distinguished legal prose. Apart from countless briefs of high quality, including some by Abraham Lincoln, but generally of ephemeral interest, and some notable oral arguments such as Robert Jackson's closing argument to the Nuremberg Tribunal, works of scholarship and polemic by law professors such as (to mention only the dead) William Prosser, Alexander Bickel, Arthur Leff, Karl Llewellyn, Henry Hart, Herbert Wechsler, Paul Bator, and Harry Kalven have occasionally scraped the rhetorical heights. Considerations of space have dissuaded me from discussing any of these works, but I shall discuss the rhetoric of several law professors' writings in Chapter 10 and I have discussed the rhetoric of Wechsler's famous "neutral principles" article in Posner, note 1 above, at 70–75.

39. See, for example, William Empson, *Milton's God* (2d ed. 1981). The orthodox view is forcefully restated in Jeffrey Burton Russell, *Mephistopheles: The Devil in the Modern World* 95–127 (1986).

mortal enemies might nevertheless have the same feelings as you. Hemingway "refuses to make villains of all the Fascists in *For Whom the Bell Tolls* or to make all the Loyalists good and decent people."[40] Stendhal, as hostile as he was to the Church and the nobility, refuses in *The Red and the Black* to romanticize liberals, peasants, republicans, bourgeois, Parisians or provincials, or Bonapartists.

Trial lawyers have trouble developing empathy with their opponents or even their clients, and judges characteristically score short-lived rhetorical triumphs by suppressing the facts and law favorable to the losing side. Yet there is no better advice to a legal advocate than to empathize—with the client (what would he say on his own behalf if he were learned in law?), with the client's adversary (what can he say in reply to my points?), and with the judge (what will appeal to him in my position, what will trouble him, and how can I limit my submission so that its acceptance would not require an unsettling change in doctrine or have untoward practical consequences?). The adversary system gives each disputant a chance to speak his part, and he can learn how to do so from the example of the great writers of imaginative literature.

The antithesis of what I am calling impartiality is illustrated by the Supreme Court's opinion in *Eisenstadt v. Baird*. The issue was whether a state could forbid the sale of contraceptives to unmarried persons. The Supreme Court had held earlier that the state could not forbid the sale of contraceptives to married persons, but now it refused to consider this a significant distinction: "The marital couple is not an independent entity with a mind and heart of its own, but an association of two individuals each with a separate intellectual and emotional makeup. If the right of privacy means anything, it is the right of the *individual,* married or single, to be free from unwarranted governmental intrusion into matters so fundamentally affecting a person as the decision whether to bear or beget a child."[41] The dice are loaded. No one is likely to describe a married couple as "an independent entity with a mind and heart of its own," or to defend "unwarranted" government intrusion. The Court is lazily knocking down straw

40. An observation by Cleanth Brooks quoted in Robert Penn Warren, "A Conversation with Cleanth Brooks," in *The Possibilities of Order: Cleanth Brooks and His Work* 1, 16 (Lewis P. Simpson ed. 1976). With the second half of Brooks's remark ("or to make all the Loyalists good and decent people") compare Shakespeare's refusal to make all the Christians in *The Merchant of Venice* good and decent people. Indeed, it has been argued (though I think with exaggeration) that "what Shakespeare is saying in *The Merchant of Venice* is that Jews are bad, but Christians are just as bad . . . The only practising Christian in the play is Portia, who, as a female barrister, cannot possibly exist." W. D. Rubinstein, *A History of the Jews in the English-Speaking World: Great Britain* 41 (1996).

41. 405 U.S. 438, 453 (1972).

men with italics. Had it said the issue was whether a state is constitutionally obligated to allow the sale of goods that facilitate fornication and adultery by making these practices less costly, its refutations would not have
sounded so convincing. The most remarkable assertion in the passage is that
if the right of privacy means "anything," it means that unmarried people
are entitled to buy contraceptives. This is to say that until 1972, when the
Supreme Court decided the case (or maybe 1970, when the court of appeals rendered its decision, which the Supreme Court affirmed), there had
been no right of privacy. One might have thought the right of privacy peripheral to, rather than centrally engaged by, the issue in *Eisenstadt.*

There is plenty of hyperbolic literary writing as well, some of it of great
distinction. When Shelley in "The Mask of Anarchy" urges the common
people of England to "shake your chains to earth like dew" and promises
that "tyrants would flee / Like a dream's dim imagery," he is inadvertently
belittling the struggle for liberty by making the enemies of liberty appear
insubstantial.[42] It is the lack of a mature awareness of the finitude of human
capability that turned so many New Critics against so much Romantic poetry. It is wonderful poetry, but it is not a good model for judges.

The second component of aesthetic integrity, "scrupulousness"—the
search for the exact word and phrase—is found in those sentences where,
as T. S. Eliot explained in Part V of "Little Gidding,"

> . . . every word is at home,
> Taking its place to support the others,
> The word neither diffident nor ostentatious,
> An easy commerce of the old and the new,
> The common word exact without vulgarity,
> The formal word precise but not pedantic,
> The complete consort dancing together.

The metaphysical poets, among many others, and their modern avatars, like
Eliot himself, illustrate this ideal in poetry. Examples from prose writers include Flaubert, James, Joyce, Woolf, Kafka, and Philip Roth (as you will
have glimpsed from my quotations from *Operation Shylock*). Contrasting
Kafka with one of his imitators, Ronald Gray shows how Kafka's power
derives in part from his refusal to strive for the sensational effects that his
frequently fantastic subject matter seems to invite—from the sobriety and
restraint of his style.[43]

---

42. Thomas R. Edwards, *Imagination and Power: A Study of Poetry on Public Themes* 167 (1971).
43. Gray, *Franz Kafka* 10–28 (1973). See also Joseph Strelka, "Kafkaesque Elements in Kafka's
Novels and in Contemporary Narrative Prose," 21 *Comparative Literature Studies* 434–435 (1984).

Or consider Hamlet's letter to Horatio, written upon Hamlet's return to Denmark following the aborted voyage to England:

> Horatio, when thou shalt have overlooked this, give these fellows some means to the king: they have letters for him. Ere we were two days old at sea, a pirate of very warlike appointment gave us chase. Finding ourselves too slow of sail, we put on a compelled valour; in the grapple I boarded them: on the instant they got clear of our ship, so I alone became their prisoner. They have dealt with me like thieves of mercy, but they knew what they did; I am to do a good turn for them. Let the king have the letters I have sent; and repair thou to me with as much haste as thou wouldst fly death. I have words to speak in thine ear will make thee dumb; yet are they much too light for the bore of the matter. These good fellows will bring thee where I am. Rosencrantz and Guildenstern hold their course for England: of them I have much to tell thee. Farewell. (IV.4.12–28)

An adventure is narrated with high drama and effortless grace, yet without any sacrifice of clarity or economy. There is no straining for effect, no bluster. This is prose at its most exact yet elegant.

As an example of the third element of what I am calling aesthetic integrity, "concreteness," consider the second stanza of "The Second Coming," which begins:

> Surely some revelation is at hand;
> Surely the Second Coming is at hand.
> The Second Coming! Hardly are those words out
> When a vast image out of *Spiritus Mundi*
> Troubles my sight . . .

My focus here is not on what all this might mean or what *Spiritus Mundi* is[44] or how these lines are going to modulate into the great closing lines of the poem. The word I invite the reader's attention to is "sight" in the fifth line. In recollection one is likely to think of it as "mind"; a vision is something in the mind. But to a poet it is something one sees, because what one sees is real but what one imagines is often imaginary, and the poet wants to make the reader believe in the reality of the vision. It is a small touch, and there is an air of unreality in talking about the concreteness of a fantasy. It is, however, a characteristic literary touch, this use of visual or tactile imagery to drive home a point. These are the touches that give literature concreteness—a quality that Holmes's writing has (remember the fluttering cherubs, the Fallopian tubes, the grub, the street lamps, and the

---

44. See Richard P. Blackmur, "Yeats: The Second Coming," in *Master Poems of the English Language* 847 (Oscar Williams ed. 1966).

evil eggs) and that modern judicial opinions could use more of. An able Supreme Court Justice may be remembered mainly for having said of pornography that he could not define it but "I know it when I see it, and the motion picture involved in this case is not that."[45] The candor (in acknowledging the limits of legal reasoning) and bluntness of this statement make a refreshing contrast to the characteristic evasions of the modern judicial opinion. It had the effect of opening a window in a stuffy room.

More typical is the opening sentence in the statement of facts in *Cox Broadcasting Corp. v. Cohn.* The case holds that the First Amendment forbids a state to allow the family of a rape victim killed by the rapist to obtain damages for the invasion of privacy caused by broadcasting the victim's name. The sentence reads, "In August 1971, appellee's 17-year-old daughter was the victim of a rape and did not survive the incident."[46] The words "did not survive the incident" are unconsciously borrowed from the standard phraseology for describing a medical procedure in the course of which the patient dies: "*X* was operated on for a tumor but did not survive the operation." No normal person says, "*X* was shot, and did not survive the incident"; he says, "*X* was killed." The Court shied away from stating the blunt truth. It euphemized, smoothing the way for the startling conclusion of the opinion, which is that the First Amendment immunizes from legal liability the public dissemination of the macabre and irrelevant detail of the victim's name.

The avoidance of the concrete is ubiquitous in legal prose. To a judge or legislator a 14-year-old pregnant girl is a "minor pregnant woman" and a 12-year-old murderer a "delinquent minor."[47] More than euphemizing is involved; the legal mind is insensitive to the imagery of language. Consider the standard legal cliché for the abortion cases: "*Roe* and its progeny."[48] A person who writes such things is "not seeing a mental image of the objects he is naming."[49] A judge (or judge's law clerk) who is comfortable using the word "progeny" to describe the "descendants" of the case that legalized abortion is, in all likelihood, a person who thinks of

---

45. Jacobellis v. Ohio, 378 U.S. 184, 197 (1964) (Stewart, J., concurring).

46. 420 U.S. 469, 471 (1975).

47. Akron Center for Reproductive Health, Inc. v. City of Akron, 651 F.2d 1198, 1205 n. 4 (6th Cir. 1981), affirmed in part and reversed in part, on other grounds, 462 U.S. 416 (1983); In re Hester, 446 N.E.2d 202, 204 (Ohio App. 1982).

48. For example, Planned Parenthood of Southeastern Pennsylvania v. Casey, 112 S. Ct. 2791, 2861 (1992) (dissenting opinion); Rust v. Sullivan, 500 U.S. 173, 216 (1991) (dissenting opinion); City of Akron v. Akron Center for Reproductive Health, Inc., 462 U.S. 416, 420 n. 1 (1983); Harris v. McRae, 448 U.S. 297, 312 (1980). The reference of course is to Roe v. Wade, 410 U.S. 113 (1973).

49. George Orwell, "Politics and the English Language," in *The Collected Essays, Journalism and Letters of George Orwell,* vol. 4, pp. 127, 134 (Sonia Orwell and Ian Angus eds. 1968).

abortion in abstract rather than concrete terms. It is dangerous for judges to lose sight of the consequences of their decisions and fool themselves into thinking that they inhabit a purely conceptual realm.

I can generalize and systematize these remarks about aesthetic integrity by noting and naming a fundamental split among judicial opinions. On one side of the divide the opinions have a lofty, formal, imperious, impersonal, "refined," ostentatiously "correct" (including "politically correct"), even hieratic tone; on the other side they tend to be forthright, conversational, intimate, even racy, even demotic. Tone depends on many things, including the choice of words and phrases and the decision to embrace or to avoid contractions, colloquialisms, humor, and jargon. By "jargon" I do not mean the names of legal doctrines, which judicial opinions could hardly dispense with. I mean turns of phrase, usually archaisms or shorthand, that lawyers use but other writers avoid.[50] These usages are eminently avoidable by lawyers too, for if they were not, they would not mark a style; styles are optional. They stamp legal prose as legalese, imparting an in-group, "professional" tone to legal writing. The disappearance of an older legal jargon, with its "aforesaids" and its substitution of "one" for a first name ("a witness, one Jones, testified that . . ."), fools some modern judges into thinking that their opinions are free from jargon.

Short sentences and sentence fragments, suppression of ornamentation and parentheticals, and simplicity and brevity all tend to "lower" the tone of a writing, to make it more like speech. But the qualification implicit in *tend* is important. The elimination of all ornamentation may impart an impersonal, bureaucratic, hence formal tone to a writing. Brevity may lend an oracular, dogmatic, imperative, and thus again a formal tone. A string of short sentences can create the impression of a harangue.

The avoidance of headings and subheadings, and of course of footnotes, has a lowering effect because they are scholarly appendages to ordinary speech—no one speaks in footnotes and headings. Paratactic (coordinate) sentence structure, in which clauses are connected by "but" and "and," lowers tone, too, while arranging clauses in hierarchies by means of sub-

---

50. Such as "absent" when used as a preposition, "implicate" (to mean relate to or invoke, as in "the due process clause implicates privacy concerns"), "ambit," "chilling effect" (to describe the effect of the regulation of speech on the marketplace of ideas and opinions), "-based" (as in "autonomy-based justification"), "habeas" (for habeas corpus), "instant" case for "present" case, "construction" (to mean interpretation), "facially" to mean "on its face," "impeach" to mean "contradict," "even had we" (for "even if we had"), "mandate" (as a verb meaning to order or require), "prong" (as meaning one element of a multifactor test or standard), and—of course— "progeny."

ordinating or concessive conjunctions such as "although" raises it. A proclivity for acronyms raises tone by making a work seem technical; a fondness for everyday speech lowers it. Tone is raised by polish, lowered by candor and spontaneity (or the pretense of these things), as illustrated by the contrast between Brutus's and Antony's funeral orations. Oddly, a predilection for rare words that are not terms of legal art can raise tone by making an opinion seem pompous and learned yet equally can lower it by making the opinion seem self-indulgent, even frivolous. Personality lowers, impersonality raises (though with an important qualification noted later). Certitude raises; dubiety and tentativeness lower, but excessive qualification raises. Configuring an opinion as a story, debate, or exploration lowers; configuring it as dogmatic announcement, *de haut en bas,* or as a logical demonstration, raises.

The metaphor of height may be misleading. Judges such as Holmes who write in what I am calling the "low" style are by and large the judges who are intimate with high culture, fussy about their style, aristocrats of writing and thought, judicial Coriolanuses even. So let me switch metaphors and borrow Robert Penn Warren's distinction between "pure" and "impure" poetry.[51] He was writing at a time when the most celebrated modern poets, such as Yeats and Eliot, were in self-conscious revolt against the characteristic style of nineteenth-century Romantic and, particularly, Victorian poetry. Tennyson's poetry, for example, is very refined, "correct," polished, sonorous—he was, after all, the poet laureate of Victoria's England. He avoids in his poetry "low" subjects and diction, upholds conventional values, expresses conventional emotions conventionally, is self-consciously "poetic" and "elevated." As a corollary of all these things, his work lacks a certain tang and texture, a conversational immediacy. Warren explains: "The pure poem tries to be pure by excluding, more or less rigidly, certain elements which might qualify or contradict its original impulse. In other words, the pure poems want to be, and desperately, all of a piece" (p. 16).

Tennyson was a great poet, but it is possible to prefer a "rougher" poetic style, a style that is more concrete, more personal, franker, wittier, more intellectual, and more like drama or conversation; one that has a wider emotional register and range of subject matter and employs a more varied diction; a style closer to that of everyday life (to prose, even). It is the style of Shakespeare,[52] of Donne and the other metaphysical poets, of Byron, and

---

51. Warren, "Pure and Impure Poetry," in his *Selected Essays* 3 (1958).

52. Shakespeare's "dialogue is level with life." Samuel Johnson, "Preface to the Plays of William Shakespeare," in *Samuel Johnson's Literary Criticism* 139, 143 (R. D. Stock ed. 1974).

among modern poets of T. S. Eliot (despite the evident resemblances between Eliot and Robert Browning, one of Tennyson's contemporaries),
Wallace Stevens, Yeats after 1910 or so, Auden, Philip Larkin, and many
others. Warren speaks of "resistances," of "the tension between the rhythm
of the poem and the rhythm of speech . . .; between the formality of the
rhythm and the informality of the language; between the particular and the
general, the concrete and the abstract; . . . between the beautiful and the
ugly; between ideas" (p. 27). Other New Critics spoke of irony, paradox,
complexity, polysemy, ambiguity, the concrete universal.

No one I suppose considers Shakespeare, or even Eliot, inferior to
Tennyson. They are merely different. And it is a difference echoed in judicial opinions. Most judicial opinions are carefully drafted to emphasize
the difference between their diction and that of ordinary speech, which is
just the sort of difference that poets like Shakespeare, Byron, and Eliot like
to blur. Yet no careful reader, making due allowance for differences in linguistic conventions between the nineteenth century and today, will fail to
note the personal, direct, and conversational tone of judges who write in
the manner of Holmes and Learned Hand—so different from the usual tone
of judicial opinions.

Judicial opinions that employ the pure style tend to be long for what
they have to say, solemn, far removed from the tone of conversation, and
predictable in the sense of conforming closely to professional expectations
about the structure and style of a judicial opinion. If we had a judicial laureate, that is how he or she would write. The standard "pure" opinion uses
technical legal terms without translation into everyday English, quotes
heavily from previous judicial opinions, includes much unnecessary detail
concerning names, times, and places, complies scrupulously with whatever
are the current conventions of citation form, avoids any note of levity, conceals the author's personality, prefers ready-made formulations to novelties,
and bows to the current norms of political correctness (corresponding to
the euphemisms for which the Victorians became notorious) at whatever
cost in stilted diction. The familiarity of the pure style makes it invisible to
its practitioners and the intended audience of lawyers. But it is not at all a
plain or transparent style. Its artificiality is revealed by a comparison with
the prose of a nonlawyer dealing with a similar issue—for example, a
philosopher writing about intention compared to a judge in a criminal case
writing about intention, or Philip Roth describing the common law of privacy compared to a judicial opinion in a privacy case.

Impure stylists like to pretend that what they are doing when they write
a judicial opinion is explaining to a hypothetical audience of lay persons
why the case is being decided in the way that it is. These judges eschew

what has been aptly termed the "rhetoric of inevitability."[53] They prefer the bolder approach (to critics, brazen) of trying to persuade without using stylistic devices intended to overawe. They write as it were for the ear rather than for the eye, and avoid long quotations from previous decisions so that they can speak with their own tongue—make it new, make it fresh. (Avoidance of the ready-made was an important element of the "wit" that Eliot admired in the metaphysical poets.) They like to be candid and not pretend to know more than they do or to speak with greater confidence than they feel. They eschew unnecessary details, however impressive the piling on of them might be, and shun clichés. They imitate the movement of thought—unfriendly critics call their style "stream of consciousness." The judicial impurists, as Warren said of the modernist poets, "have tried, within the limits of their gifts, to remain faithful to the complexities of the problems with which they are dealing . . . They have refused to take the easy statement as solution" (pp. 30–31).

Paradoxically, the impurists generally take more pains over style than the purists do; for unless one is a particularly gifted writer, it takes a great deal of effort to make an opinion seem effortless![54] The pure style, despite its artificiality, comes more easily to a legally trained person than the impure style. For one of the things that law school and legal practice teach all unconsciously—and all the more effectively for that—is to forget how one wrote before one became a lawyer.

"Voice" goes with "ear." The choice of styles is influenced by the nature of the audience at which the judge is aiming. For many judges it consists of the lower-court judge whose decision is being reviewed and the parties' lawyers; anyone else is just an authorized eavesdropper. These are the most knowledgeable and interested professional consumers of the appellate court's opinion. Consummate insiders, they are adept at reading (including reading between the lines of) a pure judicial opinion. The author wants to persuade them that in reaching its result the court has carefully considered all the points in the case and has not deviated from "the law" in the typical sense in which the lawyers and the lower-court judge will have conceived it—has not pulled any rabbits out of hats. For this rhetorical purpose the pure style is the best because this tiny, focused, homoge-

---

53. Robert A. Ferguson, "The Judicial Opinion as Literary Genre," 2 *Yale Journal of Law and the Humanities* 201, 213–216 (1990). See also Pierre Bourdieu, "The Force of Law: Toward a Sociology of the Juridical Field," 38 *Hastings Law Journal* 805, 820 (1987).

54. An English observer, noting that "Holmes's style tends to be undemonstrative, unemphatic, casual, insouciant even," argues that it exemplifies "Ovid's maxim *ars est celare artum*—the art is to conceal the art." Neil Duxbury, "When Trying Is Failing: Holmes's 'Englishness'" 7 (Nov. 1996, forthcoming in *Brooklyn Law Review*).

neous professional audience has settled expectations concerning the appropriate diction and decorum of a judicial opinion. At the other end of the stylistic spectrum, the primary audience at which the most boldly impure judicial stylists aim consists not of the legal insiders but of those, both lay people and lawyers, who can "see through" the artifice of judicial pretension.[55] Here is to be found the "one in a thousand" for whom Holmes said that he wrote. Since one in a thousand comes to a larger number than the lawyers and lower-court judge in a single case, the impure judicial stylist may have a larger audience than the pure, just as Shakespeare has a larger audience than Tennyson.

The pure tendency is illustrated by the opinions of Cardozo, Brandeis (especially his majority opinions), Frankfurter, Brennan, and the second Harlan, and the vast majority of opinions written by law clerks—which means most opinions in all American courts today. On the impure side can be found most opinions of Holmes, Douglas, Black, Jackson, and Learned Hand.[56] My inclusion of Douglas should make clear that impure judicial opinion-writing is not always superior to pure, any more than all impure poetry is superior to all pure poetry. Cardozo, mostly a purist, was one of the finest judicial writers in our history.

The two styles are correlated, though not perfectly, with two jurisprudential stances, the formalist and the pragmatic. The former emphasizes the logical, objective, and constrained character of legal reasoning. The formalist holds that the function of a judicial opinion is to demonstrate that the decision is right and true. The pragmatist, while not doubting that right and wrong and true and false have useful roles to play in a variety of "language games," doubts that the decision of finely balanced cases is one of them. The pragmatist thinks that in deciding such a case the judge is trying to come up with the most reasonable result in the circumstances, though with due regard for systemic constraints, such as the need to maintain continuity with previous decisions and respect the limitations that the language and discernible purposes of constitutional and statutory texts impose on the interpreter.

In complaining about the "impersonality" of the pure style, I risk seeming to endorse the very emotionality, sentimentality, and egoism characteristic of much Romantic and Victorian poetry that the modernists de-

---

55. Willard Hurst, "Who Is the 'Great' Appellate Judge?" in *The Writing of Judicial Biography—A Symposium,* 24 *Indiana Law Journal* 363, 394, 398 (1949), remarks Holmes's "irreverence toward judicial pretense"—a salient characteristic of Holmes's opinions.

56. Don't be fooled by the florid character of some (not all, or even most) of Hand's prose. It reflects the culture in which he grew up. He was born in 1872. With a similar adjustment in perspective, John Marshall's opinions can be seen as notable examples of the impure style.

nounced. The arch sentimentalist—possibly the arch egoist—of the modern judiciary was Justice Harry Blackmun, who did not try to disguise or, more important, to discipline the strong feelings that many of the cases that came before the Supreme Court aroused in him; who seemed (not only in his opinions but also in his public comments about the Court) to insist on "letting it all hang out." Although his opinions in these cases depart from the professional norms that I am associating with the "pure" style and are certainly not lacking in "voice," the departure is not in the direction of Donne or Eliot. The voice is rather that of Joyce Kilmer and Norman Rockwell. Whatever the merit of Blackmun's positions on such matters as abortion, capital punishment, sexual equality, the exemption of baseball from the antitrust laws, or the duty of the state to protect people from private violence, the opinions in which he expressed his heartfelt views on these subjects are embarrassing precisely because they seem the unmediated expression of self. They are maudlin (*DeShaney*[57]), melodramatic (*Webster*[58]), unreasoned (*Roe v. Wade,*[59] *Callins*[60]), narcissistic (*Casey*[61]), sophomoric (*Roe*'s history of abortion from ancient Persia on and the ode to baseball in *Flood v. Kuhn*[62]), or gratuitously indecorous (*Michael M.*[63]).

---

57. "Poor Joshua!" DeShaney v. Winnebago County Department of Social Services, 489 U.S. 189, 213 (1989) (dissenting opinion). "Poor Joshua!" is at the other end of the personal-impersonal spectrum from the "did not survive the incident" of *Cox Broadcasting*. It should be possible for judges to avoid bureaucratic euphemizing without succumbing to the opposite vice of labile sentimentalizing.

58. Webster v. Reproductive Health Services, 492 U.S. 490, 538, 560 (1989) (concurring and dissenting opinion): "I fear for the future. I fear for the liberty and equality of the millions of women who have lived and come of age in the 16 years since *Roe* was decided . . . For today, at least, the law of abortion stands undisturbed. For today, the women of this Nation still retain the liberty to control their destinies. But the signs are evident and very ominous, and a chill wind blows." His fear proved unwarranted.

59. On the rhetorical ineptitude of the opinion, see my book *Sex and Reason* 337 (1992).

60. Callins v. Collins, 114 S. Ct. 1127, 1128 (1994) (dissenting opinion). As Justice Scalia pointed out, Justice Blackmun's belief that the death penalty cannot be administered constitutionally is based on the existence of inconsistent lines of Supreme Court decisions—and the Court could eliminate the inconsistency by choosing between the lines. Id. at 1127–1128 (concurring opinion).

61. "I fear for the darkness as four Justices anxiously await the single vote necessary to extinguish the light . . . I am 83 years old. I cannot remain on this Court forever, and when I do step down, the confirmation process for my successor well may focus on the issue before us today." Planned Parenthood of Southeastern Pennsylvania v. Casey, 112 S. Ct. 2791, 2844, 2854–2855 (1992). Wrong again.

62. 407 U.S. 258, 260–264 (1972).

63. See the extended quotation, irrelevant and in places obscene, from the transcript of a statutory-rape case, in Blackmun's concurring opinion in Michael M. v. Superior Court, 450 U.S. 464, 483 n. * (1981).

Although otherwise unlike the pure style, the narcissistic style is similar in having an inward orientation—albeit inward toward the judge, rather than inward toward the professional culture. The impure style points outward, toward the world outside that culture. Samuel Johnson contrasted poets such as Shakespeare, who write from life, with lesser poets, who write from the picture of life painted by their predecessors. The former

> take their sentiments and descriptions immediately from knowledge. The resemblance is therefore just; their descriptions are verified by every eye and their sentiments acknowledged by every breast. Those whom their fame invites to the same studies copy partly them, and partly nature, till the books of one age gain such authority as to stand in the place of nature to another; and imitation, always deviating a little, becomes at last capricious and casual. Shakespeare, whether life or nature be his subject, shows plainly that he has seen with his own eyes; he gives the image which he receives, not weakened or distorted by the intervention of any other mind; the ignorant feel his representations to be just and the learned see that they are complete.[64]

Most judges, like most poets, "copy" the work of their predecessors. They make small additions to the swelling corpus of judicial opinions, which now number in the millions. A few judges, while not unmindful of the constraints imposed and the resources supplied by this corpus, look outward to the world of action that law regulates and the world of thought from which the ideas and values of the law ultimately derive. They try to conform their opinions to this outer world, and they need a style suitable to it and not merely to a hermetic professional discourse.

Granted, stance cannot automatically be inferred from style. Every writing has an implied as well as an actual author, and the two are often divergent, sometimes shockingly so. (They seem shockingly *convergent* in the case of Blackmun.[65]) A comparison of Holmes's correspondence with his opinions, or of Learned Hand's preconference memoranda with *his* opinions, shows these judges assuming a loftier, a more formal, more "grown-up," tone in their opinions than in their private writings. If the impure style became popular, perhaps because pragmatism had become the orthodox jurisprudence, formalist judges might employ it. Some nonformalist judges may be masquerading as formalists by employing the pure style. There may even be formalist judges who are employing the im-

---

64. Johnson, note 52 above, at 163. I have regularized the spelling and punctuation in this passage.

65. The "Poor Joshua!" outburst in the *DeShaney* dissent was not a piece of calculated rhetoric; Blackmun blurted it out during the oral argument of the case.

pure style because their brand of formalism is unorthodox. All that a choice of style infallibly communicates is what the judge thinks is an admirable character for a judge to have.

Can a judicial writing style, which might be adopted for reasons independent of one's jurisprudential stance—which might be adopted because one could not write any other way or because of one's aesthetic principles or because a particular style was in fashion—affect content? I think it can. While it is possible to formulate a position in pragmatic terms to oneself and then wrap it in formalism, as Cardozo appears to have done in *MacPherson v. Buick Motor Co.*,[66] his famous decision expanding products liability, there is a danger that the wrapping will make it more difficult for the writer as well as for the reader to come to grips with the essential questions. We tend to believe that words enable thought. But words can also substitute for thought. The pure style is an anodyne for thought. The impure style forces—well, invites—the writer to dig below the verbal surface of the doctrines that he is interpreting and applying. There he may find merely his own emotions, but if he is lucky, he may find the deep springs of the law.

Moreover, in thinking about a case a judge might come to a definite conclusion yet find the conclusion indefensible when he tries to write an opinion justifying it. We do not think entirely in words and certainly not entirely in sentences and paragraphs. Inarticulable or even unconscious feelings and impressions fill in around the sentence fragments that form in our minds as we think about a problem. This incompletely verbalized thinking can be insightful. But it can also be muddy, so that when we try to organize it into sentences and paragraphs we may find that our confident conclusion is wrong; it "will not write." Language is not just a medium of communication; it is an aid to thinking; and "thinking on paper" is often necessary to bring the resources of language fully to bear on a problem.[67] Writing also encourages a degree of critical detachment: in reading over what he has written, the writer may wonder how an audience would react. Writing may even be necessary to bring deep intuitions to the surface. Many writers have the experience of not knowing except in a general sense what they are going to write until they start writing. A link is somehow forged between the unconscious and the pen. The link is lost to the judge who does not write. It is not only poets who write better than they know.

66. 111 N.E. 1050 (N.Y. 1916). See Edward H. Levi, *An Introduction to Legal Reasoning* 9–25 (1949); Richard A. Posner, *Cardozo: A Study in Reputation* 108 (1990).

67. Peter Carruthers, *Language, Thought and Consciousness: An Essay in Philosophical Psychology* 51–52 (1996).

The kind of judge who thinks that the considerations that bear on judicial decision making range beyond the canonical materials of formalist legal thought will find the pure style confining, because it is not designed for the articulation of those considerations. To the impure poet, "nothing that is available in human experience is to be legislated out of poetry."[68] Substitute "law" for "poetry" and we have the credo of the impure judicial stylist, as expressed in an opinion by Learned Hand in a case in which the issue was whether a veterans' reemployment statute gave the returning veteran more seniority than nonveterans in his job classification. Among the considerations that persuaded Hand and his colleagues that the answer was "no" was that

> when we consider the situation at the time that the Act was passed— September, 1940—it is extremely improbable that Congress should have meant any broader privilege than as we are measuring it. It is true that the nation had become deeply disturbed at its defenseless position, and had begun to make ready; but it was not at war, and the issue still hung in the balance whether it ever would be at war. If we carry ourselves back to that summer and autumn, we shall recall that the presidential campaigns of both parties avoided commitment upon that question, and that each candidate particularly insisted that no troops should be sent overseas. The original act limited service to one year, and it was most improbable that within that time we should be called upon to fight upon our own soil; as indeed the event proved, for we were still at peace in September, 1941. Congress was calling young men to the colors to give them an adequate preparation for our defence, but with no forecast of the appalling experiences which they were later to undergo. Against that background it is not likely that a proposal would then have been accepted which gave industrial priority, regardless of their length of employment, to unmarried men.[69]

This effort "to reconstruct . . . the purpose of Congress when it used the words in which [the provisions in issue] were cast"[70] owes nothing to distinctively "legal" methods of reasoning and could only with difficulty be expressed in a style designed for the articulation of those methods.

Two Cultures

In emphasizing the importance of an approach to judicial composition that shows awareness of the complexity of the human condition and of per-

68. Warren, note 51 above, at 26.

69. Fishgold v. Sullivan Drydock & Repair Corp., 154 F.2d 785, 788–789 (2d Cir.), aff'd, 328 U.S. 275 (1946).

70. Id. at 789.

spectives other than the writer's own, I may seem to be arming such critics of the application of economics to law as Peter Teachout. He argues that the language of economics, in its colorlessness, lack of affect, and striving for scientific precision, distorts human reality and obliterates alternative perspectives. The economic approach to law "takes an inherited cultural rhetoric that to a certain extent is already ethically integrated and subjects it to the disintegrative pressures of radical market theory."[71] He illustrates this with my article on *Bird v. Holbrook,*[72] a suit for damages brought by a young man who had been seriously wounded by a spring gun in a garden where some valuable tulips had been stolen. The owner of the garden had expected the thief to come back for more so he set a spring gun, and hoping to wound the thief, he posted no warning signs. The young man who got wounded was not the thief, however; he had entered the garden to rescue a straying peahen. He sued the owner and won. Pouncing on my remark that "the case involved two legitimate activities, raising tulips and keeping peahens, that happened to conflict,"[73] Teachout says that "in his utter preoccupation with the efficiency question—a preoccupation required by the deepest structures of the language he has chosen to employ— [Posner] virtually steps over the body of the seriously maimed young man."[74] But shouldn't a researcher be permitted a choice of approaches to his subject, rather than being forced to use every possible approach? If, as applied to a particular problem in law, the economic approach falls short because it fails to take account of all relevant considerations, other scholars can bring these to the attention of the scholarly community.

Anyway, the argument that an economic approach to tort law dulls sensitivity to human suffering is unsound both in general and with regard to spring guns. The article that Teachout criticizes approves the result in *Bird v. Holbrook,* rejects the old common-law rule that permitted the police to kill a fleeing felon, and warns against relying entirely on tort law to regulate the use of spring guns and other traps. Elsewhere, economic analysts of law have advanced the proposition, which Teachout should find congenial, that in some circumstances the value of a human life is infinite.[75]

71. Peter Read Teachout, "Worlds beyond Theory: Toward the Expression of an Integrative Ethic for Self and Culture," 83 *Michigan Law Review* 849, 881 (1985). For similar criticisms, see James Boyd White, "Economics and Law: Two Cultures in Tension," 54 *Tennessee Law Review* 161 (1987); Margaret Jane Radin, *Contested Commodities* 83–93 (1996).

72. 4 Bing. 628, 130 Eng. Rep. 911 (C.P. 1828).

73. Posner, "Killing or Wounding to Protect a Property Interest," 14 *Journal of Law and Economics* 201, 209 (1971).

74. Teachout, note 71 above, at 882.

75. See my book *Economic Analysis of Law* 197, 199–200 (4th ed. 1992).

Nothing in either the theory or the vocabulary of economics need blind an economist or economically minded lawyer to issues of life and death, which in fact bulk large in the economic analysis of law.[76] A work of economic analysis will not have the rich texture of a poem by Donne or a play by Shakespeare, but one must not confuse dispassion with callousness. A medical paper is not deemed insensitive or "disintegrative" merely because it does not express teary, or any, sympathy for sick people.

Choice of words can have political and social consequences, and an impoverished vocabulary can impoverish thought,[77] but as Margaret Radin acknowledges in what is otherwise a reprise of Teachout's attack on the description of human behavior in economic terms, to reconceive speech as a form of action on the ground that language affects thought and, through thought, action is to invite censorship.[78] The attempt by some feminists to coerce the adoption of a gender-neutral vocabulary is an attempt at censorship, defended by reference to the effect of language in shaping thought, and through thought actual behavior, toward women.

The lesson to be drawn from the study of the effects of language is the desirability of enriching the resources of human communication—not of rejecting whole classes of discourse because they seem hard-hearted or partial. That "Newspeak" (Orwell's parody of Basic English, in *Nineteen Eighty-Four*) is false or reductive is less important than that it is the only language that the rulers of "Oceania" allow people to use. To equate the language of economics to Newspeak is to misunderstand, moreover, the purpose of a scientific vocabulary, such as that of economics: not to conceal unpleasant realities but to achieve analytical precision. Mathematicians do not talk about numbers rather than things in order to conceal the social or political consequences of mathematical theorizing. The increasingly mathematical language of economics consists largely of definitions that enable economic phenomena to be modeled in exact terms. The layman's "cost" is too vague for this purpose; the economist's "opportunity cost," "long-run marginal cost," and "average total cost" are precise. In contrast, the bureaucratic impersonality of legal prose, as illustrated by the opinion in the *Cox Broadcasting* case, may convey an impression of precision to the unschooled, but the purpose or effect is generally to obfuscate.

76. See id. at 199–200 (damages in wrongful-death cases), 221 (murder), 240 (killing in self-defense), 241 (reckless killing), 374 (regulation of life-saving drugs); also Tomas J. Philipson and Richard A. Posner, *Private Choices and Public Health: The AIDS Epidemic in an Economic Perspective* (1993).

77. Richard A. Posner, *The Economics of Justice* 44–47 (1981); Posner, note 1 above, at 321.

78. Margaret Jane Radin, "Market-Inalienability," 100 *Harvard Law Review* 1849, 1882–1887 (1987). See also Radin, note 71 above, ch. 12.

Conceptualizing does, of course, involve abstraction from the world of tangible, observed objects. The economic concept of "marginal cost," for example, is not an entry on any company's books; it is an invention of economists. But the purpose is to improve the understanding of business behavior rather than to conceal unpleasant realities. The economic approach to human behavior actually insists on the gritty realism that the New Criticism taxed some Romantic poetry with trying to evade. The economic vision of the human situation is a "constrained vision," in contrast to Romanticism's "unconstrained vision."[79] In its insistence that self-interest, and hence incentives, are important in motivating human action and that in a world of scarcity everything has a cost (there is no such thing as a free lunch, as economists like to say), and in its consequent skepticism about utopian projects, economics reflects a sense of human finitude and a decided absence of romantic uplift. This is what makes economics—the rejection of Romanticism in the sphere of government—repugnant to the heirs of Romanticism, and what should make it congenial to anti-Romantics such as Auden, from whose "Lullaby" I quote the first stanza:

> Lay your sleeping head, my love,
> Human on my faithless arm;
> Time and fevers burn away
> Individual beauty from
> Thoughtful children, and the grave
> Proves the child ephemeral:
> But in my arms till break of day
> Let the living creature lie,
> Mortal, guilty, but to me
> The entirely beautiful.

Consistent with the Audenesque anti-Romanticism of economics, the economics of household behavior is being used by feminists to demystify the family and housework and place women's welfare on a more secure foundation than a husband's love.[80]

The words and (increasingly) the mathematical formulas in which economic theory is expressed are tools for making the theory as perspicuous as possible. They should be evaluated accordingly, rather than for their

---

79. Thomas Sowell, *A Conflict of Visions* (1987).

80. See, for example, Katharine Silbaugh, "Turning Labor into Love: Housework and the Law," 91 *Northwestern University Law Review* 1 (1996); Ann Laquer Estin, "Love and Obligation: Family Law and the Romance of Economics," 36 *William and Mary Law Review* 989 (1995); Nancy C. Staudt, "Taxing Housework," 84 *Georgetown Law Journal* 1571 (1996); Elizabeth S. Scott, "Rational Decisionmaking about Marriage and Divorce," 76 *Virginia Law Review* 9 (1990).

conformity to forms of discourse that have other purposes. I share the growing concern that while the expression of economic theory in mathematical models is indispensable to analyzing complex phenomena and invaluable in forcing economic theorists to make their assumptions explicit, for many economists mathematization is becoming an end it itself. A tendency to an excessively specialized discourse incomprehensible to outsiders is a typical professional deformation illustrated in literary studies by the heavy use of an ugly, esoteric, and pretentious vocabulary inspired by European philosophers.[81] And it is true that by supplying a scientific vocabulary and a conceptual scheme in which any social practice can be analyzed, economics facilitates thinking about the unthinkable. But all that this means is that while Newspeak shrinks the possible range of thought, econospeak expands it.[82]

Although critical of discussing spring guns and other life and death matters in economic terms, Teachout makes no suggestion for a better way to discuss them. And in his mentor James Boyd White's extensive writings about the relation of law to literature you will likewise will find little in the way of proposals for improving the law's treatment of sensitive issues, beyond exhortation to the judge and the lawyer to be more sensitive, candid, empathetic, imaginative, and humane. What good is it to be told that "the language that the lawyer uses and remakes is a language of meaning in the fullest sense," or that the judicial opinion "might be far more accurately and richly understood if it were seen not as a bureaucratic expression of end-means rationality [that is, in economic terms] but as a statement by an individual mind or a group of individual minds exercising their responsibility to decide a case as well as they can and to determine what it shall mean in the language of the culture?"[83] The promise of the richer understanding (note the buried economic allusion!) has yet to be redeemed. Obviously White is unhappy with where he thinks economic analysis is leading the law; but to say that instead of steering by the light of economics judges should "decide a case as well as they can" is to beg the question. Dislike of theory[84] is not a theory.

If White is too hard on the language of "end-means rationality," he is too soft on traditional legal rhetoric. Plato's dialogue *Gorgias* is about the

81. For criticisms, see Louis Menand, "How to Make a Ph.D. Matter," *New York Times Magazine,* Sept. 22, 1996, p. 78; Wendell V. Harris, *Literary Meaning: Reclaiming the Study of Literature,* ch. 9 (1996) ("Publishing the (Highly) Perishable").

82. Robert Timothy Reagan, "Judge Posner's Formula for Preliminary Injunctions: Physics Envy or a Different Voice?" *San Francisco Barrister,* Dec. 1995, p. 2.

83. James Boyd White, *Heracles' Bow: Essays on the Rhetoric and Poetics of the Law* 36, 41 (1985).

84. See White, "Judicial Criticism," 20 *Georgia Law Review* 835, 843–845 (1986).

rhetoric used by litigants (and their forensic ghostwriters—the forerunners of the modern litigator) in the extraordinarily litigious[85] society of ancient Athens. Plato was savagely critical of this rhetoric, to which he attributed all sorts of bad things, including the condemnation of Socrates. White defends lawyers from Plato's criticisms: "The task of the lawyer is not simply to persuade, using whatever cultural devices lie at hand, but to persuade a judge or jury that one result or another is the best way to act in the cultural situation defined by these facts or this evidence and by this set of statutes and opinions and understandings . . . [The lawyer] speaks to the judge or jury not as they are defined by their individual interests, passions, and biases but as they are defined by their role, which is to do justice."[86] The forensic oratory that Plato attacked was addressed to a "tribunal" (a jury, sometimes of hundreds) not much, if at all, superior in understanding and emotions to the Roman mob in *Julius Caesar*. The audience for a modern oral argument or judicial opinion is more reflective. But so ill-defined a concept is "justice" that much room is left for appeals to "individual interests, passions, and biases," especially, of course, in jury trials; thus modern legal rhetoric is emotive too, and White's advice is bad advice to the lawyer who wants to get ahead.

White has not shown that conventional legal rhetoric is *in general* a more rational or even a more civilized mode of discourse than the language and concepts of economics. But that is in general, not in every instance. Euphemizing has a place in law. The "unscientific" language of free will in the discourse of criminal law serves the valid ethical purpose of differentiating criminals from other dangerous things, such as animals and avalanches, and by doing so of discouraging casual and unreflective invocation of the concept of dangerousness as a warrant for harsh methods of law enforcement. Concepts such as human dignity that are too vague for the economist's scientific purposes have an important function in the language game that we call law. But no economist or economically minded lawyer has advocated the wholesale substitution of the economic for the legal vocabulary. Even if law could be completely modeled and fully understood in economic terms, it would not follow that the commands of the law should be expressed in those terms.

The attack by James Boyd White and other participants in the law and literature movement (Robin West, for example) on economic analysis of law raises the question whether the two movements can coexist. If not, if

---

85. See S. C. Todd, *The Shape of Athenian Law* 147–153 (1993).

86. James Boyd White, *When Words Lose Their Meaning: Constitutions and Reconstitutions of Language, Character, and Community* 270 (1984).

a choice between them must be made by the legal profession, including its academic branch, the law and economics movement will be chosen because it offers the profession more. It not only offers an indispensable way of thinking about the economic issues that loom so large in such important bodies of law as antitrust, remedies, corporate and securities law, pension law, environmental law, labor and employment law, common carrier regulation, public utility regulation, bankruptcy law, tax law, the law of international transactions, the legislative process, the award of attorneys' fees, and commercial law; it also offers a framework for understanding and improving fields of law that had seemed to have little or nothing to do with economics, such as tort law, property law, contract law, criminal law, trust law, and procedure. The isomorphism of economic and legal concepts enables the latter to be mapped on to the former (for example, negligence on suboptimal precaution, property rights on cost internalization, the decision whether to settle or go to trial on decision under uncertainty), creating a conceptual skeleton for the superficially chaotic doctrines of American law. There is no similar isomorphism between literature (whether the works of imaginative literature themselves or the theories that have been developed about those works) and law. Copyright and defamation—and the latter to only a very limited extent—are virtually the only areas of law that regulate literature, whereas many fields of law regulate economic relations and activities, especially when "economic" is interpreted as broadly as the modern economist interprets it.

There is some complementarity between the law and literature movement and the law and economics movement. We saw in Chapter 2 that the economic analysis of revenge can help in interpreting works of revenge literature, and we shall see in the last chapter that the economic theory of copyright can help in designing an optimal regime of copyright for works of literature. I even let the word "cost" creep into my discussion of the rhetoric of Odysseus's speech to Nausicaa. Some works of literature—not I think the works of Kafka discussed by Robin West, but greater works by Shakespeare and Dostoevsky—offer a critical perspective on instrumental, including economic, rationality. But for the most part the two movements are neither complementary nor competitive but merely separate. The works of literature that I examined in Part One offer insights into jurisprudential issues that lie mostly outside the domain of economics, and the contribution that I think literature can make to judicial opinion-writing is unrelated to anything in economics. Economics is not about to annex literature, or literature vanquish economics.

The level at which economics and literature begin to merge is, surprisingly, the aesthetic. Economics is beautiful to those who know enough of it to be able to read economic books and articles and who also have an aesthetic sense. Elegance, concision, surprise, precision, form, metaphor, narrative, example, economy of expression, architectonic order, mystery, wit—from Adam Smith to Gary Becker and Robert Solow, these aesthetic virtues are to be found at the highest levels of economic scholarship, just as they are to be found in imaginative literature and in the physical sciences.[87]

87. See, for example, S. Chandrasekhar, *Truth and Beauty: Aesthetics and Motivations in Science* (1987); *The Aesthetic Dimension of Science: 1980 Nobel Conference* (Deane W. Curtin ed. 1992); Edward Rothstein, "Contemplating the Sublime," 66 *American Scholar* 513, 518–519 (1997).

part III

the $\mathcal{L}$ITERARY TURN *in* LEGAL SCHOLARSHIP

NINE

The Edifying School of Legal Scholarship

A Literary Education for Lawyers?

Oscar Wilde famously remarked that "there is no such thing as a moral or an immoral book. Books are well written, or badly written. That is all." He was echoed by Auden, who said in his poem in memory of William Butler Yeats that poetry makes nothing happen (though the poem as a whole qualifies this claim), and by Croce and other formalist critics, such as Cleanth Brooks, the doyen of New Critics, who insisted that edification was the function of religion, not of poetry.[1] George Orwell, though himself a didactic novelist, was of this view as well.[2] It is one that most critics adopt when the issue is censorship. I accept Wilde's dictum—the creed of aestheticism, of art for art's sake—understanding it to mean that the moral content and consequences of a work of literature are irrelevant to its value as literature; as Helen Vendler has put it, "treating fictions as moral pep-pills or moral emetics is repugnant to anyone who realizes the complex psychological and moral motives of a work of art."[3] This is not to deny that reading can have con-

1. Brooks, "A Note on the Limits of 'History' and the Limits of 'Criticism,'" in *Seventeenth-Century English Poetry: Modern Essays in Criticism* 352, 357–358 (William R. Keast ed. 1962). But we saw in Chapter 7 that the New Critics were not always successful in maintaining the distinction between the moral and the aesthetic responses to literature. On T. S. Eliot's views concerning this issue, which fall into the same equivocation as the New Critics whom he inspired, see Malcolm Budd, *Values of Art: Pictures, Poetry and Music* 98–99 (1995).

2. "The durability of *Gulliver's Travels* goes to show that, if the force of belief is behind it, a world-view which only just passes the test of sanity is sufficient to produce a great work of art." George Orwell, "Politics vs. Literature: An Examination of *Gulliver's Travels*," in *The Collected Essays, Journalism and Letters of George Orwell*, vol. 4, pp. 205, 222–223 (Sonia Orwell and Ian Angus eds. 1968).

3. Vendler, "The Booby Trap," *New Republic*, Oct. 7, 1996, pp. 34, 37. Compare Benedetto

sequences, including moral and political ones. Information and persuasion affect behavior, and reading is a source of both.[4] Think of the role that novels by Turgenev *(Fathers and Sons)*, Dostoevsky *(The Possessed)*, Conrad *(The Secret Agent, Under Western Eyes)*, Koestler *(Darkness at Noon)*, Orwell *(Animal Farm, Nineteen Eighty-Four)*, and, of course, Solzhenitsyn played in bringing to light the true character of anarchism and communism. Of *A Passage to India* it has been said that "as an account of the social conditions of British India it was powerful enough to have influenced events."[5] Upton Sinclair's novel *The Jungle* led to federal regulation of food processing—and who doubts the effect of *Uncle Tom's Cabin* (1852) on the abolitionist cause?[6] A book could be written, launching a new subgenre of law and literature, on the effect of works of imaginative literature on public policy. And in the last chapter I argued that the craft values of literature can help judges to think straighter as well as write better.

The aesthetic tradition is woven of three strands. The first is that immersion in literature does not make us better citizens or better people. One might be able to pick out some works of literature that have such an effect because of the information they convey or the emotional state they induce, but they would be a skewed sample of the great literary works. Second, we should not be discountenanced by morally offensive views encountered in literature even when the author appears to share them. A work of literature is not maimed or even marred by expressing unacceptable moral views; by the same token, a mediocre work of literature is not redeemed by expressing moral views of which we approve. The proper criteria for

---

Croce, *Guide to Aesthetics* 57–58 (1965 [1913]): "The artist is always unblamable morally and uncensurable philosophically, even though his art may have for subject matter an inferior morality and philosophy. Insofar as he is artist, he is not a man of action and does not reason, but poetizes, paints, sings." Roger Seamon argues in similar vein that moral values in works of literature are *assumed* by the author and help us make sense of the story, rather than being supported by evidence or argument that might persuade the reader that these are sound values. Seamon, "The Story of the Moral: The Function of Thematizing in Literary Criticism," 47 *Journal of Aesthetics and Art Criticism* 229 (1989).

4. See, for example, Peter M. Marzuk et al., "Increase in Suicide by Asphyxiation in New York City after the Publication of *Final Exit*," 329 *New England Journal of Medicine* 1508 (1993).

5. Frank Kermode, "Forster and *Maurice*," in Kermode, *The Uses of Error* 265, 268 (1991). Yet the numerous factual errors in *A Passage to India*—on which see P. N. Furbank, *E. M. Forster: A Life*, vol. 2: *Polycrates' Ring (1914–1970)*, pp. 126–130 (1978)—suggest the perils of using novels as a substitute for history and social science and even for journalism.

6. See Leon Harris, *Upton Sinclair: American Rebel*, ch. 7 (1975); Thomas F. Gossett, Uncle Tom's Cabin *and American Culture* 183–184 (1985). Actually, Gossett does doubt this. See id., ch. 10.

evaluating literature are aesthetic rather than ethical. Third, the author's moral qualities or opinions should not affect our valuation of the work.

The insistence, in short, is on the separation of the moral from the aesthetic—but with two qualifications. Some literature has little interest apart from the didactic and for it the proper criticism is didactic, as we shall see in the next chapter. And the separation of moral from aesthetic values does not imply the rejection of the former. The aesthetic outlook *is* a moral outlook, one that stresses the values of openness, detachment, hedonism, curiosity, tolerance, the cultivation of the self, and the preservation of a private sphere—in short, the values of liberal individualism.

The counter-tradition in literary criticism to the aesthetic originates with Plato and insists upon the importance, in some versions to the exclusion of anything else, of the ethical or political content and consequences of works of literature, and less commonly upon the importance of the author's own morality. Martha Nussbaum considers Greek tragedies and Anglo-American realistic novels a part of moral philosophy.[7] She argues that reading novels "develops moral capacities without which citizens *will not succeed* in making reality out of the normative conclusions of any moral or political theory, however excellent."[8] Wayne Booth, disagreeing with his illustrious predecessor in the edifying school, Tolstoy, asks: "Do[es] not *King Lear* . . . depend upon *and reinforce,* among other fixed norms, the enormous value of simple kindness and the awfulness of gratuitous cruelty?"[9] Booth doesn't enjoy Rabelais as much as he used to, having been awakened by feminism to Rabelais' misogyny.[10]

The edifying tradition is diverse. Plato, Tolstoy, Bentham, and the Puritans, among others, were deeply suspicious of literature and the arts and unwilling to grant any value to literature that contains immoral ideas. Devotees of the "naked truth," whether religious, philosophical, or scientific, these eminences despised surface and figuration.[11] At the opposite ex-

7. See Nussbaum, *Love's Knowledge: Essays on Philosophy and Literature* (1990).

8. Nussbaum, *Poetic Justice: The Literary Imagination and Public Life* 12 (1995) (emphasis added). See also id. at 2–4.

9. Booth, *The Company We Keep: An Ethics of Fiction* 152 (1988) (emphasis added). Compare Leo Tolstoy, *Shakespeare and the Drama* (1903), discussed in George Orwell, "Lear, Tolstoy, and the Fool," in *The Collected Essays, Journalism and Letters of George Orwell*, note 2 above, vol. 4, pp. 287, 290.

10. Booth, "Rabelais and the Challenge of Feminist Criticism," in Booth, note 9 above, at 383–418. Booth is explicit about the ethical consequences of literature: "everyone who has read much narrative with intense engagement 'knows' that narratives do influence behavior." Id. at 227. "Almost everyone—except for a few theorists—would agree not only that we read for instruction but that the instruction often *works.*" Id. at 229. See also id. at 232–235.

11. Russell Fraser, *The War against Poetry*, ch. 7 (1970).

treme, Nussbaum integrates literature with moral philosophy. She does not deny the importance of aesthetic values, but she is prepared to trade them off against the moral, so that the morality of the work affects its final evaluation *as literature*. Booth, the professional literary critic, being more systematic and wide-ranging in his ethical criticism, is also more censorious. He discusses works that do not meet his high standards for ethical literature as well as ones that do. Nussbaum confines herself to the latter.

Some ethical critics want a work of literature to have a tidy moral, as in Aesop's fables, while others think the moral value of literature lies in a more diffuse influence on thinking and action. Booth and Nussbaum liken the reading of imaginative literature to friendship and emphasize that the effect of a friendship on one's character and outlook is complex and uncertain, yet surely not unimportant. But they do not want to stop there. They want to extract a moral lesson from the work, albeit by consideration of the form as well as the paraphrasable content of the work.

One can imagine critics in the moralistic or didactic tradition preparing lists of edifying works of literature for judges to read. If poets are the unacknowledged legislators of the world, should not judges pay attention to the moral lessons in poetry? Should they not look to them for guidance in deciding cases in the open area where precedent and other conventional sources of legal authority run out? Might not *Buck v. Bell* have been decided differently had Holmes been steeped in William Blake and Jane Austen instead of Charles Darwin? In short, and quite apart from issues of craft, shouldn't lawyers have a literary education before, or in, or, if need be, after they attend law school? Was not the great legal scholar Wigmore on the right track, therefore, when in 1913 he compiled a list of great books for lawyers to read?[12]

That the edifying school has struck a responsive chord with legal scholars of literary bent should come as no surprise. The ratio of normative to positive scholarship is higher in law than in most other fields. Law is not a contemplative discipline and the aesthetic outlook does not come easily to its disciples. If they bring literature into law it is to contribute to what they conceive to be the normative mission of legal scholarship. Thus Robin West: "The human capacities to which study of the humanities gives rise might constitute a set of moral capacities, and hence a sphere of consciousness, sufficiently removed from the influence of law to serve as a vehicle for moral criticism of it . . . A tremendous amount of canonical literature is highly critical of law, and of the arguments typically put forward

---

12. John H. Wigmore, "Introduction," in John Marshall Gest, *The Lawyer in Literature* viii–xii (1913).

to support its moral authority . . . Literature helps us understand others. Literature helps us sympathize with their pain, it helps us share their sorrow, and it helps us celebrate their joy. It makes us more moral. It makes us better people."[13] And on a less exalted plane, "lawyers can learn how to represent lesbian clients better by studying books with lesbian characters," specifically novels "argumentatively engaged in portraying, explaining, justifying, and apologizing for the lesbian."[14] Richard Weisberg interprets the novels that he discusses as bulwarks against another Holocaust. Most of James Boyd White's essays are concerned with works of literature that have no legal theme—that would not have been eligible, therefore, for inclusion in the discussion in Part One of this book—his goal being to impart a literary education to lawyers and judges so that they will be both morally and professionally improved.[15] In the last chapter we saw him run morality and professionalism together. His aspiration for the law and literature movement, which is also Nussbaum's,[16] is "the perpetual affirmation of the individual mind as it seeks community with others."[17]

When Wilde penned the aphorism with which I began this chapter, in the preface to his shocking (though, ironically, highly moralistic) novel *The Picture of Dorian Gray*,[18] he was challenging the conventional wisdom of his time. Almost every right-thinking person would have said then that immersion in the monuments of Western civilization makes one a better person. This now strikes many people as just another exploded Victorian piety. One reason is the twentieth-century behavior of Germany, often described as the world's most cultured nation, and certainly a nation in contrast to which the United States is, or at least was at the relevant times, philistine. Germany's vaunted culture did not inoculate it against

13. West, *Narrative, Authority, and Law* 7, 13, 263 (1993) (footnote omitted).

14. Anne B. Goldstein, "Representing the Lesbian in Law and Literature," in *Representing Women: Law, Literature, and Feminism* 356, 358 (Susan Sage Heinzelman and Zipporah Batshaw Wiseman eds. 1994) (footnote omitted).

15. See White, "What Can a Lawyer Learn from Literature?" 102 *Harvard Law Review* 2014, 2028 (1989). For an example of the approach commended by White, see John Denvir, "'Deep Dialogue'—James Joyce's Contribution to American Constitutional Theory," 3 *Cardozo Studies in Law and Literature* 1 (1991), using Joyce's story "The Dead" to argue that literature shows how shame can lead to the creation of community.

16. See Nussbaum, note 8 above.

17. White, "Law and Literature: 'No Manifesto,'" 39 *Mercer Law Review* 739, 751 (1988).

18. Gray complains of being poisoned by a book (p. 246 of 1946 edition), and Wilde's latest biographer claims that *The Picture of Dorian Gray* is a criticism of aestheticism and of the view that books cannot corrupt. Richard Ellman, *Oscar Wilde* 317–318 (1988). *The Picture* itself states in the narrator's voice, "Dorian Gray had been poisoned by a book" (p. 169)—an imaginary novel about the Italian Renaissance, based loosely on Huysman's *À Rebours* (Ellman, above, at 316–317).

Kaiser[19] or Führer. Cultured Germans willingly and often enthusiastically served these regimes along with *hoi polloi*. Thomas Mann, Germany's greatest novelist, was an outspoken supporter of Imperial Germany during World War I. The German judges who served Hitler so well[20] were *Gymnasium*-educated and therefore steeped in Goethe, Schiller, and Kant. Culture was actually a tool of these regimes. As Geoffrey Hartman explains, "National Socialism used aesthetic pleasure to gild aggressive and transgressive ambitions," and he concludes that "there is no hard evidence that the altruistic personality is enhanced by exposure to higher education or 'culture.'"[21] If anything, art is antagonistic to democratic politics: "art and beauty require exaltation, ecstasy, extremes; political life is more comfortable with collaboration, consensus, and compromise."[22]

One doesn't have to raise the ghosts of Wagner, Céline, Pound, Heidegger, and de Man to be skeptical about the edifying effect of high culture in general and of literature in particular. Cultured people are not on the whole morally superior to philistines. "Despite their familiarity with the classics, professors of literature do not appear to lead better lives than other people, and frequently display unbecoming virulence on the subject of one another's shortcomings."[23] In fact, immersion in literature and art can breed rancorous and destructive feelings of personal superiority, alienation, and resentment.[24] Holmes, come to think of it, was probably the best

---

19. "The Imperial German experience cautions that the humaneness of humanism in higher education should not be taken for granted." Konrad H. Jarausch, *Students, Society, and Politics in Imperial Germany* 425 (1982). The German academic high school, the *Gymnasium*, placed heavy emphasis on Greek, Latin, and classical German literature (particularly Goethe, Schiller, and Lessing). See Margret Kraul, *Das Deutsche Gymnasium 1780–1980* 100–107, 142 (1984). Speaking of the German legal profession as it was in the years leading up to World War I, Rueschemeyer says, "The elite of the profession consisted of highly competent lawyers steeped in an idealistic conception of their profession and, strange perhaps in a[s] mundane [an] occupation as the law, in ideals of *Bildung*, of literary culture and a refined personality." Dietrich Rueschemeyer, *Lawyers and Their Society: A Comparative Study of the Legal Profession in Germany and in the United States* 178 (1973).

20. See Ingo Müller, *Hitler's Justice: The Courts of the Third Reich* (Deborah Lucas Schneider trans. 1990); Posner, *Overcoming Law* 145–159 (1995).

21. Hartman, "Is an Aesthetic Ethos Possible? Night Thoughts after Auschwitz," 6 *Cardozo Studies in Law and Literature* 135, 137, 139 (1994). There is no soft evidence either. Professors were notable by their absence from the cells of resistance to Hitler that developed during his rule. Alice Gallin, *Midwives to Nazism: University Professors in Weimar Germany 1925–1933* 4–5, 100–105 (1986).

22. Tzvetan Todorov, "Poetry and Morality," *Salmagundi*, Summer 1996, pp. 68, 71.

23. K. K. Ruthven, *Critical Assumptions* 184 (1979).

24. Recall from Chapter 3 Ian Watt's interpretation of Faust as an intellectual disappointed with the world because it does not live up to the extravagant hopes of an imagination stimulated by extensive reading.

read—and I mean best read in the literary and philosophical monuments of Western civilization—judge in the history of the Supreme Court;[25] and yet his numerous critics think *Buck v. Bell* typical of his outlook on life. We shall see that there is little evidence that pornography makes men (its principal consumers) behave worse; and this is a clue that edifying literature is not likely to make them behave better.

What holds for professors of literature holds also for the classics they teach and write about. By "classics" I do not mean the authors, for no one can believe any more that great authors are more likely than nonliterary people to be fine human beings. I mean their books. The classics are full of moral atrocities—as they appear to us today, and sometimes as they appeared to the more enlightened members of the author's own society— that the author apparently approved of. Rape, pillage, murder, human and animal sacrifice, concubinage, and slavery in the *Iliad;* misogyny in the *Oresteia* and countless other works; blood-curdling vengeance; anti-Semitism in more works of literature than one can count, including works by Shakespeare and Dickens; racism and sexism likewise; homophobia (think only of Shakespeare's *Troilus and Cressida* and Mann's "Death in Venice"); monarchism, aristocracy, caste systems and other illegitimate (as they seem to us) forms of hierarchy; colonialism, imperialism, religious obscurantism, militarism, gratuitous violence, torture (as of Iago in *Othello*), and criminality; alcoholism and drug addiction; relentless stereotyping; sadism; pornography; machismo; cruelty to animals (bullfighting, for example); snobbism; praise for fascism and communism, and for idleness; contempt for the poor, the frail, the elderly, the deformed, and the unsophisticated, for people who work for a living, for the law-abiding, and for democratic processes. The world of literature is a moral anarchy; immersion in it teaches moral relativism.

Nussbaum argues that "inegalitarianism is in a degree of tension with the structure of the genre [the novel], which invites concern and respect for any story to which it directs the reader's attention."[26] Yet a majority of the best English, French, Russian, German, and American novels fall into one of several nonegalitarian classes: novels preoccupied with private themes (as they now strike us) often archaically conceived, such as adultery and man-

---

25. Yes, he did read Jane Austen. See Letter to Frederick Pollock, Aug. 2, 1923, in *The Essential Holmes: Selections from the Letters, Speeches, Judicial Opinions, and Other Writings of Oliver Wendell Holmes, Jr.* 10 (Richard A. Posner ed. 1992).

26. Nussbaum, note 8 above, at 129 n. 34. "The novel, while permitting and even suggesting certain criticisms of its characters, promotes mercy through its invitation to empathetic understanding." Id. at 130 n. 45.

liness (for example, Lawrence, Hemingway, Ford Madox Ford, and Joyce); adventure novels (a class that overlaps the first); novels that despite surface appearances are disengaged from any serious interest in the social or political arrangements of society (which I have tried to show is true even of Kafka and Camus); novels that disparage the modern project of liberty and equality (for example, Dumas, Scott, Dostoevsky, Waugh, at times Conrad); novels that presuppose an organization of society in which a leisured, titled, or educated upper crust lives off the sweat of the brow of a mass of toilers at whose existence the novelist barely hints (for example, Austen, James, Wharton, Proust, Fitzgerald); novels preoccupied with issues more metaphysical than social (Beckett, Hesse, and much of Melville, Tolstoy, and Mann); novels that defend bourgeois values (Defoe, Galsworthy, Trollope); novels that deal with public themes yet whose "take" on them is equivocal or inscrutable (Twain and Faulkner); novels that deal with both social and private themes but in which the latter predominate (Stendhal, Flaubert, Bulgakov). Some of the works of these novelists do not fit my classifications—for example, Wharton's best novel, *The House of Mirth,* has pointed criticisms of snobbery and wealth. And many novelists of distinction have had the kind of social conscience that Nussbaum admires. But the possession of such a conscience does not define the genre.

It is true that the novel is a more bourgeois medium than Greek, Elizabethan, or French tragedy, genres preoccupied with the activities and sensibilities of kings and aristocrats. The rise of the novel coincided with the rise of the bourgeoisie, the expansion of literacy, and the growth of science and philosophical realism—developments that stimulated demand for a form of literature that would depict realistically the activities and experiences of ordinary life.[27] But bourgeois and egalitarian are not synonyms.

The prestige of a work of literature generally is little damaged by the discovery that the work condones a morality that later readers find monstrous, though radicals are trying to change this, as we glimpsed in earlier chapters. Edifying works have little advantage in the struggle for canonical status. Yet only the most disciplined, self-denying reader deliberately ignores the moral dimensions of what he reads. Great literature must somehow lull the reader into suspending moral judgment. But how? I think the answer is that the moral content of a work of literature, like the legal content of most of the "legal literary" works discussed in Part One of this book, is merely the writer's raw material—something he works up into a form to

---

27. See Ian Watt, *The Rise of the Novel: Studies in Defoe, Richardson and Fielding,* chs. 1–2 (1957).

which morality is no more relevant than the value of the sculptor's clay as a building material is relevant to the artistic value of the completed sculpture. Do we stalk out of *Hamlet* at the end of the first scene, when we discover that there is a *ghost* in an ostensibly adult play? Why then should we stalk out of *Othello* when we discover that it depicts racially mixed marriage as possibly unnatural? Or out of *The Merchant of Venice* when we discover that it traffics in ugly stereotypes of Jewish greed and blood lust? Or slam *Oliver Twist* shut when we encounter Fagin? Or *Huckleberry Finn* or *Sartoris* when we encounter the word "nigger" used matter of factly? Most readers accept the presence of obsolete ethics in literature with the same equanimity that they accept the presence of obsolete military technology or antiquated diction or vanished customs in literature, as things both inevitable given the age of so much literature and collateral to the purpose for which we read it.

Moral content is irrelevant even when it conforms to our current moral opinions. This is one more implication of the "test of time" theory of literature. No reader of *The Red and the Black* is apt to take up the cudgels on behalf of the monarchists and clerics whom Stendhal attacked. But the sociological issues that preoccupied him in what has been called the first great novel of social and political criticism[28] are passé, and the novel survives only because, aside from its social and political themes, it is a great novel about love, ambition, and living an authentic life. It is a great *realist* novel still, but the realism that we now value it for is realism about human character rather than about conditions in Restoration France. *Uncle Tom's Cabin* has not survived as literature—the only interest that it holds for us is historical—even though its author's opposition to slavery now commands universal assent.

Yet ideologues of the Left tell us that "the ideology which saturates [Shakespeare's] texts, and their location in history, are the most interesting things about them," and of the Right "that Jane Austen is a greater novelist than Proust or Joyce" and "T. S. Eliot's later, Christian poetry is much superior to his earlier."[29] The first statement is bizarre in its willingness to subordinate aesthetic to political values in evaluating the greatest poet and playwright in history. But the second is unacceptable too. And not only because the effort to rank Austen against such different writers as Proust

28. See Erich Auerbach, *Mimesis: The Representation of Reality in Western Literature,* ch. 18 (1953).

29. The first quotation is from Jonathan Dollimore and Alan Sinfield, "History and Ideology: The Instance of *Henry V,*" in *Alternative Shakespeares* 206, 227 (John Drakakis ed. 1985); the second from Irving Kristol, "Reflections of a Neoconservative," 51 *Partisan Review* 856, 859 (1984).

and Joyce—a true example of incommensurability—is misguided, or because "The Waste Land" rather than "Ash Wednesday" or *Four Quartets* is the summit of Eliot's art. To devalue a work of literature because of its politics, morality, or religion is not only to cut off one's nose to spite one's face. It is also intolerant, philistine, puritanical, illiberal (most didactic or moralistic literary critics have been antiliberals), and, when it expresses itself in an assumption of moral superiority to our predecessors, complacently ethnocentric, exemplifying the form of obnoxious political correctness that Stephen Holmes calls "temporal parochialism." It is greatly to be regretted that because "the ability to disconnect one's response to a poem [or other work of literature] from one's attitude to the beliefs it expresses varies from person to person and belief to belief,"[30] people obsessed by politics, religion, or morality are incapable of an aesthetic response to literature.

Believers in a minimal state should be especially wary about subjecting literature to tests of political orthodoxy. The separation of culture and the state, of what is properly private and what is properly public, is menaced by the didactic school. By assigning to literature the function of promoting sound moral (including political) values, it associates literature with public functions, such as the inculcation of civic virtue. By doing this it makes literature an inviting candidate for public regulation, and thus contracts the private sphere. It goes far toward accepting the claim of radicals that everything is politics.

Even if immersion in literature is unlikely to make a person more ethical, might it make him wiser? Here is the philosopher Hilary Putnam commenting on Bentham's statement that there is no difference in value between poetry and the child's game of pushpin:

> We find it virtually impossible to imagine that someone who really appreciates poetry, someone who is capable of distinguishing real poetry from mere verse, capable of responding to great poetry, *should* prefer a childish game to arts which enrich our lives as poetry and music do. We *have* a reason for preferring poetry to pushpin, and that reason lies in the felt experience of great poetry, and of the after effects of great poetry— . . . the enlargement of our repertoire of images and metaphors, and the integration of poetic images and metaphors with mundane perceptions and attitudes that takes place when a poem has lived in us for a number of years. These experiences too are *prima facie* good—and not just good, but enobling [*sic*], to use an old fashioned word.[31]

Two separate ideas are merged in this passage. The first is that people steeped in literature tend to compare their experiences with the literary

30. Budd, note 1 above, at 100.
31. Putnam, *Reason, Truth and History* 155 (1981).

counterparts of those experiences and to derive some of their expectations concerning other people's behavior from the behavior of characters in literature. They use literature as a template for life. This is consistent with Aristotle's contrast between literature and history, the former concerning itself with probabilities rather than actualities—with, as we might say today, building models of human behavior rather than merely describing behavior. Literature contains wisdom and insights (not limited to the jurisprudential issues examined in Part One), which can't be said for pushpin. A lawyer open to its appeal might sum up a career spent working for a legal-aid or public defender's office in these lines from "Easter 1916" that I quoted in Chapter 7: "Too long a sacrifice / Can make a stone of the heart." A lawyer slaving away as an associate at a large law firm might ponder instead Yeats's claim in "The Choice" that "The intellect of man is forced to choose / Perfection of the life, or of the work, / And if it choose the second must refuse / A heavenly mansion, raging in the dark." You might come to worry about committing Lear's mistake of trying to separate power from perquisites, or be sensitized to the kind of "no win" situations that Agamemnon kept stumbling into. You might ponder in light of *Doctor Faustus* and *Macbeth* the maxim that the worst thing that can happen to one is to have all one's wishes granted. Jon Elster's well-known book of social theory *Ulysses and the Sirens* finds in the story of Ulysses' instructing his crew to tie him to the mast when he came within earshot of the Sirens the prototypical case of self-commitment. Sometimes, when my judicial colleagues and I become restive as a long-winded lawyer talks into our lunch hour, I think of these lines from *The Rape of the Lock* (III.19–22):

> Meanwhile declining from the noon of day,
> The sun obliquely shoots his burning ray;
> The hungry judges soon the sentence sign,
> And wretches hang that jurymen may dine.

But it doesn't follow that because some people use literature as a source of insight into human nature and social interactions, other people, for example judges who are not already lovers of literature, should be encouraged to do so. There is neither evidence nor reason to believe that literature provides a straighter path to knowledge about man and society than writings in other fields, such as history and science, and interactions with real people as distinct from fictional characters. Some of us may prefer to acquire much of our knowledge about human nature from novels, but it doesn't follow that novels are a source superior to life and to the various genres of nonfiction. I did not argue in Part One that works of imaginative literature are the only or even the best texts for studying revenge, jurisprudence, or the romantic temperament; and I reject the implications of White's claim that "information [conveyed by findings in the natural or social sciences] may shift the sufficiency of the information I already have, but I do not expect it to change *me*."[32] More people have been changed by natural science (think only of Darwin) and social science—a body of research and writing that includes the works of Adam Smith, Marx, Freud, Keynes, Kinsey, and Hayek, among many others—than by literature. White may be inoculated against this entire body of writings, but if so it is an idiosyncrasy rather than a characteristic of educated people in general.

Rarely can readers extract from works of imaginative literature practical lessons for living. Do you think that *King Lear* teaches that you shouldn't put yourself in your children's power? Think again. People who try to retain personal control of their property in their dotage are the natural prey of con men, of dishonest personal attendants and financial advisers, of grasping physicians, and of gigolos and golddiggers. Better to be dependent on your family and hope that it doesn't harbor a Regan or a Goneril. Writers of imaginative literature are rarely practical people with practical lessons to impart. And the fact that so much literature deals with disruption and crisis makes its insights difficult to transpose to everyday life.

Putnam's second claim, that making the sorts of connections that come naturally to persons of literary sensitivity is ennobling, is neither explained (what does he *mean* by "ennobling"?) nor defended. Nussbaum makes the claim more concrete by arguing that literature can enlarge our empathetic awareness of injustice and of moral issues generally, and so she brings us back to the issue of literature's edifying force. I agree with her that literature is one path, though it is not the only path, to a better understanding of the needs, problems, and point of view of types of people whom we are unlikely to encounter in real life. But there is no reason to suppose that a better understanding of people makes a person better. Great demagogues understand people all too well. Nussbaum is echoing Socrates' unsubstantiated claim that people do wrong only out of ignorance of what is right.

Her method is illustrated by the essays in *Love's Knowledge* on Henry James's novel *The Golden Bowl*. Maggie, a very rich young American woman, marries a penniless Italian prince who, unbeknownst to her, is in love with Charlotte, a penniless American woman who happens to be Maggie's best friend. Maggie discovers that her husband is committing adultery with Charlotte, and manages deftly to reclaim him and send Charlotte (now married to Maggie's widowed father) packing. Nussbaum

---

32. White, note 17 above, at 742.

argues that the novel is "about the development of a woman. To be a woman, to give herself to her husband, Maggie will need to come to see herself as something cracked, imperfect, unsafe, a vessel with a hole through which water may pass, a steamer compartment no longer tightly sealed."[33]

This is *one* of the things *The Golden Bowl* is about. Loss of innocence has been a literary theme since the *Iliad,* and it is a recurrent theme in James's novels. I also accept Nussbaum's further point that moral dilemmas are more vividly rendered in works of imaginative literature than in books about ethics, which tend to be pious, predictable, humorless, and dull, Nietzsche's ethical writings being a stupendous counter-example (but then he's against ethics, at least in the usual sense). But I disagree that *The Golden Bowl* can help us navigate the moral dilemmas in our own lives; that "in the war against moral obtuseness, the artist is our fellow fighter, frequently our guide" (p. 164). *The Golden Bowl* invites a variety of *incompatible* moral responses. One can side with the adulterers, finding Maggie the insufferable rich girl from start to finish[34] and thinking it wrong that Charlotte should lose out to her merely because Maggie is rich and Charlotte poor. One can look upon the prince as a golddigger (for it is plain that he married Maggie for her money, his excuse being that his aristocratic status obligates him to support his relatives in Italy) and think Maggie poor-spirited both for marrying him in the first place and for condoning his adultery. It is possible to be made uncomfortable by the intimacy between Maggie and her father, so much greater than their intimacy with their spouses, and to detest their condescension, as rich people, to the prince and Charlotte, the hustlers.

The novel may be warning readers that it is a mistake for women to make marriage their whole career, that men and women alike should work rather than live off inherited wealth like Maggie and her prince. It may even be presenting a "grim parody" of the marital ideals of nineteenth-century England and America and of the capitalist system in which those ideals

---

33. Nussbaum, note 7 above, at 133–134. Cf. Daniel Brudney, "Knowledge and Silence: *The Golden Bowl* and Moral Philosophy," 16 *Critical Inquiry* 397, 431 (1990), commending Maggie's "tact" in resolving the crisis created by her husband's adultery with minimum damage to the people involved.

34. "If our sympathies are anywhere they are with Charlotte and (a little) the Prince, who represent what, against the general moral background of the book, can only strike us as decent passion; in a stale, sickly and oppressive atmosphere they represent life." F. R. Leavis, *The Great Tradition: George Eliot, Henry James, Joseph Conrad* 160 (1962). Nussbaum may be coming around to this view, for in an essay written after *Love's Knowledge* she criticizes Maggie and her father for treating their spouses "as fine antique furniture," thereby "denying them human status." Martha C. Nussbaum, "Objectification," 24 *Philosophy and Public Affairs* 249, 288 (1995).

are embedded and which they reflect.[35] Nussbaum and Brudney, the moral philosophers, are oddly insensitive to the moral dubiety of Maggie and of the marriage system of which she is the upholder. There is also merit in the suggestion that "James seems to be trying . . . to weave a web of fine, life-moral significance around characters, actions, and situations that are either dramatically too thin or morally too dubious to manifest it in themselves."[36]

The different "takes" on the novel can coexist quite happily. *The Golden Bowl* is richly ambiguous and exerts no pressure on the reader to select the one "right" reading. Ethical readings of works of literature tend to be reductive—and digressive. To focus on the moral issues in *The Golden Bowl* is to risk losing sight of the prurient and Gothic vein of James's imagination—his fascination with the lurid, the unnatural, the quasi-incestuous (Hamlet would have considered sex between the prince and Charlotte, after she becomes the prince's stepmother-in-law, incestuous), and the voyeuristic: the wife committing adultery with her stepson-in-law, the daughter condoning her husband's adultery with her stepmother, the husband committing adultery with his stepmother-in-law, the father and daughter aware of and managing the adultery, the whole weird ménage seen through the eyes of the shocked and fascinated squares (the Assinghams). James was not a moralist, but something stranger and more interesting.

Nussbaum may be arguing merely (or mainly) that *discussion* of the moral dilemmas dramatized in *The Golden Bowl,* as distinct from the dramatization itself, will make us more moral by improving our skill in ethical analysis. This approach, which reflects the revival of interest in casuistic argumentation, shifts the burden of edification from literature to literary criticism and instruction. It is not a burden likely to be carried. Literary critics have rarely achieved the status of moral leaders; the moral dilemmas depicted in canonical literature are for the most part remote from current ethical concerns; above all, there is no evidence that talking about ethical issues improves ethical performance. This is not the place to expound and test a theory of how people become moral. Genes, parental upbringing, interactions with peers, and religion all play a role. That casuistic analysis stimulated by works of imaginative literature also plays a role is unproven and implausible. Moral philosophers, their students, literary critics, and

---

35. Joseph A. Boone, "Modernist Maneuverings in the Marriage Plot: Breaking Ideologies of Gender and Genre in James's *The Golden Bowl,*" 101 *Publications of the Modern Language Association* 374, 380 (1986).

36. S. L. Goldberg, *Agents and Lives: Moral Thinking in Literature* 301 (1993).

English majors are on average no more moral in attitude or behavior than their peers in other fields. They may be less so, because more skillful at rationalization, and because moral talk is for some people a substitute for moral action and even an excuse for immoral action. Talk Left but live Right, as the French say.

Now that few people in our society consider adultery a matter suitable for public regulation, the edifying force if any (I think none) of *The Golden Bowl* is, except for those readers who find in it politically useful insights into marriage under capitalism, limited to the sphere of personal relationships. For examples of how the literary imagination can affect our thinking about public life, Nussbaum turns to social novels, three in particular—Dickens's *Hard Times,* E. M. Forster's *Maurice,* and Richard Wright's *Native Son.* From the first she asks us to learn that the instrumental rationality celebrated in economic theory is incomplete,[37] and from the second and third that homosexuals and blacks deserve our sympathy. The three books are questionable candidates for a questionable role. Although *Hard Times* is a fine novel, as a tract against economic thinking it is shallow and easily refuted. Gradgrind, the butt of the satire, comes to grief by treating everyone he deals with, including members of his own family, on the model of spot-market transactions, banishing every element of trust and affection from both personal and commercial relations. Insofar as Gradgrind is a stand-in for Bentham, the satire may have a point. Confusion of the different spheres of human activity was a feature of Bentham's thought, though as he himself never married we do not know how far he would have carried this confusion into his own personal life. It has been many years since any responsible social scientist was confused in that way, so that to preach against Gradgrind has about as much point as preaching against slavery (the safest of targets, since it has no advocates). There are homologies between firms and families, and these are stressed by economists and other social scientists in quest of general theories of social behavior. But no social scientist recommends that family members incorporate and conduct themselves as shareholders. Market relations are *substitutes* for the affective ties of the family in activities conducted among strangers, and even market relations are not always impersonal. Market relations within close-knit groups are different from the relations of buyers and sellers in spot markets. When people deal with one another on a continuing basis, trust supplements or even supplants reliance on law. That is what Gradgrind fails to see. No economist today fails to see it.

---

37. See also Josephine M. Guy, *The Victorian Social-Problem Novel: The Market, the Individual and Communal Life* 131–36 (1996). Leavis, note 34 above, at 236, describes *Hard Times* as "the confutation of Utilitarianism by life."

Here is another way to understand Gradgrind's mistake. Gradgrind thinks that rationality *means* behaving like the buyer or seller in a spot market, so if rationality is a good thing that's how we should behave in all activities of life. Economists may once have conceived of rationality so, but then they didn't recommend it as a model for all human behavior. Nowadays, as we glimpsed in Chapter 6, economists conceive rational choice more broadly, and by doing so are able to bring a fuller range of human activities under the aegis of economics; but they do not do so by forcing those activities into a Procrustean bed of short-term commercial relations.

Echoing White and Teachout (see Chapter 8), Nussbaum claims that "Dickens's economic opponent [in *Hard Times*] is not a straw man: it is a conception that even now dominates much of our public life, in a form not very different from the form presented in this novel."[38] Dominates? She cites not a single public policy advocated by economists that is flawed by Gradgrindian thinking. Most policies supported by economists, such as free trade, or the deregulation of the formerly regulated industries, or legal recognition (in tax law, tort law, and domestic-relations law) of the economic value of housework, or competition in the professions, are not heartless. Some views of economists seem heartless to people who lack economic training—opposition to the minimum wage is an example—only because such people do not understand the adverse effects of these policies on the worst-off members of society or are repelled by the vocabulary of economics. The most heartless policies extant today, such as the savage punishment of drug offenders in contemporary American law or the public redistribution of wealth from poor to rich brought about by various subsidy programs, are motivated by noneconomic concerns, opposed by most economists, or both.

Nussbaum has stronger grounds for her belief that many heterosexuals lack an empathetic awareness of the problems, or even the humanity, of homosexuals and that many whites lack an empathetic awareness of the problems, or, again, even the humanity, of the poorest black men and boys in our cities. Because homosexuality and race have become foci of legal controversy, there is an argument for trying to make lawyers and judges aware of the challenges, achievements, history, and outlook of these groups. The question is how to do it. Literature is not an apt means. One reason is that the fictional depiction of a social problem can easily be dismissed as exaggerated or inaccurate—in short, as being a fiction, as we shall see in the next chapter. Another reason—the reason we do not expect to

---

38. Nussbaum, note 8 above, at 18.

find *The Golden Bowl* or *The Merchant of Venice* (despite its female lawyer role model) featured in courses on feminism, except those that take an adversary stance toward literature, which is not Nussbaum's proposal—is that the portrayal of traditionally subordinated or marginalized groups, not only blacks and other nonwhites, and homosexuals, but also Jews, women, and people afflicted with physical or mental disorders or insufficiencies, is largely negative, reflecting the cultures in which the works were written. Almost all works of literature accepted as such are at least a few decades old, and most are far older. The sensitivities that have impelled efforts to develop among legal professionals a greater awareness of the problems of discrimination against traditionally subordinated or disadvantaged groups are very recent. Because of this temporal mismatch, it is difficult to find literary exemplars of Nussbaum's concerns.[39] Forster was a novelist of great distinction, but *Maurice* is his weakest novel, with all the earmarks of special pleading,[40] and it is made esoteric by the author's preoccupation with competing and now-forgotten schools of Edwardian homosexual thought.[41] As a tract on homosexuality, it is as dated as *Hard Times* viewed as a tract on economics.

Native Son (1940) is a landmark in the history of the black American novel. It has a timely theme—interracial violence—and is even set in the South Side of Chicago, where Martha Nussbaum teaches. Its protagonist, Bigger Thomas, a 20-year-old black from the Chicago slums who is already a hardened criminal, kills a white woman, Mary Dalton. The killing probably is accidental, but afterward Bigger decapitates her and stuffs her body into a furnace in an effort to conceal the crime. Later he rapes and murders his black girlfriend. He pleads guilty to killing Mary Dalton (he is not even charged with the murder of his girlfriend—a commentary on white indifference to black life) and is sentenced to death. The novel ends, like *The Stranger,* a near-contemporaneous work to which *Native Son* bears a resemblance,[42] with Bigger awaiting execution. We are invited to believe that his smothering of Mary, from which all else follows inexorably, is due to her patronizing efforts, and those of her Communist boyfriend and lim-

39. Difficult, but not impossible. Is there any more affecting picture of mental retardation than part one of *The Sound and the Fury* or any more harrowing depiction of sexual assault than the attempted rape of Lena by the psychopath Martin Ricardo in Conrad's novel *Victory?*

40. Kermode calls it "a fairly simple wish-fulfilling fantasy; it has symbolic patterns in the usual Forster way, and these will no doubt be made much of, but they seem to be relatively inert and self-indulgent." Kermode, note 5 above, at 271.

41. Claude Summers, "The Flesh Educating the Spirit: *Maurice,*" in *Critical Essays on E. M. Forster* 95 (Alan Wilde ed. 1985).

42. Wright moved to France after World War II, became acquainted with Camus, and wrote a novel that he called *The Outsider* and that was influenced by his reading of *L'Étranger.*

ousine-liberal father (a slumlord, of course), to befriend Bigger as part of a program of helping the black race, and that his proneness to violence is the consequence of "a mode of life stunted and distorted"[43] by white bigotry. At the sentencing hearing his lawyer goes so far as to argue: "The truth is, this boy did *not* kill! . . . He was *living,* only as he knew how, and as we have forced him to live" (p. 366). The pervasiveness of bigotry is further emphasized by the erroneous but unshakable belief of the legal establishment that Bigger raped Mary[44] and by threats of lynching.

Native Son is a period piece. Its picture of race relations is accurate for the 1930s, but not for today. The persistence into the present of violence among young black males (the black murder rate is more than seven times the white murder rate) may be a legacy of racism, but if so the causal linkage is subtle and the remedy obscure. Nussbaum argues that the moral teaching of *Native Son* is that "the stigma of racial hate and shame" is "fundamentally deforming of human personality and community."[45] This is not exactly news, and anyway it is not well presented in Wright's novel. The early chapters, with their striking portraits of mutually uncomprehending poor blacks and liberal whites, promise a superb novel of manners. But beginning with Mary's dismemberment, implausibilities crowd in on the reader, the tone becomes increasingly strident, the black characters lose their depths, the energy of the writing flags. As Harold Bloom remarks with reference to Bigger's death vigil, "Wright, in *Native Son,* essentially the son of Theodore Dreiser, could not rise always even to Dreiser's customarily bad level of writing."[46] Bloom adds, "Either Bigger Thomas is a responsible consciousness, and so profoundly culpable, or else only the white world is responsible and culpable, which means, however, that Bigger ceases to be of fictive interest and becomes an ideogram rather than a persuasive representation of a possible human being. Wright . . . was not able to choose."[47]

---

43. Page 358 of the 1966 paperback edition. The passages I quote from this edition are unchanged in the uncut version of the book. See next footnote.

44. Yet at the insistence of the Book of the Month Club, Wright cut out several sexual scenes, in one of which Bigger is sexually aroused by Mary shortly before he smothers her (see pp. 96–97 of the HarperPerennial paperback edition, 1993). These cuts were not restored until 1991. See the Rampersad, Tuttleton, and Kinnamon essays in *The Critical Response to Richard Wright* 163, 167, 173 (Robert J. Butler ed. 1995). The restoration was made after Wright's death, so we cannot be certain that the restored text is more authentic than the originally published one. This is another example of the difficulty, examined in Chapter 7, of determining authorial intention.

45. Nussbaum, note 8 above at 96–97.

46. Bloom, "Introduction," in *Richard Wright's* Native Son 1 (Harold Bloom ed. 1988). There are many parallels between *Native Son* and Dreiser's "legal" novel, *An American Tragedy*.

47. Bloom, note 46 above, at 4.

Nussbaum's choice of works of literature to discuss in *Poetic Justice* is a clue that there is nothing morally improving *in literature itself,* any more than there is in music or painting or architecture. If there were, she could choose three much greater works without having to worry about whether their overt themes were "liberal." That was the kind of thing that she tried to do with *The Golden Bowl,* but she produced a reductive interpretation. Great literature *resists* being used to edify. The reason Nussbaum chose *Native Son* (locale aside) as her racial novel rather than *Othello,* an incomparably superior work (admittedly not a novel, but so what?), may lie in the politics of education and public advocacy in our multiethnic society. *Othello* has more than enough traces of the racist and sexist attitudes that permeated Shakespeare's society to poison any attempt to use it as a vehicle for instilling an empathetic awareness of the problems of blacks and women, or for denouncing racial prejudice and sexism.[48] It is true that the play equivocates between Othello as Moor and Othello as Negro ("thick lips," I.1.68). The Elizabethans applied the word "Moor" indiscriminately to Africans, rather than distinguishing as we do between North Africans (and until their expulsion from Spain, the Muslim inhabitants, formerly conquerors, of that country) and Sub-Saharan Africans.[49] But this equivocation simply multiplies the prejudices against Othello, whose cultural as distinct from racial "Moorishness" is signaled by "his uncontrollable passion . . ., his superstitious interpretation of the handkerchief, [and] his ritualistic attempt to make the murder of Desdemona a sacrifice."[50] Images of bestial transformation—an Ovidian inversion—abound, and the beast is Othello.[51]

It is unclear whether Shakespeare intended the audience to consider interracial marriage unnatural. Some of the characters in the play do; others don't. Yet it is common for a Shakespearean tragedy to begin with an unnatural act

48. On Elizabethan hostility to blacks, see Karen Newman, "'And wash the Ethiop white': Femininity and the Monstrous in *Othello,*" in *Shakespeare Reproduced: The Text in History and Ideology* 143, 148–149, 153 (Jean E. Howard and Marion F. O'Connor eds. 1987). On racism in *Othello* itself, see John Salway, "Veritable Negroes and Circumcised Dogs: Racial Disturbances in Shakespeare," in *Shakespeare in the Changing Curriculum* 108–112, 115–122 (Lesley Aers and Nigel Wheale eds. 1991).

49. David Bevington, "Othello, the Moor of Venice," in *The Complete Works of Shakespeare* 1117 (David Bevington ed., 4th ed. 1992). Barbara Everett, in her book *Young Hamlet: Essays on Shakespeare's Tragedies,* ch. 9 (1989), argues that the play presents Othello as a distinctively Spanish Moor.

50. Edward Berry, "Othello's Alienation," 30 *Studies in English Literature 1500–1900* 315, 317–318 (1990).

51. Jonathan Bate, "Ovid and the Mature Tragedies: Metamorphosis in *Othello* and *King Lear,*" 41 *Shakespeare Survey* 133, 136–137 (1989).

that is a clue to the impending disaster, whether it is Cawdor's treachery, Gertrude's marriage to her brother-in-law, or Lear's dividing his kingdom. What is certain is that Othello is grossly deceived, forms ugly ideas about women, and commits a hideous crime that he can expiate only by his own suicide. What other Shakespearean tragic hero smothers a woman?

Granted, Othello is a heroic figure, albeit deeply flawed. White Iago is incomparably more villainous. *Othello* can be read as a tragedy about reciprocal misunderstanding between the sexes, rather than about anything to do with race. Othello's isolation from polite Venetian society by his military career and his foreignness prevents him from forming a true picture of a Venetian woman's character, while Desdemona, because of the cloistered upbringing of women of her social class, knows nothing about men.[52] Alternatively, *Othello* is a "tragedy of perceptions," like Faulkner's novel *Light in August*. Because the other characters in the play cannot accept Othello as "equally human but culturally different," he (like Faulkner's Joe Christmas, the black who passes for white) comes eventually to believe that his only choice is between assimilation and barbarism, and he oscillates between those poles.[53] *Othello* can be read most simply as a play about how the insecurity that a man feels who is married to a much younger woman makes him prone to jealousy, and how difficult jealousy is to allay when once it is aroused.

So there are "safe" readings of *Othello,* as of Faulkner and Twain, who dealt with race sympathetically but to modern ears insensitively.[54] Yet one is never completely safe with a great writer, especially Shakespeare, whose greatness, it bears repeating, "lies in the fact that, whatever univocal insights or affirmations may be expressed within any work, they are thoroughly *dramatised*—that is, set within a complex interlocutory process such that they are never the 'final vocabulary' of individual works."[55]

Another feature of Nussbaum's choice of works to discuss in *Poetic Justice,* a feature related to my earlier point that the literary canon must be drastically shrunk in order to be made edifying, is that they are, as it were, preselected.[56] Their take on the social issues they deal with corresponds to her

---

52. Gayle Greene, "'This That You Call Love': Sexual and Social Tragedy in *Othello,*" in *Shakespeare and Gender: A History* 47 (Deborah Barker and Ivo Kamps eds. 1995).

53. Berry, note 50 above, at 318.

54. On Twain, see Booth, note 9 above, at 477. Booth believes that Faulkner's works are "to some degree marred by sexism," id. at 405; he does not mention racism in connection with Faulkner.

55. David Parker, *Ethics, Theory and the Novel* 60 (1994). Even Dickens is not safe; *Hard Times* expresses his fierce antipathy to labor unions, *Oliver Twist* his anti-Semitism; most of his novels are sexist.

56. Cf. Nussbaum, note 8 above, at 10.

own; they were chosen to illustrate rather than to shape her moral stance. If literature were really believed to be a source of ethical insight, the critic would examine and compare (and the teacher would assign) works of literature that reflected different ethical stances. *Hard Times* would be matched with *Nostromo* or William Dean Howell's *The Rise of Silas Lapham*,[57] *Maurice* with "Death in Venice" or Sartre's "The Childhood of a Leader,"[58] *Native Son* with *Prester John*. Or the focus would be on works that seem to wobble around the moral center, as it now seems to us, such as *Othello*, or *Pudd'nhead Wilson*, or *Light in August*. Instead the ethical position is in place before the examination begins, and furnishes the criteria of choice and shapes interpretation.

And is it an accident that *Maurice* was written by a homosexual and *Native Son* by a black? Or is the choice of these novels a statement of identity politics—of the right of members of marginalized groups to be represented in the literary canon, so that the other members of these groups will feel proud? Representation may cheer up some of them, but it is unlikely to change anyone's prejudices or behavior.

James Boyd White's exemplary novelist is Jane Austen; and let us consider how he fits her "dark" novel, *Mansfield Park*, into the law and literature canon.[59] Fanny Price, a poor young girl, is taken into the home of wealthy and aristocratic relatives to be brought up properly but also to be patronized and even abused, Cinderella-fashion. At first she accepts and indeed internalizes the false values of her grand relatives. But gradually she sees through them, and she is rewarded at the end of the novel with marriage to the most decent—and through contact with her much improved—member of the family. The point interestingly emphasized by White is that Fanny is handicapped both by being poor and oppressed and as a result deficient in self-esteem and a sense of autonomy and by having to think as well as speak in the vocabulary of her upper-crust relatives—she has no other vocabulary. It is a vocabulary that, Newspeak-fashion, inverts the proper sense of words, substituting good manners for good morals. These circumstances delay Fanny's rejection of the false values of her grand rela-

57. In which the Gradgrind-Bentham figure, the Reverend Sewell, is treated a good deal more sympathetically than his Dickensian counterpart. See Wai Chee Dimock, *Residues of Justice: Literature, Law, Philosophy*, ch. 4 (1996).

58. In Sartre, *The Wall and Other Stories* 157 (1948). The seducer in Sartre's story is a surrealist whose objets d'art include a lifelike sculpture of a turd. The young man whom he seduces is shown embarrassedly urinating in the washbasin of their hotel room while getting ready for sex. By the piling on of such details Sartre associates homosexuality with disorder, the unnatural, and the unclean.

59. See White, *Acts of Hope: Creating Authority in Literature, Law, and Politics*, ch. 6 (1994) ("Austen's *Mansfield Park*: Making the Self out of—and against—the Culture").

tives. Although White does not quite say this, he seems to view *Mansfield Park* as an allegory of the process by which an oppressed minority struggles for emancipation. Central to that process, in White's view, is the minority's achieving enough fluency in the language that the majority has imposed upon it to turn that language right side up so that it will express the minority's needs and aspirations. Language is both the prison and the key to the prison.

There is a strong didactic element in Jane Austen's novels, and as I do not question the validity of White's interpretation, it may be parochial of me to complain that he has escaped law's gravitational pull. Lawyers must learn to master language lest they be mastered by it, but to use Jane Austen as the vehicle for imparting this lesson is as strained as using the poetry of Wallace Stevens to rebuke jurisprudential extremes. White, like Thomas Grey (see Chapter 4), loves literature and knows law and wants very much to yoke them; but they can be an unruly team.

I am obliged to consider why, if we do not read literature in order to form better or truer opinions on matters of religion or politics, of economics or morality, we read it at all. We might read it to improve our reading skills by studying texts that are difficult because of cultural distance or the density or complexity of the writing. Literature "engages" (and I would add stimulates and exercises) "a good many of our most complicated faculties of perception—our nuanced knowledge of language, people, social institutions, politics, history, morality; our ability to grasp analogies, parallelisms, antitheses, significant repetitions, ellipses, ironies, double meanings, even cryptograms."[60] The test of time is once again relevant. The writings that pass the test tend to be open-ended, and "the open-endedness of the text plays a key role in this pleasure [the pleasure of reading literature] because the reader is the recipient of a kind of communication that, unlike graffiti or bumper stickers or telegrams, offers a rich multiplicity of messages in which the mind may delight."[61]

We might read literature to learn to express ourselves better by sitting at the feet of masters of expression. Most distinguished writers in law, who include Holmes, Cardozo, and Hand, were steeped in literature, though this partly reflects the character of elite education when they were growing up. In reading literature we also learn about the values and experiences of cultures, epochs, and sensibilities remote from our own, yet not so remote as to be unintelligible. And we acquire experience vicariously by

60. Robert Alter, *The Pleasures of Reading in an Ideological Age* 228 (1996).
61. Id.

dwelling in the imaginary worlds that literature creates.[62] Literature can expand our emotional as well as our intellectual horizons. An idea can usually be encoded straightforwardly enough and transferred more or less intact to another person. It is different with emotions. I do not *feel* your pain, your losses. You can *describe* a pain, its origins, and its consequences in as comprehensive detail as you like and I still will not experience them. And so with describing your feelings about growing old, falling in love, losing a friend, failing in business, succeeding in politics. Imaginative literature can, however, engender in its readers emotional responses to experiences that they have not had. We read *King Lear* and *feel* how—or some approximation to how—a failing king feels, the wicked bastard feels, the evil daughters, the good daughter, the blinded earl, the faithful retainer, the corrupt retainer, the fool, all feel. We experience simulacra of the agony of madness and the pang of early death in *Hamlet,* the depths of reciprocal misunderstanding in *The Secret Agent,* the loneliness of command in *Billy Budd,* the triumph of the will in Yeats's late poetry.[63] This is the empathy-inducing role of literature of which Putnam and Nussbaum speak. But empathy is amoral. The mind that you work your way into, learning to see the world from its perspective, may be the mind of a Meursault, an Edmund, a Lafcadio, a Macbeth, a Coriolanus, a Tamburlaine, a torturer, a sadist, even a Hitler (Richard Hughes's *The Fox in the Attic*). And speaking of Hitler, with his unparalleled insight into the hopes and fears of tens of millions of Europeans, must not he have had one of the most highly developed empathetic capacities in history?

Because most literature, even comedic, is about disruption, about screwups, it might be thought of as a source of implicit lessons on how to keep out of trouble and be happy, even if it is not rich in practical advice. On this view, as on the moralistic, literature can change us, though in the sense of helping us to be more successful at the game of life rather than morally better. If ethics is defined broadly enough, to encompass all possible answers to the question "How should I live?" including answers grounded in egoism,[64] then a lot of amoral literature may be ethical if still amoral. But I resist even the idea that literature can tell us how to live. Literature is not

62. Kendall L. Walton, *Mimesis as Make-Believe: On the Foundations of the Representational Arts* 273 (1990).

63. Flint Schier, "Tragedy and the Community of Sentiment," in *Philosophy and Fiction: Essays in Literary Aesthetics* 73, 85 (Peter Lamarque ed. 1983). So "In the Penal Colony" can be read as an allegory of the operation of great literature on its readers!

64. See Bernard Williams, "The Point of View of the Universe: Sidgwick and the Ambitions of Ethics," in Williams, *Making Sense of Humanity, and Other Philosophical Papers 1982–1993* 153, 156 (1995).

in the advice business. It is closer to the mark to say that literature helps us, as Nietzsche would have put it, to become what we are. The characters and situations that interest us in literature are for the most part characters and situations that capture aspects of ourselves and our situation.[65] Literature helps us make sense of our lives, helps us to fashion an identity for ourselves. If you don't already believe that love is the most important thing in the world, you're not likely to be persuaded that it is by reading Donne, Stendhal, or Galsworthy. But reading them may make you realize that this *is* what you think, and so may serve to clarify yourself to yourself.

The "real you" that you discover by reading literature may not, however, be a Romantic, a tame modern liberal, or a supersensitive hyperegalitarian—the type of person whom Nietzsche ridiculed for thinking they are good because they have no claws. Yeats and Hemingway, Haggard and Buchan, Gide and Camus, Waugh and Pound, Mailer and Larkin, Rabelais and de Sade may express your innermost self more faithfully than Austen, Joyce, and Forster do. You may prefer the macho Conrad of *Nostromo* and *Lord Jim* to the feminist Conrad (as it seems to me) of *The Secret Agent* and *Victory*. Since "war is more beautiful than peace,"[66] you may revel in the war-glorifying stanza of Yeats's poem "Under Ben Bulben," written a year before the outbreak of World War II: "You that Mitchel's prayer have heard, / 'Send war in our time, O Lord!' / Know that when all words are said / And a man is fighting mad, / Something drops from eyes long blind, / He completes his partial mind, / For an instant stands at ease, / Laughs aloud, his heart at ease." The possession of knowledge, whether of oneself or of others, does not dictate its use for moral ends. Not only may we identify as readers with the egomaniacs, scamps, seducers, conquerors, psychopaths, tricksters, and immoralists who people fiction; we may conceivably improve our skills in manipulating people to selfish ends by acquiring from fiction a better understanding of the naive and vulnerable, the good, the generous human types that we also encounter there. "To be able to see the world from another's point of view may be the greatest weapon one can wield in war against that other."[67]

I have no quarrel with the analogy that Booth and Nussbaum draw be-

65. "The knowledge that literature gives us is specifically a knowledge of ourselves." Cleanth Brooks, *A Shaping Joy: Studies in the Writer's Craft* 10 (1971).

66. Todorov, note 22 above, at 71.

67. Alexander Nehamas, "What Should We Expect from Reading? (There Are Only Aesthetic Values)," *Salmagundi,* Summer 1996, pp. 27, 50. Nehamas also remarks the self-serving quality of saying that a good reader is likely to be a good person, since anyone who says such a thing is implying that *he* is a good reader and therefore a good person. Id. This could be thought an example of spiritual pride.

tween reading and friendship. Bookish people do make friends with authors and even more commonly with their characters. Just as shy, imaginative children befriend imaginary beings or anthropomorphize animals, so shy, imaginative adults befriend literary characters. But does friendship make for goodness? Are bad people characteristically friendless? Literature offers a vast choice of friendship possibilities. Many of them are with evil, dangerous, or irresponsible people—*awful* role models. To befriend them is to risk being led astray, just as by other evil companions. It's not a big risk; but neither is the opposite—the likelihood that we will become better people by imaginatively befriending the "good" implied author and his "good" characters.

To emphasize the role of literature in imparting self-knowledge is more defensible than assigning it the role of making the reader a more moral individual, but it still gives literature a too solemn and even puritanical air. Literature is one of the arts, and like the other arts yields pleasure as well as knowledge. Pleasure comes in many forms, though, and it is difficult to characterize the pleasures of literature.[68] Brian Vickers observes that "we understand works of literature far better than we understand our own lives, and they form satisfying wholes, aesthetic and ethical intellectual unities, in a way that life seldom does."[69] As his observation suggests, the pleasure that literature offers can be contemplative rather than jolly, frivolous, escapist, or sensuous. Can even be, I venture to suggest at the risk of sounding oxymoronic, sad—"sweet though in sadness" (from Shelley's "Ode to the West Wind"). Philosophers since Aristotle have puzzled over the paradox that the depiction of disaster and undeserved suffering in tragic dramas yields pleasure to the audience.[70] Maybe we enjoy these works *despite* their grimness,[71] and would like them even more with happy endings, however contrived, like the ending of *Job,* or *Lear* as played in the eighteenth century. Maybe there's something to Aristotle's idea of catharsis—tragedy is our game of death, and we are happy to see fictional characters die in our place.[72]

A distinctive pleasure (or, better perhaps, satisfaction) that literature and other arts impart, one especially foreign to a moralistic outlook, is that it

68. See, for example, Charles Altieri, "The Values of Articulation: Aesthetics after the Aesthetic Ideology," in *Beyond Representation: Philosophy and Poetic Imagination* 66 (Richard Eldridge ed. 1996).

69. Vickers, *Appropriating Shakespeare: Contemporary Critical Quarrels* 143 (1993).

70. See Budd, note 1 above, at 110–123; Walton, note 62 above, at 255–259; Schier, note 63 above; A. D. Nuttall, *Why Does Tragedy Give Pleasure?* (1996).

71. Id. at 104.

72. Id. at 76–79.

gives an echo-chamber effect to everyday life. The life depicted in works of literature is recognizably human and therefore like our own, but it is more intense, more charged with significance. When we are reading literature, whether it is a brilliant "light" work like Forster's *A Room with a View* or a brilliant depressive work like *Crime and Punishment,* whether it celebrates romantic values or sees through them, we live, for the moment anyway, more intensely. We have a vision of a life more "real"—concrete, meaningful, intelligible, coherent, conscious—than our everyday existence, a sense of immense human possibility, of exaltation (a common response of art lovers to a first-rate art museum). We feel bigger; we are transported. This is not a simple hedonism; but it is something that Nietzsche or Heidegger understood better than the most sensitive moralist can, for it has to do with a sense of power and selfhood rather than with the moral sense.[73]

It might even be *dangerous* to mine literature for moral guidance. Think of all the *violence* in literature; there are as many killings in a Shakespearean tragedy as in a television crime drama. The affinity of literature for violence and aggression is not adventitious. Literature is rich in transgressive fantasies; that is an important part of its appeal. We timid bourgeois can revel in the amoral freedom of a Meursault or a Lafcadio, a Barabbas or an Edmund, a Medea or a Cleopatra. "The language of poetry naturally falls in with the language of power. The imagination is an exaggerating and exclusive faculty . . ., which seeks the greatest quantity of present excitement by inequality and disproportion . . . The principle of poetry is a very anti-levelling principle. It aims at effect, it exists by contrast. It admits of no medium. It is every thing by excess. It rises above the ordinary standard of sufferings and crimes . . . Poetry is right royal. It puts the individual for the species, the one above the infinite many, might before right. A lion hunting a flock of sheep or a herd of wild asses, is a more poetical object than they."[74]

Literature may function as therapy,[75] and more commonly as consola-

---

73. "Where Nussbaum remains weakest, perhaps, is in her treatment of literature . . . Despite her repeated affirmation that the autonomy of literary art must be recognized and respected by the interested moral philosopher, say, or legal theorist, Nussbaum fails to persuade, here as in her previous work, that her concern with literature is a concern with something more than drawing a moral lesson from it." David Gorman, Review of *Poetic Justice,* 21 *Philosophy and Literature* 196, 198 (1997).

74. William Hazlitt, *"Coriolanus,"* in *The Collected Works of William Hazlitt,* vol. 8, pp. 347–348 (A. R. Waller and Arnold Glover eds. 1903). The point is similar to Todorov's. See text at note 21 above.

75. Morris Robert Morrison, "A Defense of Poetry Therapy," in *Poetry as Healer: Mending the Troubled Mind* 28 (Jack J. Leedy ed. 1985).

tion. This value is connected with my earlier point about literature's focus on disruption and crisis. The atheist may find a substitute for religion in the stoic values upheld in Shakespeare's plays[76] or Yeats's poetry, or simply in the sense that literature inhabits a timeless realm, is death-defying. The emotional effects of literature thus are various. It moves as well as pleases, shocks as well as delights, intoxicates as well as soothes, braces as well as relaxes. But all these effects are psychological rather than moral. Taking to heart Edgar's admonition to his father (*King Lear* V.2.8–10),

> What, in ill thoughts again? Men must endure
> Their going hence, even as their coming hither;
> Ripeness is all,

may make us stronger, or prouder (or even humbler); it is unlikely to make us better. And do not say that while Shakespeare was not an egalitarian he had insights into other moral values, such as, in the passage just quoted, steadfastness in the face of adversity, and that it is for those insights that we value him. The Stoics were moralists, and stoic values are conspicuous in many of Shakespeare's plays, but he did not *argue* for them. You might read Shakespeare and decide that you were, or should strive to become, a Stoic. But it would be just another example of how literature can help the reader become what he or she really is (that is, wants to be)—which need not be a *moral* improvement over the reader's present, less authentic self.

Particularly remote from morality is the disinterested, "art for art's sake" pleasure that much literature affords. This is closest to the pleasure that we get from the visual arts, especially abstract art, and from music, especially instrumental music. It is the pleasure that comes from being in the presence of beauty. Consider the middle stanza of Keats's "Ode to Melancholy":

> But when the melancholy fit shall fall
>   Sudden from heaven like a weeping cloud,
> That fosters the droop-headed flowers all,
>   And hides the green hill in an April shroud;
> Then glut thy sorrow on a morning rose,
>   Or on the rainbow of the salt sand-wave,
>   Or on the wealth of globèd peonies;
> Or if thy mistress some rich anger shows,
>   Emprison her soft hand, and let her rave,
>   And feed deep, deep upon her peerless eyes.

---

76. Maynard Mack, for example, sees "Shakespeare's more tragic vision [in *King Lear*] of the creature [us] whose fate it is to learn to love only to lose (soon or late) the loved one, and to reach a ripeness through suffering and struggle, only to die." Mack, King Lear *in Our Time* 79 (1965).

Or this stanza from Part V of "The Waste Land":

> A woman drew her long black hair out tight
> And fiddled whisper music on those strings
> And bats with baby faces in the violet light
> Whistled, and beat their wings
> And crawled head downward down a blackened wall
> And upside down in air were towers
> Tolling reminiscent bells, that kept the hours
> And voices singing out of empty cisterns and exhausted wells.

These two stanzas are good candidates for touchstones of literary greatness (another is Shakespeare's description of Cleopatra on her barge, which I quote in Chapter 11). Yet they have no moral or informational content to speak of. (The stanza from Keats's ode will *not* help anyone suffering from depression, and it is patronizing toward women.) They have only beauty. It is true that although musicality is an important part of their appeal, it cannot be divorced from the sense of the words, as is often possible with songs. Even nonsense verse depends for its effect on our being able to understand the words and sentences.[77] Still, it is very difficult to extract a moral of any sort from the stanzas that I have quoted, or anything that could be described as information; and even the echo-chamber effect that I described earlier seems muted.

It is not only from poetry that we derive an enjoyment fairly to be described as aesthetic; the appeal of prose works as different from each other (and from snatches of poetry) as *The Stranger*, "The Dead," *The House of Mirth*, *The Sound and the Fury*, *For Whom the Bell Tolls*, *The Golden Bowl*, and *Moby-Dick* also resides largely in the formal properties of these works—changes of pace, shifts of voice and point of view, the echoing and doubling of themes, the arousing of expectations and the deferral of their satisfaction, the creation and release of tensions, and the harmonizing of disparate elements—properties similar to those of instrumental music.[78] The more attuned we are to these properties, the less concerned we will be with the moral beliefs of the implied or the actual author. The formal properties do not exhaust the worth and appeal of literature, but the moral properties are almost sheer distraction.

---

77. "Jabberwocky" in *Through the Looking-Glass* is the limiting case; but the drift of the poem is quite intelligible, even though a number of the made-up words are purely evocative. (Likewise *Finnegans Wake*.) And right after the recitation of the poem Alice (and so the reader) is told the meaning of the made-up words.

78. On the properties of "abstract" (nonvoice, nonprogrammatic) music, see Budd, note 1 above, at 164–169.

Pornographic Literature

Those who disagree with the argument in the previous section and believe that literature can make us better people are apt also to think that the wrong kind of literature can make us worse. To quote Irving Kristol again, "if you believe that no one was ever corrupted by a book, you have also to believe that no one was ever improved by a book."[79] This outlook primes some moralistic critics[80] to support efforts at suppressing, whether by formal or informal means, literature that might be thought to encourage violence, discrimination, sexual deviance, atheism, or other reprobated behaviors and attitudes. Opposition to censorship thus is undermined by the edifying school. Of course, to anyone who thinks that literature to count as such *must* be edifying, so that immoral books are by definition not literature, the banning of such books cannot impair literary values. But I hope that I have succeeded in showing that "literature" should not be defined so narrowly.

Prosecutions for the sale of nonillustrated works of literature have become rare in this country. But public libraries, and especially the libraries of public schools, respond to community pressures in deciding what books to stock, and this official though informal censorship shows no signs of abating. Private colleges and universities practice self-censorship under the spur of angry students, sometimes whipped up by angry faculty or alumni. This form of censorship appears to be on the rise, and not only because of the political-correctness movement. The pressure for informal censorship comes from the religious right as well as the egalitarian left and is resisted by civil libertarians on the left and by libertarian conservatives on the right.

Literature with some pornographic content is just one species of writing that has invited the attention of censors, but as it has received the most attention I shall center my discussion on it. The most celebrated American judicial decision holding that a work of literature is not obscene is Judge Woolsey's decision in the *Ulysses* case. Yet Paul Vanderham has mounted a powerful attack on Judge Woolsey's reasoning. He criticizes each of its four premises: "first, that literary works like [Joyce's] *Ulysses* have nothing in common with works of pornography; second, that artistic intention precludes other intentions—moral, political or religious—that might oppose or undermine values which the law (rightly or wrongly) upholds; third, that *l'homme moyen sensuel,* the average person, responds to art in a res-

79. Kristol, "Pornography, Obscenity and the Case for Censorship," *New York Times Magazine,* March 28, 1971, p. 24.

80. Not all, by any means. Nussbaum, for example, opposes governmental censorship of pornography, at least purely verbal pornography. See Nussbaum, note 34 above, at 281–282. Booth also.

olutely esthetic and therefore static manner; and fourth, that the effect of a literary work as a whole is necessarily the effect of any one of its parts, and that because a work like *Ulysses,* taken as a whole, is not legally obscene (or otherwise harmful in the eyes of the law), it is nowhere obscene, nowhere harmful."[81] The first premise is just an inference from the last three, and rises or falls with them. The second premise Vanderham is surely right to question. There is no reason why a writer should not set out to write a book that will be at once literary and pornographic or why his aims, whether simple or multiple, consistent or inconsistent, should determine the actual character of the work. Whatever the dominant character of the work, moreover (I am moving now to the third premise), there is nothing to prevent a reader from making a use of the work that is inconsistent with that dominant character. Last, the aphrodisiacal effect of a book's pornographic passages might not be cancelled out by the anaphrodisiacal passages that surround them—might even, as we shall see, be enhanced by them.

There are better grounds for the *Ulysses* decision than those articulated in the judge's opinion. Consider who reads works of literature. Literature is read in high school, in college or university, and after graduation. The high-school and college readers are for the most part a captive, restive, and unmoved audience. A great teacher can inspire them; great teachers are rare. Anyway, no one is suggesting that pornographic literature, even so mild a specimen by current standards as *Ulysses,* should be prescribed for students. So forget the students. But who is left? Only a tiny minority of Americans continues to read serious literature—classics and candidates to become classics—after graduating from college[82]—which, incidentally, supports my claim that high-school and college readers of literature are for the most part unimpressionable. Those fired to a love of literature in childhood or young adulthood do not cool. They must be very few, since adult readers of the classics are so few. Because this is a huge country, the relative and the absolute diverge. James Joyce has thousands of fans, but even after they are added to all the rest of the literature buffs in the nation the total is probably a minute and aging fraction of the population. And quite apart from how Joyce and other literary giants are faring in the market-

81. Vanderham, "Lifting the Ban on *Ulysses*: The Well-Intentioned Lies of the Woolsey Decision," *Mosaic,* Dec. 1994, pp. 179, 194, discussing United States v. One Book Called "Ulysses," 5 F. Supp. 182 (S.D.N.Y. 1933), aff'd, 72 F.2d 705 (2d Cir. 1934).

82. Art, literature, and poetry account in the aggregate for only 2 percent of retail sales of books (both hardcover and paperback) in the United States, with 22 percent of the buyers of such books being under the age of twenty-five. This is a much higher proportion than for any other category of books, and is indicative of the importance of the student segment of the book market. Book Industry Study Group, Inc., *1990/1991 Consumer Research Study on Book Purchasing* 17, 73 (1991).

place, the print media are losing the competition with the electronic media as a source of ideas, information, and entertainment. Nowhere is the competitive struggle more one-sided in favor of the electronic media than in the domain of pornography. A verbal description or evocation of sexual activity is unlikely to produce as much arousal as a photograph or a film.

To defend works of literature against censorship on the ground that they are harmless or little read may seem to be to wield a two-edged sword. If literature is marginal to the moral and even the entertainment life of the nation, the case for granting it legal protection may seem no stronger than the case for trying to suppress the obscenity or immorality in it. But besides the knowledge and delight that literature brings to the small minority of Americans who read it out of love rather than duty, literature continues to be an important component of high-school and college education because of its effects in stretching the student's imagination, multiplying his cultural perspectives, broadening his intellectual and emotional horizons, offering him a range of vicarious experiences, and assisting him to read difficult texts, express complex thoughts, and write and speak persuasively. The study of literature will not make a young person a more decent human being, and it will probably fail to addict him to literature. But it may make him a little smarter and a little more successful. However, education in literature does not require assigning pornography to the students.

Arguing that expository prose is worthier of legal protection in the name of free speech than imaginative literature is, Frederick Schauer claims that "fiction is parasitic on nonfiction, if by nonfiction we mean simply telling the whole truth as accurately as possible."[83] It is true that without a conception of truth we would not have a conception of fiction. It is also irrelevant. Descriptive accuracy does not exhaust the concept of truth, let alone of value. Scientific models frequently purchase explanatory and predictive power at the cost of descriptive accuracy, as in Newton's law of falling bodies, which assumes, contrary to fact, that bodies fall in a vacuum. Does this counterfactual assumption make Newton's law a fiction parasitic on truth? Aristotle's conception of literature as a selection from the welter of particulars is similar to the scientist's concept of a model. Some fiction is truer than some nonfiction, even than some accurate nonfiction.

It would no doubt be worse to abolish *all* political, scientific, or religious expression than *all* literary and artistic expression. Better a technologically advanced philistine democracy than a totalitarian artocracy. But the practical choice is never that; it is always whether to suppress a *particular* political, artistic, scientific, or religious work. It is far from clear that,

83. Frederick Schauer, "Liars, Novelists, and the Law of Defamation," 51 *Brooklyn Law Review* 233, 266 (1985).

evaluated at the margin in this way, literary expression is characteristically less valuable than political, scientific, or religious expression. I am not even sure that Schauer is right in claiming that society would not suffer "nearly as much" from losing the novels of Edith Wharton as it would have suffered from being "deprived of the exposure of Watergate and its associated crimes."[84] That may just be a political science major's prejudice. Reference to the Watergate scandal, in which most of the principals from Nixon on down were lawyers, brings to mind the fact that in its wake all law schools were required by the accrediting authorities to institute compulsory courses in legal ethics. Does anyone believe that lawyers' ethics have since improved? Is this not further evidence that talking about ethics doesn't make people more ethical? The real purpose and only effect of the ethics courses is to make a few laypersons think that lawyers are more ethical than they are.

But suppose (coming back to pornography) that the question were only whether to forbid obscenity in *contemporary* "literature"—the body of works that aspire to literary status and may fit the recognized genres of literature (novels, poems, plays, or short stories)—though most of these works will never achieve literary status. We cannot be confident that the moral content of these works is irrelevant, or even secondary, to the qualities for which they are being read. Still, the difficulty, in a relativistic age and pluralistic society, of achieving a consensus on what is immoral expression, coupled with the costs of stamping out a victimless crime, the untrustworthiness of the people likely to seek appointment as public censors, the associated risk of destroying literature in its incipience—not only by suppressing particular works but also by inducing self-censorship—and the lack of convincing evidence that immoral works of fiction cause immoral conduct, argue against authorizing government to suppress nonpictorial writing of any kind on grounds of immorality.

Yet it is easy to exaggerate the threat that censorship poses to literature, which has often thrived under the censor's eye. The Elizabethan theater was censored; indeed, formal censorship of the English theater ended only recently. *Ulysses* could not be sold in England or many other countries for many years after its publication. The novels of Henry Miller, and D. H. Lawrence's *Lady Chatterley's Lover,* could not be sold legally in the United States until the 1960s. The depiction of homosexuality in a favorable light was under an informal but effective ban until recently, and only recently was the *Index Librorum Prohibitorum* abolished. It has been argued, as I noted in an earlier chapter, that censorship actually benefits literature by steering

---

84. Id. at 255.

authors away from the topical. Forster's self-censored *Maurice* is his weakest novel. And literature inflammatory enough to invite prosecution in a country that has not abolished censorship is apt to encounter devastating informal censorship by publishers, booksellers, and libraries in a country that has. Censorship in totalitarian regimes, such as the former Soviet Union, and in theocracies such as Iran, can stifle literary creativity, but the milder censorship of the Western democracies probably had little effect beyond delaying by a generation or two the incorporation of detailed descriptions of sexual acts into works of fiction. And that was yesterday. Today the limits of society's toleration of sexual description are so broad that probably no canonical literature exceeds them. The closest to doing so may be Aristophanes' plays, especially *Lysistrata* (the subject of which is a wives' sex strike), and the novels of Henry Miller—and the pressure to suppress these works is nil. Although cultural differences need not prevent one from enjoying the literature of the past (almost by definition literature *is* of the past), its aphrodisiacal effects do wane. That takes care of Aristophanes. Henry Miller illustrates the point that our licentious culture can't be shocked by shockers composed in more decorous times.

It has always been a puzzle what if any concrete harms censors apprehended from sexually explicit literature; but their main worry seems to have been that it would encourage sexual freedom and experimentation and by doing so weaken the family. Since the traditional family was patriarchal, one might have expected feminists, who want to undermine it, to rally to the defense of pornography on that score. Some have. But some radical feminists have become pornography's fiercest antagonists, on the ground that it encourages not sexual freedom but female subordination. They argue that it depicts women as enjoying sexual submission to men and that by doing so it incites men to rape, harass, and discriminate against women.[85] They thus want to shift the emphasis in the regulation of pornography from excessive frankness in the depiction of sex, the sort of thing the old-fashioned censors forbade, to harm to women. This shift is ominous because many works of literature portray with approval the subordination of women to men (though this is not the same thing as depict-

---

85. The feminist approach to pornography is sketched in K. K. Ruthven, *Feminist Literary Studies: An Introduction* 87–90 (1984). For fuller statements, see Andrea Dworkin, *Pornography: Men Possessing Women* (1981); Catharine A. MacKinnon, *Only Words* (1993); *Take Back the Night: Women on Pornography* (Laura Lederer ed. 1980). Not all radical feminists, however, wish to suppress pornography. See Carlin Meyer, "Sex, Sin, and Women's Liberation: Against Porn-Suppression," 72 *Texas Law Review* 1097 (1994); Robin West, "The Feminist-Conservative Anti-Pornography Alliance and the 1986 Attorney General's Commission on Pornography Report," 1987 *American Bar Foundation Research Journal* 681.

ing women *enjoying* that subordination—the particular concern of the feminist opponents of pornography—though there is plenty of that too). Consider Briseis and Chryseis in the *Iliad,* treated as no better than chattels. Or the humiliation of Kate in *The Taming of the Shrew.* The Bible contains many examples of misogyny, beginning with Eve's being blamed for the Fall of Man. So does *Paradise Lost,* not to mention *Eumenides*—the list is endless. Customs officers in Canada, which has enacted a version of the radical feminist position on pornography, have seized literary works by Oscar Wilde, Marguerite Duras, and others—including Andrea Dworkin.[86] Although it is unclear to what extent the seizures are powered by the new law and to what extent they reflect preexisting law, they are a warning against the dangers of censoring "pornography."

Catharine MacKinnon's position can be interpreted as not caring whether her definition of illegal pornography sweeps within it the occasional classic: "If a woman is subjected, why should it matter that the work has other value? Perhaps what redeems a work's value among men enhances its injury to women. Existing standards of literature, art, science, and politics are, in feminist light, remarkably consonant with pornography's mode, meaning, and message."[87] A more conciliatory feminist might not grasp the nettle of aesthetic value but might instead argue that as long as the only works suppressed are sexually explicit, the threat to literature is small, for how much literature is sexually explicit? The answer is, a great deal. Authors of works of literature that were sexually explicit by the standards of their times (and in some of my examples for centuries, even millennia, afterward) include Aristophanes, Boccaccio, Rabelais, Joyce, and Lawrence. John Millington Synge's *The Playboy of the Western World* was deemed obscene when first performed (1907) because it used the word "shift" for a woman's slip.[88] Some works that are sexually explicit by today's standards may someday be recognized as great literature—unless their creation is deterred by a broad definition of pornography. Conversely, standards may become more conservative. In that event, literature that is not explicit by today's liberal standards may come to be thought so in the

86. Nadine Strossen, *Defending Pornography: Free Speech, Sex, and the Fight for Women's Rights* 229–239 (1995). Margaret Atwood and Joyce Carol Oates are among other woman writers whose graphic depictions of brutal treatment of women might make their works eligible for suppression under Canadian law.

87. MacKinnon, *Toward a Feminist Theory of the State* 202 (1989) (footnote omitted). Maybe, though, "If a woman is subjected . . .?" is a genuine question rather than, as it appears to be, a rhetorical one.

88. Hugh Kenner, *A Colder Eye: The Modern Irish Writers* 20–21 (1983). On trends in the literary depiction of sex, see Charles I. Glicksberg, *The Sexual Revolution in Modern American Literature* (1971); Glicksberg, *The Sexual Revolution in Modern English Literature* (1973).

future. Shakespeare was too bawdy for the nineteenth century, and was bowdlerized; maybe Joyce will be too bawdy for the twenty-first.

In fairness to MacKinnon, she is not troubled by the portrayal of sexual activity as such, even when the portrayal is so detailed and explicit as to be deemed obscene, but rather with its being portrayed in a way calculated to incite male violence; that is why she prefers the term "pornography" to "obscenity." And the antipornography ordinance that she and Andrea Dworkin drafted requires proof on a case-by-case basis that the pornography purveyed by the defendant inflicted tangible harm on the plaintiff, as by inciting a customer to rape her. As such proof is very difficult to come by except in the rare case of a "copycat" crime, where the criminal enacts a script found in a book that he has read or, more commonly, a movie that he has seen, the ordinance might have little effect. That is rather its saving grace than an affirmative merit; to suppress pornography effectively would be a mammoth undertaking, piling enforcement costs on top of the costs to literature—and for what benefits? The evidence for the harms of sexually explicit literature that portrays women in positions of subordination to men is limited to reports of coercion and sexual abuse of pornographic models and actresses—evidence that has no relevance to nonpictorial pornography—and to laboratory studies finding that violent pornography can arouse aggressive feelings toward women in male college students. Evidence against the harmfulness of pornography is the lack of a consistent correlation between the amount or tolerance of pornography in a society and the incidence of rape and other indicators of women's status in the society.[89]

Feminists are concerned not only with the effect of pornography on violence against women but also with what they believe to be its tendency to foster sexual stereotypes, such as the stereotype of women as merely the sexual playthings of men, and with the consequences of these stereotypes for the treatment of women in the workplace. Whether pornographic books have such a tendency and such consequences is unknown, but seems unlikely. Pornography does not purport to present a realistic picture of women, and nobody expects it to do so. Nor does it always depict them as submissive or demure; often it portrays them as sexually aggressive; that is one traditional trope of pornography. Why are social conservatives so exercised over pornography if, as radical feminists believe, it serves to rein-

---

89. For a review of the evidence concerning the effects of pornography, see my books *Overcoming Law,* note 20 above, at 361–363, and *Sex and Reason* 366–374 (1992); also Paul R. Abramson and Steven D. Pinkerton, *With Pleasure: Thoughts on the Nature of Human Sexuality* 188–190 (1995). As I mentioned earlier, the lack of convincing evidence that pornography, especially nonpictorial pornography, induces immoral behavior suggests that edifying literature is unlikely to induce moral behavior.

force the conservatives' own beliefs about the woman's place? Pornography is suppressed in patriarchal societies and flourishes in egalitarian ones, a pattern that radical feminism cannot explain.

One person's stereotype, moreover, is another's truth. If the objection to pornography is that it induces false or pernicious *beliefs* that could have serious consequences,[90] the sexually explicit angle is a red herring and we are in the presence of a massive challenge to freedom of speech and of the press. Since that challenge is the logical terminus of the edifying school of literary criticism, it casts further doubt on the program of that school. If literature is to be valued for its moral content, then it is likewise to be condemned for its immoral content. The result is to deform the literary canon from two directions. The edifying works are highlighted and the unedifying cast out, with results described by David Lodge, reviewing an anthology of young American fiction writers: "An intellectual environment in which it is frowned upon or expressly forbidden to say or write anything that might offend any individual's or group's values, self-esteem, sense of cultural and ethnic identity, religious beliefs, or special interests is not one in which the budding literary imagination is likely to flourish. Important writers are often rebellious, arrogant, irreverent, even outrageous . . . Political correctness encourages caution, parochialism, and self-censorship."[91]

A pertinent example of the outrageous is Yeats's "Leda and the Swan":

> A sudden blow: the great wings beating still
> Above the staggering girl, her thighs caressed
> By the dark webs, her nape caught in his bill,
> He holds her helpless breast upon his breast.
>
> How can those terrified vague fingers push
> The feathered glory from her loosening thighs?
> And how can body, laid in that white rush,
> But feel the strange heart beating where it lies?
>
> A shudder in the loins engenders there
> The broken wall, the burning roof and tower
> And Agamemnon dead.

90. Which is not MacKinnon's objection. Her conception of pornography is of a stimulus applied directly to the penis, without being mediated by the mind. "The message of [pornography] . . . is 'get her' . . . This message is addressed directly to the penis, delivered through an erection, and taken out on women in the real world." MacKinnon, note 85 above, at 21. As with much of MacKinnon's writing, however, it is difficult to know how literally this passage should be read.

91. Lodge, "O Ye Laurels," *New York Review of Books,* Aug. 8, 1996, pp. 16, 20. See also Steven G. Gey, "The Case against Postmodern Censorship Theory," 145 *University of Pennsylvania Law Review* 193 (1996), and Alan Soble, *Sexual Investigations,* ch. 6 (1996).

> Being so caught up,
> So mastered by the brute blood of the air,
> Did she put on his knowledge with his power
> Before the indifferent beak could let her drop?

This is pretty vivid (especially the "white rush"), does not criticize rape, and can be interpreted as expressing the poet's and possibly even the victim's approval of the rape.[92] It is also a blasphemous parody of the Annunciation and thus a companion piece to the blasphemous Nativity of "The Second Coming." The poem could well be thought an outrage both to Christianity and to womanhood.[93] Yet it is a great poem. The challenge to feminist jurisprudence is to formulate a principled and reasonably definite standard for deciding when literature ought to be suppressed because of its misogynistic content or consequences.

As important as the standard is the application. I think it would work badly and offer as evidence both the recent Canadian experience and the decision by a federal court of appeals in 1953 upholding an order to destroy copies of *Tropic of Cancer* and *Tropic of Capricorn* by authority of a federal statute forbidding the importation of obscene books.[94] According to the decision, Miller's two novels are a "sticky slime" of filth and degradation. The erotic episodes are not of that "stark ugliness [which] might repel many," but rather "lure on with the cleverness of scene, skillfulness of recital, and the use of worse than gutter words" (p. 145). "Dirty word description of the sweet and sublime, especially of the mystery of sex and procreation, is the ultimate of obscenity" (p. 146). Bawdy classical authors are enigmatically distinguished on grounds of cultural relativity; there are ominous suggestions that if they were writing today they would be in deep trouble: "We are not well acquainted with Aristophanes or his times, but we know they were different from ours. We have chanced upon Chaucer and we know his times were different from ours. Boccaccio is lurid. The Bible is not free from the recounting of immoral practices. But the translators, from the languages in which The Bible was originally written, did not word-paint such practices in the lurid-Miller-morally-corrupt manner"

---

92. It also resonates with the argument that "images of the victim's physical beauty and the male's bestiality pervade legal descriptions of violent crimes against women," Lisa Binder, "Law and Literature: 'With More Than Admiration He Admired': Images of Beauty and Defilement in Judicial Narratives of Rape," 18 *Harvard Women's Law Journal* 265 (1995), although the beauty in the poem is not the rape victim herself, but a child of the rape (Helen).

93. See Elizabeth Butler Cullingford, "The Case of Yeats's 'Leda and the Swan,'" in *Representing Women,* note 14 above, at 165, 174–185.

94. Besig v. United States, 208 F.2d 142 (9th Cir. 1953).

(p. 146). Later the court seems to retract the suggestion that classical authors might be forgiven for having written in ruder times: "We risk the assertion that there is an underlying, perhaps universal, accord that there is a phase of respectable delicacy related to sex, and that those compositions which purposefully flaunt [*sic*] such delicacy in language generally regarded as indecent come under the ban of the statute" (p. 147).

At times the court appears to be suggesting that certain aspects of human experience (for example, excretion) and even dirty words are out of bounds even to the moral artist, and at other times that if only Miller had depicted his sordid subject matter with remorse or disapproval he might have avoided the morally corrupt *manner* that marks the books as obscene. In some passages the court appears to concede that Miller's novels have literary merit, though not enough to redeem them from the charge of obscenity; in other places it asserts that their literary merit makes them more dangerous; in others it implies that their only literary merit lies in a kind of sleekness, itself pornographic, in the depiction of sex; in others it concedes literary merit only to the nonerotic scenes, which however are not frequent enough to save the work; and in still others it suggests that a single offensive incident, no matter how integral to a work's literary structure, might condemn the work as obscene. We are invited to consider the prospect of elderly men incited by Henry Miller's novels to commit serious sex crimes: "Salacious print in the hands of adults, even in the hands of those whose sun is near the western horizon, may well incite to disgusting practices and to hideous crime" (p. 146).

The opinion in the *Besig* case is so goofy that had it been written as a parody of censorship we would think it overdone. Yet in content it is close to the feminist position. The judges draw a highly speculative connection between reading pornography and committing sex crimes, disparage aesthetic values,[95] and therefore easily conclude that the social costs of allowing Americans to read Miller's novels outweigh the social benefits. The court does more than merely denigrate aesthetic values. It intimates that an immoral work is worse if it is better written, because the writing disarms the reader. Judge Leval seems to have had something similar in mind in criticizing judges who try to write well (see Chapter 8); they are trying to blind the reader's rational faculty with beauty.

The history of censorship is usually presented as a tale of folly and futility, and *Besig v. United States* supports that characterization. Yet so widespread and persistent an institution cannot plausibly be ascribed merely to

---

95. Notice the complacency with which the court acknowledges its ignorance of the classics.

public stupidity and the prurient interests of would-be censors. Robert Darnton's study of illegal literature in eighteenth-century France suggests that literature can affect public opinion, and that the literature in question played a role in bringing about the French Revolution.[96] The books and pamphlets that the censors tried unsuccessfully to suppress "molded public opinion in two ways: by fixing disaffection in print (preserving and spreading the word), and by fitting it into narratives (transforming loose talk into coherent discourse)."[97] But the literature that had these effects was primarily the political rather than the pornographic literature of the period. The latter was viewed chiefly as an aid to masturbation.[98] The censors weren't worried about masturbation. Their objections to pornographic literature had mainly to do with the frequent admixture of political and anticlerical themes in that literature.[99]

These are details. The age-old practice of censorship is evidence of a prevalent and not implausible belief that books, including works of fiction, a frequent target of censorship, can have moral and political effects. This belief bears on the general issue of ethical criticism. The aesthetic tradition, I argued, does not deny that literature can have moral and political effects. But the *decline* of literary censorship is evidence that those effects have become slight. The reasons are the rise of education, which has turned people into more critical readers, and the decline in importance of the print media. From Plato on, supporters of censorship have worried about books getting into the hands of people who lack the intellectual competence to resist the subversive and blasphemous blandishments of imaginative literature. "In an era when television and radio did not challenge the supremacy of the printed word, books aroused emotions and stirred thoughts with a power we can barely imagine today."[100] Any powerful source of ideas is bound to be viewed with suspicion by a government worried about its abil-

96. Darnton, *The Forbidden Best-Sellers of Pre-Revolutionary France,* ch. 10 (1995).

97. Id. at 191. Cf. Steven L. Winter, "The Cognitive Dimension of the *Agon* between Legal Power and Narrative Meaning," 87 *Michigan Law Review* 2225, 2272 (1989).

98. Darnton, note 96 above, at 103, 222. Present-day feminist advocates of censorship are not concerned with aids to masturbation. Moreover, the eighteenth-century French pornographic novel presented the "fantasy . . . [of] a free-loving, freethinking, female *philosophe*." Id. at 114. It *promoted* the feminist and revolutionary causes, as does *Lysistrata*. Pornography has often been associated with sexual freedom rather than with patriarchy.

99. See Darnton, note 96 above, ch. 3. Consistent with one of Vanderham's criticisms of the opinion in the *Ulysses* case, the presence of political and philosophical passages in eighteenth-century French pornography appears not to have diminished the pornographic impact of these works and may actually have enhanced it by underscoring their transgressiveness.

100. Darnton, note 96 above, at 217. It was while reading a book together, a book about courtly love, that Paolo and Francesca fell in love, with fatal consequences. Julien Sorel developed his fatal ambition while reading Napoleon's memoirs. Emma Bovary and Don Quixote

ity to maintain control of the population. People may be spending as much time reading books as they used to,[101] but books of fiction are not powerful molders of values or public opinion in our society, and the government is not worried about revolution.

Dicta about the harmlessness of imaginative literature have to be qualified: they are not universals; they are time-and-place bound. But in our time and our place, works of nonpictorial imaginative literature do not have significant power for good or for evil. Lawyers and judges will not become better people by trolling in literature for ethical insights. Ordinary readers will not become worse people by seeking erotic stimulation in pornography.

---

were led astray by reading romances. And recall how Hamlet tried to use the performance of a play to unseat the king—a possible echo of an incident in 1601 in which followers of the Earl of Essex commissioned Shakespeare's company to give a special performance of *Richard II* on the eve of Essex's rebellion in an unsuccessful effort to drum up support for the rebellion. See Louis Montrose, *The Purpose of Playing: Shakespeare and the Cultural Politics of the Elizabethan Theatre,* chs. 5, 7 (1996).

101. U.S. Dept. of Commerce, Bureau of the Census, *Statistical Abstract of the United States 1995* 255, 572 (115th ed. 1995) (sers. 406, 407, 899); Malcolm Gladwell, "Six Days a Week, the Library Is Closed: Inner Cities Aren't Sharing in America's Resurgence of Reading," *Washington Post,* April 6, 1993, p. A1.

TEN

Lies like Truth?
Narrative Legal Scholarship

The Legal Narratology Movement

I remarked in the preceding chapter on the difficulty of finding literary exemplars of the desired moral outlook on contemporary social problems such as race and sex. Some law professors have decided to furnish those exemplars themselves, by writing stories. This is a bold though questionable advance over conventional law and literature scholarship that merely *argues* for a greater role of imaginative literature in legal thought. Although fiction by law professors on legal themes is not entirely new,[1] the scale of the new legal "narratology" and its predominantly "oppositional" character are new. Moreover, "story" (or "narrative") is not synonymous with "fiction." Plato's dialogues are fictions, but not stories. And a story can be true or false, while a fiction, even if not completely "made up," invariably contains false particulars, although often with a heavy admixture of literal truths—for instance a gallery of real people thinly, and sometimes not at all, disguised as fictitious.

Some legal narratologists, such as Derrick Bell, write outright fiction, in his case science-fiction stories offered as such. Others write stories that purport to be autobiographical and so are offered as literally true; yet not only are the stories unverifiable, but the story mode, and sometimes specific details, undermine their veracity.[2] Autobiographical legal scholarship shades into biographical legal scholarship, which I discuss in the second section of this

1. See, for example, Norval Morris, *Madness and the Criminal Law,* chs. 1, 3 (1982); Morris, *The Borstal Boy and Other Parables of the Law* (1992); Lon L. Fuller, "The Case of the Speluncean Explorers," 62 *Harvard Law Review* 616 (1949).

2. Anne M. Coughlin, "Regulating the Self: Autobiographical Performances in Outsider Scholarship," 81 *Virginia Law Review* 1229 (1995). Like so many developments in academic law,

chapter with reference to judicial biography, its most common form. Judicial biography is the tame cousin of legal narratology.

The stories written by legal narratologists are explicitly didactic, and so invite ethical criticism. I shall discuss the stories' aesthetic dimension only insofar as it affects the fulfillment of their didactic aims. Yet it is not those aims that make this the right approach for me to take; a great deal of literature was in its origin didactic. It is the absence from most of these stories of anything else worth attending to.

A story is a sequence of events invented, selected, emphasized, or arranged in such a way as to vivify, explain, inform, or edify. Stories "must have beginnings, middles, and ends" and must be "so constructed that the mind of the listener, viewer, or reader [can] take in the relation of beginning, middle, and end" and "see the end as entailed by a process."[3] The story need not be true, but it must be coherent, intelligible, significant— remember Darnton's comment on the role of narrative in giving coherence to loose talk.

Ubiquitous in history, biography, literature, and religion, storytelling plays a smaller but still important role in other fields as well. One of these is law. In a trial, the plaintiff and the defendant each tell a story— actually a translation of their "real" or raw stories into the narrative and rhetorical forms authorized by law—and the jury chooses the story it likes better. (If it is a criminal case and the defendant's confession is placed in evidence, there is a story within the story.) This is not how the law conceptualizes the trial process. The law requires the plaintiff to prove each element of his claim by a preponderance of the evidence, or beyond a reasonable doubt if it is a criminal case, and likewise the defendant if he pleads any affirmative defenses. But if this, the official account of the trial process, were taken literally, plaintiffs would win cases in which the likelihood that their claim was valid was actually

---

the turning to autobiography is found also in literary studies. See Adam Begley, "The I's Have It: Duke Professors Affirm Themselves," *Lingua Franca,* March/April 1994, p. 54.

3. Peter Brooks, "The Law as Narrative and Rhetoric," in *Law's Stories: Narrative and Rhetoric in the Law* 14, 17 (Peter Brooks and Paul Gewirtz eds. 1996). *Law's Stories* is a good introduction to the legal narratology movement. See also Symposium, *Legal Storytelling,* 87 *Michigan Law Review* 2073 (1989); *Pedagogy of Narrative: A Symposium,* 40 *Journal of Legal Education* 1 (1990); Nancy L. Cook, "Outside the Tradition: Literature as Legal Scholarship," 63 *University of Cincinnati Law Review* 95 (1994); William N. Eskridge, Jr., "Gaylegal Narratives," 46 *Stanford Law Review* 607 (1994); Arthur Austin, "Evaluating Storytelling as a Type of Nontraditional Scholarship," 74 *Nebraska Law Review* 479 (1995); Robert L. Hayman, Jr. and Nancy Levit, "The Tales of White Folk: Doctrine, Narrative, and the Reconstruction of Racial Reality," 84 *California Law Review* 377 (1996).

very slight.[4] What really happens in a trial is that each side tries to convince the jury that its story is more plausible.[5]

The Supreme Court has magnified the story element in the sentencing phase of capital trials by insisting that the defendant be permitted to tell a no-holds-barred story of his life in an effort to persuade the jury that he should not be put to death. Lately the Court has decided that the victim's family should be allowed to tell the jury the absent victim's story in order to balance the defendant's story.[6]

Judicial opinions have a story element—the narrative of the facts of the case that opens most opinions. Cardozo's statements of fact are justly celebrated for their literary skill, shown chiefly in the clever highlighting of some facts and the clever suppression of others.[7] Learned Hand's summations of literary plots in his copyright opinions are comparably distinguished displays of narrative skill. Some judges try to cast their whole opinion as the story of the parties' dispute, using chronology rather than a logical or analytical structure to organize the opinion. Judges must also know when *not* to tell stories. The Supreme Court in *Brown v. Board of Education* was right to forgo a narrative of the history of the oppression of black people in the South, even though that history is the essential background to understanding the harm of segregated schooling. Such a narrative would have made it even more difficult for the southern states to accept the decision. The Court's reliance in the *Brown* decision on social science in lieu of narrative has been criticized sharply and often; how ironic, but how telling, that its choice should be defended in a book on legal narrative![8]

---

4. Ronald J. Allen, "A Reconceptualization of Civil Trials," 66 *Boston University Law Review* 401 (1986); Allen, "The Nature of Juridical Proof," 13 *Cardozo Law Review* 373, 409–420 (1991). Suppose that a plaintiff in a particular tort case must prove three things to prevail on his claim for $100,000 in damages for personal injury (forget any affirmative defenses that the defendant might have): that the defendant was negligent, that his negligence caused injury to the plaintiff, and that the injury imposed a loss of at least $100,000 on the plaintiff. Suppose each proposition has a .51 probability of being true. Then the probability that all three are true (assuming they are independent of each other) is only .13 (.51 x .51 x .51). Yet, on these assumptions, according to the official version of the proof process, which requires only that the plantiff prove each element of his case by a bare preponderance of the evidence, the plaintiff has proved his case!

5. The storytelling, indeed mythmaking, potential of the criminal trial is the subject of a brilliant essay by Robert A. Ferguson, "Story and Transcription in the Trial of John Brown," 6 *Yale Journal of Law and the Humanities* 37 (1994).

6. Payne v. Tennessee, 501 U.S. 808 (1991).

7. See my book *Cardozo: A Study in Reputation* 42 (1990).

8. Sanford Levinson, "The Rhetoric of the Judicial Opinion," in *Law's Stories*, note 3 above, at 187.

Critical race theorists and radical feminists use stories of oppression to stir the reader to a more vivid awareness of the suffering of the downtrodden.[9] This literature has been linked to victim impact evidence in capital cases because that evidence "consists of stories of victimized and silenced people, who are the usual concern of many in the [legal] storytelling movement."[10] The narratologists don't like this point; they don't like capital punishment, and allowing victim impact statements is calculated to increase the number of cases in which it is imposed.[11] Yet there is powerful appeal in the argument that if the defendant is to be allowed to plead for mercy, the absent victim should be allowed to plead for justice—like the ghost of Hamlet's father, or the Commendatore in *Don Giovanni.*

Although literary theory has long concerned itself with narrative as a pervasive feature of imaginative literature,[12] legal narratologists do not much discuss the literary techniques that make narratives different from each other and from other expressive devices. The business of legal narratology is telling stories rather than reflecting on storytelling techniques. These techniques include the choice of narrator (ranging from the obtuse to the omniscient), the construction of an implied author (who may be different from both the real author and the narrator), the use or omission of description, the juxtaposition of parallel stories (in *King Lear,* for example, the story of Gloucester and his sons with the story of Lear and his daughters), and the handling of time. When narratives begin and end as they often do *in medias res,* the surface or foreground story does not coincide chronologically with the implied or background story that generates it. Even when they do coincide, the tempo of the narrative is bound to be irregular. Some events that pass quickly in "real time" are narrated in leisurely fashion, while others, which may take much longer to unfold in real time, are skipped over rapidly. Lawyers and judges could improve their writing by

9. See Cook, note 3 above. See also *Representing Women: Law, Literature, and Feminism* 357, 358 (Susan Sage Heinzelman and Zipporah Batshaw Wiseman eds. 1994); Derrick A. Bell, "Who's Afraid of Critical Race Theory?" 1995 *University of Illinois Law Review* 893, 906 (1995).

10. Paul Gewirtz, "Victims and Voyeurs: Two Narrative Problems at the Criminal Trial," in *Law's Stories,* note 3 above, at 135, 143.

11. Supporters of legal narratology who have opposed the admissibility of victim impact evidence have emphasized their opposition to capital punishment. Martha C. Nussbaum, "Equity and Mercy," 22 *Philosophy and Public Affairs* 83, 119, 121 n. 93 (1993); Susan Bandes, "Empathy, Narrative, and Victim Impact Statements," 63 *University of Chicago Law Review* 361, 392 n. 156 (1996).

12. See, for example, Wallace Martin, *Recent Theories of Narrative* (1986); Seymour Chatman, *Story and Discourse: Narrative Structure in Fiction and Film* (1978); Robert Alter, *The Pleasures of Reading in an Ideological Age,* ch. 6 (1996); Gerald Prince, "Narratology," in *The Johns Hopkins Guide to Literary Theory and Criticism* 524 (Michael Groden and Martin Kreiswirth eds. 1994).

the study of narrative techniques as of other elements of literary craft, but helping them to do so is not a focus of legal narratology.

Oppositionist legal storytelling, a large part of legal narratology, tries to illuminate the plight of the oppressed. But against a background of expanding opportunities for women and minorities, it seems whiny and self-pitying. It feeds the stereotype of women and blacks as incapable of rigorous thought, as limited to emotional talk, "mere rhetoric," and so puts them in a self-created ghetto—the ghetto of complaint. A deeper problem is the *typicality* of the stories that the oppositionists tell.[13] The significance of a story of oppression depends on its representativeness. In a nation of more than a quarter of a billion people, almost every ugly thing that can happen will happen. To react to it on the plane of policy sensibly and not just hysterically, systematically and not just episodically, we have to know its frequency—a matter that is in the domain of social science rather than of narrative. The oppositionists should realize this. They complain with some justice that the conservative opponents of the political-correctness movement and affirmative action exaggerate the frequency of the abuses that they denounce. Narrative is a two-edged sword, being a literary technique; as we saw in the preceding chapter, there is nothing inherently egalitarian in literary technique.

A related problem with the oppositionist stories is that of establishing causality. When a defendant in his plea of mercy tells a harrowing story of childhood abuse and neglect, he implicitly asserts a causal connection between the events narrated and the criminal act for which he is to be sentenced; the story has no relevance otherwise. But to assert is not to prove. The proof is crucial and is not supplied by the story, which may be appealing to credulous and sentimental intuitions about fall and redemption. Oppositionist storytellers evade issues not only of causality but also of personal responsibility, as in the following remark about the fact that black men commit a disproportionate number of rapes: "black women have simultaneously acknowledged their own victimization and the victimization of black men by a system that has consistently ignored violence against women while perpetrating it against men."[14] So black men are off the hook.[15]

---

13. Daniel A. Farber and Suzanna Sherry, "Telling Stories out of School: An Essay on Legal Narratives," 45 *Stanford Law Review* 807 (1993). Cf. Toni M. Massaro, "Empathy, Legal Storytelling, and the Rule of Law: New Words, Old Wounds," 87 *Michigan Law Review* 2099 (1989).

14. Angela P. Harris, "Race and Essentialism in Feminist Legal Theory," in *Representing Women,* note 9 above, at 106, 121 (footnote omitted).

15. Harris actually implies that white women are somehow complicit in the rape of black women by black men. See id. at 120–121.

"Victim stories . . . adhere to an unspoken norm that prefers narratives of helplessness to stories of responsibility, and tales of victimization to narratives of human agency and capacity," yet are said to have value in "disrupting these rationalizing, generalizing modes of analysis [legal doctrine, economic analysis, and philosophical theory] with a reminder of human beings and their feelings, quirky developments, and textured vitality."[16] How exactly the downtrodden are to benefit from this disruption of systematic thinking about their problems is not explained. It will not be by shaking up the oppressors' preconceptions. People read junk that does not challenge their preconceptions; they do not read junk that does. Few if any legal storytellers have a big enough literary gift to entice readers who are not already a part of the oppositionist culture. This is not said in criticism. A law professor should not be ashamed of lacking literary genius, but then he ought not to expect to find readers for his *stories* (as distinct from his theoretical or empirical scholarship) among those whom the stories are intended to shake out of their insensitivity. Writing stories without a literary gift is like doing economic analysis without knowing economics.

What white person, heretofore unsympathetic or only tepidly so to the contemporary plight of many American blacks, is going to be changed by Derrick Bell's story "The Space Traders"?[17] The story is set in the year 2000. Space aliens offer gold and other valuable resources in exchange for all the blacks in the United States. A constitutional amendment is quickly passed which provides that "without regard to the language or interpretations previously given any other provision of this document, every United States citizen is subject at the call of Congress to selection for special service for periods necessary to protect domestic interests and international needs." The story ends:

> The last Martin Luther King holiday the nation would ever observe dawned on an extraordinary sight. In the night, the Space Traders had drawn their strange ships right up to the beaches and discharged their cargoes of gold, minerals, and machinery, leaving vast empty holds. Crowded on the beaches were the inductees, some twenty million silent black men, women, and children, including babes in arms. As the sun rose, the Space Traders directed them, first, to strip off all but a single undergarment; then, to line up; and finally, to enter those holds which yawned in the morning light like Milton's 'darkness visible.' The inductees looked fearfully behind them. But, on the dunes above the beaches, guns at the ready, stood U.S. guards. There was no

16. Martha Minow, "Stories in Law," in *Law's Stories,* note 3 above, at 24, 32, 36.
17. In Bell, *Faces at the Bottom of the Well: The Permanence of Racism* 158 (1992).

escape, no alternative. Heads bowed, arms now linked by slender chains, black people left the New World as their forbears had arrived. (p. 194)

Well, not exactly, because their forbears were not sold into slavery by whites. Black people in the United States have not drawn even with whites economically, but they are in no danger of losing their citizenship. (Why, by the way, are the blacks in Bell's stories assembled on a *beach?* Because they were originally brought to America on ships? But they're not leaving by ship. And who picked Martin Luther King Day as the date of departure?) There is among whites growing resentment over affirmative action, multiculturalism, bloc voting, black hostility to whites, black victimology, and the social pathologies of the inner city—drugs, crime, gangs, gun-toting preteens, AIDS, teenage mothers, welfare dependency, crack babies, babies born out of wedlock, cynical and corrupt—sometimes crazy—political leadership, anti-Semitism, credulity, riots. But Bell has nothing to offer to the solution of these problems, from which, indeed, an emphasis on white racism and black victimhood distracts. He is in the state that psychiatrists call denial. "The Space Traders" will make some of its white readers write off Bell as a hysteric and others feel complacent about their own racial feelings because they do not support the sale of the black population of the United States. The lunatic fringe that does want to deprive blacks of citizenship has never heard of Bell, would not read a story by him, and would not be moved by it to change their minds if they did.

William Eskridge begins a book that advocates the legalization of homosexual marriage with the love story of two lesbians, plaintiffs in the lawsuit in Hawaii that has placed the issue of homosexual marriage on the policy agenda.[18] He tells us about Ninia Baehr, "fawnlike," with "brown eyes that engulf you with understanding and alert sympathy," and Genora Dancel, whose "broad, dimpled smile and friendly, easygoing disposition belie her serious work ethic." Ninia's mother tells Ninia about her friend Genora: "I hear she's a lesbian. I'd be happy if she were your friend, too. Why don't you meet her?" After a brief courtship, Genora "popped the question, 'Will you marry me?' A microsecond later Ninia answered, 'Yes!'"[19] Eskridge is an able scholar, and his book as a whole makes a powerful intellectual case for his position. But the story of Ninia and Genora is neither emotionally nor aesthetically convincing. It is a tale in which "true love" runs truer, smoother, and more clichéd ("microsecond" is a really

18. See Baehr v. Lewin, 852 P.2d 44 (Hawaii 1993).
19. William N. Eskridge, Jr., *The Case for Same-Sex Marriage: From Sexual Liberty to Civilized Commitment* 1–2 (1996).

bad touch) than anything likely to be encountered outside a Harlequin romance or Gertie MacDowell's fevered imagination.

There is enough fiction in law already. I refer not to legal fictions, which are white lies designed to disguise legal creativity as continuity, but to the self-serving and often phony stories, told by litigants and witnesses and faithfully transcribed, that find their way into appellate opinions because accepted by credulous jurors or, for procedural or tactical reasons, simply not challenged.[20] Law is deficient in fact rather than in fiction. Eskridge's book, revealingly entitled *"The Case for* Same-Sex Marriage," is a work of advocacy, but it is not constrained by the truth-forcing devices, inadequate as they are, that constrain courtroom advocacy. Only the credulous, or the already convinced, will take the story of Ninia and Genora at face value. The real art of Eskridge's book lies elsewhere—in the patient, measured, rational, unemotional tone in which he states the case for legalizing homosexual marriage. The implied author that the book creates is a more effective refutation of the homosexual stereotypes that stand athwart Eskridge's goal than the ice-cream-parlor normalcy of his model lesbian couple.

A deeper point is that "stories contribute no independent moral insight of their own."[21] As Catharine MacKinnon puts it, making my point about the two-edged character of storytelling, "Stories break stereotypes, but stereotypes are also stories, and stories can be full of them . . . [T]here is much to be said for data . . . Lies are the ultimate risk of storytelling as method. This may be embarrassingly non-postmodern, but reality exists . . . It is my view that the major conflicts of our time are over the real and only secondarily over versions of it and methods for apprehending it."[22] She is reacting to the frivolousness of postmodernism and its claim that all reality is constructed—everything is a story told from a particular viewpoint

20. A notable example is the famous right to privacy case Melvin v. Reid, 297 Pac. 91 (Cal. App. 1931). The none too plausible facts recited in the court's opinion, and ever since used as Exhibit A to the case for recognizing a broad right of privacy—see, for example, William L. Prosser, "Privacy," 48 *California Law Review* 383, 392 (1960)—were taken from the plaintiff's complaint, without any independent verification. The defendant had decided to accept the factual allegations of the complaint for the sake of argument and argue that, even if they were true, the plaintiff had no case in law. According to the complaint, a prostitute, shortly after being acquitted of murder, was completely rehabilitated, married, and became an exemplary virtuous housewife. Seven years later the defendants made a movie of her lurid past, using her maiden name, and immediately all her new friends dropped her. It is not an impossible scenario, but it is a little too pat, like the story of Ninia and Genora, to ring true. For the cynical version of Mrs. Melvin's story, see Raymond Chandler, *Farewell, My Lovely* (1940).
21. Anthony Kronman, "Leontius' Tale," in *Law's Stories,* note 3 above, at 54, 56.
22. MacKinnon, "Law's Stories as Reality and Politics," in id. at 232, 235.

("there is nothing either good or bad but thinking makes it so," *Hamlet* II.2.249–50)—which tends to occlude the perception of real suffering. The pitfall of narratology into which MacKinnon herself has fallen in writing about pornography is that of atypicality. She is a magnet for the unhappy stories of prostitutes, rape victims, and pornographic models and actresses. Even if all these stories are true (though how many are exaggerated? Does McKinnon know?), their representativeness is an essential issue in deciding what if anything the law should try to do about the suffering narrated in them. "Victimless" crimes (more precisely, crimes in which there is unlikely to be a complaining witness) are exceedingly difficult to prevent without a significant curtailment of civil liberties, so anyone who advocates a campaign of effective suppression bears the burden of establishing that the crime causes substantial rather than merely isolated harm. Anecdote and speculation are not enough to carry this burden. Critical though she is of narratology, MacKinnon is a paranarratologist, trying to make her case for legal change through other women's stories.

Emotionality is another problem for legal storytelling. Emotion complements reason in some settings but undermines it in others. Evidence is regularly excluded from jury trials because it would inflame the jury, and jury verdicts are sometimes set aside because the verdict shows that the jury was carried away by passion or prejudice. The emotional wallop of murder victim impact statements is justifiable only as an offset to the emotional wallop of the capital defendant's plea for mercy.

Legal narratologists have had difficulty specifying the appropriate role of emotion in the legal process. Those who think it fine that a criminal defendant at his sentencing hearing should use the story of his life to awaken the jury's sense of pity are appalled when the prosecutor uses the story of the victim's life to awaken the jury's retributive sense, although the prosecutor is merely restoring the emotional balance. Susan Bandes thinks the desire for retribution a bad emotion; she calls it the "crude passion for revenge . . . a thirst for undifferentiated vengeance."[23] Martha Nussbaum points out that revenge is a primitive emotion, because (she argues) it abstracts from the particulars of the individual wrongdoer.[24] Revenge *is* primitive, is instinctual, as also is love, of which compassion for a criminal is a diluted form. If primitiveness disqualifies an emotion from playing a role in sentencing, out should go the defendant's plea for mercy. Nor are emotions of repulsion categorically inferior to those of attraction. Would it have been right, had Hitler been brought to trial, to let him tell the story of his

23. Bandes, note 11 above, at 398.
24. Nussbaum, note 11 above, at 89–90. Odd that abstraction should be thought primitive.

deprived childhood and the disappointments of early adulthood and being gassed in World War I and so forth while excluding all statements by his victims concerning their sufferings at his hands? To complain that the admission of such statements would be a yielding to the primitive emotion of revenge would strike most people as being in poor taste; and likewise if the defendant were a serial killer, terrorist bomber, or other sub-Hitlerian mass murderer. The strongest objection to giving play to feelings of revenge—that revenge lacks measure or discrimination because the victim of the wrong or a member of his family is the self-appointed judge and jury (Chapter 2)—has no force when the issue is merely whether victim impact statements can be considered by a disinterested judge or jury.

Robert Weisberg emphasizes "the utility of narrative in promoting symbolic national or group identity over abstract ideological or governmental structure."[25] The trial of John Brown altered the terms of the slavery debate and paved the way for Lincoln's redefinition of national purpose. Brown "transformed himself from a man of questionable character, a feckless loser in both business and the military, into a mythic hero by artfully blending legal rhetoric, courtroom dramaturgics, and shards of junk culture from popular American romances."[26] Weisberg admires these theatrics but recognizes that they were a *misuse* of the trial process. They illustrate the trial turned into a circus, and suggest the danger of confusing trial with theater, law with literature. And in Weisberg's reference to the utility of narrative in promoting a symbolic national identity and transforming a man of questionable character into a mythic hero, we may sense an allusion to the master evil narrativist of our century. Hitler told his rapt audiences an emotion-charged story of the betrayal and humiliation of the nation.

Mention of Hitler in this connection is not hyperbole. The arguments made by the growing corps of Holocaust-deniers "powerfully evoke the rhetoric of attorneys practiced in the art of adversarial litigation . . . By casting the trial as a truth-seeking device, the [deniers] are thus able to present the most tendentious and partisan hyperbole as a proper contribution to public debate and historical instruction." Yet criminal justice "has long been dedicated to values such as protecting the dignity and autonomy of the accused that may actually disable the pursuit of truth in a particular case"[27]—the trial, in other words, suffers from the same epistemological inadequacies as narrative, which it employs and resembles. Supreme Court

25. Weisberg, "Proclaiming Trials as Narratives: Premises and Pretenses," in *Law's Stories,* note 3 above, at 61, 77.

26. Id. at 79, summarizing Ferguson's article, note 5 above.

27. These quotations are from Lawrence Douglas, "The Memory of Judgment: The Law, the Holocaust, and Denial," 7 *History and Memory* 100, 109–110 (1996).

Justices who participate in mock trials of Shakespeare's authorship[28] do not realize that by doing so they are conferring legitimacy on a misuse of trial procedure that undermines standards of historical accuracy.

The uneasy relation between storytelling and truthtelling is the overriding problem for the legal narratology movement.[29] Patricia Williams's book *The Alchemy of Race and Rights* (1991)[30] is an autobiographical account of the travails of a black woman law professor. Autobiography is a notoriously unreliable source of truth,[31] yet Williams wants the authority of literal truth as well as the emotional punch of fiction in the following description of an episode at a Benetton clothing store: "Buzzers are big in New York City. Favored particularly by smaller stores and boutiques, merchants throughout the city have installed them as screening devices to reduce the incidence of robbery: if the face at the door looks desirable, the buzzer is pressed and the door is unlocked. If the face is that of an undesirable, the door stays locked. Predictably, the issue of undesirability has revealed itself to be a racial determination," as Williams discovers one Saturday afternoon when she "was shopping in Soho and saw in a store window a sweater that I wanted to buy for my mother. I pressed my round brown face to the window and my finger to the buzzer, seeking admittance. A narrow-eyed, white teenager wearing running shoes and feasting on bubble gum glared out, evaluating me for signs that would pit me against the limits of his social understanding. After about five seconds, he mouthed 'We're closed,' and blew pink rubber at me. It was two Saturdays before Christmas, at one o'clock in the afternoon; there were several white people in the store who appeared to be shopping for things for *their* mothers" (pp. 44–45).

The power of this story lies in its compression, in its vivid contrasting of the narrator's round brown face with the sales clerk's narrow eyes and pink bubble gum, in its use of physical exclusion as a metaphor for social exclusion, in its suggestion that the least significant of whites (this gum-chewing bubble-blowing teenage sales clerk) is utterly comfortable with exercising power over an older and more accomplished black, and in its elegant summation of the clerk's reaction to her ("evaluating me for signs that would pit me against the limits of his social understanding"). But is the

---

28. Irvin Molotsky, "You-Know-Who Wrote the Plays, Judges Say," *New York Times,* Sept. 26, 1987, p. 1; Amy E. Schwartz, "Three Justices, a Poetry-Starved Crowd and Shakespeare," *Washington Post,* Oct. 14, 1987, p. A19.

29. For additional evidence, see Dan Subotnik, "What's Wrong with Critical Race Theory? Reopening the Case for Middle-Class Values" (unpublished, Touro College Law Center, 1997).

30. I discuss her book at greater length in *Overcoming Law,* ch. 18 (1995).

31. Andrew Hudgins, "An Autobiographer's Lies," 65 *American Scholar* 541 (1996).

story true? Did Williams, who is not a child, who is a mature woman, *really* press her face against the window (isn't that what "press to the window" means?). Or is she embroidering the facts for dramatic effect—making the insult to her seem graver because it shattered a childlike eagerness and innocence? And how does she *know* that the sales clerk refused to let her into the store because she's black? Her evidence is that since Christmas was approaching, it is unlikely that the store had closed, and that there were other shoppers in the store. The second point has no force. Stores normally stop admitting more customers before all the ones already in the store have left—otherwise the store might never be able to close. The first point is stronger. Although many stores close early on Saturday, the likelihood that a Benetton store in New York City during the Christmas shopping season would be one of them is slight. Yet Williams does not suggest that she has tried to find out whether the store was open or that she saw any customers admitted after she was turned away. The absence of a sign indicating that the store was closed would be some evidence that it was open, but she does not mention the presence or absence of a sign. Many stores list their hours on the front door. She makes no mention of that either.

Her anger at the episode may reflect a pervasive uncertainty that confronts blacks in their encounters with whites. Not every disappointment that a black person encounters is a result of discrimination, and yet it may be impossible to determine which ones are and which ones are not. We like to know where we stand with other people, and this is difficult for blacks in their dealings with whites (and vice versa). But if *this* is what the Benetton episode is about—the psychology of the American black— Williams should have said so.

I am not being a fusspot in insisting on the distinction between fact and fiction. Benetton is not a fiction. It is a real company. Williams has accused it in print of unlawful behavior. This is a serious accusation, especially when made by a lawyer. Indeed, it is potentially libelous. If her account of the episode departs from the literal truth, she owes it to her readers and to Benetton to tell us that.

Williams had told us at the outset of her book, in defense of doing legal scholarship in the form of storytelling, "that one of the most important results of reconceptualizing from 'objective truth' to rhetorical event will be a more nuanced sense of legal and social responsibility" (p. 11). I am wary of the scare quotes around "objective truth" and by the term "rhetorical event." Is she warning us that the difficulty of proving racial discrimination is so great that we must give up on factual inquiry and accept fictitious accounts of discrimination—accounts that present fears and suspicions as proven facts? Is she thus disclaiming the factuality of her vignettes? Or is she committing herself to getting the particulars of an event or situation right rather than submerging them in a generality, such as that whites hate blacks? If the latter is her aim, it entails an effort to find out what *really* was going on in that white teenager's mind when he told her the store was closed. Maybe, as I said, it *was* closed; maybe it wasn't but the clerk had his hands full with the customers inside. Maybe he was a disloyal employee who wanted to get his employer in trouble. Maybe he was lazy, mischievous, rude, irresponsible, or just plain dumb. These questions would not arise if the incident were offered as outright fiction, but it seems that instead Williams wants to marry the authority of truth to the charm of fiction. To such a marriage, equivocation over literal truth is fatal. The selection of facts is the narrator's prerogative; their invention, and only a little less culpably the omission of facts without which the nonfiction narrative will mislead, are the narrator's temptation and one to which oppositionist legal storytelling has too often succumbed.[32]

Judicial Biography

Biography is an old (older than Plutarch, conventionally regarded as the father of the genre), rich, various, immensely popular, philosophically controversial genre. Judicial biography is an expanding, problematic subgenre of biography and of legal scholarship[33] and a cousin to the autobiographical narratives just discussed. Biography is the most *literary* of scholarly genres. The resemblance of biography, and especially autobiography, to the novel is often remarked, so that one might imagine using the same criteria to evaluate biographies as to evaluate novels. This would require setting to one side all questions of factuality. Catherine Drinker Bowen's popular biography of Justice Holmes, *Yankee from Olympus*, is a good "read," its subject having led a life that a writer of fiction would have been proud to in-

32. See Daniel A. Farber and Suzanna Sherry, *Beyond All Reason: The Radical Assault on Truth in American Law*, ch. 5 ("The Assault on Truth and Memory") (1997); also Coughlin, note 2 above. Robin West, an admirer of Patricia Williams, acknowledges that in *The Alchemy of Race and Rights* Williams "conveyed her complex arguments about white racism with stories that purported to be historical, but which actually may not have been factually accurate." West, "Constitutional Fictions and Meritocratic Success Stories," 53 *Washington and Lee Law Review* 995, 998 (1996).

33. See, for background, Symposium, *National Conference on Judicial Biography*, 70 *New York University Law Review* 485 (1995); Michael J. Gerhardt, "The Art of Judicial Biography," 80 *Cornell Law Review* 1595 (1995). A related genre that I will not discuss, although it would provide a suitable bridge from the first section of this chapter, is feminist biographies of women lawyers. See Carol Sanger, "Curriculum Vitae (Feminae): Biography and Early American Women Lawyers," 46 *Stanford Law Review* 1245 (1994).

vent. It may be one of the best "novels" about judges that we have. But it is rarely mentioned in articles on judicial biography, because it is not "serious," that is, not scrupulously concerned with getting things right. Biography, unless rankly "popular" or sensationalistic—or downright fraudulent—aspires to be a branch of history rather than of fiction. Yet just as with the work of the legal narratologists, there is a nagging sense that its aspirations are unfulfilled, its truth content dubious.

Biography is not a homogeneous category of writing; but a stated concern with truth is common to the different types. Some biographies use a person's life as a scaffold on which to hang a narrative of historical events that the person participated in or observed, or a selection of the person's letters, or other previously unpublished documents. These biographies, respectively historical and bibliographical in their emphasis, are the least interesting from the standpoint of biography considered as a distinct genre. Other biographies cater to our curiosity, often prurient, about other people's lives, especially famous people's (Plutarch, Suetonius, and Procopius are the pioneers here). They provide a kind of vicarious acquaintanceship akin to what we get from gossip or from fiction. Some biographies tell an exciting story; A. J. A. Symons's *The Quest for Corvo* is an example. Some are critical, debunking, like Lytton Strachey's *Eminent Victorians,* and many are hagiographical.[34] I shall call both these sorts of biography *ideological,* but without any pejorative connotation. Some biographies are *edifying*: they are designed to provide models or anti-models for the reader's own life. A famous example is David Cecil's life of Melbourne. Many feminist biographies are of this character. Some biographies aim at answering specific questions, often of a causal nature: why did *X* do *a,* or where did *X* get the idea for *a,* or was *X* really the author of *a,* or, most commonly, *why* was *X* a great writer, leader, warrior, or composer? Let me call these *scientific* biographies. Psychobiography is the subgenre of scientific biographies that investigates psychological causes of people's beliefs and actions.

The most ambitious biographies seek to reveal the "inner man" (or woman), the essential self—what Walt Whitman called "the Me myself" and Leon Edel the "private self-concept that guides a given life" or equivalently the "concealed self."[35] Biographies dominated by this aim I call *essentialist* biographies, as they posit an essential self. Obviously I am not using the word in its normal philosophical sense.

34. Illustrations from judicial biography are legion. See, for example, Frank Sikora, *The Judge: The Life and Opinions of Alabama's Frank M. Johnson, Jr.* (1992).

35. Leon Edel, "Keynote Address: Biography and the Science of Man," in *New Directions in Biography* 1, 9, 10 (Anthony M. Friedson ed. 1981). See also Elisabeth Young-Bruehl, "The Writing of Biography," 50 *Partisan Review* 413 (1983).

The most common aims of *judicial* biography, other than to provide a framework for discussing an area of law, or a legal institution (usually the Supreme Court), or the history of a legal institution, are ideological and essentialist. But sometimes one finds instead or as well the aim of edification, vicarious acquaintanceship, or causal explanation: What made Judge X great?—what made him decide cases the way he did?

Ideological and essentialist biographies have different but equally uneasy relations to truth. The ideological presupposes some ideal against which to compare and by which to measure the individual who is the subject of the biography. Often it will be difficult to justify the ideal to doubters, to show that it is a worthy ideal. And in order to make the comparison between his subject and the ideal plausible, the biographer will be tempted to prune the "nonessential" features of his subject—the good features if the biographer wishes to debunk him for his failure to come up to the ideal, the bad if the biographer wishes to present the subject as an exemplar of the ideal. The subject of the biography is not an end in himself or herself but an instrument for the promotion of an ideal, and the sharper and cleaner the instrument the more effective it is. Here the resemblance between biography and fiction is particularly close, because the writer of fiction is also engaged in the pruning of details that would detract from the coherence and significance of the work.

The essentialist biographer is in quest of a self invariably assumed to be coherent,[36] a unity of some kind; if it is a disorderly aggregation of conflicting elements, the biographer and his readers will not be satisfied that the biography has penetrated beneath the surface. In the psychology implicit in essentialist biography each of us has three layers of personality. The first consists of the constructed self—the face we present to the world in an effort to foster advantageous transactions, whether commercial or personal, with other people. This is the level at which autobiography often stops and which makes it such an unreliable, self-serving, indeed self-aggrandizing genre. Below is a second self, consisting of aspects of personality that we conceal from all but our closest intimates. Below *that* self is—and this is the indispensable assumption of the essentialist's project—the essential self, the one that generates the two higher levels, that holds the key to the person and his works. This too is a constructed self, though constructed by the biographer rather than by his subject. In this respect it resembles the implied author of a work of literature.

Is this essential self a construct that captures a reality, or is it merely a dogma or perhaps a fiction, which "makes sense" of the subject in the way

36. See Ira Bruce Nadel, *Biography: Fiction, Fact and Form* 10, 155 (1984).

that avowed fiction seeks (in Aristotelian theory) to make human action coherent, intelligible, plausible, probable?[37] I think it's a fiction. People are confusing mixtures, lacking unity and coherence both over time[38] and at the same time. I do not mean that they are irrational in the sense of behaving inconsistently or even foolishly. But their preferences, values, reactions, traits of character, and personality are not reducible to an easily labeled essence—the "saint," the "villain," the "weak man," the "designing woman," the "genius," the "hero," and so forth. There is no inconsistency, no "irrationality," in having preferences that do not compose an aesthetically or emotionally pleasing unity—no inconsistency, therefore, in being a brilliant writer and a vicious anti-Semite, a brilliant doctor and a child molester, a daring warrior and an acrophobe, a lover of hairshirts and of caviar. The characters in fiction have, most of them anyway (not all—think of Hamlet), a unity and transparency not often found in real life. We are constantly being fooled about real people; they don't conform to the models we construct of them. Writers borrow generously from real life—how generously, we shall see in the next chapter—but in the recasting complexities are scraped away and a dominant trait is allowed to swallow the other traits of the real-life model, making most fictional characters more like medieval "humors" than like people you actually encounter. To the chronologist, history (including biography) is indeed just one damn' thing after another. Narrative, including the narrative of a life, turns a chronology into a story, with a beginning, middle, and end causally related to one another. By doing so it imposes coherence on a sequence of events that may have no coherence.

Even if each of us does have an essential self, the truth claims made by essentialist biographers cannot be verified. There is no technique for comparing the essential self presented in a biography to the subject's "real" essential self. Whenever truth claims cannot be verified, the claims themselves are likely to be influenced by wishful thinking generated by the claimant's, in this case the biographer's, own traits and values; this turns out to be a serious problem for judicial biography. The problem of unverifiability also attends what I am calling the *scientific* biography. For it is a general problem with attributions of causality to historical events, and biography is a branch of history. To say that Napoleon caused the diffusion of the ideas of the French Revolution throughout Europe is merely to hypothesize that had there been no Napoleon those ideas would have diffused more slowly

---

37. The danger in the writing of biography of exaggerating the unity of the self is noted in Richard H. Blum, "Psychological Processes in Preparing Contemporary Biography," 4 *Biography* 293, 301–303 (1981).

38. As I emphasize in my book *Aging and Old Age* 84–94 (1995).

or perhaps not at all. (What he did, he did; but someone or ones might have done the same in his absence.) That is a counterfactual impossible to confirm or refute through experimental or statistical methods, or any other methods objective enough to convince skeptics.

We know how things turned out, how a life turned out. We have no direct knowledge of how they would have turned out if something had been different, say in the subject's upbringing. The tendency to see the climactic events or crowning achievements of a life as latent in a person's character or early life is merely the by-product of the urge to understand. Biography is often, perhaps characteristically, the telling of a plausible story of how the events of a person's life *might* have been causally related to each other and (as both cause and effect) to earlier and later perturbations in the social environment. The most honest biography would be the one written contemporaneously with the life being lived by its subject, so that the biographer would not know how that life was going to turn out. The biographer would make predictions from his conception of his subject's essential self, and the predictions would be confirmed or falsified in the unfolding of the subject's life.

Closely related to the epistemological problems of essentialist biography is the problem of inconsequence or disconnection, which recalls the discussion of intentionalism in Chapter 7. Even if each of us has an essential self discoverable by an empathetic biographer, it is far from clear that the essential self generates what interests us about the person who is the subject of the biography. The deepest layer of personality must be connected with something in the more visible layers if the former is a responsible (even if unverifiable) inference from the latter; but that something may not be the individual's aptitudes or achievements. This point, deeply troublesome when the subject of a biography is a writer or other "intellectual worker," is obscured in the case of biographies of men of action because the interest is mainly in the actions. We might learn about Napoleon's campaigns by reading a biography of Napoleon. But we would be unlikely to read a biography of Joyce without some previous acquaintance with his writings, and our main curiosity in reading the biography would be about the source of his genius. We would be disappointed. We might learn why he was so strange, but we would not learn why he was a great writer or what his works mean. This was the basis for T. S. Eliot's wish not to have a biography written. He thought the real life of a poet is in the poetry.[39] Yeats too thought that poetry was a surrogate for, rather than an expres-

---

39. James Olney, "Where Is the Real T. S. Eliot? Or, The Life of the Poet," in *The Cambridge Companion to T. S. Eliot* 1 (A. David Moody ed. 1994).

sion of, the poet's life. As biography becomes more candid, more penetrating, more ruthless, wider-ranging,[40] the disjunction between the person and the product simply widens. We learn from biographies of T. E.
Lawrence that he derived sexual pleasure from being whipped and apparently from nothing else; the connection between his sexual taste and his
achievements as soldier, writer, translator, statesman, and self-promoter remains completely obscure. Read Lynn's highly regarded biography of
Hemingway[41] and you will encounter a creep who is the antithesis of the
implied author of Hemingway's novels.

The lesson of the best biographies of creative people, whether in the arts,
the sciences, or the professions, is precisely the disconnection of achievement
from self: "Whenever a writer, artist, musician, any mode of imagination is
made the subject of a biography, his light may be extinguished . . . Life is simply a shell, the kernel of which is creative work. There is no real nourishment
in biography. The words fly up, the lives remain below."[42] Henry James's
story "The Private Life" (1892) presses this point to its logical extreme. Vawdrey, a novelist, disappoints the narrator, along with his other acquaintances,
by the commonplace manner of his conversation. It is impossible to imagine
that he is the actual author of his novels. He is not. One night, while Vawdrey is talking to another guest on the terrace of the Swiss inn at which they
are staying, the narrator enters Vawdrey's room and sees a silent Vawdrey,
sitting at his desk in the dark,[43] writing. This *Doppelgänger* is the novelist, and
he is totally disconnected from the public Vawdrey.

I do not push the disconnection thesis quite so hard. The fact that Joyce
grew up in Dublin is related to the setting of *Ulysses*. The fact that
Napoleon became an officer at a time when the established military and
political hierarchies had been destroyed is related, along with luck and daring, to his rapid rise to power. And it is a reasonable guess that intelligence

40. See, for example, William M. Murphy, *Family Secrets: William Butler Yeats and His Relatives*
(1995).

41. Kenneth S. Lynn, *Hemingway* (1987).

42. Michael Holroyd, "Literary and Historical Biography," in *New Directions in Biography*, note
35 above, at 12, 18. The point is well illustrated by Furbank's superb two-volume biography of
E. M. Forster. In the fabulous particularity of Furbank's description of Forster, see P. N. Furbank,
E. M. Forster: A Life, vol. 2: *Polycrates' Ring (1914–1970)*, ch. 13 (1978) ("E. M. Forster
Described"), Forster the *writer* quite disappears—as he should. The writer and the man are dis-
connected. Aldous Huxley put it this way: the biographer has the Midas touch—but in reverse.
The point is made with reference to G. Edward White's effort to expose Oliver Wendell
Holmes's "inner self" in Evans Wohlforth, "The 'Essential' Holmes" (review of G. Edward
White, *Justice Oliver Wendell Holmes: Law and the Inner Self* [1993]), 47 *Rutgers Law Review* 441,
443–447 (1994).

43. Cf. Yeats's image, in the lines from "The Choice" that I quoted in the last chapter, of the
artist (he who has chosen perfection of the work over perfection of the life) "raging in the dark."

and energy are preconditions for most forms of admired achievement; again we could illustrate with Napoleon and Joyce. But we know these things without the aid of essentialist or scientific biography. The literary biography in particular seems to miss the point, and in doing so to illustrate the joke about the man who searched for his keys not where he had dropped them but where the light from the street lamp made a search possible. The New Critics were right to disparage biographical literary criticism. The essentialist approach to biography is the intentional fallacy writ large.

Not only is biography a problematic endeavor; it is also, when based on original sources rather than on previous biographies of the same person, a very costly one. Biographies of people who died long ago are highly labor-intensive, like other works of historical scholarship, because it takes a lot of digging in archives to make even a plausible reconstruction of the past. Biographies of the recently deceased or the still living are labor-intensive for a different reason—the likelihood of a superabundance of material. Although letter-writing is in decline, more copies are made of those letters that are written, so disappearance is less likely. And people are leaving their traces in all sorts of other recoverable forms, ranging from electronic mail and videotapes to oral histories and library depositories of personal papers. Then if acquaintances of the subject survive, there is much interviewing to be done.

Time is money for people who write for a living. For academics, the cost of time takes the form of forgoing other scholarly projects. Anyone mulling whether to write a biography must weigh an enormous investment of time against the likely rewards financial or otherwise. The cost of biography explains the practice of granting a biographer exclusive access to the private papers of his subject. Exclusivity performs a function similar to that of the patent monopoly. A scholar or writer may be unwilling to invest a huge amount of his time in doing a biography unless assured that his work cannot be duplicated before he has had a chance to recoup some of his costs (in time lost to other projects) through the publication and sale of a book that has no close competitors.

The financial rewards of biography are limited to biographies of the famous or the notorious. The great but unknown, or nongreat, are unlikely to find biographers anywhere but in universities. An academic must consider carefully what he is giving up by devoting years to doing the research for and writing a biography, given the uncertainty of the contribution that the biography will make to knowledge and the alternative uses for his time. In the time that Gerald Gunther took to write his 818-page biography of Learned Hand[44] he could have written dozens of law review articles, and

---

44. Gerald Gunther, *Learned Hand: The Man and the Judge* (1994).

conceivably the contribution to legal scholarship would have been greater. Of course, benefits to scholarship are not and should not be the only consideration in decisions about a career; the scholar's taste is an important consideration. Moreover, biographies can be expected to have a longer shelf life—to remain in print longer and be read longer—than an essay or (nonbiographical) book about the same person. Because they are so costly to write, fewer biographies will be written about a person than essays and nonbiographical books about him. The biographies will be spaced farther apart in time and as a result will not be superseded so quickly as the other types of writing about the person in question. Gunther's biography was the first of Hand; it may be the last.

The would-be biographer must ponder the existence of alternative genres to biography—types of study that seek to attain the aims, or some of them, of biography at a lower cost in time and sometimes a stronger claim to truth. Examples are brief lives (by Plutarch, Aubrey, Johnson, Strachey, and others); biographical studies that confine themselves to the most momentous years of the subject's life or that focus even more narrowly on specific crises or turning points in that life; group biographies (more likely of course to be biographical sketches, "profiles," so as to fit within one cover);[45] interpretive essays that seek to "explain" a historical figure; studies of a person's works with only incidental reference to his life; oral histories—autobiography midwifed by an historian; and aggregative comparative studies. By the last I mean works like the Goertzels',[46] which try to discover the springs of creativity inductively by comparing the frequency with which certain traits are found in creative people to the frequency of those traits in the population as a whole. The sampling of three hundred lives in one book seems a more *efficient* method of studying people's lives than three hundred biographies—until one realizes that the Goertzels could not have gotten to first base without the biographers; for it was the biographers who generated the data (and indeed furnished the sample) on

45. Plutarch's *Lives* and Strachey's *Eminent Victorians* remain the most famous examples. An example in law is G. Edward White, *The American Judicial Tradition: Profiles of Leading American Judges* (1976).

46. Mildren George Goertzel, Victor Goertzel, and Ted George Goertzel, *Three Hundred Eminent Personalities: A Psychosocial Analysis of the Famous* (1978). The criterion for inclusion in their list was having been the subject of two or more recent biographies. Id. at 2. For other examples of this genre, see Dean Keith Simonton, *Greatness: Who Makes History and Why* (1994); Howard Gardner, "The Creators' Patterns," in *Changing the World: A Framework for the Study of Creativity* 69 (David Henry Feldman, Mihaly Csikszentmihalyi, and Howard Gardner eds. 1994). For a hybrid of this genre and group biography, see Howard Gardner, *Creating Minds: An Anatomy of Creativity Seen through the Lives of Freud, Einstein, Picasso, Stravinsky, Eliot, Graham, and Gandhi* (1993).

which the Goertzels' study was based. Not all works in the alternative genres, however, are parasitic upon the standard full-length biography.

So: a problematic and costly genre, the biography;[47] and nowhere is this truer than in judicial biography. All the problems of biography in general, and of literary biography in particular, are present, exacerbated by additional problems. The aims of judicial biography are various. The scaffolding aim is prominent, especially in biographies of recent Supreme Court Justices.[48] The biographer's primary interest is in the workings of the Supreme Court as illuminated by the Justice's private papers (abundant only in the case of recent Justices), unless the Justice happens to be a person of exceptional qualities, which is rarely the case, or lived an exciting life, which is even more rare. Biographies of early Justices, from Marshall to Fuller, often turn out to be histories of the Supreme Court during the subject's tenure. Perhaps these should not be regarded as biographies at all, but as works of an alternative genre. The more recent the Justice, the more likely the biography is to provide, in addition to a coat rack for hanging information about the Supreme Court, a vehicle for expounding the biographer's own judicial philosophy. The biography of Hugo Black[49] does not yield to this temptation, and it maintains a good balance between the subject's pre–Supreme Court years and his Court years. But while it is a good read and a mine of interesting information, it is less analytical than adulatory and slightly breathless. Such a book, which comes closest to general biographies written for popular audiences, caters mainly to the public's curiosity about the personalities and private lives of powerful men.

A notable exception is Laura Kalman's biography of Abe Fortas,[50] a rare, perhaps unique, example of an edifying judicial biography. Kalman's book is in the tradition of medieval cautionary tales of the mutability of worldly fortune. Fortas had a rocket-fast rise followed by a meteoric fall due, as Kalman skillfully and unobtrusively demonstrates, to the arrogance, pride, loss of touch, overconfidence, closed-mindedness, and lack of self-knowledge that are the occupational hazards of the highly successful. It is the only judicial biography known to me that can be recommended to judges and

---

47. Joan Mellen, the author of a biography of Kay Boyle and a dual biography of Dashiell Hammett and Lillian Hellman, has echoed my concerns with literary biography in a recent article, "Confessions of an Ex-Biographer," forthcoming in *Biography and Source Studies,* vol. 3 (Frederick R. Karl ed. 1997). See also Mellen, "A Biographer Declares—The End of Biography," *The Sun,* Sept. 15, 1996, p. 1E.

48. See, for example, John C. Jeffries, Jr., *Justice Lewis F. Powell, Jr.* (1994); Fowler V. Harper, *Justice Rutledge and the Bright Constellation* (1965). Hutchinson's biography of Byron White, which I discuss later, is a notable counterexample.

49. Roger K. Newman, *Hugo Black: A Biography* (1994).

50. Kalman, *Abe Fortas: A Biography* (1990).

lawyers as a warning not to stray too far from the paths of virtue, humility, and prudence.

Few judges have been extraordinary individuals or have led interesting lives.[51] Few have had Fortas's Lucifer-like fall from grace. Satisfying the reading public's curiosity about the great, or about the fascinating, is thus rarely a motive for a judicial biography. The principal exception is biographies of Holmes, a judge of towering greatness who also lived an interesting life and left a huge mass of public and private papers to sift through. His biographers[52] have tried to locate his essential self in the many thousands of pages by and about him (mostly by). They have failed.[53] One reason is the diversity and even inconsistency of his thought as revealed in his writings. Another is his lack of any marked quirks. Holmes was, as far as anyone knows, physically and mentally healthy, energetic, successful, sociable without being gregarious—in short "normal"[54]—and had a generally upbeat, optimistic, serene, and even humorous outlook on life. If there was a volcanic psychic core that generated the philosophical and political vision that many have thought bleak, it was effectively concealed. Gunther has tried to find the inner self of Learned Hand and Hirsch that of Felix Frankfurter,[55] and they have had a bit more to work with, since both of these judges were quirky, and Hand in particular would have given a psychiatrist a field day. Nevertheless, Gunther has been unable to relate Hand's jurisprudence to his quirkiness.

The most common aim of judicial biography, often overlapping the essentialist, is the ideological. The judge is presented as a spokesman for a judicial philosophy of which the biographer either approves or (rarely) disapproves. (The Hand biography is an example.) Scientific judicial biographies—biographies that try to identify causal relations, for example between what a judge read and the judicial opinions that he wrote—are

51. A review of biographies of Earl Warren concludes, with impolitic candor, "he was a dull man and a dull judge." Dennis J. Hutchinson, "Hail to the Chief: Earl Warren and the Supreme Court," 81 *Michigan Law Review* 922, 930 (1983). These are not necessarily criticisms. Not all of us wish to be judged by lively, interesting people.

52. Of whom there are by now a goodly number. John F. Hagemann, "Looking at Holmes: A Review Essay," 39 *South Dakota Law Review* 433 (1994).

53. Adam J. Hirsch, "Searching inside Justice Holmes" (Review of G. Edward White, *Justice Oliver Wendell Holmes: Law and the Inner Self* [1993]), 82 *Virginia Law Review* 385 (1996). Notice the subtitle of White's book.

54. The conjecture by a recent biographer of Henry James that James had a homosexual affair with Holmes, see Sheldon M. Novick, *Henry James: The Young Master* 110 (1996), has no evidential basis whatever, as pointed out in Millicent Ball, "The Divine, the Unique," *Times Literary Supplement,* Dec. 6, 1996, p. 3. It is a *reductio ad absurdum* of the prying, prurient character of so much modern biography.

55. H. N. Hirsch, *The Enigma of Felix Frankfurter* (1981).

rare. The most pawed-over causal issue in scientific judicial biography is whether and in what way Holmes's three years' service in the Civil War, in which he was thrice wounded seriously, influenced his judicial philosophy. There is endless speculation, but no satisfactory answer. It is certainly *plausible* to attribute the "hard" side visible in some of his opinions and more of his letters to his brutal experiences in wartime, but is it right? Many of his contemporaries who had no military experience were equally "hard," a good example being Holmes's English acquaintance James Fitzjames Stephen, whom we met in Chapter 5 praising Pontius Pilate. Holmes may simply have been rebelling against his garrulous, irritating, annoyingly famous, faintly nasty father (who used to tease his son about the length of his neck). Tough-minded and militantly atheistic, Holmes wrote that "there was with him [his father] as with the rest of his generation a certain softness toward the interstitial miracle—the phenomenon without phenomenal antecedents, that I did not feel."[56]

The principal output of appellate judges (biographies of trial judges are rare) is judicial opinions. This makes judicial biography a cousin of literary biography, with all the pitfalls of confusing the real with the implied author. Emphasis on personality has done unwarranted damage to the reputation of Felix Frankfurter, an extremely accomplished judge. The relation between literary and judicial biography is particularly close for those who believe, as I do, that literary distinction is central to the reputation of the great judges. But it makes the disconnection between inner self and literary expression almost as serious a problem for judicial biography as for literary biography. We have some clues, if nothing more, to where the great "literary" judges like Holmes, Hand, and Cardozo got their judicial philosophies from, but we have no idea what it was in these judges or their environments that can explain their literary distinction. Their education was not markedly different from that of other judges of their time who wrote with no literary distinction, including judges such

---

56. Letter to Morris Cohen, Feb. 5, 1919, in *The Essential Holmes: Selections from the Letters, Speeches, Judicial Opinions, and Other Writings of Oliver Wendell Holmes, Jr.* 110 (Richard A. Posner ed. 1992). Holmes himself speculated that "probably a sceptical temperament that I got from my mother had something to do with my way of thinking." Id. Anent his father, Holmes in a letter to Felix Frankfurter made this interesting comment: "I came last night on a passage about the superiority complex that made me wonder whether my father, who certainly taught me a great deal and did me a great deal of good, didn't also do me some harm by drooling over the physical shortcomings of himself and his son and by some other sardonic criticisms. At least he made it difficult for his son to be conceited. Within limits no doubt it is good for a child to be brought down to actualities with a bump." Letter from Holmes to Frankfurter, May 21, 1926, in *Holmes and Frankfurter: Their Correspondence, 1912–1934* 214 (Robert M. Mennel and Christine L. Compston eds. 1996).

as William Howard Taft and Charles Evans Hughes, both men of formidable intellect.

If the literary dimension of judicial performance complicates judicial biography in one sense, its decline complicates it in another. Today few
judges, even the most famous (William Brennan being a notable example),
write their own opinions or speeches. The writing is delegated, often with
very little supervision, to law clerks; sometimes even the selection of the
law clerks is delegated. Increasingly, judicial output is a corporate affair. (It
always has been, though in a more limited sense, because of the heavy reliance that most judges place on the briefs of the lawyers.) The biographies
of modern judges may come to resemble histories of General Motors or
the New York Public Library.

The special problems of judicial biography can be brought into focus by
asking who can be expected to write it and who to read it. The answer to
both questions is, mainly lawyers. Few others are interested in reading
about the lives of judges, for judges by and large are obscure and faintly
forbidding figures to the public. If the readership of judicial biography is
to be composed largely of lawyers, there is a certain logic to the authors'
being lawyers as well, the better to communicate with the primary audience for the work. Moreover, it is difficult for a layman to write a judicial
biography, not only because judges deal with technical legal issues but also
because the role of the judge is difficult for the laity to understand.
Nonlawyers tend either to be credulous about judges' self-serving rhetoric
of disinterest or to assume that judges are merely politicians ("statesmen,"
if the writer shares the judge's politics) in disguise. The truth is somewhere
in between.

Although a number of well-known biographies of Supreme Court Justices, beginning with Beveridge's life of John Marshall, have been written
by nonlawyers, the results are mixed. Mason's biography of Harlan Fiske
Stone,[57] for example, shows Stone not as he was but as he would have liked
the public to think that he was.[58] Mason turned out to be a gullible member of that public. Judges are great bluffers, and it is particularly difficult for
nonlawyers to penetrate the bluff unless they are highly cynical—though it
is possible to be too cynical even about the legal profession.

57. Alpheus Thomas Mason, *Harlan Fiske Stone: Pillar of the Law* (1956).
58. Philip B. Kurland, Book Review, 70 *Harvard Law Review* 1318 (1957). See also J.
Woodford Howard, Jr., "Alpheus T. Mason and the Art of Judicial Biography," 8 *Constitutional
Commentary* 41, 48–49 (1991). The problem of a biographer's identifying with his subject is of
course not limited to judicial biography, let alone judicial biography by nonlawyers. Cf. Eva
Schepeler, "The Biographer's Transference: A Chapter in Psychobiographical Epistemology," 13
Biography 111 (1990).

Yet biographers who are lawyers usually don't do much better in piercing the façade, though for a different reason. Deference to judges is ingrained in the legal culture. This is partly because judges have power over lawyers (elected judges have less power over lawyers and so receive less deference), and partly because, like any guild or profession, lawyers tend to close ranks against outsiders. The probity and intelligence of judges are cornerstones in the "official" picture of the law that lawyers paint for laymen. Even when writing biography, lawyers are reluctant to foul their nest by depicting judges as they really are. Then too the relation of lawyers to truth is an ambivalent one; they are bound to be unreliable practitioners of a craft—the writing of biography—that itself bears a questionable relation to truth. Skilled equivocators, lawyers are more comfortable defending a position than finding out the way things really are. It comes naturally to the lawyer biographer to write a brief for, or occasionally against, his subject. These things are truer of practicing lawyers than of law professors, and it is from the ranks of the latter that most judicial biographers come.[59] But few law professors shed entirely the outlook of the lawyer they were trained to be.

The more a lawyer is a true believer in the legal profession's official, still widely believed, and even more widely propagated view of law, the less likely he is to think that writing a judicial biography is a worthwhile undertaking. In the most extreme version of legal formalism the judge is an oracle or a computing machine; his personality, life history, values, family, and politics do not enter into his decisions at all. The problem of disconnection is then at its most acute. No lawyer is *that* formalistic today, and anyway a formalist biography could be written to show that the judge's life had *not* influenced his decisions; there is a hint of this theme in Gunther's biography of Hand. Still, as one moves from the formalist to the realist pole, the attraction of biography as a mode of explaining judicial decisions grows. One reason for writing and reading biographies of Supreme Court Justices is doubt that their decisions are fully determined by the rules of law; we think that personal factors must play a significant role.[60] It is therefore odd that the legal realists did not write judicial biographies and that their successors as "rule of law" skeptics, the adherents of the critical legal studies movement, have also shown little interest in the lives of judges.

Law schools are not oriented to the demands of time-consuming scholarly projects. Historically and even today few law professors had or have

---

59. Though one of the better judicial biographies was written by a practicing lawyer: Willard L. King, *Melville Weston Fuller: Chief Justice of the United States, 1888–1920* (1950).
60. Phil C. Neal, "Introduction," in id. at vii.

the taste or training for such projects. Law professors do not have cadres of graduate students to assist them, though they can get some help from law students. They have, many of them, heavy teaching loads. They are constantly being dragooned into university governance activities for which their lawyerly talents peculiarly equip them. And they are easily tempted from their academic duties by opportunities for engaging in legal consulting, public service, and other "real world" extracurricular activities. No wonder there have been extraordinary delays in the appearance of biographies of major judges. Mark DeWolfe Howe died before he could finish his biography of Holmes, and was followed to the grave by his designated successor, Grant Gilmore. The Hand biography was published thirty years after it was commissioned. Law professors' biographies of Brandeis, Cardozo, Frankfurter, and Jackson have yet to appear. Andrew Kaufman has written a splendid biography of Cardozo, and it will be published soon. But it has been almost forty years in the making.

Worst of all, nothing in the training and experience of a lawyer or law professor equips him to write a biography. He is not trained to write narratives or to depict human beings empathetically; few academic lawyers, even those with experience as law clerks, know what being a judge *feels* like. Weakness in that area does not matter much with respect to the most popular subject for judicial biography, namely Holmes. His biographies are essentially written out of Holmes's letters and judicial opinions. The empathetic observer is Holmes himself. But in another sense a lack of empathy is a serious impediment to the writing of an adequate biography of Holmes. His outlook has proved deeply antipathetic to most of his biographers. He is not "politically correct." True, he was a philo-Semite; but that's not good enough today; his views of blacks and women were conventional for his time. He was, we know, a eugenicist—and no pacifist! He was hostile to government intervention in the economy and to the redistribution of income and wealth. He admired the robber barons. He is not the patient judicial craftsman of legend. (Remember the flaws in the *Lochner* dissent, in Chapter 8?) He is not entirely consistent. He does not seem entirely likeable. He determinedly concealed his "inner self." Read in great swatches, he becomes a little tedious, being repetitious and at times egoistic and complacent. Worst of all, his intellectual breadth exceeds that of his biographers, who thus have trouble encompassing him while at the same time feeling compelled constantly to apologize for him. There are good biographies of Holmes,[61] yet the definitive biography of Holmes has not been written, and may never be.

61. See, for example, Sheldon Novick, *Honorable Justice: The Life of Oliver Wendell Holmes* (1989); G. Edward White, *Justice Oliver Wendell Holmes: Law and the Inner Life* (1993).

The case of Holmes is special. The general challenge of judicial biography, to which few judicial biographers rise, is to write empathetically and arrestingly about dullish people who are not introspective. The writing of a biography requires great diligence and patience, which many academic lawyers have, but diligence and patience are not enough to produce a first-rate biography. *Sitzfleisch* and literary flair are not a natural pair. Lack of literary skill impedes the writing of good judicial biography in the same way that it impedes the writing of good autobiography by oppositionist legal scholars. For a biography to have the charm of fiction, its subject must be as interesting as a character in fiction, and this is rarely possible in judicial biography. Biography must usually make its way with fact, yet it has serious problems with factuality.

If dull people make for dull biographies, the handful of relatively interesting judges becomes the inevitable focus of judicial biography. The consequence, however, is to create a distorted impression of the judicial process. Most law is made by the ordinary judge, not the extraordinary one. Holmes, Brandeis, Cardozo, Hand, and a few others have each been more influential than any judges outside of that charmed circle. But the aggregate contribution of the run-of-the-mill judges to the shape of our law is greater than that of the charmed circle, because of the incremental and hierarchical nature of judge-made law and the much greater number of ordinary than extraordinary judges.[62]

It is no surprise that most judicial biographies really do not deserve the name, an example being Charles Fairman's biography of Samuel F. Miller, who served on the Supreme Court in the latter part of the nineteenth century.[63] The title of Fairman's biography is significant. He substitutes an honorific ("Mr. Justice") for the man's first name (known to few lawyers even) and makes all too clear that the only thing that interests him about Miller is his long service on the Supreme Court during a tumultuous period (are there any others?) in the Court's history. Miller never comes alive. The impression conveyed, probably unintentionally, is of a pompous ass, energetic and well-meaning but mediocre in intellect and thoroughly conventional in outlook. Dickens could make a conceited ass interesting. Fairman could not. The writing is stilted, and full of respectful gestures toward the Court and its members. It is writing by and for the guild.[64] King's biography of another Supreme Court old-timer, Chief Justice Fuller,[65] is

62. See Posner, note 30 above, ch. 3.

63. *Mr. Justice Miller and the Supreme Court, 1862–1890* (1939).

64. Cf. Morton J. Horwitz, "The Conservative Tradition in the Writing of American Legal History," 17 *American Journal of Legal History* 275 (1973).

65. See note 59 above.

better written than Fairman's book and paints a lively picture of a nice man, though a less considerable judicial figure than Miller. Fairman was a distinguished scholar, and King was not a scholar at all, and Fairman had an abler subject and a more interesting period to write about. But King's is a genuine biography, and Fairman's is a slice of Supreme Court history garnished with quotations from the not very interesting private letters of one of its not very interesting members.

Even Gerald Gunther's painstakingly thorough and beautifully written biography of Learned Hand[66] has serious deficiencies.[67] One is its ideological cast, which carries Gunther away from the true significance of Learned Hand's career. Gunther, a constitutional scholar, wishes to make Hand a spokesman for restraint in constitutional adjudication. Hand did write a few notable constitutional opinions and gave a series of lectures on constitutional interpretation, but the bulk of his judicial career was devoted to statutory and common law cases, and it is in those areas rather than in constitutional law that he made an enduring mark on American law and earned the reputation of being the greatest lower-court judge in American history. Yet Hand's nonconstitutional cases receive relatively short shrift in Gunther's long book because of their remoteness from the theme of judicial self-restraint that preoccupies him in consequence of his extrabiographical interests and commitments.

As with all ideological biographies, the author's desire to make his subject stand for (or against) an ideal causes some trimming of rough edges. The Hand portrayed by Gunther is a pretty rough diamond; the actual diamond was even rougher. A more serious problem concerning the significance of the Hand biography, a problem that a deeper or franker confrontation with Hand's foibles would only have magnified, is the disconnection between inner self and outer achievement.[68] The insecurity, the rudeness, the orneriness, the uxoriousness, the ambition, the emotionality, the neuroticism that characterized Hand the person are not visible in the judicial opinions. Although Gunther attempts to relate the skepticism that he finds at the root of Hand's philosophy of judicial self-restraint to Hand's personal insecurities, the attempt founders on the familiar problem of the difficulty of proving a counterfactual. Hand got his philosophy of

---

66. Note 44 above.

67. See my review, "The Hand Biography and the Question of Judicial Greatness," 104 *Yale Law Journal* 511 (1994). For a more generous evaluation, see Michael Boudin, "The Master Craftsman," 47 *Stanford Law Review* 363 (1995).

68. A similar point is made in a superb review of Hirsch's psychobiography of Frankfurter. George Kannar, "Representative Egos," 16 *Harvard Civil Rights-Civil Liberties Law Review* 875, 886–889 (1982).

judicial self-restraint from Holmes, who had none of Hand's insecurities. It could nevertheless be true that insecurity is a sufficient though not a necessary condition of being a restrained judge. Yet it would be easy to make a list of judicial activists who were personally insecure.

A curious property of judicial biography is that the more political a judge, the more illuminating is his biography likely to be. Appointed to the Supreme Court from the Senate, where he had been notable for his partisanship, Hugo Black was unlikely to be other than political as a Supreme Court Justice, and he was not. He was an intelligent person, an able lawyer, and a graceful writer, but *au fond* he was a politician in robes; the stamp he placed on the Constitution was an entirely personal one. Newman's biography identifies some aspects of personality and life experiences that may have shaped Black's political outlook and by doing so may help explain why Black was the kind of Supreme Court Justice that he was. This approach would not get as far with a Holmes, a Hand, or a Cardozo. Not because these judges' decisions were not influenced by extralegal knowledge and experience, but because we are interested in much more than their votes on particular cases and because even the votes cannot be mapped onto a simple pattern of ideology or personal preferences.

The two best judicial biographies have not yet been published; and perhaps this is a sign that the genre is improving and my pessimism is premature. The first is Andrew Kaufman's biography of Cardozo. A book of extraordinary thoroughness and meticulous accuracy—the work of four decades—it is definitive; I doubt that there will ever be another full-length biography of Cardozo. It is not a lively book, because Cardozo was not a very interesting person and did not lead an interesting life, and Kaufman has resisted the temptation to pad out the life with a potted history of Cardozo's times, or biographical sketches of the interesting people whom Cardozo met. The focus is on Cardozo's judging, which *was* his life. The opinions are dissected and their style and substance related persuasively to Cardozo's experiences as a lawyer before he became a judge and to his personal and professional values, temperament, and mindset.

Dennis Hutchinson, in writing his biography of Byron White, *The Man Who Once Was Whizzer White,* had the considerable advantage of writing about a judge whose career before becoming a judge was as interesting as Holmes's. Born and raised in modest circumstances in a small town in Colorado, White achieved extraordinary distinction in college and professional football, became a Rhodes Scholar, was one of the most brilliant students in the history of the Yale Law School, survived *kamikaze* attacks as a naval officer during World War II, clerked for a Supreme Court Justice, helped John Kennedy (whom he had met in England before the war and with whom he had served briefly in the Pacific) win the Presidency, served with distinction as Deputy Attorney General to Robert Kennedy (facing down the Governor of Alabama in the "Freedom Riders" crisis)—and all this *before* his appointment to the Supreme Court in 1962, at the age of 45. Now retired after more than 30 years on the Court, White is not only an authentic American hero, but a person of almost morbid modesty and of unblemished private as well as public character and, taken all in all, as admirable a person as one will find.

As Hutchinson's biography also brings out, White had, besides his legal analytic abilities, a number of traits that we value in judges, traits discernible in White's life before his appointment to the Court. He was, to begin with, smart enough and modest enough not to worry about his place in history— a worry that is the bane of the second-rate Supreme Court Justice. The Court did not go to his head. He understood the limitations of judges as legislators, administrators, political scientists, and moral tutors. He eschewed grandiosity. He was independent-minded, tough-minded, and— what we should particularly value in a Supreme Court Justice—truly indifferent to blame or praise, though this was only partly a matter of character, and partly a product of a lifelong disdain of journalists and academics. But his great strengths coexisted with great weaknesses. He had no imagination; no curiosity; no culture; no feel for history or social science; no comprehension of the importance of the judicial opinion as distinct from the outcome of the case; no writing style; above all no intellectual compass, so that there are no connecting threads in his decisions—they do not compose a coherent whole. He was very much the English judge in his resolute unintellectuality and narrowness—and English judges are fine, but they don't have the discretionary power or political responsibilities of American judges, especially Justices of the U.S. Supreme Court.

This is *my* balance sheet on White the judge, not Hutchinson's. *The Man Who Once Was Whizzer White* is resolutely and wisely nonjudgmental. It lays out the facts and lets readers draw their own conclusions. The facts include two very important negatives: that White's directionless jurisprudence was not a product of the legal realism he encountered at the Yale Law School, and that it was not a product of the New Deal, either. These points are important to an understanding of White's judicial performance. White exemplifies what is common enough—and not only in the United States—the disjunction of intellect and intellectuality. He was probably as able a legal analyst as Holmes—maybe abler. But unlike Holmes, he had no intellectual interests. Gruff and taciturn, he seems to have regarded culture, abstract thought, and fine writing as sissy-stuff. This outlook is readily understandable in light of White's provincial origins and his

Depression-, sports-, and war-shaped experiences, including the constant interruption of his schooling by professional football and by war, and the nature of his law practice (he was an office lawyer in a second-tier city). Understandable, but regrettable, for reasons that my discussion of judicial rhetoric in Chapter 8 may help to illuminate. I have emphasized the importance of rhetoric in the reputation and performance of the great judges; that importance is highlighted by the example of White, an immensely able lawyer of sterling character and fine judicial temperament who should have been a great Supreme Court Justice.

So the obstacles to successful judicial biography are not insurmountable, after all. But they are formidable, making it almost as questionable a genre of "literary" legal scholarship as oppositionist storytelling, and thereby imparting urgency to the issue of the utility of alternative genres to judicial biography.[69] There is no dearth of these. Since what is interesting about judges is mainly their opinions and their votes (sometimes their behind-the-scenes influence on their colleagues), the obvious alternative to studying the judge's life is studying the judge's opinions, philosophy, style, legacy, and influence. Each of the famous judges has accreted a large commentary of this sort—so large a commentary that asking what a biography could add to the understanding and critique of the judge qua judge is a legitimate and not merely an impertinent question. The insightful essays on Holmes's jurisprudence by Thomas Grey, G. Edward White, and others tell us more about Holmes than the biographies do.

Since appellate judges decide cases as a committee, a particularly attractive alternative to the conventional judicial biography is the study of the membership of a court in a particular period. An example is Marvin Schick's study of the Second Circuit when Learned Hand was chief judge.[70] Nastily criticized by Judge Henry Friendly,[71] Schick's book is essentially ignored by Gunther (he does cite it, however), though it deals with important aspects of Hand's work as a judge in greater depth than does the biography. Several things in Schick's fine work may have offended

69. J. Woodford Howard, Jr., "Commentary on Objectivity and Hagiography in Judicial Biography," 70 *New York University Law Review* 533 (1995), discusses some of these genres. Howard is the author both of a notable biography of Justice Frank Murphy and of a fine alternative study of the judiciary. J. Woodford Howard, *Courts of Appeals in the Federal Judicial System* (1981).

70. Schick, *Learned Hand's Court* (1970).

71. Friendly, Book Review, 86 *Political Science Quarterly* 470 (1971). The tone of the review is established in the first two sentences: "In an access of modesty Marvin Schick questions in his preface whether, in having tried to employ some techniques familiar to lawyers and some techniques used by political scientists, he has 'succeeded to the satisfaction of either' (p. xii). As a lawyer I can confirm his doubts; my guess is that political scientists also will share them."

Friendly and perhaps Gunther. First is his less than reverential, although highly respectful and on the whole highly positive, evaluation of Hand as a judge. Second is his suggestion that Hand's court contained "liberals" and "conservatives" and that the balance between the two wings determined the outcome of some cases. Third is Schick's willingness to wash the court's dirty linen in public (albeit a tiny public) by exposing the infantile feud between two of its most distinguished members, Jerome Frank and Charles Clark. Fourth is a taste for quantification, though this receives the grudging approval of Judge Friendly. In a series of tables, Schick reports each judge's "scorecard" of affirmances and reversals by the Supreme Court and shows that "liberal" Second Circuit judges and "liberal" Supreme Court Justices tended to vote the same way and the "conservatives" on both courts likewise. Fifth and last is the presumptuousness of a social scientist's undertaking to evaluate judges.

Schick's sins against the legal establishment were thus many: failing to worship at the shrine of a judicial saint, treating the judicial process as politicized and personalized, presuming that a nonlawyer can pass judgment on respected members of the legal profession, and reducing cases to statistics. Judge Friendly remarks revealingly that if the reader skips roughly the first two-thirds of the book and skims much of the remainder, "thus read, the book can be palatable to *aficionados* of the Second Circuit in its great days."[72] Should *this* be the criterion for scholarship about judges?

We need more books like Schick's and fewer judicial biographies. We learn a lot about the judicial process from Schick's book (not least how it is viewed from outside law), which is what most of us, judges or lawyers, would read a judicial biography for. Any curiosity we have about the lives of other judges can be satisfied by biographical essays, which are many.[73]

Schick's approach is only one of many alternatives to biography. The focus can remain on the individual judge rather than on his court, yet it can be the judge's work that is studied rather than his life.[74] The quantitative approach can be expanded to include the study of patterns of judicial

72. Id. at 476.

73. See, for example, Charles E. Wyzanski, Jr., "Augustus Noble Hand," 61 *Harvard Law Review* 573 (1948); and the essays by Judge Friendly on Hand, Brandeis, and Frankfurter in Henry J. Friendly, *Benchmarks* (1967). My personal favorite is Edmund Wilson's essay on Holmes in Wilson's book *Patriotic Gore: Studies in the Literature of the American Civil War,* ch. 16 (1962). See also Louis Menand, "Bet-tabilitarianism: The Principles (Sort of) of Oliver Wendell Holmes," *New Republic,* Nov. 11, 1996, p. 47.

74. For a notable example, see Stephen W. Baskerville, *Of Law and Limitations: An Intellectual Portrait of Louis Dembitz Brandeis* (1994), esp. ch. 6. Cf. David P. Bryden, "Brandeis's Facts," 1 *Constitutional Commentary* 281 (1984); Clyde Spillenger, "Elusive Advocate: Reconsidering Brandeis as People's Lawyer," 105 *Yale Law Journal* 1445 (1996).

and scholarly citations to the opinions of the judge or judges being studied.[75] If one wished to study the effects of race and gender on judicial performance, a quantitative study using race and gender as explanatory variables would produce a more objective result than biographies of individual black or female judges.

A judge's opinions should be compared with the lawyers' briefs[76] in order to determine not only the judge's "value added" but also his scrupulousness about the facts in the record and the arguments of the parties. It is also important to find out so far as possible what the judge read (because what a person reads may shape his outlook, style, and philosophy) and, more broadly, how he informed himself about what was going on in the world about him.[77] When the subject is an appellate judge, an assessment ought to be made of his colleagues because the performance of an appellate judge is both enhanced and constrained by them. Hand benefited from having unusually good colleagues; Holmes complained about the overediting of his opinions by his colleagues. The heft and composition of the caseload of the judge's court are important too, and also how cases were assigned—whether randomly, as was and remains common in state appellate courts, or by the presiding judge.

For judges active in the modern era of ghostwriting by law clerks, an attempt must be made to separate the judge's work from that of his ghosts; the polite fiction that all judges are the authors of all their opinions must be dropped, certainly for purposes of scholarly analysis. A nonbiographical study of judges that we urgently need is a study of what the disappearance of the literary judge will mean for American law.

---

75. See Posner, note 67 above, at 536–539 (tab. 1); Posner, *Cardozo: A Study in Reputation,* ch. 5 (1990).

76. See id., ch. 6.

77. This is not a new idea. See Lynford A. Lardner, "Judges as Students of American Society," 24 *Indiana Law Journal* 386, 389–390 (1949). Baskerville, note 74 above, at 274, points out that Brandeis's judicial decisions "were not determined by a uniquely 'juristic' set of values, but by generalized articles of social, economic, and political faith that derived as much from the gleanings of literature, history, and the social sciences as they did from the study of law."

the REGULATION of LITERATURE by LAW

ELEVEN

Authorship, Creativity, and the Law

What Is an "Author"?

We think of a work of imaginative literature as the work of a specific person (rarely, of two or more persons collaborating—Conrad and Ford, for example, or Beaumont and Fletcher, or the authors of the books of the Old Testament, in which multiple hands are evident). And this person, the "author," "makes it up" rather than merely copying or imitating the text of some predecessor. The laws that confer rights and impose duties upon authors are based upon this picture of the creative process. The picture is not inevitable. The attribution of specific works to specific individuals as authors, with all the ethical, interpretive, and legal implications of that attribution, is, as I noted in Chapter 7, citing Foucault, a cultural artifact.[1] Works of literature used often to be published anonymously, or their authorship was ascribed to kings or to fictitious entities such as muses.[2] Fictitious ascription survives in the practice of ascribing obviously ghost-written works to the ghost's hirer. So "authorship" is a functional rather than a natural designation—which implies that there is no natural pre-

---

1. The literature applying Foucault's insight to copyright and related matters discussed in this chapter is well illustrated by the essays in *The Construction of Authorship: Textual Appropriation in Law and Literature* (Martha Woodmansee and Peter Jaszi eds. 1994), and by Mark Rose, *Authors and Owners: The Invention of Copyright* (1993). See also James Boyle, *Shamans, Software, and Spleen: Law and the Construction of the Information Society* (1996); Cynthia J. Brown, *Poets, Patrons, and Printers: Crisis of Authority in Late Medieval France* (1995); Robert H. Rotstein, "Beyond Metaphor: Copyright Infringement and the Fiction of the Work," 68 *Chicago-Kent Law Review* 725 (1993). On the origins of copyright, see also Fedor Seifert, *Von Homer bis Richard Strauss: Urheberrecht in Geschichten und Gestalten*, chs. 1–10 (1989).

2. Similarly, too, religious art works were not signed when they were believed to emanate from or embody the divine presence. Béatrice Fraenkel, *La signature: Genèse d'un signe* 168–174 (1992).

scription for what a writer must do to be credited with authorship. The idea that a work is yours only if you made it rather than found, copied, or sponsored it is a convention of particular cultures. Shakespeare was by modern standards a plagiarist, but by the standards of his time not.[3] A strong concept of plagiarism depends on a belief that originality is the heart of creativity and on an insistence upon distinguishing between the literary, defined as the domain of fiction, and the nonliterary, defined as the domain of nonfiction. The writer of a work of nonfiction is constrained by fact, and so his work is bound to resemble those of other writers on the same subject. The writer of fiction is not so constrained, and so resemblances to previous work are suspect.

The three types of legal regulation of the literary process that I examine in this chapter all relate to the nature of authorship and creativity. The first is the tort law of defamation (and what is closely related, invasion of privacy) by fiction, committed when the author of an ostensibly fictional work incorporates real people into it in a recognizable form and tells injurious untruths about them. The second type of regulation, and the most important, is copyright law, which places limits on the kind of "creative copying" that we find in Shakespeare and many other great authors who wrote before there was copyright law in its modern sense. The third type, a subset of the second, is the application of the concept of fair use (a defense to copyright infringement) to parodies—works that depend on copying the parodied original.

Defamation by Fiction

A public statement that impugns the character of a living person and sounds credible tends to harm the person by injuring his reputation and so making other people less willing to transact with him, whether personally or commercially. This is so whether the statement is true or false, but of course the normative implications are different. A true statement about a person's character or competence promotes the efficient functioning of the

3. Though he may once have been accused of plagiarism. A competing playwright, Robert Greene, called Shakespeare "an upstart Crow, beautified with our feathers." The view that this was an accusation of plagiarism is spiritedly argued in J. Dover Wilson, "Malone and the Upstart Crow," 4 *Shakespeare Survey* 56 (1951). See also Peter Berek, "The 'Upstart Crow,' Aesop's Crow, and Shakespeare as a Reviser," 35 *Shakespeare Quarterly* 205 (1984). But most scholars disagree. See, for example, Leo Kirschbaum, "The Authorship of *1 Henry VI*," 67 *Publications of the Modern Language Association* 809, 814–815 (1952); Harold Ogden White, *Plagiarism and Imitation during the English Renaissance: A Study in Critical Distinctions* 100–106 (1933). On the difference between plagiarism and infringement, see note 36 below.

market in reputations. A false statement distorts that market, just as fraud distorts markets in goods and services.[4] The costs of such distortion are "external," in the terminology of economics: the author or publisher will not bear them unless forced to do so. The law of defamation is intended to force the author and publisher to bear ("internalize") them.

The importance of truth and falsity in the law of defamation makes the use of that law against producers of fiction problematic.[5] If the work is indeed one of fiction and is so represented to its readers, it is not intended to be believed. But by the same token, if it is believed there can be no defense of truth. The dilemma is real, but this formulation of it illustrates the fallacy of imposing arbitrary definitions on literature. Even poetry, the most "literary" of literary genres, regularly crosses the line between the real and the fictional. Much of Yeats's poetry is at one level about real people, such as Maud Gonne and Robert Gregory, and real events, such as the Easter Rising. A play, novel, or short story cannot be put into a box labeled "fiction—not intended to be believed." Some works of fiction are, or at least in their origin were, didactic (think of Swift, Orwell, and C. S. Lewis) and contain a slant—political, religious, or ethical—that the author desperately wants the reader to accept. Some are *romans à clef*—thinly disguised descriptions of real people and real events. Even works of fiction that fall into neither of these classes are often—indeed characteristically—peopled with the author's acquaintances and relatives,[6] often thinly disguised. Some of the major characters in Proust's great novel, for example, have real-life models (such as Haas for Swann and Montesquiou for Charlus), though most are composites. Many of the characters in *Ulysses* are likewise transparently modeled on real people, for example Buck Mulligan on Oliver St. John Gogarty. And often fictional characters are modeled on living persons unflatteringly characterized[7]—potential defamation plaintiffs all. An exam-

---

4. For an elaboration of this way of analyzing reputation, see my book *Overcoming Law*, ch. 25 (1995).

5. Inciting considerable law-review commentary on liability for defamation by fiction. For an example, see Mary Frances Pechtel, Comment, "Classical Malice: A New Fault Standard for Defamation in Fiction," 55 *Ohio State Law Journal* 187 (1994).

6. For a meticulous and representative account of how one great writer transformed living persons and actual events into subjects of fiction, see Norman Sherry, *Conrad's Eastern World* (1966); Sherry, *Conrad's Western World* (1971).

7. See William Amos, *The Originals: Who's Really Who in Fiction* (1985); H. M. Paull, *Literary Ethics: A Study in the Growth of the Literary Conscience,* ch. 22 (1928); Thomas Mann, *The Story of a Novel: The Genesis of Doctor Faustus* (1961), especially pp. 87–88, 199, 216, 218; Henry Ordower, "Protecting Defamatory Fiction and Reader-Response Theory with Emphasis on the German Experience," 22 *Georgia Journal of International and Comparative Law* 249 (1992); Randy F. Nelson, *The Almanac of American Letters* 181–204 (1981). The significance of "living" persons in the text is that defamation of the dead is generally not a tort.

ple is the portrayal of the Romantic poet Leigh Hunt in *Bleak House* under the name Harold Skimpole, that epitome of childish selfishness and irresponsibility who sponges off Mr. Jarndyce.[8] Leigh Hunt's feelings were badly hurt by this portrayal, and Dickens wrote him a letter of apology.[9] Casaubon, the dusty pedant who is the most riveting character in *Middlemarch,* is transparently modeled on a former patron of George Eliot, Dr. Brabant. Lady Ottoline Morrell was savaged by D. H. Lawrence in *Women in Love* under the name of Hermione Roddice, and Polonius in *Hamlet* may have been modeled on Lord Burghley.[10]

Some works of fiction add real persons to the *dramatis personae* to lend verisimilitude or for other reasons: think of Napoleon in *War and Peace,* Martin Luther in *Michael Kohlhaas,* Booker T. Washington in *Ragtime,* Aharon Appelfeld in *Operation Shylock,* Machiavelli in Marlowe's *Jew of Malta.* A number of real people appear under their proper names in *Ulysses.* Much literature was originally written as nonfiction and thus is "about" real people: such works as Boswell's *Life of Johnson,* Gibbon's *Decline and Fall,* much of Orwell's journalism. And what about Shakespeare's plays? The history (including the Roman) plays are—historical. Only one character in *Julius Caesar* (the boy Lucius) does not appear in Plutarch's lives of Caesar or Brutus.

Some works of literature are *intended* to defame.[11] Dante populated Hell with his personal enemies under their proper names, albeit only those who had died before 1300, the date of the events depicted in the *Divine Comedy.* The great, but damned, lovers, Paolo and Francesca, were real Florentines of those names. Shakespeare relentlessly libeled the House of York in his history plays. Pope's *Dunciad* is an extended libel of his literary antagonists, Dryden's *Mac Flecknoe* a savage libel of Dryden's rival Shadwell. Joyce's

---

8. Doris Alexander, *Creating Characters with Charles Dickens* 42 (1991). Several other characters in *Bleak House* are modeled on writers personally known to Dickens. Id. at 40–48. The infamous Uriah Heap of *David Copperfield* is based on Hans Christian Anderson! Id. at 78. Julien Sorel in *The Red and the Black* is a merger of two criminals of whom Stendhal had read newspaper accounts with Stendhal himself. See Wallace Fowlie, *Stendhal* 91–98 (1969). When a fictional character is a composite of several living persons, as is also common—see, for example, Albert Rothenberg, *The Emerging Goddess: The Creative Process in Art, Science, and Other Fields* 312–315, 326–327 (1979)—the risk of defamation is much less.

9. Paull, note 7 above, at 246–247; but cf. *Oxford Companion to English Literature* 485 (5th ed. Margaret Drabble ed. 1985).

10. Ruby V. Redinger, *George Eliot: The Emergent Self* 134–135, 470–471 (1975); Louise DeSalvo, *Conceived in Malice* 164–207 (1994); A. L. Rowse, *William Shakespeare: A Biography* 323 (1963).

11. DeSalvo, note 10 above, emphasizes the frequency with which writers use their fiction as a vehicle for settling scores with their enemies.

Ulysses contains a fair amount of settling scores, *Gulliver's Travels* more. Hemingway worked into *For Whom the Bell Tolls* a devastating description of his father. Some of these works defamed persons already dead when the work was written; and the heirs of a defamed person cannot (with immaterial exceptions) sue for defamation. But others defamed living persons.

It is true that because literature is not *centrally* concerned with making claims of literal truth,[12] one of the adjustments we make in reading a work as literature rather than as history or sociology is to ignore most issues of factuality. But this observation does not negate the possibility of defamation by fiction. The same work may be read by some as literature and by others as history, biography, journalism, or gossip. Or the author may, despite all his efforts, fail to create a "pure" work of literature, a work that is read as making no factual claims whatever. And a work destined to become literature may, when first created, be offered to the public—and accepted—as history or journalism rather than, or as well as, literature. So the problem of defamation by fiction is a real problem, and let us consider whether the law's efforts to prevent it could harm literary enterprise seriously.

Any case of defamation by fiction, or invasion of privacy by fiction[13] will represent a clash of two interests. One is the interest of members of the general public in not being defamed. The other is the interest of authors (which is also an interest of their readers) in being allowed both to work real people into their books and to make their fictional characters realistic. If an author does either of these things, a real person who is the model for a character or maybe just fortuitously resembles one may suffer a harm to reputation when readers confuse the real person with the fictional one.

The law's usual approach to such conflicts is to weigh the competing interests, either categorically by a system of rules or on a case by case basis, and give judgment to the injured party if his interest is the weightier. The

---

12. See Stein Haugom Olsen, *The End of Literary Theory* 156–175 (1987), and references cited there: K. K. Ruthven, *Critical Assumptions*, ch. 11 (1979); Kendall L. Walton, *Mimesis as Make-Believe: On the Foundations of the Representational Arts*, ch. 2 (1990).

13. Recall from the discussion of *Operation Shylock* in Chapter 8 that a writer or publisher can commit the tort of invasion of privacy by describing a person in a "false light" or by revealing intimate or embarrassing, though not necessarily defamatory, details of a person's life; an example of the latter type of case is *Haynes v. Alfred A. Knopf, Inc.*, 8 F.3d 1222 (7th Cir. 1993). Still another branch of the privacy tort allows a person to complain about the use of his name or likeness in advertising without his consent. One case holds that inserting a real person, under his real name, into a work of fiction (like Martin Luther in *Michael Kohlhaas*) may be tortious on this theory, especially if his name is mentioned in the advertising for the book. *Marcinkus v. NAL Publishing Inc.*, 522 N.Y.S.2d 1009 (S. Ct. 1987).

difficulty in a case of defamation by fiction is that although harm to reputation can be measured, or at least approximated, by the methods of litigation, literary merit cannot be. It is determined by a competitive process
stretching over many years. By the time the process is complete (if it can
ever be said to be complete), it will be too late to redress an injury to reputation if the defamatory work turns out to have little merit. Moreover,
the issue is not the merit of the work *tout court* but its merit if revised to
delete or modify the offending character so that the work does not defame.
The testimony of literary critics can be solicited, but the use of expert witnesses on matters of literary merit is likely to be an even more sour joke
than in other areas where expert witnesses are used, such as antitrust law
and medical malpractice.[14] Because there are no agreed-upon standards of
literary merit, it is easy to find critics of equal plausibility and credentials to
testify on opposite sides of a dispute over literary merit. Even if a work of
so-called literature is palpably meritless, some reputable critic can always be
found to testify to its merit because he believes that any imposition of a
sanction on a writer is a form or harbinger of censorship.

And it is not enough to consider whether as good or nearly as good a
work could have been produced without libeling anyone. The burden on
the author of writing the book in a way that would have avoided a libel
suit must also be considered, and it might outweigh the injury to the person libeled. It may be as difficult for an author to write without real-life
models as it is for a painter to paint the human figure without a model.
This is another issue unlikely to be illuminated by expert testimony.

The Supreme Court, acting in the name of the First Amendment, has
limited the liability of authors and publishers for defamation of public
figures by requiring proof that the author or publisher knew that the offensive characteristic that the work attributes to the public figure was false,
or did not care whether it was false or not.[15] This speech-protective approach cannot be used in a case of defamation by fiction. The people defamed are likely to be private figures—the family and acquaintances of the
author—who need only prove negligent falsehood.[16] The very falsity of the

---

14. See the analysis of expert testimony in the obscenity trials of *Tropic of Cancer* in Al Katz,
"Free Discussion v. Final Decision: Moral and Artistic Controversy and the *Tropic of Cancer*
Trials," 79 *Yale Law Journal* 209 (1969); the transcript of the expert witness's testimony in the
obscenity trial of Allen Ginsberg's poem *Howl,* in J. W. Erlich, *The Lost Art of Cross-Examination*
151–169 (1970); and Frank Kermode, "'Obscenity' and the 'Public Interest,'" 3 *New American
Review* 229 (1968), a mordant description of a distinguished critic's experience as an expert witness in an obscenity case.

15. New York Times Co. v. Sullivan, 376 U.S. 254 (1964).

16. Gertz v. Robert Welch, Inc., 418 U.S. 323 (1974).

ascription, moreover, may be essential to the author's purposes. Authors of fiction, as Aristotle taught us, aim at probability or plausibility rather than historical accuracy. Like the chronicler of history, the author of fiction is concerned with particular lives and concrete incidents; but he is concerned with the *representative* life and the *representative* incident.[17] Real people are too complicated, many novelists say, to be put into a novel without change,[18] a point supported by the discussion of biography in Chapter 10. By taking liberties with its real-life models, a work of literature can highlight aspects of human nature that are only dimly visible in real people.

These considerations not only reinforce the earlier point that liability for defamation by fiction is apt to reduce the quality and increase the cost of producing literature; they also seem to tell against the possibility that defamation by fiction could ever harm anyone's reputation. But the particular trait of a person that the writer attaches to a fictional character may so identify the person to those who know (or know of) him that readers will assume that the fictional character is he.[19] The discrepancies between the fictional character and the real person will be ascribed to the novelist's having had to make changes for the sake of his art or to ward off a libel suit. Nevertheless, the likelihood of serious damage to reputation resulting from a fictional work is less than if the work is ostensibly factual. And the danger of impeding literary creativity is significant. A mundane but important consideration is that it is difficult for a publisher to do a libel check on a fictional manuscript submitted for publication. The publisher is unlikely to know who the people are on whom the fictional characters are modeled (or even whether the characters *are* based on real people), and will therefore be unable to determine the likelihood that it contains defamatory material. Yet if, as is usually the case, the person libeled is a private figure, the publisher will be legally liable if found by the court not to have used due care in checking the manuscript for potential defamation.

But to abolish liability for defamation by fiction would create the ap-

17. "A fiction produced by the imagination and not necessarily based on fact could *also* be more or less true, since the imagination can go beyond the facts and state what is probable, how things could have happened and how they might happpen again some day." L. H. LaRue, *Constitutional Law as Fiction: Narrative in the Rhetoric of Authority* 129 (1995).

18. See, for example, *Writers on Writing* 203–204 (Walter Allen ed. 1948). Cf. E. M. Forster, *Aspects of the Novel*, ch. 3 (1927); Nadine Gordimer, *Writing and Being* 1–15 (1995).

19. If so, the standard disclaimer—"Any resemblance of the characters in this book to real persons living or dead is purely coincidental"—is unlikely to save the author's hide. See Peter Mack, "Thou Art Not He nor She: Authors' Disclaimers and Attitudes to Fiction," *Times Literary Supplement*, Dec. 15, 1995, p. 12. The disclaimer is so often false that it is no longer believed, if it ever was.

pearance of placing fiction on a pedestal that it is not entitled to occupy, like proposing that writers be exempted from the income tax.[20] That objection might be met by emphasizing how little harm defamation by fiction has been shown to do and how difficult it is for publishers to prevent such defamation—and also by invoking once again the concept of an externality, here an external benefit. Much of the benefit in pleasure and instruction that literature confers cannot be captured by the author in royalties or other income because copyright protection is limited both in time and in scope. Literary genres such as the sonnet, the novel, and tragedy, and literary techniques such as blank verse, the obtuse narrator, the *deus ex machina,* and stream of consciousness, cannot be copyrighted at all; nor can most plots,[21] characters, themes, or images. The greater a work of literature moreover, the likelier it is to last beyond the period of copyright protection. On both counts, limited duration and limited scope, even if there had been a copyright law identical to our own in Shakespeare's time he could not have captured for his own or his descendants' enjoyment more than a trivial fraction of the benefits that his literary output has conferred on society; nor could the playwrights and historians from whom he borrowed so liberally, and sometimes literally. The common law has long used the granting of immunity from tort liability to encourage the creation of external benefits.[22] This may be a better way of encouraging the production of literature than by expanding copyright protection, which, as we shall see, might deform that production.

Tort immunity must not be pushed too far. People portrayed in works primarily or ostensibly of fiction under their real names should surely be allowed to sue for defamation if they are libeled. Defamation that names names is both more harmful to the victim and easier for the publisher to prevent. But is it really possible to stop there? A different name can be an awfully thin disguise (and how different must it be?). It would be strange for the law to withhold a remedy when an author wanted to defame someone and, without naming him, used deliberate falsehoods to blacken his character and planted unmistakable clues to his identity.

20. They have in fact tussled with the Internal Revenue Service over the proper tax treatment of their expenses, seeking what might be thought special treatment. See, for example, Hadley v. Commissioner, 819 F.2d 359 (2d Cir. 1987); John Warren Kindt, "The New Assault on Freedom of Thought: Section 263A of the Internal Revenue Code," 33 *St. Louis University Law Journal* 137 (1988).

21. See June Noble and William Noble, *Steal This Plot: A Writer's Guide to Story Structure and Plagiarism* (1985)—a distillation, for aspiring writers of fiction, of thirteen plots lawfully appropriable from works of literature.

22. For examples, see Richard A. Posner, *Economic Analysis of Law* 174, 258, 684 (4th ed. 1992).

A better case might be made for liability for any defamation by fiction published in a magazine rather than in a book. The reasons that defamation by fiction is likely to cause less harm to reputation than writings that invite literal belief are that some readers will not pierce even a thin fictional disguise, others will think the resemblance between the real and the fictional person accidental, and still others will discount the defamatory aspects of the portrayal on the ground that after all the author is not an expert in truth-telling. These reasons have greater force in the case of books than in the case of magazines. Since almost all magazines publish nonfiction as well as fiction, magazine fiction that alluded to real people might be thought by many readers an extension of the publication's nonfiction section.[23] Yet the great Victorian novels were first published as serials in magazines, and even today distinguished fiction is often published first in magazines, some not noted for their good taste or scrupulous factuality.

The tort of defamation by fiction is here to stay. No blanket immunity would be appropriate. But maybe it should be narrowed; specifically, maybe nonmalicious defamation of persons who appear under fictitious names in books of ostensible fiction should be immunized.

Copyright and Creativity

The concept of external benefits illuminates the logic of copyright law. If I sow a crop but anyone can reap it, I am bearing the cost of the crop and others will be obtaining the benefit. The prospect will create incentives to shift investment from agriculture to activities that do not require as much preparatory investment, such as hunting. It has long been thought that a similar problem would arise if authors had no property rights in what they wrote. Then anyone could copy their writings; an author would not be able to secure royalties; and the amount of writing would drop as authors reallocated their time to other pursuits.

Yet, although the first copyright law in England was not enacted until 1710 and was far narrower than modern copyright laws—for instance, translations from a foreign language were not considered to infringe the author's copyright—plenty of great literature was written before 1710 and between then and the enactment of the modern laws. How is that possible? One an-

---

23. A variant of this problem was presented by the English case of Jones v. E. Hulton & Co., 2 K.B. 444 (1909), affirmed, A.C. 20 (H.L. 1910). A newspaper published malicious gossip about "Artemus Jones," whom the publisher believed to be a fictitious character. There was a real Artemus Jones, and readers took him to be the subject of the column. He sued the publisher for libel and won.

swer is that the cost of writing has always been pretty low—it is mainly the time cost to the author—so authors can afford to do some writing even if they have little or no hope of obtaining royalties or other income from their writing because they lack copyright protection. This would not be true if writing were a full-time occupation, but most writers write only part time even if they are well paid for writing. Many writers, moreover, receive non-monetary rewards from writing—fame, prestige, the hope of immortality, therapy, inner satisfaction. These rewards reduce the net cost of writing; and some of them, notably fame, can be translated into money even if intellectual property is not legally protected. A famous author will be invited to give lectures or teach, awarded prizes, asked for endorsements. A related point is that copyright protection is important only if an author is seeking payment for his writing from book buyers. He may instead have a patron who pays him to write, or may receive a public subsidy for writing, or—this is increasingly common—may be paid to teach writing or literature, with the understanding that he will use his free time to write, so that his teaching income is implicitly a writing income as well.

Of particular importance is the fact that for centuries after the invention of the printing press books continued to be very expensive to produce. More precisely, the *variable* costs of printing—the costs that varied with the number of copies printed, such as the cost of paper and ink—were high both absolutely and relative to fixed costs.[24] As a result, the copier could not take much of a free ride on the original publisher merely by avoiding having to pay a royalty to the author. The higher the cost of a copy relative to that of the original, the smaller the advantage to the copier of not having borne all the costs of creating the original, including the cost of compensating the author for his contribution to the work. For example, if that cost is only 1 percent of the total cost, the copier will derive only a 1 percent cost advantage over the original publisher from not bearing it.

In addition, cost is often inverse to time; it usually costs more to do something on an accelerated schedule. So if copying is very expensive, it may take a long time to make copies economically, and the lag will give the author and publisher of the original an interval in which to make money from the sale of the book despite the absence of legal protection against copying. This is an important consideration with drama. If most plays have only a short run (and this was true in Shakespeare's day, just as in ours, though plays were often revived sometime after their initial run), by the time a pirate acquires the script and produces the play the public may have lost interest in it.

24. Henri-Jean Martin, *The History and Power of Writing* 237–239 (1994).

Furthermore, the absence of copyright protection is, paradoxical as this may seem, a benefit to authors as well as a cost to them. It reduces the cost of writing by enabling an author to copy freely from his predecessors. Shakespeare would have had to work harder, and so might have written fewer plays, had he not been able to copy gratis from works of history and literature, sometimes, as we shall see, verbatim. A related point is that the less originality is valued, the less valuable to authors and readers is copyright protection, which encourages originality. The absence of copyright law in Imperial China despite the fact that printing had begun there centuries before it began in the West has been attributed in part to the emphasis that Chinese culture placed on continuity with the past, and its suspicion of novelty, both of which *encouraged* copying.[25] Medieval and Renaissance Europe was more hospitable to novelty, but the prevalence of censorship shows that intellectual creativity was feared as well as valued and that the encouragement of literary output by the generous bestowal of authors' rights would not have been considered a prudent aim of public policy.

Before there was formal copyright law, moreover, there were limited functional equivalents.[26] In England, publishers of particularly expensive or politically sensitive books, such as the Bible and law books, were sometimes given printing patents, the equivalent of copyright, by the Crown. Also, because the Stationers' Company had a monopoly of the books registered by it, a member of the company (which was composed, however, of printers and booksellers, not authors) could obtain the equivalent of copyright protection on a book by producing a book—or even just by buying a copy of a book—and registering it. And we know from Milton's contract for the sale of the uncopyrighted *Paradise Lost* to a publisher in 1667 that publishers would pay authors a significant sum for the author's contractual promise not to sell copies of his work to anyone else.[27] These pre-

25. William P. Alford, "Don't Stop Thinking about . . . Yesterday: Why There Was No Indigenous Counterpart to Intellectual Property Law in Imperial China," 7 *Journal of Chinese Law* 3, 29–32 (1993). Alford also mentions limited literacy and absence of corporate bodies capable of large-scale commercial innovation as factors discouraging the creation of intellectual property law. Id. at 20. These factors would have reduced the demand for copying and increased the cost, making copyright law less necessary.

26. John Feather, "From Rights in Copies to Copyright: The Recognition of Authors' Rights in English Law and Practice in the Sixteenth and Seventeenth Centuries," in *The Construction of Authorship: Textual Appropriation in Law and Literature,* note 1 above, at 191; Rose, note 1 above, 9–12, 17; David Saunders, *Authorship and Copyright* 47–51 (1992). Parallel developments in sixteenth-century France are traced in Brown, note 1 above, and in sixteenth-century Germany in Seifert, note 1 above, ch. 9.

27. Peter Lindenbaum, "Milton's Contract," in *The Construction of Authorship: Textual Appropriation in Law and Literature,* note 1 above, at 175.

cursors of formal copyright law carry us back only to the middle of the sixteenth century. Before then, however, the other considerations that I have mentioned assured a flow of books despite the absence of copyright protection.

Even today, copyright protection is limited both in time—the author's lifetime plus 50 or 75 years—and in the aspects of the copied work that are protected. In general only the exact verbal form is fully protected. A subsequent author is free, as I mentioned earlier, to copy genre, technique, style, and even—to a significant though not unlimited extent—plot and characters. The result is that copyright law discriminates among types of literary work. By doing so, it may be distorting writers' choices of which genres to work in. A lyric poem receives maximum protection because the verbal pattern is almost everything in poetry and it is verbal pattern that copyright law protects most securely. Maximum, but not complete. If the poem employs a new meter (such as dactylic hexameter) or a new form (such as the sonnet), the poet will not be able to prevent the copying of the meter or the form. Novels and plays, in which plot and character often are more important than the specific words, receive even less protection than poetry.

Since the property right is incomplete, one might suppose that literature is being underproduced and therefore copyright protection should be expanded in both scope and duration—perhaps made comprehensive and perpetual. The matter is not so simple. Consider first the difficulty of distinguishing between copying and independent inspiration when one is dealing with structural resemblances, such as similar plots. Works of literature do not endure unless they depict permanent features of the human condition. If Homer had not lived, eventually someone else would have written a poem about revenge, gods, and a war over a beautiful woman. Yet once the *Iliad* is in existence, it becomes hard to determine whether subsequent authors of works on these themes are copying the *Iliad* or copying life. The analytic problem could be solved by extending protection to all original features of a work regardless of whether the author of a subsequent work, the alleged infringer, was copying (it might be a case of independent discovery). That is the approach used in patent law; an independent discovery of the patented invention is still an infringement. It is not used in copyright law; copyright protection is confined to the specific form of the work, making independent discovery unlikely and proof of copying therefore easy in most cases. The question is whether that protection should be broader, like patent protection, or perhaps narrower, as it used to be.

One objection to broader copyright protection is that it would yield windfalls, in the sense of rewards far in excess of what is necessary to evoke literary creativity, to a genre's founders. What if Homer and his heirs had been granted an entitlement to the full perpetual stream of earnings generated by his hypothetical invention, or rather congeries of hypothetical inventions that include the epic poem, the revenge story, narration in flashbacks, plot doubling, and dactylic hexameter? This assumes that one person wrote the Homeric epics and ignores the question of Homer's predecessors. But let us put these issues to one side and assume, almost certainly falsely, that Homer was an absolute original rather than the culminating figure in a long tradition of oral epic. To give him and his heirs a perpetual copyright in his inventions would still have overcompensated him, for they are inventions that in all likelihood his genius merely accelerated. And so with the invention of tragedy by Aeschylus, if he *was* the inventor (some would say it was Homer—that the *Iliad* is the tragedy of both Achilles and Hector). Or the invention of the mystery novel by Willkie Collins (or was *Hamlet* the first detective story? Or *Oedipus Tyrannus?*). Or the inventor of the Faust legend, to whom not only Marlowe and Goethe and Mann, but also Faulkner and Yeats and countless other writers, would be literally indebted under a comprehensive regime of copyright.

The notion of "overcompensation" is vague, however, implying as it does a benchmark—but what would that be? And overcompensation is less likely when we turn from the copying of broad literary themes to the copying of specific literary techniques—the sonnet, *terza rima,* the obtuse narrator, blank verse, the rhymed couplet, the realistic depiction of sex, and so forth. These less comprehensive inventions are analogous to the sort of novelties for which the inventor of a new technological process can obtain a patent, yet the copying of them is no more an infringement of copyright than copying a genre is.

A better argument against broader copyright proceeds from the distinction that copyright law makes between "idea" and "expression"; only the second is protected. It may seem anomalous to deny legal protection to what at first blush seems the more important form of originality. But it makes sense once the nature of the "ideas" found in literature is understood. Most of what is categorized as literature is written for a mass audience—regardless of the author's intentions—because even the most esoteric writings, in order to pass the test of time, must accrue over time a substantial audience. To do this a work must be relatively impervious to cultural change. It must therefore deal, as I keep emphasizing, with the recurrent problems of the human condition—with the commonplaces of life, with stock situations, stock characters, stock narratives. That is why paraphrasing literature tends to yield merely bromides and banalities. Ideas in literature are not like the ideas of science or philosophy; they are more like painters' subjects. And as they comprise a quite limited stock of situations, narratives, and character types, to recognize property rights in them would overreward the earliest writers and deplete the stock of literary raw material available for later writers without fee.

Literary techniques (I gave examples earlier) are intermediate between ideas and expression. They may or may not be more numerous than the stock situations that are the "ideas" of literature but certainly they are highly limited in relation to the number of works of literature. Think only of the thousands of English poems written in blank verse or rhymed couplets. If the inventor of either technique enjoyed a perpetual copyright, he and his descendants would reap immense rewards.

Economists worry more about costs than about windfalls, which are not costs but transfer payments, affecting how the economic pie is sliced but not (directly anyway) the size of the pie. If the costs of administering a system of copyright licenses in a regime of comprehensive copyright protection were very low, the fact that almost every new writer would have to obtain a license from Homer's descendants might not impede the creation of new literature. The licensors would have no revenues if they charged license fees that deterred the new writers, and therefore they would have an incentive to charge reasonable, or at least bearable, fees. But in fact the administrative costs of licensing under such a regime would be very high even if the problem of identifying original inventors and their heirs (a decisive practical objection to perpetual copyright) were ignored. All property rights are costly to administer and copyrights particularly so because the infringed and infringing works lack the ready observability of conflicting uses of tangible property. You can more easily see the trespasser standing on your land than you can spot and prove plagiarism, unless it is verbatim. Remember Hamlet's aphorism that the author of imaginative literature holds a mirror up to nature? Since the authorial mirrors will be recording the same, uncopyrighted phenomena—love, war, crime, vengeance, sickness, death, folly, and so on—there are bound to be similarities among works of literature even if each author is a true "original," owing nothing to his predecessors. (As Oscar Crease acknowledges in *A Frolic of His Own,* he cannot copyright the Civil War or his grandfather.) If two photographers shoot the same scene, the resulting photographs are bound to look much alike, and if the first photograph is copyrighted, the second may be difficult to distinguish from an infringing work, that is, a photograph that copies the first photograph rather than the scene. If Ovid, Chaucer, or Shakespeare could copyright the story of star-crossed lovers, there would be endless disputes, costly to resolve, over whether subsequent stories about other lovers infringed the copyright or owed their resemblance to the copyrighted work merely to their common subject matter.

Economists use the term "rent seeking" to refer to the incentive to over-produce goods that promise a return greater than the cost of production (that return is what economists call "rent"), and to the resulting waste when rents are transformed, through competition to obtain them, into costs. This indirect effect of windfalls on costs provides a further economic argument for limiting copyright protection. Suppose that the cost of creating a new literary genre, meter, style, plot, or character type were very low, yet who-ever was the first to create it—even if he beat out his rivals by only one day—would, by virtue of copyright law, have a legally protected monopoly of exploiting it. There would be a tremendous race to be first, because the monopoly would be so lucrative. The costs consumed in the race might well exceed the social benefits of accelerated production, which in my example would be limited to having the innovation one day sooner. Literary creativity does not require as heavy an investment in training, equipment, and testing as does technological creativity—the domain of patent and trade secrets law. The principal investment is the author's time, which he could be using to make a surer income either from some other, economically more secure occupation or from some secure, more conventional form of literary endeavor. If as I am suggesting the cost of literary creativity is low, the likelihood, under a system of comprehensive copyright, of large windfalls and, as a result, of heavy rent-seeking costs would be high.

Let me illustrate. Suppose the cost of inventing a new genre by time t is $10,000 and the social value of the new genre if invented by then will be $1 million and all of it will be captured in royalties to the inventor if he is given a copyright. Suppose further that the social value of the new genre if invented at t minus one day is $999,999. Competition to obtain this lucrative monopoly (worth to the monopolist $999,999 − $10,000 = $989,000) will induce potential investors to spend heavily on inventing the genre before their rivals. If the heavy expenditures succeed merely in accelerating the invention by one day, they will be largely wasted.

There is another economic objection to expansive—indeed to any—copyright protection: it reduces the number of copies of copyrighted works that are sold, thereby deflecting potential readers to substitute products that may cost society more to produce. Unless other products (whether books or not) are perfect substitutes, the publisher of a copyrighted work can charge a price in excess of the cost of production without fear of being undercut by a copier. This is true regardless of how much of the publisher's additional profit from being able to charge a price in excess of cost goes to the author. The number of copies sold depends on the price, not on how the price is divided between author and publisher. For simplicity I shall assume that all of it goes to the author in the form of a royalty.

No seller wants to turn away a customer who will cover the seller's costs. So if an additional copy of a copyrighted book could be made and sold at a cost less than that of the best substitute product if all but one penny in royalty were forgiven (that is, if the royalty were reduced to 1¢), a reduction in the price by this amount would give the author a penny he otherwise would lose. With the reduction, he sells one extra copy, albeit at a meager royalty of 1¢, but without the reduction he does not sell the copy and thus loses the royalty. However, the costs of obtaining information about the demand schedules of different consumers, and the costs of preventing persons charged a lower price from reselling to those charged a higher price (causing the scheme of differential pricing to collapse), make it infeasible to vary the price of a book continuously over all copies and to all buyers. In technical terms, perfect price discrimination is infeasible, and imperfect price discrimination will result in a lower output of copyrighted works than if they are sold at a price equal to their cost. In the example, cutting the royalty to 5¢ on sales to a class of marginal customers will still exclude the potential customers who are unwilling to pay more than 4¢ above the zero-royalty price.

This last point ignores, however, the effect on the book industry's output if, because there is no copyright protection, fewer books are written though more copies of each one are sold. But *would* fewer books be written? Maybe more would be. An expansion of copyright protection might, as I have suggested, reduce the output of literature—the number of works, not just the number of copies—by increasing the royalty expense of writers.[28] The works of previous writers are inputs into current work, and these inputs get more expensive the more those earlier works are protected by copyright. If every author of an epic poem had to pay royalties to Homer's heirs, then Virgil, Dante, Ariosto, Milton, Pope, Goethe, and others would have had to incur an additional expense to write their epics.[29] The expense might have deflected some of them to a different literary form, or caused them to write less, resulting in a social loss. In principle, Homer's heirs would want to negotiate with each prospective writer of an epic a royalty

28. See William M. Landes and Richard A. Posner, "An Economic Analysis of Copyright Law," 18 *Journal of Legal Studies* 325 (1989), for a more rigorous treatment of this point.

29. On Homer's influence on subsequent epic writers, see Martin Mueller, *The Iliad,* ch. 7 (1984). The topic of literary influence is vast. See, for example, Göran Hermerén, *Influence in Art and Literature* (1975); Ruthven, note 12 above, ch. 8; *Influx: Essays in Literary Influence* (Ronald Primeau ed. 1977). For a painstaking examination of one great writer's influence, see Raymond Dexter Havens, *The Influence of Milton on English Poetry* (1922).

not so steep as to deter the writer, since if he were deterred there would be no royalty. But this—another example of perfect price discrimination—would be infeasible. Dante illustrates the problem that I discussed earlier of the uncertain scope of the property right when copyright is conceived broadly. He never read Homer, but he read and imitated Virgil, and the *Aeneid* is modeled on the Homeric epics.

Thus writers themselves might as a group prefer less copyright protection in order to reduce the cost to them of writing their own works, even though it would mean forgoing some income from the sale of those works because they would be less fully protected against copying. How advantageous this trade is perceived to be will depend on how much or how little the writers of a particular epoch draw on the work of their predecessors. In Shakespeare's day, it was very much. His characteristic mode of dramatic composition was to borrow the plot and most of the characters—and sometimes some of the actual language—from an existing work of history, biography, or drama and to embroider the plot, add some minor characters, alter the major ones, and write most or more commonly all of the dialogue. For example, Shakespeare made up Antony's great funeral oration; no part of it is in his source, North's translation of Plutarch. But we shall see that for the description of Cleopatra in *Antony and Cleopatra* Shakespeare merely edited North-Plutarch's description, though he did so brilliantly and vastly improved it.

Such was the extent of borrowing by the Elizabethans that some of their plays would be classified by modern copyright lawyers as "derivative" works, which infringe the original unless the author of the original has authorized them. John Gross describes a corny play by St. John Irvine, *The Lady of Belmont,* about the characters in *The Merchant of Venice* ten years later. Bassanio has run through Portia's money and is about to have an affair with Jessica, in whom Lorenzo has lost interest. Shylock, rich again after his coerced conversion to Christianity, drops in on Portia and the others and they chat about old times. If copyright were perpetual, this sequel, which appears to contain no hint of parody, would be a derivative work and so infringe *The Merchant of Venice* unless authorized by Shakespeare's heirs.[30] Shakespeare did to other writers what Irvine did to him. Alexander Lindey gives a good example of Shakespearean plagiarism in *The Tempest;* notes (with considerable exaggeration, however) that "some of the most

30. Gross, *Shylock: A Legend and Its Legacy* 228–229 (1992). A more difficult case is Jane Smiley's novel *A Thousand Acres* (1991), which is very loosely based on *King Lear*—so loosely as merely to echo rather than to infringe (were *King Lear* copyrighted). Presumably allusion is within the scope of the fair-use defense, of which more in the last section of this chapter, although I am not aware of any cases dealing with the issue.

impressive passages in the Bard's Roman plays are Sir Thomas North's prose strung into blank verse"; and reports that of the 6,033 lines in the first three parts of *Henry VI*, 1,771 were copied intact (presumably from Holinshed) and 2,373 were paraphrased from the same source.[31]

Measure for Measure illustrates the trouble Shakespeare would have been in under modern copyright law. Its main source was the play *Promos and Cassandra* written by George Whetstone in 1578 and thus recent enough to have been protected. (Apparently no copy of Whetstone's play had been registered with the Stationers' Company.) I can ignore the complications created by the fact that Whetstone himself had done some heavy borrowing from his predecessors. Even if their work was in the public domain, Whetstone would be entitled to copyright his embellishments.

Whetstone's play is set in a Hungarian city in which the law against fornication has not been enforced for a long time. Promos, the king's deputy, sentences Andrugio to death for fornication. Andrugio's sister, Cassandra, pleads with Promos for his life. Promos at first refuses but then relents on condition that she have sex with him. She agrees and they have sex, but he reneges on his part of their agreement and orders the jailer to send him Andrugio's severed head. The jailer substitutes the head of another, recently executed felon. (The literary device of substituting someone else for the condemned goes back at least as far as Ovid's rendition of the legend of Jason and Medea. Ovid's heirs would have been among the greatest all-time beneficiaries of a system of perpetual and comprehensive copyright.) Cassandra complains to the king, who orders that Promos shall marry Cassandra and then be beheaded. As soon as the marriage is solemnized, Cassandra discovers that she loves Promos, or at least that she owes him the duties of a wife; in any event she pleads movingly for his life. The king refuses till Andrugio—until then thought to be dead—steps forward; then the king pardons both Andrugio and Promos.

Shakespeare made the plot more ingenious and rewrote the dialogue completely, while retaining the theme of justice perverted by a corrupt judge. He probably used enough nonobvious details of Whetstone's plot to be guilty of copyright infringement under modern law; since the plot of

---

31. Lindey, *Plagiarism and Originality* 74–75 (1952). Lindey's book contains many other examples of plagiarism from various periods. See also Françoise Meltzer, *Hot Property: The Stakes and Claims of Literary Originality*, ch. 2 (1994); Thomas MacFarland, *Originality and Imagination* 23–26 (1985); Horace G. Ball, *The Law of Copyright and Literary Property* 1–6 (1944); Augustine Birrell, *Seven Lectures on the Law and History of Copyright in Books*, ch. 6 (1899); Paull, note 7 above, ch. 9. On Dostoevsky's heavy borrowings in *The Brothers Karamazov*, see Victor Terras, *A Karamazov Companion: Commentary on the Genesis, Language, and Style of Dostoevsky's Novel* 11–24, 27–31 (1981).

Whetstone's play was fictitious, Shakespeare could not have argued that he was copying history rather than Whetstone. I say that Shakespeare "probably" would have been guilty of infringement because the standards for infringement by paraphrase, that is, by copying that is not verbatim, are vague, as perhaps in the nature of the problem they must be.[32] Still, it is a strong probability. An influential treatise, applying the test of "substantial similarity" that many courts use, concludes that *West Side Story* would infringe *Romeo and Juliet* if the latter were copyrighted.[33] If this is right, then *Measure for Measure* would infringe *Promos and Cassandra*, *Ragtime* would infringe *Michael Kohlhaas*, and *Romeo and Juliet* itself would have infringed Arthur Brooke's *The Tragicall Historye of Romeo and Juliet*, published in 1562, which in turn would have infringed several earlier *Romeo and Juliets*,[34] all of which probably would have infringed Ovid's story of Pyramus and Thisbe—which in *A Midsummer Night's Dream* Shakespeare staged as a play within the play. If the Old Testament had been copyrighted, *Paradise Lost* would have infringed it, not to mention *Joseph and His Brothers*.

There was a notion of plagiarism in the Renaissance,[35] but it was much more limited than the modern notion.[36] The dominant theory of literary creativity in the Renaissance, as it had been in classical and medieval times, was creative imitation, or incremental improvement: the imitator was free to borrow extensively from previous writers as long as he added to what he borrowed.[37] This borrowing, to us stealing, was a way of expressing re-

---

32. "If Twelfth Night were copyrighted, it is quite possible that a second comer might so closely imitate Sir Toby Belch or Malvolio as to infringe, but it would not be enough that for one of his characters he cast a riotous knight who keeps wassail to the discomfort of the household, or a vain and foppish steward who became amorous of his mistress." Nichols v. Universal Pictures Corp., 45 F.2d 119, 121 (2d Cir. 1930) (L. Hand, J.).

33. *Nimmer on Copyright*, vol. 3, § 13.03[A], pp. 13–26 to 13–27 (1986).

34. See *Narrative and Dramatic Sources of Shakespeare*, vol. 1, pp. 269–283 (Geoffrey Bullough ed. 1957).

35. See Thomas M. Greene, *The Light in Troy: Imitation and Discovery in Renaissance Poetry* (1982).

36. On which see, for example, Thomas Mallon, *Stolen Words: Forays into the Origins and Ravages of Plagiarism* (1989), and Meltzer, note 30 above. Plagiarism and infringement, it should be noted, are not synonyms; you can copy from works that are in the public domain without violating the laws protecting intellectual property, but you can still get into trouble if you present the material as your own. Meltzer rightly emphasizes that the meaning and scope of "plagiarism" depend on the society's concept of creativity.

37. As emphasized in White, note 3 above. See also Richard McKeon, "Literary Criticism and the Concept of Imitation in Antiquity," in *Critics and Criticism: Ancient and Modern* (R. S. Crane ed. 1952); Ruthven, note 12 above, ch. 7 and pp. 123–124; Stephen Orgel, "The Renaissance Artist as Plagiarist," 48 *English Literary History* 476 (1981).

spect for illustrious predecessors in a tradition-oriented society. Such a society is more likely to look backward to a Golden Age than forward to a future made bright by progress, and more likely therefore to want to maintain continuity with the past than to break with the past for the sake of the future.[38] And this was the era of the rediscovery of classical antiquity; hence it was natural for poets and playwrights to employ classical forms as their models. Moreover, writers of imaginative literature were not yet celebrated as geniuses, so there was no expectation that they would possess a high order of originality. "Early Modern plays were only very rarely regarded as 'literature' in a sense recognisable today. They are better regarded as raw material fuelling the profitable entertainment industry of Early Modern London, much as film scripts are the raw material of today's film industry."[39] The modern equation of literary creativity with originality is largely a legacy of the Romantic era, with its cult of the artist genius as the exemplary individual—lonely, self-fashioning, Promethean.[40] "The originality of genius replaced the subordinate relation to the muse. Inspiration would well up from within instead of being imposed from the outside. Assertion would replace receptivity."[41]

This sketch of the mutation of the concept of creativity must be qualified in two respects. The first is that the absence of copyright protection could have influenced, as well as being a consequence of, the Renaissance conception of literary creativity. When copying is not forbidden, writers have an incentive to steal wholesale from their predecessors; there is nothing to stop them, and it may be a lot easier than trying to be original. Had there been a strong copyright law in sixteenth-century England, Shakespeare would have redirected some of his energies to inventing new plots.

38. One clue to the changing fashions in borrowing is that the use of quotation marks to indicate quotations (rather than for emphasis) did not become a binding norm until late in the eighteenth century. Margreta de Grazia, "Sanctioning Voice: Quotation Marks, the Abolition of Torture, and the Fifth Amendment," in *The Construction of Authorship: Textual Appropriation in Law and Literature,* note 1 above, at 290–291.

39. Jonathan Hope, *The Authorship of Shakespeare's Plays: A Socio-Linguistic Study* 3 (1994).

40. See, for example, Ruthven, note 12 above, ch. 7; Hermerén, note 29 above, at 129–144; James D. A. Boyle, "The Search for an Author: Shakespeare and the Framers," 37 *American University Law Review* 625 (1988). The conventional landmark in the emergence of the modern concept of artistic creativity is Edward Young's book *Conjectures on Original Composition* (1759), but the notion of literary genius in England goes back at least as far as Dryden, in the previous century. See also Patricia Phillips, *The Adventurous Muse: Theories of Originality in English Poetics 1650–1760* (1984).

41. Leo Braudy, *The Frenzy of Renown: Fame and Its History* 419 (1986). "The vital criticism that Stendhal makes of his hero . . . is that he is living not his own life, but a modified *copy* of another's . . . Julien does not *invent* himself, he conforms to a borrowed model." F. W. J. Hemmings, "The Dreamer," in *Stendhal, Red and Black: A Norton Critical Edition* 521, 525 (Robert M. Adams ed. 1969).

Second, because the copyright act of 1710 precedes the Romantic era, it would be a mistake to consider it solely a product of Romanticism. And anyway the act was intended primarily for the protection of publishers rather than of authors.[42] Publishers have an even greater interest in copyright when they pay their authors a modest wage or when there is no author in the picture (as in compilations or translations of work in the public domain) than when most of the profits made possible by copyright protection go to authors in royalties. Moreover, the Romantic movement was not a sudden break with the past but rather an inflection point in the more or less unbroken rise of individualism from the Middle Ages to the present day, a rise marked for example by the steady decline in the fraction of written works that are published anonymously.[43]

Although the recognition of the "author" is a signpost on the road to modern individualism, the causes of that recognition may be as much material as ideological. A medieval writer of books was plausibly viewed as a member of a team of equally skilled craftsmen (others being the binder, the copier or printer, the illustrator, the seller, perhaps the censor) engaged in the production of a book.[44] Anyway most newly published books were revisions or translations of old works. As the fraction of books that were newly written rose, as the waning of censorship made writing a less dangerous activity (and signified that it was less feared), and as the advent of labor-saving machinery "deskilled" the nonwriting contributors to book publication, the writer began to stand out from the team: became the "author."[45] This movement was greatly aided by the steady fall in the price of copies with the advent of printing and with subsequent improvements in printing technology. The fall in price led to a shift in the source of an author's income from a patron to whom he was known personally to a diffuse audience of

42. Peter Jaszi, "Toward a Theory of Copyright: The Metamorphoses of 'Authorship,'" 1991 *Duke Law Journal* 455, 468–471. So a strong sense of authorship is not a necessary condition for copyright law. Neither is it a sufficient condition. The classical world had a strong sense of individual authorship, but there were, so far as I have been able to discover, no laws against copying other people's writings. See Raymond J. Starr, "The Circulation of Literary Texts in the Roman World," 37 *Classical Quarterly* 213 (1987); Károly Visky, "Geistiges Eigentum der Verfasser im antiken Rom," 106 *Archiv für Urheber- Film- Funk- und Theaterrecht* 17 (1987); B. A. van Groningen, "Ekdosis," 16 *Mnemosyne* 1 (1963). Presumably because copying was so expensive before the invention of printing and the system for distributing books to the consuming public so undeveloped, copyright was not necessary to discourage plagiarism.

43. The parallel in the visual arts is the declining fraction of paintings unsigned by the painter. See Remi Clignet, *The Structure of Artistic Revolutions* 135 (1985).

44. Martha Woodmansee, "On the Author Effect: Recovering Collectivity," in *The Construction of Authorship: Textual Appropriation in Law and Literature*, note 1 above, at 15–16.

45. Cf. Clignet, note 43 above, at 105.

strangers, the purchasers of cheap copies for whom the author's name, like a trademark, signaled the character and quality of the book.

The older conception of creativity is illustrated by what Shakespeare did with North's translation of Plutarch in the barge scene in *Antony and Cleopatra*. Here is North:

> She disdained to set forward otherwise, but to take her barge in the river of Cydnus; the poope whereof was of gold, the sailes of purple, and the owers [oars] of silver, which kept stroke in rowing after the sounde of the musick of flutes, howboyes, citherns, violls, and such other instruments as they played upon in the barge. And now for the person of her selfe: she was layed under a pavilion of cloth of gold of tissue, apparelled and attired like the goddesse Venus, commonly drawen in picture: and hard by her, on either hand of her, pretie faire boyes apparelled as painters doe set forth god Cupide, with litle fannes in their hands, with the which they fanned wind upon her.[46]

And here is the corresponding passage in Shakespeare (II.2.201–215):

> The barge she sat in, like a burnished throne,
> Burnt on the water. The poop was beaten gold;
> Purple the sails, and so perfumèd that
> The winds were lovesick with them. The oars were silver,
> Which to the tune of flutes kept stroke, and made
> The water which they beat to follow faster,
> As amorous of their strokes. For her own person,
> It beggared all description: she did lie
> In her pavilion—cloth-of-gold of tissue—
> O'erpicturing that Venus where we see
> The fancy outwork nature. On each side her
> Stood pretty dimpled boys, like smiling Cupids,
> With divers-colored fans, whose wind did seem
> To glow the delicate cheeks which they did cool,
> And what they undid did. (II.2.201–215)

And here for good measure is T. S. Eliot's version, in Part II of "The Waste Land":

> The Chair she sat in, like a burnished throne,
> Glowed on the marble, where the glass
> Held up by standards wrought with fruited vines
> From which a golden Cupidon peeped out
> (Another hid his eyes behind his wing)

46. Plutarch, "The Life of Marcus Antonius" (translated by Sir Thomas North, 1579), in *Narrative and Dramatic Sources of Shakespeare*, vol. 5, pp. 254, 274 (Geoffrey Bullough ed. 1964).

> Doubled the flames of sevenbranched candelabra
> Reflecting light upon the table as
> The glitter of her jewels rose to meet it.

In Shakespeare's "copy" the beautifying effect is astonishingly vivid,[47] while Eliot's pastiche of Shakespeare achieves an ironic reduction. Under a regime of copyright law, Shakespeare would have had to get a license from North in order to be allowed to compose one of his most beautiful passages.[48] One cannot exclude the possibility that Shakespeare's plays would have been even better had he been induced by the expense of obtaining such licenses to be more "original." Conversely, our expansive copyright laws, by discouraging the kind of creativity that Shakespeare and his contemporaries[49] exhibited, may be impairing literary creativity. The literary imagination, as should be apparent from the earlier discussion of the use of living persons as models of fictional characters, is not a volcano of pure inspiration but a weaving of the author's experience of life into an existing literary tradition.[50] The more extensive is copyright protection, the more inhibited is the literary imagination. This is not a good reason for abolishing copyright, but it is a reason possibly for narrowing it, and more clearly for not broadening it.

In the extraordinary allusiveness of Eliot's poetry we find a concrete reason for his hostility to the Romantic movement. To the Romantic idea of creativity as originality Eliot opposed, and in his poems exemplified, the older idea of creativity as imitation with enrichment. He was not alone; the echoing of the literature of the past has been a common device of mod-

47. In like manner, Bullough remarks of Shakespeare's use of Brooke's *Romeo and Juliet* that "Brooke's poem is a leaden work which Shakespeare transmuted into gold . . . The surprising thing is that Shakespeare preserved so much of his source in vitalizing its dead stuff." Bullough, note 34 above, at 277–278.

48. If Plutarch were in the public domain, then Shakespeare (or anyone else) could translate and edit Plutarch without violating North's (hypothetical) copyright. But a translator of a public-domain work can copyright his translation; and Shakespeare obviously was copying North's translation rather than copying the original, and so infringing North's (hypothetical) copyright. If Plutarch's works were copyrighted, Shakespeare would be infringing that copyright as well. Eliot, however, might be able to get away with his pastiche under the fair-use doctrine, since he took only two lines (plus the reference to Cupid) from Shakespeare and edited them heavily.

49. And not only them, of course. As one of countless examples, the best theory of the composition of the Homeric epics is that the genius (or geniuses) whom we call Homer reorganized, and added extensive finishing touches to, existing epic works. See, for example, Seth L. Schein, *The Mortal Hero: An Introduction to Homer's Iliad,* ch. 1 (1984), and references there. Or as Rudyard Kipling put it: "When 'Omer smote 'is bloomin' lyre, / He'd 'eard men sing by land and sea; / An' what he thought 'e might require, / 'E went an' took—the same as me!"

50. For an excellent discussion of this point, see Robert Alter, *The Pleasures of Reading in an Ideological Age,* ch. 4 (1996).

ernist literature. Joyce's *Ulysses* is only the most famous example. I mentioned Kafka's borrowings from Kleist and Dickens. The first stanza of Yeat's poem "The Second Coming," which I quoted in Chapter 7, contains borrowings from two of Shelley's poems.[51] Modern writers, living in the age of copyright, are perforce limited to taking from the public domain. The more ample the copyright protection, the smaller the public domain. Eliot might have added that the Romantic equation of creativity with originality was a considerable exaggeration of the actual practice of the Romantic poets. We now know that Coleridge, seemingly the most "original" of the Romantics, borrowed heavily, to the point of plagiarism, from other writers.[52]

Yet despite the pervasiveness of borrowing in literature, vividly expressed in Northrop Frye's dictum that "poetry can only be made out of other poems; novels out of other novels,"[53] so fixated are most of us on the Romantic idea of creativity that it is hard not to sense belittlement—even a note of bardicide—in Mark Rose's avowal that "it would not be wholly inappropriate, I think, to characterize Shakespeare the playwright, though not Shakespeare the author of the sonnets and poems, in a quasi-medieval manner as a reteller of tales."[54] It may not be wholly inappropriate, but it is misleading, as if Shakespeare's principal activity had been translating Plutarch, Ovid, Holinshed, and his other sources into a contemporary idiom. The value added in his retelling greatly exceeds any debt to his predecessors. If Shakespeare is not the most original writer who ever lived, he may well be the most creative.

Rose, in the passage that I have quoted, may be too much under the influence of Northrop Frye, whose great book *Anatomy of Criticism* organizes the whole of literature into a handful of symbols, genres, modes, and myths. At that level of generality there is nothing new in literature; everyone is a reteller of someone else's tales; so copyright becomes problematic. Frye has some tart words about copyright. He notes the challenge to the assumptions underlying the copyright law of "a literature which includes Chaucer, much of whose poetry is translated or paraphrased from others; Shakespeare, whose plays sometimes follow their sources almost verbatim; and Milton, who asked for nothing better than to steal as much as possible out of the Bible."[55] The copyright law distinguishes, however, as I have

51. Harold Bloom, *Shelley's Mythmaking* 94 (1959).
52. See Norman Fruman, *Coleridge, The Damaged Archangel* (1971).
53. Frye, *Anatomy of Criticism* 97 (1957), quoted in Malcolm Budd, *Values of Art: Pictures, Poetry and Music* 2 (1995).
54. Rose, note 1 above, at 26.
55. Frye, note 53 above, at 96. See also id. at 95–104.

noted, between idea and expression, and most of Frye's examples involve the former. Frye's schematic approach and disavowal of qualitative evaluation obscures the important point that what Chaucer, Shakespeare, and Milton *did* with inherited or borrowed themes and sources, which would today be considered plagiarism or, if the originals had subsisting copyrights, copyright infringement, exemplified a higher order of creativity than is commonly attained by works of literature that are fully original in the copyright sense.

Parody

Parody and burlesque are ancient literary genres; *The Battle of Frogs and Mice* is an ancient Greek parody of the *Iliad*. These genres depend for their effect on the copying of distinctive features of the original, features without which the meaning of the parody or burlesque would be lost. Here, from Part II of "The Sweeniad" by the pseudonymous "Myra Buttle," is a parody of the opening stanza of "The Waste Land" (footnote omitted):

> Sunday is the dullest day, treating
> Laughter as profane sound, mixing
> Worship and despair, killing
> New thought with dead forms.
> Weekdays give us hope, tempering
> Work with reviving play, promising
> A future life within this one.
> Thirst overtook us, conjured up by Budweisserbrau
> On a neon sign: we counted our dollar bills.
> Then out into the night air, into Maloney's Bar,
> And drank whiskey, and yarned by the hour.
> *Das Herz ist gestorben,* swell dame, echt Bronx.
> And when we were out on bail, staying with the Dalai Lama,
> My uncle, he gave me a ride on a yak,
> And I was speechless. He said, Mamie,
> Mamie, grasp his ears. And off we went
> Beyond Yonkers, then I felt safe.
> I drink most of the year and then I have a Vichy.

This is as close a copy as Shakespeare's description of Cleopatra. And since the original work is copyrighted, why isn't the parodist an infringer? The usual answer is that the use the parodist makes of the original is a "fair use" within the meaning of the copyright law.[56] Yet many parodies have

---

56. The "fair use" defense to copyright infringement is codified at 17 U.S.C. § 107.

been held to be copyright infringements, and the Supreme Court has declined to provide authoritative guidance, ruling instead that whether a parody is a fair use depends on the circumstances of the individual case.[57]

Parody is best understood in terms of one of its synonyms: it is a "take off" on another work or on a genre of works. It takes characters, incidents, dialogue, or other aspects of the parodied work(s) and moves on from there to create a new work. Generally there is an incongruity between the borrowed and the new elements, as where the parodist sets about to "grasp the essentials of the style of a given [serious] author or a school of authors, and then proceed[s] to concoct an outlandish episode which is expressed in that style."[58] In the words of another critic, "The highest kind of parody may be defined as a humorous and aesthetically satisfying composition in prose or verse, usually written without malice, in which, by means of a rigidly controlled distortion, the most striking peculiarities of subject matter and style of a literary work, an author, or a school or type of writing, are exaggerated in such a way as to lead to an implicit value judgment of the original."[59]

So there is both a taking from a previous work and an injection of creativity, large or small. Often what is taken, however, is *none* of the copyrighted elements of the parodied work(s). This is especially likely if what is being parodied is not a single work but a writer's entire *oeuvre*—in short, his style—because style is not copyrightable; or an entire genre, since genre is not copyrightable either. So Max Beerbohm's splendid parodies of Henry James in "The Mote in the Middle Distance" and "The Guerdon" would not be within range of an infringement suit. But neither is a title copyrightable, nor stock characters, nor the standard plots, so a parodist who took only these features from a copyrighted work would not be an infringer either.

If, however, the parodist does take copyrighted elements of the parodied work, it can be argued that he infringes no matter how great his creative input. The combination of copyrighted elements with fresh creative input simply yields a derivative work, and modern copyright law assigns the exclusive right to make and sell derivative works to the owner of the copyright on the original work. It does not matter how much "better" or commercially more valuable the derivative work is. Transaction costs are

---

57. Campbell v. Acuff-Rose Music, Inc., 510 U.S. 569 (1994). See Anastasia P. Winslow, "Rapping on a Revolving Door: An Economic Analysis of Parody and *Campbell v. Acuff-Rose Music, Inc.*," 69 *Southern California Law Review* 767 (1996).

58. G. D. Kiremidjian, "The Aesthetics of Parody," 28 *Journal of Aesthetics and Art Criticism* 231, 235 (1969).

59. J. G. Riewald, "Parody as Criticism," 50 *Neophilologus* 125, 128–129 (1966).

minimized when all rights over the copyrighted work are concentrated in a single pair of hands. But the fair use doctrine sometimes permits the appropriation of parts of a copyrighted work, and we must consider whether parody should always or sometimes be deemed a fair use.

A use may be said to be "fair" when the costs of transacting with the copyright owner over permission to use the copyrighted work would exceed the benefits of transacting.[60] These benefits include not only economizing on other transactions but also, and more important, stimulating the production of intellectual property by enabling its creators to appropriate as private gain the social value of their creation. A book review that quotes at length from or minutely describes the book being reviewed, and so would be a candidate for infringement were there no concept of fair use, illustrates the social function of the privilege. Most book reviews increase the sales of the books reviewed, so that imposing transaction costs on the reviewers would harm authors. Even unfavorable reviews stimulate sales when the alternative would be no reviews at all. Book reviews are free advertising, and are especially credible advertising because not controlled by the advertiser (the publisher). Their credibility would be undermined if a reviewer needed the author's permission to quote from the book. Censored by book authors, reviews would be no more credible than paid advertising. Authors as a group would suffer from abrogation of the privilege of fair use for book reviews even if an occasional author gained. Authors *want* to be reviewed, even though they have no control over whether the reviews will be favorable.

When a review does reduce the sales of a book, it is not because it fills the demand for the book—rarely is a review a close substitute for the book—but because it identifies flaws in one specific work and so provides valuable information about it without undermining the rewards for creating *worthwhile* intellectual property. The harm to an author from drawing attention to the *lack* of value of the intellectual property he has created is not the kind of harm that the law should seek to rectify or prevent. Of course, not all books that contain errors are valueless; indeed, books can have great weaknesses yet still be socially valuable because of offsetting strengths. But such a book will not be devastated by negative book reviews that stress its weaknesses. The marketplace in ideas and opinions will produce other reviews that emphasize its strengths.

Parodies, unlike book reviews, are not intended to introduce readers to the parodied work. On the contrary, since effective parody requires that the audience have some and often considerable familiarity with the paro-

---

60. Landes and Posner, note 28 above, at 357–361.

died work, works are rarely parodied that are not already well known. The book reviewer *has* to "steal" from the copyrighted work, in order to introduce the work to its audience. The parodist labors under no such necessity, except—a big except—insofar as he must steal in order to have his work recognized as a parody.

It might seem that the criticism-protective policy of the fair-use defense would be equally applicable to parodies, because parody can be an effective method of ridicule, and ridicule is a form of criticism.[61] But parody is a confined form of criticism because of its focus on idiosyncrasy: "Parody naturally tends to be the watchdog of established forms, a correction of literary extremes . . . [It] tends to confine itself to 'writers whose style and habit of thought, being more marked and peculiar, was more capable of exaggeration and distortion.' This tendency seriously restricts the scope of critical parody because it seems to ignore the fact that the absence of any 'marked and peculiar' style and habit of thought is a symptom of mediocrity rather than of talent."[62] This is overstated. There are plenty of parodies of mediocrity, as in *Dubliners,* the Gerty MacDowell episode in *Ulysses,*[63] and *A Frolic of His Own,* among many other examples; mediocrity is often ridiculous. And parodies of the style of great writers, such as Shakespeare's parody in *Hamlet* of Marlowe[64] or Beerbohm's parodies of James and Shakespeare,[65] focus on criticizable (whether justly or not) features of the style of the writers parodied—in these examples, Elizabethan bombast and Jamesian convolution. Whether it is an individual writer or an entire culture that is being parodied, there will rarely be any question of copyright infringement, because the parodist will not have to copy the writer's actual sentences in order to evoke the writer's style. Myra Buttle could have done an effective parody of T. S. Eliot without sticking quite so closely to the meter and "story" of "The Waste Land."

Unlike a book review, a parody may supply a part of the demand for an admired original work, thus diminishing the sales of the original by substitution rather than by criticism. *Abbott and Costello Meet Frankenstein,* a par-

61. Kiremidjian, note 58 above, at 234.

62. Riewald, note 59 above, at 132–133 (footnotes omitted).

63. The style of which "owes a considerable debt of parody to the style of" Maria Cummins's novel *The Lamplighter* (1854), whose heroine is named—Gerty. Don Gifford, with Robert J. Seidman, *Ulysses Annotated: Notes for James Joyce's* Ulysses 384 n. 1 (2d ed. 1988).

64. In the player's bombastic speech narrating Priam's slaying by Pyrrhus (II.2.450–518)—a takeoff on Aeneas's narration of the same incident in Marlowe's *The Tragedy of Dido, Queen of Carthage* (II.1.518–558).

65. The latter in "'Savonarola' Brown," in Beerbohm, *Seven Men and Two Others* 233, 246 (1950).

ody of the earlier movies *Frankenstein, Dracula,* and *The Wolf Man,* reproduces the principal characters and themes of the parodied works in a full-
length movie that many viewers prefer to seeing (or, more likely, seeing
for a second or a third time) all three of the original works. *Young
Frankenstein* may do the same for *Frankenstein.* As in these examples, most
parodies are humorous, and many people prefer a humorous to a serious
version of a work, especially when the "serious" version is itself intended
purely as entertainment, having no ethical or intellectual pretensions. Some
parodies are erotic versions of a nonerotic original. They may supply the
demand for the original on the part of the segment of the population that
likes its entertainment spiced with sex.[66]

The parody that substitutes for the original is, so far as the appeal of the
fair use defense is concerned, at the opposite extreme from the book review. In economic terms, the difference is between substitution and complementarity. Goods are substitutes when a fall in the price of one results
in a fall in the demand for the other. They are complements when a fall in
the price of one results in a rise in the demand for the other. Book reviews
complement (even when they do not compliment!) books, so writers of
books benefit from the conferral of a privilege of fair use on reviewers.[67]
But parodies that substitute for the parodied works reduce the incomes of
the authors of those works.

There is still the privilege for criticism to be considered. But a parody
does not always ridicule or otherwise criticize the parodied work. On the
contrary, it may use that work—treating it as the standard of excellence—
to disparage something else. "The Waste Land" parodies Augustine, Dante,
Spenser, Marvell, and other classic authors to criticize not them but the sordidness and spiritual emptiness of modern life—they are the standard. In
this example the parodied work is the *weapon* rather than the *target.* But in
such a case, why should the owner of the original be reluctant to license
the parody and why therefore should the parodist have the benefit of the
fair-use defense? Or, as with *Abbott and Costello Meet Frankenstein,* the parody may not be a work of criticism at all; its only object may be to amuse.
Perhaps these parodies are better regarded, therefore, as burlesques.
Beerbohm's good-natured parodies of James and Shakespeare should prob-

66. This, rather than judicial prudery (as conjectured in Elliott M. Abramson, "How Much
Copying under Copyright? Contradictions, Paradoxes, Inconsistencies." 61 *Temple Law Review*
133, 172 [1988]), may explain why most of the erotic parodies that have been challenged have
been held to be infringing.

67. Cf. Gary S. Becker and Kevin M. Murphy, "A Simple Theory of Advertising as a Good
or Bad," 108 *Quarterly Journal of Economics* 941 (1993) (advertising as complement of product ad-
vertised).

ably be viewed in this light as well. The burlesque may or may not be a substitute for the original; in the case of Beerbohm surely not.

But it cannot be assumed that either the parody as weapon or the parody as burlesque, merely because it does not criticize the original, should "belong" to the copyright holder just like a normal derivative work. There may be obstacles to a well-functioning licensing system for such parodies, though whether they are obstacles that justify a broad privilege of fair use is uncertain. The copyright holder may be unwilling to license either type of parody (weapon or burlesque) at a reasonable price regardless of its literary merit and even if it poses no threat of being purchased as a substitute for the original work. Many authors are thin-skinned (though Henry James seems to have liked Beerbohm's parodies), and quick to take offense. Others are hyperserious. If the parodist wants to use the original work in a way potentially offensive to the audience for the original, even if he is not criticizing it, the copyright holder may fear a negative effect on his revenues. This has happened in the trademark context when homosexual groups tried to use popular trademarks (such as the "Pink Panther") to identify themselves.[68] In such cases the invocation of the fair-use defense might be thought degrading to the author of the original work. With the gradual spread of the "moral rights" doctrine of European copyright law into American law, degrading uses of a copyrighted work are becoming legally problematic, though presumably the critic's privilege, which has First Amendment overtones, will survive.

For now, all that is clear is that the parodist should not be allowed to copy so many of the copyrighted features of the original work as to make the parody a substitute for it. For then he could reproduce an entire copyrighted work with impunity simply by giving the characters funny names or having them speak in comical accents, enticing the silly or vulgar members of the audience of the original work—who may be a substantial fraction of the potential audience for that work. This would be the literary equivalent of multiplying both sides of an equation by -1 or transposing a musical work written in the key of A minor into a different key.

It could be argued that the parodist should be allowed to take from the original no more than is necessary to make the parody effective. If so, the fact that he appropriates only a few of the copyrighted features of the original work should not be a defense to infringement. It is true that the less he takes, the less likely he is to be siphoning off the audience for the orig-

---

68. See Rosemary J. Coombe, "Author/izing the Celebrity: Publicity Rights, Postmodern Politics, and Unauthorized Genders," in *The Construction of Authorship: Textual Appropriation in Law and Literature,* note 1 above, at 101.

inal work. But as in the law of larceny, so in the law of copyright, there should be no privilege for stealing small. The parodist should be allowed to "steal" only so much as he needs to remind his readers of the original work, and that is a criterion independent of the relative or absolute amount of the original work that he takes.

Against so tight a curtailment of the fair use privilege of parodists it can be argued that since effective parody requires that the original work be known to the audience, the only works that are ever parodied are *successful* original works, implying that the copyright holder will have reaped his just reward and should not be entitled to insist on a share of the profits of the parody, at least if there is no danger of the parody's taking audience from the original. This objection ignores, however, the distinction emphasized in Chapter 6 between the ex ante (in advance) and the ex post (after the fact) perspective. Viewed ex post, a successful work of intellectual property—a Broadway hit, a best seller, a hit song—may appear to confer a windfall gain on the creator. But ex ante the creator faces a distribution of possible outcomes, and if the upper tail of the distribution is cut off, the mean of the distribution will be lowered and the incentive to create intellectual property reduced.

Could freedom of expression be impaired by burdening the creation of parodies with the costs of transacting with and paying royalties to copyright holders? Following the reasoning that writers are not entitled to steal paper and pencils in order to reduce the cost of satire, one is hard pressed to come up with a compelling reason to subsidize social criticism by allowing writers to use copyrighted materials without compensating the copyright holder. Yet I concede that the cases are not identical. Intellectual property is a public good. A pencil is not. If you take my pencil I cannot use it, while if you take my intellectual property I can still use it, so the deprivation is less—but my incentive to create it will be diminished if I cannot make you pay for it. And recall that it is possible to parody an author, a genre, even an individual work without taking any copyrighted materials at all.

The parodist, in short, must be allowed to take enough to make his work recognizable as a parody, but not so much as to make his parody a substitute for the original. The challenge to the law is to find the point, within the range of possible fair-use configurations that is bounded by these extremes, that will optimize the mixture of parodies and original works.

This formulation presupposes, of course, the desirability of a form of literary property right that will encourage "original" writing. As we saw earlier, this premise is not inevitable, and if it were rejected there would be no reason to worry about parodies that take "too much" from the parodied works, or indeed about any other form of plagiarism. But even Shakespeare had a form or "inform" of property right—not only were his plays not published before they were performed, but the players were given only parts and cues, not the full text, possibly to make it difficult for a pirate to obtain a copy of the entire script. Clearly, it would be irresponsible to propose the repeal of copyright for literary works on the ground that it rests on culturally "local" and contestable concepts of authorship and creativity and its abolition might usher in a new Golden Age of literature. All that can be said with confidence is that proposals to expand the copyright protection of literary works, whether by statute[69] or by judicial interpretation (for example of the fair use defense, a judge-made doctrine that the Copyright Act codifies without defining), cannot be defended persuasively on the basis of literary history or literary theory. This much, at least, the operating level of law can learn from the study of literature.

69. The Copyright Term Extension Act of 1995, S. 483, H.R. 989, now pending in Congress, would if enacted extend the term of copyright protection in most cases from the life of the author plus 50 years to life plus 70 years.

Index